Canadian EXPLORATION LITERATURE

an anthology

edited by Germaine Warkentin

TORONTO   OXFORD   NEW YORK
OXFORD UNIVERSITY PRESS
1993

Oxford University Press, 70 Wynford Drive, Don Mills, Ontario M3C 1J9

Toronto   Oxford   New York
Delhi   Bombay   Calcutta   Madras   Karachi   Kuala Lumpur
Singapore   Hong Kong   Tokyo   Nairobi   Dar es Salaam
Cape Town   Melbourne   Auckland   Madrid

and associated companies in
Berlin   Ibadan

This book is printed on permanent (acid-free) paper ♾ .

Canadian Cataloguing in Publication Data

Main entry under title:

Canadian exploration literature in English

Includes bibliographical references and index.
ISBN 0-19-540989-2 (bound) ISBN 0-19-540867-5 (pbk.)

1. Canada – Discovery and exploration – Sources.
2. Frontier and pioneer life – Canada – Sources.
I. Warkentin, Germaine, 1933–

FC161.E96 1993   971   C93–093033-9
F1032.E96 1993

OXFORD is a trademark of Oxford University Press

Map illustration by Nina Price

1 2 3 4 –   96 95 94 93

Printed in the United States of America

To John, "most reverend head . . ."

Contents*

Part V   Prelude to Settlement

* The list of contents is designed to outline the chronology of explorations as well as the pages on which the selections are to be found. Authors' dates appear with the headnotes to each selection.

Acknowledgements

In compiling and annotating a large anthology like this, some of it edited from original sources, I have accumulated debts to almost every friend I have, and indeed to some I have never met. I have tried to list below all those who helped, and hope I have not forgotten anyone who assisted me in tracing a lost reference, or set me straight when I had gone astray. My first debt is to the students of my course 'Exploration Writing in English Canada' for whom the anthology was first prepared; it was their enthusiasm which convinced me it might have a wider audience. I am deeply grateful to Victoria College for material help in the form of research funds to assist my work on Radisson and Kelsey, and to the Library staff at Victoria University in the University of Toronto, especially David Brown of Readers' Services, and at Robarts Library, University of Toronto, especially Jane Lynch of Inter-Library loan, for answering many urgent requests for books no one ever looks at. The special skills of my research assistants, Lalage Grauer and John C. Parsons, made a major contribution to the project. Phyllis Wilson and Olive Koyama of Oxford University Press were unfailingly patient as I completed what turned out to be a larger task than I anticipated. Judith Hudson Beattie, Keeper of the Hudson's Bay Company Archives, and her predecessor Shirlee Anne Smith were instantly responsive to my queries, as was Edward J. Dahl, early cartography specialist in the Cartographic and Architectural Archives Division of the National Archives of Canada. Jennifer S.H. Brown and Sylvia Van Kirk were firm supporters whenever I wearied. The typists at Oxford University Press who input most of the manuscript, and Ingrid Smith of Victoria College who did the remainder, have my particular gratitude. In addition I owe thanks to (in no particular order): the New Oxford English Dictionary project at the University of Waterloo, David Galbraith of Victoria's Centre for Reformation and Renaissance Studies, George Lang, Laura Peers, Henri Pilon of the *Dictionary of Canadian Biography*, an un-named assistant in the library at Regis College, Toronto, Sean Peake, Jay Macpherson, Richard Telekey, Conrad Heidenreich, W.J. Eccles, Dennis Carter-Edwards, Ian MacLaren, Hugh MacMillan, Ian Bowring, William R. Bowen, Diana Patterson, John Noble, Joan Winearls, Rivkah Zim, W. McAllister Johnson, Glyndwr Williams, Harry Duckworth, Mary A. Gallagher, Neil Semple, and John J. McCusker. The most important debt of all is acknowledged in the dedication; this volume is a retirement present to my husband, the geographer John Warkentin, who first introduced me to the writing of the explorers when he edited an anthology of his own, *The Western Interior of Canada* (1964), and thus dispatched me on a journey of exploration that has sometimes surprised both of us.

MATTHEW COCKING. 'Matthew Cocking's Journal', ed., Lawrence J. Burpee, *Transactions of the Royal Society of Canada*, Third Series, Section II (1908). Used by permission of the Royal Society of Canada.

PETER FIDLER. 'Journal' in *The Journals of Samuel Hearne and Philip Turnor*, ed. J.B. Tyrell. Publication of the Champlain Society, XXI, Toronto, 1934. Used by permission.

SIMON FRASER. From *The Letters and Journals of Simon Fraser, 1806–1808*, ed., with an introduction by W. Kaye Lamb (1960). Used by permission of W. Kaye Lamb.

ANDREW GRAHAM. *Observations on Hudson's Bay, 1767-91*, ed. Glyndwr Williams, with an introduction by Richard Glover. Publications of the Hudson's Bay Record Society, XXVII (London, 1969). Used by permission of Keeper, Hudson's Bay Company Archives, Manitoba Provincial Archives.

ANTHONY HENDAY. '"York Factory to the Blackfeet Country": The Journal of Anthony Hendry [sic], 1754–55', *Transactions of the Royal Society of Canada*, Third Series, Section II (1907). Used by permission of the Royal Society of Canada.

DANIEL HARMON. From *Sixteen Years in the Indian Country: The Journals of Daniel William Harmon, 1800–16*, ed. W. Kaye Lamb (1957). Used by permission of W. Kaye Lamb.

LETITIA HARGRAVE. *The Letters of Letitia Hargrave*, ed. Margaret Arnett MacLeod. Publication of the Champlain Society, XXVIII, Toronto, 1947. Used by permission.

SAMUEL HEARNE. From *The Narrative of Samuel Hearne* (ms. Stowe 307). Used by permission of the British Library Board.

JAMES ISHAM. *James Isham's Observations on Hudson's Bay, 1743*, ed. E.E. Rich and A.M. Johnson. Publication of the Hudson's Bay Record Society, XII. (Published by the Champlain Society for the Hudson's Bay Record Society, 1949.) Used by permission of Keeper, Hudson's Bay Company Archives, Manitoba Provincial Archives.

ALEXANDER MACKENZIE. From *The Journals and Letters of Sir Alexander Mackenzie*, edited by W. Kaye Lamb. Used by permission of The Council of the Hakluyt Society.

JOHN PALLISER. *The Papers of the Palliser Expedition, 1857–1860*. ed. Irene M. Spry. Publication of the Champlain Society, LXIV, Toronto, 1968. Used by permission.

PETER POND. 'The Narrative of Peter Pond' was transcribed by the Minnesota Historical Society especially for publication in a reprint edition of *Five Fur Traders of the Northwest*, edited by Charles M. Gates, copyright 1965 by the Minnesota Historical Society. The original Pond document is held by Yale University. Used by permission of the Minnesota Historical Society.

PIERRE ESPRIT RADISSON. MS. Rawlinson A 329. Used by permission of Keeper of Western Manuscripts, Bodleian Library, University of Oxford.

FRANCES SIMPSON. 'Journal of a Voyage from Montreal, thro' the Interior of Canada, to York Factory on the Shores of Hudson's Bay' (1830). Winnipeg: Hudson's Bay Company Archives, D6/4. Used by permission of Keeper, Hudson's Bay Company Archives, Manitoba Provincial Archives.

SIR GEORGE SIMPSON. 'The Character Book of Governor George Simpson' in *Hudson's Bay Miscellany 1670–1870*, ed. Glyndwr Williams. Publication of the Hudson's Bay Record Society, XXX (Winnipeg, 1975). Used by permission of Keeper, Hudson's Bay Company Archives, Manitoba Provincial Archives.

DAVID THOMPSON. *David Thompson's Narrative, 1784–1812*, second edition, ed. Richard Glover. Publications of the Champlain Society, XL, Toronto, 1962. Used by permission.

GEORGE VANCOUVER. *The Voyage of Captain George Vancouver 1791–1795*, ed. W. Kaye Lamb. 4 volumes. London: The Hakluyt Society, 1984. Used by permission of The Council of the Hakluyt Society.

Introduction

On the first day of August, 1859, two elderly gentlemen, Simon Fraser the explorer and John McDonald of Garth, his fellow fur-trader, wrote and signed a letter to posterity which marked the end both of their respective careers — one shining, one obscure — and of their era. 'We are the last of the old North West partners,' they wrote,

> We have known one another for many years. Which of the two survives the other we know not. We are both aged, we have lived in mutual esteem and fellowship, we have done our duty in the stations allotted us without fear, or reproach. We have braved many dangers, we have run many risks. We cannot accuse one another of any thing mean & dirty through life, nor done any disagreeable actions, nor wrong to others. We have been feared, loved & respected by natives. We have kept our men under subordination. We have thus lived long lives. We have both crossed this continent, we have explored many new points, we have met many new Tribes, we have run our Race, & as this is probably the last time we meet on earth, we part as we have lived in sincere friendship & mutual good will.[1]

It is not surprising that two such tough old birds should bid farewell to an adventurous life in textual form; the explorers of Canada were assiduous writers, and both Fraser and McDonald left accounts of their experiences. What marks their letter is its awareness of the historical moment; almost as they wrote, H.Y. Hind and John Palliser were assessing the prairies for their settlement possibilities, and Sir George Simpson of the Hudson's Bay Company was making arrangements for transport of the Company's goods not by the old shipping route from England through York Factory, but by the new American railroad to St Paul.

The letter is marked also by the old gentlemen's belief in the validity of their task and the way they had carried it out: the values they want to be remembered by are a sense of duty, a capacity for command, and a benevolent stance towards the "many new Tribes" they encountered. Modern Canadians look back on the Frasers and McDonalds (if they look at all) with mingled feelings; the European discovery and settlement of Canada, with its horrifying effect on a long-established and vigorous native population, no longer seems a high-minded enterprise, and even its ecological consequences are being thoughtfully questioned today. Like most societies which are the product of European expansionism, we began our social existence by consuming Satan's apple. The knowledge of good — an understandable affection for our own world and the life we have built in history—brought with it the knowledge of evil—the cost of our triumph to the peoples we attempted to supplant. The textual records of this experience comprise the first body of a literature which can in any sense be called Canadian. This anthology is a record of the writing in English about that world, or what can be recaptured of it, between 1660 when the Provençal adventurer Pierre Esprit Radisson visited Lake Superior, and 1860 when Captain John Palliser of the Royal Geographical Society began to issue his vast report on the settlement prospects of the Canadian plains.

Most of the writings selected here belong to the 'classical' world of the exploration document: journals, letters, reports, even surveys have their place. Yet the effect of reading them is to contradict both the view of the trader-explorer that the old Nor-Westers' letter sought to leave, and the very notion of the classical exploration document itself. The stereotype pictures the explorer as a solitary hero, but we discover a scene crowded both with the natives whom Europeans encountered and the Europeans' own business and scientific partners and acquaintances, a scene that is as often comic or tragic as it is heroic. A world seemingly without women is revealed as full of them: first the native wives who became the dowagers of many an eminent fur-trade family, and then the British women—diverse in personality and class, but representing an important historic change—who arrived after the 1820s. A 'literature of travel' written by English speakers turns out to be reports in many different forms, devised in a multi-lingual environment which besides French, Cree, and the new creole tongues, includes the dialects of English spoken by explorers like Peter Pond, whose phonetic spelling communicates his salty Yankee twang. The old tale is one of single-minded Europeans succeeding decaying Indian tribes; a newer tale is told not only by the evidence of social conflict among the Europeans, but of the genuine variety of European response to native life, from the steely imperialism of George Vancouver to the awed response to aboriginal religious customs of George Nelson. Native life, too, emerges in all its variety and complexity. We meet not only the half-assimilated natives around Cumberland House whom John Richardson described as so wretched, but also the energetic mid-continental traders encountered by La Vérendrye and the awe-inspiring Blackfoot chief who admitted Anthony Henday into his presence, and we witness the ethnic tension between Matonabbee's Chipewyan companions and their victims, the Inuit of Bloody Fall. Complicating the picture is the evident peripheralization of the Canadien voyageur, who was fated to be canonized as a native Canadian "type" at the same time as he was forgotten as a historical reality.[2]

The very way we read the texts themselves has been transformed. Where we once assumed that an exploration document, like a literary text, was written by a single author and reflected his views and his resources as a writer, recently we have become aware that these are 'incremental' texts, often with several stages of composition of which the daily log is only the first, sometimes with additions by fellow explorers, and often revised by other hands before appearing as a grand quarto volume of 'travels' to ornament a gentleman's library. It used to be generally believed that texts like these belonged on the periphery of serious literature, and were unrelated even to each other except through the economic and geographical issues they addressed. At best this kind of writing was relegated to the domain of the historical and antiquarian, or to that of 'children's literature'. More recently we have come to realize with what complexity exploration texts testify in written form to moments of cultural crisis, and to the emergence of new cultures from such crises. One of these, in Canada at least, is the frail but coherent culture of fur trade and exploration. In the writings which emerged from it we can recognize not only the testimony of a society in the making—aboriginal and European—but of one beginning to interpret and understand itself.

To leave it at that, of course, is to risk replacing one stereotype with another, the old heroic fiction-making with a revisionism which may be just as narrow in its vision. In resistance, we might perhaps take our lead from David Thompson, the most distinguished of the writers anthologized here, who wrote, 'the Great Architect said "Let them be, and they were," but he has given to his creature the power to examine his works on our globe; and perhaps to learn the order in which he has placed them.'[3] That modest Thompsonian 'perhaps' is typical, but so too is Thompson's confidence in the idea that an order exists to be sought out, and that human beings are equipped to seek it. Today we are more likely to attribute such an order less to the universe itself than to the words we use to talk about it, to the 'order of discourse' which comprises the many ways in which we explain the world to ourselves, whether stereotyped (and thus the enemy of true exploration) or inquiring. In such a situation, the powerful tools of contemporary literary analysis—disentangling text and sub-text, recognizing the social construction of discourse, engaging in cultural analysis—are available to serve the very objectives Thompson, at once the most philosophical and the most down-to-earth of our writers, set before us. If the land-mass of Canada—if Canada itself as a community—remains a conundrum to us, commanding us to the task of investigation, the discourse of Canada invites that Thompsonian spirit of inquiry.

The writing of the explorers provokes just such an inquiry, for in poring over the narratives of the people who were living at that time and place it is we who become the explorers. This often involves a leap of the imagination, for most of them are European men, convinced—as was even the greatest of them, David Thompson— of the historic inevitability of their project. But skilled reading can unlock the sub-texts they did not recognize, and give utterance to the other voices—women, natives, labourers—which speak through them. Even in the partial and limited way which these essentially European texts permit, what emerges is a picture of great richness and complexity, and a social scene which, if re-examined with these questions in mind, may hold the key to the afterlife of their narrative of conquest, which is a matter of great interest to all of us, since we are living it.

*   *   *

In the last half of the eighteenth century, when Simon Fraser was born, the map of North America still held at its heart an enigma: the mysterious empty space which stretched north and west from Lake Superior to the Arctic and Pacific coasts. The

Atlantic coast had been mapped to North and South so early that the narrative of its discovery really belongs to the naval and mercantile history of Renaissance Europe. Between 1525 and 1700 the early inhabitants of this coast, writing in French and (as the Jesuits did) in Latin, left a parallel record of the opening up of the St Lawrence, the Saguenay, and northern New York. But as late as 1769 Moses Norton, Governor of Fort Prince of Wales, could send Samuel Hearne northwestward through the Barrens with the not very precise instructions to search for 'a river represented by the Indians to abound with copper ore, animals of the furr kind, & c. and which is said to be so far to the Northward, that in the middle of the Summer the Sun does not set, and is supposed by the Indians to empty itself into some ocean.'[4] If Europeans were deeply committed to finding out what the vast and apparently empty space west and north of the St Lawrence held, they also tended to imagine that it contained what they wanted it to contain. The French court officials with whom La Vérendrye dealt twenty-five years earlier had been sure there was a great river trending westward, or possibly a 'Western Sea'; English merchants and naval officers were just as certain that there must be a North West passage through the Arctic ice.

In both cases it was the lure of trade with China that governed their imaginings: the intervening landmass was chiefly an obstacle, though when Radisson and Des Groseilliers returned to Quebec from the interior in 1660 with a treasure in furs, information about the interior itself became a pressing economic necessity. Its 'discovery' and interpretation was to absorb the energies of seven generations of European and Canadian men and women, and eventually to sap (though as events have proved, thankfully not quite destroy) the political and cultural life of the native inhabitants of North America who were already securely inhabiting the allegedly empty space. The excerpts gathered here all focus on the first imagining of that mysterious space on the map, on how it began, on how it continued, and on how it expired, beginning with the encounter of two late-Renaissance societies: the French on one hand and the Cree and Saulteur of Lake Superior on the other, and concluding with the effective erasure of what had imperiously been named 'Rupert's Land' by the equally imperious settlement projects forecast in the reports of the Victorian explorers Hind and Palliser.

Rupert's Land is a concept as much as a place. It began as an English mercantile objective, and the old name is very much alive in the province of Manitoba today, where native leader Elijah Harper until recently served as Member of the Legislative Assembly for the constituency of Rupertsland. It persists, too, as a state of mind. For English Canadians it is the first great unimagined space in our national conscious-ness, predating the settlement history of the West itself, pre-dating the English garrisons in the Maritimes. For Québécois, it is a product of their own history of exploration, as Radisson's narrative shows, as well as that of La Vérendrye (written in French but included in this English selection also). Within the vague, immense boundaries of Rupert's Land, as Richard Davis has rightly pointed out, the problems that as Canadians we still attempt to solve today were first posed: the relation between Eurocentric traders and the aboriginal 'other', between the English cling-ing to their Bayside posts and the French at their backs in the interior, between the desire to exploit the land and the fact of its quick exhaustion, between the settler's dream of peaceful plenty and the farmer's nightmare of drought and betrayal.[5] Rupert's Land thus provides a metaphor for the whole of Canadian life, for its history since the beginning, for its abiding relationship with the land both in its 'pastoral' (David Thompson's word) and its agricultural phases, and for its intransigent social complexity, so at odds with the exclusionary principles by which societies of whatever sort announce their difference from other societies. No master narrative of the kind Americans have devised to account for their own social complexity has been possible in Canada, and in this respect the vast enigma of Rupert's Land provides a metaphor for Canadian discourse in general.

One feature of the combined coherence and mystery of the interior of Canada has been the link between the making of culture and the conduct of trade. This linkage long pre-dates the arrival of Europeans in the area; not only did the aboriginal peoples trade enthusiastically among themselves, but their cultures relied on the symbolic exchange of 'gifts' as a means of ending warfare and cementing political alliances. The Europeans who began to arrive in the interior in the seventeenth century usually recognized the exchange of gifts as an essential ceremony, though they were likely to give it a primarily economic meaning, preferring to exchange what they regarded as cheap trading commodities for the furs the natives had in such profusion (though as Hearne and Henday testify they were eagerly looking for minerals as well). As a result, the exploration of a large part of Canada is closely, though not exclusively, bound to the conduct of the fur trade. And between 1660 and 1860 the men and women of the fur trade, native and European, developed in that enigmatic space on the map what can only be called a culture: a world of shared social, linguistic, and eventually historical experience which was born when Radisson and Des Groseilliers escaped the Governor's edict to head out for the west, and died even as Fraser and McDonald parted from each other.

The map was, of course, not empty. Nor was it populated by idyllic native peoples living an upchanging existence in edenic seclusion from the conflicts of Europe. Aboriginal life was one of continuing change and transition, as modern historians and archaeologists are well aware, and the history of North America before its conquest is as complex as its history afterwards. Native nations saw the arriving Europeans as potential trading equals, and met them with the gifts appropriate to the making of useful alliances, a symbolic mode of operation which the earliest explorers, emissaries of late Renaissance cultures and themselves used to allegorical thinking, adopted if they were shrewd. One of the greatest of such meetings (staged as expertly by the natives as by the Europeans) is unself-consciously recounted in Radisson's description of French participation in the Feast of the Dead held on the south shore of Lake Superior in the winter of 1659–60. When Henry Kelsey travelled down the Hayes River in 1690, it was only partly to discover what was at the end of it; with him he bore the 'Governor's pipe' (the native calumet) and instructions to make peace among warring tribes who, the London Committee of the HBC were agreed, would be better occupied in bringing their furs down to York Fort to trade. Mariner though he was by training, Kelsey thought the moment was worth recording in laborious verse, the model for which he may have found in that 'mariner's Bible', Richard Hakluyt's *The Principall Navigations Voiages and Discoveries of the English Nation* (1589).[6]

Throughout the next two centuries the fur trade provided the central mechanism through which the fragile, thin-spun and always imperilled culture of the mysterious interior developed. It united natives and Europeans in a common purpose, given force in the marriages into which native women entered to ensure the trading alliances that brought them technologically superior domestic goods. It kept the English and French in conflict, as the Europeans vied with each other for native trade. It produced a second great trading enterprise in the North West Company, which from the late 1770s to its union with the HBC in 1821 fought the HBC with innovative flair and intellectual and economic entrepreneurship. It brought change to the natives, though other, continent-wide forces were working upon them as well, first introducing horses to the plains, as the native elder Saukamapee's wonderful chronicle relates, and then the dreaded smallpox.

As journal after journal reminds us, natives and Europeans traversing the immense empty space met and eagerly exchanged news of friends, relations and enemies. Hospitality was preserved under the stress of conflicting business partnerships, as we see in 1776 when Matthew Cocking of the Hudson's Bay Company courteously plays host at Cumberland House to the independent trader Alexander Henry the Elder. Families were established: the wife of trader John Rowand (a figure memorably described in George Simpson's *Character Book*) was the mixed-blood daughter of the irascible Edward Umfreville, whose bitter polemic against HBC policy (plagiarized in its details from the scholarly factor of Fort Severn, Andrew Graham) is excerpted here. Families were destroyed; the serene good manners of Frances Simpson's account of her arrival in Red River (1830) disguises the dismay which George Simpson's unexpected English marriage caused in society there. The Governor already had a native wife of established prestige, and his high-handed treatment of her outraged men like John Stuart who had spent a lifetime in the west and knew its customs well. Daniel Harmon's gentle journal records his love of books, his spiritual life, his friendships, and his eventual happy marriage to a native woman; it is one of the best testimonies to the strong, if thin-spun, web of the emerging culture — reliant both on the ongoing investigation of the land and on the exploitation of its economic resources — which united the people of this immense space. Another aspect of the familial experience — closely observed and with a tart sense of the prevailing absurdity of life — appears in the letters of Letitia Hargrave, Scots wife of the Chief Trader at York Fort in the 1840s. And the vitriolic biographical sketches George Simpson secretly made of the Hudson's Bay Company men who worked under him, reveal, despite their naked aggression, a lively panorama of exploration and fur trade personalities, whether of high station or low.

Two careers, those of Sir Alexander Mackenzie and Sir George Simpson, exemplify the particular strains which inevitably developed within, and then destroyed, the culture of fur trade and exploration in the interior. In some brief geographical remarks appended to his published journal, Alexander Mackenzie surveyed the land-mass of the western interior and observed,

> the whole of this country will long continue in the possession of its present inhabitants, as they will remain contented with the produce of its woods and waters for their support, leaving the earth, from various causes, in its virgin state. The proportion of it that is fit for cultivation is very small, and is still less in the interior parts; it is also very difficult of access; and whilst any land remains uncultivated to the South of it, there will be no temptation to settle it. Besides, its climate is not in general sufficiently genial to bring the fruits of the earth to maturity. It will also be an asylum for the descendants of the original inhabitants of the country to the South, who prefer the modes of life of their forefathers, to the improvements of civilisation.[7]

Here the interior of Canada is depicted as a permanent resource base beyond the periphery of civilized society. However it is not a dramatically risky and conflict-ridden frontier zone, as in the United States, but a semi-pastoral administrative fiefdom of the Hudson's Bay Company. Mackenzie's aim in his geographical notes was not to overthrow this fiefdom, but to seek a share of it on behalf of the interests which he represented. At the time Mackenzie wrote, the infrastructure of the Hudson's Bay Company had determined the social organization of the culture of the interior, with its gradations of rank from Chief Factor down to canoeman and labourer, for over a century. Religion was not a concern of the London Committee of the HBC, and missionaries came very late to Rupert's Land; as for justice, only in 1803 did the Canada Jurisdiction Act give the inhabitants of the interior access to British law. Thus the issue was never the 'conquest of the land for civilization', but how this permanently wild terrain ought to be administered, whether by the HBC, or by — in Mackenzie's words — 'an association of men of wealth to direct, with men of enter-prise to act, in one common interest' (415-16). Prince Rupert himself, the royal patron of the HBC, might have put it in just that way.

When George Simpson took up his responsibilities in 1820 the two companies were effectively at war over possession of this rich fiefdom, as we can see in the narrative of John Franklin, who had the delicate problem of negotiating for supplies with the contending parties. Pastoral fantasies notwithstanding, Simpson inherited a trapped-out domain, and one of his tasks would be to impose a moratorium on the taking of pelts in certain areas until nature could restore them. This sign of change in what had seemed to many a changeless land was the forerunner of others: part of the conflict between the HBC and the NWC was caused by the older company's willing-ness to allow agricultural settlers, under the patronage of Lord Selkirk — whose wife was the sister of Andrew Wedderburn (later Colville), a prominent figure in the Company — to establish themselves at Red River.

Once the two companies united in 1821, European missionaries, and then Euro-pean women, began to arrive at York Fort. The quantity of information which the task of exploration produced, disseminated not only in published journals but in the maps of figures like Peter Pond and David Thompson, was being quickly absorbed by a Europe looking outward after the Battle of Waterloo, and it had rapid effect in re-fashioning the ways in which not only Europeans, but the expanding population of Upper and Lower Canada, began to imagine the west. By the 1830s silk hats were replacing the beaver hats which had been made with Canadian pelts, and the new railways of industrial England were about to appear in Canada. If Simpson's first challenge was to transform a late feudal social structure (in seventeenth-century entrepreneurial form) into a modern business enterprise, his last was to face the coming absorption of his domain into an Anglo-Canadian community expanding westward, for which the agricultural settlement of a land now almost fully explored was the prime objective. A decade after his death Rupert's Land was handed over to the Canadian government, and the modern settlement history of the west began.

*   *   *

Radisson travelled west in 1659 at a time of great transition both for native peoples and Europeans. The Huron-Iroquois wars of the preceding two decades had shat-tered Huronia and dispersed the high culture of its people. The consequences affected the great aboriginal trading networks far into the interior for many years. Radisson too came from a culture in transition. As his journals show (they are written in a vivacious Francophone English, possibly his own), he understood and automati-cally used the symbolic codes of the late Renaissance. Yet when he arrived in England, the news was circulated among men involved in the foundation of the Royal Society, which would be dedicated to the scientific projects — and the rationa-listic scientific discourse — which was to dominate exploration writing over the next two hundred years. As David Thompson was to observe, 'the age of guessing is passed away, and the traveller is expected to give his reasons for what he asserts' (*Narrative*, 213). For the explorer, whether scientist or fur trader, the giving of reasons involved a close survey of the land through which he travelled searching for pelts.

There is a grain of scientific inquiry even in Radisson and Kelsey, but they are primarily early ethnographers of the societies of the interior, chiefly concerned with assessing the natives' attitudes to trade. At the French court, however, contemporary geographical theory ensured that La Vérendrye would report in detail on the unfathomable topography he was encountering. James Isham, still tied by HBC policy to his Bayside post, took the opportunity of a winter illness to record in his own lively vernacular the weather, the mineral deposits, and the botanical life around York Fort, as well as the habits of the 'Home Indians' who had already become sadly dependent on the post's activities. In the mid-eighteenth century the Hudson's Bay Company endured a Parliamentary enquiry resulting from its alleged failure to establish posts in the interior, where French traders following the trail laid down by La Vérendrye and his sons were challenging HBC hegemony. Hudson's Bay men had always kept detailed Post journals, and over the next hundred years, the logs and diaries of those who at last pressed into the interior record, step by step, the scientific as well as the human scene their writers encountered. One of the most distinguished was Andrew Graham, who in fact never travelled to the interior himself; instead he compiled at his various posts on the Bay a vast manuscript collection recording the information he was assembling. Graham struggled to give his voluminous writings 'the severe order of a treatise', but they proved almost uncontrollable; amended and re-written with each new piece of information, they told and retold the uncovering of the secrets of the immense spaces through which his men were travelling. Graham also transmitted information regularly to the scientists of the Royal Society, and seems not to have protested when an early collaborator, Thomas Hutchins, actually represented work of Graham's as his own.[8]

The rationalistic discourse of the 'age of reason' with its bias towards cold fact posed its problems for the writing of the explorers, who felt a strong obligation to record the 'true geography' (Vancouver's words) of the areas they had visited. 'Calculation is tedious reading,' David Thompson observed, 'yet without it, we cannot learn the real state of any country' (*Narrative*, 219). Though they are usually anything but tedious, the journals and letters of the explorers are full of 'calculation'. No matter how simple their own education (few of them, except perhaps Umfreville and later Palliser, came from the higher social classes), the traders tried to keep track of where they were even though no one had ever established the precise location of any place in the interior until the nineteen-year-old David Thompson did so for Cumberland House in 1789. In journals like that of the not very literate (and apparently less mathematical) Anthony Henday the very recording of these details must have been a struggle; as the manuscript tradition of his historic journal to the interior suggests, he may have had to be 'de-briefed' by James Isham in order to get all of it on paper. And their science was often mixed with earlier notions: for Isham himself, the composition of his rambling but sharply observed *Observations on Hudson's Bay* functioned as a 'cure' for his physical and psychological ills which even the physicians of ancient Rome would have recognized.

Nevertheless the newer intellectual tradition represented by the Royal Society, with its rigorous stress on scientific observation divested of personal content and literary artifice, encouraged the attitude that a proper description was one which excluded the emotive and the 'literary'. We can see Matthew Cocking struggling anxiously with this responsibility when he writes 'I have been particularly careful to be impartial in the account I have given, not exaggerating, but rather leaning to the favourable side.' With Peter Fidler, on the other hand, mathematical and scientific observations are mingled unself-consciously with a young lad's amiable and sharp-witted account of life among the women and children of a native community almost entirely isolated from the world. The task was not always easy. Two personalities whose heroism is undoubted, Simon Fraser and Alexander Mackenzie, had difficulty in drafting their reports. In a letter of 1 February 1807 Fraser wrote to his friend John Stuart complaining that the journal he was trying to write was 'exceeding ill wrote worse worded & not well spelt,' and asking his assistance in pulling it together. A letter of Mackenzie (Fort Chipewyan, 5 March 1794) is a memorable account of the affliction of 'writer's block'. Fraser never did prepare an expanded account of his extraordinary trip down the river named after him, and Mackenzie had to have the assistance of a ghost-writer to bring his to completion.

As a reading of even the best of our writers, David Thompson, shows, exploration literature is not as highly organized as the kind of writing we traditionally call literary. Much of this writing was done in a flourishing multi-lingual environment; the explorer was often a Scotsman to begin with, or might well speak a dialect of English; he was surrounded by canoe-men speaking French or one of the rapidly emerging creole languages, and he was probably trying to learn one or more native languages himself. Depending on the stage at which it reaches the reader it can be diary-like and repetitive as well as embodying a narrative of high adventure or a scientific conceptualization of great power. Whether he was a cog in the administrative machine of a trading company or a scientist on a mission, the man in the field tried to keep a daily record of his observations. These crude notes (which sometimes seemed to have been composed after the fact, rather than at the evening campfire) were then worked up into formal reports. At a later stage, and perhaps with the help of a friendly fellow-explorer or some learned man, the report would be transformed into a published volume, to add to the growing library of exploration literature from all parts of the world which from the seventeenth century onwards went to make up what P.J. Marshall and Glyndwr Williams call 'the great map of mankind'. In the nineteenth century, volumes of travels had a huge reading public, in part because young people, sometimes forbidden to read fiction because it was morally dubious, could safely be encouraged to read travels for their 'factual' content. At the same time the literature of exploration had much to do with the establishment of the novel itself as a genre dealing with 'the world as it really is', resolving science's guilt over the relationship between narrative art and factual record by the invention of an entirely new literary kind. Frances Brooke's *The History of Emily Montague* (1769), set in Quebec just after the British victory over the French, is at once the first North American novel and an exploration narrative *par excellence*, and it was read as such long after its interest as a novel was exhausted.

In the most important of the writers collected here the conflict between narrative art and factual record is overcome, but by varied and unexpected means. David Thompson, like Thoreau — with whom he can worthily be compared — in his fusion of close, often mathematical detail and social and natural observation, is taking the measure of a powerfully imagined universe, and the result is the best writing, of whatever sort, in Canada before the twentieth century. With Hearne, Mackenzie, and Franklin, the conflict between scientific impersonality and literary expression is resolved differently. Hearne's narrative is one of the great classics of exploration literature, but scholars are increasingly unsure to what extent he wrote — or at least polished — the final version himself. The same is true of Mackenzie, where we *can* be sure: two versions of Mackenzie's Arctic journal exist, one the daily record which he kept in his own rough but evocative prose, the other rewritten in a magisterial Georgian English by the hack-writer William Combe. Even Andrew Graham did not hesitate to re-write Anthony Henday's account, incorporating new material as it arrived on his own desk. In some cases this amounts to outright plagiarism (Umfreville's pillaging of Graham, for example), but in others it is evident that the exploration document could often be a corporate production; few of their authors had much sense of proprietorship, although the aging and blind David Thompson stoutly refused to sell his manuscript to the American, Washington Irving, for popularization. As a result, exploration writings sometimes present us with unstable texts, and we have to approach them free of traditional ideas about authorial identity.

Many of these concerns come together when we consider the extraordinary narrative of John Franklin's disastrous first expedition. It too is a corporate text, including (with courteous acknowledgement) excerpts from the journals of Franklin's three English companions on his initially confident, and finally tragic, journey across the barrens. Franklin, it is evident to the thoughtful reader, struggles to control his text, to give a full and fair account of his own actions, of those who betrayed him and those who were loyal, yet at the same time give expression to what he views as the natural rightness of the English project in northern Canada. Yet there are few texts which so evidently invite what is now called 'deconstruction'. At every point in the narrative there occur gaps and silences which only the voices which have been erased — those of the voyageurs who accompanied Franklin, many of whom died on the journey — could fill.

The problem of erasure is one of the most important the reader of exploration literature has to face. Looked at from the vantage point of the languages of Shakespeare or Racine, even the best exploration writing is humble, often ragged and stumbling, dominated by an obsession with factuality, either entirely without art or deeply inhibited by the problem of expression. And it is written by Europeans, almost all of them men. But as contemporary literary theory reminds us, almost every kind of writing involves decisions which exclude possible alternatives, and these very exclusions are themselves signals to the alert reader. Sometimes the task is easy, as we can see in the cheerful gossip of Letitia Hargrave, who can tell her own story with its comic disasters and at the same time that of Mrs Gladman, which despite occasional mockery she is clearly aware is not very funny. Sometimes it is difficult because the writer is genuinely distinguished; David Thompson's great account of the organization of the central plains of North America tasks our best interpretive skills, not because he is a difficult writer but because of his power of imagination and synthesis.

Elsewhere it is the silences that have to be explored, and these are chiefly those of the native population who were for a long time equal partners in the European investigation of the interior. The natives of North America communicated with each other not in a culture of the book, like the Europeans or their Meso-American relatives, but in the symbolic language of pipe, kettle, and war-hatchet, and in the diplomatic messages of the wampum-belt. It is one of the deepest ironies of exploration writing that this native discursive world with rare exceptions can only be known through the voices of explorers who either exploited it without understanding, or — however sympathetic — were certain it was destined for extinction. At the same time, the sheer variety of personalities among the explorers, and their fascinated interest in what they encountered, ensured that many notable native speeches were recorded, and in many different ways. David Thompson remarked acidly that European rhetoric tended to colour the white man's rendering of these speeches, and we may be fortunate that if Saukamapee's account had to survive in another man's words, it survived in Thompson's. But even Thompson had his blind spots; he is contemptuous of the imaginative world of his voyageurs, who have 'no scientific object in view', and if any group is excluded from this collection it is these labourers and canoe-men, who leave their traces only in the tragic narrative of Franklin, or the songs heard by Frances Simpson.

The writings of the explorers reveal four areas of deep concern to the emergence of discourse in English-speaking Canada: first there is the insight we gain into the original inhabitants of this place, whether in the kindly but dismissive observations of a James Isham or in the fascinated transformation undergone by a George Nelson. Second, there is the powerful access we have to variant ways of organizing its history, whether that of Saukamapee, who tells in the idiom of his race the essential features of a story to which the *Europeans* are peripheral, or Thompson with his capacity for synthesis, or H.Y. Hind, musing over the traces of a dying civilization like a traveller of the Romantic period contemplating the ruins of ancient Greece. Then there is the insight into power and its operation which we gain, whether from the entrepreneurship of the outrageous Radisson, from the careful deployment of courtly compliment by La Vérendrye, the uncomfortable gap between working document and ghosted best-seller in Mackenzie, the sheer imperial authority of Vancouver's introduction to his narrative, or the gentlemanly bearing of Palliser as he savours the atmosphere of a past age while relentlessly surveying the country for a new one.

Finally — and oddly, in view of what we know of the hardness of their lives — is the evident pleasure many of these writers took in the new world in which they were living. Explorers are by nature grumblers; more than many of us, they are often cold, wet, hungry and far from home, and they let us know it. 'I think it unpardonable in any man to remain in this country who can afford to leave it,' Alexander Mackenzie observes in a letter (Fort Chipewyan, 13 January 1794); Letitia Hargrave, pregnant once more, longs for home, and H.Y. Hind does not conceal his intense revulsion at the slaughter of the buffalo hunt. But like the men in H.L. Hime's photograph, who have turned their canoe into a shelter, in many writers a subtle process of naturalization took place. We can see this process in John McDonald of Garth, whose journal has never been properly edited; following a brigade of canoes on horseback, he observes, 'this was I thought the most pleasant part of our lives, the riding a swift horse in the fine Valley of the Saskatchewan abounding buffaloe, & deers and all game.' [9] We see it in Samuel Hearne's impassioned obituary tribute (in footnote form) to his country wife, Mary Norton, and in his abiding friendship with the native 'Captain' Matonabbee, whom Andrew Graham later said killed himself for shame when Hearne surrendered Fort Prince of Wales to the French admiral La Pérouse. We see it in Peter Fidler and Anthony Henday, deeply at home in the wandering life of their isolated world, and in Graham himself at his desk at Fort Severn — 'this delightful settlement' as he called it — scribbling away as furiously as his contemporary Edward Gibbon, but writing about the birth of a new empire, not the fall of an old one. A generation earlier Bishop Berkeley had written with the closed certitude of the imperial mind:

> Westward the course of Empire takes its way;
> The first four acts already past
> A fifth shall close the drama with the day:
> Time's noblest offspring is the last.
>
> "Verses on the Prospect of Planting Arts and Learning in America" (1752)

It is probable that almost all the writers collected here — Graham included — would have accepted this vision of the movement of culture without question. But a generation later the young Wordsworth, looking into the moonlit quadrangle of his Cambridge college, would observe

> The antechapel where the statue stood
> Of Newton with his prism and silent face
> The marble index of a mind forever
> Voyaging through strange seas of thought, alone.
>
> *The Prelude* (1850 text), III 60–3

Wordsworth's Newton belongs to a different visionary scheme; though a romanticised type of the solitary voyager, he also represents the more open cosmology which (distant in time though they were from controversies like those popularized by Newton's successor Stephen Hawking) the explorers helped bring to birth. The real experience of discovery, the anthropologists tell us, was when Europeans who had thought their society perfect and complete suddenly encountered the unrecognizable 'other' represented by nations beyond their ken, and were forced to reinterpret *themselves* in the light cast by this 'new world'. It is in this experience that the culture of Canada, as well as its exploration, begins.

Notes

[1] Fraser, *Letters and Journals*, ed. Lamb, 271.
[2] See Gross, 'Coureurs-de-bois, Voyageurs & Trappers'.
[3] Thompson, *Narrative*, ed. Glover, 216. All citations are to this text.
[4] Hearne, *Journey . . . to the Northern Ocean*, 1.
[5] See Davis, 'Introduction' to *Rupert's Land : A Cultural Tapestry*.
[6] See Warkentin, ' "The Boy Henry Kelsey" '.
[7] Mackenzie, *Journals and Letters*, ed. Lamb, 411.
[8] See Williams, 'Andrew Graham and Thomas Hutchins'.
[9] National Archives of Canada, MG 19 A.17, f. 58v.

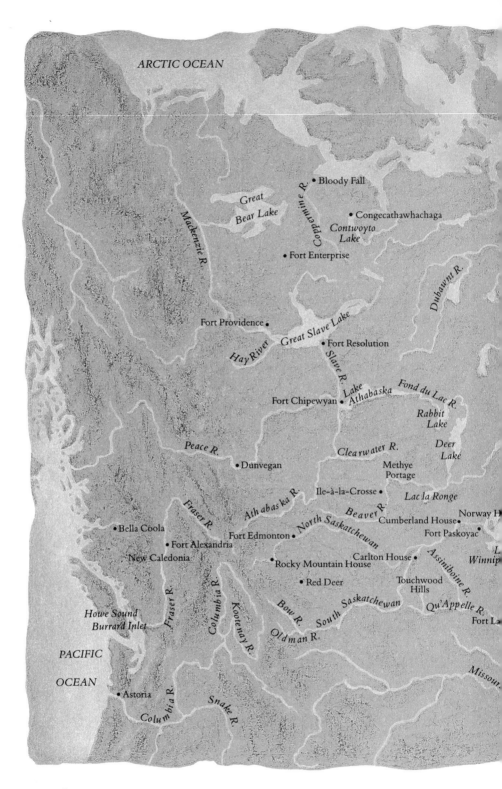

ARCTIC OCEAN

• Bloody Fall

Great
Bear Lake

Coppermine R.

• Congecathawhachaga

Contwoyto
Lake

Mackenzie R.

• Fort Enterprise

Dubawnt R.

Fort Providence •

Hay River

Great Slave Lake

• Fort Resolution

Slave R.

Fort Chipewyan •

Lake
Athabaska

Fond du Lac R.

Rabbit
Lake

Peace R.

Clearwater R.

Deer
Lake

• Dunvegan

Methye
Portage

Ile-à-la-Crosse •

Lac la Ronge

Athabaska R.

Fraser R.

Beaver R.

Cumberland House •

Norway H

• Bella Coola

North Saskatchewan

Fort Paskoyac •

• Fort Alexandria

Fort Edmonton •

New Caledonia

Carlton House •

Assiniboine R.

L

Winnip

• Rocky Mountain House

Fraser R.

Columbia R.

Kootenay R.

• Red Deer

Touchwood
Hills

Howe Sound
Burrard Inlet

Bow R.

South Saskatchewan

Qu'Appelle R.

Fort La

Oldman R.

PACIFIC

OCEAN

• Astoria

Columbia R.

Snake R.

Columbia R.

Missouri

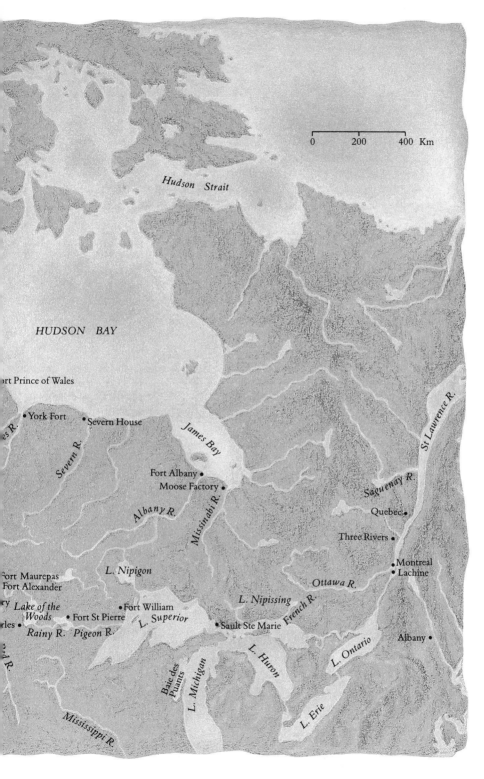

Hudson Strait

HUDSON BAY

ort Prince of Wales

es R.   • York Fort   • Severn House

Severn R.

James Bay

Fort Albany •
Moose Factory •

Albany R.

Missinabi R.

Saguenay R.

Quebec •

Three Rivers •

St Lawrence R.

L. Nipigon

ort Maurepas
Fort Alexander

y Lake of the
    Woods   • Fort St Pierre
rles •
  Rainy R. Pigeon R.

Fort William •

L. Superior

Ottawa R.

L. Nipissing

• Sault Ste Marie

French R.

Montreal
Lachine

L. Ontario

Albany •

Baie des
Puants

L. Michigan

L. Huron

L. Erie

d R.

Mississippi R.

0   200   400 Km

Part I: Discovery or Contact?

Pierre-Esprit Radisson   (c. 1640 – 1710)

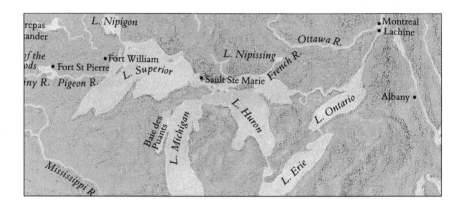

RADISSON was not French but Provençal, which perhaps explains his ambiguous record of service to the King of France. He came to New France as a youth, possibly with his half-sister, who married Médard Chouart Des Groseilliers, Radisson's partner in most of his explorations. This was the period of the Huron-Iroquois wars, which scattered the Huron from their settlements in Southern Ontario to territory in Michigan and northern Wisconsin, ravaged French settlements along the St Lawrence, and brought the fur trade to a halt. In 1651 Radisson was captured by the Iroquois and adopted into a native family, escaping in 1653 after many adventures. In 1657 his trip to the Jesuit mission at Onondaga led to another miraculous escape, which he probably engineered. And in 1659–60 he and his brother-in-law embarked on a remarkable journey to Lake Superior, which the latter had already visited in 1654–5. Radisson's account, writes Grace Lee Nute, 'is exact and convincing, with enthusiastic descriptions of the countryside and detailed reports of their strange, varied, and often harrowing experiences'. Among these are ritual cannibalism, acute famine, and a lengthy and genial account of the Feast of the Dead as it was celebrated among the Saulteur, Dakota, and Cree of the Lake Superior shore. Despite the spectacular cargo of furs with which they returned, the explorers received a cold welcome, and during the 1660s transferred their allegiance to England in search of the patronage that would make possible exploitation of the resources of the wonderful new country they had 'discovered'. The result was the foundation of the Hudson's Bay Company in 1670. Radisson wrote four journals of his early adventures at this time, all still extant in an English scribal manuscript. From its French characteristics, it appears Radisson may have been writing in the English he had learned during three years on the fringes of the Stuart court. Each of these journals presents a different aspect of the evolving explorer, but in all he remains the courageous, wily, alternatively self-mocking and self-aggrandizing figure of 'The Lake Superior Voyage'. Ever discontented with his masters, Radisson served both English and French in later life. His further adventures produced two more journals (both in French), and he died in London after three marriages, an elderly pensioner of the company which had its origin in the success of his youthful journey to Lake Superior.

Text: Bodleian Ms. Rawl. A 329; scribal contractions ('ye' for 'the' and '&' for 'and') have been expanded, punctuation and spelling slightly modernized, and repeated words omitted. Some emendations made in Gideon Scull's 1885 transcription have been retained, as have his paragraph divisions (the original is written continuously).

Radisson and Des Groseilliers are forbidden to travel to the interior

The spring following we weare in hopes to meet with some company, having ben so fortunat the yeare before.[1] Now during the winter whether it was that my brother[2] revealed to his wife what we had seene in our voyage and what we further intended, or how it came to passe, it was knowne, so much that the Father Jesuits weare desirous to find out away how they might gett downe the Castors[3] from the bay of the North by the sacgnes,[4] and so make themselves masters of that trade. They resolved to make a tryall as soone as the Ice would permitt them. So to discover our intentions they weare very earnest with me to ingage myselfe in that voyage, to the end that my brother would give over his: which I uterly denied them knowing that they could never bring it about; because I heard the wild men say that although the way be easy, the wildmen that are feed[5] att their doors would have hindred them, because they make a Livelyhood of that trade.

In my last voyage I tooke notice of that that goes to three hands,[6] which is first from the people of the North to another nation, that the French call squerells, and another nation that they call porquepicque, and from them to the Montignes and Algonquins that live in or about Quebucque; but the greatest hinderance is the scant of watter and the horrid torrents and want of Victuals, being no way to carry more then can serve fourteen dayes' or 3 weeks navigation on that River. Nevertheless the Fathers are gone with the Governors son of the three Rivers and six other French and twelve wildmen.

During that time we made our proportion [proposition?] to the governor of Quebuc[7] that we weare willing to ventur our Lives for the good of the Countrey, and goe to travell to the Remotest Countreys with two hurrons and that made their escape from the Iroquoits. They wished nothing more then to bee in those parts, where their wives and families wear[e], about the Lake of the stairing haire;[8] to that intent would stay untill august to see if any body would come from thence. My Brother, and I weare of one minde; and for more assurance my Brother went to Montroyall to bring those two men along. He came backe, being in danger. The Governor gives him leave, conditionally that he must carry two of his Servants along with him, and give them the moitie⁹ of the profit. My brother was vexed att such an unreasonable demand, to take Inexperted men to their ruine. All our knowledge and desire depended onely of this Last voyage; besides that the governor should compare two of his servants to us, that have ventured our lives so many years and maintained the Country with our generosity in the presence of all; neither was there one that had the Courage to undertake what wee have done. We made the Governor a slight answer, and tould him for our part we knewed what we weare; Discoverers before governors. If the wild men came downe, the way [was the same?] for them as for us, and that we should be glad to have the honnour of his Company, but not of that of his Servants, and that we weare both masters and Servants; The Governor was much displeased att this, and commanded us not to go without his Leave.¹⁰ We desired the Fathers to speake to him about it; our addresses were slight because of the shame was putt uppon them the yeare before of their retourne. Besides, they stayed for an opportunity to goe there themselves; for their designe is to further the Christian faith to the greatest glory of God, and indeed are Charitable to all those that are in distresse and needy, especialy to those that are worthy or industrious in their way of honesty. This is the truth, lett who he will speak otherwise, for this realy I know me selfe by experience. I hope I offend non to tell the truth. We are forc'd to goe back without doeing any thing.

The month of August that brings a Company of the Sault,¹¹ who weare come by the river of the three rivers with incredible paines, as they said. It was a Company of seven boats, we wrote the news of their arrivement to Quebuc. They send us word that they will stay untill the two fathers be turned from Sacquenes, that we should goe with them. An answer without reason. Necessity obliged us to goe. Those people are not to be inticed, for as soone as they have done their affaire they goe. The Governor of that place defends¹² us to goe. We tould him that the offense was pardonable because it was every ones interest nevertheless we knewed what we weare to doe, and that he should not be blamed for us, we made guifts to the wildmen, that wished with all their hearts that we might goe along with them. We told them that the governor minded to send servants with them, and forbids us to goe along with them. The wild men would not accept of their Company, but told us that they would stay for us two dayes in the Lake of St Peter in the grasse some Six Leagues from the three Rivers; but we did not lett them stay so long, for that very night my brother having the keyes of the Brough¹³ as being Captaine of the place, we embarqued ourselves.

We made ready in the morning, so that we went, three of us about midnight. Being come opposit to the fort: they aske who is there, my brother tells his name, every one knows what good services we had done to the Country, and loved us, the inhabitants as well as the souldiers. The sentery answers him God give you a good voyage. We went on the rest of that night. Att six in the morning we arrived to the appointed place, but found no body. We weare well armed, and had a good boat. We resolved to goe day and night to the river of the Meddows¹⁴ to overtake them. The wildmen did feare that it was somewhat else, but three Leagues beyond that of the fort of Richlieu,¹⁵ we saw them coming to us. We putt ourselves uppon our guards thinking they weare ennemy; but weare friends, and received us with Joy, and said that if we had not come in three dayes time, they would have sent their boats to know the reason of our delay. There we are in that river waiting for the night. Being come to the river of the medows, we did separat ourselves, three into three boats; the man that we have taken with us was putt into a boat of three men and a woman, but not of the same nation as the rest, but of one that we call sorcerers. They weare going downe to see some friends that lived with the Nation of the fire, that now liveth with the Ponoestigonce or the Sault.[16] It is to be understood that this river is divided much into streams very swift and small, before you goe to the river of Canada;[17] [because] of the great game that there is in it, the Ennemy is to be feared, which made us goe through these torrents. This could make any one afraid, who is inexperted in such voyages. . . .

French and Hurons battle against the Iroquois

The day following wee weare sett uppon by a Company of Iroquoits that fortified themselves in the passage where they waited of Octauack,[18] for they knewed of their going downe. Our wildmen seeing that there was no way to avoid them resolved to be together, being the best way for them to make a quick expedition, for the season of the yeare pressed us to make expedition, we resolved to give a combat. We prepared ourselves with Targetts [shields], Now the business was to make a discovery.[19] I doubt not but the ennemy was much surprised to see us so in number. The Councell was held, and resolution taken; I and a wildman wear appointed to goe and see their fort, I offered myselfe with a free will, to lett them see how willing I was to defend them: that is the onely way to gaine the hearts of those wildmen. We saw that their fort was environed with great rocks, that there was no way to mine it, because there weare no trees neere it. The mine[20] was nothing else but to cutt the nearest tree, and so by his fall make a bracke,[21] and so goe and give an assault. Their fort was nothing but trees one against another in a round, or square without sides.

The Ennemy seeing us come neere, shott att us but in vaine, for we have fore-warned ourselves before we came there. It was a pleasur to see our wildmen with their guns and arrows, which agreed not together, neverthelesse we told them when the[y] received a bracke their guns would be to no purpose, therefore to putt them by, and make use of their bows and arrows. The Iroquoits saw themselves putt to it, and the evident danger that they weare in, but to late except they would runne away, yett our wildmen weare better footemen then they. These weare Frenchmen that should give them good dirrections to overthrow them, resolved to speake for peace,[22] and throw necklaces of porcelaine[23] over the stakes of their fort. Our wildmen weare dazelled att such guifts, because that the porcelaine is very rare and costly in their Countrey, and then seeing themselves flattered with faire words, to which they gave eare, we trust them by force to putt their first design in Execution, but feared their lives and loved the porcelaine, seeing they had it without danger of any Life. They weare persuaded to stay till the next day, because now it was almost night. The Iroquoits makes their Escape. This occasion Lost, our consolation was that we had that passage free, but vexed for having lost that opportunity, and contrary wise weare contented of our side, for doubtlesse some of us had ben killed in the bataill.

The day following we embarqued ourselves quietly, being uppon our guards for feare of any surprize, for that ennemy's danger scarcely begane, who with his furour made himselfe so redoubted [dreaded], having ben there up and downe to make a new slaugter. This morning passes in assurance enough; in the afternoone the two boats that had orders to land some two hundred paces from the Landing place. One tooke onely a small bundle very light [and] tends to the other side of the Carriage [portage] imagining there to make the kettle boyle, having killed 2 staggs two houres agoe, and was scarce half way when he meets the Iroquoits, without doubt for that same business. I think both weare much surprized. The Iroquoits had a bundle of Castor that he left behind without much adoe, our wild men did the same they both runne away to their partners to give them Notice. By chance my brothers meets them in the way. The wild men seeing that they all weare frightned and out of breath they asked the matter and was told Nadouuée,[24] and so soone said, he letts fall his bundle that he had uppon his back into a bush, and comes backe where he finds all the wild men despaired. He desired me to encourag them, which I performed with all earnestnesse, we runned to the height of the Carriage. As we weare agoing they tooke their armes with all speed; in the way we found the bundle of Castors that the Ennemy had left. By this means we found out that they weare in a fright as wee, and that they came from the warrs of the upper Country, which we told the wildmen, so encouraged them to gaine the watter side to discover their forces, where wee no sooner came but two boats weare Landed and charged their guns, either to defend themselves or to sett uppon us. We prevented this affair by our diligence and shot att them with our bows and arrows, as with our guns.

They finding such an assault, immediately forsooke the place; they would have gone into their boats, but we gave them not so much time. They threwed themselves into the river to gaine the other side. This river was very narrow, so that it was very violent. We had killed and taken them all, if two boats of theirs had not come to their succour, which made us gave over to follow them, and looke to ourselves, for we knewed not the number of their men. Three of their men neverthelesse weare killed; the rest is on the other side of the river where there was a fort which was made long before. There they retired themselves with all speed. We passe our boats to augment our victory,[25] seeing that they weare many in number, they did what they could to hinder our passage, butt all in vaine, for we made use of the bundle of Castors that they left, which weare to us instead of gabbions,[26] for we putt them att the heads of our boats, and by that means gott ground in spight of their noses. They killed one of our men as we landed. Their number was not to resist ours; They retired themselves into the fort and brought the rest of their [men?] in hopes to save it. In this they were far mistaken, for we furiously gave an assault, not sparing time to make us bucklers, and made use of nothing else but of castors tyed together. So without any more adoe we gathered together. The Iroquoits Spared not their powder, but made more noise then hurt. The darknesse covered the earth, which was somewhat favorable for us, but to overcome them the sooner, we filled a barill full of gun powder, and having stoped the hole of it well and tyed it to the end of a long pole, being att the foote of the fort. Heere we lost three of our men; our machine did play with an execution.[27] I may well say that the ennemy never had seen the like. Moreover I tooke three or four pounds of powder, this I put into a rind of a tree, then a fusy[28] to have the time to throw the rind, warning the wildmen as soone as the rind made his execution that they should enter in and breake the fort upside down, with the hattchett and the sword in their hands.

In the meane time The Iroqoits did sing, exspecting death, or to their heels, att the noise of such a smoake and noise that our machines made with the slaughter of many of them; seeing themselves soe betrayed, they lett us goe free into their fort, that thereby they might save themselves; but having environed the fort, we are mingled pell mell, so that we could not know one another in that skirmish of blowes. There was such an noise that should terrifie the stoutest men. Now there falls a showre of raine and a terrible storme, that to my thinking there was something extraordinary that the Devill himselfe made that storme to give those men leave to escape from our hands, to destroy another time more of these innocents. In that darknesse every one looked about for shelter, not thinking of those braves that layd downe halfe dead. To pursue them, it was a thing impossible, yett doe believe that the ennemy was not far. As the storme was over, we came together, making a noise, and I am perswaded that many thought themselves Prisoners that weare att Liberty. Some sang their fatall song[29] albeit without any wounds, so that those that had the Confidence to come neare the others weare comforted by assuring them the victory and that the ennemy was routed. We presently make a great fire, and with all hast make upp the fort againe for feare of any surprize. We searched for those that weare missing. Those that weare dead and wounded weare visited. We found eleven of our Ennemy slain'd and two onely of ours, besides seaven were wounded, who in a short time passed all danger of life. While some weare busie in tying five of the ennemy that could not escape, the others visited the wounds of their Compagnions, who for to shew their Courage sung'd lowder then those that weare well. The sleepe that we tooke that night did not make our heads guidy, although we had need of reposeing. Many liked the occupation, for they filled their bellyes with the flesh of their ennemyes, we broiled some of it and kettles full of the rest.[30] We bourned our Comrades, being their coustome to reduce such into ashes, being slained in bataill. It is an honnour to give them such a buriall.

Att the brake of day we cooked what could accommodate us, and flung the rest away. The greatest marke of our victory was that we had ten heads and foure prisoners, whom we embarqued in hopes to bring them into our Countrey, and there to burne them att our owne leasures for the more satisfaction of our wives. We left that place of masacre with horrid Cryes. Forgetting the death of our parents, we plagued those infortunates. We plucked out their nailes one after another. . . .

The arrival at Lake Superior

Afterwards we entered into a straight which had ten leaugues in lenght full of Islands where we wanted not fish. We came after to a rapid,[31] that makes the seperation of the lake of the hurrons, that we calle Superior or upper, for that the wildmen hold it to be longer and broader besids a great many Islands, which maks appeare in a bigger extent. This rapid was formerly the dwelling of those with whome wee weare,[32] and consequently we must not aske them if they knew where the hare layed.[33] Wee made Cottages att our advantages, and found the truth of what those men had often [said], that if once we could come that that place, we should make good cheare of a fish that they call assickmack which signifieth a white fish. The beare, the Castors, and the Oriniack [moose] shewed themselves often but to their lost [loss]. Indeed it was to us like a terrestriall paradise after so long fastning [fasting], after so great paines that we had taken, [to] finde our selves so well, by choosing our dyet, and resting when we had a minde to it. Tis here that we must tast with pleasur a sweet bitt, we doe not aske for a good swace [sauce]; it's better to have it naturaly it is the way to distinguish the sweet from the bitter.

But the season was far spent, and [we] use diligence and leave that place so wished, which wee shall bewaile to the coursed Iroquoits; What hath that poore nation done to thee and being so Far from thy Country? Yett if they had the same Liberty that in former dayes they have had, we poore French should not goe further with our heads, except we had a strong army, those great Lakes had not so soone comed to our knowledge if it had not ben for those brutish people; two men had not found out the truth of these seas so cheape; the interest[34] and the glorie could not doe what terror doth att the end. We are a little better come to ourselves and furnished; we left that Inne without reckoning with our hoast. It is cheape when wee are not to put the hand to the purse, nevertheless we must pay out of Civility: the one gives thanks to the woods, the other to the river, the third to the earth, the other to the rocks that stayes the fish, in a word, there is nothing but kinekoiur[35] of all sorts; the encens of our Encens is not spared.[36] The weather was agreable when we began to navigat upon that great extent of watter. Finding it so calme and the aire so cleare we thwarted[37] in a pretty broad place, came to an Isle most delightfull for the diversity of its fruits; we called it the Isle of the foure beggars.[38] We arived about five of the Clocke in the after none that we came there, we sudainly [quickly] put the kettle to the fire, we reside there a while, and seeing all this while the faire weather and calme, we went from thence att tenne of the Clocke the same night to gaine the firme Lande, which was six leagues from us, where we arrived before day. Here we found a small river, I was so curious that I inquired my dearest friends the name of this streame, they named me it pauabickkomesibs, which signifieth a small river of copper. I asked him the reason, he told me, Come, and I shall shew thee the reason why. I was in a place which was not two hundred paces in the wood, where many peeces of copper weare uncovered, further he told me that the mountaine I saw was of nothing else. Seeing it so faire and pure, I had a minde to take a peece of it, but they hindred me, telling my brother, there was more where we weare to goe. . . .

From this place we went along the coasts, which are most delightfull, and wounderous for it's nature that made it so pleasant to the eye, the sperit, and the belly. As we went along we saw banckes of sand so high, that one of our wildmen went upp for our curiositie, being there, did shew no more then a Crow. That place is most dangerous when that there is any storme, being no Landing place so long as the sandy bancks are under watter, and when the wind blowes, that sand doth rise by a strang[e] kind of whirling that are able to choake the passengers [travellers], one day you will see fifty small mountaines att one side, and the next day, if the wind changes, on the other side. This putts me in mind of the great and vast wildernesses of Turkey Land, as the Turques makes their pylgrimages.[39]. . .

After this we came to a remarquable place. It's a banke of Rocks that the wild men made a sacrifice to, they calle it Nauitoucksinagoit which signifies the liknesse of the devill, they fling much tobacco and other things in its veneration.[40] It is a thing most incredible that that lake should be so boisterous, that the waves of it should have the strenght to doe what I have to say by this my discours, first that it's so high and Soe deepe that it's impossible to claime up to the point. There comes many sorte of birds that makes there Nest here, the goilants which is a white sea bird, of the bignesse of pigeon,[41] which makes me believe what the wildmen told me concerning the sea to be neare directly to the point; it's like a great Portall, by reason of the beating of the waves, the lower part of that oppening is as bigg as a tower, and grows bigger; in the going up there is I believe six acres of land; above it a shipp of five hundred tuns could passe by so bigg is the Arch. I gave it the name of the portall of St Peter, because my name is so called, and that I was the first Christian that ever saw it. There is in that place caves very deepe, caused by the same violence. We must looke to our selves, and take time with our small boats, the coast of rocks is five or six leagues and there scarce a place to putt a boat in assurance from the waves. When the lake is agitated the waves goeth in these concavities with force, and make a most horrible noise, most like the shooting of great guns. Some dayes afterwards we arrived to a very beautifull point of sand, where there are three beautifull Islands, that we called of the Trinity, there be three in triangle. From this place we discovered a bay very deepe, where a river empties it selfe with a noise for the quantitie and dept of the water.[42] We must stay there three dayes to wait for faire weather to make the Trainage which was about six leagues wide, soe done, we came to the mouth of a small river, where we killed some Oriniacks. We found meddows that weare squared, and ten leaugues as smooth as a boord; we went up some five leagues further, where we found some pools made by the Castors, we must breake them that we might passe. The sluce being broaken what a wounderfull thing to see the Industrie of that Animal, which had drowned more then twenty leagues in the grounds, and cutt all the Trees, having left non to make a fire if the Countrey should be dried up. Being come to the height, we must drague our boats over a trembling ground for the space of an howre. The ground became trembling by this means, the Castor drowning great soyles with dead water, herein growes mosse which is two foot thick or there abouts, and when you think to goe safe and dry, if you take not great care you sink downe to your head or to the midle of your body, when you are out of one hole you find your selfe in another. This I speake by experience for I me selfe have bin catched often. But the wildmen warned me which saved me, that is that when the mosse should breake under [me] I should cast my whole body into the watter on sudaine. I must with my hands hold the mosse, and goe soe like a frogg, then to draw my boat after me there was no danger. . . .

The fort on Chequamegon Bay

. . . we went on half a day before we could come to the Landing place, and wear forced to make another carriage a point of two leagues long and some sixty paces broad. As we came to the other sid we weare in a bay of 10 leagues about, if we had gone in. By goeing about that same point we passed a straight, for that point was very nigh the other side, which is a Cape very much elevated like piramides. That point should be very fitt to build and advantageous for the building of a fort, as we did the spring following.[43] In that bay there is a Chanell where we take great store of fishes, sturgeons of a vast biggnesse, and Pycks of seaven foot long. Att the end of this bay we Landed. The wildmen gave thanks to that which the[y] worship, we to God of Gods to see our selves in a place where we must leave our navigation and forsake our boats to undertake a harder peece of worke in hand, to which we are forced. The men told us that wee had five great dayes' Journeys before we should arrive where their wives weare. We foresee the hard task that we weare to undergoe by carrying our bundles uppon our backs. They weare used to it. Here every one for himselfe and God for all.

We finding ourselves not able to performe such a taske, and they could not well tell where to finde their wives, fearing least the Nadoueceronons had warrs against their nation and forced them from their appointed place, my brother and I we consulted what was best to doe, and declared our will to them, which was thus: Brethren, we resolve to stay here, being not accustomed to make any Cariage on our backs as yee are wont. Goe yee and Looke for your wives; we will build us a fort here. And seeing that you are not able to carry all your Marchandizes att once, we will keepe them for you, and will stay for you fourteen days. Before the time expired you will send to us if your wives be alive, and if you find them they will fetch what you leave here and what we have. For their paines they shall receive guifts of us. Soe you will see us in your Countrey. If they be dead, we will spend all, to be revenged, and will gather up the whole Countrey for the next spring, for that purpose to destroy those that weare the Causers of their death, and you shall see our strenght and vallour. Although there are seaven thousand fighting men in one Village, yoill see we will make them runne away, and you shall kill them to your best Liking by the very noise of our armes and our presence, who are the Gods of the earth among those people.

They woundered very much att our Resolution. The next day they went their way and we stay, for our assurance in the midst of many nations, being but two almost starved for want of food. We went about to make a fort of stakes, which was in this manner. Suppose that the watter side had ben in one end; att the same end there should be murtherers, and att need we made a bastion in a Triangle to defend us from an assault. The doore was neare the watter side, our fire was in the midle, and our bed on the right hand covered. There weare boughs of trees all about our fort layed a crosse, one uppon an other. Besides these boughs we had a long cord tyed with some small bells, which weare senteryes, finally, we made an ende of that fort in two dayes' time. . . .

The 12th day we perceived a far off some fifty yong men coming towards us, with some of our formest [foremost? former?] Compagnions. We gave them Leave to come into our fort, but they are astonied calling us every foot devills to have made such a machine.[44] They brought us victualls, thinking we weare halfe starved, but weare mightily mistaken, for we had more for them then they weare able to eate, having three score bustards and many sticks where was meate hanged plentifully. They offred to carry our baggage being come a purpose, but we had not so much marchandize as when they went from us, because we hid some of them that they might not have suspicion of us. We told them that for feare of the dayly multitud of people that came to see us for to have our goods would kill us. We therefore tooke a boat and putt into it our Marchandises this we brought farre into the bay, where we sunke them, biding our devill not to lett them to be wett nor rustied, nor suffer them to be taken away, which he promised faithlesse[45] that we should retourne and take them out of his hands; att which they weare astonished, believing it to be true as the Christians the Gospell. We hid them in the ground on the other sid of the river in a peece of ground. We told them that lye, that the[y] should not have suspicion of us. We made good cheere. They stayed there three dayes, during which time many of their wives came thither, and we treated them well, for they eat not fowle att all scarce because they know not how to catch them except with their arrowes. We putt a great many rind about our fort, and broake all the boats that we could have, for the frost would have broaken them or wild men had stolen them away. That rind was tyed all in length to putt the fire in it, to frighten the more these people for they could not approach it without being discovered. If they ventured att the going out we putt the fire to all the Torches, shewing them how we would have defended ourselves. We weare Cesars, being no body to contradict us, we went away free from any burden, whilest those poore miserables thought themselves happy to carry our Equipage, for the hope that they had that we should give them a brasse ring, or an awle or an needle.

A ceremonial meeting with the natives

There came above foure hundred persons to see us goe away from that place, which admired more our actions [than] the fools of Paris to see enter their King and the Infanta of Spaine, his spouse for they cry out, God save the King and Queene.[46] Those made horrid noise, and called Gods and Devils of the Earth and heavens. We marched fowre dayes through the woods. The Country is beautifull, with very few mountaines, the woods cleare. Att last we came within a leaugue of the Cabbans[47] where we layed that the next day might be for our entry. We 2 poore adventurers for the honnour of our Countrey, or of those that shall deserve it from that day. The nimblest and stoutest went before to warne before the people that we should make our entry tomorow. Every one prepares to see what they never before have seene. We weare in cottages which weare neare a litle lake some eight leagues in Circuit. Att the watter side there weare abundance of litle boats made of trees that they have hallowed, and of rind.

The next day we weare to embarque in them, and arrived att the village by watter, which was composed of a hundred Cabans without pallasados [palisades, surrounding walls]. There is nothing but cryes, the women throw themselves backwards uppon the ground thinking to give us tokens of friendship and of wellcome. We destinated[48] three presents, one for the men one for the women, and the other for the children, to the end that they should remember that journey, that we should be spoaken of a hundred years after, if other Europians should not come in those quarters and be liberal to them, which will hardly come to passe. The first present was a kettle, two hattchetts, and six knives and a blade for a sword, the kettles was to call all nations that weare their friends to the feast which is made for the remembrance of the death.[49] That is, they make it once in seaven years; it's a renewing of friendshippe. I will talke further of it in the following discours. The hattchetts weare to encourage the yong people to strengthen them selves in all places, to preserve their wives, and shew themselves men by knocking the heads of their ennemyes with the said hattchetts, the knives weare to shew that the French weare great and mighty and their Confederats and ffriends. The sword was to signifie that we would be masters both of peace and warrs, being willing to healpe and relieve them, and to destroy our Ennemyes with our armes. The second guift was of two and twenty awles, fifty needles, two gratters [graters] of castors, two Ivory Combs and two wooden ones, with red painte, six looking glasses of tin. The awles signifieth to take good courage, that we should keepe their lives, and that they with their husbands should come downe to the French when time and season should permitt, the needles for to make them robes of Castor, because the French loved them. The two gratters weare to dresse the skins; the combes, the paint, to make themselves beautifull; the looking-glasses to admire themselves. The third guift was of brasse rings, of small bells, and rasades[50] of divers coulours, and given in this maner. We sent a man to make all the children come together. When we weare there we throw these things over their heads. You would admire what a beat[51] was among them, every one striving to have the best. This was done oppon this consideration that they should be alwayes under our protection, giving them wherewithall to make them merry and remember us when they should be men.

This done, we are called to the Councell of welcome and to the feast of ffriendshipp, afterwards to the danceing of the heads. But before the danceing, we must mourne for the deceased, and then, for to forgett all sorrow to the dance. We gave them foure small guifts that they should continue such ceromonyes, which they tooke willingly, and did us good, that gave us authority among the whole nation. We knewed their councels, and made them doe whatsoever we thought best. This was a great advantage for us, you must think. Amongst such a rawish kind of people of [a?] guift is much, and well bestowed, and liberality much esteemed, but prodigalitie is not in esteeme, for they abuse it being brutish. Wee have ben using such ceromonyes three whole dayes, and weare lodged in the Cabban of the chiefest Captains[52] who came with us from the French. We liked not the Company of that blind,[53] therefore left him; he wondred at this, but durst not speake because we weare demigods. We came to a cottage of an ancient witty man, that had had a great familie and many Children, his wife old neverthelesse handsome. They weare of a nation called Malhonmines, that is, the nation of oats, graine that is much in that Country.[54] I tooke this man for my faather and the woman for my mother, soe the children consequently brothers and sisters; They adopted me. I gave every one a Guift, and they to mee.

Famine in the forest

Having so disposed of our bussinesse: The winter comes on, that warns us the snow begins to fall, soe we must retire from this place to seeke our Living in the woods. Every one getts his equipage ready, so away we goe, but not all to the Same place. Two, three att the most, went one way, and so of another. They have so done because victuals weare scant for all in a place but lett us where we will, we cannot escape the myghty hand of God that disposes as he pleases, and who chaste[n]s us as a good and a common loving father and not as our sins doe deserve. Finaly wee depart one from an other. As many as we weare in number, we are reduced to a small Company. We appointed a Rendezvous after two months and a half, to take a New road, and an advice what we should doe. During the s[ai]d tarme [term] we sent messengers every where to give speciall notice to all manner of Persons and Nation that within five moons the feast of death was to be celebrated, and that wee should apeare together, and explaine what the devill should command us to say, and then present them presents of peace and union; Now we must live on what God sends. and warre against the bears in the meane time, for we could aime att nothing else, which was the cause that we had no great cheere. . . .

. . . so the famine was among great many that had not Provided before hand, and live upon what they gett that day, never thinking for the next. It grows wors and wors dayly.

To augment our misery we receive news of the Octauaks, who weare about a hundred and fifty with their families. They had a quarell with The hurrons in the Isle where we had come from some years before[55] in the Lake of the stairing hairs, and came purposly to make warrs against them the next summer. But lett us see if they brought us anything to Subsist withall. But are worst provided then we; having no huntsmen, they are reduced to famine. But, ô Cursed Covetousnesse, what art thou going to doe. It should be farr better to see a Company of Rogues perish then see our selves in danger to perish, by that scourg so cruell. Hearing that they have had knives and hattchets the victualls of their poore children is taken away from them yea what ever they have those doggs must have their share. They are the coursedest, unablest the unfamous and cowarliest people that I have seen amongst fowr score Nations that I have frequented. O yee poore people, you shall have their booty, but you shall pay dearly for it. Every one cryes out for hungar; the women become baren, and drie like Wood.[56] You men must eate the cord, being you have no more strenght to make use of the bow, children, you must die. French, you called yourselves Gods of the earth that you should be feared, for your interest; notwithstanding you shall tast of the bitternesse, and too happy if you escape. Where is the time past? Where is the

plentinesse that yee had in all places and Countreys. Here comes a new family of
these poore people dayly to us, halfe dead for they have but the skin and boans. How
shall we have strenght to make a hole in the Snow to lay us downe seeing we have it
not to hale our racketts [snowshoes] after us nor to cutt a litle wood to make a fire to
keepe us from the rigour of the cold which is extreame in those Countreyes in its
season. Oh! if the musick that we heare could give us recreation. We wanted not any
lamentable musick nor sad specta[c]le. In the morning the husband looks uppon his
wife, the Brother his sister, the cozen the cozen, the Oncle the nevew that weare for
the most part found deade. They languish with cryes and hideous noise that it was
able to make the haire starre on the heads that have any apprehension. Good God
have mercy on so many poore innocent people, and of us that accknowledge thee,
that having offended thee punishes us. But wee are not free of that cruell Execu-
tioner. Those that have Any life seeketh out for roots which could not be done
without great difficultie, the earth being frozen two or three foote deep and the snow
five or six above it. The greatest subsistance that we can have is of rind tree[57] which
growes like Ivie about the trees, but to swallow it, we cutt the stick some two foot
long, tying it in faggot [bundles] and boyle it, and when it boyls one houre or two the
rind or skinne comes off with ease, which we take and drie it in the smoake and then
reduce it into powder betwixt two grainestoans, and putting the Kettle with the same
watter uppon the fire, we make it a kind of broath, which nourished us, but becam
thirstier and drier then the woode we eate.

The two first weeke we did eate our doggs. As we went backe uppon our stepps for to
gett any thing to fill our bellyes, we weare glad to gett the boans and carcasses of the
beasts that we killed; and happy was he, that could gett what the other did throw away
after it had been boyled three or fowre times to gett the substance out of it. We
contrived to another plott, to reduce to powder those boanes, the rest of Crows and
doggs. So putt all that together halfe foot within ground, and so makes a fire uppon it.
We covered all that very well with earth, soe feeling the heat, and boyled them againe
and gave more froth than before. In the next place, the skins that weare reserved to
make us shoose, cloath, and stokins, yea, most of the skins of our Cottages, the castors'
skins, where the children beshit them above a hundred times, We burned the haire on
the Coals. The rest goes downe throats eating heartily these things most abhorred. We
went so eagerly to it that our gumms did bleede lik[e] one newly wounded. The wood
was our food the rest of sorrowfull time. Finaly we became the very Images of death.
We mistook ourselves very often taking the living for the dead and the Dead for the
living. We wanted strenght to draw the living out of the Cabans, or if we did when we
could, it was to putt them fowr paces in the snow. Att the end the wrath of God begins
to appease it selfe, and pityes his poore Creatures. If I should expresse all that befell us
in that strange accidents, a great volume would not containe it. Here are above five
hundred dead, men, women, and children. It's time to come out of such miseryes. Our
bodyes are not able to hold out any further.

After the storme, Calme comes. But stormes favoured us, being that calme kills us.
Here comes a wind and raine, that putts a new life in us, The snow falls, the forest
cleers itselfe, att which sight, those that had strings left in their bowes takes courage to

use it. The weather continued so three dayes that we needed no racketts more, for the snow hardrned much. The Small staggs are [as] if they weare stakes in it[58] after they made seaven or eight capers. It's an easy matter for us to take them and cutt their throats with our knives. Now we see ourselves a litle fournished, but yett have not payed, ffor it cost many their lives. Our gutts became very straight by our long fasting, that they could not containe the quantity that some putt in them. I cannot omitt the pleasant thoughts of some of them wildmen. Seeing my brother all wayes in the same Condition, they said that some Devill brought him wherewithall to eate, but if they had seene his body they should be of another oppinion. The beard that covered his face made as if he had not altered his face. For me that had no beard[59] they said I loved them, because I [lived] as well as they. From the second day we began to walke.

There came two men from a strange Countrey who had a dogg, the buissinesse was how to catch him cunningly, knowing well those people love their be[a]sts. Neverthelesse wee offred guifts: but they would not, which made me stuborne. That dogge was very l[e]ane, and as hungry as we weare, but the masters have not suffered so much. I went one night neere that same Cottage to doe what discretion permitts me not to speake. Those men weare Nadoueserous.[60] They weare much Respected that no body durst not offend them: being that we weare uppon their land with their leave. The dogg comes out, not by any smell, but by good Likes.[61] I take him and bring him a litle way. I stabbed him with my dagger. I brought him to the Cottage, where [he] was broyled like a pigge and cut in peeces gutts and all, soe every one of the family had his share. The snow where he was killed was not lost, for one of our Company, went and gott it to season the kettle. We began to looke better dayly. We gave the rendezvous to the convenientest place to celebrat that great feast. . . .

The Feast of the Dead

The time was nigh that we must goe to the rendezvous. This was betwixt a small Lake and a medow.[62] Being arrived most of ours weare allready in their Cottages. In three dayes time, there arrived Eighte[e]n severall nations, and came privatly to have done the sooner. As we became to the number of five hundred we held a Councell; then the shouts and Cryes and the encouragments weare proclaimed, that a fort should be builded. They went about the worke and made a large fort; it was about six hundred and three score paces in lenght and six hundred in breadth: so that it was a square. There we had a brooke that came from the lake and emptied itselfe in those medows which had more then fowre leaugues in lenght. Our fort might be Seen afar off, and on that side most delightfull: for the great many staggs that took the boldnesse to be carried by quarters where att other times they made good cheare.[63]

In two dayes this was finished. Soone 30 yong men of the nation of the beefe arrived there, having nothing but bows and arrows, with very short garments, to be the Nimbler in chassing the stagges.[64] The Iron of their arrows weare made of staggs pointed horens very neatly. They weare all proper men, and dressed with paint. They weare the discoverers and the foreguard. We kept a round place in the midle of our Cabban, and covered it with long poles with skins over them that we might have a shelter to keepe us from the snow. The cottages weare all in good order in each ten, twelve Companies or families. That Company was brought to that place where there was wood layd for the fires. The snow was taken away, and the earth covered with deale tree bows.[65] Severall kettles weare brought there full of meate. They rested and eat above five howres without speaking one to another. The Considerablest of our Companyes went and made Speeches to them. After one takes his bow and shoots an arrow, and then cryes aloud, there speaks some few words, saying that they weare to lett them know the Elders of their Village weare to come the morrow to Renew the friendship and to make it with the French. And that a great many of their yong people came and brought them some part of their wayes to take their advice for they had a minde to goe against the Christinos[66] who weare ready for them: and they in like manner to save their wives and Children. They weare Scattered in many Cabbans that night exepecting those that weare to Come. To that purpose there was a vast large place prepared some hundred places [paces?] from the fort, where every thing was ready for the receiving of those persons. They weare to sett their tents that they bring uppon their backs. The Pearches [poles or stakes] weare putt out and planted as we received the news. The snow putt aside, and the boughs of trees covered the ground.

The day following they arrived with an incredible pomp. This made me thinke of the Intrance that the Polanders did in Paris:[67] saving that they had not so many Jewells, but instead of them they had so many feathers. The first weare yong people with their bows and arrows and Buckler on their shoulders, uppon which weare represented all manner of figures: according to their knowledge, as of the sun and moone, of terrestriall beasts, about its feathers very artificialy [artfully] painted. Most of the men their faces weare all over dabbed with severall collours. Their hair turned up, Like a Crowne: and weare Cutt very even, but rather so burned for the fire is their Cicers. They leave a tuff of haire upon their Crowne of their heads, tye it, and putt att the end of it some small pearles or some Turkey stones[68] to bind their heads. They have a role commonly made of a snakes skin where they tye severall Bears Paws, or give a forme to some bitts of buff's [buffalo] horns, and put it about the said role. They grease them selves with very thick grease and mingle it in reddish earth, which they bourne, as we our breeks:[69] With this stuffe they gett their haire to stand up. They cutt some downe of Swan or other fowle that hath a white feather and cover with it the Crowne of their heads. Their ears are pierced in five places. The holes are so bigg that your little finger might passe through. They have yellow waire that they made with Copper, made like a starre or a half moone, and there hang it. Many have Turkeys. They are cloathed with Oriniack and staggs skins, but very light. Every one had the skin of a crow hanging att their guirdles. Their stokens all inbrodered with pearles and with their own Porkepick[70] worke. They have very handsome shoose laced very thick all over with a peece sowen att the side of the heele, which was of a haire of Buff, which trailed above half a foot upon the earth, or rather on the snow. They had swords and knives of a foot and a halfe long, and hattchetts very ingeniously done, and clubbs of wood made like backswords, some made of a round head that I admired it. When they kille their ennemy they cutt off the tuffe of haire and tye it about their armes. After [over] all, they have a white robe made of Castors skins painted. Those having passed through the midle of ours that weare ranged att every side of the way. The Elders came with great gravitie and modestie covered with buff coats which hung downe to the grounde. Every one had in his hand a pipe of Councell sett with precious jowells. They had a sack on their shoulders, and that that holds it grows in the midle of their stomacks, and on their shoulders. In this sacke all the world is inclosed.[71] Their face is not painted, but their heads dressed as the foremost. Then the women laden like unto so many mules, their burdens made a greater shew then they themselves, but I supose the weight was not equipolent to its bignesse. They weare conducted to the appointed place, where the women unfolded their bundles, and flang their skins whereof their tents are made, so that they had howses [in] lesse then half an houre.

After they rested, they came to the biggest Cabbane constituted for that purpose There weare fires kindled. Our Captaine made a speech of thanksgiving, which should be long to writ it. We are called to the councell of New come Cheifes: where we came in great pompe, as you shall heare. First they come to make a sacrifice to the French, being Gods and masters of all things as of peace as warrs, making the knives the hattchetts, and the kettles rattle, etc.[72] That they came purposely to putt themselves under their protection: moreover, that they came to bring them back againe to their Country, having by their means destroyed their Ennemyes abroad and neere. So said, they present us with guifts of Castors skins, assuring us that the mountains weare elevated, the valleys risen, the ways very smooth, the bows of trees cutt downe to goe with more ease, and bridges erected over Rivers, for not to wett our feete. That the dores of their villages, Cottages of their wives and Daughters, weare upon at any time to receive us, being wee kept them alive by our marchandises. The second guift was, that they shoold die in their alliance, and that to certifie to all Nations by continuing the peace, and weare willing to receive and assist them in their Countrey, being well satisfied they weare come to celebrat the feast of the dead. The third guift was for to have one of the doors of the fort opened, if neede required, to receive and keepe them from the Christinos that come to destroy them. Being allwayes men,[73] and the heavens made them so, that they weare obliged to goe before to defend their Country and their wives, which is the dearest thing they had in the world, and in all times they weare esteemed stout and true souldiers, and that yett they would make it appeare,[74] by going to meet them, and that they would not degenerat, but shew by their actions that they weare as valiant as their fore fathers. The fourth guift was presented to us, which [was] of buff skins, to Desire our assistance, for being the masters of their lives, and could dispose of them as we would, as well of the peace as of the warrs, and that we might very well see that they did well to goe defend their owne Countrey that the true means to gett the victory was to have a thunder. They meant a gune, calling it miniskoick.

The speech being finished, they intreated us to be att the feast. We goe presently back again to fournish us with woaden bowls. We made fowre men to carry our guns afore us, that we charged of powder alone, because of their unskillfullnesse that they might have killed their fathers. We each of us had a paire of Pistoletts and sword, a daggar; we had a role of porkepick a bout our heads, which was as a Crowne, and two litle boyes that carryed the vessells that we had most need of: this was our dishes and our spoons. They made a place higher and most elevate knowing our Customs,[75] in the midle for us to sitt where we had the men lay our armes. Presently comes fowre Elders, with the calumet kindled in their hands; they present the Candles[76] to us to Smoake, and fowre beautifull maids that went before us carrying bears' skins to putt under us. When we weare together, an old man rises and throws our Callumet att our feet, and bids them, taike of the kettles from of the fire, and spoake, that he thanked the Sun, that never was aday to him so happy as when he saw those terrible men, whose words make the earth quacke, and Sang a while, having ended, came and covers us with his vestment and all naked except his feet and leggs, he saith, yee are Masters over us dead or alive you have the power over us: and may dispose of us as your pleasur. So done, takes the Callumet of the feast, and brings it; so a maiden brings us a coale of fire to kindle it. So done, we rose and [one? some?] of us begins to Sing: we had the Interpreter to tell them we should Save and keepe their lives, takeing them for our brethren, and to testify that, we shot of all our artillery which was of twelve guns. We draw our swords and long knives to our defence if need should require, which put the men in Such a terror that they knewed not what was best to run or stay. We throw a handfull of powder in the fire to make a greater noise, and Smoake.

Our Songs being finished, we begin our teeth to worke. We had there a kinde of rice, much like oats.[77] It growes in the watter in three or foure foote deepe. There is a god that shews himselfe in every Country Almighty full of goodnesse and the Preservation of those poore people who knoweth him not. They have a particular way to gather up that graine. Two takes aboat and two sticks, by which they gett the eare downe and gett the Corne out of it. Their boat being full, they bring it to a fitt place to dry it, and that is their food for the most part of the winter, and doe dresse it thus. For each man a handfull of that they putt in the pott. That swells so much that it can suffice a man. After the feast was over, there comes two maidens bringing wherewithall to smoake the one the pipes, the other the fire. They offered first to one of the Elders, that Satt downe by us. When he had smoaked, he bids them give it us. This being done, we went back to our fort as we came.

The day following, we made the principall Persons come together to answer to their guifts. Being come with great solemnity there we made our Interpreter tell them, that we weare come from the other side of the great salted lake, not to kill them but to make you live, accknowledging you for our brethren and Children whom we will love hence forth as our owne. Then we gave them a kettle.[78] The second guift, was to encourage them in all their undertakings, telling them that we liked men that generously defended themselves against all their Ennemyes, and as we weare Masters of peace and warrs we are to dispose the affairs. That we would see an universall peace all over the earth and that this time we could not goe and force the nations that weare yett further to condescend and submitt to our will, but that we would see the neighbouring Countreys in peace and Union. That the Christinos weare our brethren, and have frequented them many winters; that we adopted them for our Children and tooke them under our protextion; that we should send them Ambassadors, that I my self should make them come, and conclude a genrall peace; that we weare sure of their obedience to us; that the ffirst that should breake the peace, we would be their Ennemys, and would reduce them to powder with our heavenly fire. That we had the word of the Christinos as well as theirs, and our thunders should serve us to make warrs against those that would not submitt to our will and desire, which was to see them good ffreinds to goe and make warrs against the upper nations, that doth not know us as yett. The guift was of six hatchetts. The third was to oblige them to receive our propositions, likwise the Christinos to lead them to the dance of Union which was to be celebrated at the death's feast, and banquett of kindred. If they would continue the warrs, that was not the meanes to see us againe in their Countrey. The fourth was that we thanked them, ffor makeing us a free passage through their Countreys. The guift was of two dozen of knives; The last was of smaller triffles, six gratters 2 dozen of Awles, two dozen of Needles 6 dozens of looking-glasses made of tine [tin], a dozen of litle bells six Ivory Combs with a litle Vermillion. Butt ffor to make a recompence to the good old man that spake so favourably we gave him a hattchett and to the Elders each a blade for a sword, and to the two maidens that served us two necklaces, which putt about their necks, and two braceletts for their armes. The last guift was in generall for all the women to love us, and give us to eat when we should come to their Cottages. The Company gave us great hohoho that is thanks. Our wildmen made others for their Interrest.[79]

A Company of about 50 weare dispatched to warne the Christinos of what we have done: I went my self where we arrived the third day early in the morning. I was received with great demonstration of ffriendshippe; all that day we feasted danced and sing. I compared that place before to the Buttery of Paris,[80] for the great quantity of meat that they use to have there, but now will compare it to that of London. There I received guifts of all sorts of meate, of grease more then twenty men could carry. The Custome is not to deface[81] any thing that they present. There weare above six hundred men in a fort with a great deale of baggage on their shoulders, and did draw it upon light slids made very neatly. I have not seen them att their entrance ffor the snow blinded mee. Coming back, we passed a lake hardly frozen [frozen hard], and the sun [shone upon it?] for the most part, ffor I looked a while steadfastly on it so I was troubled with this seaven or eight dayes.

The meane while that we are there, arrived above a thousand, that had not ben therein but for those two redoubted nations that weare to see them doe what they never before had, a difference:[82] which was executed with a great deale of mirth. I ffor feare of being invied I will obmitt,[83] onely that there weare playes mirths, and bataills for sport, goeing and coming with cryes, each plaid his part. In the publick place the women danced with melody. The yong men that indeavoured to gett a pryse, indeavoured to clime up a great post very smooth and greased with oyle of Beare and Oriniack grease. The stake was att least of fifteen foot high. The price was a knife or other thing. We layd the stake there, but whoso could catch it should have it. The feast was made to eate all up. To honnour the feast many men and women did burst. Those of that place coming backe, came in sight of those of the village or fort made postures in similitud of warrs. This was to discover the ennemy by signs any that should doe soe we gave orders to take him or kill him and take his head off; The Prisoner to be tyed, to fight in retreating; To pull an arrow out of the body. To exercise and strike with a Clubbe, a buckler to their feete, and take it if neede requireth, and defende him selfe if need requirs from the Ennemy. Being in sentery to heark the Ennemy that comes neere and to heare the better lay him downe on the side. These postures are playd while the drums beate. This was a serious thing, without speaking, except by noddyng or gestures. Their drums weare earthen potts full of watter, covered with staggs skin. The sticks like hammers for the purpose. The Elders have bomkins to the end of their staves, full of small stones, which makes a ratle, to which yong men and women goe in a Cadance. The Elders are about these potts beating them and singing. The women also by [nearby] having a nose gay in their hands, and dance very modestly, not lifting much their feete from the ground, keeping their heads downewards makeing a sweet harmony. We made guifts for that while fourteen days' time. Every one brings the most exquisit things to shew what his Country affoards. The renewing of their alliances, the mariages according to their Countrey Coustoms are made; also the visit of the boans of their deceased ffriends ffor they keepe them and bestow them uppon one another. We sang in our language as they in theirs, to which they gave greate attention. We gave them severall guifts, and received many. They bestowed upon us above 3 hundred robs [robes] of Castors out of which we brought not five to the ffrench being [too] far in the Countrey. This feast ended, every one retourns to his Countrey well satisfied. . . .

Radisson alleges that he has visited Hudson Bay

We went from Isle to Isle all that Summer.[84] We pluckt abundance of Ducks as of all other sort of fowles; we wanted nor fish nor fresh meate. We weare well beloved, and weare overjoyed that we promised them to come with such Shipps as we invented.[85] This place hath a great store of Cows [Caribou]. The wildmen kill them not except for necessary use. We went further in the bay to see the place that they weare to passe that summer. That river comes from the Lake and empties itselfe in the River of Sagnes, called Tadousack, which is a hundred leaugues in the great river of Canada, as where we weare in the Bay of the North.[86] We left in this place our Marks and Rendezvous. The wildmen that brought us defended us above all things, if we would come directly to them that we should be no means Land, and to goe to the river to the other Sid that is to the North towards the Sea,[87] telling us that those people weare very Treacherous. Now whether they tould us this out of pollicy, Least we should not come to them ffirst, and so be deprived of what they thought to gett from us [I know not]. In that you may see that the envy and envy raigns every where amongst poore Barborous wild people as att Courts.[88] They made us a mapp of what we could not see, because the time was nigh to reape among the bustards and Ducks. . . .

This is a wandring nation, and containeth a Vaste Countrey.[89] In winter they Live in the Land for the hunting sake, and in Summer by the watter for fishing. They never are many together, for feare of wronging one another. They are of a good Nature, and not great whore Masters,[90] having but one wife, and are [more] satisfied then any others that I knewed. They cloath themselves all over with Castors skins in winter, in summer of staggs skins. They are the best huntsmen of all America, and scorns to Catch a Castor in a Trappe. The circumjacent nations goe all naked, when the season permitts it. But this have more modestie, for they put a piece of Copper made like a finger of a glove, which they use before their Nature. They have the same tenents [tenets, beliefs] as the nation of the beefe, and their apparell from topp to to toe. The women are tender and delicat, and takes as much paines as slaves.[91] They are of more acute wits then the men for the men are fools, but diligent about their worke. They kill not the yong Castors, but leave them in the water, being that they are sure that they will take him againe, which no other nation doth. They burne not their prisoners, but knock them in the head, or slain them with arrows, saying it's not decent for men to be so cruell. They have a stone of Turquois from the nation of the buff and beefe, with whome they had warrs. They pollish them and give them the forme of pearle long flatt round, and [hang] them at their nose. They [find] greene stones, very fine, att the side of the same bay of the sea to the norwest. There is a nation called among themselves neuter,[92] they speake the beefe and Christinos' speech, being friends to both. Those poore people could not tell what to give us, they weare overjoyed when we sayd, we should bring them commodities. We went up on another river, to the upper Lake.[93]. . .

. . . All the circumjacent neighbours do incourage us, saying that they would venter their lives with us, for which we weare much overjoyed to see them so freely disposed to goe along with us. Here nothing but Courage. Brother, doe not lye for the French will not believe thee. All men of courage and valour, lett them fetch commodities, and not stand lazing and be a beggar in the Cabbane. It is the way to be beloved of women, to goe and bring them withall to be joyfull. We present guifts to one and to another for to warne them to that end that we should make the earth quake, and give terrour to the Iroquoits if they weare so bold as to shew themselves. . . .

The explorers return to Québec

The Governour, seeing us come back with a considerable summe for our own particuler [share] and seeing that his time was expired, and that he was to goe away, made use of that excuse to doe us wrong, and to enrich himselfe with the goods that wee had so dearly bought. And by our meanes wee made the Country to subsist, that without us had been I beleeve oftentimes quite undone and ruined, and the better to say at his last breading, no Castors no ship, and what to doe without necessary commodities.[94] He made also my brother Prisoner for not having observed his Orders and to be gone without his leave although one of his Letters[95] made him blush for shame not knowing what to say, but that he would have some of them at what price soever, that he might the better maintain his Coach and horses at Paris. He fined us four thousand pounds to make a Fort at the three Rivers,[96] telling us for all manner of satisfaction that he would give us leave to put our Coat of Armes upon it, and moreover six thousand pounds for the Country, saying that wee should not take it so strangely and so bad, being wee were inhabitants and did intend to finish our dayes in the same country with our Relations and Freinds.[97] But the Bougre[98] did grease his chopps with it, and more made us pay a Custome which was the 4*th* part which came to fourteen thousand pounds, so that wee had left but 46 thousand pounds, and took away 24000£. Was not he a Tyrant to deal so with us after wee had so hazarded our lives and having brought in lesse then 2 years by that Voyage as the Factors of the said Country said, between 40 and 50 thousand pistolls[99] For they spoke to me in this manner, in which Country have you been? from whence doe you come? For wee never saw the like. From whence did come such excellent Castors, since your arrivall is come into our Magazin very near six hundred thousand pounds Tournois,[100] of that filthy [stinking] Merchandize which will be prized like Gold in France. And them were the very words that they said to me.

Notes

[1] The yeare before: the Superior voyage took place in 1659–60; this probably means the 1657–8 journey to Onondaga which Radisson undertook with Father Paul Raguenau.

[2] Médard Chouart Des Groseilliers (1618–1696?), who was married to Radisson's half-sister Marguerite Hayet. His diaries were lost in a canoe spill on their third voyage; if he ever wrote a journal, it has not been found.

[3] Radisson always uses the French word *castor* rather than the English 'beaver'. The many other French usages (see below) suggest that the manuscript is not a translation but is a copy of one written in English by a Francophone, possibly Radisson himself.

[4] The Bay of the North: Hudson Bay; Sagnes: the Saguenay river. Radisson attempts to describe this route later on (see below and note 86).

[5] Are feed: either 'feed' as in 'rewarded by the French', or 'fed', receiving food from them; in effect, the natives living near the French settlements.

[6] That that goes to three hands: trade which passes through the hands of three 'nations' before reaching the French.

[7] Pierre Voyer D'Argenson (1625–1709), governor of New France from 1658–61; his impending departure from that post is mentioned by Radisson near the end of the 'Lake Superior Voyage'.

[8] Lake of the stairing haire: Lake Michigan, where the Ottawa (Odawa) lived; they wore their hair in a brush turned up, and the French called them 'cheveux relevés'.

[9] Moitie: a 50% share.

[10] French law, which the governor had to enforce, forbade the French to travel to the interior without permission. Des Groseilliers was duly arrested when the two 'discoverers' returned (see below).

[11] A company of the Sault: the Saulteur, a branch of the Ojibwa.

[12] Defends: Fr. *défendre*, to forbid.

[13] Borough, small town (possibly from Fr. *bourgade?*).

[14] Rivière des Prairies, the channel running between Montréal Island and Isle Jésus, named after the Sieur Des Prairies who discovered it.

[15] The fort of Richlieu: built in 1642 at the mouth of Rivière Richelieu (formerly Sorel River).

[16] The sorcerers: Nipissings; the Nation of the Fire: Algonquian-speaking Mascouten, called Assistaeronon or 'fire people' by the Hurons; Ponoestigonce: Pawitikong, 'of the rapids'.

[17] The St Lawrence.

[18] Waited of Octauack: waited for the Ottawas (Odawa).

[19] The business was to make a discovery: now our job was to reveal (Fr. *se découvrir*) ourselves.

[20] Fr. *mine*, plot or secret; in the previous sentence Radisson uses the same word in its English sense of 'undermine, dig under'.

[21] Bracke: an obstacle, as in 'windbreak'. A few lines later 'bracke' seems to mean 'obstacle' in a more general sense, i.e., 'repulse' or 'rebuff'.

[22] 'The French, who should have shown them how to defeat the Iroquois, preferred a peaceful solution.'

[23] Porcelaine: made of conch or cowrie shells; such necklaces were highly valued.

[24] Nadouuée: Natowe, meaning 'great serpents' (i.e., enemies) in various Algonquin dialects (see n. 60, below).

[25] We passe our boats: we pressed onward in our boats.

[26] Wicker cylinders, filled with earth and used in building fortifications.

[27] Play with an execution: possibly from the Fr. *faire jouer*, to set in motion.

[28] Fusy: usually a musket, specifically an arquebus, which was fired with a fuse, but here Radisson appears to mean the fuse itself.

[29] Fatall song: death song.

[30] This sounds as if Radisson too feasted on the enemy's flesh. His unequivocal use of the first person plural here appears quite unselfconscious, though he may of course have been trying to shock his readers.

[31] The falls of St Mary, west of Sugar Island.

[32] Formerly the dwelling of those with whom we were: his companions were the Saulteur, who had fled west to Green Bay and Chequamegon in 1651–3.

[33] Where the hare layed: an old proverb meaning 'where the secret is' or 'what is the gist of the matter'. Radisson appears to be unwilling to ask the Saulteur for information, possibly about the whitefish.

[34] Economic advantage.

[35] Kinekoiur: meaning unknown; neither Huron or Algonquin, it may be a scribal misreading for some other word.

[36] Encens of our Encens: probably an intensifier: 'the burning of our incense produced even further incense, which we did not spare'; on his fifth voyage Radisson threatens a native opponent that he will 'eate Sagamite in the head of the head of his grandmother' (Scull, 304).

[37] Thwarted: crossed over; the location is probably Whitefish Bay.

[38] Lake Superior. The 'Isle most delightfull for the diversity of its fruits' is probably Isle Parisienne in Whitefish Bay.

[39] A few scholars think Radisson must have sailed to Turkey as a boy, but his use of the word 'pylgrimages' suggests he may have been reading some book of travels.

[40] Correctly, Nanitou cksinagoit, from Manitou (spirit) or Manitowis (a sorcerer; one who speaks with spirits) and asinaka (rocky). The Pictured Rocks, extending along the south shore of Lake Superior south of Grand Island.

[41] Goilants: the Herring Gull, *Larus argentatus*.

[42] Trinity Islands, west of Presque Isle Point. The 'Bay very deepe' is Keweenaw Bay.

[43] Chequamegon Point and Chequamegon Bay, on the south side of Lake Superior near present-day Ashland, Wisconsin.

[44] Devils labouring ceaselessly in order to have devised such a structure.

[45] Radisson and Des Groseillers pretend that a spirit under their control guards their possessions.

[46] Louis XIV and his bride, Maria Theresa of Spain. This royal 'entry' (a symbolic procession

derived from the Roman 'triumph' which was often engaged in by medieval and Renaissance rulers) took place on 26 August 1660. Radisson could only have heard about it later and at second hand. Despite his contempt for the 'fools of Paris', Radisson's account of his own and Des Groseilliers' 'entry' at the Feast of the Dead (see below) shows his awareness of the political power of allegorical pageantry.

[47] Fr. *cabane*; Radisson uses 'cabins' and 'cottages' indiscriminately to mean native dwellings.

[48] Destinated: Fr. *destiner*: to reserve for a particular purpose.

[49] Radisson is speaking of the Feast of the Dead which is shortly announced for some months later; his account is given below, following an episode of severe famine.

[50] Fr. *rassades*, glass trade beads.

[51] Beat: a fight; possibly from Fr. *se battre*, exchange blows.

[52] Captain: from the Fr. *capitaine*, or commander; here probably (as in the *Jesuit Relations*) meaning chief. For the different meaning in later Hudson's Bay Company usage see KELSEY.

[53] The manuscript says 'blind'. Adams (1967) suggests 'company of that *kind*', but Radisson may simply have been lodged with a blind man.

[54] Malhomines or Menominees, the 'Wild Rice People', immemorial inhabitants of the area around Green Bay, Wisconsin.

[55] Rock Island at the entrance of Green Bay, which Des Groseilliers had visited in 1654.

[56] According to the physiology Radisson would have known, which was based on the ancient theory of the four humours, under normal conditions the natural 'humour' or physical make-up of women was moist.

[57] Rind tree: possibly wild grape, which can be found from Ontario to Wisconsin.

[58] If they weare stakes in it: stuck fast in the snow.

[59] Unless this anecdote (in a fashion typical of Radisson) has been transposed from some earlier adventure, he still seems to have been beardless when he participated in the Lake Superior voyage in 1659–60. Radisson thought he was born in 1636, and later scholars have suggested 1640; if the story is in its correct chronological place, the date may be later yet.

[60] Nadoueserous (correctly, Nadoueserons): that is, 'snake people' or enemies. Radisson generally refers to them as 'the nation of the beef' (that is, of the bison).

[61] Because Radisson was familiar to him.

[62] There now ensues Radisson's description of the Feast of the Dead, which is devoted almost completely to the political rituals and merriment of the occasion, rather than to its spiritual significance. For the latter, described by an observer fascinated with the 'visit of the boans of their deceased friends', of which Radisson says almost nothing, see Fr. Jean de Brébeuf's 1636 *Relation* 'On the belief, manners, and customs of the Hurons', Thwaites, ed., *Jesuit Relations*, vol. 10, 279–311. The Feast of the Dead was a Huron custom, but in the late seventeenth century was also practised among Algonkian-speaking nations further inland; the natives present on this occasion appear to be Saulteur, Dakota, and Cree. The specific location of the 'rendezvous' is not known.

[63] Butchered and carried in pieces to the meal, where before they had lived in freedom.

[64] These visitors may have been from the Mdewakanton group of the Sioux, who hunted the bison on foot.

[65] Pine or fir boughs.

[66] The Nahathaway, whom the French called the Cristinaux, thus 'Cree'. They are the 'wandering nation' mentioned below.

[67] In 1573 Prince Albertus Laski came to France with a delegation of Polish ambassadors to offer the throne of Poland to Henri III; the richness of their jewels and robes impressed the French deeply, and in popular legend long remained a standard for exotic magnificence.

[68] Turkey stones: turquoises, or possibly Lake Superior amethyst.

[69] Breeches, which were greased so that they shed water.

[70] Embroidery of porcupine quills.

[71] A medicine bag.

[72] The natives' behaviour here was likely meant to exhibit ritual courtesy, rather than the political submission the Europeans thought they were receiving.

[73] Being made men by nature, and having to fulfil the obligations of men, that is, to make war and defend their families. The speakers may be making the distinction (prevalent in many cultures) between their own nation, 'the people', and beings of other cultural groups or languages (non-people by their definition).

[74] Give evidence of their manly valour.

[75] The natives have clearly been observing the Europeans as well.

[76] Candles: presumably the calumets.

[77] Wild rice, which is still harvested in the way Radisson describes.

[78] The gift of the kettle was likely carefully calculated; according to Brébeuf's *Relation*, a kettle was the central symbolic object of the Feast of the Dead.

[79] The natives accompanying us promoted our interests, supported us.

[80] Buttery of Paris: possibly *boucherie* (abbatoir, stockyards).

[81] Deface: obs., to discredit, put out of countenance.

[82] Difference: an arranged contest between two parties.

[83] . . . for fear of being envied, I will admit . . .

[84] Shortly before this passage begins, Radisson's narrative becomes suspiciously less detailed, and most scholars think he is retailing second-hand information to suggest that he and Des Groseilliers crossed Lake Superior, made their way to the Albany River, and thence to James Bay. They could not have made such a journey in the time available. See note 93 below.

[85] Fr. *inventer*, to fabricate or build.

[86] Radisson is describing from its Northern end the water route used by the Jesuits (see note 4 above) to travel from the St Lawrence, up the Saguenay, and thence via a complex of waterways to James Bay.

[87] Possibly either the Albany or Moose Rivers on the west side of James Bay.

[88] The enviousness prevalent in Court life was a standard theme of Renaissance moral satire.

[89] The 'wandring nation' are the Nahathaway (Christinaux or Cree); in the mid-seventeenth century their 'Vaste Countrey' circled Hudson Bay from the east side of James Bay to Churchill on the west; inland it reached almost to the Great Lakes in the east and well towards the present-day Alberta border in the west.

[90] Whore Masters: pimps, thus by extension, fornicators.

[91] Work as hard as slaves (which from the European point of view was true of Cree women) though this is hard to equate with his description of them as 'tender and delicat'.

[92] Neuter: an unidentified nation; they cannot be the 'Neutrals' of the Iroquois-Huron wars, who spoke Iroquois.

[93] In a single sentence, Radisson deals with the return journey down a river system like that of the Albany and back to Lake Superior. He may have been using second-hand information given to the Jesuit Father Druillettes by an Algonkian informant, in order to draw English attention to the potential of the vast new country.

[94] The better . . . commodities: thus the manuscript, but the sense is obscure; possibly 'if he had to do without the beaver we brought him through our own initiative, nothing would be forthcoming from France.'

[95] A letter of the litigious Des Groseilliers asking for just treatment. Both the explorers knew

that trade in the interior had been forbidden by Governor Lauzon on 28 April 1654, acting on instructions from the king; they could not be pardoned for the sake of the service they had rendered since others would then attempt to trade illegally.

[96] That is, to pay for the fort.

[97] Radisson is offended because the Governor assumes that the two explorers will stay in the wilderness, while he returns to Paris. Des Groseilliers probably did stay in Canada; Radisson died a settled Londoner, after three marriages and several children.

[98] Fr., scoundrel.

[99] Fr. coin, the *louis d'or*, valued at about 16–18 shillings.

[100]600,000 pounds Tournois: a very large sum; the *livre Tournois* was a 'money of account' by which the diverse coinages of Europe were give a par value. Approximately £46,000 sterling in the 1660s (about $7,100,000 in 1992 Canadian dollars).

Henry Kelsey   (*c.* 1667 – 1724)

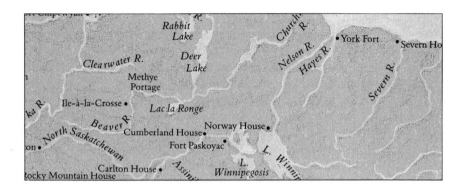

HENRY KELSEY was apprenticed to the Hudson's Bay Company about 1684, and spent most of his life on the Bay, either at York Fort or at Albany. He served as seaman, trader (often at the same time), and deputy governor at York, and was twice captured by French forces besieging Bay posts. By 1718 he had risen to the position of Governor of all the Company's settlements on the Bay. Kelsey earned his greatest renown near the beginning of his career, when in 1690, a young man of 23 accompanied by natives from around the Bay post at York Fort, he travelled down the Hayes River into the great plains and became the first European to see the Canadian prairies. In 1689 Kelsey had been part of an unsuccessful exploring party to Churchill River, making an intrepid foray inland which like other explorers he recorded in a journal. He also kept a daily record of his journey to the plains, as well as composing a 90-line poem in sturdy doggerel on his travels. His choice of the dignified genre of verse suggests how seriously he took the responsibility he had been given by Governor Geyer, 'to call, encourage, and invite the remoter Indians to a Trade with us'. When he was given a blank manuscript book in 1693, he carefully wrote out the poetical account of his thousand-mile journey to the plains on its first pages, following it immediately with a fuller prose journal of the same trip and a detailed account of 'Indian beliefs and superstitions'.

Text: *The Kelsey Papers*, ed. Arthur G. Doughty and Chester Martin (Ottawa: Public Archives of Canada and Public Record Office of Northern Ireland, 1929), compared with a microfilm of the original manuscript (N. Ireland PRO, D162/7). Scribal contractions (e.g., 'ye' for 'the', 'ym' for 'them', '&' for 'and') have been silently expanded; spelling and capitalization are Kelsey's own, but light punctuation has been added, as well as a few missing words (in square brackets) to clarify the sense.

Henry Kelsey his Book being the Gift of James Hubbud[1]
in the year of our Lord 1693

Now Reader Read, for I am well assur'd
Thou dost not know the hardships I endur'd
In this same desert where Ever that I have been,
Nor wilt thou me believe without that thou had seen
The Emynent Dangers that did often me attend,   5
But still I lived in hopes that once it would amend
And makes me free from hunger and from Cold,
Likewise many other things which I cannot here unfold;
For many times I have often been oppresst
With fears and Cares that I could not take my rest   10
Because I was alone and no friend could find;
And once that in my travels I was left behind
Which struck fear and terror into me,
But still I was resolved this same Country for to see.
Although through many dangers I did pass   15
Hoped still to undergo them, at the Last,
Now Considering that it was my dismal fate
for to repent I thought it now to late;
Trusting still unto my masters[2] Consideration
Hoping they will Except of this my small Relation   20
Which here I have pend and still will Justifie
Concerning of those Indians and their Country;
If this wont do farewell to all as I may say,
And for my living I'll seek some other way.
In sixteen hundred and ninety'th year   25
I set forth as plainly may appear
Through Gods assistance for to understand
The natives language and to see their land.
And for my masters interest I did soon
Sett from the house[3] the twealth of June,   30
Then up the River I with heavy heart
Did take my way and from all English part
To live amongst the Natives of this place
If god permits me for one two years space.
The Inland Country of Good report hath been   35
By Indians but by English yet not seen,

Therefore I on my Journey did not stay
But making all the hast I could upon our way
Gott on the borders of the stone Indian[4] Country;
I took possession on the tenth Instant[5] July   40
And for my masters I speaking for them, all
This neck of land I deerings point[6] did call;
Distance from hence by Judgement at the lest
From the house six hundred miles southwest,
Through Rivers which run strong with falls   45
thirty three Carriages, five lakes in all.
The ground begins for to be dry with wood,
Poplo[7] and birch with ash thats very good
For the Natives of that place, which knows
No use of Better than their wooden Bows.   50
According to the use and custom of this place
In September I brought those Natives to a peace,
But I had no sooner from those Natives turnd my back
Some of the home Indians[8] came upon their track
And for old grudges and their minds to fill   55
Came up with them Six tents of which they kill'd.
This ill news kept secrett was from me
Nor none of those home Indians did I see
Untill that they their murder all had done,
And the Chief acter was he thats called the Sun.   60
So far I have spoken concerning of the spoil[9]
And now will give account of that same Country soile
Which hither part is very thick of wood,
Affords small nutts with little cherryes very good;
Thus it continues till you leave the woods behind   65
And then you have beast of severall kind.
The one is a black a Buffillo great,[10]
Another is an outgrown Bear which is good meat;
His skin to gett I have used all the ways I can,
He is mans food and he makes food of man.   70
His hide they would not me it preserve
But said it was a god and they should Starve.
This plain affords nothing but Beast and grass
And over it in three days time we past,
getting unto the woods on the other side   75
It being about forty six miles wide.
This wood is poplo ridges with small ponds of water
there is beavour in abundance but no Otter,
with plains and ridges in the Country throughout;
Their Enemies many whom they cannot rout,   80

But now of late they hunt their Enemies
And with our English guns do make them flie.
At deerings point after the frost
I set up their a Certain Cross
In token of my being there,   85
Cut out on it the date of year
And Likewise for to veryfie the same
added to it my master sir Edward deerings name
So having no more to trouble you withall I am
Sir your most obedient and faithfull Servant at Command   90

HENRY KELSEY

*A Journal of a voyage and Journey undertaken
by henry Kelsey through Gods assistance to discover
and bring to a Commerce the Naywatame poets in Anno
1691*

. . . .

July the 16*th*: Today setting forward again we went through a little creek were we were forc'd to track our Cannoes into an Island within which is great ponds of water, and so padling from one to another sometimes running through long high grass which grows in near 2 foot water; this grass hath an Ear like our English Oats. Distance today 25 Miles and came to[11] in a small poplo Island. . . .

July the 18*th*: Today we paddled up the Rivers untill about noon and then we came to a small arm of the River so we concluded to sett our netts and lay up our Cannoes and Rest the remaining part of the day there which accordingly we did. So I took the Rundlett[12] which the Governor had sent me full of powder and emptyed part of it into a leather Bagg; so I put one hatchet 2 fathom of Black Tobacco 6 Knives 2 Skains of twine two nettlines one tin show[13] and other small moveables into the rundlett and headed it up again; so we made a hole in the ground and put that and other things into it; and put into it so made of it our storehouse untill we came that way the next spring dist: 8 miles 3 pikes[14] today. . . .

July the 20*th*: So setting forward again we had not gone above 9 Miles but came on the track of Indians which [I] Judged had past four Days before; so we went on till we came up with their old tents; so we seeing they had kill two Beast I thought they might have had good store of victuals and not have been farr before us; I sent an Indian before and fitted him out with my pipe and some tobacco and bid him tell them to send me some relief and likewise for to stay for me. This day we travelled about 18 Miles. . . .

July the 23*d*: Now about noon one Indian return'd back fearing lest the women would starve which were behind; so I gave him some powder and an Order to receive some shott of such a woman; so I proceeded forward along with a little slave Boy and toward night we came to good footing for all that we had passed before was heavy mossy going; so in the Evening wee came too; dist 30 Mile and nothing to eat but one wood patridge.

July the 24*th*: To day we had very good going and about noon we came up with their tents they had left to day, they having increas'd from 2 to 7; and their fire not being quite out we sat down and roasted 3 Pigeons which I had killed that morning and so went along again till about six in the afternoon we came to their tents, they having nothing but grass and Berryes to eat part of which they gave to me; but at night they're people returning from hunting one had kill'd 2 Swans and another had kill'd a Buck Muse but did not come home till in the Night. So I being asleep he sent his son to call me and when he came he told me that his father wanted me to come and smoke a pipe with him so I went and when I came he gave me a pipe to light and then presented me with the great gut of the Beast aforesaid, so when I had Eaten I returned to my rest having travelled to day 20 Miles.

July the 25*th*: This morning I made a speech desireing them for to stay for our people which was behind, but an Old man came to me and told me that it would signify nothing for to lye still, seeing that there was no victuals to Relieve them when they came up, so desired leave of me to pitch a little way that the women might fetch home the Beast which was kill'd the day before that they might have wherewithall to relieve them when they came. So I sent two women back for to help our women along with their things so we pitched about 10 Miles and came too. . . .

July the 30*th*: Now we pitched again about ten Miles and came to, our Indians making a great feast telling that they were very glad that I was returned according to my promise, for if I should be wanting they should be greatly afraid that the Nayhay-thaways Indians[15] would murder them; and so made me master of the feast. . . .

August the 4*th*: To day we lay still having strangers come to our tents from some stone Indians which was to the Southward of us. So we made a tent for our strangers and provided them something to Eat and some Tobacco for to smoak it. So they told us their news, which was that the Nayhaythaways had lost 3 of their women which the Naywattame poets[16] had killed the last spring; and withall they appointed where they themselves would meet us but as for the Naywattame poets they were fled so far that they thought I should not see them.

August the 5*th*: Now we pitched again, our strangers Likewise Returning to their tents, I telling them if by any means they could come to a speech of those Naywat-tame Indians for to give them all the Encouragements Immaginable for to come to me and not to fear that any one should do them any harm. So I gave two pieces of tobacco the one for their guang,[17] the other for the Naywatame poet if they did see any of them. Our [journey] to day 12 Miles.

August the 6*th*: To day we pitcht to that River which I have spoken of before which is not a hundred yards over and but very shoal water. This River treunts [trends?] away much to the Southward and runneth through great part of the Cuntry, and is fed by a lake which feedeth another River and Cuntry which runneth down to the South-ward of us and is called *Mith* — —.[18] Now the water which runneth down this river is of a Blood red Colour by the description of those Indians which hath seen it, which makes me to think that it may run through some mine or other. Our Journey this day by Estimation 10 Miles.

August the 7*th*: This Instant pitched up the side of this River aforesaid and in my

Journey to day in Several places I Saw slate mines along the side of this River. By *Estimation* [crossed out] dist; 10 Miles. . . .

August the 12*th*: Now we pitch again, and about noon the ground begins to grow heathy and barren in fields of about half a Mile over, Just as if they had been Artificially[19] made with fine groves of Poplo growing round them. We went to day by Estimation 10 Miles. . . .

August the 15*th*: This Instant one Indian Lying a dying, and withall a murmuring which was amongst the Indians Because I would not agree for them to go to warrs. So I taking it into Consideration cut some tobacco and call'd all the Old dons[20] to my tent, telling them that it was not the way for them to have the use of English guns and other things and that I nor they should not go near the Governor unless they ceast from warring; so lay still to day.

August the 16*th*: Now not knowing which would Conquer, life or Death, lay still to day; our people going a hunting but had small success.

August the 17*th*: Last night death ceased and this morning his body was burned according to their way, they making A great feast for him that did it. Now after that the flesh was burned, his Bones were taken and buried with Loggs set up round of about ten foot Long. So we pitcht to day near 14 Miles and came to, they holding it not good to stay by the Dead. . . .

August the 20*th*: To day we pitcht to the outtermost Edge of the woods. This plain affords Nothing but short Round sticky grass and Buffillo and a great sort of a Bear which is Bigger then any white Bear and is Neither White nor Black But silver hair'd like our English Rabbit.[21] The Buffillo Likewise is not like those to the Northward, their Horns growing like an English Ox but Black and short. Dist: 6 Miles. . . .

August the 23*d*: This Instant the Indians going a hunting Kill'd great store of Buffillo. Now the manner of their hunting these Beast on the Barren ground is when they see a great parcel of them together they surround them with men which done they gather themselves into a smaller Compass Keeping the Beast still in the middle and so shooting them till they break out at some place or other and so gett away from them.[22] Our women Likewise pitching according to order. Dist 12 Miles.

August the 24*th*: This day lay still waiting for a post which came in the afternoon from the Captain[23] of the Mountain Poets[24] Named Washa. So the Substance of their news was that he desired we would meet him when we pitcht again, so I told them I would.

August the 25*th*: So pitching again we came to altogether and in number we were 80 Tents, we having travelled to day by Estimation 12 Miles yet not reacht the woods on the other side. This plain running through great part of the Country and lyeth along near East and west.

August the 26*th*: Now we are altogether, they made a feast the which they Invited me to. So they desired leave of me for them to go to wars but I told them I could not grant them their request for the Governor[25] would not allow me so to do; so we lay still to day. . . .

August the 31*st*: This day the Indians made a feast desireing of me to be a post to a parcel of Indians[26] which was to the Northward to us, to desire them to stay for us, telling me that my word would be taken before an Indians although he went. So we lay still to day.

September the 1st: Now being in their Enemies Country I had eight Indians for my conduct one of which Could speak both Languages for to be my interpreter. So set forward and having travelled to day near 30 miles in the Evening came to in a small poplo Island which standeth out from the main Ridge of woods, because these Indians are greatly afraid of their Enemies.

September the 2d: This morning Setting forward again, it Proved very bad weather and by reason of so many beaten paths which the Buffillo makes we lost the track. So I filled two pipes of Tobacco according to their way; so I speaking to two young men to go seek for the track and when I had Ended my speech I gave Each of them a pipe to light. So they departed and it being cold we made a fire but a great parcel of Buffillo appearing in sight we gave them Chase, and by the way found the track and in the Evening came up with them. We travelled to day by Estimation 25 Miles.

September the 3d: This morning they provided a feast for me to hear what I had to say. So told them my message, which was to stay for those which I came from now, I understanding their drift was to come altogether for to go to wars. So I told them that they must not go to wars, for it will not be liked by the governer, neither would he trade with them if they did not cease from warring. . . .

September the 5th: About ten o Clock this morning the young men appearing in sight and crying out Just like a Crane, which gave a sign that they had discovered their Enemies; and as soon as they came within one hundred yards of the tent they sat all down in a Row upon the grass not speaking one word. So the old Men lighting their pipes went to them and served them round, Crying as if they had been stob'd for Joy,[27] they had found their enemies, the young men having brought some old arrows to verifie what they had been about.

September the 6th: This Instant I unclosed[28] the pipe which the governour had sent me, telling them that they must Imploy their time in Catching of beavour for that will be better liked on then their killing their Enemies when they come to the factory; neither was I sent there for to kill any Indians but to make peace with as many as I could. But all my arguments prevailed nothing with them, for they told me what signified a peace with those Indians considering they knew not the use of Cannoes;[29] and were resolved to go to wars, so I seeing it in vain I held my peace. . . .

September the 8th: Now likewise we pitched again and by the way met with those Indians which I came post from, and so came too altogether. This afternoon came four Indian strangers from those which are called Naywatame poets the which I receiv'd very kindly and made much of them, Likewise our own people returning with them. So I inquired where there Captain was, they giving me an account that he was two days Journey behind. Our Journey to day not Extending 18 Miles.

September the 9th: This morning I went to the Captain of the stone Indians tent carrying with me a piece of tobacco, I telling him to make a speech to all his Country men and tell them not to disturb nor meddle with the Naywattame poets, for I was going back to Invite and incourage them to a peace once more. So they all gave their Consent and told me that they were very free to have them to be their friends, so I took my way back along with those which came yesterday having 12 tents along with me. Our Journey to day 18 Miles. . . .

September the 12*th*: This morning having no victuals to invite the captain to, so I filled that pipe which the Governor had sent me with tobacco and then sent for the Captain. So then I made a speech to him and told him that he should not mind what had passed formerly as concerning the nayhaythaways killing Six tents of his Country men and for the future we English will seek for to prevent it going any further, for if so be they did so any more the Governor says he will not trade with them if they did not cease from killing his friends. And when I had done I presented him with a present: coat and sash, Cup and one of my guns, with knives, awls, and tobacco with small quantities of powder and shott and part of all such things as the Governor had sent me. So he seemed to be very well pleased and told me he had forgott what had past altough they had kill'd most of his kindred and relations, and likewise told me he was sorry he had not wherewithall for to make me Restitution for what I had given him but he would meet me at Deerings point the next spring and go with me to the factory. But it happened in the winter after I had parted with them the Nayhaythaways came up with them and killed two of them, which struck a new fear into them [so] that they would not venture down fearing lest the home Indians would not let them up again into their own Country. So when I was at Deerings point in the spring which is the place of resortance when they are coming down to trade, upon the arrival of some indians I had news brought me the the Captain aforesaid had sent me a pipe and steam[30] of his own making and withall the news of their being kill'd as I have spoken of before; yet if so be I would send him a piece of tobacco from the factory upon the return of the same indians he would certainly come down the next year, But if not the beavour in their Cuntry are unnumerable and will certainly be brought down every year. So having not to inlarge,[31] sir, I remain your obedient and faithfull Servant,

HENRY KELSEY

Now I shall according to the best of my knowledge give an Account of those Indians belief and Superstitions in their ways and how they make use of them.

Their first and Chiefest point is:[32] A piece of Birch rine [bark] full of Feathers of Divers sorts put on a piece of Leather which is broad at one End for to tie about their head at such a sort that the remaining part shall hang down over their back. This they put to use when their Enemies are in sight, believing it will save them from being kill'd, It being not the work of their own hands But of their father or some other old man near kind to them. This thing is called by their name Wessguaniconan,[33] which in time of use is accompanied with songs made by the same man which made the other, which songs are Called Wonny seewahiggens; so much for the first point.

Their second point is Concerning A pipe steam done with feathers of Divers sorts, and near that end which goeth into the mouth is three voulter [vulture] or Eagles feathers split and lay'd on like the feathers of an arrow. Now every one of these and all things Else belonging to the steam Aforsaid hath a speech [which] belongs to every one of them, as the makers fancy leads him. Now there is but very few Indians but what are beading [*sic*; 'leading'?] Indians that can get one of these pipes, and when he hath a mind to go to warrs or any other way he calls all of them together and tells them his mind. So then he Lights his pipe and serveth them Round, Crying.[34] Now their Custom is to take but four Whiffs of those pipes, and if any one hath not a mind to go with him nor answer his request he will Likewise refuse to smoke out of his pipe, and again if any man hath made use of a woman the last night or his wife be with Child he will pass by the pipe and give thanks if he has a Mind to go with him, for they think they shall adulterate the pipe if they should smoke out of it at such a time. Likewise they will send these pipes out upon any expedition, as when that they are in want of victuals they will fitt a young man out with a pipe steam and if it happens that it fulfills what they design, then it doth pass for a true god Ever afterwards although it hath been never so false before.

The next point being their third is when they are in want of any thing, but victuals especially, in the night they will cause the tent to be made Close and the fire to thrown out of doors. Likewise the women must be absent so all things being dark and husht one of the Indians will begin to make a speech, which Ended he will fall a singing till such time he thinks he has pleasured the Company and then will begin for to Whistle, Making his fellows believe that he hath a familiar,[35] they believing it to be so to. So by that means he will answer them to any question they shall ask him and will tell them which way they shall go to look for victuals or to find other indians, and this the Natives holds for truth but I have found it often to be lyes.

Now their fourth point is, if any of them be sick they use no other means nor know no other help but to sing to the sick, for which purpose they hire a man and he calls together some men more or less for to accompanie him in his singing. So all of them getting a piece of birch Rine and a little stick goes to the sick mans tent; then he that's hir'd begins to sing and the Rest Beats upon the Rine; the same stroke he uses with his rattle which is made of Birch rine hallow within having some stones or Beads Inclosed in it. So when he has sat and sung a while to his patient he that's hired will rise up stark naked making a hideous noise, and having there ready a Dish of Cold water, takes a mouthfull of it and spurts on the sick person. So following it Close with his mouth sucks at his skin and Rising from him again halls drugs or something out of his mouth, so makes his fellows believe he suckt it out of the sick person, and indeed is hard to be perceiv'd to the Contrary. Now in such times they will take the best things they have and hang upon Poles as an offering to him which way the cause of his sickness.[36] Likewise making along speech desiring of him to send him his health again. Now as for a woman they do not so much mind her for they reckon she is like a Slead dog or Bitch when she is living and when she dies they think she dyes to Eternity, but a man they think departs into another world and lives again.

Then their fifth point is this: If at any time they are in want of victuals they will fitt a young man out with something of their own making, as it may be half a dozen pruant [prune] stones which they have gott from the factory or Else a pipe steam. Now these pruant stones they scrape smooth and burn spots, or the shape of any thing as their fancy leads them. Now if [it] happens that this young man which is fitted out should kill a Beast that day, then they will impute it to the things he carried about him and so it passes for a God Ever afterwards. But now no Beast they kill but some part or other is allotted for mans meat, which the women are not to tast of upon no account, but more especially at this time then others by reason they think it will be a hindrance to their Killing any more Beast. Nay if a woman should eat any of this mans mans meat which is called in their Language *Crett —— tgh* [crossed out in MS] Cuttawatchetaugun and fall sick in a year or 2 afterwards and dye, they will not stick to say it was that kill'd her, for all it was so long ago she eat it.

Their sixth point I shall relate is concerning their singing of their songs and from whence they think they have them. Those that they reckon Chiefly for gods are Beast and fowl But of all Beast the Buffillo and of all fowls the voulter and the Eagle which they say they dream of in their sleep and it relates to them what they shall say when they sing and By that means whatsoever they ask or require will be granted or given them. Which by often making use of it sometimes happens to fall out Right as they say, and for that one time it will pass for a truth that he hath a familiar although he hath told never so many lies before, and so by their singing will pretend to know what the firmament of heaven is made of. Nay some Indians which I have discoursed with has told me they have been there and seen it; so likewise another has told me that he had been so near to the sun at the going down that he could take hold of it when it Cut the Horrizon. Likewise they would pretend to tell me by their singing how things stood at the factory when I was many hundred miles of along with them but I found it not true.

Now there is a Difference between the stone Indians and the Nayhaythaways although the principles of their belief is all one and the same. But I mean as to passages in their tents which I shall give some small relation of; I having been amongst the [stone] Indians of late will begin with them first. Now if they have a mind for to make a feast they will pitch a tent on purpose and after that the tent is made and fixt then no woman Kind that hath a husband or is known to have been concern'd with a man must not come within the door of the tent aforsaid. So then the master of the tent and one or two more goeth in and Cutteth out a place for the fire about three foot square in the middle of the tent, and then the fire being made they take a little sweet grass and lay at every corner of the said square and then putting fire to it they perfume the tent, so making along speech wishing all health and happiness both to founders and confounders. This being done the master burning a little more sweet grass then taketh a pipe fill'd with tobacco and perfumeth it so giveth it to another Indian telling him who he shall call to the feast. So then he goeth out of doors and those which are appointed he calls by name two or 3 times over, and then returning into the tent again lights the pipe which was given him. The pipe being lighted he turneth that end which goeth into the mouth to what place the master of the feast shall direct him which generally [is] first towards our English house and from thence moving it round gradually towards the sun rising and so about to [hole in MS] where the sun is at noon still keeping in motion to where the sun goeth down, and then turneth that end which goeth into the mouth toward the ground. So lighting it the second time handeth it round to his companions and as they receive it they give thanks. So when they are all gathered together the master will have some victuals and some tobacco ready cut with which they will sing and be merry as we do over a Cup of good liquor. Now they have but two or three Words in a song and they observe to keep time along with him that is the leader of the song, for Every man maketh his own songs by vertue of what he dreams of as I have said before, and at the Conclusion of every song they give thanks all in general to him that the song belongs too. So likewise if any one hath crost or vext them that they owe him any grudge they will pretend to set what they dream of to work and it shall kill the offender at his pleasure.

Torn out [Kelsey's note]

. . . nor step over a man boy nor Child for if at any time they should happen to stride over any one and the person fall sick at any time after they will impute it to be the reason of it. And likewise when they are sick they will call themselves to remembrance to see if that they have eat any thing which has been forbidden them to eat and if it happened by force of hunger they have eat what has been forbidden them, then presently that is the cause of their sickness, and if they should dye that fitt they still think that is the cause of it.

Notes

[1] James Hubbard: possibly the 'James Hubbald' whose affidavit was taken when the Company protested French infringement of the articles surrendering York Fort in 1694.

[2] As a 'servant' of the Hudson's Bay Company (customary usage in the Company for an employee under contract) Kelsey refers to the Governor and Committee as his 'masters'.

[3] York Fort; 'the river' in the next line is the Hayes River. Kelsey's route is hard to trace, but he seems to have travelled down the Hayes River by canoe and wintered south of The Pas, Manitoba, at a bend in the Saskatchewan River which he named Dering's Point. Next year he appears to have gone up the Saskatchewan to the Carrot River and then (on foot) across muskeg and plains country to the Touchwood Hills.

[4] Stone Indians: Assiniboines (also known as Mountain Indians; see below).

[5] Instant: this day.

[6] Sir Edward Dering (1633–1706), Deputy Governor of the Hudson's Bay Company. 'Dering's Point' is probably just south of The Pas, Manitoba.

[7] Poplo: poplar.

[8] 'Home Indians': Cree who lived near the Bay in close association with the Hudson's Bay men at York Fort; sometimes called the 'home-guard'.

[9] In the now rare sense of 'hurt' or 'damage'.

[10] Kelsey is usually regarded as the first white man to see the North American Buffalo, but the Spanish and French had already encountered bison herds elsewhere.

[11] A nautical term; Kelsey means 'camp for the night'.

[12] Kelsey often uses 'So' where we would begin a sentence; I have punctuated accordingly. A rundlett is a small barrel.

[13] Tin show: possibly a tin mirror.

[14] Pike: a variable measure (ordinarily of cloth); about two feet.

[15] Nahathaway: Cree.

[16] Naywattame poets: meaning unsure; the word *pwat* means Sioux, but Kelsey's Assiniboines

(themselves a branch of the Sioux) needed an interpreter to speak with them; perhaps the Gros Ventres, a branch of the Arapaho then living in southern Saskatchewan.

[17]Guang: gang, in the nautical sense of 'crew'; SAMUEL HEARNE (originally a naval man) and other Company men also use the word in this sense.

[18]Unreadable in the manuscript, but possibly the Mithcou or Red, known today as the Assiniboine.

[19]Made by the hand of man rather than by nature.

[20]Chiefs (from *dominus*, lord).

[21]The grizzly bear.

[22]Kelsey is describing the making of a buffalo pound.

[23]Captain (also known as 'Leader'): a 'leading Indian' or middleman (rather than a tribal chief) who organized trade between remote tribes and the Company posts; HEARNE describes the Leader's ambiguous social role as that of 'mouth-piece and beggar'. For the different French usage, see RADISSON.

[24]Mountain Sioux (*pwat*): Stone Indians or Assiniboines.

[25]Governor George Geyer at York Fort.

[26]To take a message to a group of Indians.

[27]Crying out for joy as sharply as if they had been stabbed.

[28]This day I revealed. . . . A pipe-bearer was a significant person in native society; as bearer of the Governor's pipe Kelsey was a man of some political importance.

[29]'They told me what "peace" meant to these people, considering that they were so backward they did not even know how to use canoes.' For the disdain in which the natives farther west held canoes, see HENDAY and GRAHAM; in Kelsey's day they had not yet encountered horses.

[30]A ceremonial pipe with a decorated stem.

[31]Having no more to report.

[32]The first point I want to note in connection with their practices.

[33]War-bonnet.

[34]Crying out a speech, or possibly singing.

[35]A spirit attending on and carrying out the wishes of a witch.

[36]To affect the cause of his sickness.

Pierre Gaultier de Varennes, Sieur de la Vérendrye   (1685 – 1749)

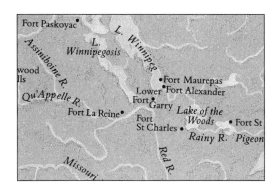

LA VÉRENDRYE was born in Canada, the son of the Governor of Trois-Rivières. His early career was spent in France as a military officer; when he returned to Canada he married, raised a family, and became a farmer who sporadically traded for furs locally. In 1728 he succeeded his brother Jacques-René as commandant of the great fur-trading area north of Lake Superior, and took up the career in exploration which occupied the last half of his life. Like the French geographers of his day La Vérendrye thought that a great Western Sea lay not far beyond Lake Superior, and he was convinced he could find this short-cut to the riches of the East. He faced immense difficulties, however; the officials of the French court with whom he had to deal had no concept of the vast spaces of North America, or of the problems of supply and provision men in the field had to face. Despite these obstacles La Vérendrye and his sons and nephew spent nearly two decades in the west, establishing forts, searching for the western sea, and preparing the way for the French fur trade which lured the natives from the Bayside posts of the English traders in the mid-eighteenth century. He sent regular journals, letters, and reports to the Governor of New France, the Marquis de Beauharnois (unstinting in his support) and through him to the Comte de Maurepas, Louis XV's minister of Marine and the Colonies, who was impatient with the explorers' failure to make rapid progress. As a writer La Vérendrye combines the exquisite tact of the experienced courtier with the questioning mind of the born traveller. He is alert to the political implications of a situation; at the same time he takes pleasure in conceptualizing the geography of a place almost unknown to Europeans. He is concerned for the careers of his sons (one of whom he lost to the Sioux) yet ready to weep with the Cree for their dead. Both his life and his writing have the sweep (and the ironies) of epic. In 1742 Maurepas began moving to exclude him from responsibility in the west; La Vérendrye retreated to an honourable retirement, and died in 1749.

Text: *Journals and Letters of Pierre Gaultier de Varennes de la Vérendrye and his Sons*, ed. Lawrence J. Burpee, with a translation by W.D. LeSueur. Toronto: The Champlain Society, 1927.

From the journal of 1729

A savage named Pako, Chief of Lake Nipigon, Lefoye, and Petit Jour his brother, Cree chiefs, reported to me that they had been beyond the height of land and reached a great river which flows straight towards the setting sun, and which widens continually as it descends;[1] that in this great river there are only two rapids about three days' journey from its source, and that wood is only found along about two hundred leagues of its course, according to the estimate they made in their travel.

They give a great account of that country, saying that it is all very level, without mountains, all fine hard wood with here and there groves of oak; that everywhere there are quantities of fruit trees, and all sorts of wild animals; that the savage tribes are there very numerous, and always wandering, never staying in any fixed place, but carrying their cabins with them continually from one place to another and always camping together to form a village. They call these nations Assiniboin and Sioux because they speak all the Sioux languages. The nations about three hundred leagues lower down are sedentary, raise crops, and for lack of wood make themselves mud huts. The wood comes to an end on the shore of a great lake[2] formed by the river about two hundred leagues from its source; on the left as you follow down, at the outlet of the lake, you come to a little river the water of which looks red like vermilion,[3] and is held in great esteem by the savages. On the same side of the river, but much lower down, there is a small mountain, the stones of which sparkle night and day. The savages call it the Dwelling of the Spirit; no one ventures to go near it. This kind of mountain and the Red river, where in places a very fine gold-coloured sand is found, seem to all the nations of the region something very precious. . . .

Tacchigis, a chief of the Cree, told me then that he had been as far as the lake of the great river of the West, and several times afterwards he told me the same story that the others had already done. I asked him if he did not know of other great rivers; he replied that he knew of several, but that the one running west exceeded all the others in width.[4] He then gave me a statement in regard to several other larger rivers that he had seen from a height of land sloping to the south-west.

He told me that four great rivers take their rise there, one of which, flowing north as far as the lake of the great river of the West, turns west at the outlet of the lake; another flowing north-east falls into a river which, flowing west-north-west, empties into the same lake. The third, flowing at first southeast and afterwards running south, goes to the country of the Spaniards. The fourth, taking its course between the last two, forms the Mississippi.[5] With a piece of charcoal he made me a map of those regions, and placed these rivers on them according to his marks.

I am expecting this spring some savages who, I am assured, have been very far down the river of the West, and who will be able to supply a map of the road to the places at which they have been.

A slave adopted by the people of the territory, and given to Vieux Crapaud, chief of the flat country, by the Cree, after having been made prisoner by the Assiniboin on the stretch of country to the left of the river of the West, reports that the villages there are very numerous, many of them being nearly two leagues in extent, and that the back country is inhabited like that fronting on the river. All the savages there, according to his report, raise quantities of grain, fruits abound, game is in great plenty and is only hunted with bows and arrows; the people there do not know what a canoe is; as there is no wood in all that vast extent of country, for fuel they dry the dung of animals.

He adds that he passed several times within sight of the mountain the stone of which shines night and day, and that from that point you begin to notice a rise and fall of tide;[6] also that from the lake near which is the Red river to far below the mountain there are no settlements of savages; that he had never heard tell whether it was far from the sea, and that he did not think there was any man bold enough to pass by the different tribes that are to be found in great number lower down in order to make an exploration.

He makes mention of all the special points contained in the Memoir which I had the honour to send you last year by the Reverend Father Gonner[7] and affirms that on the right bank of the river there is a tribe of dwarfs not over three feet or so in height, but numerous and very brave. At the place where the ebb and flow begins the river is more than three leagues in width.

With reference to the guide, the man I have chosen is one named Auchagah,[8] a savage of my post, greatly attached to the French nation, the man most capable of guiding a party, and with whom there would be no fear of our being abandoned on the way. When I proposed to him to guide me to the great river of the West he replied that he was at my service and would start whenever I wished. I gave him a collar by which, after their manner of speaking, I took possession of his will, telling him that he was to hold himself in readiness for such time as I might have need of him and indicating to him the season of the year when I might be in the flat country for the purpose of proceeding to the discovery of the Western Sea; if, Monsieur, I should have the honour of receiving your orders to do so. I then made him some presents to increase his affection for us, and make sure that he would fulfil his promises. . . .

Some Cree or Christinaux, who live towards the outlet of the Lake of the Woods, where the great River of the West has its beginning, came this spring. These savages are La Marteblanche and two other chiefs of the same tribe. They made me a map of their own country and of that of which they have knowledge, and it agrees with the first; it is in the lands that are to the left of the great river as you follow it down that minerals and metals are found in quantity. Amongst the metals, they are acquainted with lead and copper; but there is a third kind which does not flatten out, but breaks, when hammered. They do not know what it is, but its white color makes them think it is silver. According to their map, which agrees with the one made by Auchagah, the lower portion of the Western river runs west-north-west. They state that there are whites at the mouth of the river, but that they do not know to what nation they belong, the length of the journey being such that none of them venture to go there;

one would have to start from the Lake of the Woods in the month of March in order to make the journey and could not hope to get back before November. What they report is founded on hearsay. What chiefly deters them from making the journey to the sea is that on a former occasion, according to their story, two of their canoes were lost in the ice ten days' journey from Lake Winnipeg. Fear holds them back, and besides, as they can get all their wants supplied by the English of the near north, who are distant only twenty days' travel,[9] what more would they go to seek at the Western Sea? Looking at the map as they have traced it there is no appearance of the river communicating with the Northern Sea. As there are several rivers, in the latitude shown by the map, to the south-west towards Lake Winnipeg, it is probable that from the same latitude there are also some flowing to the Western Sea. To be able to settle this point, we should have to establish a post at Lake Winnipeg. La Marteblanche has promised to take me there, or, as he is old, to have me taken by his son. This lake is about five hundred leagues from the river Kaministikwia. Leaving Montreal in May, you can get to Lake Winnipeg in September. From the head of Lake Superior to the Lake of the Woods the distance is the same as from the outlet of the latter to Lake Winnipeg, with this difference that there are only two rapids requiring portages in the whole great river of the West, whereas from Lake Superior to the Lake of the Woods, a distance of a hundred leagues, you have portage after portage all the way. The two rapids I have just mentioned are in a rocky formation consisting of gun flint. The great river which goes to the sea is the discharge of the lake and of the large river which empties into it flowing west. This great river (the first mentioned) also flows west a distance of ten days' journey, after which it turns for a little west-north-west; and it is from that point that the rise and fall of the tide becomes perceptible. Such is the information given me by the Cree chiefs. This map shows all the countries they have traversed from north to south and from the Lake of the Woods to the river of the West. The whole right bank of the great river as you go down from the Lake of the Woods as far as Lake Winnipeg is held by the Cree, and it is the country of the moose and marten, while beaver is so plentiful that the savages place little value on it and only collect the large skins which they send to the English. These people dress themselves in winter in beaver skins and in spring they throw them away, not being able to sell them. The left bank of the same river is inhabited by the Assiniboin and the Sioux; the country is rich in metals, and buffalo are abundant. If they speak of places beyond it is nearly always on hearsay and without any great certainty.

After these details, Monsieur, it only remains for me to represent to you the importance, as it seems to me, of proceeding promptly with this exploration. The Cree are trading with the English, finding interpreters in the Indians of the neighbourhood, and it is natural that they should speak there of the prospect of having French among them, and that they should give the same information they have given to us here. The English have every interest in getting ahead of us, and if we allow them time they will not lose the chance of doing it. Besides, the colony will receive a new benefit independently of the discovery of the Western Sea through the quantity of furs that will be produced and which now go to waste among the Sioux and Assiniboin, or by means of the Cree go to the English. I hoped this spring to see many Cree and Assiniboin, according to the promise they made me last spring, 1729, to come to my post at Kaministikwia.[10] The death of one of their principal chiefs, a man of high consideration, has caused them to change their plan and decided them to go to war in the direction of the Spaniards to avenge his death according to their custom. I have only succeeded in getting information from two savages of the country, one of whom is a Monsoni chief, who relates that he went as far as the height of land to the north-west of the river in 1728: they state positively that there are whites, and that they have seen wood sawn into boards; these people, too, use boats, according to the description they give of their canoes.[11] This appeared to astonish them a good deal, because in all that great extent of country such a thing as an axe or a gun is never seen. There are a great many different kinds of wood there, and the animals are strange to them. Others have told me that they had seen people who said that they had gone down to the foot of the great river, and only savage tribes were met with; at the mouth of it they had seen a great island in the sea which seemed to be inhabited.

That is all, Monsieur, in the way of new information that I have been able to obtain this year.[12] If, subject to His Majesty's good pleasure, you should see fit to honour me with your instructions to go and establish a fort at Lake Winnipeg, I shall have the honour in the second year thereafter to give you positive information respecting the Sea in question.

Diplomatic negotiations; from the journal of 1733-4

I . . . began by telling them[13] that our Father, the great chief, would be very glad that they had come to see me at fort St Charles:[14] in his name I received them into the number of his children; I recommended them never to listen to any other word than his, which would be announced to them by me or by someone in my place; and not to forget the words I was speaking to them but to bring them to the knowledge of those who were absent; the French were numerous, there was no land unknown to them, and there was only one great chief among them, whose mouthpiece I was, and whom all the others obeyed. If they obeyed him also as his children, every year he would send Frenchmen to them to bring them such things as they required to satisfy their needs. And finally, if they were clever, that is to say, if they brought plenty of skins, they would benefit by what I was saying to them.

They all agreed with loud expressions of joy. I gave them news from Canada and even from France, as I had done to those who were settled at my post. I then caused the presents above mentioned to be distributed to all with the exception of the six chiefs, whom I told to come back next day with their most considerable men. I also gave some corn and some fish to all to make a feast: without the help of the pot you cannot have friendship.

On the 2nd of January, all the Frenchmen being in my room, the six chiefs and the principal men entered. In the middle of the room I had caused to be placed 12 lbs. of ball, 20 lbs. of powder, 6 axes, 6 daggers, 12 Siamese knives, two dozen awls, needles, beads, vermilion, gun-screws, six dagger hatchets, six collars of beads, six flags, 24 fathoms of tobacco, six cloaks with gilt bands, six shirts, six pairs of breeches, six pairs of leggings, the whole of which I divided among the six chiefs.

After the bestowal of the presents I thanked them several times, according to their custom, in the name of our Father, for having come to see me. 'I am ashamed,' I said, 'to have only that to give you to-day, but, if you are clever, you will come back to see me with all the people of your villages after their hunting, so that you may be in a position to have your wants supplied by the trader. Don't come with empty hands as you did the first time.' This made them smile.

I told them that the intention of the collars was to smooth all the roads to my fort, and that the flags were for all to rally under and declare themselves henceforth children of the French and not the English; that I would receive them far otherwise when I saw them coming like clever people, that is to say with plenty of packages. I added: 'My children, I have with me a blacksmith who knows how to make axes, guns, knives, kettles and everything else; but he lacks iron, and it is difficult to bring it from Montreal on account of the length of the journey. Is there no one amongst you who has some knowledge of iron? The colour of it does not matter; iron of any colour would be good to work.'

After a long deliberation amongst themselves the interpreter rose, which he had not done at other councils, and commenced in the name of all by offering many thanks, then adding that many among them, himself included, knew of several iron mines with ore of different colours; that he saw them every year, and that there was one five days' journey from our fort on a height where the iron was pure. Holding up my fire shovel, he said that the iron of that mine gave a still clearer sound, that it was very difficult to break, the outside dark like powder and the inside white; there was another further away, the pieces of which were very large, and of which they themselves made bracelets; another near to a great river towards the west, the ore of which is yellow, hard, in grains and in flakes sparkling like the sun; that a stream passes through the middle of this yellow iron and deposits a sand of the same colour; that there is no grass around any of these mines, and that it seems as if the sun had burnt everything up.

He said further, that on the bank of the same river at the foot of a hill four or five hundred yards square smoke is continually escaping and sometimes fire, which gives rise to many fables, amongst others that there is a Frenchman inside making guns, axes, knives, etc. He said that there were other places in the prairies covered as with balls of iron, black on the outside and the colour of clock metal inside, round and of various sizes, and very heavy stones which they use for lighting fire.

Finally I requested them to bring specimens to my fort next spring from all these mines; but they replied that they could not come till the winter following, because they were leaving as soon as spring opened to go to the Ouachipouennes or Caser-niers[15] to buy corn, as they had promised to do last year.

This caused me to ask them the following questions: I asked them what they thought of that tribe and whether they were savages like themselves. They replied that they took them for French; their forts and houses were much like ours, except that the roofs are flat with earth and stone over them; their forts are made of double rows of stakes with two bastions at opposite corners; their houses are large and adjoin the palisade so that you can make a tour of the fort on the tops of the houses, the latter having cellars where they keep their Indian corn in large wicker-work baskets. They never leave their fort; all alike, men and women, work in the fields, the chiefs only excepted, and these have men to serve them. . . .

After the Assiniboin had stayed seven days, during which time I had several conversations with them publicly and privately . . . I said to them: 'My children, take courage, keep well in mind the word of our Father, the great chief, fly your flags when you arrive in your villages, spread out your collars on the mats so that every one may see them, speak of the honourable manner in which I have received you in his name and of the presents he has sent you. Come next year as you have promised; you will then have new words from our Father. I want you to consider among yourselves the question of giving me next year two of your chiefs, or more if you think it advisable, to go and see our Father, in order that on their return they may relate to you the manner in which they shall have been received, and what the Frenchman is and the extent of his power.' They told me that, on their return home, the matter would be considered and the men prepared for the journey, on condition that two Cree should be taken along at the same time under the leadership of one of my sons who speaks their language. The proposition was accepted and I dismissed them. They made long harangues, according to their custom, expressive of their gratitude, and uttered shouts of joy. I gave them two bags of corn which was distributed in equal portions to all. They left on the 5th of January at noon highly pleased and satisfied with their reception and the presents I had given them after their trading was done, in which, by my orders, liberal rates of exchange were allowed them, so as to prevent their going to the English and to induce them to come back. . . .

[Fort St Pierre[16]] On the 29th at ten in the forenoon the council assembled in the house of Urtebise. I presented two collars, twelve fathoms of tobacco, white and black, and one tomahawk hidden under a beaver robe. I addressed the chief of the war party, complaining that he was thinking of going to war without consulting me. I presented him with one of the two collars and six fathoms of tobacco.

Then I rose and asked the assembly whether they recognized him as war chief, and on their assuring me that they did, I handed him a flag saying: 'By this flag I bind you to myself; by this collar I bar against you the road to the Saulteur[17] and the Sioux; and I give you this tobacco in order that your warriors may smoke it and understand my word. Have you then forgotten the word that was sent last spring to our Father and to the Saulteur and the Sioux from the Cree and the Monsoni? Why don't you wait for an answer? Peace is proposed, yet you seek to trouble the land. Do you want to strike the Saulteur and the Sioux? You needn't leave the fort; here are some (pointing to the Frenchmen), eat if you are bold enough, you and your warriors. (He hung his head.) I pity you; I know you love war.'

In presenting him with the second collar I said: 'Come down in the spring to fort St. Charles with all your warriors; — there is the road, and if you are wise you will follow my advice. I have nothing more to say to you.'

I then addressed the Cree chief who had accompanied me and told him to speak in the name of his tribe and make his sentiments known to the whole assembly.

He rose, presented a fathom of tobacco and a collar to the same chief, who still kept his head down, and addressing all present said: 'My brothers, do you reflect on what you are about to do? The Saulteur and the Sioux are our allies and children of the same Father. How can any man (speaking to the war chief) have so bad a heart as to want to kill his own relatives? Think of the words that we sent to our Father and do not make us liars. We are men who walk with our heads erect without fearing any one. I say in the name of our tribe that you are to listen to the word of our Father who gives us wisdom, and come down in the spring with all your warriors to the Lake of the Woods.'

After some deliberation the chief arose and presented me with a beaver robe which he was wearing, saying: 'This is my word. My Father, I agree to all you ask on condition, nevertheless, that you will not prevent us from going to war, and that you will let us have your son[18] as a witness of our actions.'

I then drew out the hatchet that was concealed under a robe and two fathoms of black tobacco, saying to all: 'I am not opposed to your going to war against the Mascoutens Poüanes,[19] who are your enemies.' In presenting the hatchet to him I sang the war song, after which I wept for their dead.

Having learnt that twenty men were arranging to go to the English [trading post], I presented a collar to the chief of the village in order to bar the road. I said to them that they had to be either entirely French or entirely English, and that those who went to the English would have no credit in the autumn; that if the French brought them the things they needed they ought to have some sense of obligation for being spared the trouble of going so far to get them. They seemed convinced, but it will be very difficult to keep some of them from going off.

The chief of the village made a long harangue to thank me for the trouble I had taken in going to them at so severe a season of the year to give them instruction. The war chief did the same thing, and also harangued his own people, showing them piece by piece the things I had taken the trouble to bring him. The war was put off till the spring by common accord, and the chief, resuming his discourse, said to me: 'My Father, be at ease in your mind and depart content; we will keep your word.' I stayed seven days longer to get over the fatigue of my journey, my old wounds beginning again to pain me and threatening to stop me on the road. I left fort St Pierre on the 5th of February and arrived at fort St Charles on the 14th, the weather being still intensely cold. . . .

Parting with a son

On the 7th of May seven Frenchmen who wintered at fort St Pierre arrived here with nearly 400 Monsoni armed for war, who began singing the war song the same evening. I talked to them the next day in council. The war chief presented me with four beaver robes and a collar, but he commenced by haranguing the assembly, repeating all that had been said on both sides at fort St. Pierre this winter before addressing me at all. Afterwards he said to me: 'My Father, we have come to see you, hoping that you will have pity on us because we obey your word. Here we are at your post; at whom are we to strike?'

Without waiting for me to reply he continued: 'If you wish I will tell you the thought of our warriors. I am chief, it is true, but I am not always master of their will. If you are willing to let us have your son to come with us, we will go straight wherever you tell us; but if you refuse I cannot answer for where the blow may fall. I have no doubt you know the thought of our kindred, the Cree, but I do not hide the fact from you, my Father, that there are several chiefs among us whose hearts are bitter against the Sioux and the Saulteur. You know that some of them came upon our lands until the snow fell. If they did not kill anyone it was because they were discovered. Decide what you are going to do.'

I was agitated, I must confess, and cruelly tormented by conflicting thoughts, but put on a brave front and did not boast of it. On the one hand, how was I to entrust my eldest son to barbarians whom I did not know, and whose name even I scarcely knew, to go and fight against other barbarians of whose name and of whose strength I knew nothing? Who could tell whether my son would ever return, whether he would not fall into the hands of the Mascoutens Poänes or Poüannes, the sworn foes of the Cree and the Monsoni who were asking for him?

On the other hand, were I to refuse him to them, there was much reason to fear that they would attribute it to fear and take the French for cowards, with the result of their shaking off the French yoke, which in reality makes for their happiness, but which has only been shown to them and which they do not effectually know: they appear to like it, yet they have not fully accepted it.

In this dilemma I consulted all the most intelligent Frenchmen of my post and those best able to give advice. They were all of opinion that I should grant the request of the savages, and even pressed me to do so. They said that my son would not be the first Frenchman who had gone with savages to war, and that not being chief of the war party that did not involve any consequences as regarded the tribe against which the war-cloud was forming: moreover, my son was passionately desirous of going. Several Frenchmen offered to accompany him, but, notwithstanding the pleasure this would have given me, I did not think it right to accept them for fear of consequences in the future.

These considerations determined me for the good of the colony to give my son alone to the savages for this campaign, who wanted to place him at their head and make him their first chief. This, however, I opposed for reasons above given, and only allowed him to go as their counsellor and witness of their valour, placing in his hands privately an ample instruction in writing as to the manner in which he should comport himself in the matter of speaking in the councils which ordinarily are held every evening, and even of convoking extraordinary councils according to circumstances. I gave him directions publicly, and this great affair was then concluded. I caused tobacco to be distributed to everybody, testifying the joy I had in seeing them all. . . .

I entreated them to remember the words which had been sent in their name to our

Father in favour of peace, and that they should await a reply. 'I am very glad to tell you, my children,' I said, 'that I am going down to Michilimackinac and perhaps to Montreal to carry your message to our Father and to get a supply of things that we are short of here, such as tobacco, guns and kettles, which you will get in exchange for martens and lynxes, and not for beaver, which you will use for your other needs as I promised you in the winter.'

My object in saying this was to oblige them to hunt those smaller animals which they are not accustomed to do, and at the same time to get the women to take it up, and also the children of from ten to twelve, who are quite capable of it.

'As you have obeyed the word of our Father,' I continued, 'I entrust to you my eldest son who is my dearest possession; consider him as another myself; do nothing without consulting him, his words will be mine; and as he is not as accustomed to fatigue as you, though he is equally vigorous, I depend on you to take care of him on the journey.'

The two chiefs of the two tribes rose, returned me profuse thanks, and harangued the warriors, calling upon them especially to remark the confidence I was showing in them in entrusting my son to them. A slight dispute arose, however, which was soon settled. Both tribes expressed a wish to have my son; either as a compliment to me or because they really desired it, each appeared eager to appropriate him. The Cree chief rose first and addressing me said: 'My Father, you know that your son belongs to me and that I have adopted him. His place is in my canoe. There is an escabia, that is to say a warrior, to serve him and there are two women to carry his outfit.'

My son thanked him, and addressing the Monsoni said: 'My brothers, do not be vexed, I beg of you, if I embark with the Cree; we are all marching together; your cabins are mine and we are all one.' All were then satisfied.

I gave a hatchet to the Cree chief similar to the one I had given to the Monsoni at fort St Pierre. I sang the war chant and recommended them to do their duty well. I gave them a brief account of the manner of making war in France, where men did not fight behind trees but in open country, etc. I showed them the wounds I had received in the battle of Malplaquet,[20] which astonished them. I then made them a feast, after which they continued the war chant.[21]

'The word of our Father': from the report of 1736-7

La Colle, having conferred on the spot with the chiefs of the three tribes, replies in the name of all and presents me with a collar, saying: My Father, when you came into our land you brought us things that we needed, and promised to continue doing so. For two years we lacked nothing, now we lack everything through default on the part of the traders. You forbade us to go to the English and we obeyed you, and if now we are compelled to go there to get guns, powder, kettles, tobacco, etc., you must only blame your own people.

This collar is to tell you to go yourself to see our Father at Montreal and represent our needs to him so that he may have pity on us. You will assure him that we are his true children, having all a French heart ever since we have known him. We give you the brother of La Mikouenne to accompany you; he will speak to our Father in the name of the three tribes. While awaiting your return we shall remain here with your children to keep your forts, and next spring we shall all go on a campaign against the Sioux to avenge the shedding of French blood, which is our own, and to protect your children against aggression. It is no longer you who are taking any part in it, it is I and the chiefs of the three tribes. We beg you to send us from Michilimackinac the word of our Father in order that we may obey and follow it.

The Cree chief, as deputy of the two tribes of fort Maurepas,[22] then rises and says: I thank you, my Father, for the present you are making to the warriors to stop them. I will report what you say to the men who are assembled at Pointe du Bois fort[23] and to all who may join them; but they are so inflamed against the Sioux that I don't know whether they will heed your counsels. I will, however, do my best to make them understand the matter and to stop them. I will tell them that you wish to see them this winter at your fort and ask them to bring meats and fats. . . .

From the journal in the form of a letter to the Marquis de Beauharnois, 1738–39

The chief whom I had accused [of trading with the English at York Fort] said to me: 'My Father, we thank you for having spoken well in our behalf down there to our Father. We know to-day that he has pity on us in sending Frenchmen into our country to bring us the things we need. We will keep quiet as he desires, and let the Sioux do the same. Our heart is still sore on account of your son, who was the first to come and build a fort on our land; we loved him deeply. I have already been once at war to avenge him. I only destroyed ten cabins, which is not enough to content us; but now our Father orders us to keep quiet and we shall do so.'

He asked me then where I was thinking of going, that the river of the Assiniboin was very low and that we ran a great risk of ruining our canoes; moreover that we were going among people who did not know how to kill beaver, and whose only clothing was buffalo skin, a thing we did not require. They were people without intelligence, who had never seen the French and would not be able to make anything of them.

I replied that I wanted to go in the autumn and visit that tribe of whites[24] that I had heard so much about; that I would go up the river as far as I could in order to put it in my power to pursue my journey according to your orders, and that I wanted to increase the number of your children, teach the Assiniboin to hunt, and put some intelligence into them; and that next year I would take another direction.

'You are running a great risk, my Father,' he said 'of your canoes leaving there empty. It is true the Assiniboin are a numerous people, but they do not know how to hunt beaver; I hope you will be able to sharpen their wits.'

I left on the 26th. . . . I found the water very low, as there had been no rain all the summer. The river comes from the west, winds a great deal, is wide, has a strong current and many shallows. There are fine trees along the banks, and behind these a boundless stretch of prairie in which are multitudes of buffalo and deer.

I determined to go by land across the prairie, and let the men I did not require follow in the canoes. The road is much shorter by the prairie, as you cut off several bends of the river and keep a straight road. Game is to be found along the river in great abundance. I did not walk far before meeting some Assiniboin who, having been notified that I was coming up the river, came to meet me. I pursued my way, however, deferring to speak to them till I should be on their land. The band increased in numbers day by day. I marched steadily for six days.

On the evening of October 2 the savages notified me that I could not go any higher up the river on account of the lowness of the water, that my canoes could not pass the wood; and that if it was a question of being well situated for reaching everybody, there was no better place than the portage which leads to the Lake of the Prairies,[25] for that is the road by which the Assiniboin go to the English, and being there [they said] you will stop every one on the way; and, if you wish to go to the Mandan, you are close to the road.

I held a consultation as to what we should do, our reckoning being that we were sixty leagues from the fork by water and thirty-five or forty by land across the prairies. The general opinion was, seeing that we could not go any further, and that we ran great risk of so injuring our canoes that we should not be able to get them out, the place in which we were being one in which neither gum nor resin was to be had for mending them, that the best thing to do was to stay there, as there were good facilities for building, as it was the road to the English posts, and as we had reason to expect a great many people to pass that way, and all of them people who certainly do not go to fort Maurepas.

On the morning of the 3rd I determined to choose a good spot for building a fort, which I caused to be commenced at once. I was still hoping that M. de Lamarque would come and join me. Had I gone further up the river he could not have found me.

While the men were building as hard as they could I spoke to the Assiniboin, assembling them all near my tent. I made them a present from you of powder, ball, tobacco, axes, knives, chisels, awls, these all being things which they value highly, owing to their lack of everything. They received me with much ceremony, shedding many tears in testimony of their joy. For their trouble I received them into the number of your children, fully instructing them afterwards as to your orders, which I repeated several times so that they might fully grasp them. They seemed greatly pleased, thanked me earnestly, and promised to do wonders.

I asked them to let the Assiniboin of the Red river know that they had Frenchmen among them, and that the French would never abandon them as long as they acted sensibly; they ought to recognize, I said, our kindness towards them in sending them useful things from so great a distance; their relative, the old man I had brought with me, could tell them right off all that had happened to us.

The old man then spoke and certainly he left nothing unsaid that could instruct them, or help them to understand what it is to have to do with Frenchmen. The whole was brought to a conclusion with copious tears and thanksgivings.

Notes

[1] This and the following puzzling geographical references resulted from the conflation of several native maps, which the French had not oriented correctly; they were unravelled by

Malcolm Lewis (*Cartographica* 28 (1991), 54–87); according to Pako the river which runs towards the setting sun is the Sturgeon River-English River-lower Winnipeg River system; however other informants (see below) described features which suggest the Nelson, and Lewis concurs.

2 Lake Winnipeg.

3 The Red River.

4 According to Tacchigis' account the 'Great River' would be part of the Nelson River system; then as now the Cree called the Nelson 'Keche Sipi' or 'Great River.'

5 The Saskatchewan, Red, Assiniboine, Souris, and upper Missouri.

6 The lower Nelson River is strongly tidal. The mountain of shining stones, Lewis suggests, is at Upper Limestone Rapids, where there are rocks capable of reflecting light.

7 Nicolas Degonnor (1691–1759), a Jesuit priest with experience of the interior, and deeply interested in exploration.

8 It was Auchaga who advised La Vérendrye to use the Grand Portage-Pigeon River route to the west, rather than the Kaministikwia, thus determining the route west until the Pigeon River became the international boundary in 1783 and travellers returned to the Canadian route via the Kaministikwia. Copies of the map he drew for La Vérendrye (mentioned below) still exist in the National Archives of Canada and elsewhere. For its problems, see Malcolm Lewis' article mentioned above.

9 The Hudson's Bay Company post at York Fort, where the Hayes River enters the Bay.

10 The historic trading post at the mouth of the Kaministikwia river (near present-day Thunder Bay) established in 1685 by Daniel Greysolon Dulhut or Duluth (1639–1710); the North West Company built Fort William nearby in 1801.

11 Since the Monsoni lived chiefly south-west of Hudson Bay, this must mean the English.

12 La Vérendrye's report is addressed to Charles de la Boische, Marquis de Beauharnois (1670–1749), Governor of New France between 1726 and 1747. 'His Majesty' is Louis XV.

13 Six chiefs of the Cree and Assiniboine seeking trade relations with the French. This situation required considerable diplomacy; La Vérendrye's posts were on the lands of the Cree and Assiniboine and he had to sympathize with their political position, but at the same time avoid antagonizing their enemies the Sioux and Ojibwa, with whom the French had alliances.

14 Fort St Charles, established in 1732 on the west shore of Lake of the Woods, was named after Beauharnois.

15 The Mandan Indians, on the Upper Missouri River in present-day North Dakota; for the lengthy and magnificent account of La Vérendrye's own visit to these agricultural natives, see La Vérendrye, *Journals and Letters*, 310 ff.

16 Fort St Pierre (est. 1731) on Rainy Lake, named after La Vérendrye by his nephew Christophe Dufrost de La Jemerais.

17 Saulteur Indians (dwellers by the sault): the Chippewa or Ojibwa of the Lake Huron-Lake Superior area; see RADISSON.

18 Jean-Baptiste Gaultier de La Vérendrye, eldest son of the explorer (1713–1736); he did not in fact remain with the 1734 Cree expedition which began later in the spring (see below). He died at Sioux hands in 1736 (see below).

19 Mascoutens Poüanes (prairie people): an Algonkian group (now assimilated to other tribes) then living between the upper Fox and Illinois Rivers and in the Milwaukee River area.

20 La Vérendrye was wounded and taken prisoner at the battle of Malplaquet (near the French-Belgian border; 11 September 1709) during the War of the Spanish Succession (1701–14).

21 Two years later, on 6 June 1736, Jean-Baptiste de La Vérendrye, a young Jesuit priest, Fr. Aulneau, and twenty other Frenchmen were killed by Sioux on an island in Lake of the Woods.

The bodies were retrieved by La Vérendrye and buried in the chapel at Fort St Charles, where they were found by an archaeological expedition in 1908.

[22]Fort Maurepas, built by Jean-Baptiste Gaultier de La Vérendrye near the site of present-day Selkirk, Manitoba, in 1734; named after Jean Frédéric Phélippaux, Comte de Maurepas (1701–1781), Louis XV's minister of Marine and the Colonies from 1723 to 1749.

[23]Pointe du Bois fort, in Minnesota, west of Red Lake.

[24]The Mandans.

[25]The 'Lake of the Prairies' is Lake Manitoba and Lake Winnipegosis; the portage where La Vérendrye built Fort La Reine is the site of modern-day Portage la Prairie.

Part II: The Great North-West

in the Eighteenth Century

James Isham   (1716 – 1761)

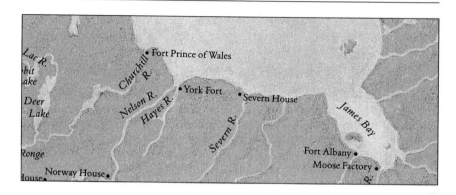

ISHAM was a Londoner by birth, but he lived on Hudson Bay with only brief visits home, from 1732 when he entered the Company's service to 1761 when he died at York Factory. He married in London in 1748, but also had a country wife; his mixed-blood son, Charles Thomas Price Isham also served the Company. He played a vital role in the Company's movement inland to contend with the French fur traders who succeeded LA VÉRENDRYE, and was a formative intellectual influence in the lives of men who served under him like ANDREW GRAHAM. It was he who sent ANTHONY HENDAY into the interior to search out the Blackfoot and urge them to come to the Bay to trade. Isham's fund of unusual knowledge and idiosyncratic spelling shows that his education had been relatively informal, but his mind was absorptive and vigorous, and despite illness and the pressure of work, he found time to document in lively fashion the Bay's flora and fauna, its people, and their language. He illustrated the manuscript of his *Observations* (in the Hudson's Bay Company Archives) with splendid primitive diagrams in colour.

Text: *James Isham's Observations on Hudson's Bay, 1743*, ed. E.E. Rich. The Champlain Society, for the Hudson's Bay Record Society, 1949.

Dedicatory Letter

To The Honourable The Governour, Deputy Governour and Committee of the Hudsons Bay Company London:

Gentlemen,

Being in a Disconsolate part of the world, where their is Little conversation or Divertisment to be had, I was dubious of that too common Malady the Vapour's,[1] which is frequent the forerunner of other Distempers, therefore to prevent such if possable, I have in cold Days and Long winter Nights, amused my self with the following Observations, which I am very Sensible the advantage the Small account of the following Language, wou'd be to any person Residing in North America. The following Vocabulary of the Language which is cheifly spoke in these parts, with some small Observations on the Country, is most Humbly presented to your honor's perusal by,

Gentlemen, Your Honor's most Obedient and Most Humble Servant, JAMES ISHAM.

from the Observations on Hudson's Bay

I observe in these Northern parts the natives have but obscure notions of a Deity &c.: however they beleive their is a good spirit which concerns himself not with them, therefore pay him no adoration. An Evill spirit they Beleive in & worship him from fear, the manner shall be seen in itt's proper place, which is all the account I can give upon this Subject, Neither is itt possable to give Indian for all the Different stiles [names] in our English Language, as itt may be observ'd that one word in the Indian tongue Stands for Severall meanings as,

The sky & clouds one word in their Language means both, as Likewise Star, or stars, they having no notion of Jupiter, mars, Venus, &c. therefore give them all one name as Just observ'd: the four corner's of the world they Stile [give names to], and observe, But have no Knowledge of all the Various points of the Compass, Neither have they any call for such, they Seldom or ever going out of Lakes, Rivers, & creeks, which they can see a cross from Land to Land, and not above five or Eight miles wide. Their Vessels indeed are not of strength or Bulk to Venture fair out of Rivers into the ocean, being very weak & thin and made of the Rhine of Berch, and of the shape & make as Lahonton,[2] and others make mention of, the Longest 18 foot in the Keel. These Boats or Cannoes are so light, that 2 men will carry them one by one a cross Land from Lake to Lake some miles, with all their household Effects upon their backs &c.

The climate may be Reckon'd a Very healthfull place with fine sweet air. I have observ'd itt Excessive hott for a Small time in the Summer, the severity of the Cold in the winter makes us fell [feel] itt so. Which summer here may be Reckon'd four month's, itt begining about the 20th of may, and Ending about the Last of august, with fine Light gales at So.So.Wt. & Wt. when the No.Wt. and Nn. winds begins to sett in, with unsufferable Cold weather, with hard snow, & great Drifts for 8 months togeather, having Known Drift banks of snow, 30 feet perpenticular. The winds and weather is very uncertain and Various in these parts, in the winter months, for itt oft'n happens we shall have fine moderate weather, in a winter morning when before night approches, a sudden gale will spring up with Drift & snow to that Degree, that if men happens to be out, and drest for warm weather, they Run a great Resque of their Lives Several having perrished by such sudden Storms. A most Shocking thing and a Dismal object to see a man when first found froze, as hard as a Rock; Notwithstanding the Cloathing hereafter mention'd. Itt's past beleif to think the Surprizing Effect the frost has in these parts. I have known men to stand at the saw for only 20 minuets when their face & hands has been froze so, they have been obligh'd to Retire to the Surgeon to have Such Cur'd or Cutt off &c. . . .

But still altho it's so excessive cold downe by the Sea shore, it's considerable more mild, & warmer, further in Land, where I think great improvment might be made, in trade &c. by making Setlements further in Land. Nay further I do not think itt unpracticible for the English to make a Setlement at the head of port Nelson River,[3] & to be supply'd from the Lower parts &c. where they might send the Indians to which place they please, or traffick with them their. Being a branch almost all Indians seperates[4] Either to go to York fort, or Churchill, — this proceeding wou'd be of great service, for by so doing they might gett double the fur's, they do now, by Reason of the Difficulty's the Indians meets with in Comming to the Lower parts, & in a few years might with god's will, be able to roat [root] the French out of that small Setlement they have at the great Lake,[5] (or Little sea so call'd by the natives which is near the fork) by advantages that might be taken. These proceedings I think reasonable, for if we was never to make such discoverys in Land, itts certain we shou'd never Reap the Benefit of what might be Discover'd. But what is the most Concern is to see us sitt quiet & unconcern'd while the french as an old saying, not only Beats the Bush but run's away with the Hair [hare] also. . . .

It's a most Surprizing thing and past belief to Imagine the force and Effects the Ice has in these parts, and could not credit such had not I been Eye witness, Large Rock stones the Ice has Lifted & Carry'd of the shores, stones of several tuns weight, has been seen Lying upon Ice at the setting in of the Rivers, much more at the Breaking up of the Rivers, when the Ice is froze fast to the ground, and the Deluges or floods of water forcing such up, thereby carrys them some Distance from their former beds. As Likewise the sand and Gravel, which is the occation of so many sholes we have in wide Large Rivers. As for my part the Very worst coulours itt's possable to Sett this part of the country off, is to[o] good, and I can not say but it's pretty nigh the truth Middletons Discription of his Journal (Page 15 Dobs.).[6]

I have observed the Indians or natives in these Northr'n parts have no Regard or Distinction of Days! sundays and workdays being all alike to them, observes the Christians Keeping the Sabbath day, which they stile a Reading Day, by Reason of the men's not being at their weekly work on that Day, as also Christmass Day, New years Day, & St George's day,[7] Which they stile the Englishmans feast, &c.

They have perticular Days they make feasts of which is at a time when several tribes meets togeather, at such a time one treats another tell all their provender is gone, Eating from morning to night. And itt's to be observ'd he who Keeps the feast obliges Every one to Eat what is alotted him, and not to make waste, or to give any of his Companians any (observation of which as follows;)

Happe'ning once to be travelling, I was Very trouthy [thirsty] so seeing an Indian tent not fair out of my way, I call at the tent to Drink some of their Shagamittee[8] which I did Very heartily, (Notwithstanding itt was full of hair's & Dirt, Like themselves, for you must Know they are none of the clenliest in their Victuals or cloathing.) To proceed, where was about 30 Indians very merry Dispos'd with two old men, one Drumming on a peice of parchment tied on an open Kettle, the other with a stek Like a Ratle, with parchment on both sides, and shott or stones on the inside to make itt Ratle. Asking the Reason of all this seeming mirth, one made answer itt was a goose feast as they styl itt, when I was immediately ask'd by the Chief of the tent to take part. Accordingly being willing to Satisfie my Curiosity, I sitts downe upon a Bundle of Ruhiggan[9] which was handed to me; when Looking round me I see them all sett to work, some a picking, & some a trussing of Geese, downe they went to the fire, some Roasted, some Boyl'd &c. when in two or three hour's, singing, Dancing & talking, Every one took their seat, round the inside of the tent, when the feast was serv'd up. Each had his goose to Devour, who was to Eat the flesh of and not break the bones. I must needs say had not I had a comming [eager] stomach, I shou'd have repented of my staying, to see them tear the flesh of with their teeth, with grease up to their Eyes, & hands as black as any Chimnly Sweepers, Spitting upon one another Cloath's &c. But I made a shift to manage my goose as fast as possable was getting up to be gone, when I was stop'd by the Chief of the tent, for which did not a Little surprize me, for their asking me to eat as welcome to w'at they had, was not the Case, they had contriv'd a sceam as soon as I appeard, for say's they, if he eats with us, he must give us Liquor in the Roome,[10] so finding itt the best way to be clear I accordingly takes them home gives them some Liquor & they Departed well pleased and I was satisfied in my curiosity and Glad I had gott Clear of my unmannerdly company.

I observe Likewise they have no names for the Days of the week, more than tomorrow Day after tomorrow, or 3 Day's to come, or 3 Days past, and as to Years they go by months (alias moons) which moons they style according to the times and Seasons of the year, as goose moon, frog moon &c. by which if itt happ'ns to be a forward winter, and an Early spring they are one month or moon out in their Reckoning, for some time afterwards, and occations their Drawing to the English forts, sooner then they otherwise wou'd do, for to hunt for the factory in the Season times. It's to be observ'd that those Indians that hunts at Seasons for the forts, can not do without the assistance of the English, any more than the English without them, for the Cheif of our Living is this Country's product &c. &c. . . .

The men are for the most part tall and thin streight & clean Lim'd Large bon'd and full breasted, their is Very few Crooked or Deform'd persons amongst them but well shap'd, neither are they of any Large Bulk or corporation, tho' very much when young which is nothing Strange considering the Quantity of water they Drink, and their unmercifull Eating & Cormotizen,[11] — a fawne, a whole or old Beaver, will make but a tollerable meal for an Indian, they observing no sett times for meals, Eating Continually if they can any way procure itt. They provide for to Day & tomorrow may provide for itt Self. They are of a Sworthy complextion, and [I] have seen Europians not so fair, Especialy those Indians that has had copulation with the English, has Brought forth into the world as fine Children as one wou'd Desire to behold, streight Lim'd, Lively active, and Indeed [they] fair exceeds the true born Indians in all things, these are most an End [generally] Light hair'd, and will Venture to say without any Disgrace to——[12] that they are pretty Numerious, for the Generality of the true born Indians, men and women, has Long black hair without curl, course and strong, hair which will Reach to their Knees, which hangs in a Careless manner, only the women, who ties itt in Knots & platts itt in Different form's, to ador'n themselves with, they being a Very ambitious sort of people. The women are for the most part short and thick, and not so Lively as the men when they are turn'd 20 Years; But very frisky when Young &c. The young women are well shap'd. Both men & women are for the most part round Visag'd with their nose flatt between the Eyes not unlike a negro, But tollerable otherways, splaw [splay] foot and Very small hands and fingers, their Eyes Large and Grey yet Lively and Sparkling very Bewitchen when Young, high forehead, white teeth, thick blubber Lip'd and mouth tollerable Large some, and some intollerable Large, Light Eye Lashes and small, their cheeks and chin well propotion'd, in the whole hansomely featur'd the woman more then the men. They are given Very much to turning their toes in and heels out, which is occation'd by the many months they wear snow shoes. The Elderly women are very Carefull in seeing the young ones Comb and Clean their hair, the girls Espetialy being given more to Vermin than the Boys; the method when they wash their hand or face is, they take a Little oyl or fatt, and Rub over their face and with their Long nails of their fingers, they Scratch to Lossing the Dirt, then wipe itt of with their garment. The men has Beards if they wou'd Let itt grow, but they have itt pulled out by the roots, as Likewise the hair in all other other parts, (Except their Eye Lids, Lashes, & hair of the head, they Destroys.) This is Chiefly the womens work, to perform, asking the Reason for so Doing, they made answer that in hard travelling they chaft much, therefore pulled itt out as before mention'd. Its very rare to see a man wear the hair of his head at full Length, some Clipping itt short, others Cutting only one side short and Leaving the other side Long, some half way their forehead Just as the fancy Leads them. . . .

We have frequent Instances among our own Countrymen of the nature not to proceed in any one thing with good words, but will with bad words or corection, and other's it's their nature to proceed with good words & no corection. So I find good usage and civility agrees well with these Natives. If they grow obstobilious [obstinate], a Little correction, then sweatning makes them pliant. They are Cunning and sly to the Last Degree, the more you give, the more they Crave. The generality of them are Loth to part with any thing they have, if at any time they give they Expect Double Satisfaction; Covetioness [covetousness] I think is a sad property to man or woman, such person Can never be Eassy but unhappy all they Days of their Life. What make's Rich misers unhappy, why! their Covetionss and mammon! they gready in getting all the Riches they Can and then a trouble to them for fear it shou'd slip out of their sight. . . .

They argue with Discretion Espetially when they are seated with the great Callimut before them, being Chiefly the Captain who is for the most part an ancient man; this Callimut (alias wus ka che) is one of their Idols, few being admitted in a meeting but those that has a Lawfull right and title to a callimut, their Nature of itt is this;

A Captain or cheif comes with a gang of Indians, in this gang they Divide themselves into Severall tents or hutts, where their is an ancient man, belonging to Each
family, who is officers under the Cheif (alias) Uka maw. When their tent is made the
Captain or Cheif, makes his Enterance with a Cheif officer, by an invitation into the
fort, where he is presented with a great many fine things and Drest as he imagin's

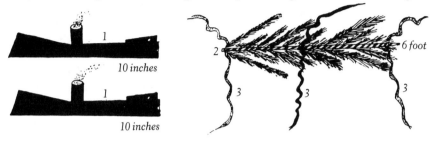

1: the Bowl, 10 inches; 2: the Stem or Callimot 6 foot —
3: Rib'n or Gartg. tied Each end & midle flyg. Loose.

Like a fine man, but in my thoughts more Like amerianderer [merry andrew, i.e.,
buffoon] and when they have satt and Smoak't a pipe for ½ an hour, the Spirit then
puts itt in their head to Speak. . . . when they have smoak'd & Gave Information, of
the Strength of his Little army, or Gang of Indians, he then Departs well Satisfied to
his Subjects or fellow Sufferers, and Divides Equally about 2 inches of tobacco and a
pipe to Each, with some Liquor tell next morning. Then the Ukemau sends his
Leuitenant to Each tent to geather his taxes or a presant for the Cheif of the fort,
which is commonly a Beaver skin, or to the Value in other furs a man [each man?].
When they have Done they give notice they want to come into the fort to smoak, in
the Callimutt &c. When the Ukemau enters with the ancients after him, and a
young man to Each who Carrys the callimutt (and itts to be observ'd the women
never smoaks out of these callimutts) — when they have enter'd the cheif is compli-
mented with a chair, where he plasses himself by the factor, the rest sitting upon
their Brich [breeches] round the table, where the Callimutts of Different makes
shapes and Coullers, are Laid upon a Clean skin upon a table in the middle of the
Roome. In this manner they sitt Very Demurr, for some time, not speak a word, tell
the Ukemau, Breaks Silence. He then takes one pipe or Callimutt and presents itt to
the factor, who Lights itt, having a Young man to hold itt as before mention'd, some
of them being 4: 5: and 6 foot Long. When Light the factor takes the Callimutt by the
midle, and points the small End first to the sun's Rising, then to the highth or midle
of the Day, then at the suns setting, then to the Ground, and with a round turn
presents itt again to the Leader, when they all and Everyone cry ho! (which signifies
thanks) the Cheif takes 4 or 5 whiffs, according to their country, then the young man
hands itt all round they taking the same whiffs Each, tell the pipe is Exhausted, they
then Deliever itt again to the factor, who is to turn it as before observ'd according to
their country three or four times round his head, by the midle of the callimutt, then
Lay itt Downe upon the skin, when the whole Assembly makes the Room Ring with

an Ecco of thanks. So by Each callimutt or pipe tell all is spent, when the Ukemaw makes a speech to the factor the Subject of which is,

'You told me Last year to bring many Indians, you See I have not Lyed. Here is a great many young men come with me, use them Kindly! use them Kindly I say! give them good goods, give them good Goods I say! We Lived hard Last winter and in want. The powder being short measure and bad, I say! Tell your Servants to fill the measure and not to put their fingers within the Brim, take pity of us, take pity of us, I say! We come a Long way to See you, the french sends for us but we will not here, we Love the English, give us good (braz[i]l tobacco)[13] black tobacco, moist & hard twisted, Let us see itt before opened, take pity on us, take pity of us I say! The Guns are bad, Let us trade Light guns small in the hand, and well shap'd, with Locks that will not freeze in the winter, and Red gun casses, (for if a gun is bad, a fine case oft'n putts it of, being great admirers of Different Colours). Let the young men have Roll tobacco cheap, Ketles thick high for the shape, and size, strong Ears, and the Baile to Lap Just upon the side. Give us Good measure, in cloth. Let us see the old measures, Do you mind me! The young men Loves you by comming to see you, take pity, take pity I say! and give them good, they Love to Dress and be fine, do you understand me!' here he Leaves of and they all say ho! But while he is making this speech Every one Else is silent Except the factor, who now and then pronounces U'h, or Ha'oko which signifies Very well. When the factor answers them with satisfaction when they Return thanks, and this is Commonly their Harrange, which is Repeated several times, over. Then another Elderly man breaks silence after two or three force[d] sighs.

'Oh, itt's very hard, itt's very hard; (sham cry) the Earchithin-nues[14] came and Kill'd severall of our Country men wherefore I will go to warr. Will you go with me, (meaning his fellow sufferers.) We do not want to Kill them but they are always Comming against us. What do yo say to itt' speaking to the factor, who perswades them from itt as much as possable, and Desires them to make peace with those Natives. But they Seldom Regard Such advice, therefore to warr they go the following year, Killing men, but chiefly women and Children, tak'n the oppurtunity when men are out a hunting not having the heart to face them, &c. . . . But to proceed, the ukamaw Exhorts his Subjects or more properly his fellow sufferers to trade quiet and not to be obstrobilious [obstinate]. If any freind or Relation is Dead they all sett up an howling for about a minuet then all is over, without Ever a tear. They then make their presant, when the Ukamaw is Deducted [led away] to see the goods. When Satisfied with this glorious Veiw of fine pleasing commoditys they then Depart and trade: when trade is over and they are Ready to be gone, the Ukamaw, after one hour's Consideration comes out of his tent, and stands at the tent Door, Leaning upon a stick if antient if not with his hands by his side, when he begins this small Speech with a Laudable Voice to all his gang of Indians.

'Do not Quarrell or Leave one another, Let the young men hunt as they go, tell they come to Such a place, their stay tell all comes and I will make a feast,' when [whereupon] they all Say very well. When this feast is over, the Cheif then again tell's them.

'I shall be the following year at the same English setlement having Been well us'd, meet me at such a place in the Spring and Bring the Rest of your country men with

you, in order to approach to the said Setlement.' This is the Cheifest Subjects of their harange tho they talk a great Deal more, of Little signification.
. . .

These Natives are not Very numerious considering the Vast track of Land, they have to Range in, we having Seldom comming Yearly to the head factory to trade more than 250 cannoes, one Year with another, which Contains 550 Indians bringing in some cannoes three Indians, besides their Goods, so that I compute their is comes Yearly to all the English setlements in these parts, or belonging to the Hudsons Bay company about 1200 Indians, being nigh as many comes to the head fort of trade as Goes to all the other Setlements.

The worst property that attends these Natives is their false information, for if you put a Question to them, as I have Done oft'n, they will answer to what I Desir'd, at the same time neither her'd see, or new[15] any thing of the matter, so by severall other casses [cases] by which they are not to be Really'd [relied] on unless all points upon the same Subject, as the proverb is, what all say's is true, but I found the Contrary by these Natives.

These Natives are given, very much to Quarrelling when in Liquor having Known two Brothers when in Liquor to Quarrell after such a manner, that they have Bitt one another nose, Ears, and finger's off, Biting being common with them when in Liquor, and no poizon so Venemous as their teeth, wheresomever they Grip. They are a cowardly people. I have frequent seen one, when in Liquior or otherwise, Beeting another which has Laid with his head downe as quiet as a Lamb, and not had the heart to rise in his own Defence. They also are Very Sulky and sullen, and if at any time one has a Resentment against another, they never show itt, tell the Spiritious Liquor's work's in their Brains, then they Speak their mind freely.

These Natives are Very Loving and fond of their Children, Never I think seen any parent or Relation strike a child in anger all the time I have been here, or in these parts, beleving itt may be the Same all over America, Observing De'la,sale[16] and Some others mentions the same, &c. And as to heaving water at them when angry, I have seen done frequent, the fondness to their children is not with them as in England, as itt's too frequent the Entire Ruing to Children and Greif to parents, when itts too Late to correct them.[17] But it's to be Regarded these son's or Daughters never Leaves their parents, tell they gett married, then the youngest son or son in Law mentains their parents as Long as they Live. . . .

Jeliousey that —— [damned?] thing that Ranges so much in all parts of the world, is Likewise very much amongst these Natives, and will be reveng'd of their antagonist some time or another, and oft'n will be the Death of such that has offended them, as I have Known both English and french by these offences. A sample of which: the french had formerly a setlement up —— River where the Natives (women) was forc'd into the fort against their will which aggravated them to that Degree, that they fixed upon Revenge. They therefore unperceived informed their husbands to be Ready upon a Signal they wou'd make, accordingly the women took an oppertunity to wett all the french fuzes[18] with their urine, and then gave the Signal, when their husbands Gott in under cover of the Night, and put their Enemies to the rout, when [whereupon] the french run to their arm's and found how they was betrayd, and was Kill'd for their prefidiousness, being 8 in Number. Some of which Indians are now alive and has told me the same by word of mouth. Notwithstanding their Jeliousy they will take wives, put them of, and take them or other's again at their pleasure, which has made me Imagine, or observe was their such methods in Europe what must be Expected. I have wonder'd oft'n they have not more misunderstandings then what they have. I have Known some to have 6 or 7 wives at a time which in process of time procure's them a Good round family the women being good Breeder's, and the Grey mair is the best horse most an End with them as well as other Nations that is more polite. . . .

The men pretends to be great Conjurer's, tho' Know nothing of any such artifice, and all I cou'd make of itt, is Very Eronious and purely Design'd to frigh'n the women and Children. I think I never was so full of mirth, then once in Seeing their Conjuring & Dancing, when in Liquor. They'l Dance hand in hand round a fire when presantly one comes up side way's, & [blank page in the manuscript] blow's another Downe with his breath, who falls Like a Dead man, so by them all, he then Blow's in their Ear's, and other parts which brings them to Life againe, their Actions being Very Umersome. If an Indians is sick or out of order, they go to singing and conjuring which they have a notion will make them well. They have also a Conceited notion, some things the Sick Keep's is the occation of their Sickness, which if put a side cures them; this is when their Conjuring won't take Effec't, they pretend to Show a hundred other tricks, which is Really not worth the observing.

Conceit has great Effect upon these natives, some having Died with such, — I have Known an Indian when in Liquor say, he wou'd be the Death of Such and Such an Indian, By which Such Indian has took itt to heart and Died, Imagining such Indians had itt in their power to put them out of the world at their pleasure. I take such to proceed from weakness they being Very timerious and fearfull. . . .

I Never knew Indians in this part to Eat raw meet, but in case of Necessity, then they do not scruple to Eat one another, to their Greif, or at Least as I imagine, having Knowne some family's that has Kill'd their Children for food. Especially one family who was Very much in want of provisions, and being a great way of from the English fort, cou'd gett no Suply, (as hungar will Enduce any man to do an unhuman action.) so they made a Dismal Slaughter of four poor Children and Eat the best part of them, which Brought them to the English setlement, in a sorryfull Condition, and of a wild Aspect, Neither do they come to their Senses and natural way of Living for nigh 3 weeks afterwards. After such a misfortune when they have Recovered their right Senses, they Commonly take other Indian's Children and bring them up as their own in Rememberance of the unfortunate Children they mascr'd. Their being starv'd and in hungar is oft'n occationed by the Quiquakatches,[19] as here after mention'd.

The generallity of these natives has some Regard in not marrying too nigh a Kind,[20] tho some few I have Known, has not Stood upon these formality's having took their own Daughters to Wife, and one man to have two Sister's is Com[m]on, tho' not so odious and Brutish in my opinion as the former.

When a Young man has a mind for a wife, they do not make Long tedious Ceremony's, nor yet use much formality's the method is this Vizt [namely]. The man goes out of his tent, to the woman's tent door, where he Looks in and Lays before her as much Cloth as will make her a smock, Sleeves, and Stockings, no words Spoke, he then Return's to his own tent, and waits for the womans Comming. In the mean time, if the woman takes this Cloth up the match is made, that she will be his wife, when she gett's up and goes and Sitts by him in his tent; as man and wife and all is over; But if the woman [refuses] to take the Cloth, some one in the tent Carry's itt and Lay's itt by the man, which Denotes she will not be his wife, when he Looks out for another and perhap's may Light of ten Disappointments, before he getts one &c. . . .

The Natives are Seldom at a Loss in their travelling, no part being Difficult for them to find, tho never was in some parts of their Country in their Lives, yet will steer by the sun, or, moon, or by notching the Bark's of the trees to see which side is thickest; w'ch is always the So. or warm side, thro woods or thickets Let itt be never so bad weather. Itt's also to be observ'd that Side of the trees which is Expos'd to the N. and N.N.Wt. winds, has Very few Branches upon them to what is on the opposite side, this I alway's observ'd when I travel'd in these parts, and Cou'd See no Sun &c.

They Live to a Very great age Both men and Women, Notwithstanding their Excessive Drinking, Which occations miscarriadges frequently. I have Known women to Bear Children at nigh 70. Their memories are sound at 100 Years, not forgetting transactions for many Years past, tho they plead ignorant if you tell them you gave them such a thing at such a time, their answer being that they do not Remember itt, But if at any time they give they will Remember such at the first mentioning. This is their nature, they are Regardless of a good Deed Done them, but will Remember or Keep in their mind a bad Deed done them as Long as they Lives. I think as others has, itts a pitty they was allow'd to taste of that Bewitching spirit called Brandy, or any other Spiritious Liquor's, which has been the Ruing of a Great many Indians, and the Cheif Cause of their Ludness [lewdness] and bad way's they are now given to, their being some few that Drinks none — what may be Called Virtious women, — but now their is no method Can be taken to break them from itt, without the Entire Ruing [ruining?] of the small fur trade in these parts. . . .

Their Robust nature and Strong Constitution is Very surprizing having seen some women that has been Brought to bed upon the Bare ground, with the Heav'ns for a Canope[y], and in an hour afterwards has took the Child upon their back's, and has gone to the woods two Long miles, Brought a Stout Load of wood, which wou'd make a stout man to flinch, and be nothing atall Consern'd or Disconsolate about itt. I can not say but in Some parts of England, Necessity obliges the Women to use almost the same methods. Therefore I think itt's only pride an ambition, that some takes in Keeping their Bed a full month, and putting a poor C— — 'n[21] to Charge and Expence for aught. . . .

These Indians which we call Northern Indians,[22] are not nigh so Numerious as them further to the Southward, believing their not to be above 1000 family's. They are for shape and complextion much the same as the other's aforemention'd, but something taller and Clean Lim'd. Itt's but of Late Years that they have been

Brought to trade at the English Setlements, and [this is a development] not Compleated Yet. They are not of that ambitious Nature as the Indians further to the Southward Dressing Very plaine; using their former Custom's, Seldom trading any finery for Such usses But what they traffick for is Chiefly necessary's for Life, such as powder shott Guns &c.

Their is one thing Very Remarkable in these Indians, which Distinguishes them from any other Country Indian's, which is, Both men and women and Children has three Long black strokes upon Each Cheek, which is Done with gunn powder or coal by pricking the Skin &c. . . . some also has a stroke upon their chin and across their nose.

Their Language is seemingly very Difficulty to understand, some words having so many meanings, Confutes [it obstructs] the Learning of their tongue, Neither is their any yet that has Learn't their tongue as to hold in conversation with the Said Indian's upon any Subject, Knowing Little more then the Names of goods they traffick in &c.

These Natives has not the conveniency of cannoes, comming chiefly by Land, and making floots to cross the Creek's, and River's, being Deep & full of Great falls, tho' do make cannoes further in Land. Their comming by Land is the occation of their bringing but few goods, being some that is nigh 24 months or moon's, advancing to the English fort to trade. These are the further most Northern Indians, next to what they call the Copper Indians, so call'd from the Copper they find upon the border's of their Country,[23] they melting the oar, and clean the Dross from itt, then beat the metle into Several form's, as hand cuffs, head pieces &c: I have seen Several pieces of this Copper and the oar, when first found, pure virgin Copper.

Upon Enquiring how many month's or moon's itt wou'd take an English man to go to their Country, or to where they gett the copper, some Inform'd me 18 month's, other's 12 months others 2 Years, so Never Cou'd Gett the truth, But this I believe a man might go one Summer and be back the summer following, by their acc't itt Lyes ab't Wt. NWt. or NNWt. of Churchill River. Where they gett this copper is nigh the Sea shore, they do not Gett itt from under the Surface of the ground, but pick the oar up Lying upon the Surface of the ground, Scattering here and there and not Very thick togeather. Itt's Low Land and Rocky, plaine Ground by the Sea shore but fine woods, Swamps, and plains further up the Country, the Lakes and Rivers near the ocean some affirm, are fast all the Summer; the Ice never breaking up, which I can not credit for in answer to Such, they come for the English Setlements, in the Spring of the year, and by then they return to their Country back againe, the winter is Sett in with the Usual freezing cold weather, which makes them Imagine the Rivers are never open, because they had been op'n while they was absent, and fast againe at their Return. This I think must be their mistake; for Even the freshes that comes out of the River's and out of the plains &c. in the Spring of the Years, wou'd break the Ice up in wide Deep River's, much more in shole narrow River's, or the Stoppage of water by the frozen Ice wou'd over flow the marshes and Low Lands, and that they say they are Seldom troubled with.

But I think there can be no true Idea given of these Copper Indians Country, or the mine unless further Discovery be made Either by Land or by Sea. And Certainly itt must consist with Reason, itt might sooner be Discover'd by Land then by Sea,[24] and not be at that immence charge and Danger ship's are at their first setting out to Discover what they never Knew ought of. My Reason for itt is this, two Experienc'd men that is of a healthy Constitution, and can Endure hardships is Suffitient for this undertaking by Land, one to converse with the Natives the other to understand Navigation in order to take observations of all Lake's, River's, &c. where and in what Latitude such River's Land mark's &c; are that proper shipping might be fitted out with a great Deal more safety and Likelywhood of Discovering the said Country, then otherwise they might, providing they did not inspect into Such by Land first, &c. It's not unlikely if a passage had been Discov'd in 1741[25] but the ships wou'd have fell in with the Copper Indians Country.

Being troublesome times in England[26] Now, must certainly be the occation why our merchants of England Does not make further Discovery's to the northward, of Churchill, having at presant anough to do to mentain & Support the Settlements already in their possession &c.

These Northern Indians being the Last Yet Discover'd to the Northward Except the Ehuskemay's, [Eskimos, i.e. Inuit] who before the English Setled here us'd frequently to come to Churchill River or Ehuskemay point so Call'd, from their graves and mark's of their Dwellings, some of which are still Remaining.

These Ehuskemays, or (Uskemaw's) are pretty Numerious towards whale cove, Sir Bybie's Island[27] &c. The Chiefest Commodity's they procure is oyl, blubber, and Whale bone &c. being not Brought to any great trade as yet, no more then the above mention'd. Beasts of Value they have in their Country of Severall sorts, Such as Wolves, Welvereen's, foxes, martins, &c. therefore it's not to be Disputed but their is fine woods with Swamp's, plains &c: further in Land, or further up their Country, martin's Seldom or Ever harbouring in plaine Rocky Ground. For which and other Reason's not here mention'd, a Setlement amongst these Natives might turn to great advantage in a few year's.

Notes

[1] Vapours: in the medicine of the time, exhalations from the region of the stomach which were thought to cause nervous depression. Illness confined Isham to Fort Prince of Wales from 23 December 1742 to 1 February 1743. During this time he wrote the *Observations* as well as routinely keeping the (still unpublished) post journal.

[2] Louis Armand de Lom d'Arce, Baron de Lahontan, published his *Nouveaux voyages . . . dans l'Amerique septentrionale* in 1703; it was immediately translated and published in English. See Letter VI, Montreal, 20 June 1684, describing native canoes.

[3] That is, inland, probably somewhere on the North Saskatchewan River near Fort Bourbon, which was on the west side of Cedar Lake.

[4] The two routes from the interior (roughly around Cumberland Lake) to the Bay, via either the Churchill River or the Hayes River.

[5] Lake Winnipeg. The 'small Setlement' was probably Fort Bourbon on Cedar Lake, which

empties into the Saskatchewan and Lake Winnipeg. For the French posts established by 1743 by Pierre Gaultier de Varennes, Sieur de La Vérendrye, and his sons, see LA VÉRENDRYE.

[6] Christopher Middleton (late 17th century–1770); Hudson's Bay Company (and later, Royal Navy) captain, navigator and climatologist. In 1741 he led the first Royal Navy expedition to search for a North-West Passage. Arthur Dobbs cites Middleton's journal in his *An Account of the Countries adjoining to Hudson's Bay, in the North-west Part of America* . . . (London, 1744), p. 15.

[7] St George's Day: April 23.

[8] Shagamittee: sagamité: broth of fish or meat.

[9] Ruhiggan: smoked, dried meat which has been pounded into a powder for long storage.

[10]The Roome: the Company's trading room.

[11]Cormotizen: possibly related to 'cormous', meaning 'gluttonous'?

[12]A dash in the text; the missing name is unknown.

[13]Brazil tobacco, which (following French example) the Company sent out to the natives after 1685 because they so evidently preferred it to English.

[14]Earchithin-nues: Archithinues: the Blackfoot.

[15]Her'd see, or new: heard say (as in hearsay) or knew.

[16]Louis Hennepin, *A Continuation of the New Discovery of a Vast Country in America* (London, 1699), pp. 120–1, quotes La Salle, 'The Children shew but small Respect to their Parents: Sometimes they will beat them without being chastised for it; for they think Correction would intimidate them, and make them bad Souldiers.'

[17]Isham's sense here is not clear, but he appears to be making a comparison between the English, who beat their children — with bad results — and the natives, who do not, and whose children revere the aged.

[18]Fuzes: muskets, (specifically the arquebus) were fired with a fuse.

[19]Quiquakatches: wolverines.

[20]Marrying too close a relative.

[21]C — — 'n: meaning unknown.

[22]The Chipewyans.

[23]For an attempt to ascertain the copper resources of the far north, see the subsequent journey of SAMUEL HEARNE.

[24]Isham has in mind Captain James Knight's ill-fated sea expedition of 1719.

[25]A reference to Christopher Middleton's unproductive expedition of 1741–2 in search of the North-West Passage.

[26]England was engaged in the War of the Austrian Succession (1740–8).

[27]Bibby Island, in Hudson Bay south of Whale Cove and Mistake Bay; named after Sir Bibye Lake, Governor of the Hudson's Bay Company from 1712–43.

Anthony Henday   (fl. 1750 – 1762)

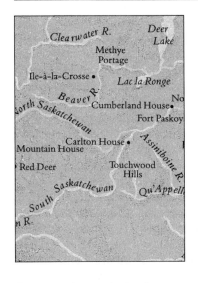

ANTHONY HENDAY emerged from among the unknown labouring men at York Fort to undertake the remarkable journey which at last brought the Hudson's Bay men into contact with the Archithinue or Blackfoot. The very spelling of his name is unsure (Hendey? Hendry?) and his birth and death dates are not known. He seems to have come from the Isle of Wight, and to have been a fisherman and perhaps a smuggler before the Company took him on as net-maker and labourer. Despite the interior journeys of HENRY KELSEY and William Stuart (1715–16) the Company had neglected the exploration of the western interior, but when LA VÉRENDRYE's successors began to establish the French as traders in the area, JAMES ISHAM proposed to send a man to the distant natives to invite them to trade. Henday volunteered, and though he was unsuccessful in encouraging the horsemen of the plains to go anywhere in a canoe, his own journey was a historic one. It lasted from 26 June 1754 to 23 June 1755, and took him down the Hayes River, past the French post at Fort Paskoyac (where he was almost stopped) and then, with a large group of natives, on foot across the prairie to the Archithinue camp near present-day Red Deer, Alberta, which he reached on 14 October. There are severe textual problems with the narrative that resulted (see textual note), but Henday's genuine appreciation of the wild and magnificent world he had happened on nevertheless is vividly apparent. Henday's humble background may have been his greatest strength; once past the French (who worried him) he enters fully into the adventure, reporting without condescension on the daily life in camp, and with genuine awe when he meets the mounted aristocracy of the plains, the Blackfoot chief and his warriors. The return trip home was frustrating; the natives he travelled with traded their best furs to the French, and it was obvious that the Company was facing serious problems in extending trade to the interior. Henday remained at York until 1762, and among other journeys made a trip to the Archithinue in 1759–60 for which no journal exists. When he was not promoted, he left the Company in 1762, and nothing more is known of him.

Text: There are four versions of Henday's journal, varying substantially in detail; for the differences, and a historian's view of their origin, see Glyndwr Williams, 'The Puzzle of Anthony Henday's Journal, 1754–55', *The Beaver* (Winter, 1978), 40–56. Williams casts doubt on the veracity of the first and most primitive version of the journal, A; the other three were made by or for Andrew Graham, B and C dating from 1767–69, D perhaps as late as 1782. The best known version (used here) is D, which is important for its effect on the historiography of the west, though it has to be read now as in part dependent on rewriting by Andrew Graham. (Text as edited by Lawrence J. Burpee, *Transactions of the Royal Society of Canada*, Section II [1907], 321–54.) Included here is a sample of Henday's observations on the landscape and the life of the explorer's camp, plus fuller excerpts from his encounter with the Blackfoot and with the French traders.

June 26, 1754. Wednesday. Took my departure from York Fort, and paddled up Hays River to Amista-Asinee or Great Stone,[1] distant from the Fort 24 miles; our course about S.W.b.W.; here we put up for the night. . . .

5. Friday. Took my departure from fortunate Fall and paddled 24 miles W.b.So. & W.S.W.: passed much shoal water, and twenty-four islands; there is not a foot of water for a mile. We are greatly fatigued with carrying and hauling the Canoes, and not very well fed, but the Natives are continually Smoking, which I already experience allays hunger. . . .

11. Thursday. Took my departure from Shad Fall and paddled two miles S.W. up the River, when it began to blow with Rain, which obliged us to put up. Here twenty Canoes of Natives passed us on their way to York Fort, with whom I sent a letter to Mr James Isham, the Chief.[2] . . .

15. Monday. Paddled 24 miles S.W.b.S. met four Canoes of Indians in the French interest the Leader's name Monkonsko. He behaved civilly and informed me that I was on the Confines of the dry inland country, called by the Natives the Muscuty Tuskee; and that I should soon see a French House. . . .

22. Monday. The Musketoes are now intolerable, giving us neither peace day nor night; paddled 14 miles up the River West, when we came to a French house.[3] On our arrival two Frenchmen came to the water-side, and in a very genteel manner, invited me into their house, — which I readily accepted. One of them asked me if I had any Letter from my Master, and where, and on what design I was going inland. I answered I had no letter, and that I was sent to view the Country, and intended to return in the Spring. He told me the Master and men were gone down to Montreal with the furs; and that they must detain me till their return. However they were very kind; and at night I went to my tent, and told Attickashish, or Little Deer, my Leader,[4] that had the charge of me, who smiled and said they dared not. I sent them two feet of tobacco, which was very acceptable to them. . . .

31. Wednesday. Travelled 13 Miles W.S.W. Level lands and burnt woods; and there are nothing but stagnated water to drink. Came to two tents of Asinepoet [Assiniboine] Indians. I smoaked with them, and talked with them to go down with me to York Fort in the summer, but they answered, 'We are conveniently supplied from the Pagua-Mistagushewuck Whiskeheginish.' That is, the Frenchman's House of Trade.

August 1. Thursday. Travelled 12 miles S.W.b.S., fine level land and tall woods; passed three small creeks of sweet water. The Indians killed two moose; I am now entering a pleasant and plentiful country. . . .

4. Sunday. Travelled 10 miles N.W. Land and Woods as yesterday. Met with 7 tents of Asinepöet Indians. I smoaked with them. — We have no hopes of getting them to the Fort, — as what cloth &c. they had were French, and, by their behaviour, I perceived they were strongly attached to the French interest, Indians killed 2 Moose.

5. Monday. Travelled 11 miles W.S.W. Level land and poor Woods; killed four Waskesew, or Red Deer, a stately animal, but the flesh coarse, and no manner equal to Moose flesh; however all is welcome to us. . . .

8. Thursday. Travelled none. All hands feasting, smoking, drinking, dancing and conjuring. . . .

13. Tuesday. Travelled 7 Miles W.S.W. Level land, short Grass, Dry-woods, and several salt water lakes. We are now entered Muscuty plains, and shall soon see plenty of Buffalo, and the Archithinue Indians[5] hunting them on Horse-back. . . .

21. Wednesday. The Indian Men made temporary Canoes of Willows, covered with parchment Moose skins.[6] The Women gathered plenty of excellent berries, and cherries. I angled a few small Trout; and in the evening we crossed the River in our Slender Canoes, without any accident happening.

22. Thursday. Travelled 12 Miles N.W. Level land and dry ridges of woods; saw no water till we put up at night; and that was fresh and good, thank God. Indians killed 6 Waskesew. They are plenty and although coarse food, yet go well down with me and my companions.

23. Friday. Travelled 12 miles West. Level land, no Woods, nor water till the evening; came to a ledge of Poplars and sweet water. The Archithinue Natives has been here lately; we know by their horses dung and foot-steps. . . .

September 5. Thursday. Travelled 12 Miles West. Level land, with plenty of fruit trees; plenty of Moose, Waskesew, Swans, Cranes, White & Grey Geese, also a few Ducks. We are yet in Muscuty plains. Here are a great many Asinepoet Indians. The Buffalo has taken the route upwards, [north] and is the reason we have not yet met with Archithinue Natives.[7]

6. Friday. Travelled W.S.W. 10 Miles. Hillocks and Dales & small ledges of woods all burnt. Indians killed 5 Moose & 2 Waskesew; met with five tents of Mekesue, or Eagle Indians. I gave their leader half a foot of Brazile tobacco, and smoked with them: they were very kind, and made me a present of some tongues, & a bladder full of fat. I could perceive no difference between them and the Asinepoet Natives with regard to the language; but one circumstance surprised me much, and that is, the men do not cover their nakedness; which are the only natives that do not attend to decency. The women are cloathed the same as the other Asinepoet Indians. The Natives inform me that they are a tribe of that brave Nation; and take their name from Eagles being plenty in the district they inhabit. The Leader promised to collect furs, and go down with me to the Fort. They never had traded with any European or Canadian. My Guides & Companions seemed afraid of them. . . .

10. Tuesday. Travelled none. The young men and I went a hunting, killed 3 Moose

& 6 Waskesew. I killed a Bull Buffalo, nothing but skin and bone; took out his tongue, and left his remains to the Wolves who were waiting around me in great numbers; they do not meddle with any person: We cannot afford to expend our ammunition on them. In the evening when we returned home, found we were joined by ten tents of different Indians, but no tidings of the Archithinue Natives. My feet are swelled, but otherwise, Thank God, in perfect health. . . .

14. Saturday. Travelled none. I went with the young men a Buffalo hunting, all armed with Bows & Arrows: killed seven, fine sport. We beat them about, lodging twenty arrows in one beast. So expert are the Natives, that they will take the arrows out of them when they are foaming and raging with pain, & tearing the ground up with their feet & horns until they fall down.

15. Sunday. Travelled 7 Miles W.S.W. Level land, no woods to be seen: passed by a lake: the Buffalo so numerous obliged to make them sheer out of our way. Also Wolves without number, lurking Indians killed a great many Buffalo; only taking what they choosed to carry. I am now well stocked with tongues. We saw a few Moose & Waskesew; but as the natives seldom kill them with the Bow & Arrows they will not expend ammunition, while Buffalo are so numerous. I hope we shall soon see the Archithinue Natives; the Horse dung, and paths being pretty fresh. Saw a large Snake but could not get at it. . . .

22. Sunday. Travelled none. Indians hunting. Indians killed 6 Moose. No Buffalo to be seen. Saw several Wild Horses. The Natives behave very kind to me, except my Guide Attickashish, who is a little out of humour because I would not lend him my gun: but I take no notice, neither do I value him.

23. Monday. Travelled none. Young Men hunting killed 4 Moose and 3 Buffalo; also a large black Bear. Saw several Toads. I cannot describe the fineness of the Weather, and the pleasant country I am now in. . . .

27. Friday. Travelled 7 Miles W.b.N. Ridgy land with hommocks of wood & small Creeks. Indians killed 6 Beaver, 3 Moose and 3 Buffalo. Saw a large smoke which we think are the Archithinue Natives. . . .

29. Sunday. Travelled none. Women dressing Skins for Shoes. Joined by more Asinepoet Indians, & two Archithinue Natives on Horseback; who informed us it is the Archithinue Smoke we saw: and that it will be eight days before we reach them. . . .

October 1. Tuesday. Travelled none. Came to us 7 tents of Archithinue Indians; the men all mounted on Horse-back, with Bows and Arrows, & bone spears & darts. I gave the Leader a foot of tobacco, one fire Steel, a string of beads, a knife; and smoked with them. By my interpreter he said that he would inform their Great Leader of my coming & so left us. . . .

5. Saturday went 6 Miles W.S.W. Level land and no woods: passed two creeks, & several Iron Mines running in large long veins. Great plenty of Buffalo. We are still in the Muscuty Country. . . .

11. Friday. Travelled 7 Miles S.W.b.W. then came to Waskesew River,[8] and crossed it on a Fall about two feet high, and much the same depth, & 20 poles wide. On both sides there are stones of different sizes & weight: quite round, and of an iron color:

and a little distance from the River, are veins of iron-ore running along the surface of the ground. No woods to be seen. Indians killed several Beaver and 2 Moose. . . .

13. Sunday. Travelled 7 Miles S.W.b.W. Level land, and ledges of woods; and numbers of Buffalo. Indians killed a great many. In the evening we were joined by 7 Archithinue Natives on Horse-back, who informed us we should see the Great Leader, & numbers of Archithinue Natives to-morrow.

14. Monday. Travelled 4 Miles S.W.b.W. Then came to us four men on Horse-back; they told us they were sent from the main body to see whether we were Friends or Enemies. We told them we were Friends. Attickasish, Canawappaw, Cokamanakisish, and the other of our Leaders walked in front about 4 Miles farther then we; came to 200 tents of Archithinue Natives, pitched in two rows, and an opening in the middle; where we were conducted to the Leader's tent; which was at one end, large enough to contain fifty persons; where he received us seated on a clear [white] Buffalo skin,[9] attended by 20 elderly men. He made signs for me to sit down on his right hand: which I did. Our Leader set on several grand-pipes, and smoked all round, according to their usual custom: not a word was yet spoke on either side. Smoking being over, Buffalo flesh boiled was served round in baskets of a species of bent, and I was presented with 10 Buffalo tongues. Attickasish my Guide, informed him I was sent by the Great Leader who lives down at the great waters, to invite his young men down to see him and to bring with them Beaver skins, & Wolves skins: & they would get in return Powder, Shot, Guns, Cloth, Beads, &c. He made little answer: only said that it was far off, & they could not paddle. Then they entered upon indifferent subjects until we were ordered to depart to our tents, which were pitched about a full quarter of a Mile without their lines.

15. Tuesday. Froze a little last night. Our women employed dressing Beaver skins for cloathing. About 10 o'clock A.M. I was invited to the Archithinue Leader's tent: when by an interpreter I told him what I was sent for, & desired of him to allow some of his young men to go down to the Fort with me, where they would be kindly received, and get Guns &c. But he answered, it was far off, & they could not live without Buffalo flesh; and that they could not leave their horses &c: and many other obstacles, though all might be got over if they were acquainted with a Canoe, and could eat Fish, which they never do. The Chief further said they never wanted food, as they followed the Buffalo & killed them with the Bows and Arrows; and he was informed the Natives that frequented the Settlements, were oftentimes starved on their journey. Such remarks I thought exceeding true. He made me a present of a handsome Bow & Arrows, & in return I gave him a part of each kinds of goods I had, as ordered by Mr. Isham's written instructions. I departed and took a view[10] of the camp. Their tents were pitched close to one another in two regular lines, which formed a broad street open at both ends. Their horses are turned out to grass, their legs being fettered: and when wanted, are fastened to lines cut of Buffalo skin, that stretches along & is fastened to stakes drove in the ground. They have hair halters, Buffalo skin pads, & stirrups of the same. The horses are fine tractible animals, about 14 hands high; lively and clean made. The Natives are good Horsemen, & kill the Buffalo on them. These Natives are drest much the same as others; but more clean &

sprightly. They think nothing of my tobacco: & I set as little value on theirs: which is dryed Horse-dung.[11] They appear to be under proper discipline, & obedient to their Leader: who orders a party of Horsemen Evening & Morning to reconitre; and proper parties to bring in provisions. They have other Natives Horsemen as well as Foot, who are their Enemies: they are also called the Archithinue Indians: & by what I can learn talk the same language, & hath the same customs. They are, like the other Natives murthering one another slyly. Saw many fine Girls who were Captives; & a great many dried Scalps with fine long black hair, displayed on poles, & before the Leader's tent. They follow the Buffalo from place to place: & that they should not be surprised by the Enemy, encamp in open plains. Their fuel is turf, & Horse-dung dryed; their cloathing is finely painted with red paint; like unto English Ochre: but they do not mark nor paint their bodies. Saw four Asses.

16. Wednesday. Women employed as yesterday. With the Leader's permission, I rode a hunting with twenty of his young men. They killed 8 Buffalo, excellent sport. They are so expert that with one, or two, arrows they will drop a Buffalo. As for me I had sufficient employ to manage my horse. When I came home I was invited to the Leader's tent again where were all the Asinepoet Leaders, etc., I thought it very curious as there were four different languages among us. The Leader gave orders to pitch away from him,[12] and that we would see him again in the Spring, when they came down after the Buffalo. He gave one of the Leaders two young slaves as a present and 40 Buffalo tongues; they were both girls. . . .

November 14. Thursday. Women making cloathing for cold weather: Some families have not got half enough of skins for cloathing them on the aproaching winter: & what surprizes me most, they never go out of their tents but when they want provisions, altho' the Beaver & Otters are swarming about us in the Creeks & Swamps, not one went out to-day but myself, & I killed two Otters. . . .

22. Friday. Travelled none. Indians killed a few Beaver. One man narrowly escaped from a Grizzle Bear that he had wounded, by throwing his Beaver coat from him; which the Bear tore to pieces, & which the Natives always do when forced to retreat. The Men & Dogs went out & killed the Bear.

23 to 27. Saturday, Sunday, Monday & Tuesday. Snow at Intervals. The men killed a few Beaver; & the Women dressing skins for cloathing. My Winter rigging is almost in readiness. Drumming, Dancing, & feasting. . . .

[December] 3 to 4. Tuesday. Frosty weather: it is now very cold: Indians pitched away from us; So that we stand in Number Viz Myself, 2 Men, 5 Women & 4 Children: killed 7 Beaver.

5 to 7. Thursday. Strong gale with freezing, drifting, weather: killed one Moose: My companions hath neither Powder nor Shot: So that we must use the gun but seldom, as they now depend on me; Women making Shoes of Moose leather: I have as yet only wore Shoes with the hair on the inside, so moderate hath the weather been. . . .

11 & 12. Wednesday. Broke open several Beaver houses but got none: The Men must look out for Beaver as they have no Ammunition & I am resolved to take care of mine, neither would it be prudent to expend Ammunition in a Beaver Country. . . .

14. Saturday. Rained all last night & this day, so that it hath left little snow or ice:

The Moose & Waskesew passing & repassing in herds, within 200 yards of our tent: The men beg Ammunition from me, but without success. . . .

18. Wednesday. Made 7 pairs of Snow-Shoes, there being no Birch the way we are to go. . . .

26 & 27. Thursday & Friday. Killed 2 Waskesew and 2 Moose: I set a Wolf-Hap [trap]. I asked the Natives why they did not Hap Wolves; they made Answer that the Archithinue Natives would kill them, if they trapped in their country: I then asked them when & where they were to get the Wolves &c, to carry down in the Spring. They made no answer; but laughed one to another.

28. Saturday. Frost & snow & very cold weather: I travelled 5 Miles N.E.b.N. Level land, & narrow ledges of poplar, Alder & trees. got a Wolf in my Hap, & set 2 more; the Wolves are numerous. An Indian told me that my tent-mates were angry with me last night for speaking so much concerning Happing, & advised me to say no more about it, for they would get more Wolves, Beaver &c. from the Archithinue Natives in the spring, than they can carry. . . .[13]

[January] 3. Friday. Ice 4 inches thick on the ponds; & the ground covered with snow; but not so deep as to wear Snow-shoes; Indians killed 6 Waskesew, saw above 300 feeding in one plain. I plainly observe all our Traders must be supplyed with Furs from the Archithinue & Asinepoet Natives; as the people that joined us had not Beaver skins to cloath them. . . .

9. Thursday. Snowy weather: travelled 5 Miles N.E.b.N.: Level land with ledges of Brush-wood & poplar: Indians killed 2 Waskesew. In the Evening we were joined by 2 more tents of our Traders, they have as few furs as the others.

10. Friday. Indians killed one Moose & 6 Waskesew: Women knitting Snow-shoes. . . .

18 to 21. Saturday, Sunday, Monday & Tuesday. Freezing weather, with snow at times: Indians employed killing Moose & Buffalo: Wolves numerous: Every Evening the Natives are employed dancing &c. I have had nothing on my feet as yet but a thin flannel sock & a Buffalo skin shoe with the hair inwards: My Horse begins to lose flesh. . . .

February 2. Sunday. The French Leader named Wappenessew[14] promises to go with me to the Fort: He hath a great sway among the Natives and is much esteemed by the French: I presented him with a little powder &c. Indians feasting, Smoking, Dancing &c. . . .

5 to 9. Wednesday, Friday, Saturday & Sunday. All hands trapping foxes. I walked in Snow-shoes for the first time this winter. In the Evening Smoked & feasted with the French Leader. . . .

11 to 27. Tuesday the eleventh to the 27th. Employed Travelling & sometimes laying by killing Buffalo, Moose &c. in a pleasant & plentiful country, our Course towards the N.E.: We were joined by different tribes of Natives, who yearly visited our Settlements: they brought with them several Archithinue Women & Children Captives, with many Scalps quite green [fresh]: We are now at Archithinue lake, about one mile broad, & a good days journey in length; with tall woods on both sides mostly pines, the largest I have yet seen.

28. Friday. Travelled 4 Miles N.E.b.E. then put up to feast &c. The Scalps were displayed on long poles round the tents; & the Captives, Boys & Girls, were given away as presents to one another. They presented to me a Boy & Girl; which I declined accepting of in as modest a manner as possible.

March 1. Saturday. Killed 3 Buffalo & 2 Moose: A Captive Girl aged about 17 years was knocked on the head with a Tomahawk by a Man's wife in a fit of jealousy: No notice was taken as such game is common amongst them: the unfortunate Girl had been presented to the Murtherer's husband yesterday. . . .

13. Thursday. Two young Natives in the french interest brought 12 Beaver skins to trade with us for Ammunition; I gave them a little & told them to go with me to York Fort with their furs, where they would receive more goods for them in barter, then they did from the French: They gave me fair promises. . . .

18. Tuesday. I went a Hunting with my Companions; Saw many Waskesew but could not come at them; the Snow so hard makes a noise under our Snow-Shoes: Ten tents came & pitched alongside of us in order to build Canoes.

19 & 20. Wednesday & Thursday. Snow almost dissolved. The Aged men making Gunwales for Canoes, & the Young Men hunting, & not yet returned. . . .

22 & 25. Saturday. Sunday. Monday. Tuesday. Snow at intervals: no walking abroad: All hands preparing Wood &c for building Canoes: The Asinepoet Natives are building Canoes below us.

26 to April 7th. Wednesday. Thursday. Friday. Saturday. Sunday. Monday. Tuesday. Wednesday. Thursday. Friday. Saturday. Sunday. Monday. All hands building Canoes & hunting; pretty good Success: Every Evening Feasting &c.

8. Tuesday. Last evening we had thunder & hail accompanyed with a N.W. Wind: Men employed as formerly: I gave my Horse to an old man who is to return him in case I should return again to this plentiful Country. Dancing. Drumming &c, and all good humoured.

9 to 12. Wednesday. Thursday. Friday & Saturday. All hands employed building Canoes & in the Evening Smoking the Grand Calimut &c: Several Asinepoet Indians pitched their tents a small distance below us; & in the Evening smoked with me, & promised not to trade with the French at Basquea Settlement, but accompany me to York Fort. . . .

20. Sunday. Each tent killed two Dogs & had a Grand feast; I must take notice they do not skin the Animal but scrape it & Roast it over a fire, two Young Men keeping turning it; for no Women hath any concern, not even to be present: The Old Men Conjuring &c. . . .

23. Wednesday. Displayed my Flag in Honour of St George; & the Leaders did the same, after acquainting them & explaining my reason:[15] In the afternoon the ice in the River broke up: a great many Geese and Swans were seen flying to the Northward: In the Evening we had a grand feast with Dancing, Drumming, Talking &c. . . .

25. Friday. Ice driving down the river. Finished the Canoes & preparing to set out for York Fort. . . .

[May] 12. Monday. Paddled 10 miles E.b.N. then came to one hundred tents of Archithinue Natives. Their Leader invited me to his tent, and gave me plenty of

Buffalo flesh: our Indians bought a great many Wolves from them, for old axes &c.[16] I could not persuade them to go to the Fort. . . .

15. Thursday. Paddled none: killed a great number of Buffalos; Indian women and children employed drying meat. One hundred and twenty seven tents of Archithinue Natives came to us: I bought 30 Wolves' skins from them, and the Indians purchased great numbers of Wolves, Beaver & Foxes etc. which proves what the Woman formerly told me, concerning the Natives getting part of their Furs from the Archithinue Indians. They told me that I should soon see their Leader. I did my Endeavour to get some of them down to the Fort; but all in vain: and altho' the Indians promised the Chief Factor at York Fort to talk to them strongly on that Subject, they never opened their mouths; and I have great reason to believe that they are a stoppage: for if they could be brought down to trade, the others would be obliged to trap their own Furs: which at present two thirds of them do not. These brave Natives swimmed their Horses across the river; they looked more like to Europeans than Indians. They shared amongst us 10 Buffalo.

16. Friday. Paddled 30 Miles N.b.E. when we came to 30 tents of Archithinue Natives: I talked with them as I did with the others; but all to no purpose. Our Indians traded a great many Furs from them. They have the finest Horses I have yet seen here, and are very kind people.

17. Saturday. Paddled none. Ten tents of Eagle Indians joined the Archithinue Indians. Five Canoes of them are going to the Fort with me. They are a tribe of the Asinepoet Nation; and like them use the Horses for carrying the baggage and not to ride on. I was invited to the Archithinue tents, where were feasting etc.: much in the same manner as our Indians practize. . . .

20. Tuesday. paddled 30 Miles N.E.b.N. a noble spacious river.

21. Wednesday. Paddled none. Seventy tents of Archithinue Natives came to us, headed by the Leader that I saw in the Muscuty Country: I used my utmost endeavors to get a few of his young men to the Fort; but to no purpose. They had very few Wolves or Furs of any kind, having traded them before with the Pegogamaw Indians who are gone to the Fort. We are above 60 Canoes and there are scarce a Gun. Kettle. Hatchet, or Knife amongst us, having traded them with the Archithinue Natives.

22. Thursday. Paddled 30 Miles North & N.b.W. the river broad and deep, no Islands. It appears to me at present to be a fine river but the Indians tell me that it is almost dry in the middle of Summer. The young men killed 4 Buffalo this morning & I gave away the remains of my powder & shot.

23. Friday. Paddled 20 Miles N.E. then came to a French Trading House[17] where were 6 men. The Master invited me to supper, but we had no bread until we were done; then He presented me with half a biscuit and a dram of French Brandy, and told me that this House was subordinate to Basquea and they heard of my passing by last Autumn.

24. Saturday. The Natives received from the Master ten Gallons of Brandy half adulterated with water; and when intoxicated they traded Cased Cats,[18] Martens, & good parchment Beaver skins, refusing Wolves and dressed Beaver. In short he received from the Natives nothing but what were prime Winter furs.

25. Sunday. Rained hard last night; I could not get the Natives away to-day; It is surprising to observe what an influence the French have over the Natives; I am certain he hath got above 1000 of the richest Skins. . . .

29. Thursday. Paddled 60 miles, then came to a French House I passed last Autumn; there were a Master & 9 men. On our arrival they gave the Natives 10 Gallons of Brandy adulterated, and they are now drunk. The Master[19] invited me in to sup with him, and was very kind: He is dressed very Genteel, but the men wear nothing but thin drawers, & striped cotton shirts ruffled at the hands & breasts. This House has been long a place of Trade belonging to the French, & named Basquea. It is 26 feet long; 12 feet wide; 9 feet high to the ridge; having a sloping roof; the Walls Log on Log; the top covered with Birch-rind, fastened together with Willows, & divided into three apartments: One for Trading goods, one for Furs, and the third they dwell in.

30. Friday. The Indians drank so much I could not get them away; nor was I capable to prevent them from trading their prime furs. I breakfasted with the French Master, and he showed me the stock of Furs Viz: A brave parcel of Cased Cats, Martens, and parchment Beaver. Their Birch-rind Canoes will carry as much as an India Ships Long-boat, and draws little water; and so light that two men can carry one several miles with ease: they are made in the same form and slight materials as the small ones; only a thin board runs along their bottom; & they can sail them when before the wind, but not else. The French talk Several Languages to perfection: they have the advantage of us in every shape; and if they had Brazile tobacco, which they have not, would entirely cut off our trade. They have white tobacco made up in Roles of 12 lb wt. each. The Master desired me to bring or send him a piece of Brazile tobacco, & a quart, or pint, japanned drinking mug.

31. Saturday. The Indians would not set out: they have kept a continued trading with the French; and I believe many would trade all if they could persuade the French to take their heavy furs. Breakfasted &c with the Master; He said he was going with the furs to one of the Chief settlements,[20] as soon as he received the Furs from the upper house, which would be in a few days hence.

June 1. Sunday. Could not paddle: Breakfasted with the Master: Several Asinepoet Natives distributed their heavy Furs and Pelts, that the French have refused, amongst our Indians with directions what to trade them for. . . .

15. Sunday. Paddled through Deer Lake and came to Steel river: here met with 4 Canoes who had been at the Fort, & who informed me of the death of Mr Skrimsheur,[21] second in Command at York Fort; and that the Governor & all the men were well. Went & found my tobacco safe that I left here last Autumn: We smoked drank out two Runlets of Brandy that the Natives had brought from the fort.

16 to 20. Monday to Friday. Sometimes had good water & sometimes dragged our Canoes; had several Canoes damaged: when on the 20th day of this month of june we arrived at the fort, where we were kindly received.

Notes

¹ In these selections, no attempt has been made to trace Henday's route in detail.

² JAMES ISHAM, Henday's superior at York Factory.

³ Basquia or The Pas in present-day Manitoba. This was Fort Paskoyac, whose strategic site was identified by a son of LA VÉRENDRYE about 1748. At the time of Henday's journey it was commanded by Louis Chapt, known as the Chevalier de La Corne (1703–61), officer and trader; Henday may have met him on May 23 (see below). He was commandant of the *poste de l'Ouest* from 1752–5, based at Fort Paskoyac.

⁴ Leading Indian, or Captain (see HENRY KELSEY).

⁵ The Blackfoot. For the arrival of horses among the natives of the plains, see SAUKAMAPEE.

⁶ The 'bull-boats' of the North and South Saskatchewan were made of skin because of the local scarcity of birchbark.

⁷ Only on the preceding day had Henday at last encountered two Archithinue.

⁸ Probably the Red Deer River.

⁹ A white buffalo skin was a costly rarity among the plains Indians, and was usually put to a religious or ceremonial purpose.

¹⁰Made a sketch, or possibly a plan; the London Committee later complained, 'we apprehend Henday is not very expert in making Drafts with Accuracy.'

¹¹Europeans often thought native tobacco weak.

¹²Henday seems to use 'pitch' in two senses; ordinarily it means 'pitch camp' but here it may simply mean 'move off.'

¹³As indeed they did; see the entry for May 12, below.

¹⁴A Leading Indian or 'Captain' operating on behalf of the French traders.

¹⁵April 23, St. George's day.

¹⁶As predicted on December 28.

¹⁷Fort St Louis, an outpost of Basquia (Fort Paskoyac) founded in 1753 by Louis Chapt, Chevalier de La Corne.

¹⁸The skin of a Canada Lynx, removed by peeling it off without slitting the body.

¹⁹Fort Paskoyac (see 22 July 1754, above). The 'Master' was possibly Louis Chapt, the Chevalier de La Corne.

²⁰Possibly Kaministikwia or Michilimackinac.

²¹Samuel Skrimsher (1721?–55), second at York 1746–8, and in charge at Flamborough House on the Nelson River from 1751 until he was killed by a native in 1755.

Alexander Henry the Elder   (1739 – 1824)

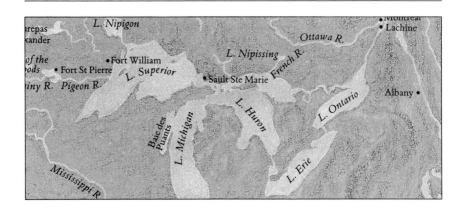

HENRY was born in New Jersey, and took up the life of a trader when he helped provision the troops of Major-General Jeffrey Amherst in 1760. Like PETER POND he was active in the period between the defeat of the French and the American Revolution, and like him traded in the area between Lake Huron and Lake Superior. The attack on the fort at Michilimackinac which he witnessed was part of the uprising against the British organized in 1763 by the Odawa chief Pontiac. Henry wrote his account of the massacre in old age, and is not always clear on the facts, but he had a born gift for story-telling and the account is a justifiably famous version of the ancient genre 'I-alone-have-escaped-alive-to-tell-you'. Between Henry's near-Gothic tale of horror and John Richardson's fictionalization of the same events in *Wacousta* (1832) the historical event itself, in which a number of interesting personalities such as Langlade and Minweweh were involved, has almost been lost to sight. Henry's narrative gifts appear in another form in his account of the journey to the prairies he made in 1775–6 with Joseph Frobisher. This is one of the periodic 'grand surveys' of the west which exploration literature produced between KELSEY and PALLISER. Like many others, Henry's narrative is fraught with potential disaster, but as befits a man who maintained his starving party with drafts of hot chocolate, his good humour always comes to the fore. The account of his reception by the Assiniboine chief Great Road deserves to stand beside HENDAY's and COCKING's record of their meetings with the Blackfoot.

Like ALEXANDER MACKENZIE, Henry was a trader born, and his later life was filled with projects for the systematization and expansion of the fur trade. He travelled widely, and made a point of contacting those who might be interested in his enterprises. A brother of La Corne ensured him an introduction to Marie Antoinette; he later presented a plan for an expedition overland to the Pacific to the great naturalist and patron of science Sir Joseph Banks, and was the host of John Jacob Astor when he came to Montreal. He settled in Montreal, where he was one of the founders of the Beaver Club, and continued to engage in trade throughout his long life.

Text: Alexander Henry, *Travels and Adventures in Canada and the Indian Territories* (1809), ed. James Bain. Boston: 1901.

I. The massacre at Fort Michilimackinac, 2 June, 1763

[I, viii] When I reached Michilimackinac, I found several other traders, who had arrived before me, from different parts of the country, and who, in general, declared the dispositions of the Indians to be hostile to the English, and even apprehended some attack. M. Laurent Ducharme[1] distinctly informed Major Etherington,[2] that a plan was absolutely conceived, for destroying him, his garrison and all the English in the upper country; but, the commandant, believing this and other reports to be without foundation, proceeding only from idle or ill-disposed persons, and of a tendency to do mischief, expressed much displeasure against M. Ducharme, and threatened to send the next person who should bring a story of the same kind, a prisoner, to Détroit.

The garrison, at this time, consisted of ninety privates, two subalterns and the commandant; and the English merchants, at the fort, were four in number.[3] Thus strong, few entertained anxiety concerning the Indians, who had no weapons but small arms.

Meanwhile, the Indians, from every quarter, were daily assembling, in unusual numbers, but with every appearance of friendship, frequenting the fort, and disposing of their peltries, in such a manner as to dissipate almost every one's fears. For myself, on one occasion, I took the liberty of observing to Major Etherington that in my judgment, no confidence ought to be placed in them, and that I was informed no less than four hundred lay around the fort.

In return, the major only rallied me [teased me], on my timidity; and it is to be confessed, that if this officer neglected admonition, on his part, so did I, on mine. Shortly after my first arrival at Michilimackinac, in the preceding year, a Chipeway, named Wa'wa'tam',[4] began to come often to my house, betraying, in his demeanour, strong marks of personal regard. After this had continued for some time, he came, on a certain day, bringing with him his whole family, and, at the same time, a large present, consisting of skins, sugar and dried meat. Having laid these in a heap, he commenced a speech, in which he informed me, that some years before, he had observed a fast, devoting himself, according to the custom of his nation, to solitude, and to the mortification of his body, in the hope to obtain, from the Great Spirit, protection through all his days; that on this occasion, he had dreamed of adopting an Englishman, as his son, brother and friend; that from the moment in which he first beheld me, he had recognised me as the person whom the Great Spirit had been pleased to point out to him for a brother; that he hoped that I would not refuse his present; and that he should forever regard me as one of his family.

I could do no otherwise than accept the present, and declare my willingness to have so good a man, as this appeared to be, for my friend and brother. I offered a present in return for that which I had received, which Wawatam accepted, and then, thanking me for the favour which he said that I had rendered him, he left me, and soon after set out on his winter's hunt.

Twelve months had now elapsed, since the occurrence of this incident, and I had almost forgotten the person of my *brother*, when, on the second day of June, Wawatam came again to my house, in a temper of mind visibly melancholy and thoughtful. He told me, that he had just returned from his *wintering-ground*, and I asked after his health; but, without answering my question, he went on to say, that he was very sorry to find me returned from the Sault; that he had intended to go to that place himself, immediately after his arrival at Michilimackinac; and that he wished me to go there, along with him and his family, the next morning. To all this, he joined an inquiry, whether or not the commandant had heard bad news, adding, that, during the winter, he had himself been frequently disturbed with the *noise of evil birds*; and further suggesting, that there were numerous Indians near the fort, many of whom had never shown themselves within it. — Wawatam was about forty-five years of age, of an excellent character among his nation, and a chief.

Referring much of what I heard to the peculiarities of the Indian character, I did not pay all the attention which they will be found to have deserved, to the entreaties and remarks of my visitor. I answered that I could not think of going to the Sault, so soon as the next morning, but would follow him there, after the arrival of my clerks. Finding himself unable to prevail with me, he withdrew, for that day; but, early the next morning, he came again, bringing with him his wife, and a present of dried meat. At this interview after stating that he had several packs of beaver, for which he intended to deal with me, he expressed, a second time, his apprehensions, from the numerous Indians who were round the fort, and earnestly pressed me to consent to an immediate departure for the Sault. — As a reason for this particular request, he assured me that all the Indians proposed to come in a body, that day, to the fort, to demand liquor of the commandant, and that he wished me to be gone, before they should grow intoxicated.

I had made, at the period to which I am now referring, so much progress in the language in which Wawatam addressed me, as to be able to hold an ordinary conversation in it; but, the Indian manner of speech is so extravagantly figurative, that it is only for a very perfect master to follow and comprehend it entirely. Had I been further advanced in this respect, I think that I should have gathered so much information, from this my friendly monitor, as would have put me into possession of the design of the enemy, and enabled me to save as well others as myself; as it was, it unfortunately happened, that I turned a deaf ear to every thing, leaving Wawatam and his wife, after long and patient, but ineffectual efforts, to depart alone, with dejected countenances, and not before they had each let fall some tears.

In the course of the same day, I observed that the Indians came in great numbers into the fort, purchasing tomahawks (small axes, of one pound weight,) and frequently desiring to see silver armbands, and other valuable ornaments, of which I had a large quantity for sale. These ornaments, however, they in no instance purchased; but after turning them over, left them, saying, that they would call again the next day. Their motive, as it afterward appeared, was no other than the very artful one of discovering, by requesting to see them, the particular places of their deposit, so that they might lay their hands on them in the moment of pillage with the greater certainty and dispatch.

At night, I turned in my mind the visits of Wawatam; but, though they were calculated to excite uneasiness, nothing induced me to believe that serious mischief was at hand. The next day, being the fourth of June, was the king's birth-day.

[I, ix] The morning was sultry. A Chipeway came to tell me that his nation was going to play at *bag'gat'iway*,[5] with the Sacs or Saäkies, another Indian nation, for a high wager. He invited me to witness the sport, adding that the commandant was to be there, and would bet on the side of the Chipeways. In consequence of this information, I went to the commandant, and expostulated with him a little, representing that the Indians might possibly have some sinister end in view; but, the commandant only smiled at my suspicions.

Baggatiway, called by the Canadians, *le jeu de la crosse*, is played with a bat and ball. The bat is about four feet in length, curved, and terminating in a sort of racket. Two posts are planted in the ground, at a considerable distance from each other, as a mile, or more. Each party has its post, and the game consists in throwing the ball up to the post of the adversary. The ball, at the beginning, is placed in the middle of the course, and each party endeavours as well to throw the ball out of the direction of its own post, as into that of the adversary's.

I did not go myself to see the match which was now to be played without the fort, because, there being a canoe prepared to depart, on the following day, for Montréal, I employed myself in writing letters to my friends; and even when a fellow-trader, Mr. Tracy, happened to call upon me, saying that another canoe had just arrived from Détroit, and proposing that I should go with him to the beach, to inquire the news, it so happened that I still remained, to finish my letters; promising to follow Mr. Tracey, in the course of a few minutes. Mr. Tracy had not gone more than twenty paces from my door, when I heard an Indian war-cry, and a noise of general confusion.

Going instantly to my window, I saw a crowd of Indians, within the fort, furiously cutting down and scalping every Englishman they found. In particular, I witnessed the fate of Lieutenant Jemette.[6]

I had, in the room in which I was, a fowling-piece, loaded with swan-shot. This I immediately seized, and held it for a few minutes, waiting to hear the drum beat to arms. In this dreadful interval, I saw several of my countrymen fall, and more than one struggling between the knees of an Indian, who, holding him in this manner, scalped him, while yet living.

At length, disappointed in the hope of seeing resistance made to the enemy, and sensible, of course, that no effort, of my own unassisted arm, could avail against four hundred Indians, I thought only of seeking shelter. Amid the slaughter which was raging, I observed many of the Canadian inhabitants of the fort, calmly looking on, neither opposing the Indians, nor suffering injury; and, from this circumstance, I conceived a hope of finding security in their houses.

Between the yard-door of my own house, and that of M. Langlade,[7] my next neighbour, there was only a low fence, over which I easily climbed. At my entrance, I found the whole family at the windows, gazing at the scene of blood before them. I addressed myself immediately to M. Langlade, begging that he would put me into some place of safety, until the heat of the affair should be over; an act of charity by which he might perhaps preserve me from the general massacre; but, while I uttered my petition, M. Langlade, who had looked for a moment at me, turned again to the window, shrugging his shoulders, and intimating, that he could do nothing for me: — *'Que voudriez-vous que j'en ferais?'*

This was a moment for despair; but, the next, a Pani[8] woman, a slave of M. Langlade's, beckoned to me to follow her. She brought me to a door, which she opened, desiring me to enter, and telling me that it led to the garret, where I must go and conceal myself. I joyfully obeyed her directions; and she, having followed me up to the garret-door, locked it after me, and with great presence of mind took away the key.

This shelter obtained, if shelter I could hope to find it, I was naturally anxious to know what might still be passing without. Through an aperture, which afforded me a view of the area of the fort, I beheld, in shapes the foulest and most terrible, the ferocious triumphs of barbarian conquerors. The dead were scalped and mangled; the dying were writhing and shrieking, under the unsatiated knife and tomahawk; and, from the bodies of some ripped open, their butchers were drinking the blood, scooped up in the hollow of joined hands, and quaffed amid shouts of rage and victory. I was shaken, not only with horror, but with fear. The sufferings which I witnessed, I seemed on the point of experiencing. No long time elapsed, before every one being destroyed, who could be found, there was a general cry, of 'All is finished!' At the same instant, I heard some of the Indians enter the house in which I was.

The garret was separated from the room below, only by a layer of single boards, at once the flooring of the one and the ceiling of the other. I could therefore hear every thing that passed; and, the Indians no sooner in, then they inquired, whether or not any Englishman were in the house? M. Langlade replied, that 'He could not say — he did not know of any;' — answers in which he did not exceed the truth; for the Pani woman had not only hidden me by stealth, but kept my secret, and her own, M. Langlade was therefore, as I presume, as far from a wish to destroy me, as he was careless about saving me, when he added to these answers, that 'They might examine for themselves, and would soon be satisfied, as to the object of their question.' Saying this, he brought them to the garret-door.

The state of my mind will be imagined. Arrived at the door, some delay was occasioned by the absence of the key, and a few moments were thus allowed me, in which to look around for a hiding-place. In one corner of the garret was a heap of those vessels of birch-bark, used in maple-sugar making. . . .

The door was unlocked, and opening, and the Indian ascending the stairs before I had completely crept into a small opening, which presented itself, at one end of the heap. An instant after, four Indians entered the room, all armed with tomahawks, and all besmeared with blood, upon every part of their bodies.

The die appeared to be cast. I could scarcely breathe; but I thought that the throbbing of my heart occasioned a noise loud enough to betray me. The Indians walked in every direction about the garret, and one of them approached me so closely that at a particular moment, had he put his hand, he must have touched me. Still, I remained undiscovered; a circumstance to which the dark colour of my clothes, and the corner in which I was must have contributed. In a word, after taking several turns in the room, during want of light, in a room which had no window, and in which they told M. Langlade how many they had killed, and how many scalps they had taken, they returned down stairs, and I, with sensations not to be expressed, heard the door, which was the barrier between me and my fate, locked for the second time.

There was a feather-bed on the floor; and, on this, exhausted as I was, by the agitation of my mind, I threw myself down and fell asleep. In this state I remained till the dusk of the evening, when I was awakened by a second opening of the door. The person, that now entered, was M. Langlade's wife, who was much surprised at finding me, but advised me not to be uneasy, observing, that the Indians had killed most of the English, but that she hoped I might myself escape. — A shower of rain having begun to fall, she had come to stop a hole in the roof. On her going away, I begged her to send me a little water, to drink; which she did.

As night was now advancing, I continued to lie on the bed, ruminating on my condition, but unable to discover a resource, from which I could hope for life. A flight, to Detroit, had no probable chance of success. The distance, from Michili-mackinac, was four hundred miles; I was without provisions; and the whole length of the road lay through Indian countries, countries of an enemy in arms, where the first man whom I should meet would kill me. To stay where I was, threatened nearly the same issue. As before, fatigue of mind, and not tranquility, suspended my cares, and procured me further sleep.

[I, x] The game of baggatiway, as from the description above will have been perceived, is necessarily attended with much violence and noise. In the ardour of contest, the ball, as has been suggested, if it cannot be thrown to the goal desired, is struck in any direction by the adversary. At such a moment, therefore, nothing could be less liable to excite premature alarm, than that the ball should be tossed over the pickets of the fort, nor that having fallen there, it should be followed on the instant, by all engaged in the game, as well the one party as the other, all eager, all struggling, all shouting, all in the unrestrained pursuit of a rude athletic exercise. Nothing could be less fitted to excite premature alarm — nothing, therefore, could be more happily devised, under the circumstances, than a stratagem like this; and this was, in fact, the stratagem which the Indians had employed, by which they had obtained possession of the fort, and by which they had been enabled to slaughter and subdue its garrison, and such of its other inhabitants as they pleased. To be still more certain of success, they had prevailed upon as many as they could, by a pretext the least liable to suspicion, to come voluntarily without the pickets; and particularly the commandant and garrison themselves.

The respite which sleep afforded me, during the night, was put an end to by the return of morning. I was again on the rack of apprehension. At sunrise, I heard the family stirring; and, presently after, Indian voices, informing M. Langlade that they had not found my hapless self among the dead, and that they supposed me to be somewhere concealed. M. Langlade appeared, from what followed, to be, by this time, acquainted with the place of my retreat, of which, no doubt, he had been informed by his wife. The poor woman, as soon as the Indians mentioned me declared to her husband, in the French tongue, that he should no longer keep me in his house, but deliver me up to my pursuers; giving as a reason for this measure, that should the Indians discover his instrumentality in my concealment, they might revenge it on her children, and that it was better that I should die, than they. M. Langlade resisted, at first, this sentence of his wife's; but soon suffered her to prevail, informing the Indians that he had been told I was in his house, that I had come there without his knowledge, and that he would put me into their hands. This was no sooner expressed than he began to ascend the stairs, the Indians following upon his heels.

I now resigned myself to the fate with which I was menaced; and regarding every attempt at concealment as vain, I arose from the bed, and presented myself full in view, to the Indians who were entering the room. They were all in a state of intoxication, and entirely naked, except about the middle. One of them, named Wenniway,[9] whom I had previously known, and who was upward of six feet in height, had his entire face and body covered with charcoal and grease, only that a white spot, of two inches in diameter, encircled either eye. This man walked up to me, seized me, with one hand, by the collar of the coat, while in the other he held a large carving-knife, as if to plunge it into my breast; his eyes, meanwhile, were fixed stedfastly on mine. At length, after some seconds, of the most anxious suspense, he dropped his arm, saying, 'I won't kill you!' — To this he added, that he had been frequently engaged in wars against the English, and had brought away many scalps; that, on a certain occasion, he had lost a brother, whose name was Musinigon, and that I should be called after him.

A reprieve, upon any terms, placed me among the living, and gave me back the sustaining voice of hope; but Wenniway ordered me down stairs, and there informing me that I was to be taken to his cabin, where, and indeed every where else, the Indians were all mad with liquor, death again was threatened, and not as possible only, but as certain. I mentioned my fears on this subject to M. Langlade, begging him to represent the danger to my master. M. Langlade, in this instance, did not withhold his compassion, and Wenniway immediately consented that I should remain where I was, until he found another opportunity to take me away.

Thus far secure, I re-ascended by garret-stairs, in order the place myself, the furthest possible, out of the reach of insult from drunken Indians; but, I had not remained there more than an hour, when I was called to the room below, in which was an Indian, who said that I must go with him out of the fort, Wenniway having sent him to fetch me. This man, as well as Wenniway himself, I had seen before. In the preceding year, I had allowed him to take goods on credit, for which he was still in my debt; and some short time previous to the surprise of the fort he had said, upon my upbraiding him with want of honesty, that 'He would pay me before long!' — This speech now came fresh into my memory, and led me to suspect that the fellow had formed a design against my life. I communicated the suspicion to M. Langlade; but he gave for answer, that 'I was not now my own master, and must do as I was ordered.'

The Indian on his part, directed, that before I left the house, I should undress myself, declaring that my coat and shirt would become him better than they did me. His pleasure, in this respect, being complied with, no other alternative was left me than either to go out naked, or to put on the clothes of the Indian, which he freely gave me in exchange. His motive, for thus stripping me of my own apparel, was no other, as I afterward learned, than this, that it might not be stained with blood when he should kill me.

I was now told to proceed; and my driver followed me close, until I had passed the gate of the fort, when I turned toward the spot where I knew the Indians to be encamped. This, however, did not suit the purpose of my enemy, who seized me by the arm, and drew me violently, in the opposite direction, to the distance of fifty yards, above the fort. Here, finding that I was approaching the bushes and sand-hills, I determined to proceed no further, but told the Indian that I believed he meant to murder me, and that if so, he might as well strike where I was, as at any greater distance. He replied, with coolness, that my suspicions were just, and that he meant to pay me, in this manner, for my goods. At the same time, he produced a knife, and held me in a position to receive the intended blow. Both this, and that which followed, were necessarily the affair of a moment. By some effort, too sudden and too little dependent on thought, to be explained or remembered, I was enabled to arrest his arm, and give him a sudden push, by which I turned him from me, and released myself from his grasp. This was no sooner done, than I ran toward the fort, with all the swiftness in my power, the Indian following me, and I expecting every moment to feel his knife. — I succeeded in my flight; and, on entering the fort, I saw Wenniway, standing in the midst of the area, and to him I hastened for protection. Wenniway desired the Indian to desist; but the latter pursued me round him, making several strokes at me with his knife, and foaming at the mouth, with rage at the repeated failure of his purpose. At length, Wenniway drew near to M. Langlade's house; and, the door being open, I ran into it. The Indian followed me; but, on my entering the house, he voluntarily abandoned the pursuit.

Preserved so often, and so unexpectedly, as it had now been my lot to be, I returned to my garret with a strong inclination to believe, that through the will of an overruling power, no Indian enemy could do me hurt; but, new trials, as I believed, were at hand, when, at ten o'clock in the evening, I was roused from sleep, and once more desired to descend the stairs. Not less, however, to my satisfaction than surprise, I was summoned only to meet Major Etherington, Mr Bostwick and Lieutenant Lesslie, who were in the room below.

These gentlemen had been taken prisoners, while looking at the game, without the fort, and immediately stripped of all their clothes. They were now sent into the fort, under the charge of Canadians, because, the Indians having resolved on getting drunk, the chiefs were apprehensive that they would be murdered, if they continued in the camp. — Lieutenant Jemette and seventy soldiers had been killed; and but twenty Englishmen, including soldiers, were still alive. These were all within the fort, together with nearly three hundred Canadians.[10]

These being our numbers, myself and others proposed to Major Etherington, to make an effort for regaining possession of the fort, and maintaining it against the Indians. The Jesuit missionary was consulted on the project; but he discouraged us, by his representations, not only of the merciless treatment which we must expect from the Indians, should they regain their superiority, but of the little dependence which was to be placed upon our Canadian auxiliaries. Thus, the fort and prisoners remained in the hands of the Indians, though, through the whole night, the prisoners and whites were in actual possession, and they were without the gates.

That whole night, or the greater part of it, was passed in mutual condolence; and my fellow-prisoners shared my garret. In the morning, being again called down, I found my master, Wenniway, and was desired to follow him. He led me to a small house, within the fort, where, in a narrow room, and almost dark, I found Mr Ezekiel Solomons, an Englishman from Détroit, and a soldier, all prisoners. With these, I remained in painful suspense, as to the scene that was next to present itself, till ten o'clock, in the forenoon, when an Indian arrived, and presently marched us to the lakeside, where a canoe appeared ready for departure, and in which we found that we were to embark.

Our voyage, full of doubt as it was, would have commenced immediately, but that one of the Indians, who was to be of the party, was absent. His arrival was to be waited for; and this occasioned a very long delay, during which were exposed to a keen north-east wind. An old shirt was all that covered me; I suffered much from the cold; and, in this extremity, M. Langlade coming down to the beach, I asked him for a blanket, promising, if I lived, to pay him for it, at any price he pleased: but, the answer I received was this, that he could let me have no blanket, unless there were some one to be security for the payment. For myself, he observed, I had no longer any property in that country. — I had no more to say to M. Langlade; but, presently seeing another Canadian, named John Cuchoise, I addressed to him a similar request, and was not refused. Naked as I was, and rigorous as was the weather, but for the blanket, I must have perished. — At noon, our party was all collected, the prisoners all embarked, and we steered for the Isles du Castor,[11] in Lake Michigan.

[I, xi] The soldier, who was our companion in misfortune, was made fast to a bar of the canoe, by a rope tied round his neck, as is the manner of the Indians, in transporting their prisoners. The rest were left unconfined; but a paddle was put into each of our hands, and we were made to use it. The Indians in the canoe were seven in number; the prisoners four. I had left, as it will be recollected, Major Etherington, Lieutenant Lesslie and Mr. Bostwick, at M. Langlade's, and was now joined in misery with Mr. Ezekiel Solomons, the soldier, and the Englishman who had newly arrived from Detroit. This was on the sixth day of June. The fort was taken on the fourth; I surrendered myself to Wenniway on the fifth; and this was the third day of our distress.

We were bound, as I have said, for the Isles du Castor, which lie in the mouth of Lake Michigan; and we should have crossed the lake, but that a thick fog came on, on account of which the Indians deemed it safer to keep the shore close under their lee. We therefore approached the lands of the Otawas, and their village of L'Arbre Croche, already mentioned as lying about twenty miles to the westward of Michilimackinac, on the opposite side of the tongue of land on which the fort is built.

Every half hour, the Indians gave their war whoops, one for every prisoner in their canoe. This is a general custom, by the aid of which all other Indians, within hearing, are apprized of the number of prisoners they are carrying.

In this manner, we reached Wagoshense,[12] a long point, stretching westward into the lake, and which the Otawas make a carrying-place, to avoid going round it. It is distant eighteen miles from Michilimackinac. After the Indians had made their war-whoop, as before, an Otawa appeared upon the beach, who made signs that we should land. In consequence, we approached. The Otawa asked the news, and kept the Chipeways in further conversation, till we were within a few yards of the land, and in shallow water. At this moment, a hundred men rushed upon us, from among the bushes, and dragged all the prisoners out of the canoes, amid a terrifying shout.

We now believed that our last sufferings were approaching; but, no sooner were we fairly on shore, and on our legs, than the chiefs of the party advanced, and gave each of us their hands, telling us that they were our friends, and Otawas, whom the Chipeways had insulted, by destroying the English without consulting with them on the affair. They added, that what they had done was for the purpose of saving our lives, the Chipeways having been carrying us to the Iles du Castor only to kill and devour us.

The reader's imagination is here distracted by the variety of our fortunes, and he may well paint to himself the state of mind of those who sustained them; who were the sport, or the victims, of a series of events, more like dreams than realities, more like fiction than truth! It was not long before we were embarked again, in the canoes of the Otawas, who, the same evening, relanded us at Michilimackinac, where they marched us into the fort, in view of the Chipeways, confounded at beholding the Otawas espouse a side opposite to their own.

The Otawas, who had accompanied us in sufficient numbers, took possession of the fort. We, who had changed masters, but were still prisoners, were lodged in the house of the commandant, and strictly guarded.

Early the next morning, a general council was held, in which the Chipeways complained much of the conduct of the Otawas, in robbing them of their prisoners; alleging that all the Indians, the Otawas alone excepted, were at war with the English; that Pontiac had taken Détroit; that the king of France had awoke, and repossessed himself of Quebec and Montréal; and that the English were meeting destruction, not only at Michilimackinac, but in every other part of the world. From all this they inferred, that it became the Otawas to restore the prisoners, and to join in the war; and the speech was followed by large presents, being part of the plunder of the fort, and which was previously heaped in the centre of the room. — The Indians rarely make their answers till the day after they have heard the arguments offered. They did not depart from their custom on this occasion; and the council therefore adjourned.

We, the prisoners, whose fate was thus in controversy, were unacquainted, at the time, with this transaction; and therefore enjoyed a night of tolerable tranquility, not in the least suspecting the reverse which was preparing for us. Which of the arguments of the Chipeways, or whether or not all were deemed valid by the Otawas, I cannot say; but, the council was resumed at an early hour in the morning, and, after several speeches had been made in it, the prisoners were sent for, and returned to the Chipeways.

The Otawas, who now gave us into the hands of the Chipeways, had themselves declared, that the latter designed no other than to kill us, and *make broth of us*. The Chipeways, as soon as we were restored to them, marched us to a village of their own, situate on the point which is below the fort, and put us into a lodge, already the prison of fourteen soldiers, tied two and two, with each a rope about his neck, and made fast to a pole which might be called the supporter of the building.

I was left untied; but I passed a night sleepless and full of wretchedness. My bed was the bare ground, and I was again reduced to an old shirt, as my entire apparel; the blanket which I had received, through the generosity of M. Cuchoise, having been taken from me among the Otawas, when they seized upon myself and the others, at Wagoshense. I was besides, in want of food, having for two days ate nothing.

I confess that in the canoe, with the Chipeways, I was offered bread — but, bread, with what accompaniment! — They had a loaf, which they cut with the same knives that they had employed in the massacre — knives still covered with blood. The blood, they moistened with spittle, and rubbing it on the bread, offered this for food to their prisoners, telling them to eat the blood of their countrymen.

Such was my situation, on the morning of the seventh of June, in the year one thousand seven hundred and sixty-three; but, a few hours produced an event which gave still a new colour to my lot.

Toward noon, when the great war-chief, in company with Wenniway, was seated at the opposite end of the lodge, my friend and brother, Wawatam, suddenly came in. During the four days preceding, I had often wondered what had become of him. In passing by, he gave me his hand, but went immediately toward the great chief, by the side of whom and Wenniway, he sat himself down. The most uninterrupted silence prevailed; each smoked his pipe, and this done, Wawatam arose, and left the lodge, saying, to me, as he passed, 'Take courage!'

[I, xii] An hour elapsed, during which several chiefs entered, and preparations appeared to be making for a council. At length, Wawatam re-entered the lodge, followed by his wife, and both loaded with merchandize, which they carried up to the chiefs, and laid in a heap before them. Some moments of silence followed, at the end of which Wawatam pronounced a speech, every word of which, to me, was of extraordinary interest:

'Friends and relations,' he began, 'what is it that I shall say? You know what I feel. You all have friends and brothers and children, whom as yourselves you love; and you — what would you experience did you, like me, behold your dearest friend — your brother — in the condition of a slave; a slave, exposed every moment to insult, and to menaces of death? This case, as you all know, is mine. See there (*pointing to myself*) my friend and brother among slaves — himself a slave!

'You all well know, that long before the war began, I adopted him as my brother. From that moment, he became one of my family, so that no change of circumstances could break the cord which fastened us together.

'He is my brother; and, because I am your relation, he is therefore your relation too: — and how, being your relation, can he be your slave?

'On the day, on which the war began, you were fearful, lest, on this very account, I should reveal your secret. You requested, therefore, that I would leave the fort, and even cross the lake. I did so; but I did it with reluctance, notwithstanding that you, Menehwehna, who had the command in this enterprise, gave me your promise that you would protect my friend, delivering him from all danger and giving him safely to me.

'The performance of this promise, I now claim. I come not with empty hands to ask it. You, Menehwehna, best know, whether or not, as it respects yourself, you have kept your word, but I bring these goods, to buy off every claim which any man among you all may have on my brother, as his prisoner.'

Wawatam having ceased, the pipes were again filled; and, after they were finished, a further period of silence followed. At the end of this, Menehwehna arose, and gave his reply:

'My relation and brother,' said he, 'what you have spoken is the truth. We were acquainted with the friendship which subsisted between yourself and the Englishman, in whose behalf you have now addressed us. We knew the danger of having our secret discovered, and the consequences which must follow; and you say truly, that we requested you to leave the fort. This we did, out of regard for you and your family; for, if a discovery of our design had been made, you would have been blamed, whether guilty or not; and you would thus have been involved in difficulties from which you could not have extricated yourself.

'It is also true, that I promised you to take care of your friend; and this promise I performed, by desiring my son, at the moment of assault, to seek him out, and bring him to my lodge. He went accordingly, but could not find him. The day after, I sent him to Langlade's, when he was informed that your friend was safe; and had it not been that the Indians were then drinking the rum which had been found in the fort, he would have brought him home with me, according to my orders.

'I am very glad to find that your friend has escaped. We accept your present; and you may take him home with you.'

Wawatam thanked the assembled chiefs, and taking me by the hand, led me to his lodge, which was at the distance of a few yards only from the prison-lodge. My entrance appeared to give joy to the whole family; food was immediately prepared for me; and I now ate the first hearty meal which I had made since my capture. I found myself one of the family; and but that I had still my fears, as to the other Indians, I felt as happy as the situation could allow.

In the course of the next morning, I was alarmed by a noise in the prison-lodge; and looking through the openings of the lodge in which I was, I saw seven dead bodies of white men dragged forth. Upon my inquiry into the occasion, I was informed, that a certain chief, called, by the Canadians, Le Grand Sable, had not long before arrived from his winter's hunt; and that he, having been absent when the war begun, and being now desirous of manifesting to the Indians at large, his hearty concurrence in what they had done, had gone into the prison-lodge, and there, with his knife, put the seven men, whose bodies I had seen, to death.

Shortly after, two of the Indians took one of the dead bodies, which they chose as being the fattest, cut off the head, and divided the whole into five parts, one of which was put into each of five kettles, hung over as many fires kindled for this purpose, at the door of the prison-lodge. Soon after things were so far prepared, a message came to our lodge, with an invitation to Wawatam, to assist at the feast.

An invitation to a feast is given by him who is the master of it. Small cuttings of cedar-wood, of about four inches in length, supply the place of cards; and the bearer, by word of mouth, states the particulars.

Wawatam obeyed the summons, taking with him, as is usual, to the place of entertainment, his dish and spoon.

After an absence of about half an hour, he returned, bringing in his dish a human hand, and a large piece of flesh. He did not appear to relish the repast, but told me, that it was then, and always had been the custom, among all the Indian nations, when returning from war, or on overcoming their enemies, to make a war-feast, from among the slain. This, he said, inspired the warrior with courage in attack, and bred him to meet death with fearlessness.

In the evening of the same day, a large canoe, such as those which came from Montréal, was seen advancing to the fort. It was full of men, and I distinguished several passengers. The Indian cry was made in the village; a general muster ordered; and, to the number of two hundred, they marched up to the fort, where the canoe was expected to land. The canoe, suspecting nothing, came boldly to the fort, where the passengers, as being English traders, were seized, dragged through the water, beat, reviled, marched to the prison-lodge, and there stripped of their clothes, and confined.

Of the English traders that fell into the hands of the Indians, at the capture of the fort, Mr. Tracy was the only one who lost his life. Mr. Ezekiel Solomons and Mr. Henry Bostwick were taken by the Otawas, and, after the peace, carried down to Montréal, and there ransomed. Of ninety troops, about seventy were killed; the rest, together with those of the posts in the Bay des Puants, and at the river Saint-Joseph, were also kept in safety by the Otawas, till the peace, and then either freely restored, or ransomed at Montréal. The Otawas never overcame their disgust, at the neglect with which they had been treated, in the beginning of the war, by those who afterward desired their assistance as allies.

II. A Journey on the Prairies in 1776

[II, x] The Plains, or, as the French denominate them, the Prairies, or Meadows, compose an extensive tract of country, which is watered by the Elk, or Athabasca, the Sascatchiwaine, the Red River and others, and runs southward to the Gulf of Mexico. On my first setting out for the north-west, I promised myself to visit this region, and I now prepared to accomplish the undertaking. Long journies, on the snow, are thought of but as trifles, in this part of the world.

On the first day of January, 1776, I left our fort on Beaver Lake, attended by two men, and provided with dried meat, frozen fish, and a small quantity of *praline*, made of roasted maize, rendered palatable with sugar, and which I had brought from the Sault de Sainte-Marie, for this express occasion. The kind and friendly disposition of Mr Joseph Frobisher,[13] induced him to bear me company, as far as Cumberland House, a journey of a hundred and twenty miles.[14] Mr Frobisher was attended by one man.

Our provisions were drawn by the men, upon sledges, made of thin boards, a foot in breadth, and curved upward in front, after the Indian fashion. Our clothing for night and day was nearly the same; and the cold was so intense, that exclusively of warm woollen clothes, we were obliged to wrap ourselves continually in beaver blankets, or at least in ox-skins, which the traders call *buffalo-robes*. At night, we made our first encampment at the head of the Maligne, where one of our parties was fishing, with but very indifferent success.

On the following evening, we encamped at the mouth of the same river. The snow was four feet deep; and we found it impossible to keep ourselves warm, even with the aid of a large fire.

On the fourth day, as well of the month as of our journey we arrived at Cumberland House. Mr Cockings[15] received us with much hospitality, making us partake of all he had, which, however, was but little. Himself and his men subsisted wholly upon fish, in which sturgeon bore the largest proportion; and this was caught near the house. The next morning, I took leave of Mr Frobisher, who is certainly the first man that ever went the same distance, in such a climate, and upon snow-shoes, to convoy a friend!

From Cumberland House, I pursued a westerly course, on the ice, following the southern bank of Sturgeon Lake, till I crossed the neck of land by which alone it is separated from the great river Pasquayah, or Sascatchiwaine.[16] In the evening, I encamped on the north bank of this river, at the distance of ten leagues from Cumberland House.

The depth of the snow, and the intenseness of the cold, rendered my progress so much slower than I had reckoned upon, that I soon began to fear the want of provisions. The sun did not rise till half past nine o'clock in the morning, and it set at half past two in the afternoon: it is, however, at no time wholly dark in these climates; the northern lights, and the reflection of the snow, affording always sufficient light for the traveller. Add to this that the river, the course of which I was ascending, was a guide, with the aid of which I could not lose my way. Every day's journey was commenced at three o'clock in the morning.

I was not far advanced, before the country betrayed some approaches to the characteristic nakedness of the Plains. The wood dwindled away, both in size and quantity, so that it was with difficulty we could collect sufficient for making a fire, and without fire we could not drink; for melted snow was our only resource, the ice on the river being too thick to be penetrated by the axe.

On the evening of the sixth, the weather continuing severely cold, I made my two men sleep on the same skin with myself, one on each side; and though this arrangement was particularly beneficial to myself, it increased the comfort of all. At the usual hour in the morning, we attempted to rise; but found that a foot of snow had fallen upon our bed, as well as extinguished and covered our fire. In this situation we remained till day-break, when, with much exertion, we collected fresh fuel. Proceeding on our journey, we found that the use of our sledges had become impracticable, through the quantity of newly fallen snow, and were now constrained to carry our provisions on our backs. Unfortunately, they were a diminished burden!

For the two days succeeding, the depth of the snow, and the violence of the winds, greatly retarded our journey: but, from the ninth to the twelfth, the elements were less hostile, and we travelled rapidly. No trace of any thing human presented itself on our road, except that we saw the old wintering-ground of Mr Finlay, who had left it some years before, and was now stationed at Fort des Prairie.[17] This fort was the stage we had to make, before we could enter the Prairies, or Plains; and on examining our provisions, we found only sufficient for five days, while, even at the swiftest rate we had travelled, a journey of twelve days was before us. My men began to fear being starved, as seeing no prospect of relief; but, I endeavoured to maintain their courage, by representing that I should certainly kill red-deer and elk, of which the tracks were visible along the banks of the river, and on the sides of the hills. What I hoped for, in this respect, it was not easy to accomplish; for the animals kept within the shelter of the woods, and the snow was too deep to let me seek them there.

On the fifteenth, our situation was rendered still more alarming, by the commencement of a fresh fall of snow, which added nearly two feet to the depth of that which was on the ground before. At the same time, we were scarcely able to collect enough wood for making a fire to melt the snow. The only trees around us were starveling willows; and the hills, which discovered themselves at a small distance, were bare of every vegetable production, such as could rear itself above the snow. Their appearance was rather that of lofty snow-banks, than of hills. We were now on the borders of the Plains.

On the twentieth, the last remains of our provisions were expended; but, I had taken the precaution to conceal a cake of chocolate, in reserve for an occasion like that which was now arrived. Toward evening, my men, after walking the whole day, began to lose their strength; but, we nevertheless kept on our feet till it was late; and, when we encamped, I informed them of the treasure where was still in store. I desired them to fill the kettle with snow, and argued with them the while, that the chocolate would keep us alive, for five days at least; an interval in which we should surely meet with some Indian at the chase. Their spirits revived at the suggestion; and, the kettle being filled with two gallons of water, I put into it one square of the chocolate. The quantity was scarcely sufficient to alter the colour of the water; but, each of us drank half a gallon of the warm liquor, by which we were much refreshed, and in its enjoyment felt no more of the fatigues of the day. In the morning, we allowed ourselves a similar repast, after finishing which, we marched vigorously for six hours. But, now, the spirits of my companions again deserted them, and they declared, that they neither would, nor could, proceed any further. For myself, they advised me to leave them, and accomplish the journey as I could; but, for themselves, they said, that they must die soon, and might as well die where they were, as any where else.

While things were in this melancholy posture, I filled the kettle, and boiled another square of chocolate. When prepared, I prevailed upon my desponding companions to return to their warm beverage. On taking it, they recovered inconceivably; and, after smoking a pipe, consented to go forward. While their stomachs were comforted by the warm water, they walked well; but, as evening approached, fatigue overcame them, and they relapsed into their former condition; and, the chocolate being now almost entirely consumed, I began to fear that I must really abandon them: for I was able to endure more hardship than they; and, had it not been for keeping company with them, I could have advanced, double the distance, within the time which had been spent. To my great joy, however, the usual quantity of warm water revived them.

For breakfast, the next morning, I put the last square of chocolate into the kettle; and our meal finished, we began our march, in but very indifferent spirits. We were surrounded by large herds of wolves, which sometimes came close upon us, and who knew, as we were prone to think, the extremity in which we were, and marked us for their prey: but, I carried a gun, and this was our protection. I fired several times, but unfortunately missed at each: for a morsel of wolf's flesh would have afforded us a banquet.

Our misery nevertheless was still nearer its end than we imagined: and the event was such as to give one of the innumerable proofs, that despair is not made for man. Before sunset, we discovered, on the ice, some remains of the bones of an elk, left there by the wolves. Having instantly gathered them, we encamped; and, filling our kettle, prepared ourselves a meal of strong and excellent soup. The greater part of the night was passed in boiling and regaling on our booty; and early in the morning we felt ourselves strong enough to proceed.

This day, the twenty-fifth, we found the borders of the Plains reaching to the very banks of the river, which were two hundred feet above the level of the ice. Watermarks presented themselves at twenty feet above the actual level.

Want had lost his dominion over us. At noon, we saw the horns of a red-deer, standing in the snow, on the river. On examination, we found that the whole carcass was with them, the animal having broke through the ice in the beginning of the winter, in attempting to cross the river, too early in the season; while his horns, fastening themselves in the ice, had prevented him from sinking. By cutting away the ice, we were enabled to lay bare a part of the back and shoulders, and thus procure a stock of food, amply sufficient for the rest of our journey. We accordingly encamped, and employed our kettle to good purpose; forgot all our misfortunes; and prepared to walk with cheerfulness the twenty leagues, which, as we reckoned, still lay between ourselves and Fort des Prairies. . . . [18]

This evening, we had scarcely encamped, when there arrived two Osinipoilles,[19] sent by the great chief of the nation, whose name was the Great Road, to meet the troop. The chief had been induced to send them through his anxiety, occasioned by their longer absence than had been expected. The messengers expressed themselves much pleased at finding strangers with their friends, and told us, that we were within one day's march of their village,[20] and that the great chief would be highly gratified, in learning the long journey which we had performed to visit him. They added, that in consequence of finding us, they must themselves return immediately, to apprise him of our coming, and enable him to prepare for our reception. . . .

At the entrance of the wood, we were met by a large band of Indians, having the appearance of a guard; each man being armed with his bow and spear, and having his quiver filled with arrows. In this, as in much that followed, there was more of order and discipline, than in anything which I had before witnessed among Indians. The power of these guards appeared to be great; for they treated very roughly some of the people, who, in their opinion, approached us too closely. Forming themselves in regular file, on either side of us, they escorted us to the lodge, or tent, which was assigned us. It was of a circular form, covered with leather, and not less than twenty feet in diameter. On the ground within, ox-skins were spread, for beds and seats. . . .

[II, xii] One half of the tent was appropriated to our use. Several women waited upon us, to make a fire, and bring water, which latter they fetched from a neighbouring tent. Shortly after our arrival, these women brought us water, unasked for, saying that it was for washing. The refreshment was exceedingly acceptable; for, on our march, we had become so dirty, that our complexions were not very distinguishable from those of the Indians themselves.

The same women presently borrowed our kettle, telling us, that they wanted to boil something for us to eat. Soon after, we heard the voice of a man, passing through the village, and making a speech as he went. Our interpreter informed us, that his speech contained an invitation to a feast, accompanied by a proclamation, in which the people were required to behave with decorum toward the strangers, and apprised, that the soldiers had orders to punish those who should do otherwise.

While we were procuring this explanation, an Indian, who appeared to be a chief, came into our tent, and invited us to the feast; adding, that he would himself show us the way. We followed him accordingly, and he carried us to the tent of the great chief, which we found neither more ornamented, nor better furnished, than the rest.

At our entrance, the chief arose from his seat, saluted us in the Indian manner, by shaking hands, and addressed us in a few words, in which he offered his thanks for the confidence which we had reposed in him, in trusting ourselves so far from our own country. After we were seated, which was on bearskins, spread on the ground, the pipe, as usual, was introduced, and presented in succession to each person present. Each took his whiff, and then let it pass to his neighbour. The stem, which was four feet in length, was held by an officer, attendant on the chief. The bowl was of red marble, or pipe-stone.

When the pipe had gone its round, the chief, without rising from his seat, delivered a speech of some length, but of which the general purport was of the nature already described, in speaking of the Indians of the Lake of the Woods.[21] The speech ended, several of the Indians began to weep, and they were soon joined by the whole party. Had I not previously been witness to a *weeping-scene* of this description, I should certainly have been apprehensive of some disastrous catastrophe; but, as it was, I listened to it with tranquillity. It lasted for about ten minutes, after which all tears were dried away, and the honours of the feast were performed by the attending chiefs. This consisted of giving to every guest a dish, containing a boiled wild ox's tongue — for preparing which, my kettle had been borrowed. The repast finished, the great chief dismissed us, by shaking hands; and we returned to our tent.

Having inquired among these people, why they always weep at their feasts, and sometimes at their councils, I was answered, that their tears flowed to the memory of those deceased relations, who formerly assisted both at the one and the other; — that their absence, on these occasions, necessarily brought them fresh into their minds, and at the same time led them to reflect on their own brief and uncertain continuance. . . .

We rose at day-break, according to the custom of the Indians, who say, that they follow it in order to avoid surprises; this being the hour at which the enemy uniformly makes his attack.

Our waiting-women arrived early, bringing wood and water. Washing appeared to me to be a ceremony of religion among the Osinipoilles; and I never saw any thing similar among other Indians.

Leaving our tent, we made a progress through the village, which consisted of about two hundred tents, each tent containing from two to four families. We were attended by four soldiers of our guard, but this was insufficient for keeping off the women and children, who crowded round us with insatiable curiosity. Our march was likewise accompanied by a thousand dogs, all howling frightfully.

From the village, I saw, for the first time, one of those herds of horses which the Osinipoilles possess in numbers. It was feeding on the skirts of the plain.[22] The masters of these herds provide them with no fodder; but, leave them to find food for themselves, by removing the snow with their feet, till they reach the grass, which is every where on the ground in plenty.

At ten o'clock, we returned to our tent, and in a short time the great chief paid us a visit, attended by nearly fifty followers of distinction. In coming in, he gave his hand to each of us, and all his attendants followed his example. When we were seated, one of the officers went through the ceremony of the pipe, after which, the great chief delivered a speech, of which the substance was as follows: — That he was glad to see us; that he had been, some time since, informed of a fort of the white-men's being established on the Pasquayah, and that it had always been his intention to pay a visit there; that we were our own masters, to remain at our pleasure in his village, free from molestation, and assured of his especial protection; that the young men had employed themselves in collecting meat and furs, for the purpose of purchasing certain articles, wherewith to decorate their wives; that within a few days he proposed to move, with his whole village, on his errand; that nothing should be omitted to make our stay as agreeable as possible; that he had already ordered a party of his soldiers to guard us, and that if any thing should occur to displease us, his ear was always open to our complaints.

For all these friendly communications, we offered our thanks. His visit to the fort it had been a principal object to invite.

After the speech, the chief presented us with twenty beaver-skins, and as many wolf. In return, we gave two pounds of vermilion, and a few fathom of twisted tobacco, assuring him, that when he should arrive at our habitation, we would endeavour to repay the benefits which we were receiving from him, and at the same time cheerfully exchange our merchandise, for the dried meat and skins of his village. It was agreed that he should strike his camp at the end of five days, and that we should remain in it so long, and accompany it to the fort. The chief now departed; and I believe that we were reciprocally pleased with each other.

Notes

[1] Laurent Ducharme (1723-after 1887) came from a Montreal family of French fur traders who had traded in the area of Michilimackinac for many years.

[2] Not much is known of Etherington, whose real name appears to have been George and who has been variously termed Major and Captain.

[3] In actuality, the garrison numbered only 35. The traders were Henry, Ezekiel Solomon, Henry Bostwick, and Mr Tracy.

[4] Wawatam, the Ojibwa chief at Michilimackinac; our only knowledge of him comes from Henry's narrative.

[5] Lacrosse.

[6] John Jamet (d. 1763) was a professional soldier who had commanded the sub-post at Sault Ste Marie until it burned down in December; he was badly injured in the fire, but evidently had recovered enough to defend himself briefly during the native attack, in which he was decapitated.

[7] Charles-Michel Mouet de Langlade (1729-c. 1800), fur trader and experienced soldier, was reputedly 'perfectly cool and fearless on the field of battle.' He was at the the siege of Quebec, and later commanded Michilimackinac until the British arrived in 1761. His mother was Odawa and his wife was native; thus from childhood on he had close relations with the natives. This may explain his careful neutrality during the massacre; it was his Odawa relatives who later helped to get the survivors to Montreal when he resumed command of the fort after the attack.

[8] The woman may or may not be Pawnee; the name also means 'slave,' since the warlike Pawnee were often sold into slavery after a tribal battle.

[9] Minweweh, 'the one with the silver tongue,' (1710–70); war chief of the Ojibwa on Mackinac Island. He was a strong ally of the French and resisted the British throughout his life. After the massacre he moved westward, and eventually died in a Fox attack on the Ojibwa.

[10] Etherington's report to his commanding officer at Detroit (13 June 1663) gives the toll as 16 soldiers and Mr Tracy killed, plus two soldiers wounded. Five prisoners were later killed.

[11]The Beaver Islands in Lake Michigan, about 45 miles from Mackinac.

[12]The name means Fox Point.

[13]Joseph Frobisher (1740–1810), born in Halifax, England, was one of three brothers who engaged in the fur trade. A partner of Simon McTavish, he was involved in the North West Company, and in later life was a socially prominent Montreal merchant and politician.

[14]Bea er Lake is 93 miles north of Cumberland House; the extra 27 miles probably resulted from detours to avoid the river which was too rapid to freeze.

[15]This was MATTHEW COCKING of the HBC; another man might not have been as hospitable to an independent trader such as Henry.

[16]This is actually Pine Island; crossing it is the Pemmican portage, which connects Cumberland House with the Saskatchewan River.

[17]James Finlay (d. 1797), an independent Scottish trader who wintered in the valley of the Saskatchewan as early as 1766. In 1768 he built Finlay's House near Neepawin, near the site of the old French fort which had been the most westerly French post on the Saskatchewan. He later operated in partnership with John Gregory; both his sons became traders.

[18]A number of different posts in the area bore this name. Henry was heading for Upper Neepawin, just below the Grand Forks of the North and South Saskatchewan.

[19]The Assiniboines, KELSEY's 'Stone Indians.'

[20]Henry is now located west and south of present-day Humboldt, on the trail between Fort Ellice and the Saskatchewan river.

[21]Great Road's people were clearly anxious for news (see above) but Henry cannot have brought them much. On his way west he had traded for wild rice (essential for provisioning the expedition) at a native village on Lake of the Woods. He reports only that his party left quickly the next morning after the general consumption of rum led to an orgy on all sides.

[22]For the arrival of horses on the plains, see SAUKAMAPEE. The Assiniboine had acquired them by 1776, but still moved camp without employing other beasts of burden than dogs, and still hunted the buffalo on foot. By the beginning of the nineteenth century all this was changed and horses were generally employed.

Andrew Graham   (mid-1730s – 1815)

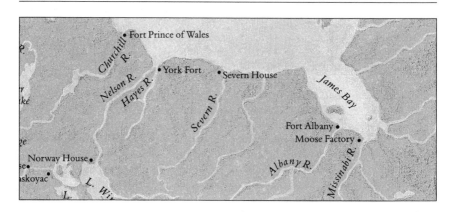

GRAHAM's contribution to the work of the Hudson's Bay Company has long been acknowledged, but his importance to science has emerged only in recent years. He joined the Company in 1749 and was posted to Fort Prince of Wales. From 1753 he was writer (clerk) at York Fort under JAMES ISHAM, whose interest in natural observation he shared; his *Observations* may have originated as a continuation of Isham's own. Graham's voluminous manuscripts narrate the events of post life, give trading information and meteorological data, record (and in ANTHONY HENDAY's case, rewrite) the journals of others, and supply early vocabularies of native languages. His natural history observations were extensive, and he collected and sent home many specimens. Graham was master at Fort Severn for over a decade, and later was acting chief at York Fort and chief at Fort Prince of Wales. It was he who sent MATTHEW COCKING to explore the interior, and he argued strongly for the establishment of the Company's first permanent inland post. He retired to Edinburgh in 1775, where he lived quietly, working on his manuscripts. Seemingly without Graham's objection, Thomas Hutchins, his early collaborator in meteorological observation, took credit for the material emerging from his pen, and for many years the remarkable scientific record amassed by Graham was attributed to Hutchins.

Text: Andrew Graham's Observations on Hudson's Bay 1769–91, ed. Glyndwr Williams, intro. Richard Glover. London: The Hudson's Bay Record Society, 1969. This is a compilation from Graham's extensive manuscripts, some of which repeat material in variant forms. Unless otherwise indicated, all material is from HBCA E.2/12 (dated 1791).

Description of Hudson Bay

On the south side of Hudson's Bay where the Company have their settlements the air is commonly sweet and serene, and the weather very warm during the months of June and July, but in the winter months extremely cold. And it appears by observations made at York Fort and Severn River the mercury on Farenheit's standard thermometer was oftentimes at 63° below the cypher and in summer it rose to 98° above the cypher.[1]

From November to March hartshorn,[2] French and British spirit, rum and the like freeze so as with difficulty to run through a brass cock. This happens not only to small quantities but to casks containing 112 gallons. We have cellars dug eight to ten feet deep under our dwellings and have an almost perpetual fire; yet even in this repository I have seen the London porter so frozen that only a few gallons have been got out of a hogshead, the remainder being converted into ice which then had no strength at all as the strength of the liquor came all off with the first draught. I have ordered a hogshead full of water to be put out into the open air and in forty-eight hours it became solid ice and burst the cask. In an hour's time the breath condenses so thick on the window that it is impossible to discern an object on the other side. Large quantities of rime adhere to the wainscoting on the inside as also to the ceiling of the rooms. The frost is never out of the ground, even in summer it is thawed only about four feet below the surface. Notwithstanding this severity I can affirm from repeated experiments (by desire of the Royal Society)[3] that the frost does not penetrate more than from eight to ten feet deep in the ground.

The soil is rich and consists of a loose fat earth for several feet deep, under which are different strata of clays, gravel and sand etc. of various colours. The lands near the coast are low and marshy, but the banks of the rivers rise gradually as they recede from the sea. I speak now of the southern and western parts of the bay where the Hudson's Bay Company have their settlements, for up to the northward and eastmain the land is rocky, barren and mountainous. . . .

Fresh water lakes are very numerous everywhere for 500 miles up the country, the largest of which is Christianeux, or French Man's Lake,[4] which is several hundred miles in length and of various breadths. Beyond this lake is a fine level country abounding with rich pasturage and meadow ground in which some salt water lakes and ponds are discovered. Several of the Company's servants who have been up in the country affirm that on the shores of the salt water lakes the salt lies in large quantities and looks like snow. Some of our men made use of the water but its cathartic quality obliged them to reject it. The learned gentlemen of Edinburgh examined a sample of the salt which I brought home and found it to answer the purpose of Glauber salt.[5] Travellers in that part of America suffer great hardships from their want of wholesome water.

Mountains are not met with nigh the sea-coast, and none have been discovered by the Company's servants who have travelled far inland to the distance of 1200 miles WSW from York Fort.[6]

Ironstone is found at Cape Churchill and other parts of Hudson's Bay. At Whale River a lead vein was discovered and some ore sent home. This mine was not prosecuted, but whether through the negligence of the Factor or the failure of the ore I know not.[7] Copper ore in large lumps is brought annually to Churchill Factory by the natives from a river which they call Copper River. In the year 1769 the Company sent an ingenious young man to examine the northern parts of the bay and to discover if there was any opening or likelihood of a north-west passage. After an absence of two years he returned having gone to Copper River in latitude 72 degrees north and 128 degrees west from London. He met with no opening or large river but brought home samples of copper[8] of which I presented specimens to several gentlemen in Edinburgh, and to the Edinburgh Royal Society.[9]

The Beaver

The country about Hudson's Bay abounds with animals of several kinds. I shall begin with the Beaver.

These animals are of a brown colour in general, though sometimes we meet with black or white ones. The fur under the long hairs is of a light colour. A full grown beaver will weigh twenty-four pounds, is two feet long to two and a half from the nose to the rump, and the tail twelve inches long and six broad, has eight teeth in each jaw, six of which masticate their food. The other two (which are placed in the front and are half an inch long in the lower and three quarters in the upper jaw) serve to cut their trees and sever their food, which consists of the rind of willow and poplar, but they eat nothing of a resinous kind. In summer they eat a root that grows about the swamps and creeks, yet too scarce to admit of laying up a winter's stock. The male beaver has besides the testes a pair of castors and a pair of oil-stones, so called from their containing a very fetid oil which they make use of occasionally to prevent the water making any impression on their fur, like the reservoir on the rump of water fowl with which they lubricate their plumage. These stones are not included in a scrotum out of the abdomen, but lie one upon another in the pubes just within the skin. The wolverenes and otters are great enemies to the beaver, preying upon them whenever it is within their power. They are generally pregnant about the middle of February and bring forth their young about the end of May, from three to six which they rarely exceed. The usual number is four, but in the inland country to the southward they are more prolific. The flesh is much esteemed by the natives either roasted or boiled, but they sometimes dry it in the smoke, all the bones being previously taken out. They harbour about creeks and lakes where there are plenty of poplars and willows for food, and in such situations they build their houses, but so that it shall be surrounded by and have a communication with the water. It is in the form of an oven-crown and composed of willows, poplars, stones and mud intermixed. Near the sea-coast these however are two feet thick to resist the intensity of the cold, but farther to the southward they decrease in thickness and strength, accommodating their habitation to the nature of the climate in which they reside. What a demonstration this of the wisdom and goodness of God who furnishes even the brute creation with instincts and strength to supply its wants. But to return to the beaver-houses. They have three apartments; one may be called the dining-room, another the bed-chamber, and the third is converted into a necessary apartment which they frequently clean out, carrying the soil and filth to a considerable distance from the house.[10] Besides these they have holes in several places on each side the creek or lake, and to these they resort when they find danger or any disturbances about their house. The number of beavers in one house is between three and thirteen. They are constantly employed during the summer in building their habitations and laying up stores of provisions for the winter. These generally consist of poplars and willows which they cut into proper lengths and range them in the water before the mouth of the house; and to this magazine they have recourse in the winter, and having stripped the stick of its rind, they set it adrift where the stream carries it off as a thing rendered unserviceable. In order to preserve a supply of water during the winter they increase its depth by means of strong dams, built with similar materials to the house. By this wise precaution they prevent the want of that useful element, which otherwise perhaps would be totally converted into ice. They are extremely vigilant, and when they repose the head always points to the opening into the water that they may immediately make an escape in case of an attack. Their dams are under such regulations, that they can increase and decrease the water at pleasure; it is an Herculean performance for so small an animal, and argues strength, activity and wisdom. They are seldom damaged even by the floods which sometimes are very great at the breaking up of the ice in the rivers. I have heard the noise of the water falling over these dams without injuring them above four hundred yards off. The forefeet and tail of this sagacious animal are employed in plastering; on the latter of which the mud is conveyed to the part desired. With their teeth they cut down trees and willows, and drag them to the house or dam. I know these creatures to have cut down trees in the neighbourhood of the Company's settlements, that measured ten inches in diameter; and what is again very surprising they cause it to fall towards the water, by which prudent management they shorten the distance of the carriage. One of their company keeps watch whilst the others are at work, and gives notice when the tree is going to fall. In a large community there are sometimes slave beavers that join them accidentally, who are made to do the drudgery work.[11]

The natives frequently lie in wait for them in summer, and kill them with the gun; but in winter they take them in or near their houses. As I have been formerly in one of those expeditions, I shall here subjoin an account of the method of proceeding.

There were eight of us in company including women. We set out early in the morning and in a few hours arrived at the place of action, which had previously been narrowly examined by an old and experienced Indian. Our first care was to stake the creek across both above and below the house to prevent the beaver from escaping. Afterwards we endeavoured to discover all the holes or cells about the creek, by thrusting a long hoop-stick under the ice; all these retreats were likewise barricaded by driving down stakes. Our next business was to cut a large hole in the ice near the mouth of the house, and set a net made of leather-thong, which is constantly watched by one of the oldest and most experienced men, who knows when the beaver approaches by the undulation of the water, whilst others make a noise, and beat upon the house; when out jumps the beaver, and it is caught in the net, which is immediately replaced. The women then break up the house with their hatchets and if any beavers are in the house they knock them on the head, and carefully watch for the return of others. They are extremely shy, are seldom hampered a second time in a net, and will almost drown themselves before they will return to their house when they have been once disturbed. We caught all that were in that house, which amounted only to two. If (as is sometimes the case) any of the beaver should get away by pushing through the stakes, or by finding a passage unguarded, they seek a fresh habitation until the summer when they build a new house, and strange beaver will take possession of the old one and repair it. The flesh of the beaver is equally distributed, but the skins are the sole property of the person who first discovered the house. We divide the beaver into three sizes. Firstly the whole or full-grown beaver, which is the standard. Secondly the three-quarter. Thirdly the half or young beaver, which last size generally belongs to the women. The skin of a full-grown beaver will weigh 36 ounces, and sells at London from eight to twenty shillings per pound. N.B. I presented one to the Edinburgh Royal Society, January 1787. . . .

The Wechepowuck Nation[12]

These Indians were entirely unknown to Europeans until the beginning of this present century, when the Hudson's Bay Company sent a person[13] into their country with presents and an invitation down to Churchill Settlement, to which place they bring their goods, never visiting any other Factory, because the distance would be increased. They come in with their furs spring and autumn; whilst the farthest tribes arrive only once in three years. They are strong, able people, have three blue strokes on each cheek, always dressed in deerskins, drink no spiritous liquors, and barter their furs and pelts only for necessaries such as ammunition, iron, cutlery-ware; never purchasing much cloth, beads or any other superfluous articles. . . . Their canoes hold only one person. The rivers which water their country have no communication with Churchill River; for which reason it reduces them to the necessity of bringing their bundles on their backs; and their women and dogs are loaded like pack-horses. They have a language peculiar to themselves and of a guttural kind. We have few Englishmen that can hold a conversation with them, understanding little more than what name they give to the different articles of trade. They hold no intercourse with any of the southern Indians; and are looked on by them in the same despicable light as the Esquimaux. With the aforesaid Wechepowuck Indians and the Esquimaux subsists an inveterate enmity, which all the power of the Factor at Churchill Fort is not capable to set aside. A specimen of their cruelty shall be given hereafter. They inhabit that extensive unknown country to the NW of Churchill Settlement.

Their customs and manners are in many cases different from all the other natives.

A savage race of people, and eat their provisions raw, fish in particular. One man will have from two to twelve women, which he keeps in a melancholy state of subjection, carrying day after day heavy burdens; although they differ from the other natives in not murthering the women, but beat them unmercifully with sticks. Nay, they seldom kill one another.

They never inter their dead, but leaves the corpse lying on the ground covered over with skins, stoning the garment all round that it may not blow off; for they say, what occasion are there for putting the remains under ground, let the wolves and foxes devour it. For which reason they hold these animals as sacred, singing and conjuring to them; and although they trap and shoot them for their skins to trade with, as yet the most urgent necessity will not compel them to eat the flesh.

Mr Samuel Hearne, a young gentleman of a good education, being employed by the Hudson's Bay Company to examine the country to the NW of Churchill River, in order to find whether or not there were any passage by water from the Bay to the South-Seas; after being absent three years returned, having travelled to Copper-mine River in latitude 71° 54' north, longitude 125° 09' west from London, without crossing any river worth notice. Even the Copper-mine River is not worthy the name of one. This great undertaking has fully proven that no passage is to be expected by the way of Hudson's Bay.[14] . . .

Last summer[15] I had in to trade nigh three hundred Wechepawuck Indians headed by the leader named Menetabee,[16] who conducted Mr Hearne to the Copper-Mine River. From him I had several pieces of copper, also two deerskins which are entirely white, and the hair firm in the pelt, and nearly as fine as ermine fur. They frequent high latitudes. N.B. Menetabee hung himself for grief that the French had destroyed Churchill Factory, Anno Domini 1782. . . .

The Company Posts

Having now given a description and natural history of the country, together with the account of the various natives, I shall take a view of the present state of the settlements made by the Company, beginning at the most northern and gradually advancing to the southward.

Prince of Wales's Fort is situated on a peninsula, at the mouth of Churchill River, on the north side. It is a regular stone fortress, mounting forty-two guns, from six to twenty-four pounders, commanding the entrance of the river. . . .

When the settlement was first fixed upon, there was a wooden fort built seven miles up the river; and here they inhabited until about forty years ago, when the present place was ready for their reception.[17] The Old Fort is standing in part, and serves for stables etc. There is a great inconveniency attending this place, and that is, the want of fresh water, which in summer is drawn some miles by horses, or else brought by a long-boat or shallop; but in winter they melt snow making several tones of water in a day. . . .

This Fort[18] is governed by a Chief Factor, who has under him a proper number of officers, and from forty to fifty servants of different trades and callings, which I shall explain; the Council who has a discretionary power given them by the Company to act for their interest taking care to follow all just and legal methods, strictly abiding by the laws of old England. The present Council of this fort are Mr John Fowler Chief, the Second vacant, Surgeon, Master of the brig, and Master of the sloop, and the Captain of the Company's ship when there. The others are a trader, an accomptant, two vessels' mates, steward, armourer, shipwright, black-smith, two masons, bricklayer, carpenter, cooper, tailor, three harpooners, and a proper number of seamen and labourers, who are all under contract not to trade with the natives upon their own account. Such person or persons being found guilty of such breach of contract are sent home and prosecuted by the Company; riotous peace breakers, and any who will not live quiet, are sent home and dismissed the Company's service, we never inflicting any punishment more than caning, and when that will not do by the advice of Council whipping, which last is inflicted always on him or them who steals or pilfers from their neighbours. The Chief and Council messes together, and are also in the Captain's mess out and home, excepting bad behaviour has rendered them incapable of being looked on as gentlemen. The inferior officers, tradesmen and all others are regularly kept at duty, and are obliged to assist and be at all calls when occasion requires, and are victualled etc. in the same manner and form as on board a King's ship, or foreign merchantman. The servants are rung out and in to duty by a bell. They work from 6 to 6 in summer, and from 9 to 2 in winter, being allowed an hour to breakfast, and the same time to dinner. A regular watch is kept in the night by two men, three hours at a time, that is, from 8 o'clock to 11, from 11 to 2, and from 2 to 5 in the morning; the first watch seeing all fires and lights out by 9 o'clock, and the morning watch lights the fires and calls the men up. In the summer a strict look-out is kept on the ramparts or house top, and when a ship, vessel of any kind, or canoe is seen, they acquaint the Chief and officers directly. The inferior officers and tradesmen are employed at their own business excepting on urgent occasions, such as procuring fire-wood, unloading the craft etc, at ship-times and keeping ourselves from being drifted up with snow in winter. All others are employed on various necessary duty by land and sea in the summer, and in the winter the sprightliest and best hunters are employed in shooting and netting partridges, snaring rabbits, and fishing. The others are falling and hauling fire-wood, so that oftentimes there are no more at the Fort than what barely does the necessary duty. This Fort is attended with many inconveniences, and country provisions are so scarce that the Company is obliged to send out more provisions to it than what they send to all the other settlements, and the officers' apartments are so small, and amongst the men's, often causes discontents between the Chief and them, so that few of them stays after the expiration of their first contract, if not sooner returns home. . . .

The salary of the labouring men which at their first contract is from £6 to £10 per annum is advanced forty shillings per annum, if they have behaved well in their former contract. The land and sea officers' salary at their first contract is from £30 to £50 per annum, and never rises peace nor war. The private seamen's salary is in peace

£15 per annum, and in war £20 per annum. The tradesmen's salary is from £20 to £36 per annum peace and war. The Chief's salary is from £50 to £100 per annum, which last sum is the highest that is ever given.[19] And if any servants belonging to the Company performs any extraordinary services for their interest, they are rewarded over and above their salary; and indeed they are an honourable set of gentlemen, no servant that has once served them needs want bread, they have only to apply and are sent out to some of the settlements. The Chief Factors when desirous to return to England for one year only, does not lose their place, the second Factor if found capable is appointed by the Company to command in his absence, and if not capable, they are at the great expense of sending out a person for one year. . . . The servants are allowed to buy goods out of the Company's warehouses to the value of not more than one third of their wages per annum, and a strict order to their Factors to prevent suttling etc. But all to no purpose — a spendthrift will find ways and means to make away with his money, although victuals and drink, and I may say clothing, is found them, very little English clothing being used here excepting waistcoats, shirts and a few other trifles, we being all of us dressed in the Company's furs in winter, and the working men in leather toggies and such like in summer.

No European women are allowed to be brought to Hudson's Bay, and no person is allowed to have any correspondence with the natives without the Chief's orders, not even to go into an Indian tent. And the natives are not permitted to come within the Forts but when their business requires, and then they are conducted to the Chief's house or trading room, where all business with them is transacted.[20] However the Factors for the most part at proper times allows an officer to take in an Indian lady to his apartment, but by no means or on any account whatever to harbour her within the Fort at night. However the Factors keeps a bedfellow within the Fort at all times, and have carried several of their children home as before observed. . . .

Graham's own post, Fort Severn

Severn Fort (Washeo Whiskiheggan).[21] It lies in fifty-six degrees ten minutes North latitude, and eighty-eight degrees West longitude from London. It is pleasantly situated on the north shore of New Severn River (Washeo Sepee), about eight miles from its mouth. It is a compact building, with four bastions, eight cannon, a petard, and other warlike stores for its defence. The river, like most others in Hudson's Bay, is full of shoals and sand-banks, that it is with the utmost difficulty that a vessel of small burden can get in or out; and even when within the point of land, obliged to wait for spring tides to get up to the Fort. The tides here are so weak, and the current so strong, that the tide is scarcely ever observed to run up; it only swells the water. But there is yearly a vast deluge at the breaking up of the ice in the latter end of May, and much damage is frequently done by it.

The whole complement of men at this delightful settlement is eighteen; and the trade about five thousand made beaver in furs and pelts. Here is a good strong sloop which annually brings the trade to York Fort to be put on board the ship, and returns again with a supply of European articles. A few miles up this river are seen the ruins of an old house, which we suppose to have been built by the French, when in possession of York and Albany Forts. Venison, American hares, ptarmigans, and fish are here in great abundance. In short, I affirm that New Severn River is the pleasantest river in Hudson's Bay. . . .

Since the year[22] 1756 several Englishmen have been sent annually inland to endeavour to promote the Company's trade, and to invite down the Archithinue Indians to trade, but have not yet succeeded, and am certain never will. In the years 1761 and 1766 when Chief Factor at York Fort, I did my utmost to endeavour to search and find out the reason why the Archithinues could not be got down to trade, and the reasons they gave me were the same as mentioned by Anthony Hendey in his Journal wrote at full in the first book of this work.[23] And in 1766 I had an opportunity of conversing with an Archithinue Indian man who was brought down to York Fort by one of our prime leaders, who seemed to be a man of some consequence by the great care the leader and his followers took of him. He could talk very little of the trading Indians' language,[24] but by an interpreter he told me that there were Indians beyond his country that see ships sailing in the sea or great waters, as the natives terms it, but never came nigh the shore, although there be good rivers to come into. I asked him if there were any beaver and wolves etc. in his country. He said there were plenty, and that our traders[25] came amongst them and bought up their furs, giving them a gun for fifty wolves or beaver, six ditto for a hatchet, twenty ditto for a kettle, four for a knife, and so on. I told him what they gave me for such goods. He presented me with thirty wolves, fifteen beaver, and a few other furs; and he told me that he wanted a part of every kind of goods, but no powder nor shot, which demand I complied with to his satisfaction. He demanded two laced hats, which made me enquire what he was going to do with two hats. He told me it was for his father, who would wear it when he rid on horse-back in pursuit of the buffalo. He was surprised to see me and the trader give a gun for fourteen beaver, a hatchet for one beaver, a large kettle for eight beaver etc. I talked, and did all in my power to get down him and his countrymen next year, but he generously told me they never would come down, and that he himself never would come down again, as he did not like to sit in the canoe and be obliged to eat fish and fowl as he had done mostly coming down. He said that he would be kind to my countrymen when he seed them inland. He was greatly surprised to see our shores covered with large heavy ice, and said that the ice in his country was but six inches thick, and the snow never so deep as to hinder them from pursuing the buffalo on horse-back. . . .

I have heard great talking off and on concerning Hudson's Bay being laid open to all adventurers. The climate will not allow it; every necessary must be brought from England excepting fish, flesh and fowl, and that could not be got without the assistance of the natives who would enhance the price according to the demands. Each Factory at present are obliged to employ forty able hunters to bring in provisions, notwithstanding the supplies yearly sent out. There are not natives sufficient inhabiting between the Forts and the muscuty country,[26] where the Archithinue and Aseenepoets inhabits, to raise the fur trade above 20,000 skins more than is now sent home yearly from the Bay. And if the trading standard was enlarged[27] in favour of the natives, would ruin it all; for I am certain if the natives were to get any more for their furs, they would catch fewer, which I shall make plainly appear viz. one canoe brings down yearly to the Fort one hundred made beaver in different kinds of furs, and trades with me seventy of the said beaver for real necessaries. The other thirty beaver shall so puzzle him to trade, that he often asks me what he shall buy, and when I make an answer, Trade some more powder, shot, tobacco and hatchets etc., his answer is, I have traded sufficient to serve me and my family until I see you again next summer; so he will drink one half, and trade the other with me for baubles.

I am certain that inland settlements would be more for the natives' interest than for the Company's advantage, as their being supplied so nigh would encourage their wretched indolence, prevent them from visiting the lower Forts, and as before observed they would catch no more furs than seventy or one hundred beaver, which fully supplies their annual wants. The natives that harbours nigh the settlements, not Home-guards, never brings above one hundred beaver at the best of years, although I am positive they may bring double the number of skins. All the discovered rivers are so shoal, full of cataracts and long land carriages, that with great difficulty, expense and attended with the utmost confusion, birch-rind canoes would not be got up to Keskachewan River with a trifle of goods in less than four months, even let us act as Canadians who are inured to such game. The long knowledge I have of the affairs in Hudson's Bay makes me affirm, that however advantageous it may be to two or three poor pedlars from Canada to drive a wretched and vagabond life after a few furs, I do not think it is, and am certain it would not be, worth the notice of an Honourable Company of Gentlemen to follow such pitiful game. . . .

I have made it my constant study[28] these twelve years past to examine into the affairs of Hudsons Bay, particularly York Fort and Severn House; and if the Standard of Trade was altered a little in favour of the natives viz. martens, cased cats and otters, and some difference made between good winter furs and damaged ones, would certainly encourage the Nakawawuck Indians to despise the Pedlars and come down with their prime furs to the Company's settlements. This alternation, with the good conduct of the Factor at York Fort by endeavouring to ingratiate himself into the good opinion of the Keskachewan Indians and Asinepoet Indians, would bring up the York Fort trade to its former state of thirty to thirty-three thousand made beaver, such it was when the late Messrs White and Isham commanded there, who were well beloved by the natives and are at present kindly remembered by them yearly at York Fort and Severn House. All gentlemen that are acquainted with the natives in Hudsons Bay know that it is not altogether by giving large presents to the leaders that will gain a trade, but by an affable, kind, easy behaviour to the whole body of natives; for as all natives are master over their own families they give no ear to the leader if they have any disgust to the fort. In short no leader has power to enforce what he would have put in execution. The trade will fluctuate a little let a person be never so careful, but when it gives way to a yearly decline it then plainly appears they don't love the usage; and that Messrs White and Isham's manner of trading and treating the Keskachewan and Asinepoet Indians should have been a pattern for their successors to go by. By experience I say so, for Mr Marten and I followed their rules with regard to the natives when we commanded at York Fort, and when Mr Marten settled Severn House he set out on their plan and I have since strictly adhered to, and have made answer well for the Company, and have great hopes to make it a place worth their Honours farther notice. In the years 1749 and 1750 the Chief at York Fort[29] altered Mr Isham's manner, by which in two summers the trade fell from 31,316 to 19,424 made beaver. The Canadian pilferers cannot make these strange alterations as it is plainly observed one man increases the trade and another decreases it. . . .

I know for truth[30] that from Nelson River to Moose River, and from the sea inland to the Great Lake,[31] the Country is thinly inhabited; and what natives there are trades yearly at the Company's settlements and nowhere else. As it is impossible to make settlements at the Great Lake etc. where number of natives inhabits, and resorts to; let we Factors exert ourselves to gain the confidence of the natives, and I am certain the trade in total will not only be kept up, but may be increased. I do allow that Moose, Albany, and Severn Settlements are injured by the Canadian pilferers, but not York Fort and Churchill. York Fort trade falling visibly since the year 1762 is occasioned by that numerous and valuable tribes of Keskachewan Indians leading an indolent life amongst the Archithinue and Asinepoet Indians, neglecting to get furs and come down as formerly. . . . I am of opinion that two diligent, sensible men sent yearly from York Fort inland would rouse the Keskachewan and Asinepoet Indians from that indolent and degenerate state they have fallen into since the death of Mr James Isham, who was greatly beloved by the natives, and is at this time kindly remembered by them. I am certain that the pilfering trade carried on this present time within the limits of the Company's Charter by the English Canadians is neither with the spirit, experience, nor profit, with which it was carried on by the French before the conquest of Canada.

Notes

[1] While he was Chief at York Factory from 1771 to 1772 Graham co-operated with the surgeon, Thomas Hutchins, in keeping a detailed set of 'Meteorological Remarks', and in his Severn House journals for 1772–3 and 1773–4 he entered daily thermometer readings and wind directions.

[2] Liquid ammonia.

[3] The archives of London's Royal Society (then, as now, England's pre-eminent organization of scientists) contain twenty-four volumes of meterological observations from Hudson Bay between 1771 and 1807, with data from inland as well as Bay-side posts; Graham also speaks of the Royal Society of Edinburgh in a later passage.

[4] One of the various names given to Lake Winnipeg.

[5] A laxative salt.

[6] ANTHONY HENDAY is generally considered to have sighted the Rocky Mountains in 1754, but his only possible reference to them occurs in the problematic first draft of his journal (version A), where in the entry for 24 December 1754 he mentions the 'Arsinie Watchie' (stony or rocky hills or mountains).

[7] Richmond Fort was established in 1750, partly to exploit the mineral deposits thought to lie

between Richmond Gulf and Little Whale River. Only sulphur and low-grade brass was produced, and in 1751 John Potts who was in command, sent home in disgust his three 'disorderly and intolerably idle' miners.

[8] The 'ingenious young man' was SAMUEL HEARNE. The correct location of the Coppermine River (about which Hearne was mistaken) is latitude 47° 48′N., longitude 115° 47′W. Hearne stated that he found only one piece of copper 'of any size', though his native companions came across 'some smaller ones'. Graham records that he received several pieces of copper from Hearne's native guide and leader, Matonabbee, together with some Eskimo implements and ornaments made of copper.

[9] Graham refers many times to presenting mineral samples, native artefacts, and wild life specimens to the Royal Society of Edinburgh; their natural history material was dispersed in 1859, and Graham's specimens, which may have gone to the Industrial Museum of Scotland, cannot now be traced.

[10] Graham's description of a beaver lodge appears to have been borrowed from the similar one in JAMES ISHAM's *Observations*.

[11] This notion again seems to come from ISHAM, and is corrected by HEARNE in his own account of the beaver.

[12] Chipewyan, the 'Northern Indians' of the Company journals of this period.

[13] This was William Stuart (*c.* 1678–1719), who in 1715–16 made an arduous journey with the notable native woman Thanadelthur to bring peace to the warring Cree and Chipewyans and (in Stuart's case) to reconnoitre mineral resources; they reached the area south-east of Great Slave Lake which SAMUEL HEARNE later passed through.

[14] After the failure of sloops from Churchill in the early 1760s to discover a sea-route to the Coppermine River, Graham had been among those to advocate a land journey by one or two Company servants helped by the 'Wechepowuck Indians'.

[15] In 1774 Graham wrote home from Churchill, 'we had two or three large gangs of Northern Indians that only comes here once in two or three years, and about fifty canoes of wretchedly gooded Southern Indians, which in the whole made our trade 15846.'

[16] The native captain Matonabbee; see SAMUEL HEARNE.

[17] The old wooden fort was established by James Knight in 1717.

[18] This description of Fort Prince of Wales is taken from HBCA E.2/4 (71ᵈ–73ʳ), *c.* 1768-9; the main document, E.2/12, resumes at the description of Fort Severn below.

[19] Graham was writing shortly before the reorganization of 1770, when officers' salaries were increased in compensation for the complete prohibition by the London Committee of private trade.

[20] This was not only for security, but to eliminate private trading.

[21] Severn House, established by Humphrey Marten in 1759 to secure the trade of the Indians of the Severn River and its tributaries. First known as James Fort, it was renamed Severn House by the London Committee when Graham took command there in 1761.

[22] The following three excerpts (pp. 106-8, up to n.30) are from HBCA E.2/5 (*c.* 1768-9), fols. 8-14.

[23] The reference is to version B of that journal (HBCA E.2/4, fols. 35-60); for Graham's role in copying the text, see the headnote to ANTHONY HENDAY.

[24] The 'trading Indians' were the Saskatchewan branch of the plains Cree; Graham elsewhere writes of them, 'since they have inhabited the buffalo country where provisions are so plentiful, they have neglected trapping and catching furs, but barter at a great advance a portion of the goods purchased at the Factories with the Archithinue and Asinepoet Indians'. (See Williams, ed., *Andrew Graham's Observations*, 193.)

[25] The 'trading Indians' above.

[26]Generally, the prairie; more specifically, the plains between the branches of the Saskatchewan River.

[27]That is, a higher price given for furs.

[28]From Huntington Library MS. HM 1720 (c. 1769), pp. 10–11.

[29]John Newton (d. 1750) was a ship-master in the Mediterranean trade until the Committee (contrary to their practice of giving responsibility only to men with experience in the Bay) appointed him in 1748 to replace James Isham, who was returning to England for the Parliamentary inquiry then underway.

[30]From HBCA E.2/7 (1771), 39ᵛ-39.

[31]Lake Winnipeg, sometimes described as the 'Grand Lac'.

Samuel Hearne   (1745 – 1792)

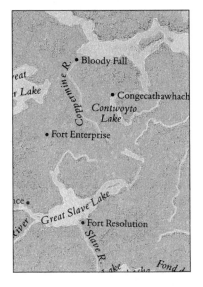

SAMUEL HEARNE joined the Royal Navy at the age of eleven and saw action during the Seven Years' War. In 1763 he went to work for the Hudson's Bay Company as a mariner. Galvanized by the parliamentary inquiry of 1749 the Company was making plans for more extensive exploration of the interior, particularly of its mineral resources. It accepted Moses Norton's plan to search for the copper which had been rumoured to exist in the north, and the young and energetic Hearne was chosen to make the expedition. Two false starts were made with guides chosen by Norton, but when Hearne found Matonabbee, he was successful at last. Hearne was not the first European to cross the Barren Lands, for William Stuart had travelled there with the native woman Thanadelthur on a peace-making mission in 1715–16. Nevertheless his journey was an extraordinary one. Between 7 December 1770 and 30 June 1772, a solitary white man moving with a shifting band of native companions, he travelled first westward in the direction of present-day Great Slave Lake, then northward down the Coppermine River. His purpose was exploration, but the Chipewyans with whom he travelled were intent on a massacre of the Inuit encamped at Bloody Fall, near the mouth of the Coppermine. Hearne witnessed the massacre, which he was powerless to prevent, and which is still recalled with horror by the Inuit today. His account not only of the bloodshed, but of the Chipewyans' initial preparations and subsequent purification rituals, has enthralled both ethnographers and ordinary readers for generations. Hearne's narrative is a fascinating mixture of geographical, biological, and ethnographical observation; he is much more interested in the lives of the natives with whom he travelled than many other explorers, and though he has many of the prejudices of his time, is particularly informative about the lives of individual natives, especially women. In describing the massacre it is the viewpoint of the Age of Sensibility that comes to his aid. But beginning with Sir John Richardson, there has been sharp debate as whether Hearne himself was responsible for the text of his published narrative. Like other exploration journals of the period (MACKENZIE's, revised by William Combe) and ANTHONY HENDAY's (several times re-written by ANDREW GRAHAM), the final version may have been produced by Hearne with the aid of a more literary friend, or revised by another hand, possibly Dr John Douglas, Bishop of Salisbury, or the astronomer William Wales.

Hearne continued with the Company, and in 1773 founded Cumberland House, the Bay's first inland post. In 1776 he was appointed chief at Fort Prince of Wales, where in 1782 he was forced by defective fortifications and small numbers to surrender to the Comte de La Pérouse. Though the Company understood his reasons for surrendering, Hearne's friend Matonabbee hanged himself for shame, so ANDREW GRAHAM alleged, and both EDWARD UMFREVILLE and DAVID THOMPSON were scornful of Hearne's action. The naval officers of the FRANKLIN expedition were equally scornful of his insecure geography and erratic observations. But Hearne's *Journey to the Northern Ocean*, posthumously published in 1795, became the first and most enduring popular classic of Canadian exploration writing.

Text: Samuel Hearne, *A Journey from Prince of Wales's Fort in Hudson's Bay to the Northern Ocean*. London, 1795.

Hearne's first and second attempts at the journey (November 1769 and February 1770) fail, but on his second return to Prince of Wales Fort, he meets Matonabbee

[September 20] In the evening of the twentieth, we were joined from the Westward by a famous Leader, called Matonabbee,[1] mentioned in my instructions; who, with his followers, or gang, was also going to Prince of Wales's Fort, with furrs, and other articles for trade. This Leader, when a youth, resided several years at the above Fort, and was not only a perfect master of the Southern Indian language, but by being frequently with the Company's servants, had acquired several words of English, and was one of the men who brought the latest accounts of the Coppermine River; and it was on his information, added to that of one I-dot-le-ezey, (who is since dead,) that this expedition was set on foot.

The courteous behaviour of this stranger struck me very sensibly. As soon as he was acquainted with our distress, he got such skins as we had with us dressed for the Southern Indians, and furnished me with a good warm suit of otter and other skins: but, as it was not in his power to provide us with snow-shoes, being then on the barren ground, he directed us to a little river which he knew, and where there was a small range of woods, which, though none of the best, would, he said, furnish us with temporary snow-shoes and sledges, that might materially assist us during the remaining part of our journey. [October] We spent several nights in company with this Leader, though we advanced towards the Fort at the rate of ten or twelve miles a day; and as provisions abounded, he made a grand feast for me in the Southern Indian stile, where there was plenty of good eating, and the whole concluded with singing and dancing, after the Southern Indian style and manner. In this amusement my home-guard Indians bore no inconsiderable part, as they were both men of some consequence when at home, and well known to Matonabbee: but among the other Northern Indians, to whom they were not known, they were held in no estimation; which indeed is not to be wondered at, when we consider that the value of a man among those people, is always proportioned to his abilities in hunting; and as my two Indians had not exhibited any great talents that way, the Northern Indians shewed them as much respect as they do in common to those of very moderate talents among themselves.

During my conversation with this Leader, he asked me very seriously, If I would attempt another journey for the discovery of the Copper-mines? And on my answering in the affirmative, provided I could get better guides than I had hitherto been furnished with, he said he would readily engage in that service, provided the Governor at the Fort would employ him. In answer to this, I assured him his offer would be gladly accepted; and as I had already experienced every hardship that was likely to accompany any future trial, I was determined to complete the discovery, even at the risque of life itself. Matonabbee assured me, that by the accounts received from his own countrymen, the Southern Indians, and myself, it was very probable I might not experience so much hardship during the whole journey, as I had already felt, though scarcely advanced one third part of the journey.

He attributed all our misfortunes to the misconduct of my guides, and the very plan we pursued, by the desire of the Governor, in not taking any women with us on this journey, was, he said, the principal thing that occasioned all our wants: 'for,' said he, 'when all the men are heavy laden, they can neither hunt nor travel to any considerable distance; and in case they meet with success in hunting, who is to carry the produce of their labour?' 'Women,' added he, 'were made for labour; one of them can carry, or haul, as much as two men can do. They also pitch our tents, made and mend our clothing, keep us warm at night; and, in fact, there is no such thing as travelling any considerable distance, or for any length of time, in this country, without their assistance.' 'Women,' said he again, 'though they do every thing, are maintained at a trifling expence; for as they always stand cook, the very licking of their fingers in scarce times, is sufficient for their subsistence.' This, however odd it may appear, is but too true a description of the situation of women in this country: it is at least so in appearance; for the women always carry the provisions, and it is more than probable they help themselves when the men are not present.

[October 23] Early in the morning of the twenty-third, I struck out of the road to the Eastward, with my two companions and two or three Northern Indians, while Matonabbee and his crew continued their course to the Factory, promising to walk so slow that we might come up with them again; and in two days we arrived at the place to which we were directed. We went to work immediately in making snowshoe frames and sledges; but notwithstanding our utmost endeavours, we could not complete them in less than four days. On the first of November we again proceeded on our journey toward the Factory; and on the sixth, came up with Matonabbee and his gang: after which we proceeded on together several days; when I found my new acquaintance, on all occasions, the most sociable, kind, and sensible Indian I had ever met with. He was a man well known, and, as an Indian, of universal knowledge, and generally respected. . . .

Hearne finally began his great journey on December 7, 1770, and by April 1771 had reached the area east of Great Slave Lake

[April 18] Having a good stock of dried provisions, and most of the necessary work for canoes all ready, on the eighteenth we moved about nine or ten miles to the North North West, and then came to a tent of Northern Indians who were tenting on the North side of Thelewey-aza River.[2] From these Indians Matonabbee purchased another wife; so that he had now no less than seven, most of whom would for size have made good grenadiers. He prided himself much in the height and strength of his wives, and would frequently say, few women would carry or haul heavier loads; and though they had, in general, a very masculine appearance, yet he preferred them to those of a more delicate form and moderate stature. In a country like this, where a partner in excessive hard labour is the chief motive for the union, and the softer endearments of a conjugal life are only considered as a secondary object, there seems to be great propriety in such a choice; but if all the men were of this way of thinking, what would become of the greater part of the women, who in general are but of low stature, and many of them of a most delicate make, though not of the exactest proportion, or most beautiful mould? Take them in a body, the women are as destitute of real beauty as any nation I ever saw, though there are some few of them, when young, who are tolerable; but the care of family, added to their constant hard labour, soon make the most beautiful among them look old and wrinkled, even before they are thirty; and several of the more ordinary ones at that age are perfect antidotes to love and gallantry. This, however, does not render them less dear and valuable to their owners, which is a lucky circumstance for those women, and a certain proof that there is no such thing as any rule or standard for beauty. Ask a Northern Indian, what is beauty? he will answer, a broad flat face, small eyes, high cheekbones, three or four broad black lines a-cross each cheek, a low forehead, a large broad chin, a clumsy hook-nose, a tawney hide, and breasts hanging down to the belt. Those beauties are greatly heightened, or at least rendered more valuable, when the possessor is capable of dressing all kinds of skins, converting them into the different parts of their clothing, and able to carry eight or ten stone[3] in Summer, or haul a much greater weight in Winter. These, and other similar accomplishments, are all that are sought after, or expected, of a Northern Indian woman. As to their temper, it is of little consequence; for the men have a wonderful facility in making the most stubborn comply with as much alacrity as could possibly be expected from those of the mildest and most obliging turn of mind; so that the only real difference is, the one obeys through fear, and the other complies cheerfully from a willing mind; both knowing that what is commanded must be done. They are, in fact, all kept at a great distance, and the rank they hold in the opinion of the men cannot be better expressed or explained, than by observing the method of treating or serving them at meals, which would appear very humiliating, to an European woman, though custom makes it sit light on those whose lot it is to bear it. It is necessary to observe, that when the men kill any large beast, the women are always sent to bring it to the tent: when it is brought there, every operation it undergoes, such as splitting, drying, pounding, &c. is performed by the women. When any thing is to be prepared for eating, it is the women who cook it; and when it is done, the wives and daughters of the greatest Captains in the country are never served, till all the males, even those who are in the capacity of servants, have eaten what they think proper; and in times of scarcity it is frequently their lot to be left without a single morsel. It is, however, natural to think they take the liberty of helping themselves in secret; but this must be done with great prudence, as capital embezzlements of provisions in such times are looked on as affairs of real consequence, and frequently subject them to a very severe beating. If they are practised by a woman whose youth and inattention to domestic concerns cannot plead in her favour, they will for ever be a blot in her character, and few men will chuse to have her for a wife. . . .

Having finished such wood-work as the Indians thought would be necessary, and having augmented our stock of dried meat and fat, the twenty-first was appointed for moving; but one of the women having been taken in labour, and it being rather an extraordinary case, we were detained more than two days. The instant, however, the poor woman was delivered, which was not until she had suffered all the pains usually felt on those occasions for near fifty-two hours, the signal was made for moving when the poor creature took her infant on her back and set out with the rest of the company; and though another person had the humanity to haul her sledge for her, (for one day only,) she was obliged to carry a considerable load beside her little charge, and was frequently obliged to wade knee-deep in water and wet snow. Her very looks, exclusive of her moans, were a sufficient proof of the great pain she endured, insomuch that although she was a person I greatly disliked, her distress at this time so overcame my prejudice, that I never felt more for any of her sex in my life; indeed her sighs pierced me to the soul, and rendered me very miserable, as it was not in my power to relieve her.

When a Northern Indian woman is taken in labour, a small tent is erected for her, at such a distance from the other tents that her cries cannot easily be heard, and the other women and young girls are her constant visitants: no male, except children in arms, ever offers to approach her. It is a circumstance perhaps to be lamented, that these people never attempt to assist each other on those occasions, even in the most critical cases. This is in some measure owing to delicacy, but more probably to an opinion they entertain that nature is abundantly sufficient to perform every thing required, without any external help whatever. When I informed them of the assistance which European women derive from the skill and attention of our midwives, they treated it with the utmost contempt; ironically observing, 'that the many humpbacks, bandy-legs, and other deformities, so frequent among the English, were undoubtedly owing to the great skill of the persons who assisted in bringing them into the world, and to the extraordinary care of their nurses afterwards.'

A Northern Indian woman after child-birth is reckoned unclean for a month or five weeks; during which time she always remains in a small tent placed at a little distance from the others, with only a female acquaintance or two; and during the whole time the father never sees the child. Their reason for this practice is, that children when first born are sometimes not very sightly, having in general large heads, and but little hair, and are, moreover, often discoloured by the force of the labour; so that were the father to see them in such great disadvantage, he might probably take a dislike to them, which never afterward could be removed. . . .

Immediately after our arrival at Clowey,[4] the Indians began to build their canoes, and embraced every convenient opportunity for that purpose: but as warm and dry weather only is fit for this business, which was by no means the case at present, it was the eighteenth of May [1771] before the canoes belonging to my party could be completed. On the nineteenth we agreed to proceed on our journey; but Matonab-bee's canoe meeting with some damage, which took near a whole day to repair, we were detained till the twentieth.

Those vessels, though made of the same materials with the canoes of the Southern Indians, differ from them both in shape and construction; they are also much smaller and lighter, and though very slight and simple in their construction, are nevertheless the best that could possibly be contrived for the use of those poor people, who are frequently obliged to carry them a hundred, and sometimes a hundred and fifty miles at a time, without having occasion to put them into the water. Indeed, the chief use of these canoes is to ferry over unfordable rivers; though sometimes, and at a few places, it must be acknowledged, that they are of great service in killing deer, as they enable the Indians to cross rivers and the narrow parts of lakes; they are also useful in killing swans, geese, ducks, &c. in the moulting season.

All the tools used by an Indian in building his canoe, as well as in making his snow-shoes, and every other kind of wood-work, consist of a hatchet, a knife, a file, and an awl; in the use of which they are so dextrous, that every thing they make is executed with a neatness not to be excelled by the most expert mechanic, assisted with every tool he could wish. . . .

During our stay at Clowey we were joined by upward of two hundred Indians from different quarters, most of whom built canoes at this place; but as I was under the protection of a principal man, no one offered to molest me, nor can I say they were very clamorous for any thing I had. This was undoubtedly owing to Matonabbee's informing them of my true situation; which was, that I had not, by any means, sufficient necessaries for myself, much less to give away. The few goods which I had with me were intended to be reserved for the Copper and Dog-ribbed Indians, who never visit the Company's Factories. Tobacco was, however, always given away; for every one of any note, who joined us, expected to be treated with a few pipes, and on some occasions it was scarcely possible to get off without presenting a few inches to them; which, with the constant supplies which I was obliged to furnish my own crew, decreased that article of my stock so fast, that notwithstanding I had yet advanced so small a part of my journey, more than one half of my store was expended. Gun-powder and shot also were articles commonly asked for by most of the Indians we met; and in general these were dealt round to them with a liberal hand by my guide

Matonabbee. I must however, do him the justice to acknowledge, that what he distributed was all his own, which he had purchased at the Factory; to my certain knowledge he bartered one hundred and fifty martins' skins for powder only, besides a great number of beaver, and other furrs, for shot, ball, iron-work, and tobacco, purposely to give away among his countrymen; as he had certainly as many of these articles given to him as were, in his opinion, sufficient for our support during our journey out and home. . . .

[May 28, 1771] In the night, one of Matonabbee's wives and another woman eloped [ran away]: it was supposed they went off to the Eastward, in order to meet their former husbands, from whom they had been sometime before taken by force. This affair made more noise and bustle than I could have supposed; and Matonabbee seemed entirely disconcerted, and quite inconsolable for the loss of his wife. She was certainly by far the handsomest of all his flock, of a moderate size, and had a fair complexion; she apparently possessed a mild temper, and very engaging manners. In fact, she seemed to have every good quality that could be expected in a Northern Indian woman, and that could render her an agreeable companion to an inhabitant of this part of the world. She had not, however, appeared happy in her late situation; and chose rather to be the sole wife of a sprightly young fellow of no note, (though very capable of maintaining her,) than to have the seventh or eighth share of the affection of the greatest man in the country. I am sorry to mention an incident which happened while we were building the canoes at Clowey, and which by no means does honour to Matonabbee: it is no less a crime than that of having actually stabbed the husband of the above-mentioned girl in three places; and had it not been for timely assistance, would certainly have murdered him, for no other reason than because the poor man had spoken disrespectfully of him for having taken his wife away by force. The cool deliberation with which Matonabbee committed this bloody action, convinced me it had been a long premeditated design; for he no sooner heard of the man's arrival, than he opened one of his wives' bundles, and, with the greatest composure, took out a new long box-handled knife, went into the man's tent, and, without any preface whatever, took him by the collar, and began to execute his horrid design. The poor man anticipating his danger, fell on his face, and called for assistance; but before any could be had he received three wounds in the back. Fortunately for him, they all happened on the shoulder-blade, so that his life was spared. When Matonabbee returned to his tent, after committing this horrid deed, he sat down as composedly as if nothing had happened, called for water to wash his bloody hands and knife, smoked his pipe as usual, seemed to be perfectly at ease, and asked if I did not think he had done right? . . .

Notwithstanding the Northern Indians are so covetous, and pay so little regard to private property as to take every advantage of bodily strength to rob their neighbours, not only of their goods, but of their wives, yet they are, in other respects, the mildest tribe, or nation, that is to be found on the borders of Hudson's Bay: for let their affronts or losses be ever so great, they never will seek any other revenge than that of wrestling. As for murder, which is so common among all the tribes of Southern Indians, it is seldom heard of among them. A murderer is shunned and detested by all the tribe, and is obliged to wander up and down, forlorn and forsaken even by his own relations and former friends. In that respect a murderer may truly be compared to Cain, after he had killed his brother Abel. The cool reception he meets with by all who know him, occasions him to grow melancholy, and he never leaves any place but the whole company say, 'There goes the murderer!' The women, it is true, sometimes receive an unlucky blow from their husbands for misbehaviour, which occasions their death; but this is thought nothing of: and for one man or woman to kill another out of revenge, or through jealousy, or on any other account, is so extraordinary, that very few are now existing who have been guilty of it. At the present moment I know not one, beside Matonabbee, who ever made an attempt of that nature; and he is, in every other respect, a man of such universal good sense, and, as an Indian, of such great humanity, that I am at a loss how to account for his having been guilty of such a crime, unless it be by his having lived among the Southern Indians so long, as to become tainted with their blood-thirsty, revengeful, and vindictive disposition. . . .

It should have been observed, that during our stay at Clowey a great number of Indians entered into a combination with those of my party to accompany us to the Copper-mine River; and with no other intent than to murder the Esquimaux, who are understood by the Copper Indians to frequent that river in considerable numbers. This scheme, notwithstanding the trouble and fatigue, as well as danger, with which it must be obviously attended, was nevertheless so universally approved by those people, that for some time almost every man who joined us proposed to be of the party. Accordingly, each volunteer, as well as those who were properly of my party, prepared a target, or shield, before we left the woods of Clowey. Those targets were composed of thin boards, about three quarters of an inch thick, two feet broad, and three feet long; and were intended to ward off the arrows of the Esquimaux. Notwithstanding these preparations, when we came to leave the women and children, as has been already mentioned, only sixty volunteers would go with us; the rest, who were nearly as many more, though they had all prepared targets, reflecting that they had a great distance to walk, and that no advantage could be expected from the expedition, very prudently begged to be excused, saying, that they could not be spared for so long a time from the maintenance of their wives and families; and particularly, as they did not see any then in our company, who seemed willing to encumber themselves with such a charge. This seemed to be a mere evasion, for I am clearly of opinion that poverty on one side, and avarice on the other, were the only impediments to their joining our party; had they possessed as many European goods to squander away among their countrymen as Matonabbee and those of my party did, in all probability many might have been found who would have been glad to have accompanied us.

When I was acquainted with the intentions of my companions, and saw the warlike preparations that were carrying on, I endeavoured as much as possible to persuade them from putting their inhuman design into execution; but so far were my intreaties from having the wished-for effect, that it was concluded I was actuated by cowardice; and they told me, with great marks of derision, that I was afraid of the Esquimaux. As I knew my personal safety depended in a great measure on the favourable opinion they entertained of me in this respect, I was obliged to change my tone, and replied, that I did not care if they rendered the name and race of the Esquimaux extinct; adding at the same time, that though I was no enemy to the Esquimaux, and did not see the necessity of attacking them without cause, yet if I should find it necessary to do it, for the protection of any one of my company, my own safety out of the question, so far from being afraid of a poor defenceless Esquimaux, whom I despised more than feared, nothing should be wanting on my part to protect all who were with me. This declaration was received with great satisfaction; and I never afterwards ventured to interfere with any of their war-plans. Indeed, when I came to consider seriously, I saw evidently that it was the highest folly for an individual like me, and in my situation, to attempt to turn the current of a national prejudice which had subsisted between those two nations from the earliest periods, or at least as long as they had been acquainted with the existence of each other. . . .

[June, 1771] Agreeably to my instructions, I smoked my calumet of peace with the principal of the Copper Indians, who seemed highly pleased on the occasion; and, from a conversation held on the subject of my journey, I found they were delighted with the hopes of having an European settlement in their neighbourhood, and seemed to have no idea that any impediment could present such a scheme from being carried into execution. Climates and seasons had no weight with them; nor could they see where the difficulty lay in getting to them; for though they acknowledged that they had never seen the sea at the mouth of the Copper River clear of ice, yet they could see nothing that should hinder a ship from approaching it; and they innocently enough observed, that the water was always so smooth between the ice and shore, that even small boats might get there with great ease and safety. How a ship was to get between the ice and the shore, never once occurred to them.

Whether it was from real motives of hospitality, or from the great advantages which they expected to reap by my discoveries, I know not; but I must confess that their civility far exceeded what I could expect from so uncivilized a tribe, and I was exceedingly sorry that I had nothing of value to offer them. However, such articles as I had, I distributed among them, and they were thankfully received by them. Though they have some European commodities among them, which they purchase from the Northern Indians, the same articles from the hands of an Englishman were more prized. As I was the first whom they had ever seen, and in all probability might be the last, it was curious to see how they flocked about me, and expressed as much desire to examine me from top to toe, as an European Naturalist would a non-descript animal. They, however, found and pronounced me to be a perfect human being, except in the colour of my hair and eyes: the former, they said, was like the stained hair of a buffaloe's tail, and the latter, being light, were like those of a gull. The whiteness of my skin also was, in their opinion, no ornament, as they said it resembled meat which had been sodden in water till all the blood was extracted. On the whole, I was viewed as so great a curiosity in this part of the world, that during my stay there, whenever I combed my head, some or other of them never failed to ask for the hairs that came off, which they carefully wrapped up, saying, 'When I see you again, you shall again see your hair.'

[June 23] The day after our arrival at Congecathawhachaga,[5] Matonabbee dispatched his brother, and several Copper Indians, to Copper-mine River, with orders to acquaint any Indians they might meet, with the reason of my visiting those parts, and also when they might probably expect us at that river. By the bearers of this message I sent a present of tobacco and some other things, to induce any strangers they met to be ready to give us assistance, either by advice, or in any other way which might be required.

As Matonabbee and the other Indians thought it advisable to leave all the women at this place, and proceed to the Copper-mine River without them, it was thought necessary to continue here a few days, to kill as many deer as would be sufficient for their support during our absence. And notwithstanding deer were so plentiful, yet our numbers were so large, and our daily consumption was so great, that several days elapsed before the men could provide the women with a sufficient quantity; and then they had no other way of preserving it, than by cutting it in thin slices and drying it in the Sun. Meat, when thus prepared, is not only very portable, but palatable; as all the blood and juices are still remaining in the meat, it is very nourishing and wholesome food; and may, with care, be kept a whole year without the least danger of spoiling. It is necessary, however, to air it frequently during the warm weather, otherwise it is liable to grow mouldy: but as soon as the chill air of the fall begins, it requires no farther trouble till next Summer.

We had not been many days at Congecathawhachaga before I had reason to be greatly concerned at the behaviour of several of my crew to the Copper Indians. They not only took many of their young women, furrs, and ready-dressed skins for clothing, but also several of their bows and arrows, which were the only implements they had to procure food and raiment, for the future support of themselves, their wives, and families. It may probably be thought, that as these weapons are of so simple a form, and so easily constructed, they might soon be replaced, without any other trouble or expence than a little labour; but this supposition can only hold good in places where proper materials are easily procured, which was not the case here: if it had, they would not have been an object of plunder. In the midst of a forest of trees, the wood that would make a Northern Indian a bow and a few arrows, or indeed a bow and arrows ready made, are not of much value; no more than the man's trouble that makes them: but carry that bow and arrows several hundred miles from any woods and place where those are the only weapons in use, their intrinsic value will be found to increase, in the same proportion as the materials which are made are less attainable.

To do Matonabbee justice on this occasion, I must say that he endeavoured as much as possible to persuade his countrymen from taking either furrs, clothing, or bows, from the Copper Indians, without making them some satisfactory return; but if he did not encourage, neither did he endeavour to hinder them from taking as many women as they pleased. Indeed, the Copper Indian women seem to be much esteemed by our Northern traders; for what reason I know not, as they are in reality the same people in every respect; and their language differs not so much as the dialects of some of the nearest counties in England do from each other.

It is not surprising that a plurality of wives is customary among these people, as it is so well adapted to their situation and manner of life. In my opinion no race of people under the Sun have a greater occasion for such an indulgence. Their annual haunts, in quest of furrs, is so remote from any European settlement, as to render them the greatest travellers in the known world; and as they have neither horse nor water carriage, every good hunter is under the necessity of having several persons to assist in carrying his furrs to the Company's Fort, as well as carrying back the European goods which he receives in exchange for them. No persons in this country are so proper for this work as the women, because they are inured to carry and haul heavy loads from their childhood and to do all manner of drudgery; so that those men who are capable of providing for three, four, five, six, or more women, generally find them humble and faithful servants, affectionate wives, and fond and indulgent mothers to their children. Though custom makes this way of life sit apparently easy on the generality of the women, and though, in general, the whole of their wants seem to be comprized in food and clothing only, yet nature at times gets the better of custom, and the spirit of jealousy makes its appearance among them: however, as the husband is always arbitrator, he soon settles the business, though perhaps not always to the entire satisfaction of the parties.

Much does it redound to the honour of the Northern Indian women when I affirm, that they are the mildest and most virtuous females I have seen in any part of North America; though some think this is more owing to habit, custom, and the fear of their husbands, than from real inclination. It is undoubtedly well known that none can manage a Northern Indian woman so well as a Northern Indian man; and when any of them have been permitted to remain at the Fort, they have, for the sake of gain, been easily prevailed on to deviate from that character; and a few have, by degrees, become as abandoned as the Southern Indians, who are remarkable throughout all their tribes for being the most debauched wretches under the Sun. So far from laying any restraint on their sensual appetites, as long as youth and inclination last, they give themselves up to all manner of even incestuous debauchery; and that in so beastly a manner when they are intoxicated, a state to which they are peculiarly addicted, that the brute creation are not less regardless of decency. I know that some few Europeans, who have had little opportunity of seeing them, and of enquiring into their manners, have been very lavish in their praise: but every one who has had much intercourse with them, and penetration and industry enough to study their dispositions, will agree, that no accomplishments whatever in a man, is sufficient to conciliate the affections, or preserve the chastity of a Southern Indian.[6]

The Northern Indian women are in general so far from being like those I have above described, that it is very uncommon to hear of their ever being guilty of incontinency, not even those who are confined to the sixth or even eighth part of a man.

It is true, that were I to form my opinion of those women from the behaviour of such as I have been more particularly acquainted with, I should have little reason to say much in their favour; but impartiality will not permit me to make a few of the worst characters a standard for the general conduct of all of them. Indeed it is but reasonable to think that travellers and interlopers will be always served with the worst commodities, though perhaps they pay the best price for what they have.

It may appear strange, that while I am extolling the chastity of the Northern Indian women, I should acknowledge that it is a very common custom among the men of this country to exchange a night's lodging with each other's wives. But this is so far from being considered as an act which is criminal, that it is esteemed by them as one of the strongest ties of friendship between two families; and in case of the death of either man, the other considers himself bound to support the children of the deceased. Those people are so far from viewing this engagement as a mere ceremony, like most of our Christian god-fathers and god-mothers, who, notwithstanding their vows are made in the most solemn manner, and in the presence of both God and man, scarcely ever afterward remember what they have promised, that there is not an instance of a Northern Indian having once neglected the duty which he is supposed to have taken upon himself to perform. The Southern Indians, with all their bad qualities, are remarkably humane and charitable to the widows and children of departed friends; and as their situation and manner of life enable them to do more acts of charity with less trouble than falls to the lot of a Northern Indian, few widows or orphans are ever unprovided for among them.

Though the Northern Indian men make no scruple of having two or three sisters for wives at one time, yet they are very particular in observing a proper distance in consanguinity of those they admit to the above-mentioned intercourse with their wives. The Southern Indians are less scrupulous on those occasions; among them it is not at all uncommon for one brother to make free with another brother's wife or daughter;[7] but this is held in abhorrence by the Northern Indians. . . .

[July 14, 1771] We had scarcely arrived at the Copper-mine River when four Copper Indians joined us, and brought with them two canoes. They had seen all the Indians who were sent from us at various times, except Matonabbee's brother, and three others that were first dispatched from Congecathawhachaga.

On my arrival here I was not a little surprised to find the river differ so much from the description which the Indians had given of it at the Factory; for, instead of being so large as to be navigable for shipping, as it had been represented by them, it was at that part scarcely navigable for an Indian canoe, being no more than one hundred and eighty yards wide, every where full of shoals, and no less than three falls were in sight at first view.

Near the water's edge there is some wood; but not one tree grows on or near the top of the hills between which the river runs. There appears to have been formerly a much greater quantity than there is at present; but the trees seem to have been set on fire some years ago, and, in consequence, there is at present ten sticks lying on the ground, for one green one which is growing beside them. The whole timber appears to have been, even in its greatest prosperity, of so crooked and dwarfish a growth as to render it of little use for any purpose but fire-wood.

Soon after our arrival at the river-side, three Indians were sent off as spies, in order to see if any Esquimaux were inhabiting the river-side between us and the sea. After walking about three quarters of a mile by the side of the river, we put up, when most of the Indians went ahunting, and killed several musk-oxen and some deer. They were employed all the remainder of the day and night in splitting and drying the meat by the fire. As we were not then in want to provisions, and as deer and other animals were so plentiful, that each day's journey might have provided for itself, I was at a loss to account for this unusual œconomy of my companions; but was soon informed, that those preparations were made with a view to have victuals enough ready-cooked to serve us to the river's mouth, without being obliged to kill any in our way, as the report of the guns, and the smoke of the fire, would be liable to alarm the natives, if any should be near at hand, and give them an opportunity of escaping.

Early in the morning of the fifteenth, we set out, when I immediately began my survey, which I continued about ten miles down the river, till heavy rain coming on we were obliged to put up; and the place where we lay that night was the end, or edge of the woods, the whole space between it and the sea being entirely barren hills and wide open marshes. In the course of this day's survey, I found the river as full of shoals as the part which I had seen before; and in many places it was so greatly diminished in its width, that in our way we passed by two more capital falls.

Early in the morning of the sixteenth, the weather being fine and pleasant, I again proceeded with my survey, and continued it for ten miles farther down the river; but still found it the same as before, being every where full of falls and shoals. At this time (it being about noon) the three men who had been sent as spies met us on their return, and informed my companions that five tents of Esquimaux were on the west side of the river. The situation, they said, was very convenient for surprising them; and, according to their account, I judged it to be about twelve miles from the place we met the spies. When the Indians received this intelligence, no farther attendance or attention was paid to my survey, but their whole thoughts were immediately engaged in planning the best method of attack, and how they might steal on the poor Esquimaux the ensuing night, and kill them all while asleep. To accomplish this bloody design more effectually, the Indians thought it necessary to cross the river as soon as possible; and, by the account of the spies, it appeared that no part was more convenient for the purpose than that where we had met them, it being there very smooth, and at a considerable distance from any fall. Accordingly, after the Indians had put all their guns, spears, targets, &c. in good order, we crossed the river, which took up some time.

When we arrived on the West side of the river, each painted the front of his target or shield; some with the figure of the Sun, others with that of the Moon, several with different kinds of birds and beasts of prey, and many with the images of imaginary beings, which, according to their silly notions, are the inhabitants of the different elements, Earth, Sea, Air, &c.

On enquiring the reason of their doing so, I learned that each man painted his shield with the image of that being on which he relied most for success in the intended engagement. Some were contented with a single representation; while others, doubtful, as I suppose, of the quality and power of any single being, had their shields covered to the very margin with a group of hieroglyphics quite unintelligible to every one except the painter. Indeed from the hurry in which this business was necessarily done, the want of every colour but red and black, and the deficiency of skill in the artist, most of those paintings had more the appearance of a number of accidental blotches, than 'of any thing that is on the earth, or in the water under the earth;' and though some few of them conveyed a tolerable idea of the thing intended, yet even these were many degrees worse than our country sign-paintings in England.

When this piece of superstition was completed, we began to advance toward the Esquimaux tents; but were very careful to avoid crossing any hills, or talking loud, for fear of being seen or overheard by the inhabitants; by which means the distance was not only much greater than it otherwise would have been, but, for the sake of keeping in the lowest grounds, we were obliged to walk through entire swamps of stiff marly clay, sometimes up to the knees. Our course, however, on this occasion, though very serpentine, was not altogether so remote from the river as entirely to exclude me from a view of it the whole way: on the contrary, several times (according to the situation of the ground) we advanced so near it, as to give me an opportunity of convincing myself that it was as unnavigable as it was in those parts which I had surveyed before, and which entirely corresponded with the accounts given of it by the spies.

It is perhaps worth remarking, that my crew, though an undisciplined rabble, and by no means accustomed to war or command, seemingly acted on this horrid occasion with the utmost uniformity of sentiment. There was not among them the least altercation or separate opinion; all were united in the general cause, and as ready to follow where Matonabbee led, as he appeared to be ready to lead, according to the advice of an old Copper Indian, who had joined us on our first arrival at the river where this bloody business was first proposed.

Never was reciprocity of interest more generally regarded among a number of people, than it was on the present occasion by my crew, for not one was a moment in want of any thing that another could spare; and if ever the spirit of disinterested friendship expanded the heart of a Northern Indian, it was here exhibited in the most extensive meaning of the word. Property of every kind that could be of general use now ceased to be private, and every one who had any thing which came under that description, seemed proud of an opportunity of giving it, or lending it to those who had none, or were most in want of it.

The number of my crew was so much greater than that which five tents could contain, and the warlike manner in which they were equipped so greatly superior to what could be expected of the poor Esquimaux, that no less than a total massacre of every one of them was likely to be the case, unless Providence should work a miracle for their deliverance.

The land was so situated that we walked under cover of the rocks and hills till we were within two hundred yards of the tents. There we lay in ambush for some time, watching the motions of the Esquimaux; and here the Indians would have advised me to stay till the fight was over, but to this I could by no means consent; for I considered that when the Esquimaux came to be surprised, they would try every way to escape, and if they found me alone, not knowing me from an enemy, they would probably proceed to violence against me when no person was near to assist. For this reason I determined to accompany them, telling them at the same time, that I would not have any hand in the murder they were about to commit, unless I found it necessary for my own safety. The Indians were not displeased at this proposal; one of them immediately fixed me a spear, and another lent me a broad bayonet for my protection, but at that time I could not be provided with a target; nor did I want to be encumbered with such an unnecessary piece of lumber.

While we lay in ambush, the Indians performed the last ceremonies which were thought necessary before the engagement. These chiefly consisted in painting their faces; some all black, some all red, and others with a mixture of the two; and to prevent their hair from blowing into their eyes, it was either tied before and behind, and on both sides, or else cut short all round. The next thing they considered was to make themselves as light as possible for running; which they did, by pulling off their stockings, and either cutting off the sleeves of their jackets, or rolling them up close to their arm-pits; and though the muskettoes at that time were so numerous as to surpass all credibility, yet some of the Indians actually pulled off their jackets and entered the lists quite naked, except their breech-cloths and shoes. Fearing I might have occasion to run with the rest, I thought it also advisable to pull off my stockings and cap, and to tie my hair as close up as possible.

By the time the Indians had made themselves thus completely frightful, it was near one o'clock in the morning of the seventeenth; when finding all the Esquimaux quiet in their tents, they rushed forth from their ambuscade, and fell on the poor unsuspecting creatures, unperceived till close at the very eves of their tents, when they soon began the bloody massacre, while I stood neuter in the rear.

In a few seconds the horrible scene commenced; it was shocking beyond description; the poor unhappy victims were surprised in the midst of their sleep, and had neither time nor power to make any resistance; men, women, and children, in all upward of twenty, ran out of their tents stark naked, and endeavoured to make their escape; but the Indians having possession of all the land-side, to no place could they fly for shelter. One alternative only remained, that of jumping into the river; but, as none of them attempted it, they all fell a sacrifice to Indian barbarity!

The shrieks and groans of the poor expiring wretches were truly dreadful; and my horror was much increased at seeing a young girl, seemingly about eighteen years of age, killed so near me, that when the first spear was stuck into her side she fell down at my feet, and twisted round my legs, so that it was with difficulty that I could disengage myself from her dying grasps. As two Indian men pursued this unfortunate victim, I solicited very hard for her life; but the murderers made no reply till they had stuck both their spears through her body, and transfixed her to the ground. They then looked me sternly in the face, and began to ridicule me, by asking if I wanted an Esquimaux wife; and paid not the smallest regard to the shrieks and agony of the poor wretch, who was twining round their spears like an eel! Indeed, after receiving much abusive language from them on the occasion, I was at length obliged to desire that they would be more expeditious in dispatching their victim out of her misery, otherwise I should be obliged, out of pity, to assist in the friendly office of putting an end to the existence of a fellow creature who was so cruelly wounded. On this request being made, one of the Indians hastily drew his spear from the place where it was first lodged, and pierced it through her breast near the heart. The love of life, however, even in this most miserable state, was so predominant, that though this might justly be called the most merciful act that could be done for the poor creature, it seemed to be unwelcome, for though much exhausted by pain and loss of blood, she made several efforts to ward off the friendly blow. My situation and the terror of my mind at beholding this butchery, cannot easily be conceived, much less described; though I summed up all the fortitude I was master of on the occasion, it was with difficulty that I could refrain from tears; and I am confident that my features must have feelingly expressed how sincerely I was affected at the barbarous scene I then witnessed; even at this hour I cannot reflect on the transactions of that horrid day without shedding tears.

The brutish manner in which these savages used the bodies they had so cruelly bereaved of life was so shocking, that it would be indecent to describe it; particularly their curiosity in examining, and the remarks they made, on the formation of the women; which, they pretended to say, differed materially from that of their own. For my own part I must acknowledge, that however favourable the opportunity for determining that point might have been, yet my thoughts at the time were too much agitated to admit of any such remarks; and I firmly believe, that had there actually been as much difference between them as there is said to be between the Hottentots and those of Europe, it would not have been in my power to have marked the distinction. I have reason to think, however, that there is no ground for the assertion; and really believe that the declaration of the Indians on this occasion, was utterly void of truth, and proceeded only from the implacable hatred they bore to the whole tribe of people of whom I am speaking.

When the Indians had completed the murder of the poor Esquimaux, seven other tents on the East side the river immediately engaged their attention: very luckily, however, our canoes and baggage had been left at a little distance up river, so that they had no way of crossing to get at them. The river at this part being little more than eighty yards wide, they began firing at them from the West side. The poor Esquimaux on the opposite shore, though all up in arms, did not attempt to abandon their tents; and they were so unacquainted with the nature of fire-arms, that when the bullets struck the ground, they ran in crowds to see what was sent them, and seemed anxious to examine all the pieces of lead which they found flattened against the rocks. At length one of the Esquimaux men was shot in the calf of his leg, which put them in great confusion. They all immediately embarked in their little canoes, and paddled to a shoal in the middle of the river, which being somewhat more than a gun-shot from any part of the shore, put them out of reach of our barbarians.

When the savages discovered that the surviving Esquimaux had gained the shore above mentioned, the Northern Indians began to plunder the tents of the deceased of all the copper utensils they could find; such as hatchets, bayonets, knives, &c. after which they assembled on the top of an adjacent high hill, and standing all in a cluster, so as to form a solid circle, with their spears erect in the air, gave many shouts of victory, constantly clashing their spears against each other, and frequently calling out *tima! tima!*[8] by way of derision to the poor surviving Esquimaux, who were standing on the shoal almost knee-deep in water. After parading the hill for some time, it was agreed to return up the river to the place where we had left our canoes and baggage, which was about half a mile distant, and then to cross the river again and plunder the seven tents on the East side. This resolution was immediately put in force; and as ferrying across with only three or four canoes took a considerable time, and as we were, from the crookedness of the river and the form of the land, entirely under cover, several of the poor surviving Esquimaux, thinking probably that we were gone about our business, and meant to trouble them no more, had returned from the shoal to their habitations. When we approached their tents, which we did under cover of the rocks, we found them busily employed tying up bundles. These the Indians seized with their usual ferocity; on which, the Esquimaux having their canoes lying ready in the water, immediately embarked, and all of them got safe to the former shoal, except an old man, who was so intent on collecting his things, that the Indians coming upon him before he could reach his canoe, he fell a sacrifice to their fury: I verily believe not less than twenty had a hand in his death, as his whole body was like a cullender. It is here necessary to observe that the spies, when on the look-out, could not see these seven tents, though close under them, as the bank, on which they stood, stretched over them.

It ought to have been mentioned in its proper place, that in making our retreat up the river, after killing the Esquimaux on the West side, we saw an old woman sitting by the side of the water, killing salmon, which lay at the foot of the fall as thick as a shoal of herrings. Whether from the noise of the fall, or a natural defect in the old woman's hearing, it is hard to determine, but certain it is, she had no knowledge of the tragical scene which had been so lately transacted at the tents, though she was not more than two hundred yards from the place. When we first perceived her, she seemed perfectly at ease, and was entirely surrounded with the produce of her labour. From her manner of behaviour, and the appearance of her eyes, which were as red as blood, it is more than probable that her sight was not very good; for she scarcely discerned that the Indians were enemies, till they were within twice the length of their spears of her. It was in vain that she attempted to fly, for the wretches of my crew transfixed her to the ground in a few seconds, and butchered her in the most savage manner. There was scarcely a man among them who had not thrust at her with his spear; and many in doing this, aimed at torture, rather than immediate death, as they not only poked out her eyes, but stabbed her in many parts very remote from those which are vital.

It may appear strange, that a person supposed to be almost blind should be employed in the business of fishing, and particularly with any degree of success; but when the multitude of fish is taken into the account, the wonder will cease. Indeed they were so numerous at the foot of the fall, that when a light pole, armed with a few spikes, which was the instrument the old woman used, was put under water, and hauled up with a jerk, it was scarcely possible to miss them. Some of my Indians tried the method, for curiosity, with the old woman's staff, and seldom got less than two at a jerk, sometimes three or four. . . .

When the Indians had plundered the seven tents of all the copper utensils, which seemed the only thing worth their notice, they threw all the tents and tent-poles into the river, destroyed a vast quantity of dried salmon, musk-oxen flesh, and other provisions; broke all the stone kettles; and, in fact, did all the mischief they possibly could to distress the poor creatures they could not murder, and who were standing on the shoal before mentioned, obliged to be woeful spectators of their great, or perhaps irreparable loss.

After the Indians had completed this piece of wantonness we sat down, and made a good meal of fresh salmon, which were as numerous at the place where we now rested, as they were on the West side of the river. When we had finished our meal, which was the first we had enjoyed for many hours, the Indians told me that they were again ready to assist me in making an end of my survey. It was then about five o'clock in the morning of the seventeenth, the sea being in sight from the North West by West to the North East, about eight miles distant. I therefore set instantly about commencing my survey, and pursued it to the mouth of the river, which I found all the way so full of shoals and falls that it was not navigable even for a boat, and that it emptied itself into the sea over a ridge or bar. The tide was then out; but I judged from the marks which I saw on the edge of the ice, that it flowed about twelve or fourteen feet, which will only reach a little way within the river's mouth. The tide being out, the water in the river was perfectly fresh; but I am certain of its being the sea, or some branch of it, by the quantity of whalebone and seal-skins which the Esquimaux had at their tents, and also by the number of seals which I saw on the ice. At the mouth of the river, the sea is full of islands and shoals, as far as I could see with the assistance of a good pocket telescope. The ice was not then broke up, but was melted away for about three quarters of a mile from the main shore, and to a little distance round the islands and shoals.

By the time I had completed this survey, it was about one in the morning of the eighteenth; but in those high latitudes, and at this season of the year, the Sun is always at a good height above the horizon, so that we had not only day-light, but sun-shine the whole night: a thick fog and drizzling rain then came on, and finding that neither the river nor sea were likely to be of any use, I did not think it worth while to wait for fair weather to determine the latitude exactly by an observation; but by the extraordinary care I took in observing the courses and distances when I walked from Congecathawhachaga, where I had two good observations, the latitude may be depended upon within twenty-miles at the utmost. For the sake of form, however, after having had some consultation with the Indians, I erected a mark, and took possession of the coast, on behalf of the Hudson's Bay Company. . . .

[September, 1771] One of the Indian's wives, who for some time had been in a consumption, had for a few days past become so weak as to be incapable of travelling, which, among those people, is the most deplorable state to which a human being can possibly be brought. Whether she had been given over by the doctors, or that it was for want of friends among them, I cannot tell, but certain it is, that no expedients were taken for her recovery; so that, without much ceremony, she was left unassisted, to perish above-ground.

Though this was the first instance of the kind I had seen, it is the common, and indeed the constant practice of those Indians; for when a grown person is so ill, especially in the Summer, as not to be able to walk, and too heavy to be carried, they say it is better to leave one who is past recovery, than for the whole family to sit down by them and starve to death; well knowing that they cannot be of any service to the afflicted. On those occasions, therefore, the friends or relations of the sick generally leave them some victuals and water; and, if the situation of the place will afford it, a little firing. When those articles are provided, the person to be left is acquainted with the road which the others intend to go; and then, after covering them well up with deer skins, &c. they take their leave, and walk away crying.

Sometimes persons thus left, recover; and come up with their friends, or wander about till they meet with other Indians, whom they accompany till they again join their relations. Instances of this kind are seldom known. The poor woman above mentioned, however, came up with us three several times, after having been left in the manner described. At length, poor creature! she dropt behind, and no one attempted to go back in search of her.

A custom apparently so unnatural is perhaps not to be found among any other of the human race: if properly considered, however, it may with justice be ascribed to necessity and self-preservation, rather than to the want of humanity and social feeling, which ought to be the characteristic of men, as the noblest part of the creation. Necessity, added to nation custom, contributes principally to make scenes of this kind less shocking to those people, than they must appear to the more civilized part of mankind. . . .

Among the various superstitious customs of those people, it is worth remarking, and ought to have been mentioned in its proper place, that immediately after my companions had killed the Esquimaux at the Copper River, they considered themselves in a state of uncleanness, which induced them to practise some very curious and unusual ceremonies. In the first place, all who were absolutely concerned in the murder were prohibited from cooking any kind of victuals, either for themselves or others. As luckily there were two in company who had not shed blood, they were employed always as cooks till we joined the women. This circumstance was exceedingly favourable on my side; for had there been no persons of the above description in company, that task, I was told, would have fallen on me; which would have been no less fatiguing and troublesome, than humiliating and vexatious.

When the victuals were cooked, all the murderers took a kind of red earth, or oker, and painted all the space between the nose and chin, as well as the greater part of their cheeks, almost to the ears, before they would taste a bit, and would not drink out of any other dish, or smoke out of any other pipe, but their own; and none of the others seemed willing to drink or smoke out of theirs.

We had no sooner joined the women, at our return from the expedition, than there seemed to be an universal spirit of emulation among them, vying who should first make a suit of ornaments for their husbands, which consisted of bracelets for the wrists, and a band for the forehead, composed of porcupine quils and moose-hair, curiously wrought on leather.

The custom of painting the mouth and part of the cheeks before each meal, and drinking and smoking out of their own utensils, was strictly and invariably observed, till the Winter began to set in; and during the whole of that time they would never kiss any of their wives or children. They refrained also from eating many parts of the deer and other animals, particularly the head, entrails, and blood; and during their uncleanness, their victuals were never sodden in water, but dried in the sun, eaten quite raw, or broiled, when a fire fit for the purpose could be procured.

When the time arrived that was to put an end to these ceremonies, the men, without a female being present, made a fire at some distance from the tents, into which they threw all their ornaments, pipe-stems, and dishes, which were soon consumed to ashes; after which a feast was prepared, consisting of such articles as they had long been prohibited from eating; and when all was over, each man was at liberty to eat, drink, and smoke as he pleased; and also to kiss his wives and children at discretion, which they seemed to do with more raptures than I had ever known them do it either before or since.

[October 6] October came in very roughly, attended with heavy falls of snow, and much drift. On the sixth at night, a heavy gale of wind from the North West put us in great disorder; for though the few woods we passed had furnished us with tent-poles and fewel, yet they did not afford us the least shelter whatever. The wind blew with such violence, that in spite of all our endeavours, it overset several of the tents, and mine, among the rest, shared the disaster, which I cannot sufficiently lament, as the but-ends of the weather tent-poles fell on the quadrant, and though it was in a strong wainscot case, two of the bubbles, the index, and several other parts were broken, which rendered it entirely useless. This being the case, I did not think it worth carriage, but broke it to pieces, and gave the brass-work to the Indians, who cut it into small lumps, and made use of it instead of ball.[9] . . .

On the eleventh of January, as some of my companions were hunting, they saw the track of a strange snow-shoe, which they followed; and at a considerable distance came to a little hut, where they discovered a young woman sitting alone. As they found that she understood their language, they brought her with them to the tents. On examination, she proved to be one of the Western Dog-ribbed Indians, who had been taken prisoner by the Athapuscow Indians in the Summer of one thousand seven hundred and seventy; and in the following Summer, when the Indians that took her prisoner were near this part, she had eloped from them, with an intent to return to her own country; but the distance being so great, and having, after she was taken prisoner, been carried in a canoe the whole way, the turnings and windings of the rivers and lakes were so numerous, that she forgot the track; so she built the hut in which we found her, to protect her from the weather during the Winter, and here she had resided from the first setting in of the fall.

From her account of the moons past since her elopement, it appeared that she had been near seven months without seeing a human face; during all which time she had supported herself very well by snaring partridges, rabbits, and squirrels; she had also killed two or three beaver, and some porcupines. That she did not seem to have been in want is evident, as she had a small stock of provisions by her when she was discovered; and was in good health and condition, and I think one of the finest women, of a real Indian, that I have seen in any part of North America.

The methods practised by this poor creature to procure a livelihood were truly admirable, and are great proofs that necessity is the real mother of invention. When the few deer-sinews that she had an opportunity of taking with her were all expended in making snares, and sewing her clothing, she had nothing to supply their place but the sinews of the rabbits legs and feet; these she twisted together for that purpose with great dexterity and success. The rabbits, &c. which she caught in those snares, not only furnished her with a comfortable subsistence, but of the skins she made a suit of neat and warm clothing for the Winter. It is scarcely possible to conceive that a person in her forlorn situation could be so composed as to be capable of contriving or executing any thing that was not absolutely necessary to her existence; but there were sufficient proofs that she had extended her care much farther, as all her clothing, beside being calculated for real service, shewed great taste, and exhibited no little variety of ornament. The materials, though rude, were very curiously wrought, and so judiciously placed, as to make the whole of her garb have a very pleasing, though rather romantic appearance.

Her leisure hours from hunting had been employed in twisting the inner rind or bark of willows into small lines, like net-twine, of which she had some hundred fathoms by her; with this she intended to make a fishing net as soon as the Spring advanced. It is of the inner bark of willows, twisted in this manner, that the Dog-ribbed Indians make their fishing-nets; and they are much perferable to those made by the Northern Indians.

Five or six inches of an iron hoop, made into a knife, and the shank of an arrow-head of iron, which served her as an awl, were all the metals this poor woman had with her when she eloped; and with these implements she had made herself complete snow-shoes, and several other useful articles.

Her method of making a fire was equally singular and curious, having no other materials for that purpose than two hard sulphurous stones. These, by long friction and hard knocking, produced a few sparks, which at length communicated to some touchwood; but as this method was attended with great trouble, and not always with success, she did not suffer her fire to go out all the Winter. Hence we may conclude that she had no idea of producing fire by friction, in the manner practiced by the Esquimaux, and many other uncivilized nations; because if she had, the above-mentioned precaution would have been unnecessary.

The singularity of the circumstance, the comeliness of her person, and her approved accomplishments, occasioned a strong contest between several of the Indians of my party, who should have her for a wife; and the poor girl was acually won and lost at wrestling by near half a score different men the same evening. My guide, Matonabbee, who at that time had no less than seven wives, all women grown, besides a young girl of eleven or twelve years old, would have put in for the prize also, had not one of his wives made him ashamed of it, by telling him that he had already more wives than he could properly attend. This piece of satire, however true, proved fatal to the poor girl who dared to make so open a declaration; for the great man, Matonabbee, who would willingly have been thought equal to eight or ten men in every respect, took it as such an affront, that he fell on her with both hands and feet, and bruised her to such a degree, that after lingering some time she died.

When the Athapuscow Indians took the above Dog-ribbed Indian woman prisoner, they, according to the universal custom of those savages, surprised her and her party in the night, and killed every soul in the tent, except herself and three other young women. Among those whom they killed, were her father, mother, and husband. Her young child, four or five months old, she concealed in a bundle of clothing, and took with her undiscovered in the night; but when she arrived at the place where the Athapuscow Indians had left their wives, (which was not far distant,) they began to examine her bundle, and finding the child, one of the women took it from her, and killed it on the spot.

This last piece of barbarity gave her such a disgust to those Indians, that notwithstanding the man who took care of her treated her in every respect as his wife, and was, she said, remarkably kind to, and even fond of her; so far was she from being able to reconcile herself to any of the tribe, that she rather chose to expose herself to misery and want, than live in ease and affluence among persons who had so cruelly murdered her infant.[10] The poor woman's relation of this shocking story, which she delivered in a very affecting manner, only excited laughter among the savages of my party.

In a conversation with this woman soon afterward, she told us, that her country lies so far to the Westward, that she had never seen iron, or any other kind of metal, till she was taken prisoner. All of her tribe, she observed, made their hatchets and ice-chisels of deer's horns, and their knives of stones and bones; that their arrows were shod with a kind of slate, bones, and deer's horns; and the instruments which they employed to make their woodwork were nothing but beavers' teeth. Though they had frequently heard of useful materials which the nations or tribes to the East of them were supplied with from the English, so far were they from drawing nearer, to be in the way of trading for iron-work, &c. that they were obliged to retreat farther back, to avoid the Athapuscow Indians, who made surprising slaughter among them, both in Winter and Summer. . . .

[February, 1772] On the twenty-fourth, a strange Northern Indian leader, called Thlew-sa-nell-ie, and several of his followers, joined us from the Eastward. This leader presented Matonabbee and myself with a foot of tobacco each, and a two-quart keg of brandy, which he intended as a present for the Southern Indians; but being informed by my companions, that there was not the least probability of meeting any, he did not think it worth any farther carriage. The tobacco was indeed very acceptable, as our stock of that article had been expended some time. Having been so long without tasting spirituous liquors, I would not partake of the brandy, but left it entirely to the Indians, to whom, as they were numerous, it was scarcely a taste for each. Few of the Northern Indians are found of spirits, especially those who keep at a distance from the Fort: some who are near, and who usually shoot geese for us in the Spring, will drink it at free cost as fast as the Southern Indians, but few of them are ever so imprudent as to buy it.

The little river lately mentioned, as well as the adjacent lakes and ponds, being well-stocked with beaver, and the land abounding with moose and buffalo, we were induced to make but slow progress in our journey. Many days were spent in hunting, feasting, and drying a large quantity of flesh to take with us, particularly that of the buffalo; for my companions knew by experience, that a few days walk to the Eastward of our present situation would being us to a part where we should not see any of those animals.

The strangers who had joined us on the twenty-fourth informed us, that all were well at Prince of Wales's Fort when they left it last; which, according to their account of the Moons past since, must have been about the fifth of November one thousand seven hundred and seventy one. These strangers only remained in our company one night before the Leader and part of his crew left us, and proceeded on their journey to the North Westward; but a few of them having procured some furrs in the early part of the Winter, joined our party, with an intent to accompany us to the Factory.

Having a good stock of dried meat, fat, &c. prepared in the best manner for carriage, on the twenty-eighth [of February] we shaped our course in the South East quarter, and proceeded at a much greater rate than we had lately done, as little or no time was now lost in hunting. The next day we saw the tracks of some strangers; and though I did not perceive any of them myself, some of my companions were at the trouble of searching for them, and finding them to be poor inoffensive people, plundered them not only of the few furrs which they had, but took also one of their young women from them.

Every additional act of violence committed by my companions on the poor and distressed, served to increase my indignation and dislike; this last act, however, displeased me more than all their former actions, because it was committed on a set of harmless creatures, whose general manner of life renders them the most secluded from society of any of the human race.

Matonabbee assured me, that for more than a generation past one family only, as it may be called, (and to which the young men belonged who were plundered by my companions,) have taken up their Winter abode in those woods, which are situated so far on the barren ground as to be quite out of the track of any other Indians. From the best accounts that I could collect, the latitude of this place must be about 63 1/2°, or 63° at least; the longitude is very uncertain. From my own experience I can affirm, that it is some hundreds of miles both from the sea-side and the main woods to the Westward. Few of the trading Northern Indians have visited this place; but those who have, give a pleasing description of it, all agreeing that it is situated on the banks of a river which has communication with several fine lakes. As the current sets to the North Eastward, it empties itself, in all probability, into some part of Hudson's Bay; and, from the latitude, no part seems more likely for this communication, than Baker's Lake, at the head of Chesterfield's inlet. This, however, is mere conjecture; nor is it of any consequence, as navigation on any of the rivers in those parts is not only impracticable, but would be also unprofitable, as they do not lead into a country that produces any thing for trade, or that contains any inhabitants worth visiting.

The accounts given of this place, and the manner of life of its inhabitants, would, if related at full length, fill a volume: let it suffice to observe, that the situation is said to be remarkably favourable for every kind of game that the barren ground produces at the different seasons of the year; but the continuance of the game with them is in general uncertain, except that of the fish and partridges. That being the case, the few who compose this little commonwealth, are, by long custom and the constant example of their forefathers, possessed of a provident turn of mind, with a degree of frugality unknown to every other tribe of Indians in this country except the Esquimaux. . . .

Hearne and Matonabbee meet other natives en route to the Bay

. . . it is an universal practice with the Indian Leaders, both Northern and Southern, when going to the Company's Factory, to use their influence and interest in canvassing for companions; as they find by experience that a large gang gains them much respect. Indeed, the generality of Europeans who reside in those parts, being utterly unacquainted with the manners and customs of the Indians, have conceived so high an opinion of those Leaders, and their authority, as to imagine that all who accompany them on those occasions are entirely devoted to their service and command all the year; but this is so far from being the case, that the authority of those great men, when absent from the Company's Factory, never extends beyond their own family; and the trifling respect which is shown them by their countrymen during their residence at the Factory, proceeds only from motives of interest.

The Leaders have a very disagreeable task to perform on those occasions; for they are not only obliged to be the mouth-piece, but the beggars for all their friends and relations for whom they have a regard, as well as for those whom at other times they have reason to fear. Those unwelcome commissions, which are imposed on them by their followers, joined to their own desire of being thought men of great consequence and interest with the English, make them very troublesome. And if a Governor deny them any thing which they ask, though it be only to give away to the most worthless of their gang, they immediately turn sulky and impertinent to the highest degree; and however rational they may be at other times, are immediately divested of every degree of reason, and raise their demands to so exorbitant a pitch, that after they have received to the amount of five times the value of all the furrs they themselves have brought, they never cease begging during their stay at the Factory; and, after all, few of them go away thoroughly satisfied.[11] . . .

[June, 1772] Just at the time we were crossing the South branch of Po-co-thee-kis-co River[12], the Indians that were sent from Egg River with a letter to the Chief at Churchill, joined us on their return, and brought a little tobacco and some other articles which I had desired. Though it was late in the afternoon before we had all crossed the river, yet we walked that evening till after ten o'clock, and then put up on one of the Goose-hunting Islands, as they are generally called, about ten miles from the Factory. The next morning [June 30, 1772] I arrived in good health at Prince of Wales's Fort, aftering having been absent eighteen months and twenty-three days on this last expedition; but from my first setting out with Captain Chawchinaha, it was two years seven months and twenty-four days.

Though my discoveries are not likely to prove of any material advantage to the Nation at large, or indeed to the Hudson's Bay Company, yet I have the pleasure to think that I have fully complied with the orders of my Masters, and that it has put a final end to all disputes concerning a North West Passage through Hudson's Bay. It will also wipe off, in some measure, the ill-grounded and unjust aspersions of Dobbs,[13] Ellis, Robson, and the American Traveller; who have all taken much pains to condemn the conduct of the Hudson's Bay Company, as being averse from discoveries, and from enlarging their trade.

Some Account of MATONABBEE, *and of the eminent Services which he rendered to his Country, as well as to the Hudson's Bay Company.*

Matonabbee was the son of a Northern Indian by a slave woman, who was formerly bought from some Southern Indians who came to Prince of Wales's Fort with furrs, &c. This match was made by Mr Richard Norton,[14] then Governor, who detained them at and near the Fort, for the same purpose as he did those Indians called Home-guard. As to Matonabbee's real age, it is impossible to be particular; for the natives of those parts being utterly unacquainted with letters, or the use of hieroglyphics, though their memories are not less retentive than those of other nations, cannot preserve and transmit to posterity the exact time when any particular event happens. Indeed, the utmost extent of their chronology reaches no farther, than to say, My son, or my daughter, was born in such a Governor's time, and such an event happened during such a person's life-time (though, perhaps, he or she has been dead many years). However, according to appearance, and some corroborating circumstances, Matonabbee was born about the year one thousand seven hundred and thirty-six or one thousand seven hundred and thirty-seven; and his father dying while he was young, the Governor took the boy, and, according to the Indian custom, adopted him as his son.

Soon after the death of Matonabbee's father, Mr Norton went to England, and as the boy did not experience from his successor[15] the same regard and attention which he had been accustomed to receive from Mr Norton, he was soon taken from the Factory by some of his father's relations, and continued with the Northern Indians till Mr Ferdinand Jacobs[16] succeeded to the command of Prince of Wales's Fort, in the year one thousand seven hundred and fifty-two; when out of regard to old Mr Norton, (who was then dead,) Mr Jacobs took the first opportunity that offered to detain Matonabbee at the Factory, where he was for several years employed in the hunting-service with some of the Company's servants, particularly with the late Mr Moses Norton,[17] (son of the late Governor,) and Mr Magnus Johnston.

In the course of his long stay at and near the Fort, it is no wonder that he should have become perfect master of the Southern Indian language, and made some progress in the English. It was during this period, that he gained a knowledge of the Christian faith; and he always declared, that it was too deep and intricate for his comprehension. Though he was a perfect bigot with respect to the arts and tricks of Indian jugglers, yet he could by no means be impressed with a belief of any part of our religion, nor of the religion of the Southern Indians, who have as firm a belief in a future state as any people under the Sun. He had so much natural good sense and liberality of sentiment, however, as not to think that he had a right to ridicule any particular sect on account of their religious opinions. On the contrary, he declared, that he held them all equally in esteem, but was determined, as he came into the world, so he would go out of it, without professing any religion at all. Notwithstanding his aversion from religion, I have met with few Christians who possessed more good moral qualities, or fewer bad ones.

It is impossible for any man to have been more punctual in the performance of a promise than he was; his scrupulous adherence to truth and honesty would have done honour to the most enlightened and devout Christian, while his benevolence and universal humanity to all the human race,[18] according to his abilities and manner of life, could not be exceeded by the most illustrious personage now on record; and to add to his other good qualities, he was the only Indian that I ever saw, except one, who was not guilty of backbiting and slandering his neighbours.

In stature, Matonabbee was above the common size, being nearly six feet high; and, except that his neck was rather (though not much) too short, he was one of the finest and best proportioned men that I ever saw. In complexion he was dark, like the other Northern Indians, but his face was not disfigured by that ridiculous custom of marking the cheeks with three or four black lines. His features were regular and agreeable, and yet so strongly marked and expressive, that they formed a complete index of his mind; which, as he never intended to deceive or dissemble, he never wished to conceal. In conversation he was easy, lively, and agreeable, but exceedingly modest; and at table, the nobleness and elegance of his manners might have been admired by the first personages in the world; for to the vivacity of a Frenchman, and the sincerity of an Englishman, he added the gravity and nobleness of a Turk; all so happily blended, as to render his company and conversation universally pleasing to those who understood either the Northern or Southern Indian languages, the only languages in which he could converse.

He was remarkably fond of Spanish wines, though he never drank to excess; and as he would not partake of spirituous liquors, however fine in quality or plainly mixed, he was always master of himself. As no man is exempt from frailties, it is natural to suppose that as a man he had his share; but the greatest with which I can charge him, is jealousy, and that sometimes carried him beyond the bounds of humanity.

In his early youth he discovered talents equal to the greatst task that could possibly be expected from an Indian. Accordingly Mr Jacobs, then Governor at Prince of Wales's Fort, engaged him, when but a youth, as an Ambassador and Mediator between the Northern Indians and the Athapuscow Tribe, who till then had always been at war with each other. In the course of this embassy Matonabbee not only discovered the most brilliant and solid parts, but shewed an extensive knowledge of every advantage that could arise to both nations from a total suppression of hostilities; and at times he displayed such instances of personal courage and magnanimity, as are rarely to be found among persons of superior condition and rank. He had not penetrated far into the country of the Athapuscow Indians, before he came to several tents with inhabitants; and there, to his great surprise, he found Captain Keelshies, (a person frequently mentioned in this Journal,) who was then a prisoner, with all his family and some of his friends, the fate of whom was then undertermined; but through the means of Matonabbee, though young enough to have been his son, Keelshies and a few others were released, with the loss of his effects and all his wives, which were six in number. Matonabbee not only kept his ground after Keelshies and his small party had been permitted to return, but made his way into the very heart of the Athapuscow country, in order to have a personal conference with all or most of the principal inhabitants. The farther he advanced, the more occasion he had for intrepidity. At one time he came to five tents of those savages, which in the whole contained sixteen men, besides their wives, children, and servants, while he himself was entirely alone, except one wife and a servant boy. The Southern Indians, very treacherous, and apparently the more kind when they are premeditating mischief, seemed to give him a hearty welcome, accepted the tenders of peace and reconciliation with apparent satisfaction, and, as a mark of their approbation, each tent in rotation made a feast, or entertainment, the same night, and invited him to partake; at the last of which they had concerted a scheme to murder him. He was, however, so perfect a master of the Southern Indian language, that he soon discovered their design, and told them, he was not come in a hostile manner, but if they attempted any thing of the kind he was determined to sell his life as dear as possible. On hearing this, some of them ordered that his servant, gun, and snow-shoes, (for it was Winter,) should be brought into the tent and secured; but he sprung from his seat, seized his gun and snow-shoes, and went out of the tent, telling them, if they had an intention to molest him, that was the proper place where he could see his enemy, and be under no apprehensions of being shot cowardly through the back. 'I am sure (said he) of killing two or three of you, and if you chuse to purchase my life at that price, now is the time; but if otherwise, let me depart without any farther molestation.' They then told him he was at liberty to go, on condition of leaving his servant; but to this he would not consent. He then rushed into the tent and took his servant by force from two men; when finding there was no appearance of farther danger, he set out on his return to the frontiers of his own country, and from thence to the Factory.

The year following he again visited the Athapuscow country, accompanied by a considerable number of chosen men of his own nation, who were so far superior to such small parties of the Southern Indians as they had met, that they commanded respect wherever they came; and having traversed the whole country, and conversed with all the principal men, peace and friendship were apparently re-established. Accordingly, when the Spring advanced the Northern Indians began to disperse, and draw out to the Eastward on the barren ground; but Matonabbee, and a few others, chose to pass the Summer in the Athapuscow country. As soon as the Southern Indians were acquainted with this design, and found the number of the Northern Indians so reduced, a superior number of them dogged and harassed them the whole Summer, with a view to surprise and kill them when asleep; and with that view twice actually approached so near their tents as fifty yards. But Matonabbee told them, as he had done when alone, that though there were but few of them, they were all determined to sell their lives as dear as possible: on which the Southern Indians, without making any reply, retired; for no Indians in this country have the courage to face their enemies when they find them apprized of their approach, and on their guard to receive them.

Notwithstanding all these discouragements and great dangers, Matonabbee persevered with courage and resolution to visit the Athapuscow Indians for several years successively; and at length, by an uniform display of his pacific disposition, and by rendering a long train of good offices to those Indians, in return for their treachery and perfidy, he was so happy as to be the sole instrument of not only bringing about a lasting peace, but also of establishing a trade and reciprocal interest between the two nations.

After having performed this great work, he was prevailed upon to visit the Copper-Mine River, in company with a famous leader, called I-dat-le-aza; and it was from the report of those two men, that a journey to that part was proposed to the Hudson's Bay Company by the late Mr Moses Norton, in one thousand seven hundred and sixty-nine. In one thousand seven hundred and seventy he was engaged as the principal guide on that expedition; which he performed with greater punctuality, and more to my satisfaction, than perhaps any other Indian in all that country would have done. At his return to the Fort in one thousand seven hundred and seventy-two, he was made head of all the Northern Indian nation; and continued to render great services to the Company during his life, by bringing a greater quantity of furrs to their Factory at Churchill River, than any other Indian ever did, or ever will do. His last visit to Prince of Wales's Fort was in the Spring of one thousand seven hundred and eighty-two, and he intended to have repeated it in the Winter following; but when he heard that the French had destroyed the Fort, and carried off all the Company's servants, he never afterwards reared his head, but took an opportunity, when no one suspected his intention, to hang himself. This is the more to be wondered at, as he is the only Northern Indian who, that I ever heard, put an end to his own existence.[19] The death of this man was a great loss to the Hudson's Bay Company, and was attended with a most melancholy scene; no less than the death of six of his wives, and four children, all of whom were starved to death the same Winter, in one thousand seven hundred and eighty-three.[20]

Notes

[1] Matonabbee (*c.* 1737–1782), a notable 'Captain' or 'leading Indian', was a Chipewyan, born and raised near Fort Prince of Wales; Hearne's biography of him concludes the main narrative of his *Journey* (see below).

[2] Sean Peake, who has tested Hearne's measurements in the field, believes this to be the Thoa River.

[3] One stone = fourteen pounds; 6.35 kg.

[4] Sean Peake suggests this is Doran Lake.

[5] Kathawachaga, at the north end of Contwoyto Lake, between the Coppermine River and Bathurst Inlet.

[6] [Hearne's long note is a biographical sketch of the woman who is believed to have been his 'country wife', Mary Norton.] Notwithstanding this is the general character of the Southern Indian women, as they are called on the coasts of Hudson's Bay, and who are the same tribe with the Canadian Indians, I am happy to have it in my power to insert a few lines to the

memory of one of them, whom I knew from her infancy, and who, I can truly affirm, was directly the reverse of the picture I have drawn.

MARY, the daughter of MOSES NORTON, many years Chief at Prince of Wales's Fort, in Hudson's Bay, though born and brought up in a country of all others the least favourable to virtue and virtuous principles, possessed them, and every other good and amiable quality, in a most eminent degree.

Without the assistance of religion, and with no education but what she received among the dissolute natives of her country, she would have shone with superior lustre in any other country: for, if an engaging person, gentle manners, an easy freedom, arising from a consciousness of innocence, an amiable modesty, and an unrivalled delicacy of sentiment, are graces and virtues which render a woman lovely, none ever had greater pretensions to general esteem and regard; while her benevolence, humanity, and scrupulous adherence to truth and honesty, would have done honour to the most enlightened and devout Christian.

Dutiful, obedient, and affectionate to her parents; steady and faithful to her friends; grateful and humble to her benefactors; easily forgiving and forgetting injuries; careful not to offend any, and courteous and kind to all; she was, nevertheless, suffered to perish by the rigours of cold and hunger, amidst her own relations, at a time when the griping hand of famine was by no means severely felt by any other member of their company; and it may truly be said that she fell a martyr to the principles of virtue. This happened in the Winter of the year 1782, after the French had destroyed Prince of Wales's Fort; at which time she was in the twenty-second year of her age.

Human nature shudders at the bare recital of such brutality, and reason shrinks from the task of accounting for the decrees of Providence on such occasions as this: but they are the strongest assurances of a future state, so infinitely superior to the present, that the enjoyment of every pleasure in this world by the most worthless and abandoned wretch, or the most innocent and virtuous woman perishing by the most excruciating of all deaths, are matters equally indifferent. But,

> Peace to the ashes, and the virtuous mind,
> Of her who lived in peace with all mankind;
> Learn'd from the heart, unknowing of disguise,
> Truth in her thoughts, and candour in her eyes;
> Stranger alike to envy and to pride,
> Good sense her light, and Nature all her guide;
> But now removed from all the ills of life,
> Here rests the pleasing friend and faithful wife.

Her father was, undoubtedly, very blamable for bringing her up in the tender manner which he did, rendering her by that means not only incapable of bearing the fatigues and hardships which the rest of her countrywomen think little of, but of providing for herself. This is, indeed, too frequent a practice among Europeans in that country, who bring up their children in so indulgent a manner, that when they retire, and leave their offspring behind, they find themselves so helpless, as to be unable to provide for the few wants to which they are subject. The late Mr Ferdinand Jacobs, many years Chief at York Fort, was the only person whom I ever knew that acted in a different manner; though no man could possibly be fonder of his children in other respects, yet as there were some that he could not bring to England, he had them brought up entirely among the natives; so that when he left the country, they scarcely ever felt the loss, though they regretted the absence of a fond and indulgent parent.

[7] In a note, Hearne comments disapprovingly on what he holds to be the 'Southern Indians' tolerance of incestuous relationships.

[8] [Hearne's note] *Tima* in the Esquimaux language is a friendly word similar to *what cheer?*

[9] An explorer's scientific instruments were among his most precious possessions, and their loss in one of the many accidents that befell expeditions was always a major disaster.

[10] Hearne's note comments disapprovingly on the Southern Indians' attitude to war captives, whom he reports were treated as slaves to be killed by the women at will. He himself was willing to employ such a slave as a domestic.

[11] [Hearne's note] As a proof of this affection I take the liberty, though a little foreign to the narrative of my journey, to insert one instance, out of many hundreds of the kind that happen at the different Factories in Hudson's Bay, but perhaps no where so frequently as at Churchill. In October 1776, my old guide, Matonabbee, came at the head of a large gang of Northern Indians, to trade at Prince of Wales's Fort; at which time I had the honour to command it. When the usual ceremonies had passed, I dressed him out as a Captain of the first rank, and also clothed his six wives from top to toe: after which, that is to say, during his stay at the Factory, which was ten days, he begged seven lieutenants' coats, fifteen common coats, eighteen hats, eighteen shirts, eight guns, one hundred and forty pounds of weight of gunpowder, with shot, ball, and flints in proportion; together with many hatchets, ice-chissels, files, bayonets, knives, and a great quantity of tobacco, cloth, blankets, combs, looking-glasses, stockings, handkerchiefs, &c. besides numberless small articles, such as awls, needles, paint, steels, &c. in all to the amount of upwards of seven hundred beaver in the way of trade, to give away among his followers. This was exclusive of his own present which consisted of a variety of goods to the value of four hundred beaver more. But the most extraordinary of his demands was twelve pounds of powder, twenty-eight pounds of shot and ball, four pounds of tobacco, some articles of clothing, and several pieces of iron-work, &c. to give to two men who had hauled his tent and other lumber the proceding Winter. This demand was so very unreasonable, that I made some scruple, or at least hesitated to comply with it, hinting that he was the person who ought to satisfy those men for their services; but I was soon answered, That he did not expect to have been denied such a trifle as that was; and for the future he would carry his goods where he could get his own price for them. On my asking him where that was? he replied, in a very insolent tone, 'To the Canadian Traders.' I was glad to comply with his demands; and I here insert the anecdote, as a specimen of an Indian's confidence.

[12] The Knife River, north of Churchill.

[13] Arthur Dobbs (1689–1765) was an Irish gentleman of property who was deeply interested not only in trade problems but in science. He was convinced of the existence of a North West Passage to the western sea (and the orient trade) which had been sought to the south by La Vérendrye. Shocked by the powers the Company exercised in the Bay, during the period 1731–49 he exercised immense pressure to limit its authority. In 1744 he published the influential *An Account of the Countries Adjoining to Hudson's Bay . . . ,* which urged that the monopoly be abolished and the country thrown open for trade and settlement. As a result, in 1745 the British government offered a reward of £20,000 to a British subject who discovered a North West passage. The arrival at York Fort of two ships engaged in the search posed serious problems of diplomacy for JAMES ISHAM. When the Crown resisted petitions to form a rival company Dobbs called for a parliamentary inquiry, which took place in 1749. However after extended testimony for and against the company Dobbs and his supporters lost the eventual vote. This controversy was one of the most formative in the history of the Company, and galvanized Company men who supported exploration of the interior.

[14]Richard Norton (1701–41); chief factor at Fort Prince of Wales 1731–41. Moses Norton (see below) was his son.

[15]This was JAMES ISHAM.

[16]Ferdinand Jacobs (*c.* 1713–1783), who was chief factor at Fort Prince of Wales 1752–62. As chief at York in 1774 he would send Hearne and MATTHEW COCKING to found Cumberland House.

[17]Moses Norton (*c.* 1735–1773), the able but controversial son of Richard Norton (see above). He was chief factor at Fort Prince of Wales 1762–73, and his interest in the reported copper mines of the north led to Hearne's dispatch on his expedition. Hearne's hostile view of Norton is reflected in the long footnote (note 6 above) on his daughter Mary.

[18][Hearne's note] I must here observe, that when we went to war with the Esquimaux at the Copper River in July 1771, it was by no means his proposal: on the contrary, he was forced into it by his countrymen. For I have heard him say, that when he first visited that river, in company with I-dot-le-aza, they met with several Esquimaux; and so far from killing them, were very friendly to them, and made them small presents of such articles as they could best spare, and that would be of most use to them. It is more than probable that the two bits of iron found among the plunder when I was there, were part of those presents. There were also a few long beads found among those people, but quite different from any that the Hudson's Bay Company had ever sent to the Bay: so that the only probable way they could have come by them, must have been by an intercourse with some of their tribe, who had dealings with the Danes in Davis's Straits. It is very probable, however, they might have passed through many hands before they reached this remote place. Had they had an immediate intercourse with the Esquimaux in Davis's Straits, it is natural to suppose that iron would not have been so scarce among them as it seemed to be; indeed the distance is too great to admit of it.

[19]ANDREW GRAHAM wrote that Matonabbee committed suicide 'for grief that the French had destroyed Churchill Factory.' His action is not surprising from a member of what enthnographers call an 'honour society,' that is, a society which places a high value on public honour and esteem. For hostile accounts of Hearne's role in the surrender, see UMFREVILLE and THOMPSON.

[20]Hearne's country wife Mary Norton (see note 6, above) died in the same hard winter. Hearne and others had been allowed to sail back to England after the surrender; he did not return until September 1783.

Matthew Cocking   (1743 – 1799)

Born in York, England, possibly the son of a tailor, COCKING joined the Hudson's Bay Company in 1765. He was well enough educated to serve as a 'writer' or accountant, and his style indicates a literate, if not literary, man. By 1770 he was second in command at York, and though he appears to have had little experience in canoes, went inland for Andrew Graham in 1772 in an attempt to sort out the incoherent accounts of the interior arriving at York Fort. Like ANTHONY HENDAY, Cocking wandered with the natives, and through much of the same country, but HENDAY was a net-maker and Cocking was a clerk, and the difference in social class shows. Between Cocking and the natives he travelled with there is always a barrier; he is convinced they are untrustworthy, and refers to their 'superstitions' and 'fancies'. He certainly produced the 'rational account' that Graham sought; as he reports, 'I have been particularly careful to be impartial in the account I have given, not exaggerating, but rather leaning to the favourable side.' And he left Graham with no illusions about the encroachments of competitive traders. At the same time Cocking is very sensitive to the dark side of life in the drifting native bands, to illness, quarrels, the sorrows of the bereaved, and the struggles of women. Like HENDAY he admires the Blackfoot deeply; these 'Equestrian natives' seem much more like Europeans to him than the natives of the Bayside posts. In 1774 Cocking helped SAMUEL HEARNE found Cumberland House, the HBC's first permanent post inland. Although he had been appointed master of Severn House, he was sent inland twice more before taking over. As acting master at York he had to confront the terrible smallpox epidemic of 1781–2 (see SAUKAMAPEE). He was relieved just before La Pérouse's capture of York Fort in 1782 (see EDWARD UMFREVILLE) and escaped the French by ship. He died in his native York, and never returned to the Bay.

Text: 'An adventurer from Hudson Bay: Journal of Matthew Cocking, from York Factory to the Blackfeet Country, 1772–73', ed. Lawrence J. Burpee, *Transactions of the Royal Society of Canada*, 3rd series, II (1908), section ii, 89–121.

June 27, 1772. Saturday. This day at noon took my departure from York Fort in Lat. 57° 00′. The Indians were unwilling to proceed, being such bad weather; and two of them becoming sickly so we put up for the night, four miles above the Fort. . . .

29. Monday. At 7 A.M. proceeded, but my Canoe mate died; we put up for the night. . . .

[July] 9. Thursday. Paddled in deep water and carryed the Canoes & Goods at intervals; Deer Lake is well stored with fish & Gulls; I laid bye a second store of tobacco. Course South 39° West. Distance 29 miles. Having left the River to-day, entered Deer Lake,[1] and paddled upwards of 20 miles in it; From the mouth of Chuckitanaw river to this lake the course is nearly S.W. by true Compass & distance 135 miles as judged; in which are innumerable quantity of Falls & carrying places.

10. Friday. Paddled & carried our Canoes at times; Spearing fish; & the sick people retarding our proceeding. Departed from Deer lake and paddled in a river. Course South 31° W. Distance 31 miles. I observe no difference of the produce of the country, only that Birch wood grows along the bank in places.

11. Saturday. This morning we discovered a poor Native seemingly at the point of death; his neighbours had left him behind, & we also did; paddled & carried the Canoes & Goods. Fish jumping in the Lake, but being cloudy, we could not spear any; paddled about 12 miles in the river, which was very shoal; then entered Pimochickomow Lake.[2] Course to-day South 46° Wt. Distance 36 miles. . . .

13. Monday. We did not proceed; men went a hunting; they saw the tracks of several but killed none; Hungry times: A quarter of an Eagle, Gull or Duck is one persons Allowance pr. day.

14. Tuesday. In the Evening proceeded: Two of our Company very sickly, lying helpless in the Canoes: One canoe overtook us, they inform'd us that four Indians are dead: One of them a Leader: others obliged to be left on the road. Paddled on the Lake South 49° West 20 miles, & came at Wethawecwakechewan River head: Tried the depth of water which was two fathoms: Many Islands in the Lake. It is about three miles broad. . . .

17. Friday. Did not proceed: The disorders of the Natives are pains in the breast & Bowels, attended with a cough, & spitting ill-coloured phlegm. . . .

23. Thursday. Paddled in the lake: a great swell very dangerous paddling; came to a noted fishing place for pike, Sturgeon, Perch, & other fish; Here I laid up my fourth reserve of Tobacco: No success in angling, so proceeded; paddled over the lake, saw several sturgeon leaping a considerable height out of the water; entered a small river. Here the Natives have a stage built across, on which they stand to spear Sturgeon, stopping the passage with long sticks stuck in the ground a small space asunder, unsupported at top: The Sturgeon, swimming against these stakes, shake them; which directs the Natives where to strike. This river is well stored with Guinaids[3] & other fish; Put up here, Kaiskatchewan river[4] in sight: We killed eleven sturgeon & a

few Tickomeg (i.e.) Guinaids & one black Bear; A seasonable supply being greatly in want: The Pedlar, Mr Currie (who intercepted great part of York Fort trade this year),[5] is one days paddling below this river, at Cedar Lake: Laid up a fifth reserve of tobacco. Sounded 6 fathoms in Oteatowan lake on the N.W. side where we paddled about S.W. 27 miles, then came at a small river named Kippahagan Sepee (i.e.) Shut up river and paddled a small distance in it. Course South 42 West, distance 30 miles.

24. Friday. We did not proceed: Busy killing Sturgeon: We are now recovering our spirits: The Natives inform me we will soon be where food of many kinds are plenty. . . .

31. Friday. Proceeded & came to Basquia.[6] Here at a small river where the Natives killed Guinaids with hand nets: Many Natives had been here lately: This is a long frequented place where the Canadians rendezvous & trade with the Natives: Many of their Superstitions & Fanciful marks are seen here: We met an Indian with his wife & Family, I present my pipe to him & make him a small present, & by strength of a little liquor prevailed on him to accompany us & hope to take him with me to the Fort next summer. He had been employed last summer & winter by the pedlars to procure them food. Our Course in Saskatchewan river Wt. 20° North, distance 20 miles.

N.B.—From York Fort to Basquia I make the Course South 46 West, Distance 450 miles.

August 1. Saturday. Proceeded: Paddled: saw several wild-fowl & Basquia hills, also an old house formerly belonging to the Canadians.[7] Paddled in a branch of Saskatchewan River & in a Lake named Manemeshahsquatanan Sakahegan[8] on the South of the main river. From the main river in the branch to the Lake is S. 76° West 5 miles and the Lake Wt. N. by 24 miles, then arrived at a river with a strong current, & paddled 5 miles W.S.W. So[uther]ly in it. Course Corrected So. 76 Wt. 27 miles distance. . . .

4. Tuesday. Proceeded: Paddled, Dragged, & Carried our Canoes & Goods at intervals. Plenty of wild fowl: Here I met with a York Fort Leader who had not been down this summer. He denied having traded with the pedlars; but the Canadians goods that were in their possession contradicted his Assertion. Paddled about a mile West in the river, then came to Maneshashsquatanan Lake again, and paddled about 2 miles N.W. in it; when after two Carriadges, & dragging Canoes thro' swamps 2 miles N.W. nearly, we entered Saskatchewan again, and paddled for about 12 miles in it W.S.W., then put up for the night. About a mile below which place, on the North side of the river, is a place where the Natives tell me that the Beaver Indians carry their goods & canoes into a Lake named Menistaquatakow:[9] this Carrying place is named Menistick-Minikqueuskow. Course corrected North 84° West, distance 16 miles.

5. Wednesday. Proceeded: Paddled in the afternoon, met with 15 canoes who had traded all their furs with the Pedlars; they are laying by waiting for their friends. The Indians inform me that we are now arrived at the dry Country, no Lakes being on either side the river. Course South 68° Wt., distance 18 miles.

6. Thursday. Proceeded: we met a Canoe going down to the Natives we saw yesterday, informed us that a Canoe was waiting a little farther on to assist us; We expect to see them to-morrow. After paddling about 4 miles nearly S.W. We passed a branch of the river which runs W.b.S. & which the Natives say joins the river again a long way up

the Country. It is named little Sturgeon river; We caught some here: a little before we put up for the night passed an opening bearing S.b.Wt. which joins the river a little above Basquia, being a small branch;[10] Course S. 32 Wt. distance 14 miles. . . .

11. Tuesday. In the afternoon came to the Families Viz, seven tents of them. Here the Natives always wait for their Friends: Formerly the French had a House here.[11] Course corrected S. 39° Wt., 14 1/2 miles distance. From Basquia to this place I make the Course to be So. 58° Wt., & distance 150 miles.

12. Wednesday. We did not proceed. I am informed that there are 18 tents of Natives a short distance off: I am also informed that Sesiwappew's son is grieved for the loss of his father, & is going to war to revenge his death: Such is the superstition & wild notions of the natives. The Natives rejoice that the journey from the Fort is ended; Indeed we have been forty-five days in performing what they used to be only twenty days other years, when healthful: Musquetoes hath been troublesome without intermission all the way, at the Carrying places especially; the Dress we were obliged to wear afforded us but little defence against them: I found it impossible to make any remarks of the force of the Currents, depth of water, &c., the Canoes not being constructed for such experiments: As to the Falls & Shoals, Vessels (i.e.) Large Canoes must be carried over: I have been particularly careful to be impartial in the account I have given, not exaggerating, but rather leaning to the favourable side.

13. Thursday. We travel to-morrow. A Child died this day. I laid by a sixth reserve of tobacco & a few ball.

14. Friday. We travelled 6 miles S.W.b.S. Country hilly, producing short Grass, low willows & ponds in places; also many vermin holes; our Course very uncertain; I found it inconvenient to use the Compass; Indian Leaders, whom the Natives say are intending to go to war, are many; but we expect to see some of them before the season for these expeditions; when I hope to prevail on them to desist. The Friends of the Child who died Yesterday, make great lamentation, pricking themselves with Arrows in the Arms, sides, thighs and legs & the women scratching their legs &c. with flints. . . .

19. Wednesday. Travelled 6 miles S.W.b.S.: The Natives are very dilatory in proceeding; their whole delight is to sit smoking and feasting: Yesterday I received invitations to no less than ten feasts. . . .

23. Sunday. Crossed the branch in temporary Canoes with bended sticks, & covered with parchment skins:[12] We put upon the opposite side: Hunters killed 2 Buffalo: The Natives all promise faithfully to go down to the Forts next year, & not to trade with the Pedlars: but they are such notorious liars there is no believing them. However, I shall preserve part of my goods until my return, to try what influence that will have: I find they consider an Englishman's going with them as a person sent to collect Furs; & not as an encouragement to them to trap furs, & come down to the Settlements. . . .

28. Friday. Travelled 12 miles W.b.S. Country rather leveller than before; very short grass, with plenty of Wild wormwood; Many Marmot[13] holes, the Indians killed several; & esteem them good eating; plenty of Buffalo in sight on all sides; Males and Females in separate herds; which the Natives inform me they always are, except in

the covering [mating] season. No wood until we pitched in a long narrow ledge of small poplar.

29. Saturday. Travelled 5 miles W.S.W. along the ledge: At two miles off a narrow ridge of high land which bore North about 8 miles distant (A branch of Saskatchewan river runs on this side) named Menachinahshew Hills. They tell me of large lake on the other side, abounding with large Jack-fish named Menawow Sakahegan; near these Hills others, named Sacketagow Hills; where the Asinepoet natives go yearly for Birch-rind to cover their Canoes: There are many large Hills beyond those where the Beaver Indians reside: this high land is the termination of the barren ground that way; the Country beyond being woody, abounding in martins, Waskesew, Moose; & farther on, Beaver. This day I laid by a seventh reserve of tobacco & Shot of sizes; also other goods for Spring use at the building of canoes. . . .

[September] 3. Thursday. We proceeded: Our Course S.W.b.W. distance 5 miles: travelling along the river. Here we met with a poor forlorn French-man, along with a few Asinepoet Natives. He tells me that He left Francois the French Pedlar[14] 7 years ago on account of ill usage; & hath been with the Natives ever since; I gave him a small supply of Tobacco & other necessaries. Course Corrected for five days past South 61° West, distance 41 miles. . . .

16. Wednesday. The Natives saw a Strange Horse to-day & suppose it belongs to the Snake Indians, their Enemies.

17. Thursday. Indians killed several Buffalo: The Natives in general are afraid of the Snake Indians & say they are nigh at hand. This day I took an observation with an artificial Horizon in water but blowing fresh it was very imperfect. Latitude Pr. Account 48° 43 North.[15]

18. Friday. Ten tents of Asinepoet Natives came to us: they say they left several tents of Asinepoet Natives & Archithinue Natives[16] (their friends) two days' journey beyond Manitow-Sakahegan N.B. — We have several pack-horses with us at present, lively clean made animals, generally about 14 hands high & of different colours.

19. Saturday. Hunters looking after Beaver but scarce: Smoked with the Asinepoet Strangers: I advised them to be diligent in trapping furs, & to go with me to the Company's Forts, most of them being strangers: but they seemed unwilling, saying, they were unacquainted with the method of building Canoes & paddling: However they would send their furs by their friends who yearly visit the forts. . . .

22 Tuesday. This day the Natives pitched a very large tent. The men singing, &c., & the Women dancing; & all dressed in their most gaudy apparel: A cold collation of berries dressed up with fat.

23. Wednesday. Indians employed: Men conjuring, & Women dancing; All this is done for the recovery of the sick. . . .

[October] 2. Friday. Snow at times. We are preparing to proceed to-morrow when we shall separate for the winter-season: This day was spent in feasting on berries, which are now going out of season; & a farewell smoking.

3. Saturday. We did not proceed: Smoking the Grand Calimut & several speeches made by the Leaders: Two looking-glasses with several other trifles were presented: these were to be given to the ground [the earth] to induce it to favour them with

plenty of furs & provisions: They have a notion that these gifts have a great effect; & when anything happens contrary to their desires they commonly use this method to appease the ill Domon [demon]. When sick they are very foolish, for they throw away many necessaries, also present to others as payment for singing their god-songs that they may recover; so that if the sick person recovers, He is a poor wretched Creature having scarce any thing to cover his nakedness.

4. Sunday. We did not proceed: The men singing their Buffalo Pound songs. . . .

6. Tuesday. Travelled 8 miles W.b.N.: Country very barren: Saw several Stone heaps on the tops of the high hills; which the Natives say were gathered by the Archithinue Natives, who used to lie behind these heaps, reconnoitering the Country round: We pitched on the side of a lake, the water disagreeable, bitterish salt taste; salt laying on the surface an inch thick (A specimen of which I have preserved) & on the shore like rime in a frosty morning: We made use of Buffalo dung for fuel & it answered very well.

7. Wednesday. We did not proceed: Buffalo at present very scarce. I found in an old tent-place belonging to the Archithinue Natives, part of an earthen vessel, in which they dress their victuals; It appeared to have been in the form of an earthen pan. Saw several Wolves. . . .

9. Friday. We did not proceed: A heavy rain last night: Male Buffalo our food at present; very poor excepting in the spring. N.B. — All over the Country where Buffalo resort are many hollow places in the ground,[17] made by the Bulls in the covering season. . . .

11 to 13. Sunday to Tuesday. We did not proceed: Busy building traps for Wolves; Numbers around us; so that we have the prospect of good luck.

14. Wednesday. This day an Indian Man, belonging to those who last separated from us, was brought to my tent, having fallen from his Horse & broke his leg: I did & shall do all in my power to get him well again.

15. Thursday. The Indians belonging to the lame man joined me.

16 to 19. Friday to Monday. The lame man doing well: Busy trapping: good success: several Smokes near us which we suppose are our Friends the Archithinue Natives: The Natives shew me a tobacco plantation belonging to the Archithinue Indians about 100 yards long & 5 wide, sheltered from the northern blasts by a Ledge of poplars; & to the Southward by a ridge of high ground.

20. Tuesday. We are preparing to proceed to-morrow, to be in readiness for pounding Buffalo at an Archithinue pound. . . .

23. Friday. Every person repairing the Beast pound. It is a circle fenced round with trees laid one upon another, at the foot of an Hill about 7 feet high & an hundred yards in Circumference: the entrance on the Hill-side where the Animal can easily go over; but when in, cannot return: From this entrance small sticks are laid on each side like a fence, in form of an angle extending from the pound; beyond these to about 1 1/2 mile distant. Buffalo dung, or old roots are laid in Heaps, in the same direction as the fence: These are to frighten the Beasts from deviating from either side. This pound was made by our Archithinue friends last spring, who had great success, many Skulls & Bones lying in the pound. Several Buffalo seen near at hand, & the Young men endeavoured to drive them beyond the pound but without success.

24. Saturday. Wolves, Foxes, the Roebuck; another Animal of the Deer kind named Pistaticoos,[18] but something less in size; plenty of Hares; pheasants; Crows; Magpies & small Birds of the same kind as to the Northward: Red Deer are scarce. Snow fell last night.

25 to 26. Sunday to Monday. Snow at times: Natives employed trapping & endeavouring to drive Buffalo to the pound but without success. We are not so expert at pounding as the Archithinue Natives.

27 to Nov. 3. Tuesday to Tuesday included the 3rd November. Snow all dissolved: Natives trapping & killing Buffalo with the Bow & Arrows: And in the Evenings Conjuring & feasting.

4. Wednesday. The expectation of seeing the Archithinue Natives is lost, which is a great disappointment to my Companions, who used to trade Horses & Buffalo skin Garments, for winter apparel; also Wolf-skins & other furs. Showed me a Coat without sleeves six fold leather quilted, used by the Snake tribe to defend them against the arrows of their adversaries. I shall be sorry if I do not see the Equestrian Natives who are certainly a brave people, & far superior to any tribes that visit our Forts: they have dealings with no Europeans, but live in a state of nature to the S.W. Westerly: draw towards the N.E. in March to meet our Natives who traffick with them. . . .

11. Wednesday. Most of the snow dissolved: Three tents of our Company unpitched this day, & proceeded back to Mikisew-Wachy: At present 3 tents of us: We are intending to remain here hoping to have greater success, now there are but few people. The Man who some time ago had his leg broke hath pitched from us, & is in a fair way of doing well. I get no rest at nights for Drumming, Dancing, &c. . . .

21. Saturday. This day two Archithinue Natives came to us from the Southward: They left their friends 28 tents early this morning: They say their people will pitch this way now they are convinced we are friends: These are the people whose smoke we saw on the 12th instant. . . .

Dec. 1. Tuesday. Our Archithinue friends came to us and pitched a small distance from us; on one side the pound 21 tents of them, the other seven are pitched another way. One of the Leaders talks the Asinepoet language well, so that we shall understand each other, as my Leader understands it also. This tribe is named Powestic-Athinuewuck (i.e.) Water-fall Indians. There are 4 Tribes, or Nations, more, which are all Equestrians Indians, Viz., Mithco-Athinuwuck or Bloody Indians, Koskitow-Wathesitock or Blackfooted Indians, — Pegonow or Muddy-water Indians & Sassewuck or Woody Country Indians.

2. Wednesday. The Archithinue Natives repairing the pound, the repair we gave it on our arrival not being sufficient. Snow within the ledge about 8 inches deep in general.

3. Thursday. This day smoked with the Archithinue Natives & presented the Leaders & principal men with tobacco, &c., As far as prudence would permit; at the same time by the mouth of my Leader I endeavoured to persuade two of them to accompany me on my return to the Fort, where they would meet with a hearty welcome, & receive many presents: but they said that they would be starved & were unacquainted with Canoes & mentioned the long distance: I am certain they never can be prevailed upon to undertake such journies.

4. Friday. The Archithinue Natives drove into the pound 3 male & one female Buffalo, & brought several considerable droves very near: They set off in the Evening; & drive the Cattle all night. Indeed not only at this Game, but in all their actions they far excell the other Natives. They are all well mounted on light, Sprightly Animals; Their Weapons, Bows & Arrows: Several have on Jackets of Moose leather six fold, quilted, & without sleeves. They likewise use pack-Horses, which give their Women a great advantage over the other Women who are either carrying or hauling on Sledges every day in the year. They appear to me more like Europeans than Americans.

5. Saturday. Our Archithinue Friends are very Hospitable, continually inviting us to partake of their best fare; generally berries infused in water with fat, very agreeable eating. Their manner of showing respect to strangers is, in holding the pipe while they smoke: this is done three times. Afterwards every person smokes in common; the Women excepted; whom I did not observe to take the Pipe. The tobacco they use is of their own planting, which hath a disagreeable flavour; I have preserved a specimen. These people are much more cleanly in their cloathing, & food, than my companions: Their Victuals are dressed in earthen pots, of their own Manufacturing; much in the same form as Newcastle pots, but without feet: their fire tackling a black stone used as flint, & a kind of Ore as a steel, using tuss balls as tinder, (i.e.) a kind of moss.

6. Sunday. No success in pounding: the Strangers say the season is past. A hungry prospect: Many of us and no great Store of provisions.

7 to 12. Monday. The Natives pounded a few Buffalo & presented to me my full share: Women, Children, & Slaves, feed on berries. The Slaves whom they have preserved alive are used with kindness, they are young people of both sexes, & are adopted into the families of those who have lost their children, either by War or sickness: They torture all the aged of both sexes in a most shocking & deliberate manner. . . . [19]

14 to 15. Monday & Tuesday. Smoked with the Hospitable Strangers & gave them what goods I could spare. Three Archithinue Natives, of the same tribe, came to us from the Westward; who say the Buffalo are scarce, & that their Countrymen are going to war with the Snake Indians.

16 to 17. Wednesday & Thursday. Snow at times: We left our Archithinue Friends & proceeded back to Mikisew-Wachee. Our Course about East and distance 6 miles. . . .

23. Wednesday. A Young man, who came to us yesterday, shot himself through the lungs; the reason very trifling. This rash action was nearly the death of two of his friends, who intended to stab themselves, but were prevented by myself, & other bystanders. The Asinepoet Natives are oftentimes guilty of Suicide, on very childish grounds. I am informed Francois the Canadian pedlar, with 15 Canoes arrived in the Autumn, at the House mentioned 19th August.

24 to Jan. 8, 1773 [Thursday, 24 Dec. to 8 January, 1773]. All hands employed making Snow-shoes, hunting for food, & such like exercises; Young Indian Men coming & going at times. I send by them presents of Tobacco: they inform me that few are gone, or intend going, to war the ensuing summer; but are to collect Furs & go down to the Company's settlements. . . .

22. Friday. Snow. We proceeded: our Course about N.b.E. & distance about 5 miles over barren & unlevel grounds: We put up in a ledge of poplars: The Natives say this place is the termination of the barren land this way. A female child born. A Young man joined us from the Beast pound to the Eastward of us, where we intended to go: He says the Buffalo are so scarce that the Indians are distressed for want of food; & therefore had unpitched intending to build a pound further on to the Eastward, where Buffalo are said to be numerous. Our Ammunition is turning scarce, and provisions must be collected & dried, to serve us on our long journey to the forts. . . .

26 to 30 [Tuesday, 26th to Saturday, 30th]. Freezing. A Horse died for want, & ourselves hard pinched for want of food. The Natives suffer hunger, &c. with surprising patience. Several stragglers from the Asinepoet Natives joined us, who all complain of want of food.

31. Sunday. We proceeded: our Course N.b.E. & distance 7 miles: Country was before: We are now entered on the side of Saketakow-Wachee. A Male child born. Hungry times. . . .

3. Wednesday. We did not proceed. Two Asinepoet Natives joined us, they left their people 7 tents this morning: They say Buffalo are very scarce; plenty of Waskesew but no Ammunition: I gave them a supply. A woman died. . . .

6 to 8. Saturday, 6th to Monday, 8th. More Asinepoet Natives arrived, & we are all now rejoicing, feasting, Dancing, Drumming, Smoking: A large tent pitched: They imagine that these merriments are a means of their being successful & living long.

9 to 14. [Tuesday, 9th, to Sunday, 14th]. Natives pitching to & from us: Busy in the Evenings smoking, &c., & advising them not to trade with the Canadians, but to go with me to the Fort, where they will receive good usage, & more in return for their goods. The Asinepoet Indians inform me they yearly build their Canoes, about 4 days moderate walking, to the N.Et. of where we are now. . . .

23. Tuesday. This morning the Indian arrived from those we intend to go to, with information that all the Natives were pitched further on, towards Waskesew-Wachee, intending to build a Beast-pound there: my Leader with eleven tents of Asinepoet Natives unpitched intending to proceed there: but I with nine tents part;[20] Asinepoet Natives lay still: they intend to build Canoes at Saketow-Wachee. The Neheathaway Natives intend to go to the pound but slowly; endeavouring to preserve provision by pitching after the Buffalo: fearing a scarcity at the Beast-pound: with these I intend to go. I expect that different tribes will be coming for supplies from the S.W. & Westward. I sent three presents of Tobacco by my Leader to the Natives at the Pound. I also sent off a Young fellow with presents of Tobacco to three Leaders in the Canadian interest, & who never have been at any of our Forts; desiring them to go down with me, where they would meet with kind treatment, & received in return more for their furs. I shall do all in my power for forwarding the Company's interest. . . .

[March] 4 to 26 [Thursday, 4th to Friday, 26th]. Freezing in the nights & thawing in the days. Nothing material happened us. Young men employed in Collecting food & myself doing all in my power, to persuade the Natives to go with me to the Fort, & not to trade their Furs with Francois, nor Curry, whom we cannot avoid seeing on our way down: Notwithstanding all their fair promises, I am credibly informed that several hath been trading with the above two pedlars for Ammunition; & in sound policy they preserve their stock of Liquor, to intercept us on our way to the Settlements: I also heard the same from the Canadian Louis Primo who is in our service. I am certain he hath a secret kindness for his old Masters, & is not to be depended on. A melancholy affair happened a few days ago: An Asinepoet Native shot his Brother in the heat of passion. Such Actions are customary amongst these people, not only being guilty of murther, but killing themselves afterwards: Nay two will deliberately fire shot about, till one falls. They are a daring, bold, morose people; but they are very civil to me.

27. Saturday. We proceeded: Our Course N.E. & distance 10 miles, through Woody hummocks, with some large Ponds: We arrived at the Beast pound, where we met with my Leader again, with 4 tents of Neheathaway & 20 tents of Asinepoet Natives; The last are most part of them unacquainted with Canoes; the others, 30 tents of Neheathaway Natives, had unpitched, intending to proceed slowly towards the place of building Canoes, hunting as they go. Two Indians, who had been at Francois, are here: They inform me that Francois, the old French pedlar, has 6 large Canoes with him, & 3 Canoes more are lying at the Shallow Lake, on this side of Basquia; which I find is the Lake I paddled in the 1st day of August last; & 2 more Canoes are lying a little below Kippahagan Sepee, mentioned 23rd July. These with the 3 above mentioned are to come to him, on the breaking up of the rivers: He says 4 Canoes more are lying in the tract of the Natives who are more Southward, & who paddled down the Chuckitanaw river in their voyage to York Fort: & that several more Pedlars are lying all along to the Grand portage, to intercept the Natives who annually trade at Severn, Albany, & Moose Settlement. The name of the Grand portage is Kechy-Wenecop. Francois hath told the Natives, that He intended wintering with a few of his men at the Fork of the river; sending down his Furs. He has at present collected as many prime furs as will load one large Canoe; traded chiefly from the Natives who are unacquainted with Canoes. . . .

[May] 5. Wednesday. An Indian came from those down the river: Informs me that many are sickly, & that we are much forewarder than they in building our Canoes; that they have been fighting, occasioned by the liquor presented to them by the pedlars.

6 to 15 [Thursday, 6th, to the 15th instant]. Musquitoes plenty & troublesome: after a shower of rain intolerable: Canoes ready; & we propose setting out to-morrow for York Fort. We have a good stock of food, Viz., Buffalo flesh & several bladders of fat. . . .[21]

20. Thursday. Arrived at Francois Settlement, where we landed: found Louis Primo tented on the Plantation, with 5 tents of Natives. I am informed that 30 Canoes are gone on before, & are to wait for us: They have traded the richest furs here. On our arrival the French man introduced the Natives unto his house, giving about 4 inches of tobacco; Afterwards they made a collection of furs, by the bulk about 100 Beaver; presenting them to the Pedler: who, in return, presented to them about 4 Gallons liquor, Rum adulterated: also cloathed 2 Leaders with a Coat & Hat. I endeavoured all in my power to prevent the Natives giving away their furs, but in

vain; Liquor being above all persuasion with them: Francois informs me, that he shall embark very soon with his furs, having expended almost his goods. His House is a long square; built log on log: half of it is appropriated to the use of a kitchen: the other half used as a trading room, & Bed-room; with a loft above, the whole length of the building where He lays his furs: also three small log houses; the Men's apartments: the whole enclosed with ten feet Stockades, forming a Square about twenty yards. The Canoes are each 24 feet long: extreme breadth 5 quarters; and 22 inches deep: I believe Francois hath about twenty men, all french Canadians.

21. Friday. We did not proceed: None of the Indians are trading with Francois, for this reason: He hath no goods left: but His Servants enter our tents with Baubles, &c., which the Natives (children like) purchase at any rate. An Indian gave four Wolves for a Tomahawk: Another a Beaver, for a small tin Breakfastplate; & a third a Beaver for ¹/₂ yard of worsted lace. A General Smoking with the Natives, when I advised them to embark; which they promised to do to-morrow. I shall remain here a few days, in hopes to see some of the Natives who have not yet come down.

22. Saturday. The Natives were unwilling to embark without me, therefore I promised to proceed to-morrow: the major part with Louis primo set off. I have been twice into Saswee's dwelling house by invitation, to eat with him; which I did not think necessary to refuse: He is an old ignorant Frenchman: I do not think that he keeps a proper distance from his men; they coming into his apartment & talking with him as one of themselves. But what I am most surprised at, they keep no watch in the night; even when the Natives are lying on their plantation. . . .

26. Wednesday. We proceeded in the morning & soon arrived at the noted Fishing place for Pike, &c. Here we met with 8 tents of Strangers; also our Indians who set off before me: The Strangers hath traded their furs with the Pedler who resides on this side Basquia. I observe plenty of french goods amongst them. It surprises me to perceive what a warm side the Natives hath to the French Canadians.

27. Thursday. Proceeded; & in the afternoon arrived at Basquia, where were six tents of Indians; also the Pedler mentioned yesterday lying in a tent with four Canadians, all French extraction: He hath only one large Canoe full of Furs: have sent two down to the Grand portage: he is going down himself in a few days: Louis primo tells me he is going down also, to see his friends: I told him that he was doing wrong as he was under a written contract to serve the Company: but all to no purpose. . . .

29. Saturday. We proceeded & arrived at Kippahagan Sepee, which we entered, leaving Saskatchewan River. Here we pitched our tents. We found one tent of Natives here who have traded all their Furs with the Canadians one days journey from here, & ten Canoes are gone by the Lake Winnipeg all bound for York Fort. . . .

31. Monday. Paddled over the Lake & came into Manihagow River. We passed over the Carrying places. The Natives are very brisk not stopping to hunt.

June 1 to 18. Tuesday. Nothing material occurred; at York Fort with my Company where we found all well.

Notes

[1] A lake 27 miles long, west of Knee Lake.

[2] Cross Lake.

[3] Whitefish.

[4] The Saskatchewan.

[5] Thomas Curry or Currie. Andrew Graham, the factor at York Fort, noted that 'Mr Currie's encroachment was the reason I sent Mr Cocking inland.'

[6] The Pas (see ANTHONY HENDAY).

[7] Fort Paskoyac (see ANTHONY HENDAY).

[8] Saskeram Lake.

[9] Cumberland Lake.

[10] Sipanok Canal.

[11] Fort La Corne (see ANTHONY HENDAY).

[12] For these skin boats, see ANTHONY HENDAY.

[13] Spermophiles or 'ground squirrels'.

[14] Evidently one of the French traders who remained in the west after the conquest. It is not clear if Francois is the Christian name or the surname; it may possibly be a corruption of the French surname Franceur.

[15] Burpee notes, 'N.B. — Very imperfect indeed'.

[16] The Blackfoot; see among others ANTHONY HENDAY and SAUKAMAPEE.

[17] Buffalo wallows; they rolled in the wallows until caked with mud and so found a measure of protection from the assaults of flies and mosquitoes.

[18] Burpee suggests these are probably antelope.

[19] At this point Cocking reaches his most westerly point — somewhere in the Great Plain between the North and South Saskatchewan. He turns back to the eastward.

[20] Possibly 'I left with nine tents'?

[21] On the 19th Cocking reached 'the joining of the branches', the forks of the Saskatchewan River.

Peter Fidler   (1769 – 1822)

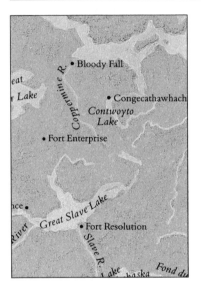

FIDLER was born in Bolsover, England, and like ANTHONY HENDAY joined the Hudson's Bay Company as a labourer, but he had some education and was quickly promoted to writer (clerk). Like DAVID THOMPSON he was trained as a surveyor by Philip Turnor. In September 1790 he set out with Malchom Ross and Turnor for a two-year stay in the Athabasca region, and from 4 September 1791 to 10 April 1792 lived alone — with almost no provisions, ammunition, or proper clothing — with the Chipewyans in the area of Great Slave Lake. His aim was to learn the language and to practise his surveying. Hampered by inadequate clothes (at one point he had to wear his blanket as a kind of petticoat, for lack of trousers) the twenty-two-year-old often stayed in camp with the women and children. As a result his *Journal* of these arduous but satisfying months is a superbly detailed account of domestic life among the northern natives who were just beginning to adapt to the arrival of the fur trade in their territory. Fidler is no ethnographer, like GEORGE NELSON; rather, he observes the personal and familial life of his native hosts with shrewd good sense and real sympathy, and is well able to tell a good story at his own expense. The following year he passed another sojourn with the Piegans and learned their language too.

Fidler spent a long life in the Company's service, trading furs, founding posts, and making important maps. He was in constant conflict with the North West Company, particularly during their resistance to the founding of the Red River Colony in 1812–16. He and his native wife Mary had 14 children. Extensive (and still unedited) journals remain in his hand, and he collected a good library, some books of which are still in the Hudson's Bay Company Archives. He died, after what appears to have been a stroke, at Dauphin Lake House.

Text: Peter Fidler, 'A Journal of a Journey with the Chepawyans or Northern Indians to the Slave Lake, & to the East & West of the Slave river in 1791 & 2 in J.B. Tyrrell, ed., *Journals of*

Samuel Hearne and Philip Turnor (Toronto: Champlain Society, 1934). Since Fidler's *Journal* is an almost daily record, elisions are indicated simply with three dots. Some punctuation and capitalization has been added.

[1791] *September 4th Sunday.* In the afternoon I embarked with 4 Canoes of Jepewyans,[1] in order to remain the whole Winter with them, & acquire their Language. These Indians have got pretty large Credits from Mr Ross,[2] & he wished a person to accompany them, to secure his Debt, & not one of the rest of our people would winter with them — I got a few articles as supplies from Mr Ross such as 6 Womens & 2 Mens Knives, 4 Awls, 2 Steels, 1/2 lb of Common beads, 2 fathems of Brazile Tobacco, 1 Quart of Gunpowder, 50 Ball, & 4 lb of Shott, 4 Flints, 1 small ax & some few other trifles, I took with me neither Leather nor stuff for Socks which made me very badly of the greatest part of the Winter for those articles for Winter's rigging. Slept upon the Island in the Bay — We have no Tent with us. The Man that I am going in care[3] of left his at the Slave Lake. In the Summer we are to proceed for that place.

5th Monday Early in the morning got away & paddled to the mouth of the Athapescow river, where we lay by till evening & killed several geese. This is now the Season that the Geese &c of all sorts return from the more northern parts & fly to the Southward where they winter as not a single Bird of the aquatic kind remain here in the winter on account of the extreme severity of that Season. In the Even[g] we paddled across the Lake & reached the outer Island quite dark at Night, the travers in that part about 20 miles We shipped much water in crossing as the Wind blew fresh at NNE.

6th Tuesday D M a[lt]. LL[4]

Lat. 58° 42′ 23″

74° 36′ 20″
+ 2′ 15″
74° 38′ 35″

Taken at the opening across the Lake at the high bare rocky point in the road to the Slave Lake when we passd July last. The Observations in this Journey are made with the small Sextant mentioned in the former part of this book of 5 inches radius with an artificial horizon of quicksilver but no parallel glasses[5] being obliged when I took an observation to seek a calm place that the Wind might not have any power to shake the Mercury which answered nearly as well as having Parallel Glasses, but oftentimes gave me trouble to fix on a proper place in a Southern direction & clear away the woods for to remove all obstructions. Sometimes I would have had an observation more frequent but either the Wind blowed too hard or else being in the midst of thick woods I had no watch with me consequently could make no Observations for the Longitude with the necessary degree of accuracy. The Nautical Almanack & requisite Tables composed the whole of my Library — with 1 Shirt besides the clothes I had on my back also composed the whole of my wardrobe. In the forenoon killed several Geese, and in the afternoon we embarked & went into the little Lake round the high rocky point where the observation was taken & obliged to put on shore too much wind to proceed. As we passed this place in July I shall not again put down the

Courses, Distances &c until we come to places we have not before seen. I have a Boats compass with me, card 3 inches Diameter. . . .

11th Sunday Early this morning we got underway & carried over the long portage at 8 AM. Fresh breezes Southerly. Lay by at the lower end of the Portage & all the men went on hunting but returned without getting any thing also on the 7th they went on hunting & had no better success. For these few days past we have gone ashore in several places in order to collect hips, being the only berry to be got, to eat in place of more substantial food — we take the Canoe & our little baggage over the portage at one trip, so that we pass them expeditiously — in the afternoon we again got underway & carried over all the portages except the Last one. We met 4 Canoes of Southern Indians[6] of the Beaver river, 7 men & 3 women, who are returning back to their own Country from War, they went in the Spring and the Cree that accompanied us all Summer was their relation & missed them in the Athapescow Lake & prevented his accompanying them; he was with us all summer. They had the Scalps of 2 Men, one quite grey-haired & the other one belonging a Young Man. They had a severe scuffle before they got the young one killed, he had nearly overpowered one of the Crees wounded him when another of his friends came to his assistance & betwixt both despatched him. They also killed one Woman. They met them coming towards the Slave Lake House[7] as they supposed to Trade as they had a few Beaver skins with them, with hatchets, Ice chisels &c marked on them. Probably these were the articles they wished to purchase. They met them to the Westward of the Slave Lake coming down a river that falls into it. They were of the Dog ribbed tribe[8] — & use Canoes They got from those they killed. Several arrows shod with a kind of hard stone resembling flint a Bow or 2 of very clumsy workmanship a small old Knife & a Bayonet made by themselves from either an Ice chisel or a Hatchet, but both of them very rudely constructed. It was 22 nights since they killed these people & they appeared very much elated at their success — barberous rascals! As they had no ammunition & Tobacco, I gave them 10 Ball (they having Powder of their own) & 14 Inches of Tobacco, & they gave me the rump of a boiled Beaver & about 1 1/2 lbs of Fatt, which they told me was every thing eatable in their possession. They had suffered great hardships for want of food during the greatest part of the time they were on this expedition. The meat I got from them was very acceptable as I much stood in need of it having these 2 days past had only the Leg of one Goose — which to an european is but small allowance. As to the Indians they all in general from their earlyest infancy used to go without for 2 or 3 days frequently & some times nearly double that time; as when they have any thing they can never rest till all is consumed, it is always with them either a feast or a famine. They Chepewyans I was with was very near killing all the Crees on account of an old Grudge as they had killed a Jepewyan 2 years ago upon a portage. I had some difficulty in pursuading them to abandon their design. The Southern Indians not knowing a single word of what the Chepewyan said they had not the least knowledge of their intent besides they having no Ball would have much favoured the success of the Jepewyans & little danger could have been received from them. At night we all slept together & the Crees made a large fire apart from us & Sang & danced with the Scalps of the unhappy sufferers upon a pole the greatest part of the Night & the Jepewyans at last was invited to partake of their general joy which they kept up till near midnight when every one sought his bed at the Foot of a Pine Tree which is our only Covering from all the inclemencies of the Season until we arrive where (Thooh or the Paps the man that has the Care of me) his Tent is at the Slave Lake. . . .

16th Friday . . . In clearing a place to take an observation for want of a Watch to advertise me when near the Meridian I noted the Compass after making a proper allowance for the variations Easterly & set up a mark in order to clear all the intervening objects away & to shew me nearly the time when I was to observe. This method I used with success all the winter. . . .

21st Wednesday . . . Men on hunting but killed nothing. The Buffalo are pretty plentiful, but the Jepewyans are such very indifferent hunters. Women employed Splitting & Drying meats. We are now living in a very plentiful manner to make up for the very short allowance we have generally have had these many days past. A variety of weather yesterday at Noon; this Day the Sky cleared & is pretty warm the country & season considered. . . .

29th Thursday Snow all night & till 1 PM In the afternoon, strong Gales from the West. Very disagreeable weather as we have nothing to protect us in the least from the inclemency of the weather which is now severe. In the Evening the Gale abated & began again to Snow. Did not move owing to the Severity of the Weather. The Men at Beaver houses to shoot them as they usually do in the fall but had no luck not coming out of their Houses until too late to see well to take good aim at them.

30th Friday . . . we were under to [the?] necessity to put a shore, it snowing so very fast as we could not see 40 yards before us at noon. Pretty good pine the latter part of last days paddle & this day. Snow all day without any intermission. Fresh breezes from the West, cold frosty weather. Our wet clothing & the cold weather makes it very bad for us & gives us all a Cold & is disagreeable in every respect. Yesterday & this Day the Ice driving in the river. Snow 8 Inches deep on the Ground. Our Canoe is become so very leaky this severe weather that we are very frequently obliged to go on shore to empty out the Water which is a disagreeable job on account of so much Snow & Cold. We have no Pitch to repair the Canoe with. Got one ³/₄ Beaver. . . .

October 3rd Monday Went to fetch the Cow that was killed yesterday SW 5¹/₂ to the edge of a very extensive plain. Not a single tree to be seen as far as the eye could reach to the W&WNW & extends probably very near the vicinity of the Slave Lake. We have now all our Canoes as full of meat as they can conveniently carry being of a very small size. Wind West, dull freezing weather. Saw a number of Buffalo on the large plain but could not approach them within shott. Very fine dry ground apparently all the Plain. . . .

October 7th Friday Snow until 3 PM then cleared up. Cold freezing weather, river driving full of Ice. In the afternoon we broke our Canoes & made a kind of Tent of them along with pine branches which is to be our habitation until we can pass over the Ice. It had a doorway or open space at each end being of an oblong form.

8th Saturday The river set fast. We slept very comfortably in our new dwelling being the first kind of shelter we have had from the weather either night or day since we left the Athapescow 4th of last month. . . .

12th Wednesday. . . Not very clear. Went round my Martin Traps & got 1 Martin. The Women employed making Bone fatt in a Birch rind kettle by beating stones red hot & frequently immersing them into it which makes a tolerable shift for want of a Metal one. We are a very poor set not having a Kettle amongst all of us. We eat our meat always roasted for want of a Kettle to boil it in. Making everything in readiness to walk towards the Slave Lake House tomorrow. . . .

15th Saturday In the morning the men went to look at the river near the Lake & found it impassable not yet being froze over on account of the late high Westerly wind. In the afternoon the men went for Birch to make sledges & very fortunately met with one of their Countrymen that was going to the side of the Lake for some Goods of his that he had left there some time ago. He informed that there were several Tents about 8 miles up the river & that the Ice opposite these Tents were passable over it.

16th Sunday Got underway at $8^1/_2$ AM & proceeded up along the river & arrived at the Tents about noon. 10 Canoes here that were stopped by the Ice on the early setting in of the Fall. They are luckily tolerably stocked with Fresh & Dry meat. They inform us that the Canadians had not arrived with Goods at their house at Slave Lake 3 Days ago & doubtly they will not as all the Smaller branches are froze over & great quantities of floating Ice driving down the larger ones. Fresh breezes at SSE with Snow most part of the day cold freezing weather. The Indians are very busy making Snow Shoes & Sledges ready against the Large Branch gets frozen over. In the afternoon we made a hut of pine branches for our habitation, the Tent &c belonging to the Indian. I am with one at Tall chu dez za[9] about 50 miles yet farther off to the Eastward along the Lake. . . .

20th Thursday The Indians burnt the Greater part of their Canoes as they said no person should receive any benefit from them & that they would not be here next year to use them. Moved 2 miles up the river. One Tent along with the others & the 2 young men that paddled with me in the Summer are gone for the Slave Lake House. The Indians killed a Black Bear in his vault about 3 miles from the Tent.

21st Friday Accompanied the Indian Men that went to fetch the meat of the Bear killed yesterday. The skin they burnt & all the large bones were cut out & thrown to all the four cardinal points — a piece of superstition of theirs. Went round my Traps but got nothing. . . .

22nd Saturday A pretty smart thaw that overflowed the Ice These several Days past. Fresh breezes at SE, clear sharp weather. Cannot purchase any Leather from the Indians for no consideration, they wanting to make Tents of it. I am in a very bad situation for the want of that very useful article at this Season having neither Toggy[10] nor Shoes. On the 10th Ins' I was under the necessity of cutting off both Sleeves of my Leather Coat to make a pair of Shoes. . . .

25th Tuesday After dark a Canadian & a chepawyan arrived here. The Canadian is come for his Wife who was remaining with these Indians all Summer during his journey to & from the Grand Portage. He says that 3 Canoes with Mr Daniel McKenzie & John Findlay[11] embarked from the Athapescow & that 2 of the Canoes got overtaken by the Ice at the upper end of the Falls & that the other one got a little way below the last carrying place. Thooh at a Beaver house & killed one.

26th Wednesday These 2 last nights slept in one of the Indians Tents being the only times I have had that comfort since I left our house at the Athapescow. At noon we all got underway & proceeded down the edge of the river very near to the Lake & there found a Canoe which we crossed the river with altho it was attended with much danger owing to the great quantity of driving Ice. . . .

28th Friday In the Morning got underway & arrived at the Canadian House at noon. Exceeding bad walking the latter part no Ice near the Shore & necessitated to carry Sledges & all thru very thick woods upon our backs a pretty good distance & had the misfortune to break the Bottle that contained my Quicksilver for the Artificial Horizon but luckily none of it was spilt being well rapped up within a Shirt. At the House I procured another bottle which held the most of it & the rest I tyed up in a bit of Leather, I being in such a very poor situation having neither Shoes, Socks Mittins nor any thing to make them off. I offered to trade a small blanket & a moose Skin from the Canadian master Mr Daniel McKenzie with Martin Skins that I had trapped & got from Indians in the fall but he would neither Trade with me or give me those necessaries that I was so great in want of. However, with frequent solicitations he at last condescended to give me a pair of Shoes two old Socks one of which was very much burnt & about 9 Inches of their worst cloth. Such was the generosity of that man. For his being so much against supplying me with those few things I cannot conceive unless it was his jealousy at my accompanying the Indians & by that means induce several of them to trade at our House.

29th Saturday Remained at the House which I eat & slept in during my short stay. The people here very poorly off for provisions. Large Ice driving on the Lake that they cannot venture to set nets & most part of their dependance is upon Fish. Strong breezes at NNW. Hazy weather. A great swell in the Lake. The Large Branch of the Slave river set fast the 27th Ins^t the day after we crossed it.

30th Sunday Mr McKenzie & Findlay with a few men that got froze in below the Lower carrying place walked down along shore sometimes upon the Ice & more frequently thru the Woods all the way to the house here. They suffered innumerable hardships both for cold hungar & hard fatigue. They have little goods here not being able to bring any along with them. When the Ice becomes firm they are to fetch it down upon sledges. At 11 AM Thooh his wife & myself got off from the House on our way to Tall chu dezza. All the others that accompanied us to the House remains there the Canadian Master has employed them to fetch goods from the rapids There. Indians & 1 Canadian accompanied us to the Eastern branch of the Slave river who are going for Goods. The Canadians were 2 Days wrong in their account having this only Friday. This is the first time I ever knew them wrong 2 days but they are one frequently. Mr McKenzie says that 2 of their Canoes are froze in a good way below the Falls & that the others are at the head of them & that those people there are very near eating one another thro' hungar. As I had in the Summer taken sketch[12] betwixt the West & Eastern branches I now ommit it & beyond to the Eastward of the Eastmost branch wait as on the other side. . . .

4th Friday At 9 AM the Men proceeded for the Slave Lake House & the Boy Woman & myself set off for the Tents, but we were obliged to carry all our things upon our backs & haul the Sledges empty, there not being a sufficient quantity of Snow upon the Ground, being quite bare upon the Rock, being blown off into the vallies. Very stony rough walking & very thicketty with windfall wood in the vallies. As the Woman & boy walked slow I set foreward by myself seeing the Track in some few places & after going about 14 miles I found several where the Indians had been thru taking Beaver houses & I unluckely took a wrong one & got lost & slept by myself. Had nothing to eat but fortunately a few Martin bates which I had in my bag of which I eat for supper very uneasy at being lost.

5th Saturday All this day I spent in a fruitless search for the right Track & in my search shot one White Partridge but eat only half of it for supper not knowing when I could get any thing else or find the Indians.

6th Sunday Before day light & a little after fired 3 Shots & as the morning was fine & calm I expected that the Indians would here them if they were nigh & return them but to my great mortification heard nothing. Left my Sledge Snow Shoes & 8 Martin Skins behind me & hung up to a Tree & my Gun Bag & Bedding I took upon my back & now determined to tread my footsteps back to the edge of the Slave Lake & waite the return of those men that went to the Canadian House the 4th Inst. There was also there one Moose & 1 Black Bear which the Indians had killed in the Fall & could not conveniently take away. They had built a small log house over it to keep if from being eaten by the wild animals & intended to return for it so soon as there was good hawling. At this place I determined to remain until I found Indians. My sleigh altho hawling it empty was very inconvenient always catching hold in the thickets which made me leave it. After having gone back thro my old Track towards the Lake 3 miles I very fortunately fell into a fresh Sleigh Track which I supposed to belong to the Woman & the Boy particularly as I could see only the footsteps of 2 people. I followed this Track & arrived at the Indians Tents about 1 PM. Course from where the last observation was taken at the Lake to the Tents about SSE 14 & SbE 7 miles. I intend going tomorrow to fetch my things that I left behind this morning. Found 1 Tent & 1 Brush hut with one family in it when I arrived. They are very badly of for provisions not knowing the proper method to take Beaver. Slept in a Tent which I have not done since I left the House 4th Sep[t] except 2 night the 24th & 25th of last month which has been very severe bad weather of late but thank God I do not find at present the least hurt from it altho' very disagreeable at the time. My Tobacco of all sorts expended that I now cannot fill a pipe to an Indian. . . .

10th Thursday The Indian & his wife at a Beaver house & fortunately killd four ¹/₂ & two old Beaver. We are all very badly of for want of a kettle to either Cook or make Water in. We are obliged to roast all & make water by immersing red hot stones into a roggan[13] of Snow — or else when the Snow is hard by sticking a lump of it upon a stick before the fire & setting a small roggan dish of Birch rind below it. I have neither Shoes Stockings Mittens or Trousers or any thing to make them off & those I am with cannot well assist me. He lent me his old Stockings & a Blanket I am obliged to rap about me like a petticoat & the other one thro over my body to preserve me from the Cold when we pitch. . . .

15th Tuesday Moved back along our old Track SWbW 2 to the Creek then WbS 2¹/₂ to another branch of the Tall chu dez za about 30 yards wide, low banks, scrubby Juniper. Very severe clear sharp weather. I was almost froze in bed in the Night. I never suffered such severe cold before. I was obliged 3 or 4 Times to get up in the night & make on a small fire, nothing but small wood we had, & that but Little, & I looked out anxiously for day Light long before it appeared.

16th Wednesday Got off pretty early and went up the same branch as the latter part of yesterday SEbS 9 miles SSW 1/3 & came to the main branch which is about 400 yards wide. Went up it SSE 3 & put up a little below a heavy rapid and at the mouth of the Gin dezza or Musk rat river[14] when we found one Tent cont^g 1 Woman & 3 Children, the men gone to the Slave Lake House for Credits. In the evening they returned. The Musk rat river at the Mouth about 60 yard wide bold banks & no rapid in it. By the Indian account about 20 miles up there is a Portage into the Slave river about 4 or 5 miles long. A great many falls in Tall chu dezza higher up. This signifies in the Northern Indian tongue *Red Knife*. All along the east side of this river very rocky ground & extends a great distance to the Eastward by the Ind^n report with woods of an inferior size such as Birch Pine Juniper & Poplar—a remarkable plentiful place for Beaver Houses all in the Small Lakes which are very numerous but are very Difficult to Kill owing to the rocky situation of the Country. The Beaver get into the fissures & hollows of rock & cannot be got at by any means that the Jepewyans are acquainted with. To the S & Westward of this river the face of the country is quite different being generally a level country clothed with good stout Timber & very seldom a stone is to be found—a plentiful place for Martins on the West side Tall chu dezza—few amongst the rocky ground. . . .

18th Friday. . . the Canadians are to remain about 10 Days or a fortnight & then return. The principal part of their errand I suppose is to endeavour to debauch the Indians & particularly the one I am with to send me home that they may get all the Skins they kill—a common custom of the Canadians. . . .

28th Monday Moved about 2 miles higher up the river. Men on hunting. Gabble Killed a Cow & one of the others shot a Wolverine which we snapped up before it was well warm thro—a delicious morsel!!!! but what cannot hungar do. We were under the necessity of leaving the Beaver Ground on the East side Tall chu dezza for want of Line to net our Snow shoes with as very few animals of that discription are to be found in those parts. No Catts on the East side where the Beaver are. Wind West, a strong Gale. Before we got away in the morning we had only one Beaver Tail amongst 10 of us—a very small share to each! River not more than 20 Yards wide. Curse this Pitching[15] WSW.

29th Tuesday Went up the river making a WSW Course 5 miles & crept thro' a point of Wood on the South side 150 yd over which saved us 2 miles walking the river making a large sweep & coming nearly to the same place again. One man went & bro't home a load of meat from the Cow that was killed yesterday. The rest will be brought Tomorrow. Got a Cap made of a Beaver Skin after the manner of the womens which is very well adapted for keeping the Snow from ones neck going thro the woods. . . .

10 Saturday The Men on hunting these 2 days past but no luck. Moved WbN 2 miles &

came to the East side. The Portage out of this into the Slave river course in the last reach joining the carrying place NW by Compass left the Musk rat river & went on the South side SW 1 mile & put up on the Portage. Paddy killed a fatt doe moose about $1/4$ mile from where we pitched our Tent Our allowance these 2 days past being reduced to a handful of Beat meat without any fatt. Such are the inconsiderate [improvident] way of the Indians that while they have any victuals they eat in a manner night & day never thinking of eating regular. The Musk rat river very crooked, short turnings all the way from its mouth to the Carrying place a little, above which it loses itself in several small swamps plenty of water in it for Indian canoes only — upon the Carrying place about $1/2$ mile from where we left the Musk rat river is the largest Beaver House that ever I saw & the Indians with me said that it also far surpassed in size any they had seen. I had on this account the curiosity to measure it & found it to be 44 yard in circumference & 18 feet high, situated in the middle of a small Swamp, but appeared to us to have had no water in it these few years back. The house was old & no Beaver in it. It was not a collection of Houses joined together as the Beaver some times make as the families of the Beaver grow up, but one single intire house & had been made in one season. On account of its prodigious size I should imagine it to have been the collective labour of nearly 20 Beaver. . . .

13th Tuesday Moved SbW 4 & came to a small Creek about 8 yards wide went along it SEbE $3^1/2$ & put up. In the morning before we started I set off to cross the Carrying place & see the Slave river. After going about 3 miles & not seeing the river I returned & tore my old Cotton trousers all to pieces that I threw them away as past all repair. Also my Drawers became quite useless thro' Long wear. Wrap a Blanket about me like a womans Petticoat to protect me from the Cold. Remarkable warm weather since the 6th Ins' the Season & Climate considered. The Men at Beaver houses & had great luck killing five $1/2$ & 3 old Beavers.

14th Wednesday Rain yesterday from $3^1/2$ to 9 PM, pretty briskly. The rain falling at this season of the year incrusts with a hard surface of Ice upon the Snow that makes a great noise walking which makes it very hard to approach animals. Consequently makes it hard hunting until another pretty large fall of Snow. The Last Night, according to the Indians invariable custom when they have any thing, we had Beaver stuck upon sticks all round the fire that we could scarcely see it & kept eating at spells the greater part of the Night. Moved along the Creek SE 1 then betwixt SWbS & SWbW $2^1/2$, along a kind of narrow swampy Lake about 100 yards wide. Got one $1/2$ Beaver. Light Airs at ENE.

15th Thursday All the Men on hunting & killed on Cow Buffalo. On account of the very wretched condition I am in for want of Trousers (having nothing of the Kind) the man I am with cut a skin out of the Bottom of his Tent to make a pair of Trousers & upon work at them. Clear & very sharp weather.

December 16th Friday Finished making my Leather Trousers which is a very great acquisition to me. Broke all my needles in making them, the leather being so stiff & hard, & went to work in the Indian manner with an awl & Sinnews before I completed them, having at first only 4 needles. Men at Beaver houses and got two $3/4$ Beaver.

17th Saturday Men at Beaver houses & only got one large Beaver. Fetched home the

Cow Yesterday & this Day Got one Wolverine. Gabble & his wife had a very severe quarrel & he knocked her down with the head of the Ax that I fancied he had killed her. The cause was that a young man in the tent & her made several private meetings together, besides the Woman pretended to have the Monthly Evacuations every 10 Days, which is a custom with the Indians at those periods not to sleep or remain in the Tent which would in their opinion infalliably pollute every things, besides having bad Luck in the Chase. They return at those times & build a small hut without in the woods for themselves till it has ceased & this pretext of hers afforded an easy & sure method to enjoy the company of her beloved paramor very frequently. This game being played a long Time the husband at Last suspected the real cause of her pretended discharges & gave her the drubbing above mentioned. All the rest of his Tent mates long knew the reason of the Wifes frequent retiring for 2 or 3 days at a time but would not acquaint him with it & he being a simple person was thus so long deluded. . . .

December 20th Tuesday Gabbles younger brother & Din na sleeny arrived at our Tent. They say that there are 40 Tents of Chepawyans a little way to the Northward of us, that they are returning from war with the Esquimeaux & had killed 5 Tents of those harmless inoffensive people. . . .

22nd Thursday Got one large & one ³/₄ Beaver. At 6¹/₂ PM the 2 men returned from the Canadian House at the Slave Lake that went from us the 19th Insᵗ but they could not get a Kettle on Credit as they expected, I suppose on account of their keeping me & would prevent them from giving them any skins this Season for any thing they might have taken upon Credit. I expect now that we shall be the remainder of the Winter without that very necessary article. The Canadian master sent the Indians about 6 Inches of Brazil Tobacco. . . .

31st Saturday Moved along the East side of the Large Island 2 miles & put up on the Main. Men all on Hunting and Killed 4 Bulls on the NE side of the Island. Wind East, clear morning, afterwards cloudy, very sharp weather. Fetched home the Buffalo killed yesterday. Put on a clean shirt, never shifted myself since I left the House 4th Sepʳ, having at first only 2 Shirts & no Soap or Kettle to wash one with.

[1792] *January 1st Sunday* Moved. Went up the river 1¹/₄ mile & then NE 1 rather within on NE side the river & put up. Brought two Buffalo to the Tents. Fresh breezes at W the forepart of the Day, latter part nearly Calm, clear & very sharp weather. I went to assist getting the 2 Bulls home being the first time I have been to fetch meat since the winter set in. It is an invariable custom with all Indians & none more so that these I am with that the more an European does of work with them the worse he is respected by them & gets generally the worst victuals & frequently but little of it when he complys to do every thing they bid him, whereas if he stiffly refuses from the first that he is with them they will be very kind to him & will give him a larger allowance of provisions than had he listened to every request of theirs. . . .

6th Friday Thooh killed an other moose upon the Big Island and one Porcupine. A Jaˢ Sutherland his wife & 2 northern Indians arrived here waiting the arrival of some other Canadian & Jepewyans who have gone a fortnight ago to fetch goods from the upper end of the Falls when one Canoe got froze in in the Fall.

7th Saturday Moved to the Big Island 1 1/2 mile where the 3 moose were killed. We are now all heavily laden with Provisions which at this Cold season of the year is very fortunate for us to have such luck. . . .

9th Monday Arrived this morning 2 Canadians & 2 Jepewyans with 4 Sledges loaded with Trading Goods as yesterday. All their faces much froze & one of the Canadians feet, which prevented their proceeding this Day. Those that arrivd yesterday proceeded on their way for the Slave Lake House & Bolyea the Carpenter went ahead with Letters from the Athapescow. He left his Sledge behind & a young Jepewyan from our Tent took it to the Lake. Also 2 more men took 2 Sledges of Meat to Trade there. They say that they will sleep 4 Nights going there. There is also a good quantity of Goods remaining up the river. People at the House very badly off for Living, very few fish to be taken owing to the severity of the weather. The like before they say that they never experienced. The Canadians made me a present of 1 1/2 lb of carrot Tobacco. Mine was all expended early in November. A little Tobacco to fill a pipe to an Indian occasionally is thought very much on by them. . . .

15th Sunday Moved up the river 3 Miles & put up on the SW wide on the main shore. The Island 1 1/2 mile from where we put up. In the evening a young Jepewyan arrived at our Tents in search of some of his Countrymen to get a supply of Provisions from. Their Tent is about 10 miles NE of us & are nearly starving thro hungar & they have not even any Ammunition to kill any animals with — he says that they will join us in a few Days.

16th Monday Moved across a point of Wood 3 miles it being a long way round about by the river. The man returned back to his Tent having been very liberally supplied by us with as much provisions as he could conveniently carry. Our Men on hunting every Day but without any success. . . .

18th Wednesday Moved 2 Miles to the river & then went up it 2 more & put up. The Indian men that went to the Slave Lake House the 9th Ins' with meat returned & brought a little Tobacco & a small quantity of Liquor for their Tent. My Tent mates had not an Inch sent them. The 2 Tents joined us that the man came from the 15th Ins'. They are all in a wretched condition, not any thing to eat & their faces much frost bit. Gabble killed a Doe Moose On account of our New Visitors, some of whom slept in our Tent that they thronged it up so very much that I was obligd the whole to lay in a manner double & could not get any Sleep — before morning I often wished our new comers at the Devil & I am afraid that they will remain with us, & eat what we should require for ourselves — as none of them are any thing of even tolerable hunters.

20th Friday A little afternoon arrived at our Tents Mr John Findlay a Canadian & 2 Jepewyans on their way to the Athapescow House with Letters from Mr Daniel to Roderic McKenzie.[16]

21st Saturday At noon Mr Findlay & party left us & about 2 hours after arrived a Canadian his Wife & 2 Children. They are to remain with Din na sleeny in his Tent. This Canadian cannot speak any English, consequently can have but little conversation together but what we can carry on in the Indian Tongue. . . .

24th Tuesday Thooh in the morning came to Gabbles Tent and begged hard with tears in his Eyes that I would return again to his Tent & remain with him as he had no ammunition of his own. I therefore consented & accompanied him back very much pleased that I had listened to what he had said. This man I had been with all the Fall & winter to this Time & the reason I left him I had very often wished him to procure me either a drest Moose skin or a Deers Skin Coat to make me a Toggy off as all the winter I have had nothing of the kind & have always been obliged to wrap myself up in a Blanket when ever we pitched. His often promising me the above & never performing it determined me to leave him & accompany Gabble (my last Winters Tent mate) who promised me faithfully that I should soon have good winters rigging. Those were my reasons that I changed the short time Tent mates & now Thooh solemnly promises that I shall directly have stuff to make a Coat off. Returned back with Thooh & they pitched 2½ miles up along side of the river a little within on the SWᵗ side. Killed one Young Bull. Slept in Dinna Sleenys Tent.

25th Wednesday Moved ¾ mile & put up. Killed 1 Cow Buffalo. The 2 Tents that we left behind the 23 Insᵗ came up, they had remained to dry meat for more convenience of carriage. 4 Tents of us now together. Thooh & myself slept in a hut of Pine branches. He now accomplished his long promise & I got from him a Deer Skin robe with the Hair on to make me a Coat which I did very soon having very frequently been near perishing by the Cold when we pitched along for want of such a useful piece of clothing. . . .

3rd Friday The other 2 Tents moved after the one that pitched yesterday to join Aw gee nah the great Chepawyan Chief who accompanied Mr Alexʳ McKenzie to the Hyperborean Sea in 1789.¹⁷ Arrived a young man from the Rabbits head who is tenting on the West side the Buffalo river. This young man is to remain with the Paps. This man, Thooh & his wife and myself moved back along our old Track in order to meet those who are hourly expected from the Big Island. We pitched no Tent.

4th Saturday Moved in the same direction as yesterday 4 miles & put up. Those 2 men that went a few days since with provisions to meet those that are near starving returned accompanied by 2 others & they bring the melancholy intelligence that a middle aged man & a boy about 12 years old had fallen victims to hungar before thy arrived back with the meat. So soon as the above relation was made known every one set up a most dismal & disagreeable crying or rather howl on account of the unfortunate death of their Countrymen. This continued all the day at frequent Intervals of 10 or 15 minutes each time. The young man who lately came to remain with us being out a hunting & did not arrive at our hut till 8 oClock at Night & when he heard the News they all began their usual chorus of howling & crying & beating themselves & tearing their hair. He appeared almost distracted far surpassing all the rest in his horrid lementations. He cut the Stockings from off his Legs which was new & threw several of his Clothes & his other necessary articles away which will render him pitiful until he can again be supplied. The Man I am with behaved with great fortitude & suppressed his agonating Grief like a true philosopher altho at the same time he was as inwardly affected as any of those who made the loudest & frequent howls. They kept up this way nearly the whole night that alarmed me not a little not knowing but in their frantic fits of desperation they might have hurt me. As I was one alone I did not get a wink of sleep the whole night for watching their motions. By good chance the Moon was nearly full & the Sky quite clear that I could see nearly as well about me as perfect day. The remainder of them will be here tomorrow.

5th Sunday I never passed a more disagreeable night than this last altho I lay quite still all night I did not sleep the least on account of the very frequent horrid crying they kept up all night. As soon as day light app^d which was joyful to me the Young Man began to cut everything he had in pieces of clothing keeping howling all the time. About 10 AM the others came up & joined us & they all got a supply of Provisions which they all stood in very much need off. Their withered imaceated skelleton like look was enough to move even the hardest heart, the deceased mans wife with 2 young Children & far advanced her pregnancy of the 3rd & her Brother with the Mans Mother. I am remaining with & his Son about 10 years old who had the misfortune to have all his toes frozen when an infant in the cradle that he has not a single toe remaining, he however walk pretty well. These with the 2 men accompany us & I suppose will remain with us the rest of the Winter. All the deceased mans property was destroyed & thrown away when they joined us.

6th Monday Moved 4 miles E towards the Slave river & put up. Before we started in the morning Thooh supplied the young man with every necessary that he could conveniently spare, the young man having destroyed all his clothing yesterday. Not to do the like & make themselves totally destitute is looked upon by their countrymen as having an unfeeling heart & the man I am along with lay under those insinuations by the rest because he did not destroy every thing he had. He was by much the wisest of them all. Had he have done like the rest some of them must have absolutely perished by the cold thro' want of clothing to protect them from the severity of the Season which in these parts at this time is uncommonly severe. Thooh on hunting & returned without success, also the young man on the like expedition but killed nothing. We are again at very short allowance notwithstanding our late superfluities, occasioned in a great measure by supplying those half starved poor creatures who have lately joined us.

7th Tuesday This night dreamed in the Chepawyan Language for the first time and I appeared to have a more extensive command of words when asleep than when awake, being so long & not hearing any thing else spoken but the Jepewyan — custom is second nature. . . .

12th Sunday Fetched home the Moose & I accompanied them. We had a roast there where the Animal was killed & I stuck a lump of Snow upon a stick before the fire which was pretty large a flame of wind blew the blaze right upon me & took off my beard as clean as if it had just been shaved altho it was pretty long being on 10 Days. This was the most expeditious shave I ever had tho' somewhat disagreeable. Thooh killed another buck Moose so that thank God we again began to set famine at defiance. . . .

29th Wednesday Got 2 martins from my Traps & I went for wood to make a Sledge for Thooh's mother as her Son has little time to do it being out hunting &^c & I having nothing to do, it is a recreation to me to be about such little jobs. Made a roast of a whole Buffalo head hair horns &^c which was hung before the fire 2 Days & 2 Nights before it was thoro'ly done.

March 1st Thursday Made a Sledge for Thoohs mother & afterwards moved ENE 4 miles. It is my constant custom all winter whenever they pitched to remain in the old Tent place till such time as I thought the women had time to arrive where they pitched to & put up the Tent & have everything done that when I arrived I had nothing else to do but put my few things into the Tent. Besides going behind I always had a good track to go thro'. Men on hunting but no luck. The Snow Birds made their first appearance an unerring harbinger of Spring.

2nd Friday Moved SSE 2 miles & put up. Got one Beaver. At Night arrived Ki an cho a Canadian 3 Coppermine Indians & one Jepowyan on their way to the Athapescow Lake House with Letters. They remained with us all night.

3rd Saturday The people that arrived here the last Night set of for the Athapescow Lake with 2 Sledges. I wrote a Letter to Mess^{r}s Philip Turnor[18] & Ross telling them of my situation & as these Indians say they will return back again to us I requested a little Tobacco Ammunition &^{c} also some Book or other to read as the Days are now become pretty long & mild, & I rather think long for want of something to read. Moved SEbE 5 miles & put up.

4th Sunday The 2 Young Men in our Tent went away by themselves to the Slave river to kill Beaver. Moved SE 4^1/$_2$ miles & put up. Thooh killed a young Buffalo at the stony ground. I had the ill luck to again break the Bottle that contained my Quicksilver but fortunately none of it was lost.

5th Monday Gave Thooh the last of my Ammunition. Made a small vessel of Buffalo horn to contain my Quicksilver for the Artificial Horizon which answers extraordinarily well being much preferable to either Grass [glass?] or earthenware as not so subject to break. . . .

13th Tuesday Very bad yesterday & the day before, having a sore throat & a violent pain in my head. Pretty well now thank god except a sore throat which I hope will soon get better. Snow yesterday. Moved NNE 2 miles & was necessitated to put up short of where we intended to go on account of the deceased mans wife being delivered in the Track when hawling a very heavy Sledge. The other womin wished to erect the small Tent for that purpose but she was too quick for them. She had a boy. Got 2 large Beaver. Warm weather.

14th Wednesday Got tolerable well thank God. To be ailing alone with the Indians is a melancholy situation for any one that ever experienced it, being ^{a}bsent from all friends & Countrymen. Arrived 2 Jepewyans from the Thay thule dezza or Stony river.[1] They slept 2 nights in coming here. Several Jepowyans are at that river. Moved NNE 6 miles to the edge of the Stony Ground about 8 miles from the Thay thule dezza bearing North. The woman that was delivered yesterday took her heavy sledge to drag as usual the same as if nothing had happened to her. She Sleeps in a small brush hut not hav^g permission to come into the Tent along with the men & other women. The 2 young men that went to Slave river to kill Beaver the 4th Ins^t set of for the Slave Lake House (Muskrat & the Monkey). Got one large & one ^{3}/$_4$ Beaver. . . .

20th Tuesday Moved NbE 4 miles. Got on ^{3}/$_4$ & 2 large Beaver. At Sunset we had the agreeable pleasure to see those return from the Athapescow who went with Letters the 3rd Ins^t. They brought me a Letter from Mess^{r}s Ross & Turner also 2 fathoms of Brazil

Tobacco as I had none of that very necessary article that the Canadian gave me in January some time ago. I also received a Bound Magazine which will pass away several long hours the remainder of the Spring or rather winter as the cold is still severe. . . .

25 Sunday Moved SbE 2 miles & put up. Thooh returned he brought with him 16 Martin Skins that his Countrymen had given him as he is still a good deal short of having Furs enough to pay our Credit. Cha ha in na a Coppermine river Indian accompanied Thooh. He is to accompany us to the House, his Wife will be here tomorrow. This is the same person who paddled in company with me in the Summer when we went down the Eg gid da zal la dezza or Buffalo river. This man very well agrees with the Jepewyans but the 2 nations has a secret jealousy for each other notwithstanding they speak the same Language and might be called with great propriety one & the same people. The Coppermine river Indians inhabit to the N & E of the Jepewyans & are the nigh neighbours to the Esquimaux with whom they are frequently at war with, principally to acquire their stone kettles for Cooking in — them & the Northern Indians has an invariable custom when at War never to take any prisoners but indiscriminately kills all of every age & Sex contrary to the manners of the Southern Indians & most other natives who very often save the young women & several Children whom the latter they adopt as their own Children. The Young Women, they take as Wives the most handsome, who are well used & the ugly ones are made Slaves off for doing all kinds of hard work such as cutting firewood fetching water &ᶜ &ᶜ. . . .

April 1st Sunday Cha ha in na & A you na taking birch rind for canoe building to make after their return from the Athapescow Lake. The Birch trees here are but a small size only fit for small Indian Canoes. The 2 Men are not yet returned from hunting & various conjectures are formed on their long absence & the tears of Sorrow & affection is upon every ones countenance. A Gentle Thaw every day since the 28th Insᵗ. The 29th there was rain at night and on the 30th rain the morning. The Snow in consequence has greatly diminished these 3 days past.

2nd Monday At Sun Set the 2 Men returned after an absence of 5 Days the sight of whom cheered up every one. They said that they had been following Buffalo tracks all the time in order to kill some for the Women & Children to live upon while they returned from the Athapescow Lake but had the luck to kill one only. . . .

4th Wednesday. . . We found 2 Canadian Canoes which had been set in last Fall. They had built a small log house to keep the Goods in. There was about 10 pieces remaining and several articles laying within in a very careless manner, these had been protected or Guarded all winter by an Image set upon a painted red pole over the house about the size of a small child. Not an Indian would go up to the House to look at it until I did, being thoroughly persuaded that if they even attempted to take any thing away the Een coz zy as they called it would acquaint the Canadians of the offender which beleefe I further confirmed the Indians in — all winter number of Indians have frequently passed this place but never one even ventured up near the place altho' with no thought of stealing. . . .

8th Sunday Got underway & met with some more Indians who are going to the House. Proceeded about 4 miles when an Old Man his Son & myself proposed to go up a small branch on the left a little way & then cut over land & fall into the Athapescow Lake which was at least 12 miles nearer than the way we paddled in the Summer & which all the other Indians are going. Proceeded till noon when the Old Mans son returned back to join the others & the Old Men went in quest of him & gave orders to me to remain where I was until he returned. I waited some time & no sight of either the old Man or his Son. Thinking that probably they would go the other way I set forward by myself having a good Track to go thro' which I proceeded about 4 miles when I found several different ones going different ways. A wrong one I unluckily took & proceeded along it till near night & found the termination of it where Indians had killed a moose & thro this Track they had hauled it to the Tent. I now returned & at dusk I got to an old Tent place where I made a fire & remained for the Night. I had no victuals with me but boiled in my Tin quart pot some Rockwood & had a little fatt which I boild with it & made a tolerable supper. About midnight as I supposed I was terribly alarmed out of my sleep by an uncommon loud noise which appeared not far off. I immediately rose & made a large fire & put my gun in order ready for an attack which I expected every moment. I thought it to have been Bears that was going to fall upon me. After the fire began to blaze much I was agreeably surprised to hear the noise recede farther from me upon both sides of me till at last when near morning it totally ceased I then lay down but durst not venture to sleep. The surprize & consternation I had lately been in prevented sleep from falling upon me. Afterwards I told the Story to the Indians describing the kind of noise & they told me that it proceeded from 2 Moose Deer calling to one another. Being lost & a stranger to the parts also but a young hand in this Country such was the cause of my great terror & consternation. . . .

10th Tuesday In the morning 3 young men accompanied me to our House where we arrived about 2 PM being absent from all European intercourse & alone with the Jepewyans ever since the 4th September last, having acquired a sufficiency of their Language to transact any business with them. Upon the whole this has been rather an agreeable winter than otherwise. The principal difficulty we laboured under was the want of a Kettle & being at some few times reduced to very short allowance in provisions which last is ever the case with any person that may accompany Indians. Cold wea[the]r & drift at NNE, fresh Gale. In crossing this wide lake free from any Shelter I got one of my Ears severely froze that it was not well for 3 weeks afterwards. Here ends my Remarks with the Jepewyans. My Tent mates arrived at our House yesterday which alarmed Mr Ross me not being there.

Notes

[1] The Chipewyans, or Northern Indians, one of the various tribes of the Dene; the same nation with whom SAMUEL HEARNE had travelled.

[2] Malchom Ross (1754–99) began as an Orkney labourer with the Hudson's Bay Company in 1744, and through sheer ability rose to the officer class. His early death by drowning occurred on his way to establish the Company as a trading power in the Athabasca region.

[3] This is Thooh or the Paps; as Fidler relates, he also stayed with a native named Gabble.

[4] Fidler's *Journal* contains a detailed record of his astronomical observations of which only a sample can be included here.

[5] Artificial horizon: a little basin filled with mercury, the surface of which is used as a mirror to reflect the images of the sun and stars in taking astronomical observations. Parallel glasses: sheets of glass used to cover the mercury to prevent the wind from disturbing its surface.

[6] The Cree.

[7] The 'Canadian House' referred to below; a North West Company trading house built during the preceding summer on the south shore of Great Slave Lake opposite Stony Island.

[8] One of the various tribes of the Dene nation.

[9] The Taltson River.

[10] From the Cree *misotaki* (coat); a calf-length beaver coat worn by natives and traders.

[11] Daniel McKenzie (1769?–1832) was one of the many McKenzies who were at one time or another in the employ of the North West Company; he served in the west from 1791 until at least 1817, and died at Brockville, Ontario. John Finlay or Findlay (1774–1833) served the North West Company from 1789, retiring as a partner in 1805; he died in Montreal, the last man to preside over a dinner of the Beaver Club.

[12] Made a sketch map; Fidler's *Journal* contains a number of such maps.

[13] From the Ojibwa *onagan*: bowl.

[14] Pierrot Creek.

[15] As in HENDAY, 'pitch' here appears to mean 'move in the direction of'.

[16] Roderick Mackenzie (1761–1844) was a first cousin of Sir Alexander Mackenzie, and closely related by blood or marriage to many fur trade figures. In 1788 he established Fort Chipewyan on Lake Athabasca. Mackenzie left the fur trade and settled in Terrebonne in 1801; however, he was an early and important collector of fur trade documents, and probably wrote the history of the trade that begins his cousin's *Voyages from Montreal* (1801).

[17] This is Aw-Gee-Nah, the native MACKENZIE called 'the English Chief'.

[18] For Philip Turnor, see DAVID THOMPSON.

[19] A tributary of the Taltson river, today spelled 'Tethul'.

Part III: Life and Letters among the Explorers

Edward Umfreville   (fl. 1771 – 1789)

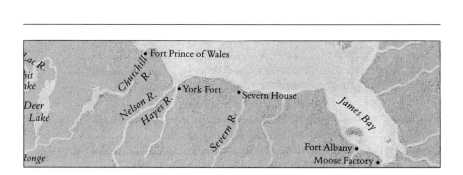

Though he seems to tell us so much of his life and opinions we know surprisingly little of UMFREVILLE, not even his birth or death dates. He is certainly not Edward Umfreville, author of *Lex Coronaria* (1761) as the British Library catalogue suggests, though his evident education suggests he might have come from the same legal family. He arrived in the Bay in 1771 as a 'writer' or clerk, and served under ANDREW GRAHAM at Severn and under Humphrey Marten (who thought he had a violent temper) at York Fort. Umfreville was serving as second to Marten when La Pérouse captured the fort in 1782, and was sent prisoner to France. When he got back to London he quarrelled with the Company over his wages, and in 1784 joined the North West Company, for whom he searched out an alternate route from Lake Nipigon to Lake Winnipeg; his journal of that exploration has been published.[1] He served on the North Saskatchewan from 1784–7, and apparently took a country wife, for a daughter — Lisette — appears in later fur trade history as the wife of the remarkable John Rowand (see GEORGE SIMPSON). By 1788 he had decided to return to the Hudson's Bay Company, but once more he disagreed with the Committee over terms. The next year he published *The Present State of Hudson's Bay*, which in fiery terms castigates the Company and all its works. Umfreville's book is a fascinating mixture of material appropriated from other writers such as ANDREW GRAHAM and diatribe in the best high style of an educated man of his age. After its publication he disappears entirely from history.

Text: Edward Umfreville, *The Present State of Hudson's Bay*. London, 1790.

from the 'Prefatory Advertisement'

In the year 1771, I entered into the service of the Hudson's Bay Company, in the capacity of writer,[2] at the Salary of fifteen pounds a year; and continued in that employ eleven years. But two of their principal settlements being taken by the French in 1782,[3] when I was made prisoner, and, upon their restoration to the Company, some disagreement arising in point of salary, I quitted their service.

Being thus disengaged, in April 1783, I made a voyage to Quebec, with a view of acquiring a knowledge of the manner in which the Fur trade was carried on from that quarter; and here I remained for four years; during which time I made the state of the country, and the trade of it, my peculiar study.

By so long a residence in that part of the world, I flatter myself I am, in a great measure, acquainted with every interesting particular relative to it; and shall lay them before the public with that truth and impartiality which ought to guide the pen of every person who attempts to inform.[4]

Of all the authors who have wrote on this extensive country, few have given a just and disinterested account of it. Some seem to be actuated by prejudice, whilst others, either through want of good information, or a proper knowledge of the subject, have led their readers into error, by misrepresentation. Among the best writers, we must rank Ellis and Robson; the former as a philosopher, and ingenious reasoner; the latter as a candid, true, and impartial writer, and who, by having resided in the country, obtained a fund of knowledge of his subject which enabled him to inform with confidence.[5] For my part, I shall only attempt to lay before the public such particulars as the above authors had not an opportunity of acquiring a knowledge of, and this I shall do in a plain unadorned manner, humbly trusting that it will be read with candour, and animadverted on with good nature.

The geographical part of my subject I shall touch very lightly on, as the extent of the country and its boundaries are sufficiently known. My intention is to exhibit to the world the value of the settlements under consideration, and how far they are capable of improvement; pointing out at the same time, the destructive effects of a baneful monopoly, which has subsisted ever since the year 1670. . . .

Though the extent of the country from North to South is pretty well known, yet to the Westward we are not so well informed. I have myself travelled as far as 120 degrees of Longitude,[6] from the meridian of London, through many different nations of Indians, and have always found them friendly, and ready to receive our commodities with avidity.

In speaking of the inland country too much cannot be said in commendation of it. Every species of food necessary for the support of man, is to be procured in the greatest plenty. The climate is much milder than on the Sea coast, and nothing seems to be wanting to the convenience and accommodation of its inhabitants. On the Sea coast, which the Hudson's Bay Company solely possess, though nature has been less kind, yet the country is not half so bad as it has been represented: the climate, though cold, is extremely healthful, and our countrymen usually enjoy a remarkable good state of health, during their residence there. I can for my own part aver, that I resided there eleven years without knowing the least ailment. If a stranger was to visit these parts, he would be induced to think, by the debilitated state of the natives, that he was in a country uncommonly unfavourable to the human species: but the use of spirituous liquors, and not the climate, is the cause of this misfortune:

they drink to such excess, that it is rather more surprizing any should be left alive to tell the tale, than that they should be found emaciated, decrepid, and slothful. It is a melancholly reflection that the poor devoted Indians are by this means considerably diminished in number, their minds are debased, their spirits dejected, their bodies enervated, and they are thereby rendered unfit to support their families, at a time of life when the tender age of their offspring stand in most need of support. . . .

the tale of Farrant, Tomson and Ross, from 'A Brief Account of the Climate, Soil, etc.'[7]

. . . The intenseness of the cold is beyond expression, and its effects are frequently productive of the most tragical events. The poor natives take every precaution to guard against its consequences; but notwithstanding their utmost care, they frequently fall a prey to its severity. Unhappy, indeed, is the fate of those creatures, who meet with this kind of death! After enduring great torment for a considerable time, the cold at length seizes the vitals, when the unfortunate person soon expires. Women have been found frozen to death, with a young infant, likewise frozen, clasping its arms round the mother's neck; others have been found dead, and the babe still alive.

The first year I wintered in Hudson's Bay, afforded an opportunity of describing the melancholy effects of the cold in the persons of three of our Factory men, whose names were John Farrant, James Tomson, and James Ross. The following account was gathered at times from the latter, who survived his unfortunate companions.

On Monday, January the 6th, 1772, these three men set out in the morning in order to hunt partridges, and to collect fresh provisions for the Factory, as is the custom of the country. They were to stay three weeks; at the conclusion of which time they were to return with what they had procured. In the early part of their journey they had a river to cross, about three miles over, which was not compleatly frozen at the time they reached it. Near this river, they slept the first night, intending to cross it the next morning.

Tuesday the 7th. About eight or nine o'clock in the morning they proceeded to cross the river, but they had not walked far on the ice before they perceived the smoke[8] of open water below them, and that they went very fast down the river; which convinced them that they were adrift. This they found to be the case, and that the ice they were on was a large smooth field. They had two dogs with sleds with them, and the ebb tide carried them out to sea.

Wednesday the 8th. The tide of flood brought them into the same river, but not so high as the place from whence they had been first carried. The weather hitherto had been very mild, and it had snowed a little during the night. In their baggage was some cake they had baked the day before they left the fort, and a bottle with near a quart of gin; of this they took a little now and then.

Thursday the 9th. The weather still continued remarkably mild and clear. They were again driven up the river with the flood, but not so high as yesterday, as the tides were falling off. As the piece of ice they were upon did not, during its thus driving up and down the river, come near the shore, they were obliged to continue on it, and were driven out again with the ebb. The cake and gin was not yet expended, and they slept together in a leathern tent upon the ice.

Friday the 10th. The weather mild as before, with small breezes of wind from the S.E. quarter. A little snow fell in the night. The flood brought them again into the river, and this day they exerted themselves very much to gain the shore. In hopes of doing this Ross took his gun, powder and shot, blanket, and a little bag containing materials for kindling a fire; Farrant took only a beaver coat. Tomson was so anxious to gain the shore that he would stay for nothing. One of the dogs accompanied them, the other stayed with the sleds. After wandering about over the ice with the greatest anxiety for the major part of the day, they found their utmost endeavours ineffectual; they therefore turned about to go to their sleds; but, to add to their misfortunes, they saw the sleds pass them on another piece of ice, and the dogs eating and tearing the tent, &c. without their being able to come at them. Their little stock of cake was expended this day. The ebb tide now carried them far out into the bay, so that they lost sight of the land, and wild geese and other sea fowls hovered over them in great numbers. Ross and Tomson lay under the blanket, and Farrant used the beaver coat.

Saturday the 11th. The weather, though colder than any of the preceding days, was yet very moderate for this frigid time of the year. The wind S.W., a moderate frost, the night over-cast, but the day clear. The unhappy men had seen land to eastward, and again to the northward. When the flood made,[9] they drew nearer to the land, and the ice closing about high water, afforded them hopes of once more getting on shore; but the attempt did not succeed. John Farrant this day had the misfortune to fall into the water, in stepping from one piece of ice to another; he was nearly carried under, before his miserable companions could drag him out. Ross having a clean shirt in his bag, they put it upon Farrant, and belted the beaver coat about him: afterwards, being nearly spent, he lay down, while Ross and Tomson gathered pieces of shelving ice, which they placed round him, as a barricade against the weather. They had a piece of sugar left, and half of it was all they subsisted on that day.

Sunday the 12th. Though it was very warm all the day, yet it was very disagreeable, as it blew very hard from the N.E. and much snow fell, which caused it to drift much during both the day and night. The piece of ice they were upon had grounded before day-break; and when the flood made, the water began to come upon it, so that they were obliged to call upon Farrant to rise; but death had freed the poor man from his troubles. Ross and Tomson continued on or near the same piece until the water had fallen away. While they sat weeping by the corps, a seal came upon the ice; it did not meddle with the body, but looked very stedfastly on them; Tomson desired Ross to shoot it, but he refused, saying, 'I myself may soon be dead.' They afterwards went from piece to piece, but the weather being thick, they knew not what course to take. The sugar which remained was their food this day, and now their whole stock was expended.

Monday the 13th. A stiff gale of wind still continued from N. to N.N.W. with thick drifting weather; the morning was mild, but as night approached it grew very sharp and cold. Tomson and Ross walked again amongst the rough ice. The hands of the former were swelled to such a size, that even with the assistance of his comrade, he could not force them into his mittens; his face was also much tumified,[10] and he became delirious; for on Ross telling him, that in two days they would reach the Factory, he answered, what—, naming a village in the Orkneys, to which he belonged. The flood confined them to the same piece of ice, and here poor Tomson died, just as the moon sunk below the horizon.

Tuesday the 14th. The gale was quite abated, but the cold increased, and though very rimy,[11] yet the sun shone early in the morning. The water flowed upon the ice that Ross remained on, and soon after it drove a large piece over Tomson's body, upon which Ross with difficulty got. The ebb running out, and the sun becoming visible, he directed his course by it, and after walking all the day over the rough ice, he reached the shore at the back of the Factory Island, where a path is cut strait, from high water mark, to the Factory. The unfortunate man imagining himself on the eastern shore, mistook this opening from some river or creek on that coast, so walked up till he came to a place which he remembered. Here he found his mistake, and returning back immediately, struck into a right path. He now broke down some sticks, and endeavoured to kindle a fire, but without effect. In this attempt he froze his fingers; he had benumbed them before in exchanging mittens and assisting Tomson: his feet were likewise benumbed before he reached the shore. This night he lay on a few sticks, he had broken down for that purpose.

Wednesday the 15th. The weather this day was very moderate. He set out for the Factory, but his extreme weakness made him fall several times, which filled his mittens with snow, and froze his fingers solid. Though the distance was no more than four miles at farthest, it was seven o'clock in the evening when he arrived at the gates, where he fired his gun off to make himself heard. The extremity of his nose was frozen, but he was perfectly sensible on his arrival. One of the dogs came home with him, having staid by him all the time.

The packet[12] for Churchill went from the Factory but the day before; had the factorymen but followed the track of these natives, all then would have been well; but the decrees of Providence are unsearchable. The other dog was slightly wounded by a setting gun[13] on the eastern shore. Poor Tomson declared the day before his death, that he could have lived much longer had he had provisions to eat.

The unfortunate survivor was obliged to suffer amputation on most of his fingers and toes, and his nose was much mutilated. But Mr. Hutchins[14] who was then the surgeon at York Fort, effected a fine cure by preserving him; and the man now lives comfortably in Orkney, the place of his nativity. On hearing of his misfortune, a subscription was set on foot for his support at every place in the Company's settlements. The people liberally contributed according to their several abilities; and the Company, actuated by the laudable example set by their servants, allowed him an annuity of 20 l.[15] for life.

Before I leave the subject of this unfortunate man, I cannot help remarking, that his ingratitude was conspicuous to a great degree; notwithstanding his mates in the Factory, chiefly his poor countrymen, affected by his misfortunes, had so liberally contributed towards his support, he had not the sensibility to thank any one of them for their humanity, though the greatest part of his benefactors had no more than 6 l. a year. . . .

from 'Some account of the Company's Officers . . . as well . . . as inferior Servants'

The chief employments of the inferior servants in the settlements, is carrying logs of wood, walking in snow-shoes, sledging the snow out of the Factory avenues, and hunting; and notwithstanding the inconveniences before recited, after a person has been a few years in the services, he generally imbibes a love for the country, unless discouraged by the bad usage of his superiors.

The hunting part of his duty he generally follows with pleasure and avidity; besides the recreation he receives from the sport on these excursions, he takes delight in being from the Factory during them, as then he becomes his own master, and is free from inspection of a too watchful overseer. Notwithstanding the customs of this country, as at present established, are rather forbidding, and seem to discourage us from wishing to live in so frigid a clime, yet, as already observed, though cold, it is exceeding healthy; and there have been many who have lived here several years not only comfortably, but happy; and have enjoyed a better state of health perhaps than they would have done in a less inhospitable country.

I cannot leave this subject without representing the lost state a youth is in, who is unfortunate enough to be bound apprentice to the Hudson's Bay Company. — The unfortunate young man is perhaps the only son of a tender and affectionate parent, who, thinking to forward the happiness of his child, articles him to his Company for seven years: I have known an instance where a boy has been bound for fourteen years.

On his arrival in the country, he knows nobody. His masters who sent him out, and to whom he is to look for support, are now many hundreds of miles distant. The Governor is quite indifferent about him, he having servants of his own. The consequence of this is, the boy associates with the common men, forms connections with them, and becomes habituated to their customs, which his tender years are not able to guard against. The education given him by his parents is now soon obliterated; he imbibes fresh vices daily; contracts a love for smoking, drinking, and swearing; and in a word, becomes a reprobate. His employment consists in cleaning the Governor's knives and shoes, running on errands for the cook, and cutting down and carrying heavy logs of wood, much beyond his years and strength. In the mean time, no care is taken to inculcate the precepts of religion and virtue in his mind, or even preserve those principles and knowledge he may have brought in the country. Every step that would make him a man fit for the world, and a useful member of society, is totally neglected.

I would ask the Hudson's Bay Company what an apprentice of their's is fit for, after having served them for seven or fourteen years? whether he has obtained a knowledge of any art of business that will enable him to get a creditable living in the world, or to support himself when the strength and vigour of youth are exhausted? — I will defy them to point out any, that has been thus acquired; as his constant employment has consisted of every species of drudgery and subordinate labour: so that on his returning home, his indulgent parents, instead of finding him instructed in anything that is praise-worthy, are lamentably convinced, that he is a proficient in nothing but idleness, swearing, and debauchery.

It may be argued by the abettors of the Company, (if they have any) that after the period of the apprentice's indentures is expired, he has an opportunity of rising in their service, if by good behaviour he has merited so much favour; that from his apprenticeship, he may be made a writer at 15 l. per year, from thence be raised to an assistant at 25 l. per year, afterwards a second at 40 l. per year; and from thence to the exalted station of a Governor, at 150 l. per year.[16] To this I would reply, that I am enabled to say, from the eleven years service which I passed through in their employ, that the prospect of ascending this important ladder is very faint indeed. But even allowing the youth to be fortunate enough, by assiduity or favour, to succeed to promotion in this service, he is not even then exempt from labour and menial duty; for every person in the Factories; except the Governor and surgeon, must occasionally go to hard work; and should he object to this usage, and beg for milder employment, in the most submissive terms, it will have no effect on the Governor, who in all probability, will not only increase the difficulties of the complainant, by every series of severe treatment, but send him home to the Company with a bad character;[17] representing that he is unfit for their service, having refused his duty.

Such is the usual progress of the servitude of their apprentices; and so little is the probability of the young men reaping any advantage from it. . . .

from a letter to the Editor of the Morning Chronicle and Daily Advertizer[18]

Mr Editor,   Churchill River.
According to my promise I now send you the account of the capture of Prince of Wales, or Churchill Fort, on the N.W. coast of Hudson's Bay, which I received from a gentleman, who was upon the spot at the time, and on whose veracity I can depend.

The French visited this place before York Fort, on account of its Northern situation, and the general prevalency of winds from that quarter, thinking to take the advantage of them in going to the Southward. Accordingly the three ships appeared before the Fort on August 8, 1782 at a time when the Governor[19] was very busy trading with some Indians who were just arrived: but the sight of such unexpected visitors did not fail to engage the attention of the Factory people, who were not used to see so many strangers in these seas.

At this time, which was about six o'clock in the evening, the enemy had cast anchor within five miles of the Fort, and in a little time afterwards appeared very industrious in sounding the river, even within musquet shot of the place; and I have heard the Governor declare, that their officers went about the Factory avenues, shooting birds, with the greatest indifference; a convincing proof that they did not conceive themselves to be in much danger. The Fort at this time mounted forty-two cannon, six, twelve, and twenty-four pounders, was provided with ammunition in great plenty, and the Factory was not in immediate want of provisions of any kind. The strength of the Fort itself was such as would have resisted the attacks of a more considerable force; it was built of the strongest materials, its walls were of great thickness, and very durable, it having been forty years in building, and attended with great expence to the Company. In short it was the opinion of every intelligent person, that it might have made an obstinate resistance when attacked had it been as well provided in other respects; but through the impolitic conduct of the Company, every courageous exertion of their servants must have been considered as imprudent temerity; for this place, which would have required four hundred men for its defence, the Company, in their consummate wisdom, had garrisoned with only thirty-nine.

About three o'clock in the morning Aug. 9, the enemy began to disembark their troops, at a place called Hare-Point; from whence they marched in a regular manner towards the Factory, until they arrived within about four hundred yards, when they made a halt, and sent two officers from the main body, with a summons to the Governor to surrender the place. The Governor and two of his officers met them half way, when all difficulties that obstructed the negotiation were speedily overcome, to the satisfaction of both parties. In consequence of this verbal agreement, the French, to the amount of about four hundred men entered the Fort, at six o'clock in the morning, when the British flag was lowered, and a table cloth from the Governor's table hoisted in its stead.

Every part now exhibited a scene of devastation and ruin; for the licentious soldiery, finding they were were not restricted by a capitulation, began to plunder whatever came in their way. It must, however, at the same time be acknowledged, that the officers took every opportunity to depress this spirit in the common soldiers, with great humanity and address; politely sympathizing with the sufferers in the inevitable distresses attending the fortune of war. The remainder of this, and the following day, were spent in demolishing the works belonging to the fortifications, shipping on board sundry articles of stores, provisions, and a valuable quantity of peltry, which if the Company had received would have indemnified them for all their other losses conjointly.

On the 11th, the three ships set sail for York-Fort; but about five o'clock in the morning, a sail was observed apparently steering for Churchill, which was now in flames. One of the frigates was ordered to chace. The experience of her commander was, however, so inadequate to the task of coping with the skill of the English Captain, that if he had persevered he would probably have been led into such a labyrinth of shoal water and rocky ground, as might have made him repent his visit to Hudson's Bay. Accordingly the Frenchman gave up the pursuit about seven o'clock in the evening, after firing a bow chace from an eighteen pounder, which he found had no other effect than, if possible, to make the Englishman go faster than before.

I would just remark, that Churchill Settlement was by much the best ever erected in Hudson's Bay. The Company usually have their Factories built with logs of pine, which are squared, and laid one upon another; but this building was entirely of free-stone; the artillery was in admirable condition; and the fortifications were most skilfully planned under the inspection of the ingenious Mr Robson, who went out in 1742 for that purpose.[20]

While the trade of the other settlements had been upon the decline for some years, this place had in general held its former medium, and of late years considerably increased. Notwithstanding the advantages of so flourishing a settlement to the Company, their extreme parsimony would not permit them to have above one man to a gun, even in the midst of a precarious war. What folly could be more egregious, than to erect a fort of such extent, strength, and expence, and only allow thirty-nine men to defend it? The force which the French sent into Hudson's Bay was more than sufficient to reduce every place in the country, weakly defended as they were. This place, in particular, with so few men, was totally incapable of withstanding the well-directed efforts of so strong an armament, especially as the depth of water in the river would admit the largest ships to lie very near the Fort; and bombs may be used with great effect.

Notwithstanding the Governor must have been sensible of his inability to make an obstinate defence, his conduct was in some respects highly reprehensible.[21] In the first place, he should have sent an express to York Fort, over land, by the Indians, with information of an enemy's arrival. Had he done so, the people at that settlement would have had five days more at least to prepare themselves for so unexpected an event. Secondly, he should have destroyed the papers of the master of the sloop, who was then to the Northward upon a trading voyage. By the possession of these papers, the enemy acquired a complete description of York Fort, with an account of its weakness on the land side, which induced them to try their success that way. Thirdly, his timidity in quietly suffering a known enemy to be sounding the river, as it were, under his nose, without opposition, was not, I think I may venture to say, consistent with that fortitude which ought to actuate a Briton, in the service of his country. . . .

from 'A Brief Account of the Present State of the Trade'

It is an uncontrovertable fact, that since the French have evacuated Canada, the fur trade from the inland parts of Hudson's Bay, has been carried on to a greater extent than ever it was before; for the Company, who till then confined themselves to the sea-shore, knew nothing of the numerous nations inland; and these again knew as little of them: that the Company, notwithstanding they had obliged themselves by their charter to explore the whole of their territories, confined themselves within a small circle. They consequently did not exert their influence to procure peltries, or to augment the consumption of British manufactures, by any other methods than through the channel of a very few Indians, comparatively speaking. These Indians however, brought down enough to enrich a few individuals, whose interest it was to prevent too great an influx of furs, which would not only lower the price at market, but probably open the eyes of an injured commercial people. In the days I am alluding to, the port of York Fort was surrounded with nations of Indians entirely unknown to the traders of the Company; and they would have remained in the same state of ignorance to this day, had they not been awakened from their reveries by the unsurmountable perseverance of a few Canadian[22] merchants, who found them out, through obstacles and impediments attended with more danger and personal hazard than a voyage to Japan. . . .

By the prosecution of this commerce from Canada, the Hudson's Bay Company found themselves effectually supplanted on the sea-shore, the natives being supplied inland with every conveniency for war and domestic uses. This induced the Company, in the year 1773, to begin their inland voyages,[23] so that the Canadians from Canada and the Europeans from Hudson's Bay met together, not at all to the ulterior advantage of the natives, who by this means became degenerated and debauched, through the excessive use of spirituous liquors imported by these rivals in commerce.

It however must be owned, that the Hudson's Bay traders have ingratiated themselves more into the esteem and confidence of the natives than the Canadians. The advantage of trade is evidently on their side; their men, whose honesty is incorruptible, being more to be depended upon. In proportion to the goods imported, the Company export a greater quantity of furs, and these in better preservation, and consequently more valuable. Their unseasonable parsimony has hitherto been proved very favourable to their Canadian Opponents; as the accumulated expences attending so distant an undertaking would overbalance the profits of the latter, if the exertions of the Company were adequate to the value of the prize contended for.

The Hudson's Bay servants being thus more in possession of the esteem of the natives, they will always have the preference of trade as long as this conduct continues. Another great advantage in their favour is, that the principal articles of their trading goods are of a superior quality to those imported from Canada. I would not by this insinuation infer, that the goods sent inland from Canada are not good enough for the Indian trade; no, I well know that the worst article imported is good enough; but while they have to contend with people who send goods of a superior kind, they evidently lie under a disadvantage, and it is my opinion, that it would be for the interest of the Canada merchants to supply goods of an equal if not superior quality to their adversaries, at every post where they have these formidable rivals to oppose them.

The great imprudence, and bad way of living of the Canadian traders have been an invincible bar to the emolument of their employers. Many of these people, who have been the greatest part of their lives on this inland service among savages, being devoid of every social and benevolent tie, are become slaves to every vice which can corrupt and debase the human mind; such as quarrelling, drunkenness, deception, &c. From a confirmed habit in bad courses of this nature, they are held in abhorrence and disgust, even by the Indians, who finding themselves frequently deceived by specious promises, never intended to be performed, imagine the whole fraternity to be impregnated with the same failing, and accordingly hold the generality of the Canadian traders in detestation and contempt.

On the contrary, the servants of the Hudson's Bay Company, imported principally from the Orkney Isles, are a close, prudent, quiet people, strictly faithful to their employers, and sordidly avaricious. When these people are scattered about the country in small parties among the Indians, the general tenor of their behaviour is conducted with so much propriety, as not only to make themselves esteemed by the natives, and to procure their protection, but they also employ their time in endeavouring to enrich themselves, and their principals, by their diligence and unwearied assiduity. By this prudent demeanor among the Indians, notwithstanding they have annually exposed themselves to all the dangers incident to the trade, for fifteen years past, they have not sustained the loss of a man; and the principal advantage of the Company over the Canadian traders, is more to be attributed to the laudable efforts of their servants, than even to the superior quality of their goods.

While the Canadian servants[24] are so far from being actuated by the same principles, that very few of them can be trusted with a small assortment of goods, to be laid out for their masters profit, but it is ten to one that he is defrauded of the whole by commerce with Indian women, or some other species of peculation. By this and various other means which lower them in the eyes of the natives, as before observed, they are become obnoxious to the Indians, their faith is not to be relied on, nor their honesty confided in; so that scarce a year elapses, without one or more of them falling victims to their own imprudence, at a time when fatal experience should teach them, that a conduct guided by caution and discretion ought to be the invariable and uniform rule of their behaviour.

It must be owned, that many of these people are possessed of abilities capable of aggrandizing their masters, and promoting their own welfare. They are very apt at learning the Indian languages, and acquiring a knowledge of the necessary Indian ceremonies, as well as customs to be observed in prosecuting the trade; but in the whole course of my observation, I have scarcely found one of them, who, for his abilities, honesty, integrity, and other necessary qualifications, could be intitled to the denomination of a good and faithful servant.

It cannot, however, be denied, but that they are excellent canoemen, and labour with surprizing dexterity, and inimitable patience, in their long inland voyages; and even when their provisions fail them, they bear their misfortunes with fortitude. But at the same time it must not be admitted that they are the *only* people on the face of the earth, who are capable of performing these voyages and undergoing the fatigues of them. Though such may be the sentiments of their employers, let these gentlemen for a while look round them, and survey without prejudice the inhabitants of our own hemisphere, and they will find people who are brought up from their infancy to hardships, and inured to the inclemency of the weather from their earliest days; they will also find people, who might be trusted with thousands, and who are too much familiarized to labour and fatigue to repine under the pressure of calamity as long as their own and their masters benefit is in view. I will further be bold to say, that the present servants of the Hudson's Bay Company may be led as far inland as navigation is practicable, with more ease and satisfaction to the owners than the same number of Canadians. The former would be always honest, tractable, and obedient, as well from inclination, as from fear of losing their pecuniary expectations; whereas the latter being generally in debt, and having neither good name, integrity, not property to lose, are always neglectful of the property committed to their charge, and whenever difficulties arise, there is never wanting some among them to impede the undertaking. . . .

To make the [North West] Company truly respectable, and at the same time to put in it their power to render the province of Canada of greater consideration to the mother country than it is, they should be legally admitted to the rights, immunities and privileges of a chartered Company; and if it were practicable, they should be united with the present Hudson's Bay Company, as we have seen an old and new East India Company united and incorporated in one joint body of merchants. And perhaps such a junction might not be unacceptable to the Hudson's Bay Company, who, for so many years, have tasted the sweets of monopoly.

I am fully persuaded that nothing is required but interest and proper application to bring about some plan of this nature. The magnitude of the object would justify the experiment; and I have no doubt that many respectable persons would be found to patronize an adventure, which would put the proprietors in possession of a greater extent of territory than what is inhabited by all the Christian States in Europe.

I again repeat, that great improvements are to be made, and much wealth acquired from the seas about Hudson's Bay; and likewise that full as much remains to done inland; but while affairs are carried on in those parts of the globe, upon the same footing they are at present, there is a probability that all these countries will remain as utterly unknown to the world, for ages to come, as the regions within the Polar Zones.

. . . No period, in my opinion, can be more favourable than the present. When so many fair provinces have been wrested from the mother country, on the same continent, it is our duty to point out every feasible method by which the parent state may cherish and bring to perfection the remainder.

Notes

[1] *Nipigon to Winnipeg: A Canoe Voyage Through Western Ontario by Edward Umfreville in 1784.* Ottawa: R. Douglas, 1929.

[2] A clerk or secretary, second-lowest (after apprentice) of the ranks of the Hudson's Bay Company (see below, note 16).

[3] The French under Admiral La Pérouse captured Fort Prince of Wales (at Churchill) on 9 August 1782, and York Fort on 24 August. For Umfreville's account of the former, see below.

[4] Phrases such as 'that truth and impartiality', 'just and disinterested account', 'plain and unadorned manner', and 'read with candour and animadverted on with good nature' are conventional in eighteenth century narrative, whether journalistic or fictional.

[5] Henry Ellis (1721–1806), author of *A Voyage to Hudson's Bay by the Dobbs Galley and California, in the Years 1746 and 1747* (1748) and Joseph Robson (fl. 1733–63), author of *An Account of Six Years Residence in Hudson's Bay* (1752); these were among the earliest published accounts of life on the Bay. Both books played a part in the debate provoked by Arthur Dobbs over the alleged inaction of the Company in failing to explore inland which culminated in a Parliamentary committee of inquiry in 1749.

[6] Longitude 120° forms the present-day border between Alberta and British Columbia. From 1784-7 Umfreville, working for the North West Company, operated out of a post on the North Saskatchewan ('Umfreville's House') near today's Frenchman Butte.

[7] This tragic mishap took place in January, 1772. Little is known of John Farrant or Ferrant, James Tomson or Thomson, and James Ross beyond what is given here or in the version in journal form by ANDREW GRAHAM (see Graham, *Observations on Hudson's Bay*, 308–15). Umfreville says he got his information 'from a gentleman who resided there [at York Fort] in

the capacity of Surgeon, [who] gathered the account from the survivor, at different times, and in consequence of it, made many useful experiments at York, and Albany Forts, which proved highly acceptable to the learned and ingenious. . . .' The 'Surgeon' may have been Thomas Hutchins (see below), but in actuality Umfreville seems to have appropriated his account from Graham. (For Hutchins' own pillaging of Graham's materials, see ANDREW GRAHAM.)

[8] Fog or mist.

[9] When the flood made: when the tide rose.

[10] Swollen.

[11] Covered with hoar-frost.

[12] Mail and messages, carried by native couriers as the next clause shows.

[13] A setting gun: one being adjusted or aligned.

[14] Thomas Hutchins (?–1790), surgeon and chief factor, collaborated with ANDREW GRAHAM in studying the natural history of the Bay area and also appears to have represented scientific observations of Graham's as his own.

[15] Twenty pounds.

[16] In the Company language of Umfreville's day, the words 'writer', 'second', or 'Governor' had a precise meaning; they denoted the ranks or managerial levels through which Company men were promoted. A writer was a clerk or accountant.

[17] Character: a letter of reference.

[18] Umfreville was present at the capture of York Fort but his second-hand account of the capture of Fort Prince of Wales is included here for its view of SAMUEL HEARNE, then the fort's Governor; the 'gentleman' who was his source has not been identified. An edited version of his letter on the capture of York Fort appeared in the *Morning Chronicle and London Advertiser* for Monday, 21 April 1783; it is not clear if the letter on Fort Prince of Wales was ever published.

[19] That is, Samuel Hearne.

[20] Joseph Robson (see above) was hired in 1733 as a stonemason to help build Prince of Wales Fort; he did not become Surveyor and Supervisor of Buildings at York Fort until his second tour of duty in 1744. Modern historians argue that Prince of Wales Fort was in fact badly planned and could not be successfully defended.

[21] Despite Umfreville's contempt, modern historians have suggested Hearne understood the odds against him and acted wisely. For more on Hearne and the French admiral, La Pérouse, see HEARNE and THOMPSON.

[22] That is, French traders operating out of post-conquest Montreal.

[23] This is not the case; besides HENRY KELSEY's journey of 1690–2, a number of other Company men had travelled inland before 1774 when Samuel Hearne founded Cumberland House on the Saskatchewan River; see for example ANTHONY HENDAY and MATTHEW COCKING.

[24] The cultural barriers between the famous 'voyageurs' of the northwest, and the English and Scots who were their masters are often reflected in exploration writings; for examples, see THOMPSON and FRANKLIN.

Peter Pond   (1740 – 1807)

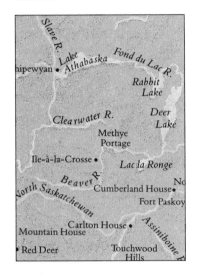

PETER POND was at one and the same time a shrewd and successful Yankee trader and a signally important explorer and map-maker. ALEXANDER HENRY speaks of 'Mr Pond, a trader of some celebrity in the northwest', but besides celebrity, Pond also had a reputation for violence. As his 'autobiography' relates, early in life he shot a man in a duel but then found that no one would arrest him. 1782 he may have shot a fellow trader, though it is not clear if he was ever tried for the crime. In Athabaska during the winter of 1786-7 another man was 'shot in a scuffle with Mr Pond's men'. In one of DAVID THOMPSON's characteristically measured verdicts, he was described as 'a person of industrious habits, a good common education, but of a violent temper and unprincipled character'. His autobiography, written about 1805, relates the events of his life up to 1775 in a phonetic spelling which rivals Haliburton's Sam Slick for its evocation of the Yankee idiom of its time. Anyone puzzling over it needs only to read it aloud and the man himself — 'a philosopher, and . . . odd in his manners' as Roderick McKenzie called him — steps immediately off the page. As a youth Pond served in the Colonial army, and participated in the taking of Montreal by Amherst. After a period taking care of his parentless brothers and sisters, he entered the fur trade in 1765, operating independently of larger trading companies. His decade of increasingly successful trading (much of it in Wisconsin) is chronicled in the autobiography, which breaks off after the 1775 grand council at Michilimackinac. The continuation (which may have been lost, or perhaps never written) would have covered Pond's subsequent career on the North Saskatchewan and in the Athabasca country. It was here he gained his reputation as a geographer; in the spring of 1779 he emerged from two years of trading (among people only HEARNE had so far visited) with a spectacular load of furs; furthermore, he had discovered the arduous but traversable Portage La Loche (Methye Portage) which linked the Hudson Bay and Athabasca watersheds. Rivalry in the rich fur trading region thus opened up to them was to dominate the Hudson's Bay and North West Companies for forty years. Pond had one share in the

North West Company when it was founded in 1783–4, and his explorations north of Lake Athabasca established the Nor-Westers firmly in this area. In 1784–5 Pond, wintering in Montreal, drew an important map of his northern explorations (see *Historical Atlas of Canada*, I, plate 67 for Pond's map and others of the period). Pond left the north in 1788, but he went on producing copies of his map. He returned to his birthplace, Milford, Connecticut; his prosperity had vanished by the time he died there in 1807.

Text: *Five Fur Traders of the Northwest*, ed. Charles M. Gates. Second edition. St Paul: Minnesota Historical Society, 1965. The transcription was prepared by June D. Holmquist, Anne A. Hage, and Lucile M. Kane of the Minnesota Historical Society especially for the second edition. The manuscript of Pond's narrative is held by Yale University Library.

[*I was born in*] Milford in the countey of New Haven in Conn [*the 18 day*] of Jany 1740 and Lived thare under the Government and [*protec*]ton of my Pairans til the year 56 a Part of the British troops which Ascaped at Bradixis Defeat on ye Bank of the Monagahaley in Rea the french fortafycation which is now Cald fort Pitmen[1] Cam to Milford toward Spring Goverment Bagan to Rase troops for the Insewing Campain aGanst Crounpoint under the Command of [G]enarel Winsloe[2] Beaing then Sixteen years of age I Gave my Parans to understand that I had a Strong Desire to be a Solge that I was Detarmend to Inlist under the Ofisers that was Going from Milford & joine the armey But thay for bid me and no wonder as my father had a Larg and young famerley I Just Began to be of Sum youse to him in his afairs Still the sam Inklanation & Sperit that my Ansesters Profest Run threw my Vanes it is well Knone that from fifth Gineration downward we ware all waryers [warriors] Ither by Sea or Land and in Dead Both So strong was the Popensatey for the arme that I [c]ould not with Stand its Temtatons One Eaveing in April [*the*] Drams an Instraments of Musick, waae all Imploid [*to th*]at Degrea that thay Charmd me I Repaird to a Publick [*hou*]se whare Marth & Gollatrey [jollity] was Highley Going on I found [*ma*]ney Lads of my Aquantans which Seamd Determined [*to*] Go in to the Sarvis I talkt with Capt Baldwin & ask him [*we*]ather he would take me in his Companey as he was the [*Recrui*]teing Offeser He Readealey a gread and I set my [*hand*] to the orders My Parans was so angry that they for[*bid me*] makeing my apearance at Home I taread [tarried] a bout the [*town*] among my fello Solgers and thought that I had made [*a profitable*] Exchange giting a Rigmintal Coate in Plase [*mss. torn*] llard Cloth at Length the time Came to Repo[*rt. Early in*] June we imbark on bord a Vasel to jion [*sic*] the [*Arme at*] the Randavuese [rendezvous] We Sald from Milford to New Y[*ork proceeded up*] North r[*iver and arrived safe*] at A[*lbany.*] I came on Smartly as I had Sum of my Bountey Money with me I did not want for Ginger Bread and Small Bear and sun forgot that I had left my Pairans who was Exseadingley trubeld in Minde for my well fair. . . .

. . . in thre[e] years while I was in the armey all Cannaday was in the Hands of the

British Nor have thay [the French] Had aney Part of it Sins all Cannaday subdued I thought thare was no bisnes left for me and turnd my atenshan to the Seas thinking to make it my Profesion and in Sixty one I went a Voige to the Islands in the West Indens and Returnd Safe but found that my father Had gon a trading Voig to Detroit and my Mother falling Sick with a feaver Dide before his Return I was Oblige to Give up the Iedea of going to Sea at that time and take Charge of a young fammaley til my father Returnd after which I Bent my Mind aftor Differant Objects and taread in Milford three years which was the Ondlay three years of my Life I was three years in One Plase Sins I was Sixteen years old up to Sixty at ye End of the three years I went into Trade first at Detroit I Continued in trade for Six years in Differant Parts of that Cuntrey But Beaing Exposed to all Sorts of Cumpaney it Hapend that a parson [person] who was in trade himSilf to Abuese me in a Shamefull manner Knowing that if I Resontd he Could Shake me in Peaceis at same tim Supposeing that I Dair not Sea him at the Pints or at Leas I could not But the Abuse was two Graie we met the Next Morning Eairley & Discharged Pistels in which the Pore fellow was unfortennt I then Came Doan the Cuntrey & Declard the fact But thare was none to Prosacute me I then Made a ture to ye West indaes & on my Return Home I Recved a Leatter from a Gentelman in New York to Cum Doan and Sea him for he was Desiaras to Go into Partner Ship with me in trade I Cumplyed and we Lade in a cargo to the amount of four thousend Six Hundred Pounds & I went into the Entearor Part of the Cuntrey first to Mishlemackenack from thenst to the Masseppay and up Sant Peters [Minnesota] River & into the Plains Betwene the Misseppey & the Miseeurea and Past my Winter a mong the NattawaySease [Sioux]³ on Such food as thay mad youse of them Selves which was Verey darteyaly [dirtily] Cooked.

The Next is to Show the Way of Convance [conveyance] of these Goods to the Most Remot Parts of ye Cuntrey for that year or Season In the first Plase thay ware Shipt at New-York for allbaney from thens thay ware takeen fooreteen Miles By Land to Sconacaday⁴ in wagens then Shipt on Bord Battoes & takeen up the Mohawk River to fort Stanwex thare Carread a Mile By Land with the Boates and Put in to Woodcrick & from thens threw the Onida Lake & Doun them waters to Lake Ontarey & Coasted aLong the South Side of that Lake till thay came to Nagarey & from the Landing Plase a fue Miles South of that fort thay ware with the Battoese⁵ Caread a Cross that Caring Plase about Nine Miles then Put into the waters that Coms out of Lake Erey into Lake Ontarey at a Plase Cald fort Slosser⁶ from that in thos Boats ware takeen to a Small fort Cald fort Erey on the north Side of Lake Earey then Coasting along North Side of that Lake til thay Cam to the Mouth of the River then up to De[t]roit from thens up them waters to Lake St Clair a Small one aBout fourteen Miles Long. from thens Proseaving these waters which Cum out of Lake Huron you com to that Lake & Coasting a Long the West Sid of it aBout five Hundread Miles thay Cam to Mishlamacneck that Lay at that on the South Side of a Strate Betwene Lake Huran & Mishagon thare was a British Garason whare all the traders aSembel yearley to arang thare afairs for the InSewing Winter But I Didnot A Cumpany My Goods mySelf Left that Part to my

Partner Mr Graham[7] I wanted Sum Small artickels in the Indan way to Cumpleat my asortment which was not to be had in New York I tharefour took my Boat threw Lake George & threw Lake Champlain to Montreal whare I found all I wanted this was in the Spring 1773 thare was a number of Canues fiting for Mishlamacanac I a Gread With Isac Tod [Todd] aSqur. [esquire] to take my Good in His Canneues an fraight and Imbark with him & James McGill Esqr[8] in one of his Canues and Seat of from Lashean [Lachine] for Mackenac By way of the Grand [Ottawa] River as you Pass the End of the Island of Montreall to Go in a Small Lake Cald the Lake of the Two Mountans thare Stans a Small Roman Church Aganst a Small Rapead this Church is Dedacateed to St Ann who Protesct all Voigeers heare is a Small Box with a Hole in the top for ye Reseption of a Lettle Muney for the Hole father or to Say a Small Mass for those who Put a small Sum in the Box Scars a Voigeer but Stops Hear and Puts in his mite and By that Meanes thay Suppose thay are Protacted while absant the C[h]urch is not Locked But the Munney Box is well Sacured from theaves after the Saremony of Crossing them selves and Rapeting [?] a Short Prayer we Crost the Lake and Entard the Grand River so Calld which Lead us to the Waters which Cams in to that River from the Southwest we a Sended these waters & Makeing Sum Caring Plaseis [portages] we Came to a Small Lake Cald Nipasank [Nipissing] whos Waters fall into Lake Huron By the french River we Desended that River and Coasted a Long the North Side of that Lake til we Came Oppaseat to Mackenac then Crost the Strat to the Garreason whare I found my Goods from New York Had A Rived Safe Hear I Met with a Grate meney Hundred People of all Denomanatons Sum trading with the tribes that Came a Grate Distans with thare furs Skins & Mapel Suge[r] &c to Marke[t] to these May be adead Dride Venson Bares Greas and the Like which is a Considerabel Part of trade Others ware Imployd in Makeing up thare Ecipments for to Send in to the Differant Parts of the Cuntry to Pas the winter among ye Indan tribes and trade what thay Git from the Hunt of ye Winter Insowing I was one of this Discription I Devided my Good in to twelve Parts and fited out twelve Large Canues for Differant Part of the Massasippey River Each cannew was mad of Burch Bark & white Seader [cedar] thay would Carry seven Thousand wate. . . .

. . . the white fish are another Exqiuseat fine fish thay will way from $2^{1}/_{2}$ to 9 & 10 Pound wt Baran La Huntan[9] who was the first that made an Excirtion from Mackanac Into the Masecipey By the Rout of the fox River, tho his Ideas ware Rong in Sum things as I have Proved Sins his say that Buter spild the flave[r] of white fish was Right the Sturge[on] are the Best in these Lakes & the Harens [herring] Exsead in flaver the waters are transParant and fine I return to my one [own business.] In Septr I Had my Small fleat Readey to Cross Lake Mishegon on my way to Grean Bay at the Mouth of the fox river I Engaged Nine Clarks for Differant Parts of the Sourthan & Westarn Cantrey and Beaing Mand we Imbarkt & Crost the Lake without Seaing an Indan or Eney Parson Except our Ome [own] in three or four Days we arive at the Mouth of the Bay which is two or three Miles Brod in the Mouth is Sum Islands which we follow in Crosing to the South west Sid, and then follow ye shore to the Bottom which is Seventey Miles whare the fox River Emptey in to the Bay, we went a Short Distans up the River whare is a Small french villege and thare Incampt for two Days this Land is Exalent, the InHabatans Rase fine Corn and Sum Artickels for fammaley youse in thare Gardens, Thay Have Sum trad with ye Indians which Pas that way on the North Part of this Bay is a Small Villeag of Indans Cald the Mannamaneas[10] who Live By Hunting Chefeley thay Have anothe[r] Resors [resource] the Bottom of the Bay Produsus a Large Quantity of Wilde Rice which thay Geather in Septr for food I ort to have Menshand that the french at ye Villeg whare we Incamt Rase find Black Cattel & Horseis with Sum swine. . . .

. . . we asendead that River til we Cam to a High Pece of Groand Whare that Nation yous to Entair thar Dead whin thay Lived in that Part[11] we stopt hear a while finding Sum of that Nation on the Spot who Came thare to Pay yare Resepct to thar Departed frend thay Had a small Cag of Run and seat Around the Grave thay fild thar Callemeat [calumet] and Began thar Saremony By Pinting the Stem of the Pipe upward then giveing it a turn in thare and then toward ye head of the Grave then East & West North & South after which thay smoake it out and fild it a Gane & Lade [it] By then thay toock Sum Rum Out of the Cag in a Small Bark Vessel and Pord it on the Head of the Grave By Way of giveing it to thar Departed Brother then thay all Drank them Selves Lit the Pipe Smokd and seam to Injoie themselves Verey well thay Repeated this till thay the Sperit Began to Operrate and thare harts Began to Soffon then thay Began to Sing a Song or two But at the End of Everey Song thay Soffend the Clay after Sum tim Had Relapst the Cag hat Bin Blead often thay Began to Repete the Saisfaction thay had with that frind while he was with them and How fond he was of his frinds while he Could Git a Cag of Rum and how thay youst to Injoy it togather thay amused them selves in this manner til thay all fell a Crying and a woful Nois thay Mad for a while til thay thought wiseley that thay Could not Bring him Back and it would not Due to Greve two much that an application to the Cag was the Best way to Dround Sorrow & Wash away Greafe The Moshan was sun Put in Execution and all Began to be marey as a Partey Could Bea thay Contineued til Near Nite Rite wen thay ware More then Half Drunk the men began to aproach the femals and Chat frelay and apearantly frindley at Length thay Begin to Lean on Each other Cis & apeared Virey amoras at Length two would Steapt a Sid in ye Eag [edge] of the Bushis Prasently two more would Steapt of But I could Obsarve Clearley this Bisnes was first Pusht on By the women who mad thare Viseat to the Dead a Verey Pleaseing one in thare way Wone of them who was Quit Drunk as I was By [my] Self Seating on the Ground obsarveing thare Saremones Came to me and ask me to take Share of her Bountey in the Eag of the Bishis But I thought it was time to Quit and went about Half a mile up the Rive[r] to my Caneuees whare My men was Incampt But the Indans Neaver Came Nigh us thar the Men Menshan that thre[e] of the Women had bin at the Camp In the Night In Quest of Imploy. . . .

. . . An acount of the fox River and its Neghbering Cuntrey A Long its Shores from the Moath to the Peuans Lake is A good Navagation One or two Small Rapeds from that Lake the Water up to the Caring plase is Verey Gental But Varey Sarpentine In Meney Parts In Going three Miles you due not advans one the Bank is all most Leavel With the Water and the Madoes on Each Side are Clear of wood to a Grate Distans and Cloth with a Good Sort of Grass the Ope[n]ings of this River W[h]ich are Cald Lakes But thay are no more than Large Opening [In] these Plaseis the water is aboat four or five feet deap with a Soft Bottom these Plaseis Produseis the Grateest Quantateys of Wild Rise of Which the Natives Geather Grat Quantateys and Eat what they Have Ocation for & Dispose of the Remainder to People that Pas & Repass on thare trade this Grane Looks in its Groth & Stock & Ears Like Ry and the Grane is of the Same Culler But Larger and Slimer when it is Cleand fit for youse thay Boile it as we Due Rise and Eat [it] with Bairs Greas and Suger But the Greas thay ad as it is Bileing which Helps to Soffen it and make it Brake in the same maner as Rise When thay take it out of thare Cittels [kettles] for yous thay ad a Lettle suger and [it] is Eaten with fres Vonsen [venison] or fowls we youosed it in the Room of Rise and it Did verey well as a Substatute for that Grane as it Busts it tarns Out Parfectly White as Rise Back from this River the Lands are as Good as Can be Conseaved and Good timber But not Overthick it is Proverbel that the fires Which Ran th[r]ew these woo[d]s and Meadoes Stops the Groth of ye wood and Destroise Small wood I Have Menshand the Vast Numbers of Wild Ducks which faten on ye Wild Rise Eaverey fall it would Sound two much Like a travelers Storey[12] to Say What I Rearley Beleve from what I Have Sean you Can Parchis them Verey Cheape at the Rate of two Pens Per pese if you Par[fer] Shuteing them your Self you may Kill what you Plese — An acound of the Portage of Osisconstan the South End of this Caring plase is Verey Leavel But in wet wather it is Bad On acount of the Mud & Water which is two thirds of a Mile and then the Ground Riseis to a Considerabel Hith and Cloth with fine Open Wood & a Hansum Varder [verdure] this Spot is Abot the Senter of ye Portage and take up about a Quorter Part of it the North End is Low flat and Subject to Weat it was on this Spot that Old Pinneshon a french Man Imposed apon Carve[r][13] Respecting the Indan haveing a Rattel Snake at His Call which the Indand Could order into a Box for that Purpas as a Peat [pet]. . . .

He found Carver on this Spot Going on Dissoverey in an Obscur[?] Mananer without undirstanding orther [either] french or Indan & full of Enquirey threw his Man who Sarved him as an Enterprar thought it a Proper Opertunetey to ad Sumthing more to his adventers and Make his Bost of it after which I have Haird Menea times it hirt Cairver much hearing such things & Puting Confadens in them While he is Coruect [correct?] He Give a Good a Count of the Small Part of the Westarn Cuntrey he Saw But when he a Leude to Hearsase he flies from factes in two meney Instansis — . . .

the Land is E[x]alant & Clear of wood Sum Distans from the Villeage thare [are] Sum Hundreds of InHabbatan thare amusements are Singing Dan[c]ing Smokeing matches Gameing and Feasting Drinking Playing the Slite of Hand Hunting & thay are famas in Mageack Thay are Not Verey Gellas [jealous] of thare women In Genaral the women find Meanes to Grattafy themSelves with out Censent of the

men the Men often jion war parteies with Other nations and Go aganst the Indans
on the Miseeure and west of that Sume time thay Go Near St Fee [Santa Fe] in
New Maxeco and Bring with them Spanish Horseis; I have sean Meney of them
the River aford But a fue fish thare woods aford Partragis a fue Rabeat Bairs &
Deear are Plentey In thare Seasons, wild foul thay have But fue thar Religan is Like
Most of the tribes thay a Low thare is two Sperits One Goods Who Swelve a Bove
the Clouds Superintends over all and helps to all the Good things we have and Can
Bring Sicknes on us if He pleaseis and another Bad one who dwelves in the fire and
air Eaverey whare among m[en] & Sumtimes Dose Mischef to Mankind Cortship &
Mareages — [two words illegible] At Night when these People are Seating Round
thare fiuer [fire] the Elderly one will be teling what thay Have Sean and Hard or
Perhaps that may be on SumIntrest[ing] Subg[ec]t the famley are lis[ten]ing if
thare be any Young Garles in this Lodg or hut that any Man of a Differan Hut has a
Likeing for he will Seat among the Parson of his Arrant [errand] Being Prasent hea
will watch an Opertunety & through [throw] a Small Stick at Hair if she Looks up
with a Smile it is a Good Omen he Repets a Sacond time Perhaps ye Garle will
Return the Stick the Simtam [symptoms] ar Still Groing Stronger and when they
think Proper to Ly doun to Slepe Each Parson Raps himself up in his One Blanket
he takes Notis whar the Garl Seats for thare [she] sleep when all the famaley are
Qui[e]t and Perhaps a Sleap he Slips Soffley in to Hut and Seats himself Down By
her Side PresantLey he will Begin to Lift her Blanket in a Soft maner Perhaps she
may twish it Out of his hand with a Sort of a Sie & Snore to Gather But this is no
Kiling Matter he Seats a while and Makes a Sacond Atempt She may Perhaps
Hold the Blankead Doun Slitely at Length She turns Over with a Sith [sigh?] and
Quits the Hold of the Blanket He then Creapes under and Geats as Close as he
Can til allmost and than of[f] to his one Hut this Meathard [method] is Practest a
Short [time] then ye yong Indan will Go ahanting and [if] he is Luckey to Git meat
he Cums and Informs the famely of it and whare it is he Brengs the tung and hart
with him thay Seat of after the Meat and Bring it Home this Plesis [pleases] and he
Begins to Go Bold in the famerly The Garl after that will not Refuse him under the
Blanket he Will then Perhaps Stay about the famerly a Year and Hunt for the Old
father But in this Intram [interim] he Gives his Consent that thay may Sleap
toogther and when thay Begin to have Children thay Save what thay Can git for
thare One youse and Perhaps Live In a Hut apart afte[r] I had Giveen them a
number of Cradeat [credits] to Recve Payment the Next Spring I Descended to the
fox Villeage On the Same River and Same Sid about fiftey Miles Distans hear I
meat a Differant Sort of People Who was Bread at Detroit under the french Government and Clarge [clergy]; till that By Chrisanissing Grew so Bad that ware Oblige to
Go to war a Ganst them, tho thay Lived within thre Miles of the Gairsean [garrison]
and among the Inhabatans; thay Was Obligd To fite them and killd Grate Numbers
of them, the Remander flead to the fox River whare thay made a Stand and treated
the traders Going to the Misseappey Verey Ill, and Pilleaged them; at Lengh thay
went a Strong Partey against them and Beat them back to whare they Now are But
in Sad Sarkamstanis [circumstances] to what they ware Before thay took So much

on themSelves— As I Aprocht the Banks of the Villeage I Perseaved a number of Long Pa[i]nted Poles on which Hung a Number of Artickels Sum Panted Dogs and a Grate Number of Wampum Belts with a Number of Silver Braslets and Other artickels in the Indan way I Inquird the Cause they told me thay Had a Shorte time Before had a Sweaping Sicknes among them which Had Caread of Grate Numbers of Inhabetans & thay had offerd Up these Sacrafices to Apease that Beaing who was Angrey with them and Sent the Sicknes that it was Much Abateed tho that was Sum Sick Still I told them that had Dun Right and to take Cair that thay Did not Ofend him agane for fear a Grater Eavel myte befall them. . . .

we Desended the fox River to th[e] Batam of Grean Bay So cald and thare joind the Hole of ye Canues Bound to Mackenaw the way ther was fair and Plesant we all Proseaded to gather Across Lake Misheagon at the end of two Days we all apeared on the Lake, about five Miles from Mecanac, and aproach it in Order We had flags on the Masts of our Canewes Eaverey Cheafe his flock My Canew Beaing the Largest in that Part of the Cuntrey and haveing a larg[e] Youan [Union] flageI I Histed it, and when within a Mile & a half I took ye lead and the Indans followed Close behind, the flag in the fort was histed ye Cannen of the Garresen Began to Play Smartley the Shores was lind with Peaple of all sorts, who Seat up Such a Crey and hooping which Seat the Tribes in the fleat a Going to that Degrea that you Could not Hear a Parson Speak, at Length we Reacht ye Shore and the Cannen Seast I then toock My Partey to the Commander[14] who treated us verey well I Seat with them an Our and Relateed the afare and what I had Dun & what Past Dureing the Winter, after Interreduseing the Chiefs I went to my one House what I found a nunter [number] of Old frind [with] whom I spent the Remander of the Day, the People from Lake Superior Had arived Befour us and Next Day the Grand Counsel was Held Before Cumander in the Grate Counsel Chamber, Befour a Vast Number of Spectaters whare the artickels of Pece ware Concludeed and Grate Promises ware Mad on Both Sides for Abideing and Adhearing Closely to the artickels to Provent farthar BludShead . . . . the Next Day thare was a Large fat Ox Kild and Coked by the Solgers; all of these nations ware Biden to the feast thay Dined to Geather in Harmoney and finished the Day in Drinking Moderately— Smokeing to Gather Singing & Briteing[15] the Chane of frindShip in a Verey Deasant way, this was Kept up for Four Days when the Offiser Mad them Each a Present and thay all Imbark for thare One Part of thair Cuntrey

Notes

[1] In Rea: with respect to; the french fortification: Fort Duquesne [Pittsburgh]. General Edward Braddock was defeated by the French at Fort Duquesne in 1755.

[2] General John Winslow, who had earlier supervised the expulsion of the Acadians from Nova Scotia, commanded the campaign against Crown Point and Ticonderoga in 1756.

[3] A general summary of the travels which the journal will describe.

[4] Schenectady, N.Y.

[5] Bateaux, river-boats.

[6] A British fort about two miles above Niagara Falls.

[7] Felix Graham, a merchant trading out of New York; Pond was in partnership with him in 1771 and they renewed the arrangement in 1773, but Pond did so well that year that he bought out Graham when they met at Michilimackinac in 1774.

[8] Isaac Todd (*c.* 1742–1819) and James McGill (1744–1813) of the Montreal firm of Todd and McGill, which supplied goods for the Indian trade and in turn marketed furs in England and Europe. For two decades their resources backed the 'pedlars from Montreal', the predecessors of the North West Company; James McGill left a large bequest to found the university which bears his name.

[9] Louis Armand de Lom d'Arce de Lahontan, Baron Lahontan (1666-before 1716), author of *Nouveaux Voyages dans l'Amérique septentrionale* (1703, and two additional volumes published in the same year). The authenticity of certain details of the journey (supposed to have been in 1688–9) has been questioned, but his volumes were immensely popular; there were 25 editions or condensations in 55 years.

[10]The Menominees, the 'wild rice people' encountered by Radisson more than a century earlier.

[11]Present-day Butte des Mortes, Wisconsin.

[12]Proverbially, travellers have a reputation for telling tall tales.

[13]Jonathan Carver (1710–80), American-born author of *Travels through the Interior Parts of North-America in the Years 1766, 1767, and 1768* (London, 1778). Its many editions created intense interest in America among Europeans. Old Pinneshon is thought to have been Pennesha George, a trader.

[14]Captain Arent Schuyler de Peyster commanded at Mackinac, 1774–9.

[15]Possibly 'braiding'?

David Thompson (1770 – 1857)

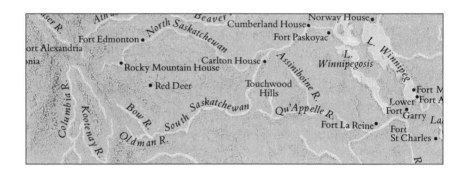

THOMPSON described himself as 'a solitary traveller unknown to the world', but his first editor, J.B. Tyrrell, frankly termed him 'the greatest practical land geographer that the world had produced'. He is also the most outstanding of Canadian exploration writers in English, possessing the most reflective cast of mind and the greatest powers of synthesis. His writing moves from the closest attention to details to the largest issues raised by their significance, and his systematization of areas such as 'the Great Plains' is both factual and conceptually very powerful. Thompson says almost nothing of himself, yet is a benevolent and amused chronicler of exploration life. His relations with the natives were characterized by courteous inquiry, but he was intolerant of those of his own race (particularly the voyageurs) who did not share his scientific spirit.

Born in London, Thompson attended the Grey Coat School in Westminster, which educated boys for careers in trade and navigation. He came to Canada at the age of fourteen, and never left. During his years in the west he travelled, often with his mixed-blood wife (Charlotte Small) and his growing family, over 50,000 miles by canoe and on foot, trading furs on behalf first of the Hudson's Bay Company and then in 1797 for the North West Company, and surveying as he went. In fact he parted from the HBC for intellectual reasons, in order to pursue his interest in surveying more fully. When he finally left the west in 1812 in order to educate his children, he had assembled the materials for his Great Map of the West, which he spent the next few years drafting and which is now in the Ontario Archives. In later life Thompson worked as a surveyor in Eastern Canada, corresponded with persons of eminence, and found his finances depleted by his sons' business failures. In 1846 he began to write his *Narrative* in hopes that its publication would enable him to support his family. Two drafts exist, but he was unable to finish owing to the onset of blindness. He died in 1857 and is buried in Mount Royal Cemetery next to his wife of nearly sixty years.

Text: *David Thompson's Narrative 1784–1812*, ed. Richard Glover. Toronto: The Champlain Society, 1962. The narrative of SAUKAMAPEE, recorded by Thompson, appears on pp. 234–42 under his own name.

I,i: Thompson, aged fourteen, joins the Hudson's Bay Company

In the month of May 1784 at the Port of London, I embarked in the ship Prince Rupert belonging to the Hudson's Bay Company, as apprentice and clerk to the said company, bound for Churchill Factory, on the west side of the bay. . . .

On the sixth day about nine PM. we anchored in the harbour of Stromness, where the three ships bound for Hudsons Bay had to wait for final instructions and sailing orders, as there were no telegraphs in those [days] we were delayed three weeks. Until this Voyage I had passed my life near to Westminster Abbey, the last seven year in the grey coat school on royal foundation. . . .

During the year our holidays at different times were about eighteen to twenty days, the greatest part of which I spent in this venerable Abbey and it's cloisters, reading the monumental inscriptions and [as] often as possible [in] Henry the seventh chapel. My strolls were to London Bridge, Chelsea, and Vauxhall and S' James's Park. Books in those days were scarce and dear and most of the scholars got the loan of such books as his parents could lend him. Those which pleased us most were the Tales of the Genii, the Persian, and Arabian Tales, with Robinson Crusoe and Gullivers Travels: these gave us many subjects for discussion and how each would behave on various occasions.

With such an account of the several regions of the Earth and on such credible authority, I conceived myself to have knowledge to say something of any place I might come to, and the blue hills of Scotland were so distant as to leave to imagination to paint them as she pleased. When I woke in the morning and went upon deck, I could not help staring to see if [what] was before me was reality for I had never read of such a place. And at length exclaimed I see no trees, to which a Sailor answered No no, people here do not spoil their clothes by climbing up trees. One of the first objects that drew my attention were several kelp kilns for burning sea weed into a kind of potash. The sea weeds were collected by a number of Men and Women their legs appeared red and swelled. The sea weeds were collected into baskets, the rope handles of which were passed round their breasts, each helped up the load for one another, and as they carried it over rough rocky shore left by the ebb tide to the kilns, the sea water streamed down their backs. . . . I could not help comparing this hard, wet labour for tenpence a day where not even a whistle was heard, with the merry songs of the ploughboys in English.

This place was to me a new world, nothing reminded me of Westminster Abbey, and my strolls to Vauxhall, Spring Gardens and other places, where all was beauty to the eye, and verdure to the feet; here all was rock with very little soil, everywhere loose stones that hurt my feet; not a tree to be seen. I sadly missed the old Oaks, under whose shade I sat, and played. I could not conceive by what means the people lived; they appeared comfortable, and their low dark houses, with a peat fire, the smoke of which escaped by a small hole, contained all they required. . . .

. . . Churchill River where it enters the Sea, is an noble stream of about one and a half mile in width; on the south side it is bounded by a low point of rock and sand; on the north side by a low neck of sand with rock appearing through it; at the extremity of which the Point is about an acre in width, on which was erected about the year 1745 a regular, well constructed Fort of Granite:[1] having about thirty cannon of six to eighteen pound shot. There was no approach to it but by the narrow isthmus of sand. The water was too shoal for three fourths of a mile to the middle of the River for Ships, and this was the only place a ship could come to. (It was at this Fort that Mr. Wales the Astronomer observed the Transit of Venus over the Sun in 1769.)[2] In the war with the United States, and with France; in the year 1782 the celebrated Navigator De la Peyrouse was sent from France, with one Ship of seventy four Guns, and two Frigates to take and destroy the Forts of the Hudson's Bay Company. In the month of August these vessels anchored in the Bay, about four miles north of the Fort; and the next day sent a boat well manned, to sound the River; at this time the Fort was under the command of the well known traveller Mr. Samuel Hearne; who had been in the naval service. He allowed the french Boat to sound the River to their satisfaction; without firing a single shot at them; from this conduct Admiral De la Peyrouse judged what kind of a Commander of the Fort he had to contend with; accordingly next day, on the narrow isthmus of sand and rock of a full mile in length which leads to the Fort, he landed four hundred men, who marched direct on the Fort with only small arms. The men in the Fort begged of Mr. Hearne to allow them to mow down the French Troops with the heavy guns loaded with grape shot, which he absolutely refused; and as they approached he ordered the gates to be opened, and went out to meet them, and surrendered at discretion; all the goods, stores, with a large quantity of valuable Furrs fell into their hands. The Fort was destroyed and burnt; but the stone walls of the Fort were of such solid masonry [that] the fire scarcely injured them. The french Commander declared, that had his sounding Boat been fired at, he would not have thought of attacking such a strong Fort so late in the season, when there was not time for a regular siege. Mr. Hearne was received with cold politeness, and looked upon with contempt by the french Officers.[3] (Note. Mr. Samuel Hearne was a handsome man of six feet in height, of a ruddy complexion and remarkably well made, enjoying good health; as soon as the Hudson's Bay Company could do without his services they dismissed him for cowardice. Under him I served my first year. It was customary of a Sunday for a Sermon to be read to the Men, which was done in his room, the only comfortable one in the Factory; one Sunday, after the service, Mr. Jefferson[4] the reader and myself staid a few minutes on orders, he then took Voltaire's Dictionary,[5] and said to us, here is my belief, and I have no other. In the Autumn of 1785 he returned to England, became a member of the Bucks Club[6] and in two years was buried:) The present Factory is about five miles above the Fort, in a small Bay formed by a ledge of rocks which closes on the river about five hundred yards below the Factory, above which for seven miles is an extensive marsh to the lower rapids of the River. The Factory is supplied once a year with goods and provisions, by a Ship which arrives on the last days of August, or early in September, and in about ten days is ready for her homeward voyage; the severity of the climate requiring all possible dispatch. The cold weather now comes rapidly on, but as there was no Thermometer, we could only judge of the intensity of the cold by our sensations, and it's action on the land and water. On the fifteenth day of November this great and deep River was frozen over from side to side. . . . From the end of October to the end of April every step we walk is in Snow Shoes. The Natives walk with ease and activity, and also many of us: but some find them a sad incumbrance, their feet become sore and their ankles sprained; with many a tumble in the snow from which it is sometimes difficult to rise. . . . The country, soil, and climate in which we live, have always a powerful effect upon the state of society, and the movements and comforts of every individual, he must conform himself to the circumstances under which he is placed, and as such we lived and conducted ourselves in this extreme cold climate. All our movements more, or less, were for self-preservation: All the wood that could be collected for fuel, gave us only one fire in the morning, and another in the evening.[7] The rest of the day, if bad weather, we had to walk in the guard room with our heavy coats of dressed Beaver; but when the weather was tolerable we passed the day in shooting Grouse.[8] The interior walls of the House were covered with rime to the thickness of four inches, pieces of which often broke off, to prevent which we wetted the whole extent, and made it a coat of ice, after which it remained firm, and added to the warmth of the House, for the cold is so intense, that everything in a manner is shivered by it, continually the Rocks are split with a sound like the report of a gun. Everywhere the rocks are fractured from the well known effects of freezing water. This is very well for winter, but in the summer season the Rocks are also fractured; although more than half of their surface is covered with Ponds and rills of water, I could not believe that water thawing could produce this effect; but in the month of July I was sitting on a rock to shoot Curlews as they passed, when a large rock not ten yards from me split, I went to it, the fracture was about an inch in width. In looking down it, about ten feet from the surface, was a bed of solid ice, the surface of which appeared damp as if beginning to thaw; a few days after another large Rock split close to me, by the fracture, at the depth of about twenty feet was a bed of ice in the same state: these rocks are not isolated, they are part of an immense extent to the westward and northward, every where with innumerable fractures; among these rocks are narrow vallies of rolled granite pebbles, now twenty to fifty feet above the level of the sea; which was once the beach of the sea: has the land been elevated, or the sea retired; who can tell what has passed in ancient times. By the early part of October all the birds of passage have left us for milder climes, and winter commences, the pools of water are frozen over and ice [is] on the river side. The polar Bear now makes his appearance, and prowls about until the ice at the sea shore is extended to a considerable distance; when he leaves to prey on the Seal, his favourite food: during his stay he is for plunder and every kind of mischief, but not willing to fight for it. . . .

The Esquimaux are a people with whom we are very little acquainted, although in a manner surrounding us, they live wholly on the sea coast, which they possess from the gulph of the St Lawrence, round the shores of Labrador to Hudsons Straits, these Straits and adjacent Islands, to Hudson's Bay, part of it's east shores; but on the west side of this Bay, only north of Churchill River, thence northward and westward to the Coppermine River; thence to the McKenzie and westward to Icy Cape, the east side of Behring's Strait. Along this immense line of sea coast they appear to have restricted themselves to the sea shores, their Canoes give them free access to ascend the Rivers, yet they never do, every part they frequent is wholly destitute of growing Trees, their whole dependence for fuel and other purposes is on drift wood, of which, fortunately there is plenty. . . .

The Esquimaux are of a square, plump make, few of them exceed five feet eight inches in height, the general stature is below this size, and the women are in proportion to the men, their features though broad are not unpleasing, with a tendency to ruddy, they appear cheerful and contented, they are supple active and strong; from the land, in the open season, they have berries, and a few rein-deer, but it is to the sea they look for their subsistence: the sea birds, the seal, morse,[9] beluga, and the whale; living on these oily foods, they are supposed not to be clean, but the fact is, they are as cleanly as people living as they do, and without soap can be expected [to be], all their cooking utensils are in good order. In summer part of them dwell in tents made of the dressed skins of the reindeer, these are pitched on the gravel banks, and kept very neat, they make no fire in them to prevent [them] being soiled with smoke, which is made near the tent. The salmon and meat of the reindeer they cure by smoke of drift wood of which they have plenty. They are very industrious and ingenious, being for eight months of the year exposed the glare of the snow, their eyes become weak; at the age of forty years almost every man has an impaired sight. The eyesight of the women is less injured at this age. They make neat goggles of wood with a narrow slit, which are placed on the eyes, to lessen the light. . . . Whale Bone is part of their trade, but whether they procure it by attacking the Whale as they do the Morse or it is the spoils of those thrown ashore, is somewhat uncertain. They are dextrous in throwing the dart, although their Canoes allow only the motion of the upper part of their bodies, and seldom miss a sea bird at thirty yards distance. Their Bows and Arrows are employed on the Rein Deer, Wolf and Fox, they draw the Arrow well and sure, whatever they make displays a neatness and ingenuity that would do honor to a first rate european workman if he had no other tools than those poor people have. All along the sea coast where the Esquimaux are found, there are no standing woods of any kind, the whole country is rock and moss, the drift wood is what they wholly depend on for every purpose for which wood is required, and fortunately it is plentiful; brought down by the rivers from the interior countries, and thrown ashore by the waves and tides of the sea; their country everywhere exhibits

Rocks, Ponds, and Moss, a hundred miles has not ground for a garden, even if the climate allowed it; . . . Their canoes are made of sealskins sewed together, and held to a proper shape by gunwales, and ribs made of drift Larch, and sometimes whale-bones added; they are very sharp at both ends and no wider in the middle than to admit a man; their length from twelve to sixteen feet, they are decked with seal skins so as to prevent any water getting into the canoe, the place to admit the man is strengthened by a broad hoop of wood, to the upper part of which is sewed a sealskin made to draw around the man like a purse, this the Esquimaux tightens round his waist so that only the upper part of the body is exposed to the waves and weather; they urge along their canoes with great swiftness, by a paddle having a blade at both ends; the handle is in the middle. Early habit has rendered him expert in balancing himself on the waves of the sea in these sharp canoes called kaijack. I never saw a european who could balance himself in these canoes for three minutes. Their weapons for killing sea birds, seals &c. are placed on the deck of the canoe, quite at hand, secured by small cords of sinew. . . .

In their conduct to each other they are sociable, friendly, and of a cheerful temper. But we are not sufficiently acquainted with their language to say much more; in their traffic with us they are honest and friendly. They are not of the race of the north american Indians, but of european descent. Nothing can oblige an Indian to work at anything but stern necessity; whereas the Esquimaux is naturally industrious, very ingenious, fond of the comforts of life so far as they can attain them, always cheerful, and even gay; it is true that in the morning, when he is about to embark in his shell of a Canoe, to face the waves of the sea, and the powerful animals he has to contend with, for food and clothing for himself and family, he is for many minutes very serious, because he is a man of reflection, knows the dangers to which he is exposed, but steps into his canoe, and bravely goes through the toil and dangers of the day. . . .

After passing a long gloomy, and most severe winter, it will naturally be thought with what delight we enjoy the Spring, and Summer; of the former we know nothing but the melting of the snow and the ice becoming dangerous; Summer such as it is, comes at once, and with it myriads of tormenting Musketoes; the air is thick with them, there is no cessation day nor night of suffering from them. Smoke is no relief, they can stand more smoke than we can, and smoke cannot be carried about with us. The narrow windows were so crowded with them, they trod each other to death in such numbers, we had to sweep them out twice a day; a chance cold northeast gale of wind was a grateful relief, and [we] were thankful for the cold weather that put an end to our sufferings. The Musketoe Bill, when viewed through a good microscope, is of a curious formation, composed of two distinct pieces; the upper is three sided, of a black color, and sharp-pointed, under which is a round white tube, like clear glass, the mouth inverted inwards; with the upper part the skin is perforated, it is then drawn back, and the clear tube applied to the wound, and the blood sucked through it into the body, till it is full; thus their bite are two distinct operations, but so quickly done as to feel as only one; different Persons feel them in a different manner; some are swelled, even bloated, with intolerable itching; others feel only the smart of the minute wounds; Oil is the only remedy and that frequently applied; the Natives rub themselves with Sturgeon Oil, which is found to be far more effective than any other oil. All animals suffer from them, almost to madness, even the well feathered Birds suffer about the eyes and neck. The cold nights of September are the first, and most steady relief. A question has often been asked to which no satisfactory answer has ever been given; where, and how, do they pass the winter, for on their first appearance they are all full grown, and the young brood does not come forward until July. The opinion of the Natives, as well as many of ourselves, is, that they pass the winter at the bottom of ponds of water, for when these ponds are free of ice, they appear covered with gnats in a weak state; and two, or three days after the Musketoes are on us in full force. This theory may do very well for the low countries, where except the bare rock, the whole surface may be said to be wet, and more, or less, covered with water, but will not do for the extensive high and dry Plains, where, when the warm season comes on, they start up in myriads a veritable full grown plague. We must conclude that wherever they find themselves when the frost sets in, there they shelter themselves from the winter, be the country wet or dry; and this theory appears probable, for all those countries where they were in myriads, and which are now under cultivation by the plough, are in a manner clear of them, and also the Cities and Towns of Canada. But in America there always has been, and will be Woods, Swamps, and rough ground, not fit for the plough, but admirably adapted to produce Musketoes, and the Cows turned out to graze, when they return to be milked bring with them more than enough to plague the farmer. . . .

While these insects are so numerous they are a terror to every creature on dry lands if swamps may be so called, the dogs howl, roll themselves on the ground, or hide themselves in the water; the Fox seems always in a fighting humour; he barks, snaps on all sides, and however hungry and ready to go a birdsnesting, of which he is fond, is fairly driven to seek shelter in his hole. A sailor finding swearing of no use, tried what Tar could do, and covered his face with it, but the musketoes stuck to it in such numbers as to blind him, and the tickling of their wings were worse than their bites; in fact Oil is the only remedy. I was fortunate in passing my time in the company of three gentlemen the officers of the factory, Mr. Jefferson the deputy governor, Mr. Prince the captain of the Sloop, that annually traded with the Esquimaux to the northward, and Mr. Hodges the Surgeon; they had books which they freely lent to me, among them were several on history and on animated nature, these were what I paid most attention to as the most instructive. Writing paper there was none but what was in the hands of the Governor, and a few sheets among the officers. On my complaining that I should lose my writing for want of practice, Mr. Hearne employed me a few days on his manuscript entitled 'A journey to the North,'[10] and at another time I copied an Invoice.

It had been the custom for many years, when the governors of the factory required a clerk, to send to the school in which I was educated to procure a Scholar who had a mathematical education to send out as Clerk, and, to save expenses, he was bound apprentice to them for seven years. To learn what; for all I had seen in their service neither writing nor reading was required, and my only business was to amuse myself, in winter growling at the cold; and in the open season shooting Gulls, Ducks, Plover and Curlews, and quarelling with Musketoes and Sand flies.

The Hudsons Bay Company annually send out three Ships to their Factories, which generally arrive at their respective ports in the latter end of August or the early part of September, and this year (1785) the Ship arrived as usual. When the Captain landed, I was surprised to see with him Mr. John Charles,[11] a school fellow and of the same age as myself, whom I had left to be bound out to a trade. I enquired of him what had made him change his mind, he informed me that shortly after my departure, from what he could learn some maps drawn by the fur traders of Canada had been seen by Mr. Dalrymple,[12] which showed the rivers and lakes for many hundred miles to the westward of Hudsons Bay. That he applied to the Company to send out a gentlemen well qualified to survey the interior country, all which they promised to do, and have [a] gentleman fit for that purpose to go out with their ships next year; they accordingly sent to the School to have one ready. As he was the only one of age, he was placed in the mathematical school, run quickly over his studies, for which he had no wish to learn, for three days, for a few minutes each day, taught to handle Hadley's quadrant,[13] and bring down the Sun to a chalk mark on the wall [and] his education was complete, and pronounced fit for the duties he had to perform; he was very much disappointed at all he saw, but he could not return. Hudson's Bay, is certainly a country that Sinbad the Sailor never saw, as he makes no mention of Musketoes.

I, iia: Trading on the Saskatchewan; the Bow River country

The fur traders from Canada[14] for several years past had so far extended their trading posts through the interior country as almost to cut off the trade from the Factories. The whole of the furs collected at Churchill barely loaded the ships long boat. The Hudson's Bay [Company] therefore found it necessary to make trading houses in a few different places, and as the Kisiskatchewan[1] is the great leading river of the country, these trading houses were situated on it's [banks] or the branches which flow into it. This inland trade was still in its infancy. The company had only two houses, Cumberland House built by Mr. Samuel Hearne and Hudson House about 300 miles above it. . . . It was now thought proper to make a trading house about 200 miles higher up the River, leave Hudson House for the present and instead to build a house about 40 miles to the southward, on the right bank of the Bow River, the great South Branch of the Kisiskatchewan; the latter to be under the charge of Mr. Mitchel [Mitchell] Oman, a native of the Isle of Orkney. He had no education, but a fine looking manly powerful man of a tenacious memory and high moral qualities, and much respected by the Indians and whose language he had acquired. I was appointed to be his clerk and embarked with him. . . . Everything being ready, our provisions for the Voyage was given to each canoe, being 60 lbs. of Oatmeal, 20 lbs. of Flour and about 30 lbs. of Bacon. The salt pork and beef called junk were of too low a quality to bear carriage. In the latter end of July we set off with the tide which took us four miles and there left us to contend with a strong current of 300 yards in width but somewhat shoal. The current could not be stemmed by paddles and two men from each canoe went on shore and took the tracking line, leaving one man to steer the canoe. Although the whole weight of cargo and baggage did not exceed 800 lbs. yet it required a strong steady pull to advance two miles an hour. This was performed on the left side of the River which has generally the best beach, and the deepest water near the shore. The labor is not more than common but rendered almost dreadful by the heat and torment of Musketoes. To alleviate this latter the men make for themselves wide loose caps of cotton with a piece of green bunting in the front, but the sweat from toil and heat makes it unbearable in the day time, but [it] serves well at night.... The River now formed Lakes and small streams with several carrying places over which we passed to a low winding ridge of land which separates the waters that flow eastward into Hudson's Bay, and those that run westward into Lake Winepeg. This ridge continues all along the east side of this Lake to the River Winipeg, which it crosses and forms one of its falls. On the short carrying place by which we crossed this ridge the Indians time out of mind had placed a manito stone in shape like a cobless [cobbler's] lap stone but three times its size to which they make some trifling offerings; but the Stone and offerings were all kicked about by our tolerant people.[16] ... The west side [of Cedar Lake] is formed of immense alluvials of the Kisiskatchewan, which passes through the Lake. These alluvials have many channels of the River, one of which in about three days brought us to Cumberland Lake, so named from the House on its south east bank. It was in charge of Mr. George Hudson who had been brought up in the same school in which I had received my education, but had left it several years before I entered. The canoes stopped for a few minutes to take in dried provisions and proceeded, and gave not time for conversation. Passing this Lake we continued for three days to proceed with the paddle up the alluvial channels to their end, where the River is one stream. There the current is strong and we had to bind the tracking line to the Canoes and as Clerk to take my share of the labor; but everything was now very different from the wretched labor from York Factory. We were here in a high and dry country, the beach was wide and dry the season the latter end of August, the Musketoes were not numerous, the weather fine and as we advanced the Red Deer became in plenty and the call of the stag made the forest resound and be answered by other stags. Each day we marched fourteen hours averaging 25 miles a day. On the evening of the fourth day we camped at the entrance of the Bow River. The next morning four canoes under the charge of Mr. Mitchell Oman crossed to and proceeded up this River, the other canoes with Mr. Tomison went up the main River to their wintering houses. With the tracking line we followed up the left bank of the River, every hour appeared to bring us to a better country, instead of dark pine forests the woods were of well grown Poplar, Aspen and white Birch and for the first time saplings of Ash. The whistling and calls of the Red Deer echoed through the woods, and we often heard the battling of the Staghorns battling which should be lord of the herd of Does, for these Stags are all Turks. On the evening of the third day up the River we came opposite to where houses were building for the furr trade and next morning crossed over and placed ourselves eighty yards above them. These houses were on account of two companies from Canada; one of them of the firm of McTavish and company; under the charge of a Scotch gentleman of the name of Thorburn.[17] The other was of the firm of Gregory and company under the care of a french gentleman. The men were all french canadians with long red or blue caps, half of which hung down the head; they wore grey capots or blanket coats belted round their waist, their trowsers of grey cloth or dressed leather and their shoes the same. Our dresses were a coarse hat; tight blue jacket with leather trowsers and shoes, to which in winter was added a leather coat. We now cleared the ground to build a log house of thirty six feet in length by twenty in breadth; which when carried up to seven feet in height was roofed with split logs. The ridgepole was placed on two upright logs of twelve feet and gave to each side a slope of five feet. The whole was mudded and covered with earth. The two chimneys were built of mud mixed with chopped coarse grass. The floors were of split logs; the house divided into three by walls of logs with doors cut in them. One of twelve feet by twenty for the goods, furs and provisions; ten feet for a hall for business and trading with the Indians; the other fourteen feet for the men called the guardroom. The indian hall was occupied by Mr. Oman and myself. Under such able architects as we were, we had raised a doric building, which might suit a painter of rustic scenery.[18] The Indians who traded at these houses were of the tribes of Nahathaways and Stone Indians called Assine poetwak [Assiniboine], or people of stony lands. They appeared to be equally numerous. They were all moderately tall, manly looking men with prominent features well dressed in leather with a bison robe, the women dressed in much the same manner. They were friendly to us and by no means troublesome, axes and tools lying about, yet nothing was stolen and we builded and finished everything with as much ease and safety as if we had been alone. The french gentleman paid us a visit. He was well dressed his behaviour easy mild and polite. He understood english and spoke sufficient for common business; every sentence he spoke or answer he made was attended by a smile and a slight bow, our men grave and stiff as pokers; on leaving us he gave us his best smile and a low bow in compliment to which our men nodded their heads which was all they could do. Our other neighbour Mr. Thorburn had been some time in the naval service, and had the frank manners of an english gentleman. He was about 35 years of age and had seen much of the world; he was glad to see us and have the pleasure of speaking english. From him during winter we obtained information on the fur trade of Canada. . . . We soon found our neighbours had greatly the advantage of us in carrying on the furr trade, five men in their large canoes brought twenty four pieces of goods, of which full one fourth was high wines (strong whisky) to which four times the quantity of water was added to make grog for the Indians. With us three men brought six pieces of goods of which one fourth was english brandy, a vile spirit to which only two waters could be added, a pint of which was reckoned of the value of a beaver skin whether in furs or in provisions, all expences were thus paid yet nearly have [half] of it was given away.

The Indians are fond of long clothing, one of our men was a tailor and made a great part of the cloth into coats that came to the knee. The natives had but few horses which were kept for hunting and bringing the meat to their tents. The Nahathaway women placed their goods in a kind of saddle bags which they tied on the dogs. The Stone Indians make a kind of sled of two pieces of short poles which they fasten onto the dogs on which they laid their baggage; and thus they marched when the tents were moved from place to place. The tents being of dressed leather were carried on horses, being too heavy for dogs. As the pitching track[19] often passed near ponds of water the dogs made a rush to drink and lie down to cool themselves. The women ran to prevent their wetting their baggage; and with a big stick drove them back, but more than half got in the pond, and when the women came to avoid a beating tried to swim out and would have drowned if the women had not taken them out, the old men laughing at the sport. . . . By the beginning of April the trade with the Indians was over and they pitched away for the plains to hunt the Bison and Deer, to make dried provisions and dressed leather for tents and clothing. As we expected the ice of the River soon to break up from the mildness of the weather and rising from the melting of the snow, the furrs were assorted and made into packs of 90 pounds under a wedge press, the provisions examined and the beat meat mixed with rendered grease of the Bison made into pimmecan, and placed in bags of well dried parchment skin, each bag weighing 90 pounds. Of this strong and wholesome food an englishman requires little more than a pound a day, but a Canadian eats nearly two pounds a day. About the tenth of April the ice gave way and we prepared to embark, but our neighbours told us the latter end of the month would be soon enough, as the ice below would not break up before the beginning of May. Each party appeared satisfied with the returns of the trade and early in May we all left for our several destinations; our neighbours for the Great carrying place on Lake Superior and our party for York Factory. When arrived at Cumberland House Mr. Tomison left three men and myself to pass the summer under the command of Mr. Hudson, who had been educated in the same mathematical school in which I was and like myself bound apprentice to the Hudson's Bay Company. He had been here about thirteen years, had lost all his education except reading and writing and the little of this, for the accounts of the trade appeared labor to him: he appeared in a state of apathy smoking tobacco mixed with weed, had no conversation with any person; the little business he had was done with few words and took no exercise. I was sadly disappointed in him.[20] When we left school a Hadley's quadrant and Robertson's elements of navigation in two volumes were presented to each scholar. These I had brought out with me, but when I left Churchill Factory, my blankets, gun and ammunition was a load enough for me to carry one hundred and fifty miles of marsh and mud to York Factory, and they were left to be forwarded by the first opportunity which never happened: they would have been invaluable to me. I enquired if he had his, he said they had vanished long ago: here again no book, not even a bible. During the winter at times we had much leisure and we employed it in playing at Draughts for which we had two chequer boards, one with twelve, the other with twenty four men on each side; it is a game of skill and I became expert at it. Having nothing to do, it was my constant employment; and for want of a companion frequently played by myself. A strange incident now happened to me and which some [times] happens to mankind which brings with it a strong influence on their conduct for the rest of their lives. I was sitting at a small table with the chequer board before me, when the devil sat down opposite to me,[21] his features and color were those of a Spaniard, he had two short black horns on his forehead which pointed forwards; his head and body down to his waist (I saw no more) was covered with glossy black curling hair, his countenance mild and grave; we began playing, played several games and he lost every game, kept his temper but looked more grave; at length he got up or rather disappeared. My eyes were open it was broad daylight, I looked around, all was silence and solitude, was it a dream or was it reality? I could not decide. Young and thoughtless as I was, it made a deep impression on my mind. I made no vow but took a resolution from that very hour never to play a game of chance, or skill or anything that had the appearance of them and I kept it. It is now upwards of sixty three years since and yet the whole of this strange incident is plain before me. I now assisted the men in their labors, learned to make and mend nets and set them for our livelihoods depended on our success in fishing. . . .

. . . The trading house from which we started was near the east side of the plains and we passed on the west side of the Eagle Hills from the river they rise about four hundred feet in undulating grassy ascents with very little wood. They are thus named from their west side having several isolated conical knowls on the tops of which the natives made shallow pits which they covered with slender willows and grass under which they lay with a large piece of fresh meat opposite their breasts; thus arranged they patiently await the flight of the eagle which is first seen very high, scaling in rude circles but gradually lowering till at length he seems determined to pounce upon the meat, his descent is then very swift and his claws extended, the moment he touches the meat the Indians grasp his two legs in his hands and dashes them through the slender willows to the bottom of the pit and strikes his head until he is dead. Lying in this position and frequently somewhat benumbed, it requires an active man to pull down an eagle with his wings expanded, and dash him to the ground. As the Eagle never loses his courage, the whole must be quickly done, or the Eagle will dart his beak in the man's face and thus get away, which sometimes happens. Hawks also are frequently taken in the same manner. The greatest plague to the Eagle catchers are the grey Foxes of the plains; they are almost as tame as dogs, and while the Indian is lying patiently looking at the sky watching the Eagle one or two of these Foxes suddenly jump on his breast and seize the piece of meat; a battle ensues in which his covering of willows and grass is destroyed. As the Foxes will be sure to return the Indian is obliged to shift his place to some other knoll, several miles off and there try his chance. . . . At length the Rocky Mountains came in sight like shining white clouds in the horizon but we doubted what our guide said, but as we proceeded they rose in height, their immense masses of snow appeared above the clouds and formed an impassible barrier, even to the Eagle. . . . A few miles beyond the Bow River about a dozen Peeagans met us; some of their scouts had seen us but could not say who were; they were well mounted and armed with Bows and quivers of arrows. They gave us a hearty welcome, told us to camp where they met us, and could soon bring us good cow meat, and next morning show us to the camp. Awhile after sunset they brought us two horse-loads of fat cow meat, we were hungry, and sat up part of the night roasting and eating: as it was a long month since we had a good meal.

Two of them passed the night with us and were an anxious for news as any people could be, it was on affairs more or less connected with the tribe to which they belonged, the situation and numbers of the tribes of other Indians; whether at peace or war, or any malady among them. Early the next morning the rest of the party came and conducted us to their camp, where we arrived about noon. All the elderly men came and gave us their left hand[22] and said they were thankful we had come, as they were in want of ammunition and tobacco. We separated ourselves two by two to three different tents where the most respectable men lived. William Flett and myself were lodged in the tent of an old man whose hair was grey with age, his countenance grave but mild and open; he was full six feet in height, erect and of a frame that shewed strength and activity.[23] When we related the scarcity of the Bison and Deer they were pleased at it and said it would be to them a plentiful winter. Their argument was; the Bison and Deer have passed the latter part of the summer and the fall of the leaves upon the Missisouri, and have made the ground bare of grass and can no longer live there; they must come to us for grass to live on in our country (the Bow River) and to the northward to the Kisiskatchewan where the snow is beginning to be on the ground. The winter proved that they reasoned right for by the beginning of December, the herds of bulls which always preceded the herds of cows began to pass us for the northward; and shortly after the Stags and small herds of Doe red Deer followed by Wolves and Foxes. After a few days the old man spoke to me in the Nahathaway language and asked me if I understood it and how long since I had left my own country. I answered this is my fourth winter, and the Nahathaways are the people we trade with, and I speak the tongue sufficiently for common purposes. Upon which, with a smile, he said I am not a Peeagan of these plains I am a Nahathaway of the Pasquiau River (a River that joins the Kisiskatchewan about fifty miles below Cumberland House) that is my native country and of my fathers for many many winters. I should have forgotten my mother's tongue were it not that some of my father's people come among us to buy horses and aid us in war. I told him I knew the country, had wintered near it and hunted Geese and Ducks in the Rivers he mentioned. He said it is many winters since I last saw the ground where my parents lie. I came here as a young man and my name is still the same I then received (Sark a map pee young man) as you know my country you can name the old men that now live there. I named three old men, but he knew nothing of them. I enquired if the Nahathaways did not give him news of his native country; he replied, they knew nothing of it and enquired what people were now hunting there. I informed him that the sons of those he left there hunted on the north bank of the River, many days march above it, that the lowest of them were on the west side of the Eagle Hills and that his country was now hunted upon by the Indians whom in his time were eastward of Lake Winipeg. He remained silent for some time and then said, What a stranger I now find myself in the land of my fathers. Although erect and somewhat active, and in full possession of his faculties, yet from the events he related and upon comparing them with the accounts of the french writers on the furr trade of Canada he must have been near ninety years of age, or more, for his relation of affairs went back to near the year one thousand seven hundred and this was now the year 1789.[24] (Note Between three and four years after this he died of old age). He was fond of conversation in his native tongue, and recounting the events of his life, the number and positions of the different tribes of Indians, how they were allied and the battles they had fought to gain the country of the Bow River (a distance in a direct line of about 800 miles in the direction of S54W).

Almost every evening for the time of four months I sat and listened to the old man without being in the least tired, they were blended with the habits customs and manners, politics and religion such as it was, anecdotes of Indian chiefs, and the means of their gaining influence in war and peace that I always found something to interest me. Upon the dreadful malady of the Small Pox whose ravages had ceased only a few years he did not wish to speak he said it was brought by a war party of their people who had attached a small party of the Snake Indians that had it and it spread from tent to tent and camp to camp. He appeared to have no Idea of contagion and expressed himself that his belief was the good Spirit had forsaken them for a time, during which the evil spirit destroyed them and this appeared the prevalent opinion amongst these people. . . .

One afternoon, early in January, there was a stir in the camp; and soon after we had the war song of victory sung by the young men one of whom entered the tent and spoke to the old man for a few minutes. After he went out the old man informed me that a large war party which had been absent for more than two moons had arrived at the frontier camp, and part of them would be here the morrow that they had seen no enemy but the Black People (the name they give to the Spaniards) from whom they had taken a great many horses and mules. I enquired if any battle had been fought; he smirked and said, No, they never fight they always ran away. I saw at a loss what to think on so brave a people as the Spaniards running away, and when some of the Horses and Mules were brought to us, I examined them but not the least trace of blood or any injury from weapons could be seen. A few days after Kootanne Appee paid a visit to the old man, on entering the tent he gave me his left hand, and I gave him my right hand, upon which he looked at me and smiled as much as to say a contest would not be equal; at his going away the some [same] took place. He passed about half an hour conversing on the late campaign and went away. No ceremony took place between them there behaviour was as if they had always lived in the same tent. The old man recommended me to his protection which he promised. He was apparently about forty years of age and his height between six feet two to four inches, more formed for activity then strength yet well formed for either; his face a full oval, high forehead and nose somewhat aquiline; his large black eyes, and countenance, were open, frank but somewhat stern; he was a noble specimen of the Indian warrior of the great plains. The old man told me he first gained his now high reputation by conducting the retreats of the war parties of his people when pressed on by superior numbers. Before he became head warrior, when obliged to retreat, each Chief with his party shifted for themselves and great distress often happened, this he had prevented by his speeches and conduct. His plan was to keep together round him a band of bold and resolute men with which he guarded the rear; and on perceiving the enemy becoming confident and not sufficiently cautious to lay an ambuscade, let some of the foremost pass, attack them in the rear; it was an onset of a very few minutes and in the confusion and dismay march off and join his people who stood ready to protect them. This checked the advance of the enemy and gave safety to the retreating party, and has thus gained the confidence of the people. On meeting the enemy he places his people according to the number of guns they have separating them along his post so that between each gun they should have the same number of archers. The great plains on which these encounters take place are too open for an ambuscade except by lying down in undulating grounds. The old man now remarked to me that as we proceed on we should see a great many Indians who had never seen a white man, as very few of them went to the trading houses. If one of our people offers you his left hand, give him your left hand, for the right hand is no mark of friendship. This hand wields the spear, draws the Bow and the trigger of the gun; it is the hand of death. The left hand is next to the heart and speaks truth and friendship, it holds the shield of protection and is the hand of life. . . .

. . . These fine plains will in time become the abode of Mankind, probably some civilized leading pastoral life tending Cattle and Sheep. The Farmer requires a considerable quantity of wood for buildings, fences and fuel and it is only in chance places even along the river side where such can be found. The farmer must place himself on the north side of these plains where he will have abundance of wood, and extend his farm into the plains as far as he pleases, say two miles. All the rest of these plains of 350 miles in length by about 38 [?] miles in breadth will be pastoral and inhabited by herdsmen and shepherds dwelling in round leather tents; moving from place to place as circumstances require, and finding in hollows and banks of brooks the little wood they want. . . . In the early part of August the Bison came form the southward and crossed the river to the north side, herd after herd, day and night, until these solitary plains where a chance deer was all that was to be seen became literally a moving mass of black cattle; they appeared very hungry and devoured the tender grass; even when started they ran only a short distance, then stopped and grazed. The Cows were fat and excellent meat. The younger Bulls kept near the cows, and were in tolerable order, but the old Bulls fed separate, poor and fero-cious. . . . The next year in the early part of March ['January' crossed out][25] on coming down a rude steep bank I fell and broke the large bone of my right leg and had to be hauled home, which by the mercy of God turned out to be the best thing that ever happened to me. Mr. Tomison behaved with the tenderness of a father to me and alleviated my sufferings all he could. As soon as the mild weather came on, and the river clear of ice, the furrs and canoes were got ready to proceed to York Factory and I descended the river to Cumberland House which at that time (1789) was not a depot and where I was left with two men to pass the summer and fish for our livelihood; . . . In the beginning of October two canoes arrived from York Factory, bringing Mess[s] Philip Turnor,[26] Hudson and Isham,[27] the former to survey the coun-try to the west end of the Athabasca Lake with Mr. Hudson for his assistant, the latter to take his [Hudson's] place as a furr trader. This was a fortunate arrival for me, as Mr. Turnor was well versed in mathematics, was one of the compilers of the nautical Almanacs and a practical astronomer. Under him I regained my mathematical education and during the winter became his only assistant and thus learned practical astronomy under an excellent master of the science. Mr. Hudson unfortunately for himself was too fond of an idle life, became dropsical and soon died.

By too much attention to calculations in the night with no other light than a small candle my right eye became so much inflamed that I lost its sight, and in the early part of May when the rivers and lakes became navigable, my health and strength were thought too weak to accompany Mr. Turnor as his assistant and a Mr. Peter Fidler took my place.[28] With the canoes and furrs I descended the Rivers and crossed the lakes &c. to York Factory, then under the charge of Mr. Humphrey Martin and took my station as clerk and accountant of the Factory.[29] A few days sufficed for all the writing and accounts. The rest of the year was spent in shooting Geese, Ducks and white Grouse.

I, iv: the Nahathaway Indians

Having passed six years[30] in different parts of this Region, exploring and surveying it, I may be allowed to know something of the natives, as well as the productions of the country. It's inhabitants are two distinct races of Indians; North of the latitude of fifty six degrees, the country is occupied by a people who call themselves 'Dinnie', by the Hudson Bay Traders 'Northern Indians' and by their southern neighbours 'Cheepawyans'. . . . Southward of the above latitude the country is in the possession of the Nahathaway Indians their native name (Note. These people by the French Canadians, who are all without the least education, in their jargon call them 'Krees' a name which none of the Indians can pronounce; this name appears to be taken from 'Keethisteno' so called by one of their tribes and which the french pronounce 'Kristeno', and by contraction Krees (R, rough, cannot be pronounced by any Native)[31] these people are separated into many tribes or extended families, under different names, but all speaking dialects of the same language, which extends over this stony region, and along the Atlantic coasts southward to the Delaware River in the United States, (the language of the Delaware Indians being a dialect of the parent Nahathaway) and by the Saskatchewan River westward, to the Rocky Mountains.[32] The Nathaway, as it is spoken by the southern tribes is softened and made more sonorous, the frequent th of the parent tongue is changed to the letter y as Neether (me) into Neeyer, Keether (thou) into Keeyer, Weether (him) into Weeyer, and as it proceeds southward [it] becomes almost a different language. It is easy of pronunciation, and is readily acquired by the white people for the purposes of trade, and common conversation.

The appearance of these people depends much on the climate and ease of subsistence. Around Hudson's Bay and near the sea coasts, where the climate is very severe, and game scarce, they are seldom above the middle size, of spare make, the features round, or slightly oval, hair black, strong and lank; eyes black and of full size, cheek bones rather high, mouth and teeth good, the chin round; the countenance grave yet with a tendency to cheerful, the mild countenances of the women make many, while young, appear lovely; but like the labouring classes[33] the softness of youth soon passes away. In the interior where the climate is not so severe, and hunting more successful, the Men attain to the stature of six feet; well proportioned, the face more oval, and the feature good, giving them a manly appearance; the complexion is of a light olive, and their colour much the same as a native of the south of Spain; the skin soft and smooth. They bear cold and exposure to the weather better than we do and the natural heat of their bodies is greater than ours, probably from living wholly on animal food. They can bear great fatigue but not hard labor, they would rather walk six hours over rough ground than work one hour with the pick axe and spade, and the labor they perform, is mostly in an erect posture as working with the ice chissel piercing holes through the ice or through a beaver house, and naturally they are not industrious; they do not work from choice, but necessity; yet the industrious of both sexes are praised and admired; the civilized man has many things to tempt him to an active life, an Indian has none, and is happy sitting still, and smoking his pipe. . . .

The natives in their manners are mild and decent, treat each other with kindness and respect, and very rarely interrupt each other in conversation; after a long separation the nearest relations meet each other with the same seeming indifference, as if they had constantly lived in the same tent, but they have not the less affection for each other, for they hold all show of joy, or sorrow to be unmanly; on the death of a relation, or friend, the women accompany their tears for the dead with piercing shrieks, but the men sorrow in silence, and when the sad pang of recollection becomes too strong to be borne, retire into the forest to give free vent to their grief. Those acts that pass between man and man for generous charity and kind compassion in civilized society, are no more than what is every day practised by these Savages; as acts of common duty; is any one unsuccessful in the chase, has he lost his little all by some accident, he is sure to be relieved by the others to the utmost of their power, in sickness they carefully attend each other to the latest breath decently . . . the dead. . . . [manuscript torn].

Of all the several distinct Tribes of Natives on the east side of the mountains, the Nahathaway Indians appear to deserve the most consideration; under different names the great families of this race occupy a great extent of country, and however separated and unknown to each other, they have the same opinions on religion, on morals, and their customs and manners differ very little. They are the only Natives that have some remains of ancient times from tradition. In the following account I have carefully avoided as their national opinions all they have learned from white men,[34] and my knowledge was collected from old men, whom with my own age extend backwards to upwards of one hundred years ago, and I must remark, that what [ever] other people may write as the creed of these natives, I have always found it very difficult to learn their real opinion on what may be termed religious subjects. Asking them questions on this head, is to no purpose, they will give the answer best adapted to avoid other questions, and please the enquirer. My knowledge has been gained when living and travelling with them and in times of distress and danger in their prayers to invisible powers, and their view of a future state of themselves and others, and like most of mankind, those in youth and in the prime of life think only of the present but declining manhood, and escapes from danger turn their thoughts on futurity.

After a weary day's march we sat by a log fire, the bright Moon, with thousands of sparkling stars passing before us, we could not help enquiring who lived in those bright mansions; for I frequently conversed with them as one of themselves; the brilliancy of the planets always attracted their attention, and when their nature was explained to them, they concluded them to be the abodes of the spirits of those who had led a good life.

A Missionary has never been among them, and my knowledge of their language has not enabled me to do more than teach the unity of God, and a future state of rewards and punishments; hell fire they do not believe, for they do not think it possible that any thing can resist the continued action of fire: It is doubtful if their language in its present simple state can clearly express the doctrines of Christianity in their full force. They believe[35] in the self existence of the Keeche Keeche Manito (The Great, Great Spirit) they appear to derive their belief from tradition, and [believe] that the visible world, with all it's inhabitants must have been made by some powerful being: but have not the same idea of his constant omnipresence, omniscience and omnipotence that we have, but [think] that he is so when he pleases, he is the master of life, and all things are at his disposal; he is always kind to the human race, and hates to see the blood of mankind on the ground, and sends heavy rain to wash it away. He leaves the human race to their own conduct, but has placed all other living creatures under the care of Manitos (or inferior Angels) all of whom are responsible to Him; but all this belief is obscure and confused, especially on the Manitos, the guardians and guides of every genus of Birds and Beasts; each Manito has a separate command and care, as one has the Bison, another the Deer; and thus the whole animal creation is divided amongst them. On this account the Indians, as much as possible, neither say, nor do anything to offend them, and the religious hunter, at the death of each animal, says, or does, something, as thanks to the Manito of the species for being permitted to kill it. At the death of a Moose Deer, the hunter in a low voice, cries 'wut, wut, wut'; cuts a narrow stripe of skin from off the throat, and hangs it up to the Manito. The bones of the head of a Bear are thrown into the water, and thus of other animals; if this acknowledgment was not made the Manito would drive away the animals from the hunter, although the Indians often doubt their power or existence yet like other invisible beings they are more feared than loved. They believe in ghosts but as very rarely seen, and those only of wicked men, or women; when this belief takes place, their opinion is, that the spirit of the wicked person being in a miserable state comes back to the body and round where he used to hunt; to get rid of such a hateful visitor, they burn the body to ashes and the ghost then no longer haunts them. The dark Pine Forests have spirits, but there is only one of them which they dread, it is the Pah kok, a tall hateful spirit, he frequents the depths of the Forest; his howlings are heard in the storm, he delights to add to its terrors, it is a misfortune to hear him, something ill will happen to the person, but when he approaches a Tent and howls, he announces the death of one of the inmates; of all beings he is the most hateful and the most dreaded. The Sun and

Moon are accounted Divinities and though they do not worship them, [they] always speak of them with great reverence. They appear to think [of] the Stars only as a great number of luminous points perhaps also divinities, and mention them with respect; they have names for the brightest stars, as Serius, Orion and others, and by them learn the change of the seasons, as the rising of Orion for winter, and the setting of the Pleiades for summer. The Earth is also a divinity, and is alive, but [they] cannot define what kind of life it is, but say, if it was not alive it could not give and continue life to other things and to animated creatures.

The Forests, the ledges and hills of Rock, the Lakes and Rivers have all something of the Manito about them, especially the Falls in the Rivers, and those to which the fish come to spawn. The Indians when the season is over, frequently place their spears at the Manito stone at the Fall, as an offering to the Spirit of the Fall, for the fish they have caught. These stones are rare, and sought after by the natives to place at the edge of a water fall; they are of the shape of a Cobler's lap stone, but much larger, and polished by the wash of the water. The 'Metchee Manito,' or Evil Spirit, they believe to be evil, delighting in making men miserable, and bringing misfortune and sickness on them, and if he had the power would wholly destroy them; he is not the tempter,[36] his whole power is for mischief to, and harrassing of, them, to avert all which they use many ceremonies, and other sacrifices, which consists of such things as they can spare, and sometimes a dog is painted and killed; whatever is given to him is laid on the ground, frequently at the foot of a pine tree. They believe in the immortality of the soul, and that death is only a change of existence which takes place directly after death. The good find themselves in a happy country, where they rejoin their friends and relations, the Sun is always bright, and the animals plenty; and most of them carry this belief so far, that they believe whatever creatures the great Spirit has made must continue to exist somewhere, and under some form; But this fine belief is dark and uncertain; when danger was certain, and it was doubtful if we saw the day, or if we saw it, whether we should live through it, and a future state appeared close to them, their minds wavered, they wished to believe what they felt to be uncertain, all that I could do was to show the immortality of the soul, as necessary to the reward of the good and punishment of the wicked but all this was the talk of man with man. It wanted the sure and sacred promise of the Heavenly Redeemer of mankind, who brought life and immortality to light.[37]

There is an important being, with whom the Natives appear better acquainted with than the other, whom they call 'Weesarkejauk' (the Flatterer) he is the hero of all their stories always promising them some good, or inciting them to some pleasure, and always deceiving them. They have some tradition of the Deluge, as may be seen from the following account related by the old men. After the Great Spirit made mankind, and all the animals, he told Weesarkejauk to take care of them and teach them how to live, and not to eat of bad roots; that would hurt and kill them; but he did not mind [obey] the Great Spirit; became careless and incited them to pleasure, mankind and the animals all did as they pleased, quarelled and shed much blood, with which the Great Spirit was displeased; he threatened Weesarkejauk that if he did not keep the ground clean he would take everything from him and make him miserable but he did not believe the Great Spirit and in a short time became more careless; and the quarrels of Men, and the animals made the ground red with blood, and so far from taking care of them he incited them to do and live badly; this made the Great Spirit very angry and he told Weesarkejauk that he would take every thing from him, and wash the ground clean; but still he did not believe; until the Rivers and Lakes rose very high and over flowed the ground for it was always raining; and the Keeche Gahme (the Sea) came on the land, and every man and animal were drowned, except one Otter, one Beaver and one Musk Rat. Weesarkejauk tried to stop the sea, but it was too strong for him, and he sat on the water crying for his loss, the Otter, the Beaver and the Musk Rat rested their heads on one of his thighs.

[The Otter and Beaver are sent to seek for solid land, but without success]. . . . Weesarkejauk was now very sad, for what the active Otter and strong Beaver could not do, he had little hopes the Musk Rat could do; but this was his only resource: He now praised the musk rat and promised him plenty of roots to eat, with rushes and earth to make himself a house; the Otter and the Beaver he said were fools, and lost themselves, and he would find the ground, if he went straight down. Thus encouraged he dived, and came up, but brought nothing; after reposing, he went down a second time, and staid a long time, on coming up Weesarkejauk examined his fore paws and found they had the smell of earth, and showing this to the Musk Rat, promised to make him a Wife, who should give him a great many children, and become more numerous than any other animal, and telling him to have a strong heart; and go direct down, the Musk Rat went down the third time and staid so long that Weesarkejauk feared he was drowned. At length seeing some bubbles come up, he put down his long arm and brought up the Musk Rat, almost dead, but to his great joy with a piece of earth between his fore paws and his breast, this he seized, and in a short time extended it to a little island, on which they all reposed. Some say Weesarkejauk procured a bit of wood, from which he made the Trees, and from bones, he made the animals; but the greater number deny this, and say, the Great Spirit made the rivers take the water to the Keeche gahma of bad water (the salt sea) and then renovated Mankind, the Animals, and the Trees; in proof of which, the Great spirit deprived him of all authority over Mankind and the animals, and he has since had only the power to flatter and deceive. It has been already noticed that this visionary being is the hero of many stories, which the women relate to amuse away the evenings. They are all founded upon the tricks he plays upon, and the mischief he leads the animals into, by flattering and deceiving them, especially the Wolf and the Fox. But the recital of the best of these stories would be tameness itself to the splendid Language and gorgeous scenery of the tales of the oriental nations.[38]

The Nahathaway Indians have also another tradition relative to the Deluge to which no fable is attached. In the latter end of May 1806, at the Rocky Mountain House,[39] (where I passed the summer) the Rain continued the very unusual space of full three weeks, the Brooks and the River became swollen, and could not be forded, each stream became a torrent, and [there was] much water on the ground: A band of these Indians were at the house, waiting [for] the Rain to cease and the streams to lower, before they could proceed to hunting; all was anxiety, they smoked and made speaches to the Great Spirit for the Rain to cease, and at length became alarmed at the quantity of water on the ground; at length the rain ceased, I was standing at the door watching the breaking up of the clouds, when of a sudden the Indians gave a loud shout, and called out 'Oh, there is the mark of life, we shall yet live.' On looking to the eastward there was one of the widest and most splendid Rainbows I ever beheld; and joy was now in every face. The name of the Rainbow is Peeshim Cappeah (Sun lines). I had now been twenty two years among them, and never before heard the name of the Mark of Life given to the rainbow (Peemah tisoo nan oo Chegun) nor have I ever heard it since; upon enquiring of the old Men why they kept this name secret from me, they gave me the usual reply, You white men always laugh and treat with contempt what we have heard and learned from our fathers, and why should we expose ourselves to be laughed at; I replied I have never done so, our books also call the Rainbow the mark of life; what the white sometimes despise you for, is your one day, making prayers to the Good Spirit for all you want; and another shutting yourselves up, making speeches with ceremonies and offerings to the Evil Spirit; it is for the worship of the Evil Spirit that we despise you, you fear him because he is wicked, and the more you worship him, the more power he will have over you; worship the Good Spirit only and the bad spirit will have no power over you. Ah, said they; he is strong, we fear for ourselves, our wives and our children. Christianity alone can eradicate these sad superstitions, and who will teach them. Where the Natives are in villages, or even where they occasionally assemble together for two, or three months; a Missionary may do some good, but the Natives who in a hard country live by hunting, scattered by three, or four families over a wide extent of forest, are beyond the labors of a Missionary; yet the influence of the white people have done much to lessen the worship and offerings to the Evil Spirit. From the french Canadians they cannot add to their morality, and the dreadful oaths and curses they make use of, shocks an Indian. The Indian, altho' naturally grave is fond of cheerful amusements, and listening to stories, especially of a wonderful cast; and [is] fond of news, which he listens to with attention, and his common discourse is easy and cheerful. Like the rest of mankind, he is anxious to know something of futurity, and [where] he shall take up his wintering ground. . . .

I found many of the Men, especially those who had been much in company with white men, to be all half infidels, but the Women kept them in order; for they fear the Manito's; All their dances have a religious tendency, they are not, as with us, dances of mere pleasure, of the joyous countenance: they are grave, each dancer considers it is a religious rite for some purpose; their motions are slow and graceful; yet I have sometimes seen occasional dances of a gay character; I was at their Tents on business, when the Women came and told me they wanted Beads and Ribbons, to which I replied I wanted Marten Skins; early the next morning, five young women set off to make Marten Traps; and did not return until the evening. They were rallyed [teased] by their husbands and brothers; who proposed they should dance to the Manito of the Martens, to this they willingly consented, it was a fine, calm, moonlight night, the young men came with the Rattle and Tambour, about nine women formed the dance, to which they sung with their fine voices, and lively they danced hand in hand in a half circle for a long hour; it is now many years ago, yet I remember this gay hour.

Every man believes or wishes to believe that he has a familiar being who takes care of him, and warns him of danger, and other matters which otherwise he could not know; this imaginary being he calls his Poowoggan; upon conversing with them on the Being on whom they relied; it appeared to me to be no other than the powers of his own mind when somewhat excited by danger or difficulty, especially as they suppose their dreams to be caused by him, 'Ne poo war tin' (I have dreamed); too often a troubled dream from a heavy supper; but at times they know how to dream for their own interest or convenience; and when one of them told me he had been dreaming it was for what he wished to have, or to do, for some favor, or as some excuse for not performing his promises, for so far as their interests are concerned they do not want policy.

When injured they are resentful, but not more than the lower classes of europeans. They frequently pass over injuries, and are always appeased with a present, unless blood has been shed, in this case however they may seem to forgive, they defer revenge to a more convenient opportunity; courage is not accounted an essential to the men, any more than chastity to the women, though both are sometimes found in a high degree. The greatest praise that one Indian can give to another is, that he is a man of steady humane disposition, and a fortunate hunter, and the praise of the women is to be active and good humoured; their marriages are without noise or ceremony. Nothing is requisite but the consent of the parties, and Parents: the riches of a man consists solely in his ability as a Hunter, and the portion of the woman is good health, and a willingness to relieve her husband from all domestic duties. Although the young men appear not to be passionate lovers, they seldom fail of being good husbands, and when contrariety of disposition prevails, so that they cannot live peaceably together, they separate with as little ceremony as they came together, and both parties are free to attach themselves to whom they will, without any stain on their characters; but if they have lived so long together so as to have children, one, or both, are severely blamed. Polygamy is allowed, and each may have as many wives as he can maintain, but few indulge themselves in this liberty, yet some have even three; this is seldom a matter of choice, it is frequently from the death of a friend who has left his wife, sister, or daughter to him, for every woman must have a husband. The children are brought up with great care and tenderness. They are very seldom corrected, the constant company and admonition of the old people is their only education, whom they soon learn to imitate on gravity as far as youth will permit; they very early and readily betake themselves to fishing and hunting, from both men and women impressing on their minds, that the man truly miserable is he, who is dependent on another for his subsistence. They have no genius for mechanics, their domestic utensils are all rude, their snow shoes and canoes show ingenuity which necessity has forced on them, the state of every thing with them rises no higher than absolute necessity, and in all probability their ancestors some hundred years ago, were equal to the present generation in the arts of life.

I, vi: *Thompson and his companions*

It may now [be well to] say something of myself, and of the character the Natives and the french Canadians entertained of me, they were almost my only companions. My instruments for practical astronomy, were a brass Sextant of ten inches radius, an achromatic Telescope of high power for observing the Satellites of Jupiter and other phenomena, one of the same construction for common use, Parallel glasses and quicksilver horizon for double Altitudes; Compass, Thermometer, and other requisite instruments,[40] which I was in the constant practice of using in clear weather for observations on the Sun, Moon, Planets and Stars; to determine the positions of the Rivers, Lakes, Mountains and other parts of the country I surveyed from Hudson Bay to the Pacific Ocean. Both Canadians and Indians often inquired of me why I observed the Sun, and sometimes the Moon, in the day time, and passed whole nights with my instruments looking at the Moon and Stars. I told them it was to determine the distance and direction from the place I observed to other places; neither the Canadians nor the Indians believed me; for both argued that if what I said was truth, I ought to look to the ground, and over it; and not to the Stars. Their opinions were, that I was looking into futurity and seeing every body, and what they were doing; how to raise the wind; but did not believe I could calm it, this they argued from seeing me obliged to wait the calming of the wind on the great Lakes, to which the Indians added that I knew where the Deer were, and other superstitious opinions. During my life I have always been careful not to pretend to any knowledge of futurity, and [said] that I knew nothing beyond the present hour; neither argument, nor ridicule had any effect, and I had to leave them to their own opinions and yet inadvertingly on my part, several things happened to confirm their opinions One fine evening in February two Indians came to the house to trade; the Moon rose bright and clear with the planet Jupiter a few degrees on it's east side; and the Canadians as usual predicted that Indians would come to trade in the direction of this star. To show them the folly of such predictions, I told them the same bright star, the next night, would be as far from the Moon on it's west side; this of course took place from the Moon's motion in her orbit; and is the common occurence of almost every month, and yet all parties were persuaded I had done it by some occult power to falsify the predictions of the canadians. Mankind are fond of the marvelous, it seems to heighten their character by relating they have seen such things. I had always admired the tact of the Indian in being able to guide himself through the darkest pine forests to exactly the place he intended to go, his keen, constant attention on every thing; the removal of the smallest stone, the bent or broken twig; a slight mark on the ground, all spoke plain language to him. I was anxious to acquire this knowledge, and often being in company with them, sometimes for several months, I paid attention to what they pointed out to me, and became almost equal to some of them; which became of great use to me. . . . The fact is Jean Baptiste will not think, he is not paid for it; when he has a minute's respite he smokes his pipe, his constant companion and all goes well; he will go through hardship, but requires a belly full, at least once a day, good Tobacco to smoke, a warm Blanket, and a kind

Master who will take his share of hard times and be the first in danger. Naval and Military Men are not fit to command them in distant countries,[41] neither do they place confidence in one of themselves as a leader; they always prefer an Englishman, but they ought always to be kept in constant employment however light it may be.

I, xi: The Great Plains

Hitherto the Reader has been confined to the sterile Stony Region and the great Valley of the Lakes.[42] My travels will now extend over countries of a very different formation; there are [called] the Great Plains as a general name, and are supposed to be more ancient than the Stony Region and the great Valley of the Lakes.

By a Plain I mean lands bearing grass, but too short for the Scythe; where the grass is long enough for the Scythe, and of which Hay can be made, I name [them] meadows. These Great Plains may be said to commence at the north side of the Gulph of Mexico, and extend northward to the latitude of fifty four degrees; where these plains are bounded by the Forests of the north, which extend unbroken to the arctic Sea.[43] On the east they are bounded by the Mississippe River, and northward of which by the valley of the lakes; and on the west by the Rocky Mountains. The length of these Plains from South to North is 1240 miles; and the breadth from east to west to the foot of the Mountains, from 550 to 800 miles giving an area to the Great Plains of 1,031,500 square miles, in which space the Ozark Hills are included. The perpetual snows and Glaciers of the Mountains, which everywhere border the west side of these Plains, furnish water to form many Rivers; all these south of the latitude of forty nine degrees flow into the Mississippe River, the most northern of which is the Missisourie River. Close northward to the sources of the Missisourie, are the south branches of the Saskatchewan River, which descends to Hudson's Bay. The next great Rivers northward are the Athabasca and Peace Rivers, which with other lesser streams form McKenzie's River, which empties itself into the Arctic Sea. It may be remarked among other great differencies between the Stoney Region and the Great Plains, that all the Rivers of the former Region, or that pass through it, meet with, and also form many Lakes and Falls, while all the Rivers in their courses through the Great Plains, and the northward forest lands, do not form a single Lake. Thus the three great Rivers of North America[44] enter different seas. . . .

So different are the courses of these Rivers on the same side of the Rocky Mountains from which they take their rise; and on entering the different seas into which they discharge their waters, they all appear of about equal magnitude. The east side of these Great Plains have a fine appearance, the soil is rich, with many extensive Meadows. A range of fine low Hills sufficiently well wooded, with many springs of fine water and Rivulets, which for small Rivers navigable to Canoes and Boates as the Dauphine, Swan, Mouse, and Stone Indian Rivers, with several Rivulets all flowing through a rich soil. The Hills are the Turtle Hill, the most southern, and not far from the Missisourie River. The next northward are the Hair, the Nut, the Touchwood, the Dauphine, the Eagle, and the Forrest Hills. The west side of these Hills, as seen from the Plains have gentle elevations of about two hundred fet; but as seen from the eastward, present an elevation of five to eight hundred feet above the common level, and have very fine Forrests of well grown trees of Birch, several kinds of Pine, Poplar, Aspin, and small Ash and Oaks. These Hills are the favourite resort of the Moose and the Red Deer, with two or three species of the Antelope.[45] The Black, Brown, and Yellow Bears feed on the Berries, the Nuts and any thing else they can catch; one of them was shot that was guarding part of an Antelope, which he had killed and partly eaten; how this clumsy brute could have caught so fleet an animal as the Antelope was a matter of wonder. The Bears lay up nothing for their subsistence in winter, and are then mostly dormant. As we travelled through the fine forests we were often amazed with the activity of the Squirrels collecting hazel nuts for their supply in winter, and of which each collects more than a bushel, whereas the Squirrels of the Pine Forests of the north seem to lay up nothing, but are out every day feeding on the cones of the White Pine. The Field Mice are also equally active in laying in store provisions for the winter. The climate is good, the winters about five months, the summers are warm, and autumn has many fine days. The soil is rich and deep, and [there is] much vegetable mould from the annual decay of the leaves of the Forest Trees, and the grass of the Meadows: Civilization will no doubt extend over these low hills; they are well adapted for raising of cattle; and when the wolves are destroyed, also for sheep; and agriculture will succeed to a pastoral life, so far as Markets can be formed in the country, but no further; for Canada is too distant and difficult of access. The only Port open to them is York Factory on the dismal shores of Hudson's Bay, open four months in the year. And to go to York Factory and return will require all that part of the summer which cannot be spared: but when a civilized population shall cover these countries, means will be found to make it's produce find a Market.[46]

From the gulph of Mexico to the Latitude of 44 degrees north, these Great Plains may be said to be barren for great spaces, even of coarse grass, but the cactus grows in abundance on a soil of sand and rolled gravel; even the several Rivers that flow through these plains do not seem to fertilise the grounds adjacent to them; These rivers are too broad in proportion to their depth and in autumn very shallow; the Mountains are comparatively low and therefore sooner exhausted of their winter snows, and travellers often suffer for want of water. But as one advances northward the soil becomes better, and the Missisourie River through its whole length to it's confluence with the Mississippe carries with it lands of deep soil, on which are many Villages of the Natives, who subsist partly by agriculture and partly by hunting. The course of the Missisourie is through an elevated part of these Plains, and it's great body of water has a swift current for about four miles an hour, which makes the ascent of this River in boats very laborious, although there are neither rapids, nor falls: Although the heads of this River give several passages across the Mountains yet from the labor being so great, and also [the being] exposed to attacks from hostile Indians, [it seems] that Steam Vessels are the only proper craft for this River; and even to these, it's many shoals and sands offer serious impediments, for it's waters are very turbid. From these there arises more vexation than danger; this latter is incurred every day by what are called Sawyers, Planters, and Snags,[47] names which have been ridiculed without offering better in their stead. But however these things may be laughed at, they are very serious obstacles to the navigation of this River, and also of the Mississippe. They all proceed from trees torn up by the roots, by the freshets from heavy rains, or the melting of the Snow. . . .

The Bow River[48] flows through the most pleasant of the Plains, and is the great resort of the Bison and the Red Deer, and also of the Natives; the soil appears good along it's whole extent, but for the most part is bare of Woods, and those that remain are fast diminishing by fire. The soil of the plains appears to continue increasing in depth, and the same through the Forests. In Latitude 56 degrees north, is the Smoke River, the great south branch of the Peace River; by the Gullies and Ravines the earth appears to have a depth of about 300 feet; Those who wish to find a material cause for this apparent increasing depth of earth from south to north; are led to suppose a great flood of water from the gulph of Mexico rushed northwards along the Mountains, denuded all the south parts of it's earth, leaving sand and rounded gravel for a soil; and carried the earth northward, where it has settled in great depth; here is a grand cause with a great effect. But how came the Rivers not to be defaced. The Rivers that roll through this immense unbroken body of land of Plains and Forests, are so beautifully distributed; all their banks so admirably adjusted to the volumes of water that flow between them, that neither the heaviest rains nor the melting Snows of the Mountains inundate the adjacent country. In all seasons, the Indians, the Bisons and Deer, repose on their banks in perfect security. Who ever calmly views the admirable formation and distribution of the Rivers so wonderfully conducted to their several seas; must confess the whole to have been traced by the finger of the Great Supreme Artificer for the most benevolent purposes, both to his creature Man, and the numerous Animals he has made, none of whom can exist without water. Water may be said to be one of the principal elements of life. . . .

Not a single fossil bone of an Elephant, Rhinocerous, or Mammoth has been found in all Canada nor about any of the Great Lakes, and valley of the [St.] Lawrence, and northward to the Arctic Circle, although almost all these countries are sufficiently known;[49] nor has the travels of Captain Franklin in the Arctic Regions been attended with any success on this subject. On the west side of the Rocky Mountains, I passed six years[50] of discovery, yet not a vestige that these great Animals once existed in those parts could be found. We may therefore conclude, that the great animals of North America were limited to the east and west sides of the Allegany Hills, and the east side of the valley of the Mississippe, and no farther to the northward and westward on this Continent: and that these were all destroyed by the Deluge, which also put an end to other races of animals and thus the Great Creator made the Earth more habitable for his favourite creature Man.

I, xii: Change on the Great Plains

. . . [We] journeyed to the Upper House on the Red Deer River . . . but the Ponds formed by the Beaver, and their Dams which we had to cross lengthened our Road to 150 miles; these sagacious animals were in full possession of the country, but their destruction had already begun, and was now in full operation. All the above Trading

Houses of the North West Company from Canada were on the south west sides of
the range of low Hills which border the east side of the Great Plains and hitherto all
my journeys were those of pleasure: The Moose Deer of these Hills, although always
a very wary animal, yet from their being more numerous, also from the Forests being
more open, were not the same cautious, timid, animal that it is in the close, dark,
Pine Forests of the north: aided perhaps, by being accustomed to see other species of
Deer and Horses; but the Stag[51] with his half dozen of Does, which he as carefully
guards, and is as ready to fight for, as any Turkish Pacha for his Harem, that is the
pride of these forests and meadows. But when the season of love is over, as now, his
Does leave him, his head droops, and [he] is no longer the lordly animal that appeared
as light on the ground as a Bird on the wing. On such a variety of Hill and Plain, of
Forests and Meadows I expected to have found several mineral Springs, which are so
frequent in other countries; but neither my attention to this object, nor my enquiries
could find one single Spring: all my information led only to the saline Brooks of the
Red River, from some of which salt is made by boiling the saline water. All those fine
countries are the hunting grounds of the Nahathaway Indians.

Previous to the discovery of Canada (about 320 years ago,) this Continent from the
Latitude of forty degrees north to the Arctic Circle, and from the Atlantic to the
Pacific Ocean, may be said to have been in the possession of two distinct races of
Beings, Man and the Beaver. Man was naked and had to procure clothing from the
skins of animals; his only arms were a Stake, pointed and hardened in the fire, a Bow
with Arrows, the points hardened with fire, or headed with stone or bone of the legs
of the Deer, a Spear headed in the same manner, and a club of heavy wood, or made
of a rounded stone of four, or five pounds weight, inclosed in raw hide, and by the
same bound round a handle of wood of about two feet in length, bound firm to the
Stone. Such were the weapons Man had for self defence and with which to procure
his food and clothing. Against the bones of an Animal his Arrows and Spear had little
effect; the flank of every animal is open, and thither, into the bowels, the Indian
directed his fatal and unerring Arrows. (Note. Every Hunter is acquainted with the
effects of wounds in the different parts of an animal; with an arrow in, or a ball
through, the bowels, an animal if pursued will go a long way: but if let alone, soon
becomes as it were sick, lies down on it's belly and there dies.) Besides his weapons,
the Snare was much in use, and the Spear to assist it for large animals, and by all
accounts the Deer and furr bearing animals were very numerous, and thus Man was
Lord of all the dry land and all that was on it. The other race was the Beaver, they
were safe from every animal but Man, and the Wolverine. Every year each pair
having from five to seven young, which they carefully reared, they become innumerable, and except the Great Lakes, the waves of which are too turbulent, occupied all
the waters of the northern part of the Continent. Every River where the current was
moderate and sufficiently deep, the banks of the water edge were occupied by their
houses. To every small Lake, and all the Ponds they builded Dams, and enlarged and
deepened them to the height of the dams, and made them permanent Ponds, and as
they heightened the dams [they] increased the extent and added to the depth of the
water; Thus all the low lands were in possession of the Beaver, and all the hollows of

the higher grounds. Small Streams were dammed across and Ponds formed; the dry land with the dominions of Man contracted, every where he was hemmed in by water without the power of preventing it: he could not diminish the numbers half so fast as they multiplied, and their houses were proof against his pointed stake, and his arrows could seldom pierce their skins. (Note. In my travels, several thousands of the Natives were not half so well armed.) In this state Man and the Beaver had been for many centuries, but the discovery of Canada by the French, and their settlements up the St Lawrence soon placed the Natives far superior to the Beaver.

Without Iron, man is weak, very weak, but armed with Iron, he becomes the Lord of the Earth, no other metal can take it's place. For the furrs which the Natives traded, they procured from the French Axes, Chissels, Knives, Spears and other articles of iron, with which they made good hunts of furr bearing animals and procured woollen clothing. Thus armed the houses of the Beavers were pierced through, the Dams cut through, and the water of the Ponds lowered, or wholly run off, and the houses of the Beaver and their Borrows laid dry, by which means they became an easy prey to the Hunter. . . .

. . . I return to my travels in the Nut Hill; on a fine afternoon in October, the leaves beginning to fall with every breeze, a season to me of pleasing melancholy, from the reflections it brings to the mind; my guide informed me that we would have to pass over a long beaver Dam; I naturally expected we should have to load our Horses carefully over it; when we came to it, we found it a narrow stripe of apparently old solid ground, with short grass, and wide enough for two horses to walk abreast: we passed on, the lower side showed a descent of seven feet, and steep, with a rill of water from beneath it. The side of the dam next to the water was a gentle slope. To the southward was a sheet of water of about one mile and a half square of area, surrounded by moderate, low grassy banks, the Forests mostly of Aspin and Poplar but very numerous stumps of the trees cut down and partly carried way by the Beavers. In two places of this Pond were a cluster of Beaver Houses, like miniature villages. When we had proceeded over more than half way of the Dam, which was a full mile in length, we came to an aged Indian, his arms folded across his breast; with a pensive countenance, looking at the Beavers swiming in the water, and carrying their winter's provisions to their houses, his form tall and erect, his hair almost white, which was almost the only effect that age appeared to have on him, though we concluded he must be about eighty years of age, and in this opinion we were afterwards confirmed by the ease and readiness with which he spoke of times long past. I enquired of him how many beaver houses there were in the pond before us, he said, There are now fifty two, we have taken several of their houses; they are difficult to take, and those we have taken were by means of the noise of the water on their houses from a strong wind which enabled us to stake them in, otherwise they would have retired to their burrows, which are very many. He invited us to pass the night at his tent which was close by, the Sun was low, and we accepted the offer.

In the Tent was an old man, almost his equal in age with women and children; we preferred the open air, and made a good fire to which both of the old men came, and after smoking a while conversation came on. As I had always conversed with the

Natives as one Indian with another, and been attentive to learn their traditions on the animals on Mankind, and on other matter in ancient times, and the present occasion appeared favorable for this purpose. Setting aside questions and answers which would be tiresome; they said, by ancient tradition of which they did not know the origen the Beavers had been an ancient people, and then lived on the dry land; they were always Beavers, not Men, they were wise and powerful, and neither Man, nor any animal made war on them.

They were well clothed as at present, and as they did not eat meat, they made no use of fire, and did not want it. How long they lived this way we cannot tell, but we must suppose they did not live well, for the Great Spirit became angry with them, and ordered Weesaukejauk to drive them all into the water and there let them live, still to be wise, but without power; to be food and clothing for man, and the prey of other animals, against all which his defence shall be his dams, his house and his burrows: You see how strong he makes his dams, those that we make for fishing wiers are often destroyed by the water, but his always stands. His House is not made of sand, or loose stones, but of strong earth with wood and sometimes small stones; and he makes burrows to escape from his enemies, and he always has his winter stock of provisions secured in good time. When he cuts down a tree, you see how he watches it, and takes care that it shall not fall on him. 'But if so wise, for what purpose does the Beaver cut down large trees of which he makes no use whatever.' We do not know, perhaps an itching of his teeth and gums.

The old Indian paused, became silent, and then in a low tone [they] talked with each other; after which he continued his discourse. I have told you that we believe in years long passed away, the Great Spirit was angry with the Beaver, and ordered Weesaukejauk (the Flatterer) to drive them all from the dry land into the water; and they became and continued very numerous; but the Great Spirit has been, and now is, very angry with them and they are now all to be destroyed. About two winters ago Weesaukejauk showed to our brethren, the Nepissings and Algonquins the secret of their destruction; that all of them were infatuated with the love of the Castorum of their own species, and more fond of it than we are of fire water. We are now killing the Beaver without any labor, we are now rich, but [shall] soon be poor, for when the Beaver are destroyed we have nothing to depend on to purchase what we want for our families, strangers now over run our country with their iron traps, and we, and they will soon be poor:[52]

The Indian is not a materialist, nor does he believe in Instinct, a word of civilized man, which accounts for great part of the actions of Mankind, and of all those of animated nature; the Indian believes that every animal has a soul which directs all it's motions, and governs all it's actions; even a tree, he conceives must somehow be animated, though it cannot stir from it's place. Some three years ago (1797)[53] the Indians of Canada and New Brunswick, on seeing the Steel Traps so successful in catching Foxes and other animals, thought of applying it to the Beaver, instead of [using] the awkward traps they made, which often failed; At first they were set in the landing paths of the Beaver, with about four inches of water on them, and a piece of green aspin for a bait, and in this manner more were caught than by the common way; but the beaver paths made their use too limited and their ingenuity was employed to find a bait that would allure the Beaver to the place of the trap; various things and mixtures of ingredients were tried without success; but chance made some try if the male could not be caught by adding the Castorum of the female; a mixture of this Castorum beat up with the green buds of the aspin was made. A piece of dry willow of about eight inches in length beat and bruised fine, was dipped in the mixture, it was placed on the water edge about a foot from the steel trap, so that the Beaver should pass direct over it and be caught; this bait proved successful, but to the surprise of the Indians, the females were caught as well as the males: The secret of this bait was soon spread, every Indian procured from the Traders four to six steel traps, and weight of one was about six to eight pounds, all labor was now at an end, the Hunter moved about at pleasure with his traps and infallible bait of Castorum. . . .

The Nepissings, the Algonquins and Iroquois Indians having exhausted their own countries, now spread themselves over these countries, and as they destroyed the Beaver, moved forwards to the northward and westward; the Natives, the Nahathaways, did not in the least molest them; the Chippaways and other tribes made use of Traps of Steel; and of the Castorum. For several years all these Indians were rich, the Women and Children, as well as the Men, were covered with silver brooches, Ear Rings, Wampum, Beads and other trinkets. Their mantles were of fine scarlet cloth, and all was finery and dress. The Canoes of the Furr Traders were loaded with packs of Beaver, the abundance of the article lowered the London prices. Every intelligent Man saw the poverty that would follow the destruction of the Beaver, but there were no Chiefs to controul it; all was perfect liberty and equality. Four years afterwards (1797)[54] almost the whole of these extensive countries were denuded of Beaver, the Natives became poor, and with difficulty procured the first necessaries of life, and in this state they remain, and probably for ever. A worn out field may be manured, and again made fertile; but the Beaver, once destroyed cannot be replaced: they were the gold coin of the country, with which the necessaries of life were purchased.

I, xxiii: The Piegans and Kootenae Appe[55]

The Peeagans, with the tribes of the Blood, and Blackfeet Indians, who all speak the same language, are the most powerful of the western and northern plains, and by right of conquest have their west boundary to the foot of the Rocky Mountains, southward to the north branches of the Missisourie, eastward for about three hundred miles from the Mountains and northward to the upper part of the Saskatchewan. Other tribes of their allies also at times hunt on part of the above, and a great extent of the Plains, and these great Plains place them under different circumstances, and give them peculiar traits of character from those that hunt in the forests. These latter live a peaceable life, with hard labor, to procure provisions and clothing for their families, in summer they make use of canoes, and in winter haul on sleds all they have, in their frequent removals from place to place. On the other hand the Indians of the Plains make no use of canoes, frequently stay many days in a place, and when they remove have horses and dogs, both in summer and winter to carry their baggage and provisions: they have no hard labor, but have powerful enemies which keep them constantly on the watch and are never secure but in large camps. The manners and customs of all these tribes of the Plains, are much alike, and in giving those of the Peeagans, it may serve for all the others. Being the frontier tribe, they lead a more precarious and watchful life than other tribes, and from their boyhood are taught the use of arms, and to be good warriors, they become martial and more moral than the others, and many of them have a chivalrous bearing, ready for any enterprise. They have a civil and military Chief. The first was called Sakatow, the orator, and [the office] appeared hereditary in his family, as his father had been the civil Chief, and his eldest son was to take his place at his death and occasionally acted for him. The present chief was now about sixty years of age (1800) about five feet ten inches in height, remarkably well made, and in his youth a very handsome man. He was always well dressed, and his insignia of office, was the backs of two fine Otter skins covered with mother of pearl, which from behind his neck hung down his breast to below the belt; When his son acted for him, he always had this ornament on him. In every council he presided, except one of War. He had couriers which went from camp to camp, and brought the news of how things were, of where the great herds of Bisons were feeding, and of the direction they were taking. The news thus collected, about two or three hours after sun set, walking about the camp, he related in a loud voice, making his comments on it, and giving advice when required. His language was fluent, and he was admired for his eloquence, but not for his principles and his advice could not be depended on, being sometimes too violent, and more likely to produce quarrels than to allay them yet his influence was great.

The War Chief was Kootanae Appe (Kootanae Man) his stature was six feet six inches, tall and erect, he appeared to be of Bone and Sinew with no more flesh, than absolutely required; his countenance manly, but not stern, his features prominent, nose somewhat aquiline, his manners kind and mild; his word was sacred, he was both loved and respected, and his people often wished him to take a more active part in their affairs but he confined himself to War, and the care of the camp in which he was, which was generally of fifty to one hundred tents, generally a full day's march nearer to the Snake Indians than any other camp. It was supposed he looked on the civil Chief with indifference as a garrulous old man more fit for talking than any thing else, and they rarely camped together. Kootanae Appe by his five wives had twenty two sons and four daughters. His grown up sons were as tall as himself and the others promised the same. He was friendly to the White Men, and in his speeches reminded his people of the great benefit of [which] the Traders were to them, and that it was by their means they had so many useful articles, and guns for hunting, and to conquer their enemies. He had acquired his present station and influence from his conduct in war. He was utterly averse to small parties, except for horse stealing, which too often brought great hardships and loss of life. He seldom took the field with less than two hundred warriors but frequently with many more; his policy was to get as many of the allies to join him as possible, by which all might have a share of the honour and plunder, and thus avoid those jealousies and envying so common amongst the Chiefs. He praised every Chief that in the least deserved it, but never appeared to regard fame as worth his notice yet always took care to deserve it, for all his exped[it]ions were successful. . . .

II, i: *Thompson crosses the Rocky Mountains*

I believe that I have said enough [about the country] on the east side of the Mountains; I shall therefore turn to the west side; I have already related how the Peeagans watched us to prevent our crossing the Mountains and arming the Natives on that side; in which for a time they succeeded, and we abandoned the trading Post near the Mountains in the spring of 1807; the murder of two Peagan Indians by Captain Lewis of the United States, drew the Peagans to the Mississouri to revenge their deaths; and thus gave me an opportunity to cross the Mountains by the defiles of the Saskatchewan River, which led to the head waters of the Columbia River, and we there builded Log Houses, and strongly stockaded it on three sides, the other side resting on the steep bank of the River. . . . The Stockades were all ball proof, as well as the Logs of the Houses. . . .

In my new dwelling I remained quiet hunting the wild Horses, fishing, and examining the country; two Canoes of goods arrived for trade, on Horses, by the defiles of the Saskatchewan River; half of these goods under the charge of Mr. Finan McDonald I sent to make a trading Post at a considerable Lake in McGillivray's River; the season was late, and no more could be done; about the middle of November two Peeagans crossed the Mountains on foot and came to the House, to see how I was situated; I showed the strength of the Stockades, and Bastions, and told them I know you are come as Spies, and intend to destroy us, but many of you will die before you do so; go back to your countrymen and tell them so; which they did, and we remained quiet for the winter; I knew the danger of the place we were in, but could not help it: As soon as the Mountains were passable I sent off the Clerk and Men with the Furrs collected, among which were one hundred of the Mountain Goat Skins with their long silky hair, of a foot in length of a white color, tinged at the lower end with a very light shade of yellow. Some of the ignorant self sufficient partners of the Company ridiculed such an article for the London Market; there they went and sold at first sight for a guinea a skin, and half as much more for another Lot, but there were no more. These same partners then wrote to me to procure as many as possible, I returned for [as my] answer, the hunting of the goat was both dangerous and laborious, and for their ignorant ridicule I would send no more, and I kept my word.

I had now to prepare for a more serious visit from the Peagans who had met in council, and it was determined to send forty men, under a secondary Chief to destroy the trading Post, and us with it, they came and pitched their Tents close before the Gate, which was well barred. I had six men with me, and ten guns, well loaded, the House was perforated with large augur holes, as well as the Bastions, thus they remained for three weeks without daring to attack us. We had a small stock of dried provisions which we made go as far as possible; they thought to make us suffer for want of water as the bank we were on was about 20 feet high and very steep, but at night, by a strong cord we quietly and gently let down two brass Kettles each holding four Gallons, and drew them up full; which was enough for us: They were at a loss what to do, for Kootanae Appee the War Chief, had publickly told the Chief of this party, (which was formed against his advice) to remember he had Men confided to his care, whom he must bring back, that he was sent to destroy the Enemies not to lose his Men: Finding us always on the watch, they did not think proper to risque their lives, when at the end of three weeks they suddenly decamped; I thought it a ruse de guerre, I afterwards learned that some of them hunting saw some Kootanaes who were also hunting, and as what was done was an act of aggression, something like an act of War; they decamped to cross the mountains to join their own Tribe while all was well with them: the return of this party without success occasioned a strong sensation among the Peeagans. The Civil Chief harangued them, and gave his advice to form a strong war party under Kootanae Appe the War Chief and directly to crush the white Men and the Natives on the west side of the Mountains, before they became well armed, They have always been our slaves (Prisoners) and now they will pretend to equal us; no, we must not suffer this, we must at once crush them. We know them to be desperate Men, and we must destroy them, before they become too powerful for us; the War Chief coolly observed I shall lead the battle according to the will of the Tribe, but we cannot smoke to the Great Spirit for success, as we usually do, it is now about ten winters since we made peace with them, they have tented and hunted with us, and because they have guns and iron headed Arrows, we must break our word of peace with them: We are now called upon to go to war with a people better armed than ourselves; be it so, let the Warriors get ready; in ten nights I will call on them. The old, and the intelligent Men, severely blamed the speech of the Civil Chief, they remarked, 'the older he gets, the less sense [he possesses].' On the ninth night the War Chief made a short speech, to have each man to take full ten days of dried provisions, for we shall soon leave the country of the Bison, after which we must not fire a shot, or we shall be discovered: On the tenth night he made his final speech, and exhorting the Warriors and their Chiefs to have their Arms in good order, and not forget dried provisions, he named a place; there I shall be the morrow evening, and those who now march with me, there I shall wait for you five nights, and then march to cross the Mountains; at the end of this time about three hundred Warriors under three Chiefs assembled; and took their route across the Mountains by the Stag River, and by the defiles of another River of the same name, came on the Columbia, about full twenty miles from me; as usual, by another pass of the Mountains, they sent two Men to see the strength of the House; I showed them all round the place, and they staid that night. I plainly saw that a War Party was again formed, to be better conducted than the last; and I prepared Presents to avert it: the next morning two Kootanae Men arrived, their eyes glared on the Peagans like Tigers, this was most fortunate; I told them to sit down and smoke which they did; I then called the two Peagans out, and enquired of them which way they intended to return. They pointed to the northward. I told them to go to Kootanae Appee and his War Party, who were only a days journey from us, and delivering to them the Presents I had made up, to be off directly, as I could not protect them, for you know you are on these lands as Enemies; the Presents were six feet of Tobacco to the Chief, to be smoked among them, three feet with a fine pipe of red porphyry and an ornamented Pipe Stem; eighteen inches to each of the three Chiefs, and a small piece to each of themselves, and telling them they had no right to be in the Kootanae Country: to haste away; for the Kootanaes would soon be here, and they will fight for their trading Post: In all that regarded the Peeagans I chanced to be right, it was all guess work. Intimately acquainted with the Indians, the Country and the Seasons, I argued and acted on probabilities; I was afterward informed that the two Peeagans went direct to the camp of the War Party, delivered the Presents and the Message and sat down, upon which the War Chief exclaimed, what can we do with this man, our women cannot mend a pair of shoes, but he sees them, alluding to my Astronomical Obser-vations; then in a thoughtful mood he laid the pipe and stem, with the several pieces of Tobacco on the ground, and said, what is to be done with these, if we proceed, nothing of what is before us can be accepted; the eldest of [the] three Chiefs, wistfully eyeing the Tobacco, of which they had none; at length he said, You all know me, who I am, and what I am; I have attacked Tents, my knife could cut through them, and our enemies had no defence against us, and I am ready to do so again, but to go and fight against Logs of Wood, that a Ball cannot go through, and with people we cannot see and with whom we are at peace, is what I am averse to, I go no further. He then cut the end of the Tobacco, filled the red pipe, fitted the stem, and handed it to Kootanae Appee, saying it was not you that brought us here, but the foolish Sakatow (Civil Chief) who, himself never goes to War; they all smoked, took the Tobacco, and returned, very much to the satisfaction of Kootanae Appe my steady friend; thus by the mercy of good Providence I averted this danger; Winter came on, the Snow covered the Mountains, and placed us in safety: The speeches of the Indians on both sides of the Mountains are in plain language, sensible and to the purpose; they sometimes repeat a few sentences two or three times, this is to impress on the hearers the object of the speech; but I never heard a speech in the florid, bombastic style, I have often seen published as spoken to white men, and upon whom it was intended to have an effect. Although through the mercy of Providence we had hitherto escaped, yet I saw the danger of my situation. I therefore in the early part of the next spring took precautions to quit the place.

II, vi: Thompson passes over the Continental divide

November 2nd.[56] . . . Our whole attention for the present was turned to hunting and securing provisions; having now made Snow Shoes, and Sleds, on the 30th day of December [1810] we commenced our journey to cross the Mountains and proceeded up the Athabasca River, sometimes on it's shoals and ice, and at times through the woods of it's banks. The soil was sandy and a Gale of Wind drifted it to lie on the low branched pines, of wretched growth, for Snow does not lie on Sand Hills; On the 31st December we proceeded but slowly and I had to reduce the weight of the Loads of the Dogs to less than two thirds, and make a Log Hoard to secure what we left. This, the work of two hours the men took five hours to finish, during which time they cooked twice a four gallon Kettle full of Meat, which they devoured, although they had had a hearty breakfast, in fact a french Canadian has the appetite of a Wolf, and glories in it; each man requires eight pounds of meat p^r day, or more; upon my reproaching some of them with their gluttony, the reply I got was, 'What pleasure have we in Life but eating'. A French Canadian if left to himself, and living on what his Master has, will rise very early make a hearty meal, smoke his pipe, and lie down to sleep, and he will do little else through the day: to enumerate the large animals that had been killed, and I may say devoured by my men would not be credible to a man of a regular life, yet these same hardy canadians, as future years proved to me, could live upon as little as any other person. In their own houses in Canada a few ounces of Pork, with plenty of coarse bread and Potatoes is sufficient for the day, and [they are] contented. Yet the same Men when with me on government surveys, where the allowance was one pound of mess Pork (the best) one and a half pound of good fresh Biscuit and a half a pound of pease, did not find it too much, and the evening of each day left nothing. Thus ended the year [1810]. . . .

Jany 5th. Thermometer –26 very cold. Having secured the goods and provisions we could not take with us, by 11 AM set off with eight Sleds, to each two dogs, with goods and Provisions to cross the Mountains, and three Horses to assist us as far as the depth of Snow will permit. We are now entering the defiles of the Rocky Mountains by the Athabasca River, the woods of Pine are stunted, full of branches to the ground, and the Aspin, Willow &c not much better: strange to say, here is a strong belief that the haunt of the Mammoth, is about this defile, I questioned several, none could positively say, they had seen him, but their belief I found firm and not to be shaken. I remarked to them, that such an enormous heavy Animal must leave indelible marks of his feet, and his feeding. This they all acknowledged, and that they had never seen any marks of him, and therefore could show me none. All I could say did not shake their belief in his existence.

January 6th. We came to the last grass for the Horses in Marshes and along small Ponds, where a herd of Bisons had lately been feeding; and here we left the Horses poor and tired, and notwithstanding the bitter cold, [they] lived through the winter, yet they have only clothing of close hair, short and without any furr. . . .

Janu[ar]y 8th. A fine day. We are now following the Brooks in the open defiles of the secondary Mountains; when we can no longer follow it, the road is to cross a point of high land, very fatigueing, and come on another Brook, and thus in succession; these secondary Mountains appear to be about 2 to 3000 feet above their base, with patches of dwarf pines, and much snow; we marched ten miles today; and as we advance we feel the mild weather from the Pacific Ocean. This morning at 7 AM Ther +6 at 9 PM +22. One of my men named Du Nord beat a dog to death, he is what we call a 'flash' man, a showy fellow before the women but a coward in heart, and would willingly desert if he had courage to go alone; very glutinous and requires full ten pounds of meat each day. And as I am constantly ahead [I] cannot prevent his dog flogging and beating: We saw no tracks of Animals.

January 9th. Ther + 32. SE wind and snowed all day which made hauling very bad. We could proceed only about four miles, this partly up a brook and then over a steep high point with dwarf pines. We had to take only half a load and return for the rest. The snow is full seven feet deep, tho' firm and wet, yet the Dogs often sunk in it, but our snow shoes did [not] sink more than three inches; and the weather so mild that the snow is dropping from the trees, and everything wet; here the Men finished the last of the fresh and half dried Meat, which I find to be eight pounds for each man p^r day. Ther + 22.

January 10th. Ther + 16. A day of Snow and southerly Gale of wind, the afternoon fine, the view now before us was an ascent of deep snow, in all appearance to the height of land between the Atlantic and Pacific Oceans, it was to me a most exhilarating sight, but to my uneducated men a dreadful sight, they had no scientific object in view, their feelings were of the place they were; our guide Thomas told us, that although we could barely find wood to make a fire, we must now provide wood to pass the following night on the height of the defile we were in, and which we had to follow; my men were the most hardy that could be picked out of a hundred brave hardy Men, but the scene of desolation before us was dreadful, and I knew it, a heavy gale of wind much more a mountain storm would have buried us beneath it, but thank God the weather was fine, we had to cut wood such as it was, and each took a little on his sled, yet such was the despondency of the Men, aided by the coward Du Nord, sitting down at every half mile, that when night came, we had only wood to make a bottom, and on this to lay wherewith to make a small fire, which soon burnt out and in this exposed situation we passed the rest of a long night without fire, and part of my men had strong feelings of personal insecurity, on our right about one third of a mile from us lay an enormous Glacier, the eastern face of which quite steep, of about two thousand feet in height, was of a clean fine green color, which I much admired but whatever was the appearance, my opinion was, that the whole was not solid ice, but formed on rocks from rills of water frozen in their course; westward of this steep face, we could see the glacier with it's fine green color and it's patches of snow in a gentle slope for about two miles; eastward of this glacier and near to us, was a high steep wall of rock, at the foot of this, with a fine south exposure had grown a little Forest of Pines of about five hundred yards in length by one hundred in breadth, by some avalanche they had all been cut clean off as with a scythe, not one of these trees appeared an inch higher than the others. My men were not at their ease, yet when night came they admired the brilliancy of the Stars, and as one of them said, he thought he could almost touch them with his hand: as usual, when the fire was made I set off to examine the country before us, and found we had now to descend the west side of the Mountains; I returned and found part of my Men with a Pole of twenty feet in length boring the Snow to find the bottom; I told them while we had good Snow Shoes it was no matter to us whether the Snow was ten or one hundred feet deep. On looking into the hole they had bored, I was surprised to see the color of the sides of a beautiful blue; the surface was of a very light color, but as it descended the color became more deep, and at the lowest point was of a blue, almost black. The altitude of this place above the level of the Ocean, by the point of boiling water is computed to be eleven thousand feet (Sir George Simpson). Many reflections came on my mind; a new world was in a manner before me, and my object was to be at the Pacific Ocean before the month of August, how were we to find Provisions, and how many Men would remain with me, for they were dispirited, amidst various thoughts I fell asleep on my bed of Snow.

Early next morning we began our descent, here we soon found ourselves not only with a change of climate, but more so of Forest Trees, we had not gone half a mile before we came to fine tall clean grown Pines of eighteen feet girth. The descent was so steep that the Dogs could not guide the Sleds, and often came across the Trees with some force, the Dogs on one side and the Sled on the other, which gave us some trouble to disentangle them; after a hurried day's march down the mountain we came, on a Brook and camped on the Snow, it being too deep to clear away.

Janu[ar]y 13th. . . . Thus we continued day after day to march a few miles, as the Snow was too wet and too deep to allow the dogs to make any progress; on the 26th we put up on the banks of the Columbia River, my Men had become so disheartened, sitting down every half mile, and perfectly lost at all they saw around them so utterly different from the east side of the Mountains, four of them deserted to return back; and I was not sorry to be rid of them, as for more than a month past they had been very useless, in short they became an incumbrance on me, and the other men were equally so to be rid of them; having now taken up my residence for the rest of the winter I may make my remarks on the countries and the climates we have passed. . . .

The east side of the Mountains is formed of long slopes, very few in this defile that are steep; but the west side is more abrupt, and has many places that require steady sure footed Horses, to descend it's banks in the open season: one is tempted to enquire what may be the volume of water contained in the immense quantities of snow brought to, and lodged on, the Mountains, from the Pacific Ocean, and how from an Ocean of salt water the immense evaporation constantly going on is pure fresh water; these are mysterious operations on a scale so vast that the human mind is lost in the contemplation.

II, xx: Thompson reviews his own work, July 14, 1811[57]

Thus I have fully completed the survey of this part of North America from sea to sea, and by almost innumerable astronomical Observations have determined the positions of the Mountains, Lakes and Rivers, and other remarkable places of the northern part of this Continent; the Maps of all of which have been drawn, and laid down in geographical position, being now the work of twenty-seven years.

Notes

[1] Fort Prince of Wales; see UMFREVILLE, HEARNE.

[2] William Wales (c. 1734–1798) was the first scientist to winter in Hudson Bay; he spent a year at Churchill in 1768–9 to observe the transit of Venus over the sun on 3 June 1769. During his

later distinguished career (which included teaching mathematics to Charles Lamb, Leigh Hunt, and Coleridge) he remained a source of contact between men of the Company and British scientific life.

³ For the capture of Fort Prince of Wales by Jean-François de Galoup, Comte de La Pérouse see UMFREVILLE, HEARNE. Thompson's contempt for Hearne is apparent in the early pages of his narrative, and its justice has been debated; they seem to have been of very different temperaments.

⁴ HEARNE's second-in-command at Fort Prince of Wales.

⁵ François Marie Arouet de Voltaire (1694–1778), *Dictionnaire philosophique portatif* (1764). Thompson's objections to Hearne's views can be guessed from the subtitle added to the English translation published in 1765, 'containing a refutation of such passages as are in any way exceptionable in regard to religion'.

⁶ One of the gentlemen's clubs of London, some of which originated in early eighteenth-century societies of rakes and free-thinkers.

⁷ Tyrrell observes that wood was scarce on the Churchill, where the traders had been burning trees faster than they could grow since the fort's foundation.

⁸ Grouse: Thompson means the Willow Ptarmigan (*Lagopus lagopus*) and the Rock Ptarmigan (*Lagopus motus*).

⁹ Walrus.

¹⁰See SAMUEL HEARNE.

¹¹Thompson has confused his school-mate George Charles (who apparently never made any surveys of the interior) with the later John Charles, who was a Company trader from 1799 to 1842.

¹²Alexander Dalrymple (1737–1808), hydrographer to the Admiralty from 1795 until his death, had an important influence on geographical theory in his time. He was a severe critic of Hearne's geographical work.

¹³The reflecting quadrant was invented in 1730 by the British mathematician John Hadley (1682–1744), who had already made an important contribution to astronomy by improving Newton's reflecting telescope.

¹⁴Thompson soon encounters these Montreal traders; see below.

¹⁵The Saskatchewan, including, for Thompson, the Nelson, by which its waters reach Hudson Bay.

¹⁶Thompson himself has been accused of intolerance, but as his sarcasm here shows it was the Canadians he tended to judge harshly, not the natives.

¹⁷William Thorburn (fl. 1789–1805), a North West Company trader.

¹⁸A building in the Doric or Greek manner, of the kind which figures in landscapes in the manner of Claude Lorrain (1600–82).

¹⁹The direction in which they were going.

²⁰As George Hudson died of a dropsy on 19 April 1790, it is likely that he was already a sick man when Thompson was so disappointed by his lethargy.

²¹All efforts to explain this hallucination suffered by the normally thoughtful and rational Thompson have failed.

²²Thompson explains the significance of this gesture below.

²³This is the native whom Thompson later calls SAUKAMAPEE; the account he gave Thompson of Plains Indian life before contact with whites changed it irrevocably has been included under his own name.

²⁴Thompson's memory fails here; he is still dealing with the winter of 1787–88.

²⁵William Tomison's Manchester House Journal dates Thompson's accident as Tuesday, 23 December 1788; judging from later entries the injury was a serious one, as the youth needed night nursing until mid-January.

[26]Philip Turnor (*c.* 1751–1799 or 1800), the Company's first official surveyor, appointed on the recommendation of William Wales (see above). During the winter of 1789–90 he taught mathematics and surveying to Thompson and PETER FIDLER.

[27]Charles Price Isham (1754/55–1814), son of JAMES ISHAM and a native woman. He served inland in minor capacities, and during the 1790s was master at several houses, possibly the first native of Hudson Bay to attain such responsibility.

[28]PETER FIDLER (1769–1822). Thompson does not mention that during the winter of 1789–90 Fidler too had been studying surveying with Philip Turnor; he may have been jealous because in his illness Fidler took what he evidently felt should have been his place beside Turnor in the field.

[29]Humphrey Martin or Marten (*c.* 1789–1790/92), Chief at York in 1775–6. His memory evidently failing, Thompson confuses events of 1785–86 with those five years later; in actuality he did not stay at York but went back to the Saskatchewan.

[30]Four years in the service of the Hudson's Bay Company and two with the North West Company.

[31]J.B. Tyrrell notes 'Kristeno, the name by which this great tribe was usually known to the early traders, and of which the word Cree is a corruption, was the name which the Chippewa [Ojibwa] applied to them, and as the white people came in contact with, and learned to speak the language of, the Chippewa first, they naturally adopted the Chippewa name.'

[32]Thompson is describing the Algonkian linguistic family.

[33]Thompson probably has in mind the London poor of his youth.

[34]Compare Thompson as a self-taught ethnographer with Dr James Richardson (see FRANKLIN).

[35]For more details about Cree religious personages, see GEORGE NELSON.

[36]I.e., Satan.

[37]Thompson, as a believing Christian, sees the natives as people who have not yet received Christ's promise of redemption embodied in the New Testament.

[38]*The Arabian Nights*, which Thompson earlier reports was a favourite book of his boyhood.

[39]Rocky Mountain House was built by John McDonald of Garth in 1799; it was situated on the north bank of the North Saskatchewan river a mile and a quarter above the mouth of Clearwater river. Thompson wintered there in 1800–1, 1801–2, and 1806–7. J.B. Tyrrell notes 'when I visited the place in 1886, some of the bastions of the old fort were still standing.'

[40]'1 Brass Compass, 1 Fahrenheit Thermometer' are specially mentioned, along with '1 Case of Instruments' as presented 'to you as a reward for your assiduity' in a letter of 25 May 1792, from the Hudson's Bay Company's secretary to Thompson.

[41]Thompson may be thinking of the criticisms of FRANKLIN which were wide-spread among experienced fur traders; clearly, however, he shared Franklin's impatience with the voyageurs.

[42]The sterile Stony Region: the Canadian Shield; the great Valley of the Lakes: the line of lakes trending north-west from Lake Winnipeg in Manitoba to Great Bear Lake in the Northwest Territories.

[43]Thompson's description of the Great Plains is the first attempt to conceptualize it as a region, and as such is of enduring importance; he was wrong, of course, about the northern forests extending to the Arctic Ocean.

[44]The Mississippi, the Saskatchewan, and the Mackenzie.

[45]Since there is only one species of antelope in North America, *Antilocapra americana*, Thompson must be including deer.

[46]Thompson drafted his narrative in the 1840s, but his views reflect a much earlier period. By the time he wrote, GEORGE SIMPSON was already beginning to adapt the Hudson's Bay Company to the arrival of railways in the United States, and within a decade the expeditions of

HIND and PALLISER were being planned with the objective of assessing the possibilities of prairie settlement.

[47]These very specific terms signify trees of various sizes with their roots caught in the river mud; some can been seen and some cannot, but all are hazards to the canoeist.

[48]Tyrrell notes, 'Bow river is the translation of the Cree Indian name Manachaban Sipi. It is so called on account of the growth of Douglas fir on its banks, as from this wood, if it could be obtained, bows were made.'

[49]Tyrrell notes that this locality is now one of the most famous collecting grounds of these fossil bones in North America. The reason for Thompson's ignorance was doubtless that these bones are not found on the banks of the North Saskatchewan river, which was the ordinary line of travel at that time, and that the streams to the south of it, on which they do occur, were practically unknown to the white men.

[50]1817–1823 inclusive.

[51]Thompson probably means Wapiti or elk (*Cervus elaphus canadensis*), not moose; bull moose do not normally collect the cows into harems during mating season.

[52]In the 1840s GEORGE SIMPSON instituted a policy of 'rest and recuperation' for exhausted fur territory; see LETITIA HARGRAVE.

[53]Apparently this passage was not revised after 1800; the date may be approximate (see note 5).

[54]That is, 'four years after 1797'? See note 4; the date may be approximate.

[55]Thompson spells this name indifferently 'Appe' and 'Appee'.

[56]The entries in the latter part of Thompson's draft are more frequently in journal form; he had been able to revise the earlier part to develop a connected narrative. However, it is worth pointing out that he thought some experiences better narrated that way, for example his journey to the Mandans.

[57]Thompson had just travelled by boat and horseback, in part via the Columbia River, to Astoria (later Fort George) in present-day Washington State.

Saukamapee (fl. 1730 – 1788)

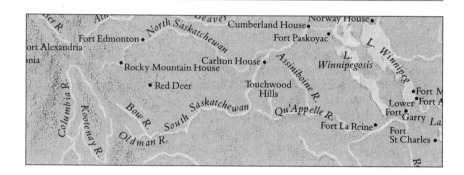

One of the rare accounts by a native of life on the prairies in the eighteenth century comes from the Piegan chief SAUKAMAPEE with whom DAVID THOMPSON spent the winter of 1787–8. It tells of the coming of horses to the Blackfoot, and the terrible small-pox epidemic of 1781. Though Thompson presented Saukamapee's story as continuous narration, he must have pieced it together from many evenings of conversation. It is unlikely, however, that he altered its tone substantially. Thompson was a fine story-teller himself, but is on record as observing that native oratory was not nearly as florid as it was usually portrayed, and it is likely he would have tried to adhere as closely as he could to the words of the speaker. Thompson begins, 'The Peeagan in whose tent I passed the winter was an old man of at least 75 to 80 years of age; his height about six feet, two or three inches, broad shoulders, strong limbed, his hair gray and plentiful, forehead high and nose prominent, his face slightly marked with the small pox, and alltogether his countenance mild, and even, sometimes playfull; although his step was firm and he rode with ease, he no longer hunted, this he left to his sons; his name was Saukamapee (Young Man); his account of former times went back to about 1730 and was as follows.'

Text: David Thompson's Narrative 1784–1812, ed. Richard Glover. Toronto: The Champlain Society, 1962; Chapter XXII.

The Peeagans[1] were always the frontier Tribe, and upon whom the Snake Indians[2] made their attacks, these latter were very numerous, even without their allies; and the Peeagans had to send messengers among us to procure help. Two of them came to the camp of my father, and I was then about his age (pointing to a Lad of about sixteen years) he promised to come and bring some of his people, the Nahathaways [Crees] with him, for I am myself of that people, and not of those with whom I am. My father brought about twenty warriors with him. There were a few guns amongst us, but very little ammunition, and they were left to hunt for the families; Our weapons was a Lance, mostly pointed with iron, some few of stone, A Bow and a quiver of Arrows; the Bows were of Larch, the length came to the chin; the quiver had about fifty arrows, of which ten had iron points, the others were headed with stone. He carried his knife on his breast and his axe in his belt. Such was my fathers weapons, and those with him had much the same weapons. I had a Bow and Arrows and a knife, of which I was very proud. We came to the Peeagans and their allies. They were camped in the Plains on the left bank of the River (the north side) and were a great many. We were feasted, a great War Tent was made, and a few days passed in speeches, feasting and dances. A war chief was elected by the chiefs, and we got ready to march. Our spies had been out and had seen a large camp of the Snake Indians on the Plains of the Eagle Hill, and we had to cross the River in Canoes, and on rafts, which we carefully secured for our retreat. When we had crossed and numbered our men, we were about 350 warriors.[3] They had their scouts out, and came to meet us. Both parties made a great show of their numbers, and I thought that they were more numerous than ourselves.

After some singing and dancing, they sat down on the ground, and placed their large shields before them, which covered them: We did the same, but our shields were not so many, and some of our shields had to shelter two men. Theirs were all spaced touching each other; their Bows were not so long as ours, but of better wood, and the back covered with the sinews of the Bisons which made them very elastic, and their arrows went a long way and whizzed about us as balls do from guns. They were all headed with a sharp, smooth, black stone (flint) which broke when it struck anything. Our iron headed arrows did not go through their shields, but stuck in them; On both sides several were wounded but none lay on the ground; and night put an end to the battle, without a scalp being taken on either side, and in those days such was the result, unless one party was more numerous than the other. The great mischief of war then, was as now, by attacking and destroying small camps of ten to thirty tents, which are obliged to separate for hunting: I grew to be a man, became a skilfull and fortunate hunter, and my relations procured me a Wife. She was young and handsome and we were fond of each other. We had passed a winter together, when Messengers came from our allies to claim assistance.

By this time the affairs of both parties had much changed; we had more guns and iron headed arrows than before; but our enemies the Snake Indians and their allies had Misstutim (Big Dogs, that is Horses)[4] on which they rode, swift as the Deer, on which they dashed at the Peeagans, and with their stone Pukamoggan knocked them on the head, and they had thus lost several of their best men. This news we did not well comprehend and it alarmed us, for we had no idea of Horses and could not make out what they were. Only three of us went and I should not have gone, had not my wife's relations frequently intimated, that her father's medicine bag would be honored by the scalp of a Snake Indian. When we came to our allies, the great War Tent [was made] with speeches, feasting and dances as before; and when the War Chief had viewed us all it was found between us and the Stone [Assiniboine] Indians we had ten guns and each of us about thirty balls, and powder for the war, and we were considered the strength of the battle. After a few days march our scouts brought us word that the enemy was near in a large war party, but had no Horses with them, for at that time they had very few of them. When we came to meet each other, as usual, each displayed their numbers, weapons and shiel[d]s, in all which they were superior to us, except our guns which were not shown, but kept in their leathern cases, and if we had shown [them], they would have taken them for long clubs. For a long time they held us in suspense; a tall Chief was forming a strong party to make an attack on our centre, and the others to enter into combat with those opposite to them; We prepared for the battle the best we could. Those of us who had guns stood in the front line, and each of us [had] two balls in his mouth, and a load of powder in his left hand to reload.

We noticed they had a great many short stone clubs for close combat, which is a dangerous weapon, and had they made a bold attack on us, we must have been defeated as they were more numerous and better armed than we were, for we could have fired our guns no more than twice; and were at a loss what to do on the wide plain, and each Chief encouraged his men to stand firm. Our eyes were all on the tall Chief and his motions, which appeared to be contrary to the advice of several old Chiefs, all this time were about the strong flight of an arrow from each other. At length the tall chief retired and they formed their long usual line by placing their shields on the ground to touch each other, the shield having a breadth of full three feet or more. We sat down opposite to them and most of us waited for the night to make a hasty retreat. The War Chief was close to us, anxious to see the effect of our guns. The lines were too far asunder for us to make a sure shot, and we requested him to close the line to about sixty yards, which was gradually done, and lying flat on the ground behind the shields, we watched our opportunity when they drew their bows to shoot at us, their bodies were then exposed and each of us, as opportunity offered, fired with deadly aim, and either killed, or severely wounded, every one we aimed at.

The War Chief was highly pleased, and the Snake Indians finding so many killed and wounded kept themselves behind their shields; the War Chief then desired we would spread ourselves by two's throughout the line, which we did, and our shots caused consternation and dismay along their whole line. The battle had begun about Noon, and the Sun was not yet half down, when we perceived some of them had crawled away from their shields, and were taking to flight. The War Chief seeing this went along the line and spoke to every Chief to keep his Men ready for a charge of the whole line of the enemy, of which he would give the signal; this was done by himself stepping in front with his Spear, and called on them to follow him as he rushed on their line, and in an instant the whole of us followed him, the greater part of the enemy took to flight, but some fought bravely and we lost more than ten killed and many wounded; Part of us pursued, and killed a few, but the chase had soon to be given over, for at the body of every Snake Indian killed, there were five or six of us trying to get his scalp, or part of his clothing, his weapons, or something as a trophy of the battle. As there were only three of us, and seven of our friends, the Stone Indians, we did not interfere, and got nothing.

The next morning the War Chief made a speech, praising their bravery, and telling them to make a large War Tent to commemorate their victory, to which they directly set to work and by noon it was finished.

The War Chief now called on all the other Chiefs to assemble their men and come to the Tent. In a short time they came, all those who had lost relations had their faces blackened; those who killed an enemy, or wished to be thought so, had their faces blackened with red streaks on the face, and those who had no pretensions to the one, or the other, had their faces red with ochre. We did not paint our faces until the War Chief told us to paint our foreheads and eyes black, and the rest of the face of dark red ochre, as having carried guns, and to distinguish us from all the rest. Those who had scalps now came forward with the scalps neatly stretched on a round willow and with a handle to the frame; they appeared to be more than fifty, and excited loud shouts and the war whoop of victory. When this was over the War Chief told them that if any one had a right to the scalp of an enemy as a war trophy it ought to be us, who with our guns had gained the victory, when from the numbers of our enemies we were anxious to leave the field of battle; and that ten scalps must be given to us; this was soon collected, and he gave to each of us a Scalp. All those whose faces were blackened for the loss of relations, or friends, now came forward to claim the other scalps to be held in their hands for the benefit of their departed relations and friends; this occasioned a long conversation with those who had the scalps; from the head of the enemy they had killed, said the Souls of the enemy that each of us has slain, belong to us, and we have given them to our relations which are in the other world to be their slaves, and we are contented. Those who had scalps taken from the enemy that were found dead under the shields were at a loss what to say, as not one could declare he had actually slain the enemy whose scalp he held, and yet wanted to send their Souls to be the slaves of their departed relations. This caused much discussion; and the old Chiefs decided it could not be done, and that no one could send the soul of an enemy to be a slave in the other world, except the warrior who actually killed him; the scalps you hold are trophies of the Battle, but they give you no right to the soul of the enemy from whom it is taken, he alone who kills an enemy has a right to the soul, and to give it to be a slave to whom he pleases. This decision did not please them, but they were obliged to abide by it. The old Chiefs then turned to us, and praising our conduct in the battle said, each of you have slain two enemies in battle, if not more, you will return to your own people, and as you are young men, consult with the old men to whom you shall give the souls of those you have slain; until which let them wander about the other world. The Chiefs wished us to stay, and promised to each of us a handsome young wife, and [to] adopt us as their sons, but we told them we were anxious to see our relations and people, after which, perhaps we might come back. After all the war ceremonies were over, we pitched away in large camps with the women and children on the frontier of the Snake Indian country, hunting the Bison and Red Deer which were numerous, and we were anxious to see a horse of which we had heard so much. At last, as the leaves were falling we heard that one was killed by an arrow shot into his belly, but the Snake Indian that rode him, got away; numbers of us went to see him, and we all admired him, he put us in mind of a Stag that had lost his horns; and we did not know what name to give him. But as he was slave to Man, like the dog, which carried our things; he was named the Big Dog.

We set off for our people, and on the fourth day came to a camp of Stone Indians, the relations of our companions, who received us well and we staid a few day[s]. The Scalps were placed on poles, and the Men and Women danced round them, singing to the sound of Rattles, Tambours and flutes. When night came, one of our party, in a low voice, repeated to the Chief the narrative of the battle, which he in a loud voice walking about the tents, repeated to the whole camp. After which, the Chiefs called those who followed them to a feast, and the battle was always the subject of the conversation and driving the Snake Indians to a great distance. There were now only three of us to proceed, and upon enquiry, [we] learned a camp of our people, the Nahathaways were a day's journey from us, and in the evening we came to them, and all our news had to be told, with the usual songs and dances; but my mind was wholly bent on making a grand appearance before my Wife and her Parents, and presenting to her father the scalp I had to ornament his Medicine Bag: and before we came to the camp we had dressed ourselves, and painted each other's faces to appear to the best advantage, and were proud of ourselves. On seeing some of my friends I got away and went to them, and by enquiries learned that my parents had gone to the low countries of the Lakes, and that before I was three Moons away my wife had given herself to another man, and that her father could not prevent her, and they were all to the northward there to pass the winter.

At this unlooked for news I was quite disheartened; I said nothing, but my heart was swollen with anger and revenge, and I passed the night scheming mischief. In the morning my friends reasoned with me upon my vexation about a worthless woman, and that it was beneath a warrior['s] anger, there were no want of women to replace her, and a better wife could be got. Others said, that if I had staid with my wife instead of running away to kill Snake Indians, nothing of this would have happened. My anger moderated, I gave my Scalp to one of my friends to give to my father, and renouncing my people, I left them, and came to the Peeagans who gave me a harty welcome; and upon my informing them of my intention to remain with them the great Chief gave me his eldest daughter to be my wife, she is the sister of the present Chief, and as you see, now an old woman.

The terror of that battle and of our guns has prevented any more general battles, and our wars have since been carried by ambuscade and surprize, of small camps, in which we have greatly the advantage, from the Guns, arrow shods of iron, long knives, flat bayonets and axes from the Traders. While we have these weapons, the Snake Indians have none, but what few they sometimes take from one of our small camps which they have destroyed, and they have no Traders among them. We thus continued to advance through the fine plains to the Stag River when death came over us all, and swept away more than half of us by the Small pox, of which we knew nothing until it brought death among us.[5] We caught it from the Snake Indians. Our Scouts were out for our security, when some returned and informed us of a considerable camp which was too large to attack and something very suspicious about it; from a high knowl they had a good view of the camp, but saw none of the men hunting, or going about; there were a few Horses, but no one came to them, and a herd of Bisons [were] feeding close to the camp with other herds near. This somewhat alarmed us as a stratagem of War; and our Warriors thought this camp had a larger not far off; so that if this camp was attacked which was strong enough to offer a desperate resistance, the other would come to their assistance and overpower us as had been once done by them, and in which we lost many of our men.

The council ordered the Scouts to return and go beyond this camp, and be sure there was no other. In the mean time we advanced our camp; The scouts returned and said no other tents were near, and the camp appeared in the same state as before. Our Scouts had been going too much about their camp and were seen; they expected what would follow, and all those that could walk, as soon as night came on, went away. Next morning at the dawn of day, we attacked the Tents, and with our sharp flat daggers and knives, cut through the tents and entered for the fight; but our war whoop instantly stopt, our eyes were appalled with terror; there was no one to fight with but the dead and the dying, each a mass of corruption. We did not touch them, but left the tents, and held a council on what was to be done. We all thought the Bad Spirit had made himself master of the camp and destroyed them. It was agreed to take some of the best of the tents, and any other plunder that was clean and good, which we did, and also took away the few Horses they had, and returned to our camp.

The second day after this dreadful disease broke out in our camp, and spread from one tent to another as if the Bad Spirit carried it. We had no belief that one Man could give it to another, any more than a wounded Man could give his wound to another. We did not suffer so much as those that were near the river, into which they rushed and died. We had only a little brook, and about one third of us died, but in some of the other camps there were tents in which every one died. When at length it left us, we moved about to find our people, it was no longer with the song and the dance; but with tears, shrieks, and howlings of despair for those who would never return to us. War was no longer thought of, and we had enough to do to hunt and make provision for our families, for in our sickness we had consumed all our dried provisions; but the Bisons and Red Deer were also gone, we did not see one half of what was before, whither they had gone we could not tell, we believed the Good Spirit had forsaken us, and allowed the Bad Spirit to become our Master. What little we could spare we offered to the Bad Spirit to let us alone and go to our enemies. To the Good Spirit we offered feathers, branches of trees, and sweet smelling grass. Our hearts were low and dejected, and we shall never be again the same people. To hunt for our families was our sole occupation and kill Beavers, Wolves and Foxes to trade our necessaries; and we thought of War no more, and perhaps would have made peace with them for they had suffered dreadfully as well as us and had left all this fine country of the Bow River to us.

We were quiet for about two or three winters, and although we several times saw their young men on the scout we took no notice of them, as we all require young men, to look about the country that our families may sleep in safety and that we may know where to hunt. But the Snake Indians are a bad people, even their allies the Saleesh and Kootanaes cannot trust them, and do not camp with them, no one believes that they say, and [they] are very treacherous; every one says they are rightly named Snake People, for their tongue is forked like that of a Rattle Snake, from which they have their name. I think it was about the third falling of the leaves of the trees, that five of our tents pitched away to the valleys of the Rocky Mountains, up a branch of this river (the Bow) to hunt the Big Horn Deer (Mountain Sheep) as their horns make fine large bowls, and are easily cleaned; they were to return on the first snow. All was quiet and we waited for them until the snow lay on the ground, when we got alarmed for their safety; and about thirty warriors set off to seak them. It was only two days march, and in the evening they came to the camp, it had been destroyed by a large party of Snake Indians, who left their marks, of snakes heads painted black on sticks they had set up. The bodies were all there with the Women and Children, but scalped and partly devoured by the Wolves and Dogs.

The party of their return related the fate of our people, and other camps on hearing the news came and joined us. A War Tent was made and the Chiefs and Warriors assembled, and red pipes were filled with Tobacco, but before being lighted an old Chief arose, and beckoning to the Man who had the fire to keep back, addressed us, saying, I am an old man, my hair is white and [I] have seen much: formerly we were healthy and strong and many of us, now we are few to what we were, and the great sickness may come again. We were fond of War, even our Women flattered us to war, and nothing was thought of but scalps for singing and dancing. Now think of what has happened to us all, by destroying each other and doing the work of the bad spirit; the Great Spirit became angry with our making the ground red with blood: he called to the Bad Spirit to punish and destroy us, but in doing so not to let one spot of the ground, to be red with blood, and the Bad Spirit did it as we all know. Now we must revenge the death of our people and make the Snake Indians feel the effects of our guns, and other weapons; but the young women must all be saved, and if any has a babe at the breast it must not be taken from her, nor hurt; all the Boys and Lads that have no weapons must not be killed, but brought to our camps, and be adopted amongst us, to be our people, and make us more numerous and stronger than we are. Thus the Great Spirit will see that when we make war we kill only those who are dangerous to us, and make no more ground red with blood than we can help, and the Bad Spirit will have no more power on us. Everyone signified his assent to the old Chief, and since that time, it has sometimes been acted on, but more with the Women than the Boys, and while it weakens our enemies makes us stronger. A red pipe was now lighted and the same old Chief taking it, gave three whiffs to the Great Spirit praying him to be kind to them and not forsake them, then three whiffs to the Sun, the same to the Sky, the Earth and the four Winds; the Pipe was passed round, and other pipes lighted. The War Chief then arose, and said Remember my friends that while we are smoking the bodies of our friends and relations are being devoured by wolves and Dogs, and their Souls are sent by the

Snake Indians to be the slaves of their relations in the other world. We have made no war on them for more than three summers, and we had hoped to live quietly until our young men had grown up, for we are not many as we used to be; but the Snake Indians, that race of liars, whose tongues are like rattle snakes, have already made war on us, and we can no longer be quiet. The country where they now are is but little known to us, and if they did not feel themselves strong they would not have dared to have come so far to destroy our people. We must be courageous and active, but also cautious; and my advice is, that three scout parties, each of about ten warriors with a Chief at their head, take three different directions, and cautiously view the country, and not go too far, for enough of our people are already devoured by wolves and our business is revenge, without loosing our people.
. . . .

. . . the narrative [of the] old man having given us the above information, he lighted his pipe; and smoking it out said, the Snake Indians are no match for us; they have no guns and are no match for us, but they have the power to vex us and make us afraid for the small hunting parties that hunt the small deer for dresses and the Big Horn for the same and for Bowls. They keep us always on our guard.
. . . .

[Thompson then relates that Saukamapee's people gathered a party of young warriors to examine the country a few days journey ahead. '. . . in the evening the principal War Chief addressed the Chief at the head of the party; reminding him that the warriors now accompanying him would steadily follow him, that they were sent to destroy their enemies, not to be killed themselves, and made the slaves of their enemies, that he must be wise and cautious and bring back the Warriors entrusted to his care. Among them was the eldest son of the Old Man [Saukamapee] in whose tent we lived. They all marched off very quietly as if for hunting.']

After they were gone; the old man said it was not a war party, but one of those they frequently sent, under guidance of those who had showed courage and conduct in going to war, for we cannot afford to lose our people, we are too few, and these expeditions inure our men to long marches and to suffer hunger and thirst. At the end of about twenty days they returned with about thirty five Horses in tolerable condition, and fiteen fine mules, which they had brought away from a large camp of Snake Indians. The old Man's son gave him a long account of the business. On the sixth evening the scouts came ahead and informed the Chief, that we[6] must be near a camp, as they had seen horses feeding: night came on, and we went aside to a wood of cotton and poplar trees on the edge of a brook, in the morning some of us climbed the trees and passed the day, but saw nothing. In the night we went higher up the brook, and as it was shoal, we walked in it for some distance, to another wood, and there lay down. Early the next morning, a few of us advanced through the wood, but we had not gone far, before we heard the women with their dogs come for wood for fuel. Some of us returned to the Chief, and the rest watched the women, it was near midday before they all went away, they had only stone axes and stone clubs to break the wood; they took only what was dry, and cut none down. Their number showed us the camp must be large, and sometimes some of them came so close to us, that we were afraid of being discovered. The Chief now called us round him, and advised us to be very cautious, as it was plain we were in the vicinity of a large camp, and manage our little provisions, for we must not expect to get any more until we retreated; if we fire a gun at the Deer it will be heard; and if we put an arrow in a deer and he gets away, and they see the deer, it will alarm them, and we shall not be able to get away. My intention is to have something to show our people, and when we retreat, take as many horses as we can with us, to accomplish which, we must have a fair opportunity, and in the mean time be hungry, which we can stand some time, as we have plenty of water to drink. We were getting tired, and our solace was of an evening to look at the horses and mules. At length he said to us to get ready, and pointing to the top of the Mountains, [said] see the blue sky is gone and a heavy storm is there, which will soon reach us; and so it did: About sunset we proceeded thro' the wood, to the horses, and with the lines we carried, each helping the other, we soon had a horse or a mule to ride on. We wanted to drive some with us, but the Chief would not allow it; it was yet daylight when we left the wood, and entered the plains, but the Storm of Wind was very strong and on our backs, and at the gallop, or trot, so as not to tire our horses, we continued to midnight, when we came to a brook, with plenty of grass, and let them get a good feed. After which we held on to sun rising, when seeing a fine low ground, we staid the rest of the day, keeping watch until night, when we continued our journey. The storm lasted two days and greatly helped us.

The old Man told his son, who, in his relation had intimated he did not think the Chief very brave; that it was very fortunate that he was under such a Chief, who had acted so wisely and cautiously; for had he acted otherwise not one of you would have returned, and some young men coming into the tent whom he supposed might have the same opinions as his son, he told them; 'that it required no great bravery for a War Party to attack a small camp, which they were sure to master; but that it required great courage and conduct, to be for several days in the face of a large camp undiscovered; and each of you to bring away a horse from the enemy, instead of leaving your own scalps.'

Notes

[1]The Piegans are one of the three tribes of the Blackfoot or Siksika; the others are the Bloods and the Blackfoot proper.
[2]Snake Indians: the Shoshone.
[3]Thompson: 'this he showed by counting every finger to be ten, and holding up both hands three times and then one hand.'
[4]Saukamapee's narrative shows that the Blackfoot first encountered horses during this war with the Snake Indians in 1730; by 1754 (see ANTHONY HENDAY) they were fully mounted, and the Assiniboines were also beginning to use horses.
[5]This was the smallpox epidemic of 1781.
[6]That is, Saukamapee's son and his companions.

Daniel Harmon   (1778 – 1843)

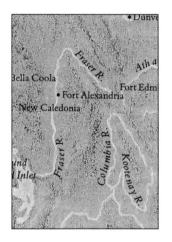

DANIEL HARMON was born into a prosperous and cultured family in Bennington, Vermont in 1778; his ancestors had arrived in New England in 1616. His entry into the fur trade as a warehouseman for McTavish, Frobisher and Company in Montreal was thus an unusual departure. In 1800 he joined the North West Company as a clerk, and travelled west, where he remained until 1819. Harmon was a courageous and resourceful trader, and indeed described himself as of a 'roving disposition', but his journal is that of a bookish, happily domestic man who valued his friendships and was devoted to his family. He was also devout; in 1813 he underwent a 'conversion experience' which he duly recorded. Strictly speaking Harmon did no exploration himself, but many of those who did passed through the posts where he served, joined his lengthening list of friends, or — like DAVID THOMPSON — wrote to him of their discoveries. Harmon's writing represents, more accurately than many other exploration documents, the developing social and intellectual culture of the fur trade as it became by the early nineteenth century an established way of life for generations of men and their families.

Text: Based on W. Kaye Lamb, ed., *Sixteen Years in the Indian Country: The Journal of Daniel Williams Harmon 1800–1816.* Toronto: Macmillan Company of Canada, 1957.

The journey west

April 30, 1800, Wednesday. Point Claire. Rainy evening and I for the first time am to pass the night in a Tent. . . . [The voyageurs] I am told have many of the Sailors customs, and the following is one of them: — from all who have not passed certain places they expect a *treat* or some thing to drink, and should you not comply with their whims, you might be sure of getting a Ducking which they call *baptizing*, but to avoid that ceremony I gave the People of my Canoe a few Bottles of Spirits and Porter, and in drinking which they got rather merry and forgot their Relations, whom they had but a few Days before left with heavy hearts and eyes drowned in tears. After being encamped, an Irish Gentleman invited me to go and take a cup of Tea at his House which was nigh bye. . . .

May 24 [1800], Saturday. Lake Huron. . . . The Canadian Voyagers when they leave one stream to follow another have a custom of pulling off their Hats and making the sign of the Cross, and one in each Brigade if not in every Canoe repeats a short Prayer. The same ceremonies are also observed by them whenever they pass a place where any one has been buried or a Cross erected, consequently those who are in the habit of voyaging up this way are obliged to say their prayers perhaps oftener than when at home, for at almost every Rapid that we have passed since we left Montreal, we have seen a number of Crosses erected, and at one I counted no less than thirty! It is truly melancholy and discouraging when I seriously reflect on the great number of my fellow creatures who have been brought to untimely ends by voyaging up this way, and yet notwithstanding such dismal spectacles which are almost constantly before our eyes, we with all the eagerness of youth press forward to follow the same route, and all in hopes of gaining a little Gold! . . .

June 13 [1800], Friday. Grand Portage,[1] where we arrived late this evening. This place I am informed lies in the 48° North Latitude and is said to be about nine hundred Miles from the *Sault St Maries* and eighteen hundred from Montreal. The Fort which is twenty four Rods by thirty is built in a Bay at the foot of a considerable Hill or Mountain. Within the Fort there are a number of Dwelling Houses, Shops & Stores &c. all of which appear to be temporary buildings, just to serve for this moment. The Bay is so shoal that the vessel must be almost light before she can approach the shore, and directly opposite the Fort there is a considerable Island, which shelters the vessel from feeling the wind from off the Lake, and therefore makes this a tolerable convenient harbour. There also is another Fort which stands within two hundred Rods of this belonging to Parker, Gerard, Forsyth, Richardson, Ogilvy & Coy.,[2] but who have been in this Country only three years & have not as yet met with much success, and it is said they must fail for want of *Capital*. As this is the Head-Quarters or General Rendezvous for all who commerce in this part of the World, therefore every summer the Proprietors and many of the Clerks who Winter in the Interior come here with the Furs that they have been able to collect in course of the last Season, and I am told this is the time when they generally arrive, but some of them are already here. Those who bring the Goods from Montreal go no farther than this, except a few who takes Goods to the Rainy Lake, intended for Athabasca, as that place lies at too great a distance from this, for the People of that quarter to come this far & return before the Winter sets in — and those who bring the Goods from Montreal on their return take the Returns of the North. . . .

June 15 [1800], Sunday. I have another fit of the Ague & Fever. The People here pass the Sundays like the Natives, with this only difference, *we* change our Cloathes but *they* do not. The labouring People have all Day been employed in making & pressing Packs of Furs to be sent to Canada. To me who has never been accustomed to see People labour on the Sabbath it appears very wrong, but I perceive that those who have been any length of time in this Savage Country pay but little regard to it. However I hope that I shall never forget the Sabbath is the Lords Day. . . .

July 4 [1800, Friday]. In the Day time the Indians were allowed to Dance in the Fort, & to whom the Coy. made a present of thirty six Gallons of Shrub[3] &c. and this evening the Gentlemen of the place dressed[4] & we had a famous Ball in the Dining Room, and for musick we had the Bag-Pipe the Violin, the Flute & the Fife, which enabled us to spend the evening agreeably. At the Ball there were a number of this Countries *Ladies*, whom I was surprised to find could behave themselves so well, and who danced not amiss. . . .

Fort Alexandria[5]

January 4 [1801], Sunday. In the morning the greater part of our People (Men, Women & Children) were sent to go and pass the remainder of the Winter in the Plains about two Days march from this, and where they will live upon the flesh of Buffaloe which they will kill themselves, and during their stay there, their Dwellings Will be Tents or Lodges made of the Skins of either Buffaloe, Moose, or Red Deer after being dressed or tanned & then sewed together, one of which contains from ten to twenty of those Skins and when erected assume the form of a Sugar-Loaf, and in one of those tents ten or fifteen persons will find sufficient space, for when they are there they are always either seated or lying down.

The Indians who come to this Establishment are *Crees & Assiniboins*, and I am told both of them are numerous Tribes. The former generally remain in the strong or thick Woods and hunt the Beaver, Moose & Red Deer &c. but most of the latter live out in the spacious Plains and hunt the Wolves (of different species) Foxes, Bears & Buffaloe &c. As both Tribes often meet their customs & manners are nearly the same, however there is no resemblance in their Dialects. Neither of them want for Horses but the *Assiniboins* are the best Horse-Men, for they never go any distance a foot, and with those Animals they often run down & kill the Buffaloe with their Bows & Arrows, which they find full as convenient for that purpose as fire arms, but the *Crees* always when they can purchase them [and] make use of the latter to kill their Game. Their Cloathing consists of a pair of Leggins, a kind of Shirt or Frock, with a Robe of dressed Buffaloe Skin which they wrap about their bodies and tie around their waists. Last evening I wrote Letters to my old fellow travellers from Montreal, Messrs. Henry & Clarke which will be taken them by the Winter Express that leaves this tomorrow and is to pass by the way of Fort des Prairies, from thence to the English River and then directly to Athabasca. And I am informed that there is an Express that every year leaves Athabasca in the Month of December and passes throughout the whole Country called the North West and reaches *Soult St Maries* towards the latter end of March, and thus the Gentlemen who come up in the Spring from Montreal get the news of the preceeding Summer much earlier than they would otherwise have done and [this] often is of great service to them and attended with a very little expense to the Concern. . . .

February 11 [1801], Wednesday. On the 1st Inst. I accompanied by eight of our People & one of the natives (who served as Guide) sat off with a small assortment of Goods to go and trade with about fifty Families of Crees & Assiniboins and in going to their Camp or Village we were three Days always in a Plain Country. . . . When we got within a Mile of the Natives Camp, ten or a dozen of their Chiefs and most respectable Men, came a Horse back to meet & conduct us to their dwellings, and immediately after our arrival there, one of the Chiefs sent his Son to invite me & my Interpreter to go to his Lodge & as soon as we were seated, the old Man caused Meat and Berries &c. (in short the best of everything he had) to be set before us, for Savages pride themselves in being hospitable to Strangers, but before we had ate much, we were sent for to go & do the same at another Lodge, and from his to another, and so on till we had been to more than half a dozen at all of which we ate a little (and smoaked our pipe) for (as my Interpreter informed me) they would think we dispised them, and look upon it as an affront should we not taste of every thing they sat before us — in fact during several Days that we remained with those People, we met with more real politeness (in this way) than is often shown to Strangers in the civilized part of the World, and much more than I had expected [to] meet with from *Savages* as the Indians are generally called, but I think wrongfully. . . .

In our excursion we saw Buffaloe in abundance, and when on a small rise of ground I may with truth say that we could see grazing in the Plains below at least five thousand of which Animals we killed what we wanted for ourselves & Dogs, and this evening returned to the Fort loaded with Furs & Provisions without having received the least affront or the smallest injury from the Natives, notwithstanding the most of them were intoxicated with the Rum we gave them. . . .

February 19 [1801], Thursday. This Day I am twenty three years of age, and how rapidly does it now appear that that space of time has past away! For it seems as if it was but yesterday that I was a Child! In fact the time is so short that we remain in this fleeting world that a person can scarcely begin to live ere he must *set his House in order to Die!* And of this truth we are all well convinced, yet are continually laying plans as though we expected to always live. But Man is so made that he cannot be idle, if not doing good a doing harm. However we always ought to strive to be so employed as to be useful to ourselves as well as to others while here below and then we may with some reason have cause to hope that hereafter we shall be happy. . . .

April 4 [1801], Saturday. Swan River Fort,[6] where I this afternoon arrived and am come to pass the remainder of the Spring here. During the time I was at Alexandria I past those Days agreeably in the company of Mr. McLeod,[7] who is a sensible Man & an agreeable Companion, but he like most others also gives in too much to the ways and customs of the Country he is in and therefore does not lead so moral a life as I am persuaded he would were he in the civilized part of the World. Yet truth as well as gratitude obliges me to say this much in his behalf that he appeared desirous of instructing me in what was most necessary for me to know concerning the affairs of this Country as well as what would make me more virtuous and good — and it was also from the example he sat me that I became fond of reading and for which I hope & trust I shall ever have a grateful heart, as well as for the many other favors he was pleased to shew me. But now I am as it were alone there being not a person here able to speak a word of English and as I have not often been in the Mens company I cannot as yet speak much of their Language. However fortunately I have a few Books here and in perusing them I shall pass most of my leisure moments . . . .

April 10 [1801], Friday. Fine pleasant weather. This afternoon I took a solitary yet a pleasing walk to the ruins of a Fort which was a few years since abandoned by the Hudson's Bay People to whom it belonged, but now they do not come into this part of the Country. After examining for some time where the Fort stood but now most of the Houses are fallen to the Ground, I could not help reflecting on the short duration of every thing that is in this perishable & fleeting World, and after I had thus meditated for a considerable time, I then went to visit a piece of Ground where a number of their People had been interred far from their Native Country, their Friends and Relations! And while lamenting their sad fate I must acknowledge my blood chilled as I thought that what had happened to them might in all probability befall me also! For I am following the same path and leading the same life as they were! But let my earnest prayers ever be that our merciful God will in due time restore me to my Friends & Relations in good health and an unblemished Character. . . .

June 1 [1801], Monday. [Fort] Alexandria, where I accompanied by two Men arrived this afternoon, and find Six Families of Crees encamped about the Fort — & here I am to pass a long Summer, but have with me one Clerk, two Interpreters & five labouring Men, Six Women & thirteen Children belonging to our People, also a number of Women & Children belonging to the Natives, whose Husbands have gone to war upon the Rapid Indians (a Tribe who remain a considerable distance out into the large Plains and near the upper part of the Missisours [Missouri] River).[8] In short there are nearly one hundred mouths to be filled out of our Store for the greater part of the Summer — but we have two good Hunters & Moose & Deer are not scarce, but the Buffaloe are gone to the large Plains again.

June 11 [correctly, 10, 1801], Wednesday. As we have been informed that the Rapid Indians intend to form a war party and come against the Indians of this quarter, (and if they come this way they will as soon fall upon us as upon the Natives themselves, for we furnish them with fire arms which they do not like) I have therefore thought it proper to set our People to build Block Houses over the Fort Gates and put the Bastions in order, so that we may be prepared to defend ourselves in case of attack. . . .

July 30 [1801], Thursday. . . . Mr. A.N. McLeod has a son here named also Alexander[9] who is about five years of age & whose Mother is of the Tribe of the Rapid Indians, and I in my leisure moments am teaching him the rudiments of the English Language. He speaks the Sauteux & Cree Dialects well for a Child his age, and makes himself understood tolerably well in the Assiniboin & French Languages. In short he is like the most of the Children in this Country blessed with a retentive memory and apt to learn. We have made about ten tuns of Hay to serve our Horses that work during the winter season, but the others pass that part as well as all the rest of the year upon Grass which they find in the Plains by taking away about a foot and a half of Snow, for I am told they seldom have more hereabouts, and on the hills the wind soon takes the greater part into the valleys.

August 28 [20, 1801], Thursday. All the Provisions that we now have in Store consists of only about fifteen pounds of Pimican [pemmican], and when or from whince we shall be able to procure a supply God only knows, for all our dependence is on the success of our Hunters, and it is now some time since they have killed an Animal, yet Moose & Deer are plentiful hereabouts. . . .

September 29 [27, 1801], Sunday. Snowed and Rained by turns all Day, and this afternoon Mr. McLeod &c. arrived from the Grand Portage & delivered me a number of Letters from my friends below, and I am happy to learn they left them all blessed with good health, which is news highly grateful to my feelings, than which nothing could give me half the real satisfaction, while thus *self-banished* in this dreary Country an [and] at such a great distance from all I hold dear in this World. I also received several Letters from Gentlemen in this Country. . . .

[Bird Mountain[10]] *October 29 [1801], Thursday.* On the 22nd Inst. Mr. McLeod & ten Men all a Horse back arrived & the Day following I accompanied them to the lower Fort, where I saw Mr. William Henry brother to Mr. A. Henry[11] who last year came up to the Grand Portage with me but the latter came up this Season. Mr. McLeod also brought in another Clerk by the name of Frederick Goedike.[12] This evening Messrs. McLeod Henry and myself returned but left our People behind whose Horses are loaded with Goods for this place & Alexandria. . . .

December 23 [1801], Wednesday. Clear and cold. On the 16th Inst. I left this for Alexandria, where I passed several Days agreeably in the company of Messrs. McLeod, Henry & Goedike, and the evening before our separation we had a Ball or rather a Dance, and Mr. Goedike played the Violin. . . .

December 28 [1801], Monday. Payet one of my Interpreters, has taken one of the Natives Daughters for a Wife, and to her Parents he gave in Rum & dry Goods &c. to the value of two hundred Dollars, and all the cerimonies attending such circumstances are that when it becomes time to retire, the Husband or rather Bridgegroom (for as yet they are not joined by any *bonds*) shews his Bride where his Bed is, and then they, of course, both go to rest together, and so they continue to do as long as they can agree among themselves, but when either is displeased with their choice, he or she will seek another Partner, and thus the Hymenial [Hymeneal] Bond, without any more ado is broke asunder — which is *law* here & I think reasonable also, for I cannot conceive it to be right for a Man & Woman to cohabit when they cannot agree, but to live in discontent, if not downright hatered to each other, as many do. . . .

[Fort Alexandria] *August 8 [1802], Sunday.* We now have a considerable quantity of Provisions in the Store and for such a blessing we endeavour to be thankful as well as may be after having passed the most of the Summer so miserably in regard to that necessary article of life. What a merciful God we have! who is constantly bestowing upon us His richest blessings, while we like the Children of Israel of old, who when their *Bellies* were not full were ever ready to complain and deny their God! Would to God that I could be sufficiently thankful for the favours I am daily and hourly receiving from the hands of an ever bountiful Providence, but my heart is so depraved that I cannot set the right value on such infinite blessings. But by whom was it thus corrupted? or was it in this forlorn condition when I first entered into this World? or has it been brought to its present depraved state by my own wiked deeds? The latter most assuredly is the case! Then since I have been able to change my heart from good to bad: why shall I not be able to bring it back to its original state? I have it most undoubtedly in my power.*

[*When I wrote the above I could not conceive the necessity of a Saviour: but thought all depended on my own natural exertions, whether I should be Saved or Damned!! What a deluded and unhappy condition! surely the most deplorable that a person could possibly be in, but thanks be to our Merciful God who has been graciously pleased to cause my deluded eyes to be opened that I might behold the awful condition I was then in.]

August 11 [1802], Wednesday. On the 9th Inst. a Chief among the Crees came to the Fort accompanied by a number of his relations who appeared very desirous that I should take one of his Daughters to remain with me, but to put him off I told him that I could not then take a Woman however in the fall perhaps I might for I added that I had no dislike of her. But he pressed me to keep her at once as he said he was fond of me and he wished to have his Daughter with the white people and he almost persuaded me to accept of her, for I was sure that while I had the Daughter I should not only have the Fathers hunts but those of his relations also, of course [this] would be much in the favor of the Company & perhaps in the end of some advantage to me likewise — so that interest (and perhaps a little natural inclination also) I find was nigh making me commit another folly, if not a sin, — but thanks be to God alone if I have not been brought into a snare laid no doubt by the Devil himself. . . .

[Bird Mountain] *November 11 [9], Tuesday. Bird Mountain* where I am come to pass another Winter and have with me one Interpreter & Six labouring Men — and thus I am continually shifting about from one place to another and when I shall have a home of my *own* God only knows. However I hope the Day *will* arrive when I shall have it in my power either to be settled down where I can pass the remainder of my Days in quietness or in travelling about in the different parts of the Civilized World. . . .

[Fort Alexandria] *May 19 [1803], Thursday.* Yesterday the most of our People sat off for the Grand Portage & today Mr. McGillis[13] &c. followed them, but I am to pass another Summer here and have with me Mr. F. Godike, one Interpreter & several labouring Men, besides Women & Children. As Mr. Goedike will be absent from the Fort the greater part of the Summer, I shall as it were therefore be left alone, for the ignorant Canadians make very indifferent Companions, and with whom I cannot associate. However fortunately for me I have *dead* Friends (my Books) who will never abandon me, till I first neglect them.

June 2 [1803], Thursday. Our People are making a Garden which they surround with Palisads in the same manner as our Forts are built. The X.Y. People are building a Fort about five Miles up this River. One of our Men gave me his Son (a Lad of about thirteen years of age) whom I in the name of the North West Coy. agree to feed and furnish with Clothing until he becomes able to earn something more. His Mother is a Sauteux Woman & he is to serve me as Cook &c.

June 21 [1803], Tuesday. This afternoon we had a heavy Shower of Hail and Rain. Yesterday I sent Mr. Goedike accompanied by two Men, with a small assortment of Goods to go about a Days march beyond where the X.Y.[14] People are building, where they will remain till the Natives return from their hunting excursion, therefore I now have with me only two Men and a Woman, which renders this a solitary place, & nothing but the perusal of the Book[15] we fortunately have here, could keep up my drooping spirits. At such moments as these I cannot help reflecting how happy I should be were it possible for me to pass a few Days or even hours in the company of my Friends below! Ant [and at] such melancholy seasons I almost regret having left my native land & all I hold dear in this World, and where I might if I had not had such a roving disposition been comfortably situated and happy in the enjoyment of the company of that Society of Friends and Relations from whom I now am at such an immense distance *self-banished!* But Providence has brought me into this Wilderness, and it therefore now becomes me to bear up under my lot with resignation, perseverance & fortitude, hoping in the mean time the Day is not far distant when I shall have it in my power to return and mingle once more in that happy circle of Friends on whose conversation I so highly and so justly lay so much value. . . .

October 16 [1803], Sunday. This afternoon there fell a little Snow and the first we have had this fall. It is now several Days since the X.Y. People arrived from the Grand Portage, but give us no news of Mr. McGillis &c. neither would they let their conditions be ever so bad—for so *well* do we agree, that neither Company will convey the other the least news that can [in] any way concern their affairs in this Country. In a word the North West Co. look upon their opponents the X.Y. Co. as encroachers of *their* territories, while the latter People consider that the former have no better right to commerce in this part of the World than they themselves have, but if the truth must be told, as they are weaker, that is have not been in this country long enough to gain much footing, *we would wish to crush them at once,* before they have too much strength, when it will be more difficult if not impossible. And this jarring of interests keep up continual misunderstandings and occasions frequent broils between the two contending parties, and some times the enmity that exists between them rises to such an unbecoming height as to cause bloodshed, and in several instance's even lives have been sacrificed! But I am of the opinion that those who have committed Murder in this Savage Country, would if a favorable occasion had offered been guilty of the like horrid crime in the Civilized part of the World—yet there are many in this Country who appear to be of a different opinion. Here it is true they have one advantage if indeed it may be thought one, that they have not below, is: here a Murderer escapes the Gallows, as there are no human laws that can reach or have any effect on the People of this Country. However I understand they are, in England about passing laws which will equally affect the People of this Country as those in the Canadas or any other part of the British Dominion[16]—and it is high time it should be so, or the most of us soon should have cut one anothers throats! . . .

December 28 [27, 1803] Tuesday. As Messrs. Henry & Goedike my Companions & Friends are both absent on excursion in two different parts of the Country, I as might be expected pass now & then a solitary hour, but when they are here, they being such agreeable mesmates [messmates] the moments glide away unperceptably by either of us, and so well do we agree, that when People live happily together, it might be said, they live like Henry, Goedike & Harmon! But when we are separated I pass the greater part of my time either reading or writing, and now & then take a ride about the Fort, or to see our neighbours, frequently a Horse back, but some times in a *Cariol* [carriole], drawn by a Horse when there is not much Snow, but when the depth is too great by Dogs, the latter being light do not sink much into the Snow, and in the above mentioned vehicle I this afternoon accompanied Mr. McGillis to pay a visit to our X.Y. Neighbours. . . .

[Fort Alexandria] *April 29 [1804], Sunday.* Yesterday the most of our people left this for Swan River, and to Day Mr. McGillis &c. set off for the same place, and are on their way to the Grand Portage, or rather the New Fort [Fort William], which stands about forty five miles north west of the above mentioned place — and I shall pass another Summer at this place and am happy in having with me my two friends Messrs Henry & Goedike, also are here one Interpreter and several labouring Men besides Women and Children. We are preparing a piece of ground for a Garden & where I hope to pass many an agreeable hour in the company of my two companions. As Mr. Goedike plays the violin well, he now and then will give us an air to enliven our spirits, and thus make the minutes pass away more pleasantly than they otherwise could. However the most of our leisure moments (and which is nearly nine tenths of our time) will be spent in reading, conversing on what we have read & meditation. We have the same neighbours as last year. . . .

July 12, [1805] Friday. The Plain Portage.[17] In the fore part of the Day we met Mr. A.N. McLeod on his way to Athabasca, which place he left the beginning of June last. We put ashore and took breakfast with him and he has taken from me my friend Mr. Goedike, who had past nearly four years with me, and all that time we lived on the most friendly terms, therefore both of us were very loth to separate. He it is true had romantic[18] Ideas, but I believe him to have a generous humane heart — and susceptible of the strictest ties of friendship. He has good natural parts, and has had a tolerable education, which he strives to improve by reading — but I can without boasting say that it was me who taught him to be fond of books (as Mr. McLeod had done to me) and I am as willing to acknowledge that he assisted me greatly in learning me to read and speak the French Language, which was his Mother tongue, but received the most of his education in the English Language. He is not master of this, but knows enough of both for common business. He has an even temper and is fond of his Mother. . . .

[South Branch House[19] *October 10 [1805], Thursday.* This Day a Canadians Daughter (a Girl of about fourteen years of age)[20] was offered me, and after mature consideration concerning the step I ought to take I finally concluded it would be best to accept of her, as it is customary for all the Gentlemen who come in this Country to remain any length of time to have a *fair* Partner, with whom they can pass away their time at least more sociably if not more agreeably than to live a lonely, solitary life, as they must do if single. In case we can live in harmony together, my intentions now are to keep her as long as I remain in this uncivilized part of the world, but when I return to my native land shall endeavour to place her into the hands of some good honest Man, with whom she can pass the remainder of her Days in this Country much more agreeably, than it would be possible for her to do, were she to be taken down into the civilized world, where she would be a stranger to the People, their manners, customs & Language. Her Mother is of the Tribe of the Snare Indians, whose Country lies about the Rocky Mountain. The Girl is said to be of a mild disposition & even tempered, which are qualities very necessary to make an agreeable Woman and an effectionate Partner. . . .

[South Branch House] *August 28 [1806], Thursday.* [Mistakenly dated June 28 in the manuscript.] The Hudson's Bay People are returned from their Factory, and if they have news of consequence from England they are determined to keep all to themselves for they give us none. . . .

[Fort Chipewyan[21] *September 21 [1808], Wednesday.* Cold raw wind. Ever since my arrival at this place, People from almost every corner of this extensive Department have been flocking in — one of whom is a Mr. Simon Fraser from New Caledonia (on the West side of the Rocky Mountain) who accompanied by Messrs. John Stuart[22] and J.M. Quesnel[23] and a Dozen of Canadians as well as two of the Natives, is just returned from a voyage to the Pacific Ocean, and for which place they early last Spring left New Caledonia, in two Canoes.[24] He says they met with some ill treatment from the Indians who live along the Sea-coast, but were hospitably received by all those they saw further up the Country, who he says are not scattered about here and there a Lodge as in the other parts of this Country, but live in villages and have Houses or Huts made of Wood. Mr. Stuart also says the Country they past through is far from being well stocked with Beaver or any other kind of Animals — of course the Natives live principally upon Fish. . . .

October 10 [1808], Monday. Dunvegan[25], which is a well built Fort and stands in a pleasant situation, with Plains on either side of the River. Here is where my friend Mr. A.N. McLeod used to Winter, while in Athabasca and here I find my former companion & friend Mr. Frederick Goedike &c. who past last Summer here — and about the Fort are encamped a number of Iroquois-Hunters[26] and Beaver Indians, who have been waiting our arrival. And at long last I have reached the place where I shall pass, God willing, the ensuing Winter, also Messrs. Donald McTavish,[27] J.G. McTavish[28] & Joseph McGillivray[29] and thirty two labouring Men, nine Women & several Children, which make it differ much from the solitary place where I was last Winter.[30] Here our principal food will be the Flesh of Buffaloe, Moose, Red Deer & Bears. We also have a tolerable Kitchen Garden, therefore we have what would make the most of People contented — that is those who only think of filling their greedy Bellies. As I have mentioned what we have to nourish our *bodies,* I must also add that we have a very good collection of Books to satisfy our *minds,* and if we are so disposed will make us grow wiser & consequently better. And to complete the whole the above mentioned Gentlemen are sociable & agreeable Companions — and now if I do not pass a pleasant & profitable winter it must be my fault. This evening I have past in agreeable chat with my friend Goedike of our transactions together in the Red River &c. &c. . . .

January 10 [1809], Tuesday. On the 6th Inst. Mr. McLeod &c. left us to return home and this morning Messrs Fraser and Goedike &c. set off also for their respective abodes, but in their agreeable company the few Days they were here I past many an agreeable moment, espetially with the latter Gentleman my old friend and messmate for nearly three years, and we had (as may be supposed after so long a separation) much to say in relating the most material circumstances that had occurred to each other since our separation in 1805, as well as talk over many, many things that took place while we were together at Alexandria. And in our conversation we had (I imagine) much the same satisfaction and delight that two old Soldiers have when they meet after a long separation in relating what might have befallen them in a later campaigne. What is there in this changeable World to be prefered to a *real* friend? . . .

June 2 [Friday, 1809]. The Seeds that we sewed in the Garden have sprung up & grow remarkably well — and if we may judge of the future from the present appearances of things, we shall be blessed with Berries in abundance — such as Red-Rasp-Berries, Straw-Berries, Poires and Cherries &c. &c. This River since the beginning of May has risen twelve feet & still continues to rise, which is in part owing to the late Rains we have had, but more so to the dissolving of the great quantity of Snow on the Rocky Mountain. . . .

July 19 [Thursday, 1809]. Mr. Stuart &c. have left this to return to New Caledonia —but the few Days he was here were by me past much to my satisfaction. We rambled about together in the adjacent Plains, and conversed as we walked, but now and then we would stop to eat a few Berries, which are plentiful everywhere. He I perceive has read much & reflected not a little — and how happy should I be to have such a Companion for the whole Summer! But such is the nature of this Country, that we meet but seldom and the time we can remain together is never long. We only have time to begin to form an acquaintance, when we must separate perhaps not to meet again for years to come! Baptiste La Fleur (my Interpreter) will accompany them as far as St Johns, in hopes of getting some tidings of his Brother, who it is supposed has been killed by a rascally Indian, while on his way last Spring from the Rocky Mountain Portage to St Johns. . . .

[Stuart's Lake[31] *May 8 [1811], Wednesday.* People arrived from Stuarts Lake and inform me that my Woman on the 25th Ult. was brought to bed of a Daughter— whom I name Polly Harmon. As the Ice in the River begins to be bad, it is expected that a few Days hence the navigation will be open, when Messrs. Stuart & Quesnel &c. will embark with the Returns for the Rainy Lake. Dallaire remains here and tomorrow I shall set off for Stuarts Lake where God willing I shall pass the ensuing Summer — but all my most serious thoughts are taken up on reflecting on the separation which is so soon to take place with me and my beloved Son[32] — who a few months hence will be at such an immense distance from his affectionate Father! And it is very probable I shall never see him again in this World! What can be more trying to the feelings of an affectionate Parent than thus to be separated from so young and so tender a Darling Child? There is no consideration that could induce me to send him down (especially while so young) but the thoughts that he soon will be in the arms of my kind Relations who will make it more in their power to bring him up in the paths of virtue in the civilized part of the World, than it could be possible for me to do in this Savage Country — and as I do what I flatter myself will in the end be to his advantage, so I also earnestly pray our Gracious God to protect him while in this world of trouble and sin & bless him in the next. Amen. . . .

April 6, Monday. 1812. Six Indians arrived from Frasers Lake and delivered me a Letter wrote by Mr. David Thompson, dated August 28th, 1811, *Ilk-koy-ope* Falls [Kettle Falls] Columbia River — which informs me that he accompanied by Seven Canadians last Spring descended the above mentioned River to where it empties itself into the Pacific Ocean,[33] and where they arrived on the 16th of July and found a number of people building a large Fort for the American Company or rather Astor & Co. [meaning the Pacific Fur Company][34] and that Mr. Alexander McKay[35] &c. (one of the Partners but formerly for the North West Co.) had gone to the Northward, in the vessel [the *Tonquin*] that brought them out, on a coasting-trade. Mr. Thompson Writes that after having remained Seven Days with the American People he set off to return to his Establishments which are nigh the source of the Columbia River and from whence he wrote the above mentioned letter, and delivered it to an Indian to bring it to the next Tribe, that they might forward it to the next and so on till it reached this place, which manner of conveyance accounts for the great length of time it has been on its way, for the distance is not so great but that People might come from there in a Months time at most. . . .

May 13 [1813], Thursday. Fine weather. In the fore part of the Day Mr. Stuart Six Canadians and two of the Natives embarked aboard two Canoes, and took with him a small assortment of Goods (as pocket money) and Provisions for a Month and a half, in order to go and join Mr. J.G. McTavish &c. at some place on the Columbia River, and there with them proceed down to the Sea — and should Mr. Stuart be so fortunate as to discover a water communication between this and the Columbia, we shall for the future get our yearly supply of Goods from that quarter, and send our Returns out that way, which will be shipped there directly for the China Market[36] in Vessels which the Concern intends building on that Coast — but while those deep-laid plains are putting in execution, I in a more humble sphere it is true, but full as sure of succeeding in my undertakings shall attend to the little affairs of New Caledonia! and pass the Summer at this place. Perhaps there is no Country in the World, where people have business to attend to in order to gain their livelyhood, who have so much time to themselves as we in this Savage Country — for few of us here are employed more & many much less than one fifth of our time in transacting the business of the Concern — therefore we have at least four fifths at our disposal, and if we do not employ those leisure moments in improving our understandings it must be our fault. . . .

September 1 [1813], Wednesday. Mr. McDougall[37] who a few Days since arrived from McLeods Lake has now gone to accompany all the People of the Fort to Pinchy who are gone there to gather Berries and I am left entirely alone, not a soul in the Fort except myself. I therefore have a favourable opportunity of turning my thoughts inwards and examine my past life — but in so doing I am struck with astonishment and grieved to find it has been so different from that of a true Christian! And those reflections bring on remorse of conscience, and as I connive I have had a more wicked life than the most of my fellow creatures, I therefore consider it both proper and necessary that I shall henceforward *Fast & Pray* the first Day of every Month — that is to eat nothing in the morning and to pass the whole Day in prayer, reading the Bible or some other good Book and in meditation — and thus shall keep *that* fresh in my memory for which I must (on the appointed Day) render an account to my Creator — and I pray God that through His infinite goodness, that this way of living for the future may in some manner serve to blot out my past Sins (or rather He will forgive my trespasses thro' the merits of our Blessed Redeemer) which I know to be without number — as well as be a means (with the aid of His Holy Spirit without which I am conscious I can do nothing) of keeping me in the path of virtue & holiness. . . . [38]

[In retrospect,[39] Harmon evidently regarded this day as the date of his conversion, for the heavily revised account in the printed text includes the following: 'Until this day, I have always doubted whether such a Saviour as the scriptures describe, every really existed, and appeared on earth! . . . As I was praying to-day, on a sudden, the faith, respecting which I was so solicitous, was, I trust, graciously granted to me. My views of the Saviour, underwent a total change. I was enabled, not only to believe in his existence, but to apprehend his superlative excellency; and now he appears to be, in truth, what the scriptures describe him to be, the chiefest among ten thousand, and one altogether lovely. May the grace of God enable me to follow his heavenly example through life, that I may dwell with him in glory, forever!']. . . .

April 15 [1816], Monday. My desire to return to my native Country in hopes of seeing my aged Mother and my expiring Brothers ere they meet their dissolutions never was so great as at the present moment, and yet I cannot think of doing it this Season as it is thought absolutely necessary that I shall pass this ensuing Summer at this place. However a few Days hence I shall write my Friends below — and knowing as I do that there is little except disappointments & Death certain in this World of Disappointments and sorrows, I therefore am resolved to forward to them, by my Friend Mr. John Stuart, a copy of this Journal, in order that they (in case I never have the inexpressible pleasure and gratification of seeing them myself) may know the satisfaction I presume it will prove to be to them of knowing how their long absent Relative has been employed both as to Body & Mind while in this Savage Country. . . .

February 28 [1819], Sunday.[40] Mr. George McDougall[41] has arrived here from Frazer's Lake, to remain, as I am going to McLeod's Lake, to prepare for a departure for Head Quarters; and my intention is, during the next summer, to visit my native land. I design, also, to take my family with me, and leave them there, that they may be educated in a civilized and christian manner. The mother of my children will accompany me; and, if she shall be satisfied to remain in that part of the world, I design to make her regularly my wife by a formal marriage. It will be seen by this remark, that my intentions have materially changed, since the time that I first took her to live with me; and as my conduct in this respect is different from that which has generally been pursued by the gentlemen of the North West Company, it will be proper to state some of the reasons which have governed my decision, in regard to this weighty affair. It has been made with the most serious deliberation; and I hope, under a solemn sense of my accountability to God.

Having lived with this woman as my wife, though we were never formally contracted to each other, during life, and having children by her, I consider that I am under a moral obligation not to dissolve the connexion, if she is willing to continue it. The union which has been formed between us, in the providence of God, has not only been cemented by a long and mutual performance of kind offices, but, also, by a more sacred consideration. Ever since my own mind was turned effectually to the subject of religion, I have taken pains to instruct her in the great doctrines and duties of christianity. My exertions have not been in vain. Through the merciful agency of the Holy Spirit, I trust that she has become a partaker with me, in the consolations and hopes of the gospel. I consider it to be my duty to take her to a christian land, where she may enjoy Divine ordinances, grow in grace, and ripen for glory. — We have wept together over the early departure of several children, and especially, over the death of a beloved son. We have children still living, who are equally dear to us both. How could I spend my days in the civilized world, and leave my beloved children in the wilderness? The thought has in it the bitterness of death. How could I tear them from a mother's love, and leave her to mourn over their absence, to the day of her death? Possessing only the common feelings of humanity, how could I think of her, in such circumstances, without anguish? On the whole, I consider the course which I design to pursue, as the only one which religion and humanity would justify.

Notes

[1] Located near where the Pigeon River enters Lake Superior south of Fort William (Kaministikwia). The distances which follow are over-estimated.

[2] This was the 'New North West Company', popularly known as the XY Company (see below).

[3] A kind of punch made with citrus fruits, sugar, and rum.

[4] That is, wore evening dress; the ladies mentioned in the next sentence were native and Métis.

[5] On the Assiniboine River, west of Fort Dauphin on Lake Winnipegosis.

[6] On the Swan River, west of Lake Winnipegosis.

[7] Archibald Norman McLeod (fl. 1785–1837/45) was an influential partner in the North West Company. His diary for 1800–1 (which mentions Harmon several times) has been published; see Charles N. Gates, ed. *Five Fur Traders of the Northwest* (2nd. ed.) St Paul: Minnesota Historical Society, 1965. He retired in 1821 when the two companies united.

[8] Actually these natives were from the rapids on the Saskatchewan River.

[9] A.N. McLeod's first name was actually Archibald.

[10] On the Swan River, south-west of Swan River post.

[11] Alexander Henry the Younger (b.?-d.1814); fur trader and explorer; nephew of ALEXANDER HENRY the Elder. The younger Henry left an important exploration journal covering the years 1779–1814.

[12] Beyond Harmon's affectionate portrait of Frederick Goedike little is known of him.

[13] Hugh McGillis (1767?–1848) served the North West Company in many posts between 1790 and 1816. He was one of the partners arrested by Lord Selkirk at Fort William in 1816, and was tried at York (Toronto) but acquitted. Like many old traders he lived in retirement at Williamstown near Cornwall.

[14] The XY or New North West Company was founded after the NWC reorganization of 1795

when Simon McTavish came into conflict with some of his wintering partners; the two companies amalgamated after McTavish's death in 1804.

[15]Probably the Bible.

[16]This was the *Canada Jurisdiction Act* (1803), which provided for the appointment of Justices of the Peace in the 'Indian Territories'; crimes committed there could be dealt with by the courts in Upper and Lower Canada.

[17]Meadow Portage, between Lake Winnipegosis and Lake Manitoba.

[18]Harmon may mean either 'impractical', 'visionary', or — more specifically — given to the ideas of the Romantic movement, that is preferring grandeur and irregular beauty to classical order and proportion.

[19]On the South Branch of the Saskatchewan River, about 70 miles west of the point where the river separates into North and South Branches.

[20]Harmon's 'country wife', to whom he became devoted, was Elizabeth Duval, daughter of a Canadian father and Cree mother; they had twelve (or possibly fourteen) children. They were legally married at Fort William in 1819. After Harmon's death of smallpox in 1843 she continued to live in Montreal until her death in 1862.

[21]On the west shore of Lake Athabasca.

[22]The notable fur trader and explorer John Stuart (1780–1847), seen from varying points of view, appears in a number of fur trade and exploration journals (see SIMON FRASER, LETITIA HARGRAVE, GEORGE SIMPSON).

[23]Jules-Maurice Quesnel (1786–1842), fur trader, and later soldier, businessman and politician; he accompanied SIMON FRASER on his 1808 journey down the Fraser River.

[24]For the historic descent of the Fraser River, see SIMON FRASER.

[25]On the Peace River east of Fort St John.

[26]Harmon's entry for 13 October 1818 states, 'For several years past, Iroquois from Canada, have been in the habit of coming into different parts of the North West country, to hunt the beaver, &c. The Natives of the country, consider them as intruders. As they are mere rovers, they do not feel the same interest, as those who permanaently reside here, in keeping the stock of animals good, and therefore they make great havock among the game, destroying alike the animals which are young and old'.

[27]Donald McTavish (1771/2–1814), North West Company trader and partner; he was in charge at Fort Dunvegan 1808–11.

[28]For J.G. McTavish, see LETITIA HARGRAVE.

[29]Joseph McGillivray (1790–1832), a son of the influential North West Company partner William McGillivray, after whom Fort William was named. Joseph was made partner in 1813 and retired in 1831.

[30]Sturgeon Lake Fort, west of Lake Nipigon.

[31]West of the Parsnip River, about 30 miles from modern Fort Fraser, B.C.

[32]Harmon's son George, born in 1807, was sent by his father to be educated by his brother Argalus in Vermont; his death after a brief illness in March, 1813 caused his father great sorrow.

[33]For THOMPSON's account of this journey see *David Thompson's Narrative 1784-1812*, ed. Richard Glover (Toronto: Champlain Society, 1962), 339–59.

[34]Fort Astoria, at the mouth of the Columbia River, renamed Fort George when it was purchased by the North West Company in 1813.

[35]For Alexander McKay, see MACKENZIE; he was his lieutenant on the expedition to the Pacific.

[36]Between 1792 and 1823 (except for 1802–3 and 1810–12) the North West Company shipped

substantial quantities of lower-grade beaver pelts to China through American firms, saving 50% on the cost of sending them by British ships going round the Horn.

[37]Harmon's close friend James McDougall (1783?–1851) brother of George (see below) spent his life as a clerk first in the North West Company and after union in the Hudson's Bay Company; he died, apparently impoverished, in Montreal in 1851.

[38]Harmon then includes a morning and an evening prayer which he has written for himself.

[39]W. Kaye Lamb's note, in his edition of 1957.

[40]Harmon's manuscript journal covers only the period to 1816, but he must have added to it in another copy, as entries continue to 1819 in the printed version edited by Daniel Haskel, Andover, Mass., 1820.

[41]George McDougall (fl. 1815–1843); brother of James (see above). He was briefly a Hudson's Bay Company clerk in 1815, but joined his brother in the North West Company in 1816. He returned to the HBC when the companies united in 1821, and remained a clerk, serving chiefly at Lesser Slave Lake.

Part IV: An Imperial Enterprise

Alexander Mackenzie   (1764 – 1820)

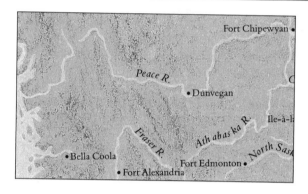

MACKENZIE, the first person of European origin to make a complete crossing of the North American continent, did so less as an explorer than as a commercial entrepreneur. If his contemporary GEORGE VANCOUVER represents the archetype of the imperialist scientific explorer, Mackenzie is his commercial twin. As such he is a profoundly different exploration writer either from DAVID THOMPSON, his other great contemporary, or from SIMON FRASER, who both shared his commercial culture and transcended it. Forthright, unphilosophical, and with no high opinion of the natives he worked with, Mackenzie set himself the task of expanding Montreal economic power to cover the whole continent. In the course of doing so he completed two arduous journeys, one by accident to the Arctic Ocean, and the second deliberately to the Pacific. He also made an early attempt (at least by one who knew the land well) to synthesize what was known about Canada into a general geographical view of the country. Too long to reprint here, this synthesis makes an interesting comparison with THOMPSON's parallel attempt to draw a general picture of the Great Plains.

Born on the Isle of Lewis, Mackenzie emigrated with his father to the United States at the age of 10, and when he was orphaned was eventually sent north by his Loyalist aunts. He entered the firm of Gregory, MacLeod in 1779, when the 'peddlers from Montreal' were beginning to give the Hudson's Bay Company serious competition in the west. The formation of the North West Company in 1783–4 tested the mettle of the smaller companies in the field; when violence erupted (centring on the unpredictable PETER POND) Gregory, MacLeod and the NWC amalgamated, and though Mackenzie in later years was deeply involved with other trading enterprises, when he made his two trips in search of a route west, it was in the North West Company's interest. Plans for the expedition of 1789 were based on information from PETER POND who was convinced that what is now the Mackenzie River would lead west, but at Camsell Bend Mackenzie faced the fact that the river he was following led inexorably northward. By the time of his second expedition of 1792 Mackenzie had improved geographical information. He made the journey to the coast with matchless energy, speed, and administrative brilliance. Though the new landscape and the lives of the people he met play a role in his narrative, Mackenzie had neither geographical nor ethnographical instincts. Instead, no matter at what point we take up his account, we experience the expedition as *system*, as a series of interacting activities with the leader always at their centre, whether in achievement or, as often happened, near-defeat. This capacity to systematize was of course the key to his economic vision.

The personal cost to Mackenzie was very great; physically strong, he was nevertheless restless in temperament and inclined to nervous depression. Back at Fort Chipewyan he suffered a bad case of writer's block in attempting an account of his expeditions. His journals were revised before publication by William Combe, a capable English literary hack with an entertaining history, who often assisted authors from his cell in debtor's prison. Besides excerpts from the final version of the Pacific journey (the log of which has not been found) two passages from the *Arctic Journal* have been included, one from Mackenzie's own log, still extant, and one from Combe's version. They illustrate the magisterial tone and pacing with which Combe endowed Mackenzie's rough but nevertheless expressive prose. Mackenzie's *Voyages from Montreal* were published in 1801 and were quickly issued in the U.S. and translated into French and German; the explorer was knighted in 1802. After a decade of unsuccessful attempts to reorganize the fur trade, Mackenzie retired to Scotland, where he died in 1820, just before the union of the two great trading companies made his continent-wide schemes practical at last.

Texts: *(I) Arctic Journal*: 1) *Journal of a Voyage from Fort Chipewyan to the Arctic Ocean* (1789); entries for 11–13 August 1789, as edited by W. Kaye Lamb (see II, below) from the scribal transcript, British Library: Stowe 793, ff. 1–81; and 2) the published version of 1801, as rewritten by William Combe. *(II) Pacific Journal*: Combe's version (the only one now extant) as edited by W. Kaye Lamb, *The Journals and Letters of Sir Alexander Mackenzie*. Cambridge University Press, for the Hakluyt Society, 1970.

I. *The Arctic Journey (1789)*

(1) from a scribal transcript of Mackenzie's journal; a few helpful emendations from the 1801 edition are in ⟨angle⟩ brackets.

Tuesday, August 11.[1] We observed several Tracks along the Beach & a Camp[men]t in the Edge of the Wood which appeared to be 5 or 6 Days old. We would have continued our Rout along this Side the River were it not that we have not seen our Hunters since Yesterday Morning. We embark'd before 3 A.M. & travers'd.[2] At 5 we see two of them coming down the River in search of us, as they were surprized what detained us. They kill'd no large Animals, only one Beaver & a few Hares, & they said that the Wood was so thick near the River that it was impossible to hunt. They had seen several of the Natives Campments not far from the River, & they were of Opinion that they were here when we passed downwards, & their having discovered us is the Reason that we meet with none of them now. I asked the English Chief[3] to return with me to the other Side to endeavour to find those whose Track & Campments we had seen, which he was not willing to do, he wanted to send the Young Men but I cou'd not trust them & am very doubtful me himself. They are still afraid that I may meet with the Natives who might give me Accounts of the other River & that I should go over Land to it, & bring them along with me. I was told to Day by one of my Men that the English Chief his wives & Brother were to leave me, this Side of the Slave Lake to go to the Land of the Beaver Indians, & again the Middle of the Winter wou'd be back to the Slave Lake where he was to meet some of his Relations who went to War last Spring to whom he had given Rendezvous. This he learn'd from one of the young Men. We traversed and continued tracking the Indians till past 12 o'Clock when we lost their Tracks. We supposed they must have crossed to the East side. We saw several Dogs on each side of the River. The young Indians killed a Wolf, which is fat, the Men eat it and declared it to be very good. Killed 15 young Geese which are big and begin to fly. It was 8 o'Clock when we camp'd.[4] Lost upwards of 4 Hours to day traversing, fine Weather all Day.

Wednesday, August 12. All embarked at 3 this Morning. Sent the young Indians across, that we might not miss any of the Natives should there be any along the River. We saw many places where they had made Fire along the Beach, none of them old and fire running in the Wood in many places. At 4 oClock we came to a Campment which the People had left this Morning, we found there Tracks in several Places in the Wood. As I thought they could not be far off, I asked the English Chief to go and try, if he could find them which he seemed to loath to do. I told him I intended to go with him, and he could not be off, we parted and went several Miles into the wood but we could not find any thing of them. The fire had ran all over the country, burnt about 3 Ins. of black light soil, which covered a cold body of Clay and which was so hard that the Feet left no Track. At 10 o'Clock we returned from our fruitless Excursion. The young Men kill'd 7 Geese. Had several Showers of Rain with Gusts of Wind and Thunder. The Men set Nets during my Absence.

Thursday, August 13. Rose our Nets without a single Fish and embark'd at half past 3 A.M. Fine weather. Pass a No. of Places where the Natives had made Fires, and many Tracks along the Beach. At 7 o'Clk we came opposite the Island where we had hid our Pemmican,[5] 2 of the young Indians went for it, and found it as we had left it, and is very acceptable to us, as it will enable us to get out of the River without losing much time to hunt. Shortly after we perceived a smoak on the S.W. Shore, 3 Leagues distant, it did not appear to be a running fire. The Indians were a little way ahead of us, and paid no attention to this smoak. They saw a flock of Geese ahead which they fired several Shot on, and we immediately perceived that the smoak disappeared, and soon after saw the Natives run along the Shore and soon embarking in their small Canoes. Tho' we were almost opposite to them, we could not think of traversing without going further upon account of the Strength of the Current. I ordered the Indians to make all the haste they could to go and speak with and make them wait our arrival. As soon as our small Canoe struck off we could see the Natives that were in their Canoes landing, drawing their Canoes on the Beach and making for the Wood. It was past 10 A.M. before we landed at where they left a Number of their Things on the Beach. They did not wait the arrival of our Indians, the latter I found busy running among the things and looking for more in the Wood. I was very vex'd at them, that instead of looking for the Natives, they were separating ⟨dividing⟩ their Property for which I severely rebuked the English Chief. I ordered him, his young Men and my own Men to go and look out for the Indians. I went also, but they were too much frightened and had too much the Start of us to over take them. We saw several Dogs in the Woods, some of which followed us to the Water side. The English Chief was very much displeased that I had reproach'd him, and told me so. I [had] waited [for] such an Opportunity to tell him [what I thought of] his Behaviour to me for some time past, told him that I had more reason to be angry than he, that I had come a great way at great Expence to no Purpose, and that I thot. he hid from me ⟨a principal⟩ part of what the Natives told him respecting the Country &c. for fear that he should have to follow me, and that his Reason for not killing ⟨game, &c.⟩ was his Jealousy, which likewise kept him from looking for the Natives. as he ought, and that we never had given him any reason for such Suspicion.

He got into a most violent Passion, and said, we spoke ill, that he was not jealous, that he had not concealed any thing from us, and that till now there were no Animals, and that he would not accompany us any further tho' he was without Ammunition, he cou'd live the same as the Slaves ⟨the name given to the inhabitants of that part of the country⟩, and that he would remain among them &c. &c. As soon as he was done his Harrangue he began to cry bitterly, and his Relations help'd him. They said they cried ⟨for their⟩ dead Friend. I did not interrupt them in their Grief for two Hours. As I could not well [do] without them, I was obliged to use every method to make the English Chief change his mind. At last he consented with a great ⟨apparent⟩ Reluctance, and we embark'd. . . .

(2) *the same passage as re-written by William Combe, from the edition of 1801; dates in that edition are in the margin, which increased the effect of continuous narrative.*

[Tuesday 11.] We observed several tracks along the beach, and an encampment at the edge of the woods, which appeared to be five or six days old. We should have continued our route along this side of the river, but we had not seen our hunters since yesterday morning. We accordingly embarked before three, and at five traversed the river, when we saw two of them coming down in search of us. They had killed no other animals than one beaver, and a few hares. According to their account, the woods were so thick that it was impossible to follow the game through them. They had seen several of the natives encampments, at no great distance from the river; and it was their opinion that they had discovered us in our passage down it, and had taken care to avoid us; which accounted for the small number we had seen on our return.

I requested the English chief to return with me to the other side of the river, in order that he might proceed to discover the natives, whose tracks and habitations we had seen there; but he was backward in complying with my desire, and proposed to send the young men; but I could not trust to them, and at the same time was become rather doubtful of him. They were still afraid lest I should obtain such accounts of the other river as would induce me to travel overland to it, and that they should be called upon to accompany me. I was, indeed, informed by one of my own people, that the English chief, his wives and companions, had determined to leave me on this side of the Slave Lake, in order to go to the country of the Beaver Indians; and that about the middle of the winter he would return to that lake, where he had appointed to me some of his relations, who, during the last spring, had been engaged in war.

We now traversed the river, and continued to track the Indians till past twelve, when we lost all traces of them; in consequence, as we imagined, of their having crossed to the Eastern side. We saw several dogs on both shores; and one of the young Indians killed a wolf, which the men ate with great satisfaction: we shot, also, fifteen young geese that were now beginning to fly. It was eight when we took our evening station, having lost four hours in making our traverses. There was no interruption of the fine weather during the course of this day.

[Wednes. 12.] We proceeded on our voyage at three this morning, and dispatched the two young Indians across the river, that we might not miss any of the natives that should be on the banks of it. We saw many places where fires had been lately made along the beach, as well as fire running in the woods. At four we arrived at an encampment which had been left this morning. Their tracks were observable in several places in the woods, and as it might be presumed that they could not be at any great distance, it was proposed to the chief to accompany me in search of them. We accordingly, though with some hesitation on his part, penetrated several miles into the woods, but without discovering the objects of our research. The fire had spread all over the country, and had burned about three inches of the black, light, soil, which covered a body of cold clay, that was so hard as not to receive the least impression of our feet. At ten we returned from our unsuccessful excursion. In the mean time the hunters had killed seven geese. There were several showers of rain, accompanied with gusts of wind and thunder. The nets had been set during our absence.

[Thursd. 13.] The nets were taken up, but not one fish was found in them; and at half past three we continued our route, with very favourable weather. We passed several places, where fires had been made by the natives, and many tracks were perceptible along the beach. At seven we were opposite the island where our Pemmican had been concealed: two of the Indians were accordingly dispatched in search of it, and it proved very acceptable, as it rendered us more independent of the provisions which were to be obtained by our fowling pieces, and qualified us to get out of the river without that delay which our hunters would otherwise have required. In a short time we perceived a smoke on the shore to the South-West, at the distance of three leagues, which did not appear to proceed from any running fire. The Indians, who were a little way ahead of us, did not discover them, being engaged in the pursuit of a flock of geese, at which they fired several shots, when the smoke immediately disappeared; and in a short time we saw several of the natives run along the shore, some of whom entered their canoes. Though we were almost opposite to them, we could not cross the river without going further up it, from the strength of the current; I therefore ordered our Indians to make every possible exertion, in order to speak with them, and wait our arrival. But as soon as our small canoe struck off, we could perceive the poor affrighted people hasten to the shore, and after drawing their canoes on the beach, hurry into the woods. It was past ten before we landed at the place where they had deserted their canoes, which were four in number. They were so terrified that they had left several articles on the beach. I was very much displeased with my Indians, who instead of seeking the natives, were dividing their property. I rebuked the English chief with some severity for his conduct, and imme-diately ordered him, his young men, and my own people, to go in search of the fugitives, but their fears had made them too nimble for us, and we could not overtake them. We saw several dogs in the woods, and some of them followed us to our canoe.

The English chief was very much displeased at my reproaches, and expressed himself to me in person to that effect. That was the very opportunity which I wanted, to make him acquainted, with my dissatisfaction for some time past. I stated to him that I had come a great way, and at a very considerable expence, without having obtained the object of my wishes, and that I suspected he had concealed from me a principal part of what the natives had told him respecting the country, lest he should be obliged to follow me: that his reason for not killing game, &c was his jealousy, which likewise prevented him from looking after the natives as he ought; and that we had never given him any cause for any suspicions of us. These suggestions irritated him in a very high degree, and he accused me of speaking ill words to him; he denied the charge of jealousy, and declared that he did not conceal any thing from us; and that as to the ill success of their hunting, it arose from the nature of the country, and the scarcity, which had hitherto appeared, of animals in it. He concluded by informing me that he would not accompany me any further; that though he was without ammunition, he could live in the same manner as the slaves, (the name given to the inhabitants of that part of the country), and that he would remain among them. His harangue was succeeded by a loud and bitter lamentation; and his relations assisted the vociferations of his grief; though they said that their tears flowed for their dead friends. I did not interrupt their grief for two hours, but as I could not well do without them, I was at length obliged to sooth it, and induce the chief to change his resolution, which he did, but with great apparent reluctance when we embarked as we had hitherto done.

II. *The Pacific Journey (1793)*

Mackenzie prepares to set out from Fort Fork[6]

[1793] The month of April being now past, in the early part of which I was most busily employed in trading with the Indians, I ordered our old canoes to be repaired with bark, and added four new ones to them, when with the furs and provisions I had purchased, six canoes were loaded and dispatched on the 8th of May for Fort Chepewyan. I had, however, retained six of the men who agreed to accompany me on my projected voyage of discovery. I also engaged my hunters, and closed the business of the year for the company by writing my public and private dispatches.

Having ascertained, by various observations,[7] the latitude of this place to be 56.9 North, and longitude 117.35.15 West, on the 9th day of May, I found, that my acrometer[8] was one hour forty-six minutes slow to apparent time; the meaning going of it I had found to be twenty-two seconds slow in twenty-four hours. Having settled this point, the canoe was put into the water: her dimensions were twenty-six feet long within, exclusive of the curves of stem and stern, twenty six inches hold, and four feet nine inches beam. At the same time she was so light, that two men could carry her on a good road three or four miles without resting. In this slender vessel, we shipped provisions, goods for presents, arms, ammunition, and baggage, to the weight of three thousand pounds, and an equipage of ten people; viz. Alexander Mackay,[9] Joseph Landry, Charles Ducette,[10] François Beaulieux, Baptist Bisson, François Courtois, and Jacques Beauchamp, with two Indians as hunters and interpreters. One of them, when a boy, was used to be so idle, that he obtained the reputable name of Cancre,[11] which he still possesses. With these persons I embarked at seven in the evening. My winter interpreter, with another person, whom I left here to take care of the fort, and supply the natives with ammunition during the summer, shed tears on the reflection of those dangers which we might encounter in our expedition, while my own people offered up their prayers that we might return in safety from it. . . .

Attempts to get information about the country ahead

[Sunday, May 12] The greater part of this band[12] being Rocky Mountain Indians, I endeavoured to obtain some intelligence of our intended route, but they all pleaded ignorance, and uniformly declared, that they knew nothing of the country beyond the first mountain: at the same time they were of opinion, that, from the strength of the current and the rapids, we should not get there by water; though they did not hesitate to express their surprise at the expedition we had already made.

I inquired, with some anxiety, after an old man who had already given me an account of the country beyond the limits of his tribe, and was very much disappointed at being informed, that he had not been seen for upwards of a moon. This man had been at war on another large river beyond the Rocky Mountain, and described to me a fork of it between the mountains; the Southern branch of which he directed me to take: from thence, he said, there was a carrying-place of about a day's march for a young man to get to the other river. To prove the truth of his relation, he consented, that his son, who had been with him in those parts, should accompany me; and he accordingly sent him to the Fort some days before my departure; but the preceding night he deserted with another young man, whose application to attend me as a hunter, being refused, he persuaded the other to leave me. I now thought it right to repeat to them what I had said to the chief of the first band, respecting the advantages which would be derived from the voyage, that the young men might be encouraged to remain with me; as without them I should not have attempted to proceed. . . .

Dangers along the route

[Monday, May 20.] The weather was clear with a sharp air, and we renewed our voyage at a quarter past four, on a course South-West by West three quarters of a mile. We now, with infinite difficulty passed along the foot of a rock, which, fortunately, was not an hard stone, so that we were enabled to cut steps in it for the distance of twenty feet; from which, at the hazard of my life, I leaped on a small rock below, where I received those who followed me on my shoulders. In this manner four of us passed and dragged up the canoe, in which attempt we broke her. Very luckily, a dry tree had fallen from the rock above us, without which we could not have made a fire,[13] as no wood was to be procured within a mile of the place. When the canoe was repaired, we continued towing it along the rocks to the next point, when we embarked, as we could not at present make any further use of the line, but got along the rocks of a round high island of stone, till we came to a small sandy bay. As we had already damaged the canoe, and had every reason to think that she soon would risk much greater injury, it became necessary for us to supply ourselves with bark, as our provision of that material article was almost exhausted; two men were accordingly sent to procure it, who soon returned with the necessary store.

Mr Mackay, and the Indians who had been on shore, since we broke the canoe, were prevented from coming to us by the rugged and impassable state of the ground. We, therefore, again resumed our course with the assistance of poles, with which we pushed onwards till we came beneath a precipice, where we could not find any bottom; so that we were again obliged to have recourse to the line, the management of which was rendered not only difficult but dangerous, as the men employed in towing were under the necessity of passing on the outside of trees that grew on the edge of the precipice. We, however, surmounted this difficulty, as we had done many others, and the people who had been walking over land now joined us. They also had met with their obstacles in passing the mountain.

It now became necessary for us to make a traverse,[14] where the water was so rapid, that some of the people stripped themselves to their shirts that they might be the better prepared for swimming, in case any accident happened to the canoe, which they seriously apprehended; but we succeeded in our attempt without any other inconvenience, except that of taking in water. We now came to a cascade, when it was thought necessary to take out part of the lading. At noon we stopped to take an altitude, opposite to a small river that flowed in from the left:[15] while I was thus engaged, the men went on shore to fasten the canoe, but as the current was not very strong, they had been negligent in performing this office; it proved, however, sufficiently powerful to sheer her off, and if it had not happened that one of the men, from absolute fatigue had remained and held the end of the line, we should have been deprived of every means of prosecuting our voyage, as well as of present subsistence. But notwithstanding the state of my mind on such an alarming circumstance, and an intervening cloud that interrupted me, the altitude which I took has been since proved to be tolerably correct, and gave 56 North latitude. Our last course was South-South-West two miles and a quarter.

We now continued our toilsome and perilous progress with the line West by North, and as we proceeded the rapidity of the current increased, so that in the distance of two miles we were obliged to unload four times, and carry every thing but the canoe: indeed, in many places, it was with the utmost difficulty that we could prevent her from being dashed to pieces against the rocks by the violence of the eddies. At five we had proceeded to where the river was one continued rapid. Here we again took every thing out of the canoe, in order to tow her up with the line, though the rocks were so shelving as greatly to increase the toil and hazard of that operation. At length, however, the agitation of the water was so great, that a wave striking on the bow of the canoe broke the line, and filled us with inexpressible dismay, as it appeared impossible that the vessel could escape from being dashed to pieces, and those who were in her from perishing. Another wave, however, more propitious than the former, drove her out of the tumbling water, so that the men were enabled to bring her ashore, and though she had been carried over rocks by these swells which left them naked a moment after, the canoe had received no material injury. The men were, however, in such a state from their late alarm, that it would not only have been unavailing but imprudent to have proposed any further progress at present, particularly as the river above us, as far as we could see, was one white sheet of foaming water.[16]

That[17] the discouragement, difficulties, and dangers, which had hitherto attended the progress of our enterprize, should have excited a wish in several of those who were engaged in it to discontinue the pursuit, might be naturally expected; and indeed it began to be muttered on all sides that there was no alternative but to return.

Instead of paying any attention to these murmurs, I desired those who had uttered them to exert themselves in gaining an ascent of the hill, and encamp there for the night. In the mean time I set off with one of the Indians, and though I continued my examination of the river almost as long as there was any light to assist us, I could see no end of the rapids and cascades: I was, therefore, perfectly satisfied, that it would be impracticable to proceed any further by water.[18] We returned from this reconnoitring excursion very much fatigued, with our shoes worn out and wounded feet; when I found that, by felling trees on the declivity of the first hill, my people had contrived to ascend it.

From the place where I had taken the altitude at noon, to the place where we made our landing, the river is not more than fifty yards wide, and flows between stupendous rocks, from whence hugh fragments sometimes tumble down, and falling from such an height, dash into small stones, with sharp points, and form the beach between the rocky projections. Along the face of some of these precipices, there appears a stratum of a bitumenous substance which resembles coal; though while some of the pieces of it appeared to be excellent fuel, other resisted, for a considerable time, the action of fire, and did not emit the least flame. The whole of this day's course would have been altogether impracticable, if the water had been higher, which must be the case at certain seasons. We saw also several encampments of the Knisteneaux along the river, which must have been formed by them on their war excursions: a decided proof of the savage, blood-thirsty disposition of that people; as nothing less than such a spirit could impel them to encounter the difficulties of this almost inaccessible country, whose natives are equally unoffending and defenceless.

Mr Mackay informed me, that in passing over the mountains, he observed several chasms in the earth that emitted heat and smoke, which diffused a strong sulphureous stench. I should certainly have visited the phænomenon, if I had been sufficiently qualified as a naturalist, to have offered scientific conjecture or observations thereon.[19]

[Tuesday, May 21.] It rained in the morning, and did not cease till about eight, and as the men had been very fatigued and disheartened, I suffered them to continue their rest till that hour. Such was the state of the river, as I have already observed, that no alternative was left us; nor did any means of proceeding present themselves to us, but the passage of the mountain over which we were to carry the canoe as well as the baggage. As this was a very alarming enterprize, I dispatched Mr Mackay with three men and the two Indians to proceed in a straight course from the top of the mountain, and to keep the line of the river till they should find it navigable. If it should be their opinion, that there was no practicable passage in that direction, two of them were instructed to return in order to make their report; while the others were to go in search of the Indian carrying-place. While they were engaged in this excursion, the people who remained with me were employed in gumming the canoe, and making handles for the axes. At noon I got an altitude, which made our latitude 56.0.8. At three o'clock had time, when my watch was slow 1.31.32 apparent time.

At sunset, Mr Mackay returned with one of the men, and in about two hours was followed by the others. They had penetrated thick woods, ascended hills and sunk into vallies, till they got beyond the rapids, which, according to their calculation, was a distance of three leagues. The two parties returned by different routes, but they both agreed, that with all its difficulties, and they were of a very alarming nature, the outward course was that which must be preferred. Unpromising, however, as the account of their expedition appeared, it did not sink them into a state of discouragement; and a kettle of wild rice, sweetened with sugar, which had been prepared for their return, with their usual regale of rum, soon renewed that courage which disdained all obstacles that threatened our progress: and they went to rest, with a full determination to surmount them on the morrow. I sat up, in the hope of getting an observation of Jupiter and his first satellite, but the cloudy weather prevented my obtaining it.

[Wednesday, May 22.] At break of day we entered on the extraordinary journey which was to occupy the remaining part of it. The men began, without delay, to cut a road up the mountain, and as the trees were but of small growth, I ordered them to fell those which they found convenient, in such a manner, that they might fall parallel with the road, but, at the same time, not separate them entirely from the stumps, so that they might form a kind of railing on either side. The baggage was now brought from the waterside to our encampment. This was likewise from the steep shelving of the rocks, a very perilous undertaking, as one false step of any of the people employed in it, would have been instantly followed by falling headlong into the water. When this important object was attained, the whole of the party proceeded with no small degree of apprehension, to fetch the canoe, which, in a short time, was also brought to the encampment; and, as soon as we had recovered from our fatigue, we advanced with it up the mountain, having the line doubled and fastened successively as we went on to the stumps; while a man at the end of it, hauled it round a tree, holding it on and shifting it as we proceeded; so that we may be said, with strict truth, to have warped the canoe up the mountain: indeed by a general and most laborious exertion, we got every thing to the summit by two in the afternoon. At noon, the latitude was 56.0.47 North. At five, I sent the men to cut the road onwards, which they effected for about a mile, when they returned.

The weather was cloudy at intervals, with showers and thunder. At about then, I observed an emersion of Jupiter's second satellite; time by the achrometer 8.32.20 by which I found the longitude to be 120.29.30 West from Greenwich.

[Thursday, May 23.] The weather was clear at four this morning, when the men began to carry. I joined Mr Mackay, and the two Indians in the labour of cutting a road. The ground continued rising gently till noon, when it began to decline; but though on such an elevated situation, we could see but little, as mountains of a still higher elevation and covered with snow, were seen far above us in every direction. In the afternoon the ground became very uneven; hills and deep defiles alternately presented themselves to us. Our progress however, exceeded my expectation, and it was not till four in the afternoon that the carriers overtook us. At five, in a state of fatigue that may be more readily conceived than expressed, we encamped near a rivulet or spring that issued from beneath a large mass of ice and snow.

Our toilsome journey of this day I compute at about three miles. . . .

News of the 'Stinking Lake'

[Sunday, June 9.] . . . we perceived a smell of fire; and in a short time heard people in the woods, as if in a state of great confusion, which was occasioned, as we afterwards understood, by their discovery of us. At the same time this unexpected circumstance produced some little discomposure among ourselves, as our arms were not in a state of preparation, and we were as yet unable to ascertain the number of the party. I considered, that if there were but few it would be needless to pursue them, as it would not be probable that we should overtake them in these thick woods; and if they were numerous, it would be an act of great imprudence to make the attempt, at least during their present alarm. I therefore ordered my people to strike off to the opposite side, that we might see if any of them had sufficient courage to remain; but, before we were half over the river, which, in this part, is not more than an hundred yards wide, two men appeared on a rising ground over against us, brandishing their spears, displaying their bows and arrows, and accompanying their hostile gestures with loud vociferations. My interpreter did not hesitate to assure them, that they might dispel their apprehensions, as we were white people, who meditated no injury, but were, on the contrary, desirous of demonstrating every mark of kindness and friendship. They did not, however, seem disposed to confide in our declarations, and actually threatened, if we came over before they were more fully satisfied of our peaceable intentions, that they would discharge their arrows at us. This was a decided kind of conduct which I did not expect; at the same time I readily complied with their proposition, and after some time had passed in hearing and answering their questions, they consented to our landing,[20] though not without betraying very evident symptoms of fear and distrust. They, however, laid aside their weapons, and when I stepped forward and took each of them by the hand, one of them, but with a very tremulous action, drew his knife from his sleeve, and presented it to me as a mark of his submission to my will and pleasure. On our first hearing the noise of these people in the woods, we displayed our flag, which was now shewn to them as a token of friendship. They examined us, and every thing about us, with a minute and suspicious attention. They had heard, indeed, of white men, but this was the first time that they had ever seen an human being of a complexion different from their own. The party had been here but a few hours; nor had they yet erected their sheds; and, except the two men now with us, they had all fled, leaving their little property behind them. To those which had given us such a proof of their confidence, we paid the most conciliating attentions in our power. One of them I sent to recall his people, and the other, for very obvious reasons, we kept with us. In the mean time the canoe was unloaded, the necessary baggage carried up the hill, and the tents pitched.

Here I determined to remain til the Indians became so familiarized with us, as to give all the intelligence which we imagined might be obtained from them. . . .

When I thought that they were sufficiently composed, I sent for the men to my tent, to gain such information respecting the country as I concluded it was in their power to afford me. But my expectations were by no means satisfied: they said that they were not acquainted with any river to the Westward, but that there was one from whence they were just arrived, over a carrying-place of eleven days march, which they represented as being a branch only of the river before us. Their iron-work they obtained from the people who inhabit the bank of that river, and an adjacent lake, in exchange for beaver skins, and dressed moose skins. They represented the latter as travelling, during a moon, to get to the country of other tribes, who live in houses, with whom they traffic for the same commodities; and that these also extend their journies in the same manner to the sea coast, or, to use their expression, the Stinking Lake, where they trade with people like us, that come there in vessels as big as islands.[21] They added, that the people to the Westward, as they have been told, are very numerous. Those who inhabit the other branch they stated as consisting of about forty families, while they themselves did not amount to more than a fourth of that number; and were almost continually compelled to remain in their strong holds, where they sometimes perished with cold and hunger, to secure themselves from their enemies, who never failed to attack them whenever an opportunity presented itself.

This account of the country, from a people who I had every reason to suppose were well acquainted with every part of it, threatened to disconcert the project on which my heart was set, and in which my whole mind was occupied. It occurred to me, however, that from fear, or other motives, they might be tardy in their communication; I therefore assured them that, if they would direct me to the river which I described to them, I would come in large vessels, like those that their neighbours had described, to the mouth of it and bring them arms and ammunition in exchange for the produce of their country; so that they might be able to defend themselves against their enemies, and no longer remain in that abject, distressed, and fugitive state in which they then lived. I added also, that in the mean time, if they would, on my return, accompany me below the mountains, to a country which was very abundant in animals, I would furnish them, and their companions, with every thing they might want; and make peace between them and the Beaver Indians. But all these promises did not appear to advance the object of my inquiries, and they still persisted in their ignorance of any such river as I had mentioned, that discharged itself into the sea.

In this state of perplexity and disappointment, various projects presented themselves to my mind, which were no sooner formed than they were discovered to be impracticable, and were consequently abandoned. At one time I thought of leaving the canoe, and every thing it contained, to go over land, and pursue that chain of connexion by which these people obtain their iron-work; but a very brief course of reflection convinced me that it would be impossible for us to carry provisions for our support through any considerable part of such a journey, as well as presents, to secure us a kind reception among the natives, and ammunition for the service of the hunters, and to defend ourselves against any act of hostility. At another time my solicitude for the success of the expedition incited a wish to remain with the natives, and go to the sea by the way they had described; but the accomplishment of such a journey, even if no accident should interpose, would have required a portion of time which it was not in my power to bestow. In my present state of information, to proceed further up the river was considered as a fruitless waste of toilsome exertion; and to return unsuccessful, after all our labour, sufferings, and dangers, was an idea too painful to indulge. Besides, I could not yet abandon the hope that the Indians might not yet be sufficiently composed and confident, to disclose their real knowledge of the country freely and fully to me. Nor was I altogether without my doubts respecting the fidelity of my interpreter, who being very much tired of the voyage, might be induced to withhold those communications which would induce me to continue it. I therefore continued my attentions to the natives, regaled them with such provisions as I had, indulged their children with a taste of sugar, and determined to suspend my conversation with them till the following morning. On my expressing a desire to partake of their fish, they brought me a few dried trout, well cured, that had been taken in the river which they lately left. One of the men also brought me five beaver skins, as a present.

[Monday, June 10.] The solicitude that possessed my mind interrupted my repose; when the dawn appeared I had already quitted my bed, and was waiting with impatience for another conference with the natives. The sun, however, had risen before they left their leafy bowers, whither they had retired with their children, having most hospitably resigned their beds, and the partners of them, to the solicitations of my young men.

I now repeated my inquiries, but my perplexity was not removed by any favourable variation in their answers. About nine, however, one of them, still remaining at my fire, in conversation with the interpreters, I understood enough of his language to know that he mentioned something about a great river, at the same time pointing significantly up that which was before us. On my inquiring of the interpreter respecting that expression, I was informed that he knew of a large river that runs towards the midday sun, a branch of which flowed near the source of that which we were now navigating; and that there were only three small lakes, and as many carrying places, leading to a small river, which discharged itself into the great river, but that the latter did not empty itself into the sea. The inhabitants, he said, built houses, lived on islands, and were a numerous and warlike people. I desired him to describe the road to the other river, by delineating it with a piece of coal, on a strip of bark, which he accomplished to my satisfaction. The opinion that the river did not discharge itself into the sea, I very confidently imputed to his ignorance of the country. . . .

Mackenzie's personal daring

[Friday, June 21] . . . Here we perceived a small new canoe, that had been drawn up to the edge of the woods, and soon after another appeared, with one man in it, which came out of a small river.[22] He no sooner saw us than he gave the whoop, to alarm his friends, who immediately appeared on the bank, armed with bows and arrows, and spears. They were thinly habited, and displayed the most outrageous antics. Though they were certainly in a state of great apprehension, they manifested by their gestures that they were resolved to attack us, if we should venture to land. I therefore ordered the men to stop the way of the canoe, and even to check her drifting with the current, as it would have been extreme folly to have approached these savages before their fury had in some degree subsided. My interpreters, who understood their language, informed me that they threatened us with instant death if we drew nigh the shore; and they followed the menace by discharging a volley of arrows, some of which fell short of the canoe, and others passed over it, so that they fortunately did us no injury. As we had been carried by the current below the spot where the Indians were, I ordered my people to paddle to the opposite side of the river, without the least appearance of confusion, so that they brought me abreast of them. My interpreters, while we were within hearing, had done every thing in their power to pacify them, but in vain. We also observed that they had sent off a canoe with two men, down the river, as we concluded, to communicate their alarm, and procure assistance. This circumstance determined me to leave no means untried that might engage us in a friendly intercourse with them, before they acquired additional security and confidence, by the arrival of their relations and neighbours, to whom their situation would be shortly notified.

I therefore formed the following adventurous project, which was happily crowned with success. I left the canoe, and walked by myself along the beach, in order to induce some of the natives to come to me, which I imagined they might be disposed to do, when they saw me alone, without any apparent possibility of receiving assistance from my people, and would consequently imagine that a communication with me was not a service of danger. At the same time, in order to possess the utmost security of which my situation was susceptible, I directed one of the Indians to slip into the woods, with my gun and his own, and to conceal himself from their discovery; he also had orders to keep as near me as possible, without being seen; and if any of the natives should venture across, and attempt to shoot me from the water, it was his instructions to lay him low; at the same time he was particularly enjoined not to fire till I had discharged one or both of the pistols that I carried in my belt. If, however, any of them were to land, and approach my person, he was immediately to join me. In the mean time my other interpreter assured them that we entertained the most friendly disposition, which I confirmed by such signals as I conceived would be comprehended by them. I had not, indeed, been long at my station, and my Indian in ambush behind me, when two of the natives came off in a canoe, but stopped when they had got within an hundred yards of me. I made signs for them to land, and as an inducement, displayed looking glasses, beads, and other alluring trinkets. At length, but with every mark of extreme apprehension, they approached the shore, stern foremost, but would not venture to land; I now made them a present of some beads, with which they were going to push off, when I renewed my entreaties, and, after some time, prevailed on them to come ashore, and sit down by me. My hunter now thought it right to join me, and created some alarm in my new acquaintance. It was, however, soon removed, and I had the satisfaction to find that he, and these people perfectly understood each other. I instructed him to say every thing that might tend to sooth their fears and win their confidence. I expressed my wish to conduct them to our canoe, but they declined my offer; and when they observed some of my people coming towards us, they requested me to let them return; and I was so well satisfied with the progress I had made in my intercourse with them, that I did not hesitate a moment in complying with their desire. During their short stay, they observed us, and everything about us, with a mixture of admiration and astonishment. We could plainly distinguish that their friends received them with great joy on their return, and that the articles which they carried back with them were examined with a general and eager curiosity; they also appeared to hold a consultation, which lasted about a quarter of an hour, and the result was, an invitation to come over to them, which was cheerfully accepted. Nevertheless, on our landing, they betrayed evident signs of confusion, which arose, probably from the quickness of our movements, as the prospect of a friendly communication had so cheered the spirits of my people, that they paddled across the river with the utmost expedition. The two men, however, who had been with us, appeared, very naturally, to possess the greatest share of courage on the occasion, and were ready to receive us on our landing; but our demeanour soon dispelled all their apprehensions, and the most familiar communication took place between us. When I had secured their confidence, by the distribution of trinkets among them, and treated the children with sugar, I instructed my interpreters to collect every necessary information in their power to afford me.

According to their account, this river, whose course is very extensive, runs towards the mid-day sun; and that at its mouth, as they had been informed, white people were building houses. They represented its current to be uniformly strong, and that in three places it was altogether impassable, from the falls and rapids, which poured along between perpendicular rocks that were much higher, and more rugged, than any we had yet seen, and would not admit of any passage over them.[23] But besides the dangers and difficulties of the navigation, they added, that we should have to encounter the inhabitants of the country, who were very numerous. They also represented their immediate neighbours as a very malignant race, who lived in large subterraneous recesses:[24] and when they were made to understand that it was our design to proceed to the sea, they dissuaded us from prosecuting our intention, as we should certainly become a sacrifice to the savage spirit of the natives. These people they described as possessing iron, arms, and utensils, which they procured from their neighbours to the Westward, and were obtained by a commercial progress from people like ourselves, who brought them in great canoes. . . .

Native map-making

[Saturday, June 22] . . . I now proceeded to request the native, whom I had particularly selected, to commence his information, by drawing a sketch of the country upon a large piece of bark, and he immediately entered on the work, frequently appealing to, and sometimes asking the advice of, those around him. He described the river as running to the East of South, receiving many rivers, and every six or eight leagues encumbered with falls and rapids, some of which were very dangerous, and six of them impracticable. The carrying-places he represented as of great length, and passing over hills and mountains. He depicted the lands of three other tribes, in succession, who spoke different languages. Beyond them he knew nothing either of the river or country, only that it was still a long way to the sea; and that, as he had heard, there was a lake, before they reached the water, which the natives did not drink.[25] As far as his knowledge of the river extended, the country on either side was level, in many places without wood, and abounding in red deer, and some of a small fallow kind. Few of the natives, he said, would come to the banks for some time; but that at a certain season they would arrive there in great numbers, to fish. They now procured iron, brass, copper, and trinkets, from the Westward; but formerly these articles were obtained from the lower parts of the river, though in small quantities. A knife was produced which had been brought from that quarter. The blade was ten inches long, and an inch and an half broad, but with a very blunted edge. The handle was of horn. We understood that this instrument had been obtained from white men, long before they had heard that any came to the Westward. One very old man observed, that as long as he could remember, he was told of white people to the Southward; and that he had heard, though he did not vouch for the truth of the report, that one of them had made an attempt to come up the river, and was destroyed.[26]

These people describe the distance across the country as very short to the Western ocean; and, according to my own idea, it cannot be above five or six degrees. If the assertion of Mr Mears be correct, it cannot be so far, as the inland sea which he mentions within Nootka, must come as far East as 126 West longitude.[27] They assured us that the road was not difficult, as they avoided the mountains, keeping along the low lands between them, many parts of which are entirely free from wood. According to their account, this way is so often travelled by them, that their path is visible throughout the whole journey, which lies along small lakes and rivers. It occupied them, they said, no more than six nights, to go to where they meet the people who barter iron, brass, copper, beads, &c. with them,[28] for dressed leather, and beaver, bear, lynx, fox, and marten skins. . . .

Mackenzie the strategist

[Sunday, June 23.] . . . I was very much surprised by the following question from one of the Indians: 'What,' demanded he, 'can be the reason that you are so particular and anxious in your inquiries of us respecting a knowledge of this country: do not you white men know every thing in the world?' This interrogatory was so very unexpected, that it occasioned some hesitation before I could answer it. At length, however, I replied, that we certainly were acquainted with the principal circumstances of every part of the world; that I knew where the sea is, and where I myself then was, but that I did not exactly understand what obstacles might interrupt me in getting to it; with which, he and his relations must be well acquainted, as they had so frequently surmounted them. Thus I fortunately preserved the impression in their minds, of the superiority of white people over themselves.

It was now, however, absolutely necessary that I should come to a final determination which route to take; and no longer interval of reflection was employed, before I preferred to go over land; the comparative shortness and security of such a journey, were alone sufficient to determine me. I accordingly proposed to two of the Indians to accompany me, and one of them readily assented to my proposition.

I now called those of my people about me, who had not been present at my consultation with the natives; and after passing a warm eulogium on their fortitude, patience, and perseverance, I stated the difficulties that threatened our continuing to navigate the river, the length of time it would require, and the scanty provision we had for such a voyage: I then proceeded for the foregoing reasons to propose a shorter route, by trying the over-land road to the sea. At the same time, as I knew from experience, the difficulty of retaining guides and as many circumstances might occur to prevent our progress in that direction, I declared my resolution not to attempt it, unless they would engage, if we could not after all proceed over land, to return with me, and continue our voyage to the discharge of the waters, whatever the distance might be. At all events, I declared, in the most solemn manner, that I would not abandon my design to reaching the sea, if I made the attempt alone, and that I did not despair of returning in safety to my friends.

This proposition met with the most zealous return, and they unanimously assured me, that they were as willing now as they had ever been, to abide by my resolutions, whatever they might be, and to follow me wherever I should go. I therefore requested them to prepare for an immediate departure, and at the same time gave notice to the man who had engaged to be our guide, to be in readiness to accompany us. When our determination to return up the river was made known, several of the natives took a very abrupt departure; but to those who remained, I gave a few useful articles, explaining to them at the same time, the advantages that would result to them, if their relations conducted me to the sea, along such a road as they had described. I had already given a moose skin to some of the women for the purpose of making shoes, which were now brought us; they were well sewed but ill shaped, and a few beads were considered as a sufficient remuneration for the skill employed on them. Mr Mackay, by my desire, engraved my name, and the date of the year on a tree. . . . [29]

[Wednesday, July 3.] It had rained hard in the night, and there was some small rain in the morning. At four we entered our canoe, and at ten we came to a small river,[30] which answered to the description of that whose course the natives said, they follow in their journies towards the sea coast; we therefore put into it, and endeavoured to discover if our guide had landed here; but there were no traces of him or of any others. My former perplexities were now renewed. If I passed this river, it was probable that I might miss the natives; and I had reason to suspect that my men would not consent to return thither. As for attempting the woods, without a guide, to introduce us to the first inhabitants, such a determination would be little short of absolute madness. At length, after much painful reflection, I resolved to come at once to a full explanation with my people, and I experienced a considerable relief from this resolution. Accordingly, after repeating the promise they had so lately made me, on our putting back up the river, I represented to them that this appeared to me to be the spot from which the natives took their departure for the sea coast, and added, withal, that I was determined to try it; for though our guide had left us, it was possible that, while we were making the necessary preparations, he or some others might appear, to relieve us from our present difficulties. I now found, to my great satisfaction, that they had not come to any fixed determination among them-selves, as some of them immediately assented to undertake the woods with me. Others, however, suggested that it might be better to proceed a few leagues further up the river, in expectation of finding our guide, or procuring another, and that after all we might return hither. This plan I very readily agreed to adopt, but before I left this place, to which I gave the name of the West-Road River,[31] I sent some of the men into the woods, in different directions, and went some distance up the river myself, which I found to be navigable only for small canoes. Two of the men found a good beaten path, leading up an hill just behind us, which I imagined to be the great road. At four in the afternoon we left this place. . . . [The canoes are left behind]

[Thursday, July 4.] At an early hour this morning, and at the suggestion of our guide, we proceeded to the landing-place that leads to the strangers'[32] lodges. Our great difficulty here was to procure a temporary separation from our company, in order to hide some articles we could not carry with us, and which it would have been imprudent to leave in the power of the natives. Accordingly Mr Mackay, and one of our Indians embarked with them, and soon run out of our sight. At our first hiding-place we left a bag of pemmican, weighing ninety pounds, two bags of wild rice, and a gallon keg of gunpowder. Previous to our putting these articles in the ground, we rolled them up in oil cloth, and dressed leather. In the second hiding-place, and guarded with the same rollers, we hid two bags of Indian corn, or maize, and a bale of different articles of merchandise. When we had completed this important object, we proceeded till half past eight, when we landed at the entrance of a small rivulet, where our friends were waiting for us.

Here it was necessary that we should leave our canoe, and whatever we could not carry on our backs. In the first place, therefore, we prepared a stage, on which the canoe was placed bottom upwards, and shaded by a covering of small trees and branches, to keep her from the sun. We then built an oblong hollow square, ten feet by five, of green logs, wherein we placed every article it was necessary for us to leave here, and covered the whole with large pieces of timber.

While we were eagerly employed in this necessary business, our guide and his companions were so impatient to be gone, that we could not persuade the former to wait till we were prepared for our departure, and we had some difficulty in persuading another of the natives to remain, who had undertook to conduct us where the guide had promised to wait for our arrival.

At noon we were in a state of preparation to enter the woods, an undertaking of which I shall not here give any preliminary opinion, but leave those who read it to judge for themselves.

We carried on our backs four bags on an half of pemmican, weighing from eighty-five to ninety pounds each; a case with my instruments, a parcel of goods for presents, weighing ninety pounds, and a parcel containing ammunition of the same weight. Each of the Canadians had a burden of about ninety pounds, with a gun, and some ammunition. The Indians had about forty-five pounds weight of pemmican to carry, besides their gun, &c. with which they were very much dissatisfied, and if they had dared would have instantly left us. They had hitherto been very much indulged, but the moment was now arrived when indulgence was no longer practicable. My own load, and that of Mr Mackay, consisted of twenty-two pounds of pemmican, some rice, a little sugar, &c. amounting in the whole to about seventy pounds each, besides our arms and ammunition. I had also the tube of my telescope swung across my shoulder, which was a troublesome addition to my burthen. It was determined that we should content ourselves with two meals a-day, which were regulated without difficulty, as our provisions did not require the ceremony of cooking.

In this state of equipment we began our journey, as I have already mentioned, about twelve noon, the commencement of which was a steep ascent of about a mile; it lay along a well-beaten path, but the country through which it led was rugged and ridgy, and full of wood. When we were in a state of extreme heat, from the toil of our journey, the rain came on, and continued till the evening, and even when it ceased the underwood continued its drippings upon us. . . .

Contact with the peoples of the coast

[July 4, cont.] At sun-set an elderly man and three other natives joined us from the Westward. The former bore a lance that very much resembled a serjeant's halberd.

He had lately received it, by way of barter, from the natives of the Sea-Coast, who procured it from the white men. We should meet, he said, with many of his country-men who had just returned from thence. According to his report, it did not require more than six days journey, for people who are not heavily laden, to reach the country of those with whom they bartered their skins for iron, &c. and from thence it is not quite two day's march to the sea. They proposed to send two young men on before us, to notify to the different tribes that we were approaching, that they might not be surprised at our appearance, and be disposed to afford us a friendly reception. This was a measure which I could not but approve, and endeavoured by some small presents to prepossess our couriers in our favour. . . .

[Friday, July 5.] We had no sooner laid ourselves down to rest last night, than the natives began to sing, in a manner very different from what I had been accustomed to hear among savages. It was not accompanied either with dancing, drum, or rattle; but consisted of soft, plaintive tones, and a modulation that was rather agreeable: it had somewhat the air of church music. . . .

[Saturday, July 6.] . . . we came to a family of natives, consisting of one man, two women, and six children, with whom we found them. These people betrayed no signs of fear at our appearance, and the man willingly conversed with my interpreter, to whom he made himself more intelligible, than our guides had been able to do. They, however, had informed him of the object of our journey. He pointed out to us one of his wives, who was a native of the sea coast, which was not a very great distance from us. This woman was more inclined to corpulency than any we had yet seen, was of low stature, with an oblong face, grey eyes, and a flattish nose. She was decorated with ornaments of various kinds, such as large blue beads, either pendant from her ears, encircling her neck, or braided in her hair: she also wore bracelets of brass, copper, and horn. Her garments consisted of a kind of tunic, which was covered with a robe of matted bark, fringed round the bottom with skin of sea otter. None of the women whom I had seen since we crossed the mountain wore this kind of tunic; their blankets being merely girt round the waist. She had learned the language of her husband's tribe, and confirmed his account, that we were at no great distance from the sea. They were on their way, she said, to the great river to fish. Age seemed to be an object of great veneration among these people, for they carried an old woman by turns on their backs who was quite blind and infirm from the very advanced period of her life. . . .

[Sunday, July 14.] . . . We now left a small lake on our left,[33] then crossed a creek running out of it, and at one in the afternoon came to an house, of the same construction and dimensions as have already been mentioned, but the materials were much better prepared and finished. The timber was squared on two sides, and the bark taken off the two others; the ridge pole was also shaped in the same manner, extending about eight or ten feet beyond the gable end, and supporting a shed over the door: the end of it was carved into the similitude of a snake's head. Several hieroglyphics and figures of a similar workmanship, and painted with red earth, decorated the interior of the building.[34] The inhabitants had left the house but a short time, and there were several bags or bundles in it, which I did not suffer to be disturbed. Near it were two tombs, surrounded in a neat manner with boards, and covered with bark. Beside them several poles had been erected, one of which was squared, and all of them painted. From each of them were suspended several rolls or parcels of bark, and our guide gave the following account of them; which, as far as we could judge from our imperfect knowledge of the language, and the incidental errors of interpretation, appeared to involve two different modes of treating their dead; or it might be one and the same ceremony, which we did not distinctly comprehend: at all events, it is the practice of these people to burn the bodies of their dead, except the larger bones, which are rolled up in bark and suspended from poles, as I have already described. According to the other account, it appeared that they actually bury their dead; and when another of the family dies, the remains of the person who was last interred are taken from the grave and burned, as has been already mentioned; so that the members of the family are thus successively buried and burned, to make room for each other; and one tomb proves sufficient for a family through succeeding generations. There is no house in this country without a tomb in its vicinity. Our last course extended about ten miles. . . .

[Monday, July 15.] . . . At eleven we came up with [the old man[35] and] . . . five men, and part of their families. They received us with great kindness, and examined us with the most minute attention. They must, however, have been told that we were white, as our faces no longer indicated that distinguishing complexion. They called themselves Neguia Dinais,[36] and were come in a different direction from us, but were not going the same way, to the Anah-yoe Tesse or River,[37] and appeared to be very much satisfied with our having joined them. They presented us with some fish which they had just taken in the adjoining lake.

Here I expected our guides, like their predecessors, would have quitted us, but, on the contrary, they expressed themselves to be so happy in our company, and that of their friends, that they voluntarily, and with great cheerfulness proceeded to pass another night with us. Our new acquaintance were people of a very pleasing aspect. The hair of the women was tied in large loose knots over the ears, and plaited with great neatness from the division of the head, so as to be included in the knots. Some of them had adorned their tresses with beads, with a very pretty effect. The men were clothed in leather, their hair was nicely combed, and their complexion was fairer, or perhaps it may be said, with more propriety, that they were more cleanly, than any of the natives whom we had yet seen. Their eyes, though keen and sharp, are not of that dark colour, so generally observable in the various tribes of Indians; they were, on the contrary, of a grey hue, with a tinge of red. There was one man amongst them of at least six feet four inches in height; his manners were affable, and he had a more prepossessing appearance than any Indian I had met with in my journey; he was about twenty-eight years of age, and was treated with particular respect by his party. Every man, woman, and child, carried a proportionate burden, consisting of beaver coating and parchment, as well as skins of the otter, the marten, the bear, and lynx, and dressed moose-skins. The last they procure from the Rocky-Mountain Indians. According to their account, the people of the sea coast prefer them to any other article. Several of their relations and friends, they said, were already gone, as well provided as themselves to barter with the people of the coast; who barter them in their turn, except the dressed leather, with white people who, as they had been informed, arrive there in large canoes.

Such an escort was the most fortunate circumstance that could happen in our favour. They told us, that as the women and children could not travel fast, we should be three days in getting to the end of our journey; which must be supposed to have been very agreeable information to people in our exhausted condition. . . .

We all sat down on a very pleasant green spot, and were no sooner seated, than our guide and one of the party prepared to engage in play.[38] They had each a bundle of about fifty small sticks, neatly polished, of the size of a quill, and five inches long: a certain number of these sticks had red lines round them; and as many of these as one of the players might find convenient were curiously rolled up in dry grass, and according to the judgment of his antagonist respecting their number and marks, he lost or won. Our friend was apparently the loser, as he parted with his bow and arrows, and several articles which I had given him. . . .

The expedition crosses the Rocky mountains

[Wednesday, July 17.] . . . We now gained the summit of the mountain, and found ourselves surrounded by snow. But this circumstance is caused rather by the quantity of snow drifted in the pass, than the real height of the spot, as the surrounding mountains rise to a much higher degree of elevation.[39] The snow had become so compact that our feet hardly made a perceptible impression on it. We observed, however, the tracks of an herd of small deer which must have passed a short time before us, and the Indians and my hunters went immediately in pursuit of them. Our way was now nearly level, without the least snow, and not a tree to be seen in any part of it. The grass is very short, and the soil a reddish clay, intermixed with small stones. The face of the hills, where they are not enlivened with verdure, appears, at a distance, as if fire had passed over them. It now began to hail, snow, and rain, nor could we find any shelter but the leeward side of an huge rock. The wind also rose into a tempest, and the weather was as distressing as any I had ever experienced. After an absence of an hour and an half, our hunters brought a small doe of the reindeer species, which was all they had killed, though they fired twelve shots at a large herd of them. Their ill success they attributed to the weather. I proposed to leave half of the venison in the snow, but the men preferred carrying it, though their strength was very much exhausted. We had been so long shivering with cold in this situation that we were glad to renew our march. Here and there were scattered a few cranberry bushes and stinted willows; the former of which had not yet blossomed.

Before us appeared a stupendous mountain,[40] whose snow-clad summit was lost in the clouds; between it and our immediate course, flowed the river to which we were going.[41] The Indians informed us that it was at no great distance. As soon as we could gather a sufficient quantity of wood, we stopped to dress some of our venison; and it is almost superfluous to add, that we made an heartier meal than we had done for many a day before. To the comfort which I have just mentioned, I added that of taking off my beard, as well as changing my linen, and my people followed the humanising example. We then set forwards, and came to a large pond,[42] on whose bank we found a tomb, but lately made, with a pole, as usual, erected beside it, on which two figures of birds were painted, and by them the guides distinguished the tribe to which the deceased person belonged. One of them, very unceremoniously opened the bark and shewed us the bones which it contained, while the other threw down the pole, and having possessed himself of the feathers that were tied to it, fixed them on his own head. I therefore conjectured, that these funeral memorials belonged to an individual of a tribe at enmity with them.

We continued our route with a considerable degree of expedition, and as we proceeded the mountains appeared to withdraw from us. The country between them soon opened to our view, which apparently added to their awful elevation. We continued to descend till we came to the brink of a precipice, from whence our guides discovered the river to us, and a village on its banks.[43] This precipice, or rather succession of precipices, is covered with large timber, which consists of the pine, the spruce, the hemlock, the birch, and other trees. Our conductors informed us, that it abounded in animals, which, from their description, must be wild goats. In about two hours we arrived at the bottom, where there is a conflux of two rivers, that issue from the mountains.[44] We crossed the one which was to the left. They are both very rapid, and continue so till they unite their currents, forming a stream of about twelve yards in breadth. Here the timber was also very large; but I could not learn from our conductors why the most considerable hemlock trees were stripped of their bark to the tops of them. I concluded, indeed, at that time that the inhabitants tanned their leather with it. Here were also the largest and loftiest elder [Alder] and cedar trees that I had ever seen. We were now sensible of an entire change in the climate, and the berries were quite ripe.

The sun was about to set, when our conductors left us to follow them as well as we could. We were prevented, however, from going far astray, for we were hemmed in on both sides and behind by such a barrier as nature never before presented to my view. Our guides had the precaution to mark the road for us, by breaking the branches of trees as they passed. This small river must, at certain seasons, rise to an uncommon height and strength of current most probably on the melting of the snow; as we saw a large quantity of drift wood lying twelve feet above the immediate level of the river. This circumstance impeded our progress, and the protruding rocks frequently forced us to pass through the water. It was now dark, without the least appearance of houses, though it would be impossible to have seen them, if there had been any, at the distance of twenty yards, from the thickness of the woods.

The 'Friendly Village'

My men were anxious to stop for the night; indeed the fatigue they had suffered justified the proposal, and I left them to their choice; but as the anxiety of my mind impelled me forwards, they continued to follow me, till I found myself at the edge of the woods; and, notwithstanding the remonstrances that were made, I proceeded, feeling rather than seeing my way, till I arrived at an house, and soon discovered several fires, in small huts, with people busily employed in cooking their fish.[45] I walked into one of them without the least ceremony, threw down my burden, and, after shaking hands with some of the people, sat down upon it. They received me without the least appearance of surprize, but soon made signs for me to go up to the large house, which was erected, on upright posts, at some distance from the ground. A broad piece of timber with steps cut in it, led to the scaffolding even with the floor, and by this curious kind of ladder I entered the house at one end; and having passed three fires, at equal distances in the middle of the building, I was received by several people, sitting upon a very wide board, at the upper end of it. I shook hands with them, and seated myself beside a man, the dignity of whose countenance induced me to give him that preference. I soon discovered one of my guides seated a little above me, with a neat mat spread before him, which I supposed to be the place of honour, and appropriated to strangers. In a short time my people arrived, and placed themselves near me, when the man by whom I sat, immediately rose, and fetched, from behind a plank of about four feet wide, a quantity of roasted salmon. He then directed a mat to be placed before me and Mr Mackay, who was now sitting by me. When this ceremony was performed, he brought a salmon for each of us, and half an one to each of my men. The same plank served also as a screen for the beds, whither the women and children were already retired; but whether that circumstance took place on our arrival, or was the natural consequence of the late hour of the night, I did not discover. The signs of our protector seemed to denote, that we might sleep in the house, but as we did not understand him with a sufficient degree of certainty, I thought it prudent, from the fear of giving offence, to order the men to make a fire without, that we might sleep by it. When he observed our design, he placed boards for us that we might not take our repose on the bare ground, and ordered a fire to be prepared for us. We had not been long seated round it, when we received a large dish of salmon roes, pounded fine and beat up with water so as to have the appearance of a cream. Nor was it without some kind of seasoning that gave it a bitter taste. Another dish soon followed, the principal article of which was also salmon-roes, with a large proportion of gooseberries, and an herb that appeared to be sorrel. Its acidity rendered it more agreeable to my taste than the former preparation. Having been regaled with these delicacies, for such they were considered by that hospitable spirit which provided them, we laid ourselves down to rest with no other canopy than the sky; but I never enjoyed a more sound and refreshing rest, though I had a board for my bed, and a billet for my pillow.

[Thursday, July 18.] At five this morning I awoke, and found that the natives had lighted a fire for us, and were sitting by it. My hospitable friend immediately brought me some berries and roasted salmon, and his companions soon followed his example. The former, which consisted among many others, of gooseberries, whortleberries and raspberries, were the finest I ever saw or tasted, of their respective kinds. They also brought the dried roes of fish to eat with the berries.

Salmon is so abundant in this river, that these people have a constant and plentiful supply of that excellent fish. To take them with more facility, they had, with great labour, formed an embankment or weir across the river for the purpose of placing their fishing machine, which they disposed both above and below it. I expressed my wish to visit this extraordinary work, but these people are so superstitious, that they would not allow me a nearer examination that I could obtain by viewing it from the bank. The river is about fifty yards in breadth, and by observing a man fish with a dipping net, I judged it to be about ten feet deep at the foot of the fall. The weir is a work of great labour, and contrived with considerable ingenuity. It was near four feet above the level of the water, at the time I saw it, and nearly the height of the bank on which I stood to examine it. The stream is stopped nearly two thirds by it. It is constructed by fixing small trees in the bed of the river of a slanting position (which could be practicable only when the water is much lower than I saw it) with the thick part downwards; over these is laid a bed of gravel on which is placed a range of lesser trees, and so on alternately till the work is brought to its proper height. Beneath it the machines are placed, into which the salmon fall when they attempt to leap over. On either side there is a large frame of timber-work six feet above the level of the upper water, in which passages are left for the salmon leading directly into the machines, which are taken up at pleasure. At the foot of the fall dipping nets are also success-fully employed. . . .

These people indulge an extreme superstition respecting their fish, as it is appar-ently their only animal food. Flesh they never taste, and one of their dogs having picked and swallowed part of a bone which we had left, was beaten by his master till he disgorged it. One of my people also having thrown a bone of the deer into the river, a native, who had observed the circumstance, immediately dived and brought it up, and, having consigned it to the fire, instantly proceeded to wash his polluted hands.

As we were still at some distance from the sea,[46] I made application to my friend to procure us a canoe or two, with people to conduct us thither. After he had made various excuses, I at length comprehended that his only objection was to the embark-ing venison in a canoe on their river, as the fish would instantly smell it and abandon them, so that he, his friends, and relations, must starve. I soon eased his apprehen-sions on that point, and desired to know what I must do with the venison that remained, when he told me to give it to one of the strangers whom he pointed out to me, as being of a tribe that eat flesh. I now requested him to furnish me with some fresh salmon in its raw state: but, instead of complying with my wish, he brought me a couple of them roasted, observing at the same time, that the current was very strong, and would bring us to the next village, where our wants would be abundantly supplied. In short, he requested that we would make haste to depart. This was rather unexpected after so much kindness and hospitality, but our ignorance of the lan-guage prevented us from being able to discover our cause. . . .

The 'Great Village'

[Thursday, July 18] . . . At one in the afternoon we embarked, with our small baggage, in two canoes, accompanied by seven of the natives. The stream was rapid, and ran upwards of six miles an hour. We came to a weir, such as I have already described, where the natives landed us, and shot over it without taking a drop of water. They then received us on board again, and we continued our voyage, passing many canoes on the river, some with people in them, and others empty. We proceeded at a very great rate for about two hours and an half, when we were informed that we must land, as the village⁴⁷ was only at a short distance. I had imagined that the Canadians who accompanied me were the most expert canoe-men in the world, but they are very inferior to these people, as they themselves acknowledge, in conducting those vessels.

Some of the Indians ran before us, to announce our approach, when we took our bundles and followed. We had walked along a well-beaten path, through a kind of coppice, when we were informed of the arrival of our couriers at the houses, by the loud and confused talking of the inhabitants. As we approached the edge of the wood, and were almost in sight of the houses, the Indians who were before me made signs for me to take the lead, and that they would follow. The noise and confusion of the natives now seemed to increase, and when we came in sight of the village, we saw them running from house to house, some armed with bows and arrows, others with spears and many with axes, as if in a state of great alarm. This very unpleasant and unexpected circumstance, I attributed to our sudden arrival, and the very short notice of it which had been given them. At all events, I had but one line of conduct to pursue, which was to walk resolutely up to them, without manifesting any signs of apprehension at their hostile appearance. This resolution produced the desired effect, for as we approached the houses, the greater part of the people laid down their weapons, and came forward to meet us. I was, however, soon obliged to stop from the number of them that surrounded me. I shook hands, as usual with such as were the nearest to me, when an elderly man broke through the crowd, and took me in his arms; another then came, who turned him away without the least ceremony, and paid me the same compliment. The latter was followed by a young man, whom I understood to be his son. These embraces, which at first rather surprised me, I soon found to be marks of regard and friendship. The crowd pressed with so much violence and contention to get a view of us, that we could not move in any direction. An opening was at length made to allow a person to approach me, whom the old man made me understand was another of his sons. I instantly stepped forward to meet him, and presented my hand, whereupon he broke the string of a very handsome robe of sea-otter skin, which he had on, and covered me with it. This was as flattering a reception as I could possibly receive, especially as I considered him to be the eldest son of the chief. Indeed it appeared to me that we had been detained here for the purpose of giving him time to bring the robe with which he had presented me.

The chief now made signs for us to follow him, and he conducted us through a narrow coppice, for several hundred yards, till we came to an house built on the ground, which was of larger dimensions, and formed of better materials than any I had hitherto seen; it was his residence. We were no sooner arrived there, than he directed mats to be spread before it, on which we were told to take our seats, when the men of the village, who came to indulge their curiosity, were ordered to keep behind us. In our front other mats were placed, where the chief and his counsellors took their seats. In the intervening space, mats, which were very clean, and of a much neater workmanship than those on which we sat were also spread, and a small roasted salmon placed before each of us. When we had satisfied ourselves with the fish, one of the people who came with us from the last village approached, with a kind of ladle in one hand, containing oil, and in the other something that resembled the inner rind of the cocoa-nut, but of a lighter colour; this he dipped in the oil, and, having eat it, indicated by his gestures how palatable he thought it. He then presented me with a small piece of it, which I chose to taste in its dry state, though the oil was free from any unpleasant smell. A square cake of this was next produced, when a man took it to the water near the house, and having thoroughly soaked it, he returned and, after he had pulled it to pieces like oakum, put it into a well-made trough, about three feet long, nine inches wide, and five deep; he then plentifully sprinkled it with salmon oil, and manifested by his own example that were we to eat of it. I just tasted it, and found the oil perfectly sweet, without which the other ingredient would have been very insipid. The chief partook of it with great avidity, after it had received an additional quantity of oil. This dish is considered by these people as a great delicacy; and on examination, I discovered it to consist of the inner rind of the hemlock tree, taken off early in summer, put into a frame, which shapes it into cakes of fifteen inches long, ten broad, and half an inch thick; and in this form I should suppose it may be preserved for a great length of time. This discovery satisfied me respecting the many hemlock trees which I had observed stripped of their bark.

In this situation we remained for upwards of three hours, and not one of the curious natives left us during all that time, except a party of ten or twelve of them, whom the chief ordered to go and catch fish, which they did in great abundance, with dipping nets, at the foot of the Weir.

At length we were relieved from the gazing crowd, and got a lodge erected, and covered in for our reception during the night. I now presented the young chief with a blanket, in return for the robe with which he had favoured me, and several other articles, that appeared to be very gratifying to him. I also presented some to his father, and amongst them was a pair of scissors, whose use I explained to him, for clipping his beard, which was of great length; and to that purpose he immediately applied them. My distribution of similar articles was also extended to others, who had been attentive to us. The communication, however, between us was awkward and inconvenient, for it was carried on entirely by signs, as there was not a person with me who was qualified for the office of an interpreter.

We were all of us very desirous to get some fresh salmon, that we might dress them in our own way, but could not by any means obtain that gratification, though there were thousands of that fish strung on cords, which were fastened to stakes in the river. They were even averse to our approaching the spot where they clean and prepare them for their own eating. They had, indeed, taken our kettle from us, lest we should employ it in getting water from the river; and they assigned as the reason for this precaution, that the salmon dislike the smell of iron. At the same time they supplied us with wooden boxes, which were capable of holding any fluid. Two of the men that went to fish, in a canoe capable of containing ten people, returned with a full lading of salmon, that weighed from six to forty pounds, though the far greater part of them were under twenty. They immediately strung the whole of them, as I have already mentioned, in the river.

I now made the tour of the village, which consisted of four elevated houses, and seven built on the ground, besides a considerable number of other buildings or sheds, which are used only as kitchens, and places for curing their fish. The former are constructed by fixing a certain number of posts in the earth, on some of which are laid, and to others are fastened, the supporters of the floor, at about twelve feet above the surface of the ground: their length is from an hundred and twenty feet and they are about forty feet in breadth. Along the centre are built three, four, or five hearths, for the two-fold purpose of giving warmth, and drying their fish. The whole length of the building on either side is divided by cedar planks, into partitions or apartments of seven feet square, in the front of which there are boards, about three feet wide, over which, though they are not immovably fixed, the inmates of these recesses generally pass, when they go to rest. The greater part of them are intended for that purpose, and such are covered with boards, at the height of the wall of the house, which is about seven or eight feet, and rest upon beams that stretch across the building. On those also are placed the chests which contain their provisions, utensils, and whatever they possess. The intermediate space is sufficient for domestic purposes. On poles that run along the beams, hang roasted fish, and the whole building is well covered with boards and bark, except within a few inches of the ridge pole; where open spaces are left on each side to let in light and emit the smoke. At the end of the house that fronts the river, is a narrow scaffolding, which is also ascended by a piece of timber, with steps cut in it; and at each corner of this erection there are openings, for the inhabitants to ease nature. As it does not appear to be a custom among them to remove these heaps of excremental filth, it may be supposed that the effluvia does not annoy them.

The houses which rest on the ground are built of the same materials, and on the same plan. A sloping stage that rises to a cross piece of timber, supported by two forks, joins also to the main building, for those purposes which need not be repeated.

When we were surrounded by the natives on our arrival, I counted sixty-five men, and several of them may be supposed to have been absent; I cannot, therefore, calculate the inhabitants of this village at less than two hundred souls.

The people who accompanied us hither, from the other village, had given the chief a very particular account of everything they knew concerning us: I was, therefore, requested to produce my astronomical instruments; nor could I have any objection to afford them this satisfaction, as they would necessarily add to our importance in their opinion.

Near the house of the chief I observed several oblong squares, of about twenty feet by eight. They were made of thick cedar boards, which were joined with so much neatness, that I at first thought they were one piece. They were painted with hieroglyphics, and figures of different animals, and with a degree of correctness that was not be expected from such an uncultivated people. I could not learn the use of them, but they appeared to be calculated for occasional acts of devotion or sacrifice, which all these tribes perform at least twice in the year, at the spring and fall. I was confirmed in this opinion by a large building in the middle of the village, which I at first took for the half finished frame of an house. The ground-plot of it was fifty feet by forty-five; each end is formed by four stout posts, fixed perpendicularly in the ground. The corner ones are plain, and support a beam of the whole length, having three intermediate props on each side, but of a larger size, and eight or nine feet in height. The two centre posts, at each end, are two feet and an half in diameter, and carved into human figures, supporting two ridge poles on their heads, at twelve feet from the ground. The figures at the upper part of this square represent two persons, with their hands upon their knees, as if they supported the weight with pain and difficulty: the others opposite to them stand at their ease, with their hands resting on their hips. In the area of the building there were the remains of several fires. The posts, poles, and figures, were painted red and black; but the sculpture of these people is superior to their painting.

[Friday, July 19.] Soon after I had retired to rest last night, the chief paid me a visit to insist on my going to his bed-companion, and taking my place himself; but, notwithstanding his repeated entreaties, I resisted this offering of his hospitality.

At an early hour this morning I was again visited by the chief, in company with his son. The former complained of a pain in his breast; to relieve his suffering, I gave him a few drops of Turlington's Balsam on a piece of sugar; and I was rather surprised to see him take it without the least hesitation. When he had taken my medicine, he requested me to follow him, and conducted me to a shed, where several people were assembled round a sick man, who was another of his sons. They immediately uncovered him, and shewed me a violent ulcer in the small of his back, in the foulest state that can be imagined. One of his knees was also afflicted in the same manner. This unhappy man was reduced to a skeleton, and, from his appearance, was drawing near to an end of his pains. They requested that I would touch him, and his father was very urgent with me to administer medicine; but he was in such a dangerous state, that I thought it prudent to yield no further to the importunities than to give the sick person a few drops of Turlington's balsam in some water. I therefore left them, but was soon called back by the loud lamentations of the women, and was rather apprehensive that some inconvenience might result from my compliance with the chief's request. On my return I found the native physicians busy in practising their skill and art on the patient. They blew on him, and then whistled; at times they pressed their extended fingers, with all their strength on his stomach; they also put their fore fingers doubled into his mouth, and spouted water from their own with great violence into his face. To support these operations the wretched sufferer was held up in a sitting posture; and when they were concluded, he was laid down and covered with a new robe made of the skins of the lynx. I had observed that his belly and breast were covered with scars, and I understood that they were caused by a custom prevalent among them, of applying pieces of lighted touch wood to their flesh, in order to relieve pain or demonstrate their courage. He was now placed on a broad plank, and carried by six men into the woods, where I was invited to accompany them. I could not conjecture what would be the end of this ceremony, particularly as I saw one man carry fire, another an axe, and a third dry wood. I was, indeed, disposed to suspect that, as it was their custom to burn the dead, they intended to relieve the poor man from his pain, and perform the last sad duty of surviving affection. When they had advanced a short distance into the wood, they laid him upon a clear spot, and kindled a fire against his back, when the physician began to scarify the ulcer with a very blunt instrument, the cruel pain of which operation the patient bore with incredible resolution. The scene afflicted me and I left it.

. . . I paid a visit to the chief, who presented me with a roasted salmon; he then opened one of his chests, and took out of it a garment of blue cloth, decorated with brass buttons; and another of a flowered cotton, which I supposed were Spanish; it had been trimmed with leather fringe, after the fashion of their own cloaks. Copper and brass are in great estimation among them, and of the former they have great plenty: they point their arrows and spears with it, and work it up into personal ornaments; such as collars, ear-rings, and bracelets, which they wear on their wrists, arms, and legs. I presume they find it the most advantageous article of trade with the more inland tribes. They also abound in iron. I saw some of their twisted collars of that metal which weighed upwards of twelve pounds. It is generally in bars of fourteen inches in length, and one inch three quarters wide. The brass is in thin squares; their copper is in larger pieces, and some of it appeared to be old stills cut up. They have various trinkets; but their iron is manufactured only into poniards and daggers. Some of the former have very neat handles, with a silver coin of a quarter or eighth of a dollar fixed on the end of them. The blades of the latter are from ten to twelve inches in length, and about four inches broad at the top, from which they gradually lessen into a point.

When I produced my instruments to take an altitude, I was desired not to make use of them. I could not then discover the cause of this request, but I experienced the good effect of the apprehension which they occasioned, as it was very effectual in hastening my departure. I had applied several times to the chief to prepare canoes and people to take me and my party to the sea, but very little attention had been paid to my application till noon; when I was informed that a canoe was properly equipped for my voyage, and that the young chief would accompany me. I now discovered that they had entertained no personal fear of the instruments, but were apprehensive that the operation of them might frighten the salmon from that part of the river. The observation taken in this village gave me 52.25.52 North latitude.

In compliance with the chief's request I desired my people to take their bundles, and lay them down on the bank of the river. In the mean time I went to take the dimensions of his large canoe, in which, it was signified to me, that about ten winters ago he went a considerable distance towards the mid-day sun, with forty of his people, when he saw two large vessels full of such men as myself, by whom he was kindly received: they were, he said, the first white people he had seen. They were probably the ships commanded by Captain Cook.[48] This canoe was built of cedar, forty-five feet long, four feet wide, and three feet and a half in depth. It was painted black and decorated with white figures of fish of different kinds. The gunwale, fore and aft, was inlaid with the teeth of the sea-otter.

When I returned to the river, the natives who were to accompany us, and my people, were already in the canoe. The latter, however, informed me that one of our axes was missing. I immediately applied to the chief, and requested its restoration; but he would not understand me till I sat myself down on a stone, with my arms in a state of preparation, and made it appear to him that I should not depart till the stolen article was restored. The village was immediately in a state of uproar, and some danger was apprehended from the confusion that prevailed in it. The axe, however, which had been hidden under the chief's canoe, was soon returned. Though this instrument was not, in itself, of sufficient value to justify a dispute with these people, I apprehended that the suffering them to keep it, after we had declared its loss, might have occasioned the loss of everything we carried with us, and of our lives also. My people were dissatisfied with me at the moment; but I thought myself right then, and, I think now, that the circumstances in which we were involved, justified the measure which I adopted.

Mackenzie reaches the sea

[Friday, July 19] . . . The navigation of the river now became more difficult, from the numerous channels into which it was divided, without any sensible diminution in the velocity of its current. We soon reached another house of the common size, where we were well received; but whether our guides had informed them that we were not in want of any thing, or that they were deficient in inclination, or perhaps the means, of being hospitable to us, they did not offer us any refreshment. They were in a state of busy preparation. Some of the women were employed in beating and preparing the inner rind of the cedar bark, to which they gave the appearance of flax. Others were spinning with a distaff and spindle. One of them was weaving a robe of it, intermixed with stripes of the sea-otter skin, on a frame of adequate contrivance that was placed against the side of the house. The men were fishing on the river with drag-nets between two canoes. These nets are forced by poles to the bottom, the current driving them before it, by which means the salmon coming up the river are intercepted, and give notice of their being taken by the struggles they make in the bag or sleeve of the net. There are no weirs in this part of the river, as I suppose, from the numerous channels into which it is divided. The machines, therefore, are placed along the banks, and consequently these people are not so well supplied with fish as the village which has been already described, nor do they appear to possess the same industry. The inhabitants of the last house accompanied us in a large canoe. They recommended us to leave ours here, as the next village was but at a small distance from us, and the water more rapid than that which we had passed. They informed us also, that we were approaching a cascade. I directed them to shoot it, and proceeded myself to the foot thereof, where I re-embarked, and we went on with great velocity, till we came to a fall, where we left our canoe, and carried our luggage along a road through a wood for some hundred yards, when we came to a village,[49] consisting of six very large houses, erected on palisades, rising twenty-five feet from the ground, which differed in no one circumstance from those already described, but the height of their elevation. They contained only four men and their families. The rest of the inhabitants were with us and in the small houses which we passed higher up the river. These people do not seem to enjoy the abundance of their neighbours, as the men who returned from fishing had no more than five salmon; they refused to sell one of them, but gave me one roasted of a very indifferent kind. In the houses there were several chests or boxes containing different articles that belonged to the people whom we had lately passed. If I were to judge by the heaps of filth beneath these buildings, they must have been erected at a more distant period than any which we passed. From these houses I could perceive the termination of the river, and its discharge into a narrow arm of the sea. . . .[50]

[Sunday, July 21.] At forty minutes past four this morning it was low water, which made fifteen feet perpendicular height below the high-water mark of last night. Mr Mackay collected a quantity of small muscals which we boiled. Our people did not partake of this regale, as they are wholly unacquainted with sea shell-fish. Our young chief being missing, we imagined that he had taken his flight, but, as we were preparing to depart, he fortunately made his appearance from the woods, where he had been to take his rest after his feast of last night. At six we were upon the water, when we cleared the small bay, which we named Porcupine Cove, and steered West-South-West for seven miles, we then opened a channel about two miles and an half wide at South-South-West, and had a view of ten or twelve miles into it.[51] As I could not ascertain the distance from the open sea, and being uncertain whether we were in a bay or among inlets and channels of islands. I confined my search to a proper place for taking an observation. We steered, therefore, along the land on the left, West-North-West a mile and an half;[52] then North-West one fourth of a mile, and North three miles to an island;[53] the land continuing to run North-North-West, then along the island, South-South-West half a mile, West a mile and an half, and from thence directly across to the land on the left, (where I had an altitude,) South-West three miles.[54] From this position a channel, of which the island we left appeared to make a cheek, bears North by East.[55]

Under the land we met with three canoes, with fifteen men in them, and laden with their movables, as if proceeding to a new situation, or returning to a former one. They manifested no kind of mistrust or fear of us, but entered into conversation with our young man, as I supposed, to obtain some information concerning us. It did not appear that they were the same people as those we had lately seen, as they spoke the language of our young chief, with a different accent. They then examined every thing we had in our canoe, with an air of indifference and disdain. One of them in particular made me understand, with an air of insolence, that a large canoe had lately been in this bay, with people in her like me, and that one of them, whom he called Macubah, had fired on him and his friends, and that Bensins had struck him on the back, with the flat part of his sword.[56] He also mentioned another name, the articulation of which I could not determine. At the same time he illustrated these circumstances by the assistance of my gun and sword; and I do not doubt but he well deserved the treatment which he described. He also produced several European articles, which could not have been long in his possession. From his conduct and appearance, I wished very much to be rid of him, and flattered myself that he would prosecute his voyage, which appeared to be in an opposite direction to our course. However, when I prepared to part from them, they turned their canoes about, and persuaded my young man to leave me, which I could not prevent. . . .

. . . When we were in mid-channel, I perceived some sheds, or the remains of old buildings, on the shore; and as, from that circumstance, I thought it probable that some Europeans might have been there, I directed my steersman to make for that spot. The traverse is upwards of three miles North-West.

We landed, and found the ruins of a village, in a situation calculated for defence.[57] The place itself was over grown with weeds, and in the centre of the houses there was a temple, of the same form and construction as that which I described at the large village. We were soon followed by ten canoes, each of which contained from three to six men. They informed us that we were expected at the village, where we should see many of them. From their general deportment I was very apprehensive that some hostile design was meditated against us, and for the first time I acknowledged my apprehensions to my people. I accordingly desired them to be very much upon their guard, and to be prepared if any violence was offered to defend themselves to the last.

We had no sooner landed, than we took possession of a rock, where there was not space for more than twice our number, and which admitted of our defending ourselves with advantage, in case we should be attacked. The people in the three first canoes, were the most troublesome, but, after doing their utmost to irritate us, they went away. They were, however, no sooner gone, than an hat, an handkerchief, and several other articles, were missing. The rest of our visitors continued their pressing invitations to accompany them to their village, but finding our resolution to decline them was not to be shaken, they, about sun-set relieved us from all further importunities, by their departure.

Another canoe, however, soon arrived, with seven stout, well-looking men. They brought a box, which contained a very fine sea-otter skin, and a goat skin, that was beautifully white. For the former they demanded my hanger,[58] which as may well be supposed, could not be spared in our present situation, and they actually refused to take a yard and an half of common broad cloth, with some other articles, for the skin, which proves the unreflecting improvidence of our European traders. The goat-skin was so bulky that I did not offer to purchase it. These men also told me that Macubah had been there, and left his ship behind a point of land in the channel, South-West from us; from whence he had come to their village in boats, which these people represented by imitating our manner of rowing.[59] When I offered them what they did not choose to accept for the otter-skin, they shook their heads, and very distinctly answered 'No, no.' And to mark their refusal of any thing we asked of them, they emphatically employed the same British monosyllable. In one of the canoes which had left us, there was a seal, that I wished to purchase, but could not persuade the natives to part with it. They had also a fish which I now saw for the first time. It was about eighteen inches in length, of the shape and appearance of a trout, with strong, sharp teeth. We saw great numbers of the animals which we had taken for sea otters, but I was now disposed to think that a great part of them, at least, must have been seals.

The natives having left us, we made a fire to warm ourselves, and as for supper, there was but little of that, for our whole daily allowance did not amount to what was sufficient for a single meal. The weather was clear throughout the day, which was succeeded by a fine moon-light night. I directed the people to keep watch by two in turn, and laid myself down in my cloak.

[Monday, July 22.] . . . Two canoes now arrived from the same quarter as the rest, with several men, and our young Indian along with them. They brought a very few small sea-otter skins, out of season, with some pieces of raw seal's flesh. The former were of no value, but hunger compelled some of my people to take the latter, at an extravagant price. Mr Mackay lighted a bit of touch wood with a burning-glass, in the cover of his tobacco-box, which so surprised the natives, that they exchanged the best of their otter skins for it. The young man was now very anxious to persuade our people to depart, as the natives, he said, were as numerous as musquitoes, and of very malignant character. This information produced some very earnest remonstrances to me to hasten our departure, but as I was determined not to leave this place, except I was absolutely compelled to it, till I had ascertained its situation, these solicitations were not repeated.

While I was taking a meridian, two canoes, of a larger size, and well manned, appeared from the main South-West channel. They seemed to be the fore-runners of others, who were coming to co-operate with the people of the village, in consequence of the message sent by the two boys, which has been already mentioned; and our young Indian, who understood them, renewed his entreaties for our departure, as they would soon come to shoot their arrows, and hurl their spears at us. In relating our danger, his agitation was so violent that he foamed at the mouth. Though I was not altogether free from apprehensions on the occasion, it was necessary for me to disguise them, as my people were panic struck, and some of them asked if it was my determination to remain there to be sacrificed? My reply was the same as their former importunities had received, that I would not stir till I had accomplished my object; at the same time, to humour their fears, I consented that they should put every thing into the canoe, that we might be in a state of preparation to depart. The two canoes now approached the shore, and in a short time five men, with their families, landed very quietly from them. My instruments being exposed, they examined them with much apparent admiration and astonishment. My altitude, by an artificial horizon, gave 52° 21′ 33″; that by the natural horizon was 52° 20′ 48″ North latitude.[60]

These Indians were of a different tribe from those which I had already seen, as our guide did not understand their language. I now mixed up some vermilion in melted grease, and inscribed, in large characters, on the South-East face of the rock on which we had slept last night, this brief memorial—'Alexander Mackenzie, from Canada, by land, the twenty-second of July, one thousand seven hundred and ninety-three.'[61]

As I thought that we were too near the village, I consented to leave this place, and accordingly proceeded North-East three miles, when we landed on a point, in a small cove, where we should not be readily seen, and could not be attacked except in our front. . . .[62]

I observed an emersion of Jupiter's third satellite, which gave 8° 32′ 21″ difference in longitude. I then observed an emersion of Jupiter's first satellite, which gave 8.31.48. The mean of these observations is 8° 32′ 2″ which is equal to 128.2 West of Greenwich."

I had now determined my situation, which is the most fortunate circumstance of my long, painful, and perilous journey, as a few cloudy days would have prevented me from ascertaining the final longitude of it.[63]

At twelve it was high water, but the tide did not come within a foot and an half of the high water mark of last night. As soon as I completed my observation, we left this place: it was then ten o'clock in the afternoon. We returned the same way that we came, and though the tide was running out very strong, by keeping close in with the rocks, we proceeded at a considerable rate, as my people were very anxious to get out of the reach of the inhabitants of this coast. . . .

The return journey[64]

[Sunday, July 28] . . . We continued our route with fine weather, and without meeting a single person on our way, the natives being all gone, as we supposed, to the Great River.[65] We recovered all our hidden stores of provisions, and arrived about two in the afternoon of Sunday, August the 4th, at the place which we had left a month before. . . .

On examining the canoe, and our property, which we had left behind, we found it in perfect safety; nor was there the print of a foot near the spot. We now pitched our tent, and made a blazing fire, and I treated myself, as well as the people, with a dram; but we had been so long without tasting any spirituous liquor, that we had lost all relish for it. The Indians now arrived from above, and were rewarded for the care they had taken of our property with such articles as were acceptable to them.

[Monday, August 5.] At nine this morning I sent five men in the canoe, for the various articles we had left below, and they soon returned with them, and except some bale goods, which had got wet, they were in good order, particularly the provisions, of which we were now in great need.

Many of the natives arrived both from the upper and lower parts of the river, each of whom was dressed in a beaver robe. I purchased fifteen of them; and they preferred large knives in exchange. It is an extraordinary circumstance, that these people, who might have taken all the property we left behind us, without the least fear of detection, should leave that untouched, and purloin any of our utensils, which our confidence in their honesty gave them a ready opportunity of taking. In fact, several articles were missing, and as I was very anxious to avoid a quarrel with the natives, in this stage of our journey, I told those who remained near us, without any appearance of anger, that their relations who were gone, had no idea of the mischief that would result to them from taking our property. I gravely added, that the salmon, which was not only their favourite food, but absolutely necessary to their existence, came from the sea which belonged to us white men; and that as, at the entrance of the river, we could prevent those fish from coming up it, we possessed the power to starve them and their children. To avert our anger, therefore, they must return all the articles that had been stolen from us. This finesse succeeded. Messengers were dispatched to order the restoration of every thing that had been taken. We purchased several large salmon of them and enjoyed the delicious meal which they afforded. . . .

[Tuesday, August 6.] . . . The morning was cloudy, with small rain, nevertheless I ordered the men to land the canoe, and we proceeded in high spirits on finding ourselves once more so comfortably together in it. . . .

[Friday, August 23.] We were on the water before day-light; and when the sun rose a beautiful country appeared around us, enriched and animated by large herds of wild cattle [buffalo]. The weather was now so warm, that to us, who had not of late been accustomed to heat, it was overwhelming and oppressive. In the course of this day we killed a buffalo and a bear, but we were now in the midst of abundance, and they were not sufficiently fat to satisfy our fastidious appetites, so we left them where they fell. We landed for the night, and prepared ourselves for arriving at the Fort[66] on the following day.

[Saturday, August 24.] The weather was the same as yesterday, and the country increasing in beauty; though as we approached the Fort, the cattle appeared proportionably to diminish. We now landed at two lodges of Indians, who were as astonished to see us, as if we had been the first white men whom they had ever beheld. When we had passed these people not an animal was to be seen on the borders of the river.

At length, as we rounded a point, and came in view of the Fort, we threw out our flag, and accompanied it with a general discharge of our fire-arms; while the men were in such spirits, and made such an active use of their paddles, that we arrived before the two men whom we left here in the spring, could recover their senses to answer us. Thus we landed at four in the afternoon, at the place we left on the ninth of May. Here my voyages of discovery terminate. Their toils and their dangers, their solicitudes and sufferings, have not been exaggerated in my description. On the contrary, in many instances, language has failed me in the attempt to describe them. I received, however, the reward of my labours, for they were crowned with success.

As I have now resumed the character of a trader, I shall not trouble my readers with any subsequent concern, but content myself with the closing information, that after an absence of eleven months, I arrived at Fort Chepewyan, where I remained, for the purposes of trade, during the succeeding winter.

Notes

[1] Mackenzie is at or near the Camsell Bend in the Mackenzie River, at about mile 285.

[2] Crossed the river.

[3] Aw-Gee-Nah, 'The English Chief' (fl. 1771–1821) came from a family of Chipewyans centring on Great Slave Lake; PETER FIDLER calls him a 'great Chipewyan Chief'. He was among the followers of Matonabbee during SAMUEL HEARNE's journey to the Arctic Ocean in 1770–72. Aw-Gee-Nah, like Mackenzie, was a trader by profession, which may account for some of the conflict between them. Most of his life, before and after his journey to the northern ocean was spent as a native middleman operating first between the NWC and natives to the north, and then with the HBC as hunter and advisor.

[4] Probably somewhere near mile 260 of the channel, which is 20 miles upstream from the North Nahanni River — a substantial tributary which Mackenzie does not mention.

[5] Probably one of the two islands between miles 236 and 238 of the channel, above Trail Creek; the pemmican had been hidden on July 1.

[6] Peace River Landing, near the intersection of the Peace River and the Smoky.

[7] Mackenzie's observations are not always correct; for more accurate measurements in some cases, see the notes to Lamb's edition.

[8] Chronometer.

[9] Born in the Mohawk Valley, Alexander MacKay (*c.* 1770–1811) was the son of Loyalists who moved to Glengarry County; he joined the NWC at an early date and was posted to Fort Chipewyan. After serving as Mackenzie's lieutenant on the expedition to the Pacific, he continued with the company and was made partner in 1800, but like some North-Westers wearied of company policies and in 1808 became involved with John Jacob Astor's project to found a post at the mouth of the Columbia. He was on the *Tonquin* on its conflict-ridden voyage to the Pacific Coast in 1810–11, and was one of those killed when natives attacked it because the brutal Captain Thorn (against MacKay's advice) had treated them badly.

[10] Mackenzie notes that Landry and Ducette were with him on the Arctic expedition.

[11] A familiar French term meaning dunce or duffer.

[12] Beaver Indians, whom Mackenzie had encountered the previous day.

[13] To soften the resin so as to waterproof the canoe patches.

[14] To cross the river.

[15] Johnson Creek.

[16] This was at Ferro Point, at the foot of the most turbulent part of the Peace River Canyon.

[17] Combe divided Mackenzie's narrative into chapters; this is the beginning of Chapter IV, which directly follows the preceding passage.

[18] Mackenzie had come so far up the vast curve of the Peace River Canyon that he could proceed further only by climbing out of it and cutting a portage trail along the southern slope of Portage Mountain.

[19] Smouldering coal seams are still found in the Canyon.

[20] At or near the sharp twists in the river downstream from the Table River.

[21] These were Sekani Indians; they traded with their western neighbours, the Carriers, who in turn traded with those on the coast.

[22] Narcosli Creek, which Mackenzie was later to name 'Deserter's River or Creek'.

[23] This is a fair description of the canyon of the Fraser River, which SIMON FRASER was to find all but impassable in 1808.

[24] They mean the Shuswap Indians.

[25] Probably one of the coastal salt-water inlets.

[26] There had been trading vessels along the coast since 1785; if one of them attempted to ascend the Fraser, there is no record of it.

[27] Mackenzie had evidently seen a copy of the *Voyages* of Captain John Meares (London, 1790), who had visited the coast in 1786 and 1788. The 'inland sea' was Georgia Strait, far to the south and much further east than Mackenzie thought.

[28] The Bella Coola Indians, who acted as middlemen between coastal trading ships and the tribes inland.

[29] This inscription was never found.

[30] The West Road River.

[31] This is the official name, but it is sometimes known locally as the Blackwater River.

[32]Mackenzie calls these people the Nascud Denee; they are the Naskotin, a branch of the Carrier Indians.

[33]Malaput Lake.

[34]This house was on Gatcho Lake. G.M. Dawson, the geologist, believed that it was still standing when he explored this country in 1876.

[35]One of Mackenzie's many native guides along the route.

[36]The Ntshaautin, a Carrier tribe.

[37]Probably the Bella Coola River.

[38]This appears to be a gambling game.

[39]The point where Mackenzie crossed the mountains is now known as Mackenzie Pass. The altitude is 6000 feet, the highest point reached on his journey.

[40]Now actually named Stupendous Mountain.

[41]The Bella Coola River.

[42]Sitkatapa Lake.

[43]They were on the rim of the Bella Coola Gorge, over 3000 feet deep.

[44]The junction of Burnt Bridge Creek and the Bella Coola River.

[45]This settlement Mackenzie named Friendly Village.

[46]They were about 31 miles away.

[47]The village of Nooskulst, on the north side of the Bella Coola River, at the mouth of the Noosgulch River. Mackenzie later refers to it as the Great Village; it was 8 or 9 miles downstream from Friendly Village.

[48]Cook visited the coast in 1778 but storms kept him well out to sea, and he was never anywhere near the area in question.

[49]Near the mouth of the Bella Coola, on the south shore; Mackenzie later refers to it as Rascal's Village.

[50]This singularly undramatic sentence marks the completion of the first European crossing of the full width of the mainland of North America.

[51]Burke Channel.

[52]Around Mesachie Nose, into Labouchere Channel.

[53]Actually a peninsula; also, the preceding measurement of one fourth mile should read 'four miles'.

[54]Point Edward.

[55]Dean Channel.

[56]'Macubah' is clearly VANCOUVER; 'Bensins' is probably Archibald Menzies, the expedition's botanist. VANCOUVER notes meeting natives in Dean Channel on 3 June 1793, but mentions no difficulties with them.

[57]The village and the rock were on the east side of the entrance to Elcho Harbour. The area around it now forms Sir Alexander Mackenzie Park.

[58]A short sword.

[59]See VANCOUVER for his party's use of ships' boats inshore, rather than sea-going craft.

[60]Mackenzie's note: 'This I found to be the cheek of Vancouver's Cascade Channel' [about four miles up Dean Channel from Mackenzie's Rock].

[61]The site was marked by the Historic Sites and Monuments Board in 1926; the inscription there is a modern re-creation.

[62]Just west of Cape MacKay, at the entrance to Cascade Inlet.

[63]Mackenzie comments in a long note, 'Mr. Meares was undoubtedly wrong in the idea, so earnestly insisted on by him in his voyage, that there was a North-West practicable passage to

the Southward of sixty-nine degrees and a half of latitude, as I flatter myself has been proved by my former voyage. . . .'

[64]Mackenzie's journal of his return home is very much briefer than that of the journey outwards.

[65]The Fraser.

[66]Fort Fork.

George Vancouver   (1757 – 1798)

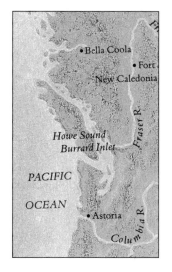

GEORGE VANCOUVER, born at King's Lynn, England, entered the Royal Navy in 1771. He served with Captain James Cook on his second (1772–5) and third (1776–80) expeditions to the Pacific, and first visited British Columbia when Cook refitted at Nootka Sound in 1778. Vancouver's admiration for his great commander marks the account of his own remarkable voyage, but his training as a naval explorer, under the astronomer William Wales on the second voyage and under Cook himself, was only put to use after a decade of service on warships, where, however, he met many of the men later chosen for his expedition. The product of awakening British interest in the west coast fur trade, this project breathed an imperial spirit with which Vancouver was totally in sympathy; his 'Introduction' to the published *Voyage of Discovery* is a forceful and unquestioning statement of the right — and obligation — of the British to rule the world commercially and culturally.

Vancouver was initially second in command of the expedition, which had to be put off when the Spanish — not without imperial ideals of their own — seized British ships at Nootka Sound in 1789; Britain armed for war, but diplomacy prevailed, and when preparations resumed Vancouver was put in charge; he set sail in April 1791. The result was a minute exploration of the continental shore of North America, designed to exhaust every possibility of navigation to the Atlantic by sea-going ships through one of its long inlets; experience quickly showed this was best done in small boats, and by living off the land. In June 1792, Vancouver encountered Spanish ships off Point Grey, with whose leaders he attempted to preserve cordial relations, but by summer's end he had not succeeded in persuading the genial Quadra to yield to the British more than a small plot of the seized territory. Vancouver's exploration of the North American coast continued until 1795; when he returned to England he was a sick man, but could claim that he had put an end to the idea that a north-west passage existed between the Pacific and the interior of the continent.

A gifted explorer, worthy of his mentor Cook, Vancouver demanded much of himself and others; he followed Cook's practice — innovative in the navy — of taking good care of his men's health, but he was not afraid to have his sailors flogged, and as his health grew worse, he was irritable and quarrelsome. In the three years between his retirement and death he worked tirelessly on the narrative and charts of his voyage, but the last 100 pages had to be completed by his brother, John.

Text: *The Voyage of Captain George Vancouver 1791–1795*, ed. W. Kaye Lamb. 4 volumes. London: The Hakluyt Society, 1984. Based on the second edition of 1801, edited by John Vancouver; for his editorial practices, see Lamb, I, 246.

From the 'Introduction'

In contemplating the rapid progress of improvement in the sciences, and the general diffusion of knowledge, since the commencement of the eighteenth century, we are unavoidably led to observe, with admiration, that active spirit of discovery, by means of which the remotest regions of the earth have been explored; a friendly communication opened with their inhabitants; and various commodities, of a most valuable nature, contributing either to relieve their necessities, or augment their comforts, introduced among the less-enlightened part of our species. A mutual intercourse has been also established, in many instances, on the solid basis of a reciprocity of benefits; and the productive labour of the civilized world has found new markets for the disposal of its manufactures. Nor has the balance of trade been wholly against the people of the newly-discovered countries; for, whilst some have been enabled to supply their visitors with an abundance of food, and the most valuable refreshments, in exchange for iron, copper, useful implements, and articles of ornament; the industry of others has been stimulated to procure the skins of animals, and other articles of a commercial nature; which they have found to be eagerly sought for by the traders who now resort to their shores from Europe, Asia, and the eastern side of North America.

The great naval powers of Europe, inspired with a desire not only of acquiring, but also of communicating, knowledge, had extended their researches, in the 16th and 17th centuries, as far into the Pacific Ocean as their limited information of the geography of the earth, at that time, enabled them to penetrate. Some few attempts had also been made by this country towards the conclusion of each of those centuries, but it was not until the year 1764[1] that Great Britain, benefiting by the experience of former enterprizes, laid the foundation for that vast accession of geographical knowledge, which she has since obtained by the persevering spirit of her successive distinguished circumnavigators.

By the introduction of nautical astronomy into marine education, we are taught to sail on the hypothenuse, instead of traversing two sides of a triangle, which was the usage in earlier times; by this means, the circuitous course of all voyages from place to place is considerably shortened. . . .

This great improvement, by which the most remote parts of the terrestrial globe

are brought so easily within our reach, would, nevertheless, have been comparatively of little utility, had not those happy means been discovered, for preserving the lives and health of the officers and seamen engaged in such distant and perilous undertakings; which were so successfully practised by Captain Cook, the first great discoverer of this salutary system, in all his latter voyages round the globe. But in none have the effects of his wise regulations, regimen, and discipline, been more manifest, than in the course of the expedition of which the following pages are designed to treat. To an unremitting attention, not only to food, cleanliness, ventilation, and an early administration of antiseptic provisions and medicines, but also to prevent, as much as possible, the chance of indisposition, by prohibiting individuals from carelessly exposing themselves to the influence of climate, or unhealthy indulgences in times of relaxation, and by relieving them from fatigue and the inclemency of the weather the moment the nature of their duty would permit them to retire; is to be ascribed the preservation of the health and lives of seafaring people on long voyages. Instead of vessels returning from parts, by no means very remote, with the loss of one half, and sometimes two-thirds of their crews, in consequence of scorbutic,[2] and other contagious disorders; instances are now not wanting of laborious services having been performed in the most distant regions, in which, after an absence of more than three or four years, during which time the vessels had been subjected to all the vicissitudes of climate, from the scorching heat of the torrid zone to the freezing blasts of the arctic or antarctic circles, the crews have returned in perfect health, and consisting nearly of every individual they had carried out; whilst those who unfortunately had not survived, either from accident or disease, did not exceed in number the mortality that might reasonably have been expected, during the same period of time, in the most healthy situations of this country. To these valuable improvements, Great Britain is, at this time, in a great measure indebted, for her present exalted station amongst the nations of the earth; and it should seem, that the reign of George the Third had been reserved, by the Great Disposer of all things, for the glorious task of establishing the grand key-stone to that expansive arch, over which the arts and sciences should pass to the furthermost corners of the earth, for the instruction and happiness of the most lowly children of nature. Advantages so highly beneficial to the untutored parts of the human race, and so extremely important to that large proportion of the subjects of this empire who are brought up to the sea service, deserve to be justly appreciated; and it becomes of very little importance to the bulk of our society, whose enlightened humanity teaches them to entertain a lively regard for the welfare and interest of those who engage in such adventurous undertakings for the advancement of science, or for the extension of commerce, what may be the animadversions or sarcasms of those few unenlightened minds that may peevishly demand, 'what beneficial consequences, if any, have followed, or are likely to follow, to the discoverers, or to the discovered, to the common interests of humanity, or to the increase of useful knowledge, from all our boasted attempts to explore the distant recesses of the globe?'[3]
. . .

Although the ardour of the present age, to discover and delineate the true geography of the earth, had been rewarded with uncommon and unexpected success, particularly by the persevering exertions of this great man, yet all was not completed; and though, subsequent to his last visit to the coast of North-West America, no expedition had been projected by Government, for the purpose of acquiring a more exact knowledge of that extensive and interesting country; yet a voyage was planned by His Majesty for exploring some of the Southern regions; and in the autumn of the year 1789, directions were given for carrying it into effect.

. . .

For some time previous to this period the Spaniards, roused by the successful efforts of the British nation, to obtain a more extended knowledge of the earth . . . had not only ventured to visit some of the newly-discovered islands in the tropical regions of the Pacific Ocean, but had also, in the year 1775, with a spirit somewhat analogous to that which prompted their first discovery of America, extended their researches to the northward, along the coast of North-West America.[4] But this undertaking did not seem to have reached beyond the acquirement of a very superficial knowledge of the shores; and though these were found to be extremely broken, and divided by the waters of the Pacific, yet it does not appear that any measures were pursued by them for ascertaining the extent to which those waters penetrated into the interior of the American continent.

This apparent indifference in exploring new countries, ought not, however, to be attributed to a deficiency in skill, or to a want of spirit for enterprize, in the commander of that expedition;[5] because there is great reason to believe, that the extreme caution which has so long and so rigidly governed the court of Madrid, to prevent, as much as possible, not only their American, but likewise their Indian, establishments from being visited by any Europeans, (unless they were subjects of the crown of Spain, and liable to a military tribunal) had greatly conspired, with other considerations of a political nature, to repress that desire of adding to the fund of geographical knowledge, which has so eminently distinguished this country. And hence it is not extraordinary, that the discovery of a north-western navigable communication between the Atlantic and Pacific oceans, should not have been considered as an object much to be desired by the Spanish court. Since that expedition, however, the Spaniards seem to have considered their former national character as in some measure at stake; and they have certainly become more acquainted than they were with the extensive countries immediately adjoining to their immense empire in the new world; yet the measures that they adopted in order to obtain that information, were executed in so defective a manner, that all the important questions to geography still remained undecided, and in the same state of uncertainty.

. . .

The extensive branches of the fisheries, and the fur trade to China, being considered as objects of very material importance to this country [Great Britain], it was deemed expedient, that an officer should be sent to Nootka to receive back, in form, a restitution of the territories on which the Spaniards had seized,[6] and also to make an accurate survey of the coast, from the 30th degree of north latitude north-westward toward Cook's river; and further, to obtain every possible information that could be collected respecting the natural and political state of that country.

The outline of this intended expedition was communicated to me, and I had the honor of being appointed to the command of it. . . .

. . .

It was with infinite satisfaction that I saw, amongst the officers and young gentlemen of the quarter-deck, some who, with little instruction, would soon be enabled to construct charts, take plans of bays and harbours, draw landscapes, and make faithful portraits of the several head-lands, coasts, and countries, which we might discover; thus, by the united efforts of our little community, the whole of our proceedings, and the information we might obtain in the course of the voyage, would be rendered profitable to those who might succeed us in traversing the remote parts of the globe that we were destined to explore, without the assistance of professional persons, as astronomers or draftsmen.

Botany, however, was an object of scientific inquiry with which no one of us was much acquainted; but as, in expeditions of a similar nature, the most valuable opportunities had been afforded for adding to the general stock of botanical information, Mr. Archibald Menzies,[7] a surgeon in the royal navy, who had before visited the Pacific Ocean in one of the vessels employed in the fur trade, was appointed for the specific purpose of making such researches; and had, doubtless, given sufficient proof of his abilities, to qualify him for the station it was intended he should fill. For the purpose of preserving such new or uncommon plants as he might deem worthy of a place amongst His Majesty's very valuable collection of exotics at Kew, a glazed frame was erected on the after part of the quarter-deck, for the reception of those he might have an opporunity of collecting.

The Board of Admiralty, greatly attentive to our personal comforts, gave directions that the Discovery and Chatham[8] should each be supplied with all such articles as might be considered in any way likely to become necessary, during the execution of the long and arduous service in which we were about to engage. Our stores, from the naval arsenals, were ordered to be selected of the very best sorts, and to be made with materials of the best quality. In addition to the ordinary establishment, we were supplied with a large assortment of seines and other useful fishing tackle of various kinds. The provisions were furnished at the victualling-office with the greatest care, all of which proved to be excellent, and manifested the judgment which had been exercised in the selection and preparations of the several articles. To these were added a large proportion of sour-krout, portable soup,[9] wheat instead of the usual supply of oatmeal for breakfast, the essense of malt and spruce, malt, hops, dried yeast, flour, and seed mustard; which may all be considered as articles of food. Those of a medicinal nature, with which we were amply supplied, were Dr. James's powders,[10] vitriolic elixir; the rob of lemons and oranges,[11] in such quantities and proportions as the surgeon thought requisite; together with an augmentation to the usual allowance, amounting to a hundred weight, of the best peruvian bark.[12]

To render our visits as acceptable as possible to the inhabitants of the islands or continent in the Pacific Ocean, and to establish on a firm basis a friendly intercourse with the several tribes with which we might occasionally meet, Lord Grenville directed that a liberal assortment of various European commodities, both of a useful and ornamental nature, should be sent on board from the Secretary of State's office. From the Board of Ordnance the vessels were supplied with every thing necessary for our defence, and amongst other articles were four well-contrived three-pound field pieces, for the protection of our little encampment against any hostile attempts of the native Indians, amongst whom we should necessarily have frequent occasion to reside on shore; and for the amusement and entertainment of such as were peaceably and friendly disposed towards us, we were furnished with a most excellent assortment of well-prepared fireworks. So that nothing seemed to have been forgotten, or omitted, that might render our equipment as complete as the nature of the service we were about to execute could be considered to demand. . . .

From Chapter VII: exploring the area around present-day Vancouver

A Light breeze springing up from the N.W. about seven in the morning of Tuesday the 5th June [1792], we sailed down Possession sound. This wind brought with it, as usual, serene and pleasant weather. Whilst we were passing gently on, the chief, who had shewn so much friendly attention to Mr. Whidbey and his party, with several of his friends came on board, and presented us with some fruit and dried fish. He entered the ship with some reluctance, but was no sooner on deck than he seemed perfectly reconciled; and with much inquisitive earnestness regarded the surrounding objects, the novelty of which seemed to fill his mind with surprise and admiration. The unaffected hospitable attention he had shewn our people, was not likely upon this occasion to be forgotten. After he had visited the different parts of the ship, at which he expressed the greatest astonishment, I presented him and his friends with an assortment of such things as they esteemed to be most valuable; and then they took their leave, seemingly highly pleased with their reception. . . .

Having reached its [the inlet's] entrance, we were met by several canoes from the westward. Some of the headmost, when they had advanced near to the ship made signs of peace, and came alongside, giving us to understand that their friends behind wished to do the same, and requesting we would shorten sail for that purpose. They seemed very solicitous to dissuade us from proceeding to the northward by very vociferous and vehement arguments; but as their language was completely unintelligible, and their wishes not appertaining to the object of our pursuit, so far as we were enabled to comprehend their meaning, we treated their advice with perfect indifference, on which they departed, joined the rest of their countrymen, and proceeded up Admiralty inlet, whose north point, called by me POINT PARTRIDGE,[13] is situated in latitude 48° 16', longitude 237° 31', and is formed by a high white sandy cliff, having one of the verdant lawns on either side of it. Passing at the distance of about a mile from this point we very suddenly came on a small space of ten fathom water, but immediately again increased our depth to 20 and 30 fathoms. After advancing a few miles along the eastern shore of the gulph, we found no effect either from the ebb or flood tide, and the wind being light and variable from the northward, at three in the afternoon we were obliged to anchor in 20 fathoms water, sandy bottom. . . .

On reflecting that the summer was now fast advancing, and that the progress of the vessels occasioned too much delay, I determined, rather than lose the advantages which the prevailing favorable weather now afforded for boat expeditions, to dispatch Mr. Puget[14] in the launch, and Mr. Whidbey[15] in the cutter, with a week's provisions, in order that the shores should be immediately explored to the next intended station of the vessels, whither they would proceed as soon as circumstances would allow. In this arrangement I was well aware, it could not be considered judicious to part with our launch, whilst the ship remained in a transitory unfixed state in this unknown and dangerous navigation; yet she was so essentially necessary to the protection of our detached parties, that I resolved to encounter some difficulties on board, rather than suffer the delay, or lose so valuable an opportunity for the prosecution of the survey. In directing this, orders were given not to examine any openings to the north-eastward, beyond Strawberry bay, but to determine the boundaries of the continental shore leading to the north and eastward, as far as might be practicable to its parallel, whither they were to resort after performing the task assigned. On this service they departed, and directed their course for the first opening on the eastern shore about 3 or 4 leagues distant, bearing by compass from the ship N. by E. . . . [16]

When due attention is paid to the range of snowy mountains that stretch to the southward from the base of mount Rainier, a probability arises of the same chain being continued, so as to connect the whole in one barrier along the coast, at uncertain distances from its shores; although intervals may exist in the ridge where the mountains may not be sufficiently elevated to have been discernible from our several stations. The like effect is produced by the two former mountains, whose immense height permitted their appearing very conspicuously, long before we approached sufficiently near to distinguish the intermediate range of rugged mountains that connect them, and from whose summits their bases originate. . . .

This country presented a very different aspect from that which we had been accustomed to behold further south. The shores now before us, were composed of steep rugged rocks, whose surface varied exceedingly in respect to height, and exhibited little more than the barren rock, which in some places produced a little herbage of a dull colour, with a few dwarf trees.

With a tolerably good breeze from the north, we weighed about three in the afternoon, and with a flood tide, turned up into Strawberry bay, where, in about three hours, we anchored in 16 fathoms, fine sandy bottom. This bay is situated on the west side of an island, which, producing an abundance of upright cypress, obtained the name of CYPRESS ISLAND. The bay is of small extent, and not very deep; its south point bore by compass S. 40 E.; a small islet,[17] forming nearly the north point of the bay, round which is a clear good passage west; and the bottom of the bay east, at the distance of about three quarters of a mile. This situation, though very commodious, in respect to the shore, is greatly exposed to the winds, and sea in a S.S.E. direction. . . .

From the officers [of the *Chatham*], I became acquainted, that the first inlet communicated with port Gardner, by a very narrow and intricate channel, which, for a considerable distance, was not forty yards in width, and abounded with rocks above and beneath the surface of the water. These impediments, in addition to the great rapidity and irregularity of the tide, rendered the passage navigable only for boats or vessels of very small burthen. This determined all the eastern shore of the gulph, from the S.W. point of this passage, in latitude 48° 27', longitude 237° 37', to the north point of entrance into Possession sound, in latitude 47° 53', longitude 237° 47', to be an island, which, in its broadest part, is about ten miles across; and in consequence of Mr. Whidbey's circumnavigation, I distinguished it by the name of WHID-BEY'S ISLAND: and this northern pass, leading into port Gardner, DECEPTION PASSAGE.

Hence they proceeded to the examination of the continental coast leading to the northward, and entered[18] what appeared to be a spacious sound, or opening, extending widely in three directions to the eastward of our present station. One, leading to the southward, and another, to the eastward,[19] they examined, and found them to terminate alike in deep bays affording good anchorage, though inconvenient communication with the shores; particularly towards the head of each bay, on account of a shallow flat of land or mud, which met them at a considerable distance from the land. Having fixed the boundaries of the continent as far to the north as the latitude of this island, agreeably to their directions, they returned, leaving unexplored a large opening which took a northern direction, as also the space that appeared to be the main arm of the gulph, to the north-westward, where the horizon was unbounded, and its width seemed very considerable. The country they had seen to the north-east of Deception passage, is much divided by water, and bore nearly the same steril appearance with that of our present situation; excepting near the heads of the two large bays, which they had examined on the continental shore. There the land was of a moderate height, unoccupied by rocky precipices, and was well wooded with timber. In the course of this expedition, several deserted villages had been seen, and some of the natives met with, who differed not, in any material particular, as to their persons, nor in their civil and hospitable deportment, from those we had been so happy, on former occasions, to call our friends.

As our present anchorage was much exposed, and supplied us with no sort of refreshment, excepting a few small wild onions or leeks, I determined, on this information, to proceed with the vessels up the gulph, to the N.W. in quest of a more commodious situation, from whence Mr. Whidbey might be dispatched, to complete the examination of the arm which had been left unfinished, and another party, to prosecute their inquiries to the N.W., or in such other direction as the gulph might take.

With a light breeze from the S.E., about four o'clock in the morning of Monday the 11th, we quitted this station, and passed between the small island and the north point of the bay to the north-westward, through a cluster of numerous islands, rocks, and rocky islets. On Mr. Broughton's first visit hither, he found a great quantity of very excellent strawberries, which gave it the name of Strawberry bay; but, on our arrival, the fruit season was passed. The bay affords good and secure anchorage, though somewhat exposed; yet, in fair weather, wood and water may be easily procured. . . .

As soon as the ship was secured, I went in a boat to inspect the shores of the bay, and found, with little trouble, a very convenient situation for our several necessary duties on shore; of which the business of the observatory was my chief object, as I much wished for a further trial of the rate of the chronometers, now that it was probable we should remain at rest a sufficient time to make the requisite observations for that purpose. Mr. Broughton[20] received my directions to this effect, as also, that the vessels should be removed, the next morning, about a mile further up the Bay to the N.E. where they would be more conveniently stationed for our several operations on shore; and as soon as the business of the observatory should acquire a degree of forwardness, Mr. Whidbey in the Discovery's cutter, attended by the Chatham's launch, was to proceed to the examination of that part of the coast unexplored to the S.E.; whilst myself, in the yawl, accompanied by Mr. Puget in the launch, directed our researches up the main inlet of the gulph.

Matters thus arranged, with a week's provision in each boat, I departed at five o'clock in the morning of Tuesday the 12th. The most northerly branch, though attracting our first attention, caused little delay; it soon terminated in two open bays; the southernmost,[21] which is the smallest, has two small rocks lying off its south point; it extends in a circular form to the eastward, with a shoal of sand projecting some distance from its shores. This bay affords good anchorage from seven to ten fathoms water: the other is much larger, and extends to the northward;[22] these, by noon, we had passed round, but the shoals attached to the shores of each, and particularly to those of the latter, prevented our reaching within four or five miles of their heads. The point constituting the west extremity of these bays, is that which was seen from the ship, and considered as the western part of the main land, of which it is a small portion, much elevated at the south extremity of a very low narrow peninsula; its highest part is to the S.E. formed by high white sand cliffs falling perpendicularly into the sea; from whence a shoal extends to the distance of half a mile round it, joining those of the larger bay; whilst its south-west extremity, not more than a mile in an east and west direction from the former, is one of those low projecting sandy points, with ten to seven fathoms water, within a few yards of it. From this point, situated in latitude 48° 57′, longitude 237° 20′, (which I distinguished by the name of POINT ROBERTS, after my esteemed friend and predecessor in the Discovery[23]) the coast takes a direction N. 28 W., and presented a task of examination to which we conceived our equipment very unequal. That which, from hence, appeared the northern extreme of the continental shore, was a low bluff point, that seemed to form the southern entrance into an extensive sound,[24] bearing N. 25 W., with broken land stretching about 5° farther to the westward. Between this direction and N. 79 W., the horizon seemed uninterrupted, excepting by the appearance of a small though very high round island, lying N. 52 W., apparently at the distance of many leagues.[25] Having thus early examined and fixed the continental shore to the furthest point seen from the ship, I determined to prosecute our inquiries to the utmost limits that care and frugality could extend our supplies; and, having taken the necessary angles,[26] we proceeded, but soon found our progress along the eastern or continental shore materially impeded by a shoal that extends from point Roberts N. 80 W. seven or eight miles, then stretches N. 35 W. about five or six miles further, where it takes a northerly direction towards the above low bluff point.[27] Along the edge of this bank we had soundings from ten to one fathom, as we increased or decreased our distance from the eastern shore; to approach which all our endeavours were exerted to no purpose, until nine in the evening, when the shoal, having forced us nearly into the middle of the gulph, we stood over its western side, in order to land for the night, and to cook our provisions for the ensuing day, which being always performed by those on watch during the night, prevented any delay on that account, in the day time. As we stood to the westward, our depth soon increased to 15 fathoms, after which we gained no bottom until we reached the western shore of the gulph, where, on our arrival about one o'clock in the morning, it was with much difficulty we were enabled to land on the steep rugged rocks that compose the coast, for the purpose of cooking only, and were compelled, by this unfavorable circumstance, to remain and sleep in the boats.[28]

At five in the morning of Wednesday the 13th, we again directed our course to the eastern shore, and landed about noon, on the above-mentioned low bluff point. This, as was suspected, formed the south point of a very extensive sound, with a small arm leading to the eastward: the space, which seemed to be its main direction, and appeared very extensive, took a northerly course.[29] The observed latitude here was 49° 19', longitude 237° 6', making this point (which, in compliment to my friend Captain George Grey of the navy,[30] was called POINT GREY) seven leagues from point Roberts. The intermediate space is occupied by very low land, apparently a swampy flat, that retires several miles, before the country rises to meet the rugged snowy mountains, which we found still continuing in a direction nearly along the coast. This low flat being very much inundated, and extending behind point Roberts, to join the low land in the bay to the eastward of that point; gives its high land, when seen at a distance, the appearance of an island: this, however, is not the case, notwithstanding there are two openings between this point and point Grey. These can only be navigable for canoes, as the shoal continues along the coast to the distance of seven or eight miles from the shore, on which were lodged, and especially before these openings, logs of wood, and stumps of trees innumerable.[31]

From point Grey we proceeded first up the eastern branch of the sound,[32] where, about a league within its entrance, we passed to the northward of an island which nearly terminated its extent, forming a passage from ten to seven fathoms deep, not more than cable's length in width.[33] This island lying exactly across the canal, appeared to form a similar passage to the south of it,[34] with a smaller island lying before it. From these islands, the canal, in width about half a mile, continued its direction about east. Here we were met by about fifty Indians, in their canoes, who conducted themselves with the greatest decorum and civility, presenting us with several fish cooked, and undressed,[35] of the sort already mentioned as resembling the smelt. These good people finding we were inclined to make some return for their hospitality, shewed much understanding in preferring iron to copper.

For the sake of the company of our new friends, we stood on under an easy sail, which encouraged them to attend us some little distance up the arm.[36] The major part of the canoes twice paddled forward, assembled before us, and each time a conference was held. Our visit and appearance were most likely the objects of their consultation, as our motions on these occasions seemed to engage the whole of their attention. The subject matter, which remained a profound secret to us, did not appear of an unfriendly nature to us, as they soon returned, and if possible, expressed additional cordiality and respect. This sort of conduct always created a degree of suspicion, and should ever be regarded with a watchful eye. In our short intercourse with the people of this country we have generally found these consultations take place, whether their numbers were great or small; and though I have ever considered it prudent to be cautiously attentive on such occasions, they ought by no means to be considered as indicating at all times a positive intention of concerting hostile measures; having witnessed many of these conferences, without our experiencing afterwards any altera-tion in their friendly disposition. This was now the case with our numerous attendants, who gradually dispersed as we advanced from the station where we had first met them, and three or four canoes only accompanied us up a navigation which, in some places, does not exceed an hundred and fifty yards in width.

We landed for the night about half a league from the head of the inlet,[37] and about three leagues from its entrance. Our Indian visitors remained with us until by signs we gave them to understand we were going to rest, and after receiving some acceptable articles they retired, and by means of the same language, promised an abundant supply of fish the next day; our seine having been tried in their presence with very little success. A great desire was manifested by these people to imitate our actions, espe-cially in the firing of a musket, which one of them performed, though with much fear and trembling. They minutely attended to all our transactions, and examined the colour of our skins with infinite curiosity. In other respects they differed little from the generality of the natives we had seen: they possessed no European commodities, or trinkets, excepting some rude ornaments apparently made from sheet cooper; this circumstance, and the general tenor of their behaviour, gave us reason to conclude that we were the first people from a civilized country they had yet seen. Nor did it appear that they were nearly connected, or had much intercourse with other Indians, who traded with the European or American adventurers.

The shores in this situation were formed by steep rocky cliffs, that afforded no convenient space for pitching our tent, which compelled us to sleep in the boats. Some of the young gentlemen, however, preferring the stony beach for their couch, without duly considering the line of high water mark, found themselves incom-moded by the flood tide, of which they were not apprized until they were nearly afloat; and one of them slept so sound, that I believe he might have been conveyed to some distance, had he not been awakened by his companions.

Perfectly satisfied with our researches in this branch of the sound, at four in the morning of Thursday the 14th, we retraced our passage in; leaving on the northern shore, a small opening extending to the northward[38] with two little islets before it of little importance, whilst we had a grander object in contemplation; and more particularly so, as this arm or channel could not be deemed navigable for shipping. The tide caused no stream; the colour of its water, after we had passed the island the day before, was green and perfectly clear, whereas that in the main branch of the sound, extending nearly half over the gulph, and accompanied by a rapid tide, was nearly colourless, which gave us some reason to suppose that the northern branch of the sound might possibly be discovered to terminate in a river of considerable extent. . . .

The shores of this channel, which after Sir Harry Burrard of the navy I have distinguished by the name of BURRARD'S CHANNEL,[39] may be considered, on the southern side, of a moderate height, and though rocky, well covered with trees of large growth, principally of the pine tribe. On the northern side, the rugged snowy barrier, whose base we had now nearly approached, rose very abruptly, and was only protected from the wash of the sea by a very narrow border of low land. By seven o'clock we had reached the N.W. point of the channel, which forms also the south point of the main branch of the sound[40]: this also, after another particular friend,[41] I called POINT ATKINSON, situated north from point Grey, about a league distant. Here the opposite point of entrance into the sound bore by compass west, at the distance of about three miles;[42] and nearly in the center between these two points, is a low rocky island producing some trees, to which the name of PASSAGE ISLAND was given. We passed in an uninterrupted channel to the east of it, with the appearance of an equally good one on the other side. . . .

The gap we had entered in the snowy barrier seemed of little importance, as through the vallies caused by the irregularity of the mountain's tops, other mountains more distant, and apparently more elevated, were seen, rearing their lofty heads in various directions. In this dreary and comfortless region, it was no inconsiderable piece of good fortune to find a little cove in which we could take shelter, and a small spot of level land on which we could erect our tent; as we had scarcely finished our examination, when the wind became excessively boisterous from the southward, attended with heavy squalls and torrents of rain which continuing until noon the following day, Friday the 15th, occasioned a very unpleasant detention. But for this circumstance we might too hastily have concluded that this part of the gulph was uninhabited. In the morning we were visited by near forty of the natives,[43] on whose approach, from the very material alteration that had now taken place in the face of the country, we expected to find some difference in their general character. This conjecture was however premature, as they varied in no respect whatever, but in possessing a more ardent desire for commercial transactions; into the spirit of which they entered with infinitely more avidity than any of our former acquaintances, not only in bartering amongst themselves the different valuables they had obtained from us, but when that trade became slack, in exchanging those articles again with our people; in which traffic they always took care to gain some advantage, and would frequently exult on the occasion. Some fish, their garments, spears, bows and arrows, to which these people wisely added their copper ornaments, comprized their general stock in trade. Iron, in all its forms, they judiciously preferred to any other article we had to offer.

The weather permitting us to proceed, we directed our route along the continental or western shore of the sound, passing within two small islands and the main land,[44] into the opening before mentioned, stretching to the westward from Anvil island.[45] As the distance of an hundred yards from the shore, the bottom could not be reached with 60 fathoms of line, nor had we been able to gain soundings in many places since we had quitted point Atkinson with 80 and 100 fathoms, though it was frequently attempted; excepting in the bason at the head of the sound, where the depth suddenly decreased from sixty fathoms to two. We had advanced a short distance only in this branch, before the colour of the water changed from being nearly milk white, and almost fresh, to that of oceanic and perfectly salt. By sun-set we had passed the channel which had been observed to lead into the gulph, to the southward of Anvil island; and about nine o'clock landed for the night, near the west point of entrance into the sound, which I distinguished by the name of HOWE'S SOUND, in honor of Admiral Earl Howe; and this point, situated in latitude 49° 23', longitude 236° 51', POINT GOWER[46]; between which and point Atkinson, up to Anvil island, is an extensive group of islands of various sizes. The shores of these, like the adjacent coast, are composed principally of rocks rising perpendicularly from an unfathomable sea; they are tolerably well covered with trees, chiefly of the pine tribe, though few are of a luxuriant growth. . . .

We had seen about seventeen Indians in our travels this day, who were much more painted than any we had hitherto met with. Some of their arrows were pointed with slate, the first I had seen so armed on my present visit to this coast; these they appeared to esteem very highly, and like the inhabitants of Nootka, took much pains to guard them from injury. They however spoke not the Nootka language, nor the dialect of any Indians we had conversed with; at least the few words we had acquired were repeated to them without effect; in their persons they differed in no other respect, and were equally civil and inoffensive in their behaviour.[47] The shores we passed this day are of a moderate height within a few miles of this station, and are principally composed of craggy rocks, in the chasms of which a soil of decayed vegetables has been formed by the hand of time; from which pine trees of an inferior dwarf growth are produced, with a considerable quantity of bushes and under-wood. . . .

The next morning, Monday the 18th, as usual, at four o'clock, we proceeded up the inlet about 3 miles in a N.N.W. direction, whence its width increases about half a league in a direction nearly N.E. to a point which towards noon we reached, and ascertained its latitude to be 50° 1', longitude 236° 46'.[48] The width of this channel still continuing, again flattered us with discovering a breach in the eastern range of snowy mountains notwithstanding the disappointment we had met with in Howe's sound; and although since our arrival in the gulph of Georgia, it had proved an impenetrable barrier to that inland navigation, of which we had heard so much, and had sought with sanguine hopes and ardent exertions hitherto in vain, to discover. . . .

. . . Through a small space of low land, which extended from the head of the inlet to the base of the mountains that surrounded us, flowed three small streams of fresh water, apparently originating from one source in the N.W. or left hand corner of the bay, formed by the head of this inlet; in which point of view was seen an extensive valley, that took nearly a northerly uninterrupted direction as far as we could perceive, and was by far the deepest chasm we had beheld in the descending ridge of the snowy barrier, without the appearance of any elevated land rising behind. This valley much excited my curiosity to ascertain what was beyond it. But as the streams of fresh water were not navigable, though the tide had risen up to the habitations of six or seven Indians, any further examination of it in our boats was impracticable, and we had no leisure for excursions on shore. From the civil natives who differed not in any respect from those we had before occasionally seen, we procured a few most excellent fish, for which they were compensated principally in iron, being the commodity they most esteemed and fought after. In all these arms of the sea we had constantly observed, even to their utmost extremity, a visible, and sometimes a material rise and fall of the tide, without experiencing any other current than a constant drain down to seaward, excepting just in the neighbourhood of the gulph. . . .

Not a little mortified that our progress should be so soon stopped,[49] it became highly expedient to direct our way towards the ships, to whose station, by the nearest route we could take, it was at least 114 miles. This was now to be performed, after the time was nearly expired for which our supply of provisions had been calculated. Necessity directed that no time should be lost; especially as I was determined to seek a passage into the gulph by the branch of this inlet that we had passed the preceeding day, leading to the N.W. conceiving there was a great probability that this branch might lead into the gulph at some distance beyond where we had entered this inlet; in which course we should have an opportunity of fixing the boundaries of the continent to the utmost extent that our present equipment would afford. . . .

The boundary of the continental shore I now considered as determined to this point, from a full conviction that the inlet under the examination of Mr. Whidbey, would terminate like those we had visited. Presuming our time to have been not ill spent, we directed our course to the station where we had left the ships now at the distance of 84 miles, steering for the opposite shore, being the land before adverted to, as appearing to form an extensive island, or peninsula; the nearest part of which was about five miles across from Scotch-fir point; and which the continental shore still formed a passage, to all appearance, of the same width, in a direction N. 62 W., with an uninterrupted horizon in that point of view; so that, whether it was an island or peninsula, remained still to be determined. . . .

As we were rowing, on the morning of Friday the 22d, for point Grey, purposing there to land and breakfast, we discovered two vessels at anchor under the land.[50] The idea which first occurred was, that, in consequence of our protracted absence, though I had left no orders to this effect, the vessels had so far advanced in order to meet us; but on a nearer approach, it was discovered, that they were a brig and a schooner, wearing the colours of Spanish vessels of war, which I conceived were most probably employed in pursuits similar to our own; and this on my arrival on board, was confirmed. These vessels proved to be a detachment from the commission of Sen' Malaspina, who was himself employed in the Philippine islands; the Sen' Malaspina had, the preceding year, visited the coast; and that these vessels, his Catholic Majesty's brig the Sutil, under the command of Sen' Don D. Galiano, with the schooner Mexicana, commanded by Sen' Don C. Valdes, both captains of frigates in the Spanish navy, had sailed from Acapulco on the 8th of March, in order to prosecute discoveries on this coast.[51] Sen[r] Galiano, who spoke a little English, informed me, that they had arrived at Nootka on the 11th of April, from whence they had sailed on the 5th of this month, in order to complete the examination of this inlet, which had, in the preceding year, been partly surveyed by some Spanish officers whose chart they produced.[52]

I cannot avoid acknowledging that, on this occasion, I experienced no small degree of mortification in finding the external shores of the gulph had been visited, and already examined a few miles beyond where my researches during the excursion, had extended; making the land, I had been in doubt about, an island; continuing nearly in the same direction, about four leagues further than had been seen by us; and, by the Spaniards, named Favida.[53] The channel, between it and the main, they had called Canal del Neustra Signora del Rosario,[54] whose western point had terminated their examination; which seemed to have been entirely confined to the exterior shores, as the extensive arms, and inlets, which they had occupied so much of our time, had not claimed the least of their attention.

The Spanish vessels, that had been thus employed last year, had refitted in the identical part of port Discovery, which afforded us similar accommodation. From these gentlemen, I likewise understood, that Sen[r] Quadra, the commander in chief of the Spanish marine at St. Blas and at California, was, with three frigates and a brig, waiting my arrival at Nootka, in order to negotiate the restoration of those territories to the crown of Great Britain. Their conduct was replete with that politeness and friendship which characterizes the Spanish nation; every kind of useful information they cheerfully communicated, and obligingly expressed much desire, that circumstances might so concur as to admit our respective labours being carried on together;[55] for which purpose, or, if from our long absence and fatigue in an open boat, I would wish to remain with my party as their guest, they would immediately dispatch a boat with such directions as I might deem necessary for the conduct of the ships, or, in the event of a favorable breeze springing up, they would weigh and sail directly to their station; but being intent on losing no time, I declined their obliging offers, and having partaken with them a very hearty breakfast, bad them farewell, not less pleased with their hospitality and attention, than astonished at the vessels in which they were employed to execute a service of such a nature.[56] . . . I shewed them the sketch I had made of our excursion, and pointed out the only spot which I conceived we had left unexamined, nearly at the head of Burrard's canal:[57] they seemed much surprized that we had not found a river said to exist in the region we had been exploring, and named by one of their officers Rio Blancho, in compliment to the then prime minister of Spain; which river these gentlemen had sought for thus far to no purpose. They took such notes as they chose from my sketch, and promised to examine the small opening in Burrard's channel, which, with every other information they could procure, should be at my service on our next meeting.

From these new and unexpected friends we directed our course along the shoal already noticed, which I now called STURGEON BANK, in consequence of our having purchased of the natives some excellent fish of that kind, weighing from fourteen to two hundred pounds each. . . . In the morning of Saturday the 23d, against a strong easterly breeze, about ten in the forenoon we reached the ships, after having traversed in our boats upwards of 330 miles.

Notes

[1] The 1764 expedition commanded by the Hon. John Byron marks the beginning of Britain's interest in Pacific exploration at the end of the Seven Years' War.

[2] Scurvy, caused by lack of Vitamin C, was common among sailors on long voyages. A 1753 discovery led Captain Cook to employ citrus fruits as a preventative on his first Pacific voyage (1768–71).

[3] The quotation is from the Introduction, by Dr John Douglas, Bishop of Salisbury, to his edition of Captain Cook's last voyage.

[4] The Spanish made voyages to the Northwest Coast in 1774 and 1775; the latter was commanded by Quadra.

[5] The unnamed commander was Juan Francisco de la Bodega y Quadra (1743–1794), Peruvian naval officer and explorer, who commanded the Spanish base at Nootka in 1792; he and Vancouver became good friends.

[6] For the 'Nootka Sound' affair, see the headnote.

[7] The surgeon-botanist Archibald Menzies (1754–1842) was the only trained scientist on the expedition; he was appointed through influence exerted by the eminent patron of science Sir Joseph Banks, and towards the end of the voyage he and Vancouver were sometimes in conflict. Menzies made extensive and distinguished botanical collections, and gave the Douglas fir its name.

[8] The *Discovery* was a sloop of war, with an authorized complement of 100 men; the *Chatham* was an 'armed tender', a smaller ship carrying 45.

[9] Portable soup, invented by a Mrs Dubois, consisted of vegetables mixed with liver, kidney, heart, etc., all boiled to a pulp; when cool and hard it was cut into slabs. It was also carried on the FRANKLIN expedition. Pioneers moving westward carried portable soup as well; an 1857 recipe is given by James Beard in *American Cookery* (1972), 82–4.

[10] A popular remedy.

[11] Fruit syrup.

[12] Cinchona bark, the source of quinine, used in cases of malaria.

[13] Possibly after John Vancouver's wife, Martha Partridge. A number of the places given names by Vancouver had already been named by previous Spanish explorers; in many cases the English names have prevailed.

[14] Peter Puget (1762?–1822), lieutenant on the *Discovery*. He later had a distinguished naval career, and was promoted Rear Admiral in 1821.

[15] Joseph Whidbey, master on the *Discovery* (that is, captain of the ship itself, as opposed to leader of the expedition).

[16] Deception Pass.

[17] Strawberry Island.

[18] Through Guemes Channel.

[19] Fidalgo Bay and Padilla Bay, respectively.

[20] Lieutenant William R. Broughton, Commander of the Chatham.

[21] Semiahmoo Bay.

[22] Boundary Bay.

[23]Captain Henry Roberts was appointed to command the expedition before the Nootka Sound controversy; Vancouver took his place when preparations resumed at the end of 1790.

[24]Point Grey, the south point of entrance to Burrard Inlet.

[25]Mount Shepherd, on Texada Island.

[26]Surveying the shore-line with instruments.

[27]Roberts Bank and Sturgeon Bank, two extensive alluvial deposits from the Fraser River, extending from Point Roberts to Point Grey.

[28]They probably spent the night off Gabriola Island.

[29]Probably Burrard Inlet 'leading to the eastward', and Howe Sound, trending north.

[30]George, third son of the first Earl Grey.

[31]This is the estuary of the Fraser River, which was probably in flood.

[32]Burrard Inlet.

[33]The First Narrows, the entrance to Vancouver's inner harbour. Stanley Park, on the south side, with the high bluff of Prospect Point, could easily have been mistaken for an island.

[34]False Creek.

[35]Without sauce or accompaniments.

[36]The 'arm' is now Vancouver's inner harbour, with the city on its south shore.

[37]They spent the night on the south shore opposite Indian Arm, which is about four miles from the end of the inlet at Port Moody, not 'half a league'.

[38]Indian Arm.

[39]Burrard's Canal in the first edition, now Burrard Inlet. Vancouver may have been honouring either the first baronet, who died 12 days after the *Discovery* sailed from England, or more likely his nephew, Sir Harry Burrard, later Burrard-Neale, who had earlier been his shipmate.

[40]Howe Sound.

[41]The 'particular friend' has not been identified.

[42]Point Cowan, on Bowen Island.

[43]Squamish Indians; Vancouver had met others earlier in his journey.

[44]Defence Island, and the smaller island near it.

[45]Thornbrough Channel.

[46]Probably after Captain (later Admiral) Sir Erasmus Gower.

[47]These natives were Coast Salish; Vancouver met many more in the next two weeks. The many dialects of the Salishian language were not all mutually intelligible.

[48]Patrick Point.

[49]By a shallow bank which his boats could not cross.

[50]That is, west and south of Point Grey, and offshore so as to be clear of the shallows west of the point.

[51]Alejandro Malaspina (1754–1810), Spanish naval officer and explorer, was engaged in a round-the-world expedition on the model of Captain Cook's; the survey of Vancouver Island and the Sound was planned by Malaspina, but as a separate project. Dionisio Alcalá-Galiano (1762–1805), Spanish naval officer and explorer, published a journal in 1802 praising the beauty and possibilities of the area; he died at the battle of Trafalgar, in which Cayetano Valdés y Flores Bazán also took part.

[52]The chart of Eliza's discoveries drawn by Juan Carrasco; Vancouver was evidently given a copy or permitted to make one.

[53]Texada Island; Favida or Feveda is a misreading of 'Texada', which is clearly marked on Carrasco's chart.

[54]Present-day Malaspina Strait.

[55]The journal of Galiano and Valdés puts a different light on this statement; it relates that Vancouver put forward 'his argument that our vessels should join his so as to be able to work together. He did this in such terms that not only were we obliged to agree but we comprehended that it would be discreditable, not only as far as we were concerned, but even for the public credit of the nation.' Vancouver did not succeed in persuading Quadra to yield more than a fraction of the territory Britain claimed.

[56]Vancouver observes that the Spanish ships had few officers and were small and cramped, yet provided with many ordinary comforts.

[57]That is, Indian Arm.

Simon Fraser   (1776 – 1862)

SIMON FRASER was born in Vermont of a Scottish Catholic emigrant family with strong connections to the Canadas and the fur trade. His father died in prison during the American revolution and his Loyalist mother moved north with her children in 1789. By 1792 Simon was apprenticed to the North West Company, and though little is known of his early life, he seems to have been sent to the Athabasca country; he was made a partner in 1802 at the early age of 25. In 1805 he was given the task of extending the NWC's trade routes across the Rockies; his great journey down the river which bears his name was only one part of this arduous enterprise. Besides the hair-raising physical difficulty of descending the river Fraser had to cope with constant political problems as the party passed almost daily from one native territory to another. Though nominally in charge of the expedition, Fraser was very much in the hands of the natives who were his guides and did not always share his objectives. Like Mackenzie, of whose early eminence he may have been jealous (elsewhere he refers to him as 'the Knight') Fraser repeatedly had to dominate events by sheer personality. Unlike Mackenzie, however, he was an alert observer of native culture and trading practices, as indeed he needed to be if the NWC was to succeed in planting trading posts west of the Rockies. His leadership abilities were tested both at the mouth of the Fraser, where he encountered strong native resistance, and a few days later when, harassed beyond their strength, his own men almost deserted. The journey from Fort George to the Strait of Georgia and back lasted from 28 May 1808 to 6 August; but it was a failure; as Jules Quesnel lamented in a letter to a friend, 'This journey did not meet the needs of the company and will never be of any advantage to them, this river not being navigable.'

Fraser spent the years from 1808 to 1817 first in the Athabasca department and then at Red River, where he was unwillingly involved in the NWC's opposition to Lord Selkirk's settlement. He was among those tried and acquitted at York (Toronto) after the Seven Oaks massacre of 1816. Like other retired fur traders he settled on a farm near Cornwall, but did not prosper, having been injured in the rebellion of 1837–8. The journal of 1808 exists in two forms; a fragment (the 'Second Journal') which appears to reproduce Fraser's own notes as taken down in travel, and a diary of the whole journey which was certainly polished by more than one hand. To this Fraser would have had no objection; in 1807 he had sent his 1806 journal to John Stuart, saying amiably 'it is exceeding ill wrote worse worded and not well spelt. But there I know you can make a good Journal of it, if you expunge some Parts & add to others and make it out in the manner you think most Proper. . . . I think it necessary to send it to headquarters in the light canoe as it will give our Gentlemen a good deal of information about the country.'

Text: 'Journal of a voyage from the Rocky Mountains to the Pacific Ocean performed in the Year 1808', in *The Letters and Journals of Simon Fraser 1806–1808*, ed. W. Kaye Lamb (Toronto: Macmillan Company of Canada, 1960); see pp. 35–6 for Lamb's account of the problems of the text, which is a careless scribal copy, not Fraser's autograph.

Saturday, May 22 [28], 1808.[1] Having made every necessary preparation for a long voyage, we embarked at 5 o'clock, A.M. in four canoes, at Fraser's River.[2] Our crew consisted of nineteen men,[3] two Indians, Mr Steward,[4] Mr Quesnil,[5] and myself; in all twenty four. At this place [the] Columbia[6] is about 300 yards wide. It overflows its banks, and has a very strong current.

After having proceeded eighteen miles we came to a strong rapid which we ran down. One of the canoes came near striking against a precipice which forms the right bank. A little lower down the channel it contracts to about 70 yards, and passes between two rocks.

After running down several considerable rapids, we put a shore at 11 A.M. to breakfast. In the mean[time] Mr Stewart took a meridian altitude, O.L.L. 115° 9' 45" by artificial Horizon. Error of Sextant 7' 30" +. We saw many fresh tracts of Red Deer. Reembarked at one. Fine going; a smooth Current interspersed with small Islands. Several houses & tombs along the left bank. . . .

Monday, May 30. We embarked at 5 A.M. Experienced a strong current. The country all along is charming, & apparently well inhabited; having seen a large number of houses. At 6 we put to shore at a large house; found a *cache* of fish. After taking a few salmons and leaving the value we secured the rest for the owners. Observed some vestiges of horses at this place. A little below we put a shore again, and left a bale of salmon in *cache*. This caused some delay. Passed several rapids [in] the afternoon. This country, which is interspersed with meadows and hills, dales & high rocks, has upon the whole a *romantic* but *pleasant* appearance.

Continuing our course expeditiously, on a sudden we perceived some of the Natives on the left shore seemingly in great confusion. We crossed to the right and landed at a large house. Our Indians then called out to the strangers on the opposite shore, informing them that we were *white people* going to the sea. . . .[7]

According to the accounts we received here, the river below was but a succession of falls and cascades, which we should find impossible to pass, not only thro the badness of the channel, but also thro the badness of the surrounding country, which was rugged and mountainous. Their opinion, therefore, was that we should continue our voyage and remain with them. I remarked that our determination of going on was fixed. They, then, informed us that at the next camp, the great Chief of the Atnaugh [Atnah] had a slave who had been to the sea, who perhaps we might procure as guide. . . .

Tuesday, May 31 . . . After inquiring repeatedly for the slave, who had a knowledge of the country below, he was at last introduced, and to form an estimate of his capacity, I had two oil cloths[9] spread out for the ground of a chart, upon which I desired him to sketch the country towards the sea. This he readily undertook, but his endeavours soon convinced me that his stock of knowledge was very slender indeed, for his lines were entirely directed by an elderly man, a relative of the Chief. However, in his sketch, we could plainly see a confirmation of the badness of the navigation, and thereby the necessity of leaving [our] canoes, and as much of our baggage as we could spare, in order to prosecute our journey by land.

The Chief who had been an advocate in our cause spoke much in our favour to his own people, and assured us that the next nation were good Indians and would be kind to white strangers. Having given to our new friend a hint that trading posts should be established in his country within a short period, he immediately offered to accompany us all the way, remarking at the same time that he was well known, and that his experience and influence would be of great consequence to the security of our success. Then his brother presented me with a fine beaver skin, and a well dressed deer skin, and then recommended the Chief to our particular protection. I thanked him for his presents, and assured him that every attention should be paid to his relation, and that he should be handsomely rewarded for his trouble on our return. When this ceremony was over, the Chief, his slave, and our Too-how-tin [Tauten] interpreter having got ready, took their departure; but the last was unwilling to proceed, alledging for an excuse that his wife and children would starve in his absence, but notwithstanding this strong argument he was prevailed upon to proceed. . . .

Wednesday, June 1. This morning at an early hour all hands were ready, and the Natives began to appear, from every quarter, in numbers. Mr Stuart, six men and myself went again to visit the rapid. We found it about two miles in length, with high & steep banks, which contracted the channel in many places to the breadth of 40 or 50 yards. The immense body of water passing through this narrow space in a turbulent manner, forming numerous gulphs and cascades, and making a tremendous noise, had an awful and forbidden appearance. Nevertheless since it was considered as next to impossible to carry the canoes across the land, on account of the heigth and steepness of the Hills, it was resolved to venture them down this dangerous pass.

Leaving Mr Stuart and two men at the lower end of the rapid, in order to watch the motions of the Natives, I returned with the other four men to the camp. Immediately upon my arrival I ordered the best five out of the crews into a canoe lightly loaded. This was no sooner given than obeyed; and the canoe in a moment was underway. After passing the first cascade the canoe lost her course, and was drawn to the eddy, where it was whirled about for a considerable time, and seemingly in suspense whether to sink or to swim. The men had no power over her. However it took a favourable turn and by degrees was led from this dangerous vortex again into the stream. It then continued flying from one danger to another, untill the cascade near the last where in spite of every effort, the whirlpools forced it against a projecting rock, which happened to be a low point. Upon this the men debarked, and saved their own lives, and contrived to save the property; for the greatest danger was still a head. Of course to continue on the water would be certain destruction.

During this distressing scene we were on shore, looking on, anxiously concerned; and seeing our poor fellows once more safe gave us as much happiness as to themselves. We hastened to their assistance, but their situation rendered our approach perilous and difficult. The bank was extremely high and steep, and we had to plunge our daggers at intervals into the ground to check our speed as otherwise we might be impelled to slide into the river.

When we joined the party we lost no time, but set to work immediately. We cut steps into the declivity of the hill, fastened a line to the front of the canoe with which some of the men ascended in order to haul it up, while the others supported the canoe upon their arms. In this manner our situation was extremely precarious; our lives hung as it were upon a thread; for failure of the line or a false step of one of the men might have hurled the whole of us into eternity. However we fortunately cleared the bank before dark.

The men who had the rest of the baggage in charge, perceiving from these difficulties, the impossbility of attempting the rapid with safety, began to carry it, and had immense high hills to ascend with heavy loads on their backs.

Numbers of the Natives came to see us in [the] course of the day and remained. They all assured us that the navigation for a certain distance below was impractible and advised us to leave our canoes in their charge and proceed on our journey by land to a great river that flows from the left into this communication [river].[9] The country they said consisted of plains, and the journey could be performed with horses in four or five days; thence we should have smooth water all the way to the sea.

But going to the sea by an indirect way was not the object of the undertaking. I therefore would not deviate and continued our route according to my original intention. . . .

Friday, June 3 . . . The Indians made us understand that within a couple of days more, we should come to a plentiful country where the Indians were hospitable, but having by this time acquired sufficient acquaintance with the character of our new councillors, we did as we were done by, we gave them civil, but evasive answers, and in all followed the dictates of our own judgement.

This is called the *Atnah Nation*. Their country is well stocked with large animals, and they consequently pay very little attention to fishing. In summer they reside in shades[10] and their winter quarters which are built under ground, are square below diminishing gradually in size to the top, where there is a small aperture which serves the double purpose of door & chimney, while a post with notches answers for a pair of stairs.

The Atnahs wish to be friendly to strangers but they do not know how. The men are tall and slender, of a serious disposition and inclined to industry. They say they never sing nor dance; but we observed them play at hazard, a [gambling] game well known among the Indians of Athabasca. They besmear their bodies with oil and red earth, and paint their faces in different colours. Their dress is leather. They are great travellers; have been at war beyond the Mountains going by the name of *Rocky Mountains,* where they saw Buffaloes; for seeing our powder horns they knew them to be of that animal.

They informed us that white people had lately passed down the first large river to the left. These we supposed to be some of our friends from the department of *Fort des Prairies.*[11]

Sunday [Saturday], June 4. . . . At 6 A.M. we were on the water and crossed to the Indians, who were on the opposite sides. Here we observed a precipice of immense heighth a head, which seemed to bar the River. Continued our course with a strong current; ran down several Rapids & Came to a dangerous one, in which the Canoes having shipped much water & being nearly upset, we landed.

Visited the lower part [of the rapid]; having found it strong and full of tremendous Whirlpools we were greatly at a loss how to act. However the nature of our situation left us no choice, for we were under the necessity either to run down the Canoes or to abandon them. The first having been preferred they were unloaded & then manned with five men each. One canoe went first, and having succeeded, the other two immediately followed. The struggle which the men on this trial experienced between the whirlpools and rocks almost exhausted their strength; the canoes were in perpetual danger of sinking or being broken to pieces. It was a desperate undertaking.

After escaping this danger the men returned by land for the baggage. This task was as difficult and dangerous as going by the water, being obliged to pass on a declivity, which formed the brink of a huge precipice, among loose stones, and gravel that constantly gave way from under their feet. One of them who had lost the path of the others got into a most intricate and perilous situation. With a large package on his back he got so engaged among the rocks that he could neither move forward nor backward, nor yet unload himself without imminent danger. Seeing the poor fellow in this predicament, I crawled to his assistance; but not without great risk, and saved him, however his load dropped off his back over the precipice into the river. . . .

Friday [Thursday], June 9. This morning the men put [on] their best cloathes. Our two Indians having only a Beaver Robe and an orignal [moose] skin, I gave each a blanket and a *braillet.*[12] All this was done that we might appear to advantage in the eyes of the new Indians whom we were to find at the *Rapide Couverte.* At 7 A.M. our arms and every thing being in due order, we embarked and [a] few hours after arrived at *Rapide Couverte.*[13] Here [the] channel contracts to about forty yards, and is inclosed by two precipices of great heighth which bending towards each other make it narrower above than below. The water which rolls down this extraordinary passage in tumultuous waves and with great velocity had a tremendous appearance.

It being absolutely impossible to carry the canoes by land, yet sooner than to abandon them, all hands without hesitation embarked, as it were a *corp perdu*[14] upon the mercy of this Stygian[15] tide. Once engaged the die was cast, and the great difficulty consisted in keeping the canoes in the medium, or *fil d'eau*[16] that is to say, clear of the precipice on one side, and of the gulphs formed by the waves on the other. However, thus skimming along like lightning, the crews cool and determined, followed each other in awful silence. And [when] we arrived at the end we stood gazing on our narrow escape from perdition. After breathing a little, we continued our course to a point where the Indians were encamped. Here we were happy to find our old friends, the Chief and the Interpreter, who immediately joined our party.

The Indians of this place drew a chart of the riverbed which to our view represented it as a dreadful chain of difficulties apparently unsurmountable, and they blamed us for venturing so far with our canoes, & for not going by land as advised by the Old Chief on a former occasion, asserting this communication both by land & by water will in some places be found impracticable to strangers, as we shall have to ascend and descend mountains and precipices by means of rope ladders &c. Here Mr Stuart had a mer[idian]. alt[itude]. of O.L.L. 112° 58′ 30″ art[ificial]. Hor[izo]n.

I prevailed upon another Indian to embark with us as pilot. We then continued our course until late in the evening when our pilot ordered us ashore for the night.[17] This afternoon the rapids were very bad; two in particular were worse, if possible, than any we had hitherto met with, being a continual series of cascades, mixt with rocky fragments and bound by precipices and mountains, that seemed at times to have no end. I scarcely ever saw any thing so dreary, and seldom so dangerous in any country; and at present while I am writing this, whatever way I turn, mountains upon mountains, whose summits are covered with eternal snows, close the gloomy scene. . . .

Sunday [Saturday] June 11. . . . The path which we followed was along the declivity of Mountains, across many ravines, and we experienced a good deal of fatigue and disagreeable walking; yet, generally speaking, we were much better of than we had reason to expect. At sunset we encamp on the side of a small river. Mr Stuart and myself still indulging the fond hopes of discovering an opening for making use of canoes went to visit the big river, which we found, as we were taught to expect, impassable. The channel was deep, cut through rocks of immense heighth and forming eddies and gulphs, which it was impossible for canoes even to approach with safety. . . .

These Indians[18] say that the sea is about ten nights from their village. One of the old men, a very talkative fellow, and we understand a great warrior, had been at the sea; saw *great canoes*[19] and white men. He observed that the chiefs of the white men were well dressed and very proud, for, continued he, getting up and clapping his two hands upon his hips, then strutting about with an air of consequence, 'This the way they go.'

Tuesday [Monday], June 13. . . . The country through which we passed this day was the most savage that can be imagined, yet we were always in a beaten path and always in Sight of the river, which, however, we could not approach, its Iron-bound banks having a very forbidden appearance. . . .

Having shaved and dressed in our best apparel, we resumed our march, followed by our retinue of yesterday, but recruiting as we went. Halting a little, a stranger, taking up our Interpreter's gun & examining it through curiosity touched the trigger; which one of our men observing just in time, threw up the muzzle as the shot was going off; thus saved the lives of some natives who otherwise would have received the contents. Such a misfortune would have at once put an end to our journey if not to our lives.

When we came to the forks,[20] the chief men dressed in their coats of mail advanced to meet us, in order, to know our disposition before we could be admitted into their camp. Our Chief harangued them in his language; they answered him in theirs; and we were obliged to employ three different interpreters, on the occasion to settle the business. These ambassadors are of the Askittih nation; they looked manly, and had really the appearance of warriors. They seemed to speak with fluency; and all was attention marked with signs of applause. Our Chief conveyed our sentiments with great animation. He assured the Askitteh Nation that we were good people and had nothing to do with the quarrels of Indian Nations.

When the conference was over, the Ambassadors returned to their camp, running as fast as their legs could carry them. We immediately followed, and encamped on the right bank opposite the village, being the best position we could find for a defence. The Natives without loss of time began to cross over in wooden canoes, and I had to shake hands with a least one hundred & thirty seven men, while the Old Chief was haranguing them about our good qualities, wishing to persuade some of them to accompany us part of the journey to which several did assent. In the meantime Mr Stuart and myself spared no pains to impress upon their minds the numberless advantages which all the nations in that quarter would derive from an open communication with the white people. . . .

Thursday [Wednesday], June 15. . . . Here we are, in a strange Country, surrounded with dangers, and difficulties, among numberless tribes of savages, who never saw the face of a white man. Our situation is critical and highly unpleasant; however we shall endeavour to make the best of it; what cannot be cured, must be endured.

Some of the Indians, who had joined us yesterday forenoon & whom we were happy to acknowledge now as old acquaintance, drew at my request a chart of the Country below this to the sea. By this sketch the navigation seems still very bad, and difficult. At some distance to the East appears another large river which runs parallel to this to the sea.[21]

After obtaining this information we prevailed upon the Indians to ferry us over to the village. They employed but one canoe which made three trips, and took up a considerable time. The village is a fortification of 100 by 24 feet, surrounded with palisades eighteen feet high, slanting inwards, and lined with a shorter row that supports a shade covered with bark, and which are the dwellings. This place, we understand, is the metropolis of the Askettih Nation. . . . We observed several European articles among them, particularly a new copper Tea Kettle, and a gun of a large size and which, perhaps, are of a Russian manufacture. . . .

Friday [Thursday], June 16. . . . Here we met some of a neighbouring nation called Hakamaugh — with these were two of another Tribe called *Suihonie;*[22] all were exceedingly well dressed in leather, and were on horseback. They have a great quantity of shells and blue beads, and we saw a broken silver broach such as the Sauteus[23] wear, among them. They were kind to us, and assisted us at the carrying place with their horses. We put up at the lower end near their camp.

Here we got acquainted with a man of the *Chilkcotin* [Chilcotin] tribe who had left his own country when a boy but still retaining a little of his mother tongue, we made a shift to understand. He observed that he had been at the sea by this communication, where he had seen men like us, who lived in a wooden enclosure upon an Island, and who had tents for the purpose of trading with the Natives in furs. He gave us a good account of the navigation, and he consented to accompany us as pilot. Since the departure of our Tha-how-tin Interpreters, this was the only man with whom we could converse to any advantage.

At this place I saw a shield different from any I had hitherto seen. It was large enough to cover the whole body, composed of splinters of wood like the ribs of stays and neatly inclosed with twine made of hemp. . . .

Monday [Sunday], June 19. . . . At 8 A.M. set out, divided as yesterday. A mile below, the natives ferried us over a large rapid river.[24] I obtained, for an awl, a passage to the next village, a distance of three miles through strong rapids. The others who went by land met some of the Indians on the way who were happy to see them. This was the village of the Chief who had left us in the morning.[25] We were told here that the road a head was very bad, and consequently we should meet with difficulty for most part of the way.

The Indians of this village may be about four hundred souls and some of them appear very old; they live among mountains, and enjoy pure air, seem cleanly inclined, and make use of wholesome food. We observed several European articles among them, viz. a copper Tea Kettle, a brass camp kettle, a strip of common blanket, and cloathing such as the Cree women wear. These things, we supposed, were brought from our settlements beyond the Mountains. Indeed the Indians made us understand as much.

After having remained some time in this village, the principal chief invited us over the river. We crossed, and He received us at the water side, where, assisted by several others, he took me by the arms and conducted me in a moment up the hill to the camp where his people were sitting in rows, to the number of twelve hundred; and I had to shake hands with all of them. Then the Great Chief made a long harangue, in course of which he pointed to the sun, to the four quarters of the world and then to us, and then he introduced his father, who was old and blind, and was carried by another man, who also made a harangue of some length. The old [blind] man was placed near us, and with some emotion often stretched out both his hands in order to feel ours.

The Hacamaugh nation are different both in language and manners from their neighbours the Askettels. They have many chiefs and great men, appear to be good orators, for their manner of delivery is extremely handsome. We had every reason to be thankful for our reception at this place; the Indians shewed us every possible attention and supplied our wants as much as they could. We had salmon, berries, oil and roots in abundance, and our men had six dogs. Our tent was pitched near the camp, and we enjoyed peace and security during our stay.

Thursday [Monday], June 20. The Indians sung and danced all night. Some of our men, who went to see them, were much amused. With some difficulty we obtained two wooden canoes; the Indians, however, made no price, but accepted of our offers.

Shortly after a tumult arose in the camp. I was writing in the tent; hearing the noise, I went to the door and observed an elderly man running towards me, but [he] was stopped by some of the others who were making a loud noise. I enquired into the cause; they crowded around me. They [the] chief spoke and all was quiet. I, then, learned that Mr Quesnel having walked in the direction of a canoe that was at some distance on the beach, the Old man in question, who was the owner, thought he was going to lose it.

This affray over, we prepared for our departure. The Chief pointed out three elderly men who were to accompany us to the next nation. In the mean time, I was presented with berries, roots and oil in abundance. Notwithstanding these tokens of friendship, the impression, which the late disturbance made on my mind, still remained. However kind savages may appear, I know that it is not in their nature to be sincere in their professions to strangers. The respect and attention, which we generally experience, proceed, perhaps, from an idea that we are superior beings, who are not to be overcome; at any rate, it is certain the less familiar we are with one another the better for us. . . .

These forks[26] the natives call *Camchin*, and are formed by a large river which is the same spoken of so often by our friend the old chief. From an idea that our friends of the *Fort des Prairies* department are established upon the sources of it, among the mountains we gave it the name of Thomson's River.[27]

Wednesday [Tuesday], June 21. Early in the morning the men made a trip with two of the canoes and part of the things which they carried more than a mile and returned for the rest. I sent Mr Quesnel to take charge of the baggage in the absence of the men. About this time Indians appeared on the opposite bank. Our guides harangued them from our side, and all were singing and dancing.

After breakfast the men renewed their work, and Mr Stuart and I remained in the tent writing. Soon after we were alarmed by the loud bawling of our guides, whom upon looking out we observed running full speed towards where we were, making signs that our people were lost in the rapids. As we could not account for this misfortune we immediately ran over to the baggage where we found Mr Quesnel all alone. We inquired of him about the men, and at the same time we discovered that three of the canoes were missing, but he had seen none of them nor did he know where they were. On casting our view across the river, we remarked one of the canoes and some of the men ashore there. From this incident we had reason to believe that the others were either a head or perished, and with increased anxiety we directed our speed to the lower end of the rapids.

At the distance of four miles or so, we found one of our men, La Chapelle, who had carried two loads of his own share [of the baggage] that far; he could give us no account of the others, but supposed they were following him with their proportions. We still continued; at last growing fatigued and seeing no appearance of the canoes of which we were in search, we considered it advisable to return and keep along the bank of the river.

We had not proceeded far when we observed one of our men D'Alaire walking slow with a stick in his hand from the bank, and on coming up to him we discovered that he was so wet, so weak, and so exhausted that he could scarcely speak. However after leaning a little while upon his stick and drawing breath, he informed us that unfortunately he and the others finding the carrying place too long and the canoes too heavy, took it upon themselves to venture down by water — that the canoe in which he was happened to be the last in setting out.

'In the first cascade,' continued he, 'our canoe filled and upset. The foreman and steersman got on the outside, but I, who was in the centre, remained a long while underneath upon the bars [thwarts]. The canoe still drifting was thrown into smooth current, and the other two men, finding an opportunity sprang from their situation into the water and swam ashore. The impulse occasioned by their fall in leaping off raised one side of the canoe above the surface, and I having still my recollection, though I had swallowed a quantity of water, seized the critical moment to disentangle myself, and I gained but not without a struggle the top of the canoe. By this time I found myself again in the middle of the stream. Here I continued astride [the canoe], humouring the tide as well as I could with my body to preserve my balance, and although I scarcely had time to look about me, I had the satisfaction to observe the other two canoes a shore near an eddy, and their crews safe among the rocks. In the second or third cascade (for I cannot remember which) the canoe from a great height plunged into the deep eddy at the foot, and striking with violence against the bottom splitted in two. Here I lost my recollection, which however, I soon recovered and was surprised to find myself on a smooth easy current with only one half of the canoe in my arms. In this condition I continued through several cascades, untill the stream fortunately conducted me into an eddy at the foot of a high and steep rock. Here my strength being exhausted I lost my hold; a large wave washed me from off the wreck among the rocks, and another still larger hoisted me clear on shore, where I remained, as you will readily believe, some time motionless; at length recovering a little of my strength I crawled up among the rocks, but still in danger, and found myself once more safe on firm ground, just as you see.'

Here he finished his melancholy tale, and pointed to the place of his landing, which we went to see, and we were lost in astonishment not only at his escape from the waves, but also at his courage and perseverence in effecting a passage up through a place which appeared to us a precipice. Continuing our course along the bank we found that he had drifted three miles among rapids, cascades, whirlpools, &c. all inconceivably dangerous.

Mr Quesnel being extremely anxious and concerned left his charge and joined us. Two men only remained on shore carrying the baggage, and these were equally ignorant with ourselves of the fate of the others. Some time after upon advancing towards the camp, we picked up all the men on our side of the river. The men that had landed on the other side, joined us in the evening. They informed us that the Indians assisted to extricate them from their difficulties. Indeed the natives shewed us every possible attention in the midst of our misfortunes on this trying occasion.[28]

Being all safe we had the happiness of encamping together as usual with our baggage. However we lost one of our canoes, and another we found too heavy to be carried such a distance. . . .

Thursday [Wednesday], June 22. . . . I sent two men to visit the rapids; but the Indians, knowing our indiscretion yesterday, and dreading a like attempt, voluntarily transported our canoes over land to a little river beyond the rapids. We encamped some distance from the village. The Chief went before to inform the Indians of the next village of our approach. He promised to accompany us until we should have passed all the dangerous places — and the Little Fellow[29] assured us that he would not leave us untill our return. . . .

Friday [Thursday], June 23. Rained this morning. One of the men was sick. We perceived that one way or other our men were getting out of order. They prefered walking to going by water in wooden canoes, particularly after their late sufferings in the rapids. Therefore I embarked in the bow of a canoe myself and went down several rapids. . . .

Sunday [Saturday], June 25. Fine weather. The Chief of [the] Camshins[30] returned this morning to his own home, but his people continued with us. This man is the greatest chief we have seen; he behaved towards us uncommonly well. I made him a present of a large silver broach which he immediately fixed on his head, and he was exceedingly well pleased with our attention.

We embarked at 5 A.M. After going a considerable distance, our Indians ordered us a shore, and we made a portage. Here we were obliged to carry up among loose Stones in the face of a steep hill, over a narrow ridge between two precipices. Near the top where the ascent was perfectly perpendicular, one of the Indians climbed to the summit, and with a long pole drew us up, one after another. This took three hours. Then we continued our course up and down, among hills and rocks, and along the steep declivities of mountains, where hanging rocks, and projecting cliffs at the edge of the bank made the passage so small as to render it difficult even for one person to pass sideways at times.

Many of the natives from the last camp, having accompanied us, were of the greatest service to us on these intricate and dangerous occasions. In places where we were obliged to hand our guns from one to another, and where the greatest precaution was required to pass even singly, the Indians went through boldly with loads. About 5 P.M. we encamped at a rapid. . . .

Monday [Sunday], June 26. This morning all hands were employed the same as yesterday. We had to pass over huge rocks, in which we were assisted by the Indians. Soon after [we] met Mr Stuart and the man. They reported that the navigation was absolutely impracticable. That evening they [had] slept on the top of a mountain in sight of our smoke.

As for the road by land we scarcely could make our way in some parts even with our guns. I have been for a long period among the Rocky Mountains, but have never seen any thing equal to this country, for I cannot find words to describe our situation at times. We had to pass where no human being should venture. Yet in those places there is a regular footpath impressed, or rather indented, by frequent travelling upon the very rocks. And besides this, steps which are formed like a ladder, or the shrouds of a ship, by poles hanging to one another and crossed at certain distances with twigs and withes [tree boughs], suspended from the top of the foot of precipices, and fastened at both ends to stones and trees, furnished a safe and convenient passage to the Natives — but we, who had not the advantages of their experience, were often in imminent danger, when obliged to follow their example. . . .[31]

Tuesday [Monday], June 27. . . . We came to a small camp of Indians consisting about 60 persons. The name of the place is Spazum [Spuzzum], and is the boundary line between the Hacamaugh and Ackinroe Nations.[32] Here as usual we were hospitably entertained, with fresh Salmon boiled and roasted, green and dried berries, oil and onions.

Seeing tombs of a curious construction at the forks on the opposite side,[33] I asked permission of the Chief to go and pay them a visit. This he readily granted, and he accompanied us himself. These Tombs are superior to any thing of the kind I ever saw among savages. They are about fifteen feet long and of the form of a chest of drawers. Upon the boards and posts are carved beasts and birds, in a curious but rude manner, yet pretty well proportioned. These monuments must have cost the workmen much time and labour, as they were destitute of proper tools for the execution of such a performance. Around the tombs were deposited all the property of the deceased.

Ready for our departure, our guides observed that we had better pass the night here and that they would accompany us in the morning. Sensible, from experience, that a hint from these people is equal to a command, and that they would not follow, if we Declined, we remained.

Wednesday [Tuesday], June 28. . . . This nation is different in language and manners from the other nations we had passed. They have rugs made from the wool of *Aspai*, or wild goat, and from Dog's hair, which are equally as good as those found in Canada. We observed that the dogs were lately shorn.[34]

We saw few or no christian goods among them, but from their workmanship in wood they must be possessed of good tools at least for that purpose. Having been newly arrived they had not as yet erected their shades. They have a gallery of smoked boards upon which they slept. Their bows and arrows are very neat.

At 1 P.M. we renewed our march, the natives still carrying part of our baggage. At the first point we observed a remarkable cavern in a rock which upon visiting we found to be 50 feet deep by 35 wide. A little above it is an excellent house 46 by 33 feet, and constructed like American frame houses. The planks are 3 or 4 inches thick, each passing the adjoining one a couple of inches. The posts, which are very strong, and rudely carved, receive the beam across. The walls are 11 feet high, and covered with a slanting roof. On the opposite wide of the river, there is a considerable village with houses similar to the one upon this side.

About 4 P.M. arrived to a camp containing about 150 souls. Here we had plenty of Salmon cooked by means of hot stones in wooden vessels.

Here we understood that the river was navigable from this place to the sea. We had of course to provide canoes if possible. We saw a number of new ones, which seemed to have been hollowed with fire, and then polished.

Their arms consist of bows and arrows, spears and clubs, or horn Powmagans. They have scarcely any leather, so that large animals must be scarce. Their ornaments are the same as the Hacamaugh nation make use of; that is to say, shells of different kinds, shell beads, brass made into pipes hanging from the neck, or across the shoulders, bracelets of large brass wire, and some bracelets of horn. Their hats, which are made of wattap [roots], have broad rims and diminish gradually to the top. Some make use of cedar bark, painted in various colours, resembling ribbands which they fix around their heads. Both sexes are stoutly made, and some of the men are handsome; but I cannot say so much for the women, who seem to be slaves, for in course of their dances, I remarked that the men were pillaging them from one another. Our Little Fellow, on one of these occasions, was presented with another man's wife for a bed fellow. . . .

Friday [Thursday], June 30. It was [hour omitted] A.M. before we could procure canoes and take our departure. At 11 we came to a camp containing near 400 souls. Here we saw a man from the sea, which they said was so near that we would see it tomorrow. Mr Stuart took a mer[idian]. alt[itude]. O.L.L. 127° 23′. The Indians of this place seem dirty and have an unpleasant smell; they were surprised at seeing men different from Indians and extremely disagreeable to us through their curiosity and attention. . . .

Saturday [Friday], July 1. . . . At 8 A.M. we arrived at a large village. After shaking hands with many, the Chief invited us to his house, and served us with fish and berries; our Indians also were treated with fish and berries, and dried oysters in large troughs. Our Hacamaugh commonly stiled Little Fellow, so often mentioned here, and who has been highly serviceable to us all along, has assumed an air of consequence from his being of our party; he ranks now with Mr Stuart, Mr Quesnel, and myself. The Chief made me a present of a coat of mail to make shoes. For this we may thank our little friend, who also received a present of white shells. I gave the Chief in return a calico gown, for which he was thankful and proud.

The Indians entertained us with songs and dances of various descriptions. The chief stood in the centre of the dance or ring giving directions, while others were beating the drum against the walls of the house, and making a terrible racket — which alarmed our men who were at a distance, and who came to see what caused the noise.

The Indians, who favoured us with a passage to this place, went off with the canoes. We had to look out for others, but none could be procured for any consideration whatever. At last the Chief consented to lend us his large canoe & to accompany us himself on the morrow.

The number of Indians at this place is about 200 who appeared at first view to be fair, but afterwards we discovered that they made use of white paint to alter their appearance. They evinced no kind of surprise or curiosity to seeing us, nor were they afraid of our arms, so that they must have been in the habit of seeing white people.

Their houses are built of cedar planks, and in shape similar to the one already described. The whole range, which is 640 feet long by 60 broad, is under one roof. The front is 18 feet high, and the covering is slanting. All the apartments, which are separated in portions, are square, excepting the Chief's which is 90 feet long. In this room the posts or pillars are nearly 3 feet diameter at the base, and diminish gradually to the top. In one of these posts is an oval opening answering the purpose of a door, thro' which to crawl in and out. Above, on the outside, are carved a human figure large as life, and there are other figures in imitation of beasts and birds. These buildings have no flooring. The fires are in the centre, and the smoke goes out an opening at [the] top. . . .

Sunday [Saturday], July 2. . . . I applied to the Chief in consequence of his promise of yesterday for his canoe, but he paid no attention to my request. I, therefore, took the canoe and had it carried to the water side. The Chief got it carried back. We again laid hold of it. He still resisted, and made us understand that he was the greatest of his nation and equal in power to the sun. However as we could not go without [the canoe] we persisted and at last gained our point. The chief and several of the tribe accompanied us. At 11 A.M. arrived at a village where we were received with the usual ceremony of shaking hands, but we were not well entertained. The houses at this place are plain and in two rows. I received two coats of mail in a present which are so good [for] shoes.

The Indians advised us not to advance any further, as the natives of the coast or Islanders were at war with them, being very malicious, and will destroy us. Upon seeing us slight their advice and going to embark, they gathered round our canoe and hauled it out of the water, and then invited us for the first time to the principal house of the village.

Leaving Mr Quesnel with most of the men to guard the canoe and baggage, Mr Stuart with two men and myself accepted the invitation. As soon as we were in the house, the Indians began singing and dancing, & making a terrible noise. Mr Stuart went to see what caused this seeming disturbance; he found the one of the natives had stolen a Jacket out of the canoe, which upon application to the Chief, was returned, and all was quiet again. Then we made a motion to embark accompanied by the Chief. His friends did not approve of his going, flocked about him, embracing him with tenderness, as if he was never to return. Our followers seeing this scene of apparent distress between the Chief and his friends changed their minds and declined going further. Even our Little Fellow would not embark, saying that he was also afraid of the people at the sea. Then some of them laid violent hands upon the canoe, and insisted upon putting it out of the water. We paid no attention to their arguments, made them desist, and we embarked.

We proceeded on for two miles, and came to a place where the river divides[35] into several channels. Seeing a canoe following us we waited for its arrival. One Indian of that canoe embarked with us and conducted us into the right channel.[36] In the meantime several Indians from the village followed in canoes, armed with bows and arrows, clubs, spears &c. Singing a war song, beating time with their paddles upon the sides of the canoes, and making signs and gestures highly inimicable. The one that embarked with us became very unruly singing and dancing, and kicking up the dust. We threatened him with the effect of our displeasure and he was quiet.

This was an alarming crisis, but we were not discouraged: confident of our superiority, at least on the water, we continued.

At last we came in sight of a gulph or bay of the sea;[37] this the Indians called *Pas-hil-roe.* It runs in a S.W. & N.E. direction. In this bay are several high and rocky

Islands whose summits are covered with snow. On the right shore we noticed a village called by the Natives *Misquiame* [Musqueam]; we directed our course towards it. Our turbulent passenger conducted us up a small winding river to a small lake to the village. . . .[38]

. . . Having spent one hour looking about this place we went to embark, [when] we found the tide had ebbed, and left our canoe on dry land. We had, therefore, to drag it out to the water some distance. The natives no doubt seeing our difficulty, assumed courage, and began to make their appearance from every direction, in their coats of mail, howling like so many wolves, and brandishing their war clubs. At last we got into deep water, and embarked. Our turbulent fellow, who embarked in our canoe before, no sooner found himself on board then he began his former impertinences. He asked for our daggers, for our cloathes, and in fine for every thing we had. Being convinced of his unfriendly disposition, we turned him out and made him and the others, who were closing in upon us, understand, that if they did not keep their distance we would fire upon them.

After this skirmish we continued untill we came opposite the second village. Here our curiosity incited us to go a shore; but reflecting upon the reception we experienced at the first, and the character of the Natives, it was thought neither prudent nor necessary to run any risk, particularly as we had no provisions, and saw no prospect of procuring any in that hostile quarter. We, therefore, turned our course and with the intention of going back to the friendly Indians for a supply, then to return and prosecute our design. When we came opposite the hostile village [Musqueam] the same fellows, who had annoyed us before, advanced to attack us which was echoed by those on shore. In this manner they approached so near that we were obliged to adopt a threatening position, and we had to push them off with the muzzles of our guns. Perceiving our determination their courage failed, and they gave up the pursuit and crossed to the village. The tide was now in our favour, the evening was fine, and we continued our course with great speed until 11, when we encamped within 6 miles of the Chief's village. The men being extremely tired, went to rest; but they were not long in bed before the tide rushed upon the beds and roused them up.

Monday [Sunday], July 3. . . . Our Little Fellow, whom we left yesterday at the village below, made his appearance. He informed us that the Indians after our departure had fixed upon our destruction; that he himself was pillaged, his hands and feet tied, and that they were about to knock him on the head when the Chief of the Ackinroe appeared, released him and secured his escape to this place, where he was now detained as a slave.

This unpleasant recital served to warn us more and more of our danger. Still we were bent upon accomplishing our enterprise, to have a sight of the main [ocean] which was but a short distance from whence we had returned;[39] but unfortunately we could not procure a morsel of provisions, & besides the Chief insisted upon having his canoe restored to him immediately. This demand we were obliged to supress. The Chief then invited us to his house. We went, but were not above five minutes absent, before one of the men came running to inform us that the Indians had seized upon the canoe and were pillaging our people. Alarmed at this report we hastened to their assistance. We found that some of the Indians from below having arrived had encouraged the others in these violent proceedings. Sensible from our critical situation that mild measures would be improper and of no service, I pretended to be in a violent passion, spoke loud, with vehement gestures and signs exactly in their own way; and thus peace and tranquillity were instantly restored.

From these specimens of the insolence and ill nature of the Natives we saw nothing but dangers and difficulties in our way. We, therefore, relinquished our design and directed our thoughts towards home — but we could not proceed without the canoe, and we had to force it away from the owner leaving a blanket in its place. Thus provided, we pushed off. . . .

Here I must again acknowledge my great disappointment in not seeing the *main ocean*, having gone so near it as to be almost within view. For we wished very much to settle the situation by an observation for the longitude. The latitude is 49° nearly, while that of the entrance of the Columbia is 46° 20'. This River, therefore, is not the Columbia. If I had been convinced of this fact where I left my canoes, I would certainly have returned from thence.

Tuesday [Monday], July 4. . . . We hurried out of the tent, and at our appearance all was quiet; yet we could not feel free of alarm seeing the whole village assembled round our baggage, armed with all kinds of hostile weapons and seemingly determined upon mischief.

It was then, that our situation might really be considered as critical. Placed upon a small sandy Island, few in number, without canoes, without provisions, and surrounded by upwards of 700 barbarians. However our resolution did not forsake us. On the contrary all hands were of one mind, ready for action, and fully determined to make our way good at all hazards.

We now applied for canoes in every direction, but could not procure any either for love or money, so that we had to regret the inadvertency committed on our arrival by parting with the one we had before. There being no alternative we had again recourse to the chief, notwithstanding our experience of his illiberality. He asked his price — I consented — he augmented his demand — I again yielded — he still continued to increase his imposition. Feeling highly provoked at the impertinence of his conduct, I exclaimed violently. He then ordered the canoe to be brought.

We immediately prepared to embark, but when we began to load, the Indians crowded about the baggage and attempted to pillage. But as they laid hold upon any of our things we pulled it from them, and had to place ourselves in a posture of defence, and to threaten them with our pieces [guns] before they desisted. . . .

Thursday [Wednesday] July 6. . . . other Indians made us signs to follow them. Doubting their sincerity we pushed from them and took a different channel. Upon this they doubled their speed. By and by we discovered a large camp of Indians, who soon taught us that they were not assembled there for any good purpose. When we came opposite all were in motion — some were in canoes, others lined the shore, and all were advancing upon us. At last it was with difficulty we could prevent them with the muzzles of our guns from seizing upon the canoe. They, however, contrived to give us such a push with the intention of upsetting us, that our canoe became engaged in the strong current which in spite of all our efforts carried us down to the rapids. However we gained the shore at the foot of a high hill, where we tied the canoe to a tree with a line. Here I ordered Mr. Stuart with some of the men to debark in order to keep the Indians in awe. The Indians perceiving our preparations for defence retired, but still kept a head.

I then directed the men, who were on shore, to enbark, but Mr. Stuart came to inform me that several of them refused, saying that they were bent upon going by land across the Mountains to the place where we had slept the 24th June. Considering this as a desperate resolution, I debarked and endeavoured to persuade them out of their infatuation; but two of them declared in their own name and in that of others, that their plan was fixed, and that they saw no other way by which they might [save] themselves from immediate destruction, for continuing by water, said they, surrounded by hostile nations, who watched every opportunity to attack and torment them, created in their minds a state of suspicion, which was worse than death.

I remonstrated and threatened by turns. The other gentlemen joined my endeavours in exposing the folly of their undertaking, and the advantages that would accrue to us all by remaining as we had hitherto done in perfect union for our common welfare. After much debate on both sides, our delinquents yielded and we all shook hands, resolving never to separate during the voyage; which resolution was immediately confirmed by the following oath taken on the spot by each of the party: 'I solemnly swear before Almighty God that I shall sooner perish than forsake in distress any of our crew during the present voyage.' After this ceremony was over all hands dressed in their best apparel, and each took charge of his own bundle. . . .

By this time it was near sun set. We, however, decamped full of spirits, singing and making a great noise. The Indians, who were waiting a head, observing us so cheerful, felt disheartened, kept their distance, and some of them thought proper to paddle down the stream. At dusk we encamped on a small Island below a village. . . .[40]

Friday [Thursday], July 7. In the morning the residue of the unfriendly Indians, who had passed the night in the vicinity of our Island, directed their course down the current, and we saw nothing of them afterwards.

Notes

[1] The first entry in the scribal copy of Fraser's journal is wrongly dated, and the days of the week are incorrect in later entries.

[2] From Fort George (Prince George), at the mouth of the Nechako River, here called Fraser's River.

[3] Eight of the French-Canadians are named in the complete journal: La Chapelle, Baptiste, D'Alaire, La Certe, Waka or Wacca (the nickname of Jean Baptiste Boucher), Borboné (probably Bourbonnais), Gagnier, and La Garde.

[4] John Stuart (1780–1847), still a young man in 1808, appears in later life in many of these excerpts (see LETITIA HARGRAVE, FRANCES SIMPSON, DANIEL HARMON). He joined the NWC in 1796 and was sent to Fort Chipewyan. From 1805 he worked with Fraser extending NWC trade

routes into British Columbia; on the journey down the Fraser it was he who kept the official log. As a NWC man he fought the HBC in Athabasca, but at union became an HBC Chief Factor. GEORGE SIMPSON, in one of his better moods, called him 'the Father . . . of New Caledonia' but mocked him in his *Character Book*. Stuart retired in 1839 and died in Scotland in 1847. His own journals have disappeared, and his extant letters suggest this may have been a major loss to exploration writing.

[5] Jules-Maurice Quesnel (1786–1842) came from a cultivated merchant family in Montreal. He joined the NWC in 1804, and was with DAVID THOMPSON in the Rocky Mountains in 1805. After his historic journey down the Fraser he stayed in New Caledonia until 1811, despite his dislike of the isolation. (See DANIEL HARMON.) He left the NWC in that year and established himself as a prosperous businessman in Montreal, where he also served in various public offices until his death.

[6] Fraser believed he was about to travel down the Columbia River.

[7] From this point to the first sentence of the entry dated June 10, the text is paralleled by the rough notes of the 'Second Journal'. See pages 131–61 of Lamb's edition.

[8] Canoes usually carried two oil cloths to protect goods and furs from spray and rain.

[9] The 'great river' is the Thompson.

[10] A shelter.

[11] One of the posts of this name on the North Saskatchewan River. The 'friends' were DAVID THOMPSON and his men, who in 1807 had crossed the Rocky Mountains by way of Howse Pass and established Kootenae House on the upper waters of the Columbia River. Fraser apparently thought the Thompson River might be the lower portion of that river.

[12] *Brayette*: pair of breeches.

[13] French Bar Canyon.

[14] À *corps perdu*: i.e., recklessly.

[15] The Styx, a river in the Greek province of Arcadia, with an aspect quite as forbidding as the Fraser; in mythology it was the chief river of the underworld.

[16] The river current.

[17] Almost certainly Leon Creek.

[18] The Askettihs or Lillooets.

[19] Deep sea ships.

[20] Where the Seton River enters the Fraser.

[21] This was the Columbia River.

[22] The first were the Thompson Indians, the second possibly Shoshoni.

[23] The Saulteaux or Ojibwa, much farther east.

[24] The Stein River.

[25] Near modern Lytton, B.C.

[26] At the junction of the Fraser and the Thompson rivers.

[27] THOMPSON, in his turn, named the Fraser River in honour of Simon Fraser.

[28] The accident probably occurred near Jackass Mountain, a dozen miles downstream from Lytton, where the river is an almost continuous series of rapids and canyons.

[29] As this 'little fellow' is referred to frequently, and as Fraser used the phrase as if it were his name, it is spelled with capitals hereafter.

[30] The Indians living in the area around the junction of the Thompson and Fraser rivers.

[31] Fraser was now in the most difficult and dangerous part of the Fraser Canyon, which centres upon Hell's Gate and the Black Canyon. His description of the return journey through this same region is equally vivid (see the entry dated 10 July in Lamb, ed., *Letters and Journals*.)

[32] Between the areas occupied by the Interior Salish (*Hacamaugh* is Fraser's name for the

Thompson Indians, an Interior Salish tribe) and the Coast Salish Indians (he calls the first Coast Salish Indians that he met *Ackinroe*).

[33] On the west side, at the mouth of Spuzzum Creek.

[34] Rugs or blankets characteristic of the Coast Salish Indians of the Fraser River. A special breed of dog, now believed to be extinct, was raised to supply hair for weaving.

[35] At New Westminster.

[36] The North Arm of the Fraser River.

[37] The Strait of Georgia.

[38] Musqueam Indian village still exists. A small stream flows through the present Indian reserve, but there is no lake; it may have been caused by high water at the time Fraser visited the place.

[39] The 'main ocean' was actually about 140 miles away.

[40] These events seem to have occurred between Hope and Yale.

John Franklin   (1786 – 1847)

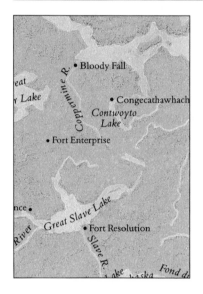

JOHN FRANKLIN joined the Royal Navy at the age of 14. Except for an interval when he participated in his uncle Matthew Flinders' circumnavigation of Australia (1802–3) he served on warships until he was discharged on half-pay at the end of the Napoleonic Wars, by which time he had survived six weeks on a sandbank after a shipwreck only days out of Sydney, and had taken part in the battle of Trafalgar (1805) and the British offensive against New Orleans in the War of 1812. English exploration of the Arctic was soon to be revived in the Royal Navy's search for a north-west passage, and among half-pay officers eager to participate Franklin's record made him a logical candidate. Franklin and his party left England in 1819, and returned in 1822 after a tragic and exhausting ordeal.

Their expedition had been hampered by poor preparation, by the rivalry of the two fur-trading companies which was at its height, and by Franklin's high-handed manner. The narrative which he immediately published is a classic of exploration literature both for its detailed account of events and its unconscious revelation of the weaknesses and strengths of those in the party. It incorporates long excerpts from the journals of Dr John Richardson and LieutenantsRobert Hood and George Back, and is lavishly illustrated with watercolours, maps, and charts by Hood (who near the end had been slain by an Iroquois voyageur) and Back. Of the nine participating natives and voyageurs who died on the journey, Franklin's *Narrative* is almost the only record; in *Playing Dead* (1989) Rudy Wiebe, with justified sarcasm, reviews the harrowing journey from their point of view.

Franklin, Richardson, and Back lived long and interesting lives; all were knighted, and Richardson in particular made important contributions to Victorian science. The three made a second and triumphantly successful journey to the Arctic in 1825–7, which also produced a journal. After a career as naval officer and Governor of Van Dieman's land (Tasmania) Franklin returned to the Arctic in 1845 on a voyage which produced no journal, but made his name legend. He died, his ships fixed in the ice-pack off King William Island, on 11 June 1847. His fate was unknown for many years; partly as a result of the activity of his wife, about 30 expeditions were sent to search for him. The mystery of Franklin's disappearance had a lasting effect on the nineteenth century imagination: Thoreau, writing of his own two years' 'exploration' of Walden Pond, mused 'is Franklin the only man who is lost, that his wife should be so earnest to find him?' and the young Joseph Conrad, while reading of Leopold McClintock's successful search for relics of the expedition, first conceived the germ of *Heart of Darkness* (1902).

Text: John Franklin, *Narrative of a Journey to the Shores of the Polar Sea in the Years 1819, 20, 21, and 22,* London: 1823.

Captain John Franklin, R.N., arrives in Hudson's Bay

[*August* 30, 1819] The opening of the morning of the 30th presented to our view the anchorage at York Flats. . . . Immediately after our arrival Mr. Williams, the Governor of the Hudson's Bay Company's posts, came on board. . . . The Governor acquainted me that he had received information from the Committee of the Hudson's Bay Company of the equipment of the Expedition, and that the officers would come out in the first ship. In the evening Dr. Richardson,[1] Mr. Hood,[2] and I, accompanied the Governor to York Factory, which we reached after dark; it is distant from the Flats seven miles. Early next morning the Governor conferred the honour of a salute on the members of the Expedition.

Having communicated to the Governor the objects of the Expedition, and that I had been directed to consult with him and the senior servants of the Company as to the best mode of proceeding towards the execution of the service, I was gratified by his assurance that his instructions from the Committee directed that every possible assistance should be given to forward our progress, and that he should feel peculiar pleasure in performing this part of his duty. He introduced me at once to Messrs. Charles, Swaine, and Snodie, masters of districts, who, from long residence in the country, were perfectly acquainted with the different modes of travelling, and the obstructions which might be anticipated. At the desire of these gentlemen, I drew up a series of questions on the points on which we required information; to which they had the kindness to return very explicit and satisfactory answers two days afterwards; and on receiving them I requested the Governor to favour me with his sentiments on the same subject in writing, which he delivered to me on the following day.

Having learned that Messrs. Shaw, McTavish, and several other partners of the N.W. Company, were under detention at this place,[3] we took the earliest opportunity of visiting them; when, having presented the general circular, and other introductory letters, with which I had been furnished by their agent Mr. Simon McGillivray, we received from them the most friendly and full assurance of the cordial endeavours of the wintering partners of their Company to promote the interests of the Expedition.

The knowledge we had now gained of the state of the violent commercial opposition existing in the country, rendered this assurance highly gratifying; and these gentlemen added to the obligation by freely communicating the information respecting the interior of the country, which their intelligence and long residence so fully qualified them to give.

I deemed it expedient to issue a memorandum to the officers of the Expedition, strictly prohibiting any interference whatever in the existing quarrels, or any that might arise, between the two Companies; and on presenting it to the principals of both the parties, they expressed their satisfaction at the step I had taken.

Cumberland House, winter 1819–20; Dr Richardson writes a lengthy description of the local Cree and Métis.

. . . The original character of the Crees must have been much modified by their long intercourse with Europeans; hence it is to be understood, that we [that is Richardson himself] confine ourselves in the following sketch to their present condition, and more particularly to the Crees of Cumberland House. The moral character of a hunter is acted upon by the nature of the land he inhabits, the abundance or scarcity of food, and we may add, in the present case, his means of access to spirituous liquors. In a country so various in these respects as that inhabited by the Crees, the causes alluded to must operate strongly in producing a considerable difference of character amongst the various hordes. It may be proper to bear in mind also, that we are about to draw the character of a people whose only rule of conduct is public opinion, and to try them by a morality founded on divine revelation; as we are not aware that it is in the power of anyone, who has been educated in a land to which the blessings of the Gospel have extended, to use any other standard.[4]

Bearing these considerations in mind, then, we may state the Crees to be a vain, fickle, improvident, and indolent race, and not very strict in their adherence to truth, besides being great boasters; but on the other hand they strictly regard the rights of property, are susceptible of the tender affections, capable of friendship, very hospitable, tolerably kind to their women, and withal inclined to peace. . . .

It might be thought that the Crees have benefited by their long intercourse with civilized nations. That this is not so much the case as it ought to be, is not entirely their own fault. They are capable of being, and I believe willing to be, taught; but no pains have hitherto been taken to inform their minds, and their white acquaintances seem in general to find it easier to descend to the Indian customs, and modes of thinking, particularly with respect to women, than to attempt to raise the Indian to theirs. Indeed, such a lamentable want of morality has been displayed by the white traders in their contests for the interests of their respective companies, that it would require a long series of good conduct to efface from the minds of the native population the ideas they have formed of the white character. Notwithstanding the frequent violations of the rights of property they have witnessed, and but too often experienced, in their own persons, these savages, as they are termed, remain strictly honest. During their visits to a post, they are suffered to enter every apartment in the house, without the least restraint, and although articles of value to them are scattered about, nothing is ever missed. They even scrupulously avoid moving anything from its place, although they are often prompted by curiosity to examine it. In some cases, indeed, they carry this principle to a degree of self-denial which would hardly be expected. It often happens that meat, which has been paid for, (if the poisonous draught it procures them can be considered as payment,)[5] is left at their lodges until a convenient opportunity occurs of carrying it away. They will rather pass several days without eating than touch the meat thus intrusted to their charge, even when there exists a prospect of replacing it.

The hospitality of the Crees is unbounded. They afford a certain asylum to the half-breed children when deserted by their unnatural white fathers; and the infirm, and indeed every individual in an encampment, share the provisions of a successful hunter as long as they last. Fond too as a Cree is of spirituous liquors, he is never happy unless all his neighbours partake with him. . . .

Many of the labourers, and a great many of the agents and clerks employed by the two Companies, have Indian or half-breed wives, and the mixed offspring thus produced has become extremely numerous.

These métifs, or as the Canadians term them, *bois-brulés*, are upon the whole a good looking people, and where the experiment has been made, have shewn much aptness in learning, and willingness to be taught; they have, however, been sadly neglected. The example of their fathers has released them from the restraint imposed by the Indian opinions of good and bad behaviour; and, generally speaking, no pains have been taken to fill up the void with better principles. Hence it is not surprising that the males, trained up in a high opinion of the authority and rights of the Company to which their fathers belonged, and unacquainted with the laws of the civilized world, should be ready to engage in any measure whatever, that they are prompted to believe will forward the interests of the cause they espouse. . . .

[Between January, 1820 and June 1821, Franklin established a base at Fort Providence, and then moved further north to build Fort Enterprise. He negotiated with Akaitcho[6] and his small band of Copper Indians for support during his proposed journey to the Arctic sea, and explored the neighbourhood. On 14 June 1821 the expedition travelled northward, and during the next months explored on foot and by boat the Coppermine River and (with a smaller group) the coast of the Arctic sea east as far as Cape Turnagain. On 17 August this party turned south to begin the desperate and famished journey back across the barren lands to Fort Enterprise which occupies all of Chapter XI of Franklin's *Narrative*.]

[*August 25*] The wind continued in the same direction until we had rounded Point Wollaston, and then changed to a quarter, which enabled us to steer for Hood's River, which we ascended as high as the first rapid and encamped. Here terminated our voyage on the Arctic sea, during which we had gone over six hundred and fifty geographical miles. Our Canadian voyagers could not restrain their expressions of joy at having turned their backs on the sea, and they passed the evening talking over

their past adventures with much humour and no little exaggeration. The consideration that the most painful, and certainly the most hazardous, part of the journey was
yet to come, did not depress their spirits at all. It is due to their character to mention
that they displayed much courage in encountering the dangers of the sea, magnified
to them by their novelty.

The shores between Cape Barrow and Cape Flinders, including the extensive
branches of Arctic and Melville Sounds, and Bathurst's Inlet, may be comprehended
in one great gulf, which I have distinguished by the appellation of George IV's
Coronation Gulf, in honour of His Most Gracious Majesty, the latter name being
added to mark the time of its discovery. The Archipelago of islands which fringe the
coast from Copper-Mine River to Point Turnagain, I have named in honour of His
Royal Highness the Duke of York. . . .

August 26. — Previous to our departure this morning, an assortment of iron materials, beads, looking-glasses, and other articles were put up in a conspicuous situation
for the Esquimaux, and the English Union [Jack] was planted on the loftiest sand-
hill, where it might be seen by any ships passing in the offing. Here also, was
deposited in a tin box, a letter containing an outline of our proceedings, the latitude
and longitude of the principal places, and the course we intended to pursue towards
Slave Lake. . . .

. . . In the evening we encamped at the lower end of a narrow chasm through
which the river flows for upwards of a mile. The walls of this chasm are upwards of
two hundred feet high, quite perpendicular, and in some places only a few yards
apart. The river precipitates itself into it over a rock, forming two magnificent and
picturesque falls close to each other. The upper fall is about sixty feet high, and the
lower one at least one hundred, but perhaps considerably more, for the narrowness
of the chasm into which it fell prevented us from seeing its bottom, and we could
merely discern the top of the spray far beneath our feet. The lower fall is divided into
two, by an insulated column of rock which rises about forty feet above it. The whole
descent of the river at this place probably exceeds two hundred and fifty feet. The
rock is very fine felspathose sandstone. It has a smooth surface and a light red colour.
I have named these magnificent cascades 'Wilberforce Falls,' as a tribute of my
respect for that distinguished philanthropist and christian.[7] Messrs. Back[8] and Hood
took beautiful sketches of this majestic scene. . . .

The leather which had been preserved for making shoes[9] was equally divided
among the men, two pairs of flannel socks were given to each person, and such
articles of warm clothing as remained, were issued to those who most required them.
They were also furnished with one of the officers' tents. This being done, I communicated to the men my intention of proceeding in as direct a course as possible to
the part of Point Lake, opposite to our spring encampment, which was only distant
one hundred and forty-nine miles in a straight line. They received the communication cheerfully, considered the journey to be short, and left me, in high spirits, to
arrange their own packages. The stores, books, &c., which were not absolutely
necessary to be carried, were then put in boxes to be left *en cache* here, in order that
the men's burdens might be as light as possible.

The next morning was warm, and very fine. Every one was on the alert at an early hour, being anxious to commence the journey. Our luggage consisted of ammunition, nets, hatchets, ice chisels, astronomical instruments, clothing, blankets, three kettles, and the two canoes, which were each carried by one man. The officers carried such a portion of their own things as their strength would permit: the weight carried by each man was about ninety pounds,[10] and with this we advanced at the rate of about a mile an hour, including rests. In the evening the hunters killed a lean cow, out of a large drove of musk-oxen; but the men were too much laden to carry more than a small portion of its flesh. The alluvial soil, which towards the mouth of the river spreads into plains, covered with grass and willows, was now giving place to a more barren and hilly country; so that we could but just collect sufficient brush wood to cook our suppers. The part of the river we skirted to-day was shallow, and flowed over a bed of sand; its width about one hundred and twenty yards. About midnight our tent was blown down by a squall, and we were completely drenched with rain before it could be re-pitched. . . .

[*September 4*] Having walked twelve miles and a half, we encamped at seven P.M., and distributed our last piece of pemmican, and a little arrow-root for supper, which afforded but a scanty meal. This evening was warm, but dark clouds overspread the sky. Our men now began to find their burdens very oppressive, and were much fatigued by this day's march, but did not complain. One of them was lame from an inflammation in the knee. Heavy rain commenced at midnight, and continued without intermission until five in the morning, when it was succeeded by snow on the wind changing to north-west, which soon increased to a violent gale. As we had nothing to eat, and were destitute of the means of making a fire, we remained in our beds all the day; but the covering of our blankets was insufficient to prevent us from feeling the severity of the frost, and suffering inconvenience from the drifting of the snow into our tents. There was no abatement of the storm next day: our tents were completely frozen, and the snow had drifted around them to a depth of three feet, and even in the inside there was a covering of several inches on our blankets. Our suffering from cold, in a comfortless canvass tent in such weather, with the temperature at 20°, and without fire, will easily be imagined; it was, however, less than that which we felt from hunger.

The morning of the 7th cleared up a little, but the wind was still strong, and the weather extremely cold. From the unusual continuance of the storm, we feared the winter had set in with all its rigour, and that by longer delay we should only be exposed to an accumulation of difficulties: we therefore prepared for our journey, although we were in a very unfit condition for starting, being weak from fasting, and our garments stiffened by the frost. We had no means of making a fire to thaw them, the moss, at all times difficult to kindle, being now covered with ice and snow. A considerable time was consumed in packing up the frozen tents and bed clothes, the wind blowing so strong that no one could keep his hands long out of his mittens.

Just as we were about to commence our march, I was seized with a fainting fit, in consequence of exhaustion and sudden exposure to the wind; but after eating a morsel of portable soup,[11] I recovered, so far as to be able to move on. I was unwilling at first to take this morsel of soup, which was diminishing the small and only remaining meal for the party; but several of the men urged me to it, with much kindness. The ground was covered a foot deep with snow, the margin of the lakes was incrusted with ice, and the swamps over which we had to pass were entirely frozen; but the ice not being sufficiently strong to bear us, we frequently plunged knee-deep in water. Those who carried the canoes were repeatedly blown down by the violence of the wind, and they often fell, from making an insecure step on a slippery stone; on one of these occasions, the largest canoe was so much broken as to be rendered utterly unserviceable. This was felt as a serious disaster, as the remaining canoe having through mistake been made too small, it was doubtful whether it would be sufficient to carry us across a river. Indeed we had found it necessary in crossing Hood's River, to lash the two canoes together. As there was some suspicion that Benoit,[12] who carried the canoe, had broken it intentionally, he having on a former occasion been overheard by some of the men to say, that he would do so when he got it in charge, we closely examined him on the point; he roundly denied having used the expressions attributed to him, and insisted that it was broken by his falling accidentally; and as he brought men to attest the latter fact, who saw him tumble, we did not press the matter further. I may here remark that our people had murmured a good deal at having to carry two canoes, though they were informed of the necessity of taking both, in case it should be deemed advisable to divide the party; which it had been thought probable we should be obliged to do, if animals proved scarce, in order to give the whole the better chance of procuring subsistence, and also for the purpose of sending forward some of the best walkers to search for Indians, and to get them to meet us with supplies of provision. The power of doing this was now at an end. As the accident could not be remedied, we turned it to the best account, by making a fire of the bark and timbers of the broken vessel, and cooked the remainder of our portable soup and arrow-root. This was a scanty meal after three days' fasting, but it served to allay the pangs of hunger, and enabled us to proceed at a quicker pace than before. The depth of the snow caused us to march in Indian file, that is in each other's steps; the voyagers taking it in turn to lead the party. A distant object was pointed out to this man in the direction we wished to take, and Mr. Hood followed immediately behind him, to renew the bearings, and keep him from deviating more than could be helped from the mark. It may be here observed, that we proceeded in this manner throughout our route across the barren grounds. . . .

We started at six on the 9th, and at the end of two miles regained our hunters, who were halting on the borders of a lake amidst a clump of stunted willows. This lake stretched to the westward as far as we could see, and its waters were discharged by a rapid stream one hundred and fifty yards wide. Being entirely ignorant where we might be led by pursuing the course of the lake, and dreading the idea of going a mile unnecessarily out of the way, we determined on crossing the river if possible; and the canoe was gummed for the purpose, the willows furnishing us with fire. But we had to await the return of Junius[13] before we could make the traverse. In the mean time we gathered a little *tripe de roche*, and breakfasted upon it and a few partridges that were killed in the morning. St. Germain[14] and Adam[15] were sent upon some recent tracks of deer. Junius arrived in the afternoon, and informed us that he had seen a large herd of musk-oxen on the banks of Cracroft's River, and had wounded one of them, but it had escaped. He brought about four pounds of meat, the remains of a deer that had been devoured by the wolves. The poor fellow was much fatigued, having walked throughout the night, but as the weather was particularly favourable for our crossing the river, we could not allow him to rest. After he had taken some refreshment we proceeded to the river. The canoe being put into the water was found extremely ticklish [unsteady], but it was managed with much dexterity by St. Germain, Adam, and Peltier,[16] who ferried over one passenger at a time, causing him to lie flat in its bottom, by no means a pleasant position, owing to its leakiness, but there was no alternative. The transport of the whole party was effected by five o'clock, and we walked about two miles further, and encamped, having come five miles and three quarters on a south-west course. Two young alpine hares were shot by St. Germain, which, with the small piece of meat brought in by Junius, furnished the supper of the whole party. There was no *tripe de roche* here. The country had now become decidedly hilly, and was covered with snow. The lake preserved its western direction, as far as I could see from the summit of the highest mountain near the encampment. We subsequently learned from the Copper Indians, that the part at which we had crossed the river was the *Congecatha wha chaga* of Hearne,[17] of which I had little idea at the time, not only from the difference of latitude, but also from its being so much farther east of the mouth of the Copper-Mine River, than his track is laid down. He only making one degree and three quarters' difference of longitude, and we, upwards of four. Had I been aware of the fact, several days' harassing march, and a disastrous accident would have been prevented by keeping on the western side of the lake, instead of crossing the river. . . .

September 10. . . . We halted at ten to gather *tripe de roche*, but it was so frozen, that we were quite benumbed with cold before a sufficiency could be collected even for a scanty meal. On proceeding our men were somewhat cheered, by observing on the sandy summit of a hill, from whence the snow had been blown, the summer track of a man; and afterwards by seeing several deer tracks on the snow. About noon the weather cleared up a little, and, to our great joy, we saw a herd of musk-oxen grazing in a valley below us. The party instantly halted, and the best hunters were sent out; they approached the animals with the utmost caution, no less than two hours being consumed before they got within gun-shot. In the mean time we beheld their proceedings with extreme anxiety, and many secret prayers were, doubtless, offered up for their success. At length they opened their fire, and we had the satisfaction of seeing one of the largest cows fall; another was wounded, but escaped. This success infused spirit into our starving party. To skin and cut up the animal was the work of a few minutes. The contents of its stomach were devoured upon the spot, and the raw intestines, which were next attacked, were pronounced by the most delicate amongst us to be excellent. A few willows, whose tops were seen peeping through the snow in the bottom of the valley, were quickly grubbed, and tents pitched, and supper cooked, and devoured with avidity. This was the sixth day since we had had a good meal. The *tripe de roche*, even where we got enough, only serving to allay the pangs of hunger for a short time. After supper, two of the hunters went in pursuit of the herd, but could not get near them. . . .

We set out on the 13th, in thick hazy weather, and, after an hour's march, had the extreme mortification to find ourselves on the borders of a large lake, which we subsequently learned from the Indians was named Contwoy-to, or Rum Lake; neither of its extremities could be seen, and as the portion which lay to the east seemed the widest, we coasted along to the westward portion in search of a crossing-place. This lake being bounded by steep and lofty hills, our march was very fatiguing. Those sides which were exposed to the sun, were free from snow, and we found upon them some excellent berries. We encamped at six P.M., having come only six miles and a half. Crédit[18] was then missing, and he did not return during the night. We supped off a single partridge and some *tripe de roche*; this unpalatable weed was now quite nauseous to the whole party, and in several it produced bowel complaints. Mr. Hood was the greatest sufferer from this cause. This evening we were extremely distressed, at discovering that our improvident companions, since we left Hood's River, had thrown away three of the fishing-nets, and burnt the floats; they knew we had brought them to procure subsistence for the party, when the animals should fail, and we could scarcely believe the fact of their having wilfully deprived themselves of this resource, especially when we considered that most of them had passed the greater part of their servitude in situations where the nets alone had supplied them with food. Being thus deprived of our principal resource, that of fishing, and the men evidently getting weaker every day, it became necessary to lighten their burthens of every thing except ammunition, clothing, and the instruments that were required to find our way. I, therefore, issued directions to deposit at this encampment the dipping needle, azimuth compass, magnet, a large thermometer, and a few books we had carried, having torn out of these such parts as we should require to work the observations for latitude and longitude. I also promised, as an excitement to the efforts in hunting, my gun to St. Germain, and an ample compensation to Adam, or any of the other men who should kill any animals. Mr. Hood, on this occasion, lent his gun to Michel, the Iroquois, who was very eager in the chase, and often successful.[19]

September 14. — This morning the officers being assembled round a small fire, Perrault[20] presented each of us with a small piece of meat which he had saved from his allowance. It was received with great thankfulness, and such an act of self-denial and kindness, being totally unexpected in a Canadian voyager, filled our eyes with tears. . . . Having searched for a part where the current was most smooth, the canoe was placed in the water at the head of a rapid, and St. Germain, Solomon Belanger,[21] and I, embarked in order to cross. We went from the shore very well, but in mid-channel the canoe became difficult to manage under our burden as the breeze was fresh. The current drove us to the edge of the rapid, when Belanger unfortunately applied his paddle to avert the apparent danger of being forced down it, and lost his balance. The canoe was overset in consequence in the middle of the rapid. We fortunately kept hold of it, until we touched a rock where the water did not reach higher than our waists: here we kept our footing, notwithstanding the strength of the current, until the water was emptied out of the canoe. Belanger then held the canoe steady whilst St. Germain placed me in it, and afterwards embarked himself in a very dexterous manner. It was impossible, however, to embark Belanger, as the canoe would have been hurried down the rapid, the moment he should have raised his foot from the rock on which he stood. We were, therefore, compelled to leave him in his perilous situation. We had not gone twenty yards before the canoe, striking on a sunken rock, went down. The place being shallow, we were again enabled to empty it, and the third attempt brought us to the shore. In the mean time Belanger was suffering extremely, immersed to his middle in the centre of a rapid, the temperature of which was very little above the freezing point, and the upper part of his body covered with wet clothes, exposed in a temperature not much above zero, to a strong breeze. He called piteously for relief, and St. Germain on his return endeavoured to embark him, but in vain. The canoe was hurried down the rapid, and when he landed he was rendered by the cold incapable of further exertion, and Adam attempted to embark Belanger, but found it impossible. An attempt was next made to carry out to him a line, made of the slings of the men's loads. This also failed, the current acting so strongly upon it, as to prevent the canoe from steering, and it was finally broken and carried down the stream. At length, when Belanger's strength seemed almost exhausted, the canoe reached him with a small cord belonging to one of the nets, and he was dragged perfectly senseless through the rapid. By the direction of Dr. Richardson, he was instantly stripped, and being rolled up in blankets, two men undressed themselves and went to bed with him; but it was some hours before he recovered his warmth and sensations. As soon as Belanger was placed in his bed, the officers immediately sent over my blankets, and a person to make a fire. Augustus[22] brought the canoe over, and in returning he was obliged to descend both the rapids, before he could get across the stream; which hazardous service he performed with the greatest coolness and judgment. It is impossible to describe my sensations as I witnessed the various unsuccessful attempts to relieve Belanger. The distance prevented my seeing distinctly what was going on, and I continued pacing up and down upon the rock on which I landed, regardless of the coldness of my drenched and stiffening garments. The canoe, in every attempt to reach him, was hurried down the rapid, and was lost to the view amongst the rocky islets, with a rapidity that seemed to threaten certain destruction; once, indeed, I fancied that I saw it overwhelmed in the waves. Such an event would have been fatal to the whole party. Separated as I was from my companions, without gun, ammunition, hatchet, or the means of making a fire, and in wet clothes, my doom would have been speedily sealed. My companions too, driven to the necessity of coasting the lake, must have sunk under the fatigue of rounding its innumerable arms and bays, which, as we have learned from the Indians, are very extensive. By the goodness of Providence, however, we were spared at that time, and some of us have been permitted to offer up our thanksgivings, in a civilized land, for the signal deliverances we then and afterwards experienced.

By this accident I had the misfortune to lose my port-folio, containing my journal from Fort Enterprise, together with all the astronomical and meteorological observations made during the descent of the Copper-Mine River, and along the sea-coast, (except those for the dip and variation.)[23] I was in the habit of carrying it strapped across my shoulders, but had taken it off on entering the canoe, to reduce the upper weight. The results of most of the observations for latitude and longitude, had been registered in the sketch books, so that we preserved the requisites for the construction of the chart. The meteorological observations, not having been copied, were lost. My companions, Dr. Richardson, Mr. Back, and Mr. Hood, had been so careful in noting every occurrence in their journals, that the loss of mine could fortunately be well supplied. These friends immediately offered me their documents, and every assistance in drawing up another narrative, of which kindness I availed myself at the earliest opportunity afterwards. . . .

[*September 19*] Our blankets did not suffice this evening to keep us in tolerable warmth: the slightest breeze seeming to pierce through our debilitated frames. The reader will, probably, be desirous to know how we passed our time in such a comfortless situation: the first operation after encamping was to thaw our frozen shoes, if a sufficient fire could be made, and dry ones were put on; each person then wrote his notes of the daily occurrences, and evening prayers were read; as soon as supper was prepared it was eaten, generally in the dark, and we went to bed, and kept up a cheerful conversation until our blankets were thawed by the heat of our bodies, and we had gathered sufficient warmth to enable us to fall asleep. On many nights we had not even the luxury of going to bed in dry clothes, for when the fire was insufficient to dry our shoes, we durst not venture to pull them off, lest they should freeze so hard as to be unfit to put on in the morning, and, therefore, inconvenient to carry.

On the 20th we got into a hilly country, and the marching became much more laborious, even the stoutest experienced great difficulty in climbing the craggy eminences. Mr. Hood was particularly weak, and was obliged to relinquish his station of second in the line, which Dr. Richardson now took, to direct the leading man in keeping the appointed course. I was also unable to keep pace with the men, who put forth their utmost speed, encouraged by the hope, which our reckoning had led us to form, of seeing Point Lake in the evening, but we were obliged to encamp without gaining a view of it. We had not seen either deer or their tracks through the day, and this circumstance, joined to the disappointment of not discovering the lake, rendered our voyagers very desponding, and the meagre supper of *tripe de roche* was little calculated to elevate their spirits. They now threatened to throw away their bundles, and quit us, which rash act they would probably have done, if they had known what track to pursue. . . .

[*September 23*] Our progress . . . was extremely slow, from the difficulty of managing the canoe in passing over the hills, as the breeze was fresh. Peltier, who had it in charge, having received several severe falls, became impatient, and insisted on leaving his burden, as it had already been much injured by the accidents of this day; and no arguments we could use were sufficient to prevail on him to continue carrying it. Vaillant[24] was, therefore, directed to take it, and we proceeded forward. Having found he got on very well, and was walking even faster than Mr. Hood could, in his present debilitated state, I pushed forward to stop the rest of the party, who had got out of our sight during the delay which the discussion about the canoe had occasioned. I accidentally passed the body of the men, and followed the tracks of two persons, who had separated from the rest, until two P.M., when, not seeing any person, I retraced my steps, and on my way met Dr. Richardson, who had also missed the party whilst he was employed gathering *tripe de roche*, and we went back together in search of them. We found they had halted among some willows, where they had picked up some pieces of skin, and a few bones of deer that had been devoured by the wolves last spring. They had rendered the bones friable by burning, and eaten them, as well as the skin; and several of them had added their old shoes to the repast. Peltier and Vaillant were with them, having left the canoe, which, they said, was so completely broken by another fall, as to be rendered incapable of repair, and entirely useless. The anguish this intelligence occasioned may be conceived, but it is beyond my power to describe it. Impressed, however, with the necessity of taking it forward, even in the state these men represented it to be, we urgently desired them to fetch it; but they declined going, and the strength of the officers was inadequate to the task. To their infatuated obstinacy on this occasion, a great portion of the melancholy circumstances which attended our subsequent progress may, perhaps, be attributed. The men now seemed to have lost all hope of being preserved; and all the arguments we could use failed in stimulating them to the least exertion. After consuming the remains of the bones and horns of the deer we resumed our march, and, in the evening, reached a contracted part of the lake, which perceiving to be shallow, we forded and encamped on the opposite side. Heavy rain began soon afterwards, and continued all the night. On the following morning the rain had so wasted the snow, that the tracks of Mr. Back and his companions, who had gone before with the hunters, were traced with difficulty; and the frequent showers during the day almost obliterated them. The men became furious at the apprehension of being deserted by the hunters, and some of the strongest throwing down their bundles, prepared to set out after them, intending to leave the more weak to follow as they could. The entreaties and threats of the officers, however, prevented their executing this mad scheme: but not before Solomon Belanger was despatched with orders for Mr. Back to halt until we should join him. Soon afterwards a thick fog came on, but we continued our march and overtook Mr. Back, who had been detained in consequence of his companions having followed some recent tracks of deer. After halting an hour, during which we refreshed ourselves with eating our old shoes and a few scraps of leather, we set forward in the hope of ascertaining whether an adjoining piece of water was the Copper-Mine River or not, but were soon compelled to return and encamp, for fear of a separation of the party, as we could not see each other at ten yards' distance. . . .

The bounty of Providence was most seasonably manifested to us next morning, in our killing five small deer out of a herd, which came in sight as we were on the point of starting. This unexpected supply reanimated the drooping spirits of our men, and filled every heart with gratitude. . . .

We set out early on the 26th, and, after walking about three miles along the lake, came to the river, which we at once recognised, from its size, to be the Copper-Mine. It flowed to the northward, and after winding about five miles, terminated in Point

Lake. Its current was swift, and there were two rapids in this part of its course,[25] but in a canoe we could have crossed with ease and safety. These rapids, as well as every other part of the river, were carefully examined in search of a ford; but finding none, the expedients occurred, of attempting to cross on a raft made of the willows which were growing there, or in a vessel framed with willows, and covered with the canvass of the tents; but both these schemes were abandoned, through the obstinacy of the interpreters and the most experienced voyagers, who declared that they would prove inadequate to the conveyance of the party, and that much time would be lost in the attempt. The men, in fact, did not believe that this was the Copper-Mine River, and so little confidence had they in our reckoning, and so much had they bewildered themselves on the march, that some of them asserted it was Hood's River, and others that it was the Bethe-tessy. . . . In short, their despondency had returned, and they all despaired of seeing Fort Enterprise again. However, the steady assurances of the officers, that we were actually on the banks of the Copper-Mine River, and that the distance to Fort Enterprise did not exceed forty miles, made some impression upon them, which was increased upon our finding some bear-berry plants, (*arbutus uva ursi*), which is reported by the Indians not to grow to the eastward of that river. Then they deplored their folly and impatience in breaking the canoe, being all of opinion, that had it not been so completely demolished on the 23d, it might have been repaired sufficiently to take the party over. We again closely interrogated Peltier and Vaillant as to its state, with the intention of sending for it; but they persisted in the declaration, that it was in a totally unserviceable condition. St. Germain being again called upon, to endeavour to construct a canoe frame with willows, stated that he was unable to make one sufficiently large. It became necessary, therefore, to search for pines of sufficient size to form a raft; and being aware that such trees grow on the borders of Point Lake, we considered it best to trace its shores in search of them; we, therefore, resumed our march, carefully looking, but in vain, for a fordable part, and encamped at the east end of Point Lake. . . .

We had this evening the pain of discovering that two of our men had stolen part of the officers' provision, which had been allotted to us with strict impartiality. This conduct was the more reprehensible, as it was plain that we were suffering, even in a greater degree than themselves, from the effects of famine, owing to our being of a less robust habit, and less accustomed to privations. We had no means of punishing this crime, but by the threat that they should forfeit their wages, which had now ceased to operate. . . .

[September 28] Eight deer were seen by Michel and Crédit, who loitered behind the rest of the party, but they could not approach them. A great many shots were fired by those in the rear at partridges, but they missed, or at least did not choose to add what they killed to the common stock. We subsequently learned that the hunters often secreted the partridges they shot, and ate them unknown to the officers. Some *tripe de roche* was collected, which we boiled for supper, with the moiety of the remainder of our deer's meat. The men commenced cutting the willows for the construction of the raft. As an excitement to exertion, I promised a reward of three hundred livres to the first person who should convey a line across the river, by which the raft could be managed in transporting the party.

September 29. . . . we hoped the whole party might be transported, by hauling it [the raft] from one side to the other, provided a line could be carried to the other bank. Several attempts were made by Belanger and Benoit, the strongest men of the party, to convey the raft across the stream, but they failed for want of oars. . . . At this time Dr. Richardson, prompted by a desire of relieving his suffering companions, proposed to swim across the stream with a line, and to haul the raft over. He launched into the stream with the line round his middle, but when he had got a short distance from the bank, his arms became benumbed with cold, and he lost the power of moving them; still he persevered, and turning on his back, had nearly gained the opposite bank, when his legs also became powerless, and to our infinite alarm we beheld him sink. We instantly hauled upon the line and he came again on the surface, and was gradually drawn ashore in an almost lifeless state. Being rolled up in blankets, he was placed before a good fire of willows, and fortunately was just able to speak sufficiently to give some slight directions respecting the manner of treating him. He recovered strength gradually, and by the blessing of God was enabled in the course of a few hours to converse, and by the evening was sufficiently recovered to remove into the tent. We then regretted to learn, that the skin on his whole left side was deprived of feeling in consequence of exposure to too great heat. He did not perfectly recover the sensation of that side until the following summer. I cannot describe what every one felt at beholding the skeleton which the Doctor's debilitated frame exhibited. When he stripped, the Canadians simultaneously exclaimed, 'Ah que nous sommes maigres.' I shall best explain his state and that of the party, by the following extract from his journal: 'It may be worthy of remark that I would have had little hesitation in any former period in my life, of plunging into water even below 38° Fahrenheit; but at this time I was reduced almost to skin and bone, and like the rest of the party, suffered from degrees of cold that would have been disregarded whilst in health and vigour. During the whole of our march we experienced that no quantity of clothing could keep us warm whilst we fasted, but on those occasions on which we were enabled to go to bed with full stomachs, we passed the night in a warm and comfortable manner.' . . .

[*October 1*] . . . On the following morning the ground was covered with snow to the depth of a foot and a half, and the weather was very stormy. These circumstances rendered the men again extremely despondent; a settled gloom hung over their countenances, and they refused to pick *tripe de roche*, choosing rather to go entirely without eating, than to make any exertion. The party which went for gum returned early in the morning without having found any; but St. Germain said he could still make the canoe with the willows covered with the canvass, and removed with Adam to a clump of willows for that purpose. Mr. Back accompanied them to stimulate his exertion, as we feared the lowness of his spirits would cause him to be slow in his operations. Augustus went to fish at the rapid, but a large trout having carried away his bait, we had nothing to replace it.

The snow storm continued all the night, and during the forenoon of the 3d. Having persuaded the people to gather some *tripe de roche*, I partook of a meal with them; and afterwards set out with the intention of going to St. Germain to hasten his operations, but though he was only three quarters of a mile distant, I spent three hours in a vain attempt to reach him, my strength being unequal to the labour of wading through the deep snow; and I returned quite exhausted, and much shaken by the numerous falls I had got. My associates were all in the same debilitated state, and poor Hood was reduced to a perfect shadow, from the severe bowel complaints which the *tripe de roche* never failed to give him. Back was so feeble as to require the support of a stick in walking; and Dr. Richardson had lameness superadded to weakness. The voyagers were somewhat stronger than ourselves, but more indisposed to exertion, on account of their despondency. The sensation of hunger was no longer felt by any of us, yet we were scarcely able to converse upon any other subject than the pleasures of eating. We were much indebted to Hepburn[26] at this crisis. The officers were unable from weakness to gather *tripe de roche* themselves, and Semandrè [sic],[27] who had acted as our cook on the journey from the coast, sharing in the despair of the rest of the Canadians, refused to make the slightest exertion. Hepburn, on the contrary, animated by a firm reliance on the beneficence of the Supreme Being, tempered with resignation to his will, was indefatigable in his exertions to serve us, and daily collected all the *tripe de roche* that was used in the officers' mess. Mr. Hood could not partake of this miserable fare, and a partridge which had been reserved for him was, I lament to say, this day stolen by one of the men.

October 4. — The canoe being finished, it was brought to the emcampment, and the whole party being assembled in anxious expectation on the beach, St. Germain embarked, and amidst our prayers for his success, succeeded in reaching the opposite shore. The canoe was then drawn back again, and another person transported, and in this manner by drawing it backwards and forwards, we were all conveyed over without any serious accident. . . .

It is impossible to imagine a more gratifying change than was produced in our voyagers after we were all safely landed on the southern banks of the river. Their spirits immediately revived, each of them shook the officers cordially by the hand, and declared they now considered the worst of their difficulties over, as they did not doubt of reaching Fort Enterprise in a few days, even in their feeble condition. We had indeed every reason to be grateful, and our joy would have been complete were it not mingled with sincere regret at the separation of our poor Esquimaux, the faithful Junius.

Back, with St. Germain, Solomon Belanger and Beauparlant[28] *is sent ahead to search for the natives at Fort Enterprise*

[*October 5*] . . . Our advance from the depth of the snow was slow, and about noon coming to a spot where there was some *tripe de roche*, we stopped to collect it, and breakfasted. Mr. Hood, who was now very feeble, and Dr. Richardson, who attached himself to him, walked together at a gentle pace in the rear of the party. I kept with the foremost men, to cause them to halt occasionally, until the stragglers came up. . . .

About noon Samandrè coming up, informed us that Crédit and Vaillant could advance no further. Some willows being discovered in a valley near to us, I proposed to halt the party there, whilst Dr. Richardson went back to visit them. I hoped too, that when the sufferers received the information of a fire being kindled at so short a distance, they would be cheered, and use their utmost efforts to reach it, but this proved a vain hope. The Doctor found Vaillant about a mile and a half in the rear, much exhausted with cold and fatigue. Having encouraged him to advance to the fire, after repeated solicitations he made the attempt, but fell down amongst the deep snow at every step. Leaving him in this situation, the Doctor went about half a mile farther back, to the spot where Crédit was said to have halted, and the track being nearly obliterated by the snow drift, it became unsafe for him to go further. Returning he passed Vaillant, who having moved only a few yards in his absence, had fallen down, was unable to rise, and could scarcely answer his questions. Being unable to afford him any effectual assistance, he hastened on to inform us of his situation. When J.B. Belanger[29] had heard the melancholy account, he went immediately to aid Vaillant, and bring up his burden. Respecting Crédit, we were informed by Samandrè, that he had stopped a short distance behind Vaillant, but that his intention was to return to the encampment of the preceding evening.

When Belanger came back with Vaillant's load, he informed us that he had found him lying on his back, benumbed with cold, and incapable of being roused. The stoutest men of the party were now earnestly entreated to bring him to the fire, but they declared themselves unequal to the task; and, on the contrary, urged me to allow them to throw down their loads, and proceed to Fort Enterprise with the utmost speed. A compliance with their desire would have caused the loss of the whole party, for the men were totally ignorant of the course to be taken, and none of the officers, who could have directed the march, were sufficiently strong to keep up at the pace they would then walk; besides, even supposing them to have found their way, the strongest men would certainly have deserted the weak. Something, however, was absolutely necessary to be done, to relieve them as much as possible from their burdens, and the officers consulted on the subject. Mr. Hood and Dr. Richardson proposed to remain behind, with a single attendant, at the first place where sufficient wood and *tripe de roche* should be found for ten days' consumption; and that I should proceed as expeditiously as possible with the men to the house, and thence send them immediate relief. They strongly urged that this arrangement would contribute to the safety of the rest of the party, by relieving them from the burden of a tent, and several other articles; and that they might afford aid to Crédit, if he should unexpectedly come up. I was distressed beyond description at the thought of leaving them in such a dangerous situation, and for a long time combated their proposal; but they strenuously urged, that this step afforded the only chance of safety for the party, and I reluctantly acceded to it. The ammunition, of which we had a small barrel, was also to be left with them, and it was hoped that this deposit would be a strong inducement for the Indians to venture across the barren grounds to their aid. We communicated this resolution to the men, who were cheered at the slightest prospect of alleviation of their present miseries, and they promised with great appearance of earnestness to return to those officers, upon the first supply of food. . . .

[*October 6*] The weather was mild next morning. We left the encampment at nine, and a little before noon came to a pretty extensive thicket of small willows, near which there appeared a supply of *tripe de roche* on the face of the rocks. At this place Dr. Richardson and Mr. Hood determined to remain, with John Hepburn, who volunteered to stop with them. The tent was securely pitched, a few willows collected, and the ammunition and all other articles were deposited, except each man's clothing, one tent, a sufficiency of ammunition for the journey, and the officer's journals. I had only one blanket, which was carried for me, and two pair of shoes. The offer was now made for any of the men, who felt themselves too weak to proceed, to remain with the officers, but none of them accepted it. Michel alone felt some inclination to do so. After we had united in thanksgiving and prayers to Almighty God, I separated from my companions, deeply afflicted that a train of melancholy circumstances should have demanded of me the severe trial of parting from friends in such a condition, who had become endeared to me by their constant kindness, and co-operation, and a participation of numerous sufferings. This trial I could not have been induced to undergo, but for the reasons they had so strongly urged the day before, to which my own judgement assented, and for the sanguine hope I felt of either finding a supply of provision at Fort Enterprise, or meeting the Indians in the immediate vicinity of that place, according to my arrangements with Mr. Wentzel[30] and Akaitcho. Previously to our starting, Peltier and Benoit repeated their promises, to return to them with provisions, if any should be found at the house, or to guide the Indians to them, if any were met. . . .

Jean-Baptiste Belanger and Michel return to Hood and Richardson

. . . Belanger and Michel were left far behind, and when they arrived at the encampment appeared quite exhausted. The former, bursting into tears, declared his inability to proceed with the party, and begged me to let him go back next morning to the tent, and shortly afterwards Michel made the same request. I was in hopes they might recover a little strength by the night's rest and therefore deferred giving any permission until the morning. The sudden failure of the strength of these men cast a gloom over the rest, which I tried in vain to remove, by repeated assurances that the distance to Fort Enterprise was short, and that we should, in all probability, reach it in four days. Not being able to find any *tripe de roche*, we drank an infusion of the Labrador tea plant, (*ledum palustre*), and ate a few morsels of burnt leather for supper. We were unable to raise the tent, and found its weight too great to carry it on: we, therefore, cut it up, and took a part of the canvass for a cover. The night was bitterly cold, and though we lay as close to each other as possible, having no shelter, we could not keep ourselves sufficiently warm to sleep. A strong gale came on after midnight, which increased the severity of the weather. In the morning Belanger and Michel renewed their request to be permitted to go back to the tent, assuring me they were still weaker than on the preceding evening, and less capable of going forward; and they urged, that the stopping at a place where there was a supply of *tripe de roche* was their only chance of preserving life; under these circumstances, I could not do otherwise than yield to their desire. I wrote a note to Dr. Richardson and Mr. Hood, informing them of the pines we had passed, and recommending their removing thither. Having found that Michel was carrying a considerable quantity of ammunition, I desired him to divide it among my party, leaving him only ten balls and a little shot, to kill any animals he might meet on his way to the tent. This man was very particular in his inquiries respecting the direction of the house, and the course we meant to pursue; he also said, that if he should be able, he would go and search for Vaillant and Crédit; and he requested my permission to take Vaillant's blanket, if he should find it, to which I agreed, and mentioned it in my notes to the officers. . . .

The party was now reduced to five persons, Adam, Peltier, Benoit, Samandré, and myself. Continuing the journey, we came, after an hour's walk, to some willows, and encamped under the shelter of a rock, having walked in the whole four miles and a half. We made an attempt to gather some *tripe de roche*, but could not, owing to the severity of the weather. Our supper, therefore, consisted of tea and a few morsels of leather.

Augustus did not make his appearance, but we felt no alarm at his absence, supposing he would go to the tent if he missed our track. Having fire, we procured a little sleep. Next morning the breeze was light and the weather mild, which enabled us to collect some *tripe de roche*, and to enjoy the only meal we had for four days. We derived great benefit from it, and walked with considerably more ease than yesterday. Without the strength it supplied, we should certainly have been unable to oppose the strong breeze we had in the afternoon. After walking about five miles, we came upon the borders of Marten Lake, and were rejoiced to find it frozen, so that we could continue our course straight for Fort Enterprize [sic]. . . . There was no *tripe de roche*, and we drank tea and ate some of our shoes for supper. Next morning, after taking the usual repast of tea, we proceeded to the house. Musing on what we were likely to find there, our minds were agitated between hope and fear, and, contrary to the custom we had kept up, of supporting our spirits by conversation, we went silently forward.

[*October 10*] At length we reached Fort Enterprise, and to our infinite disappointment and grief found it a perfectly desolate habitation. There was no deposit of provision, no trace of the Indians, no letter from Mr. Wentzel to point out where the Indians might be found. It would be impossible for me to describe our sensations after entering this miserable abode, and discovering how we had been neglected; the whole party shed tears, not so much for our own fate, as for that of our friends in the rear, whose lives depended entirely on our sending immediate relief from this place.

I found a note, however, from Mr. Back, stating that he had reached the house two days ago, and was going in search of the Indians, at a part where St. Germain deemed it probable they might be found. If he was unsuccessful, he purposed walking to Fort Providence, and sending succour from thence. But he doubted whether either he or his party could perform the journey to that place in their present debilitated state. It was evident that any supply that could be sent from Fort Providence would be long in reaching us, and could not be sufficient to enable us to afford any assistance to our companions behind, and that the only relief for them must be procured from the Indians. I resolved, therefore, in going also in search of them; but my companions were absolutely incapable of proceeding, and I thought, by halting two or three days they might gather a little strength, whilst the delay would afford us the chance of learning whether Mr. Back had seen the Indians. . . .

[*October 11*] When I arose the following morning, my body and limbs were so swollen that I was unable to walk more than a few yards. Adam was in a still worse condition, being absolutely incapable of rising without assistance. My other companions fortunately experienced this inconvenience in a less degree, and went to collect bones, and some *tripe de roche* which supplied us with two meals. The bones were quite acrid, and the soup extracted from them excoriated the mouth if taken alone, but it was somewhat milder when boiled with *tripe de roche*, and we even thought the mixture palatable, with the addition of salt, of which a cask had been fortunately left here in the spring. Augustus to-day set two fishing lines below the rapid. On his way thither he saw two deer, but had not strength to follow them. . . .

Franklin attempts to travel to Fort Providence with Benoit and Augustus, but broken snowshoes prevent him from continuing and he returns to Fort Enterprise.

[*October 21*] On my arrival at the house, I found Samandrè very dispirited, and too weak, as he said, to render any assistance to Peltier; upon whom the whole labour of getting wood and collecting the means of subsistence would have devolved. Conscious, too, that his strength would have been unequal to these tasks, they had determined upon taking only one meal each day; under these circumstances I considered my return as particularly fortunate, as I hoped to stimulate Samandrè to exertion, and at any rate I could contribute some help to Peltier. I undertook the office of cooking, and insisted they should eat twice a-day whenever food could be procured, but as I was too weak to pound the bones, Peltier agreed to do that in addition to his more fatiguing task of getting wood. We had a violent snow storm all the next day, and this gloomy weather contributed to the depression of spirits under which Adam and Samandrè were labouring. Neither of them would quit their beds, and they scarcely ceased from shedding tears all day; in vain did Peltier and myself endeavour to cheer them. We had even to use much entreaty before we prevailed upon them to take the meals we had prepared. Our situation was indeed distressing, but in comparison with that of our friends in the rear, we considered it happy. Their condition gave us unceasing solicitude, and was the principal subject of our conversation. . . .

[*October 26*] We perceived our strength decline every day, and every exertion began to be irksome; when we were once seated the greatest effort was necessary in order to rise, and we had frequently to lift each other from our seats; but even in this pitiable condition we conversed cheerfully, being sanguine as to the speedy arrival of the

Indians. We calculated indeed that if they should be near the situation where they had remained last winter, our men would have reached them by this day. Having expended all the wood which we could procure from our present dwelling, without endangering its falling, Peltier began this day to pull down the partitions of the adjoining houses. Though these were only distant about twenty yards, yet the increase of labour in carrying the wood fatigued him so much, that by the evening he was exhausted. On the next day his weakness was such, especially in the arms, of which he chiefly complained, that he with difficulty lifted the hatchet; still he persevered, Samandrè and I assisting him in bringing in the wood, but our united strength could only collect sufficient to replenish the fire four times in the course of the day. As the insides of our mouths had become sore from eating the bone-soup, we relinquished the use of it, and now boiled our skin, which mode of dressing we found more palatable than frying it, as we had hitherto done.

On the 29th, Peltier felt his pains more severe, and could only cut a few pieces of wood. Samandrè, who was still almost as weak, relieved him a little time, and I assisted them in carrying in the wood. We endeavoured to pick some *tripe de roche*, but in vain, as it was entirely frozen. In turning up the snow, in searching for bones, I found several pieces of bark, which proved a valuable acquisition, as we were almost destitute of dry wood proper for kindling the fire. We saw a herd of rein-deer sporting on the river, about half a mile from the house; they remained there a considerable time, but none of the party felt themselves sufficiently strong to go after them, nor was there one of us who could have fired a gun without resting it.

[*October 29*] Whilst we were seated round the fire this evening, discoursing about the anticipated relief, the conversation was suddenly interrupted by Peltier's exclaiming with joy, '*Ah! le monde!*' imagining that he heard the Indians in the other room; immediately afterwards, to his bitter disappointment, Dr. Richardson and Hepburn entered, each carrying his bundle. Peltier, however, soon recovered himself enough to express his joy at their safe arrival, and his regret that their companions were not with them. When I saw them alone my own mind was instantly filled with apprehensions respecting my friend Hood, and our other companions, which were immediately confirmed by the Doctor's melancholy communication, that Mr. Hood and Michel were dead. Perrault and Fontano[31] had neither reached the tent, nor been heard of by them. This intelligence produced a melancholy despondency in the minds of my party, and on that account the particulars were deferred until another opportunity. We were all shocked at beholding the emaciated countenances of the Doctor and Hepburn, as they strongly evidenced their extremely debilitated state. The alteration in our appearance was equally distressing to them, for since the swellings had subsided we were little more than skin and bone. The Doctor particularly remarked the sepulchral tone of our voices, which he requested us to make more cheerful if possible, unconscious that his own partook of the same key.

Hepburn having shot a partridge, which was brought to the house, the Doctor tore out the feathers, and having held it to the fire a few minutes, divided it into seven portions. Each piece was ravenously devoured by my companions, as it was the first morsel of flesh any of us had tasted for thirty-one days, unless indeed the small gristly particles which we found occasionally adhering to the pounded bones may be termed flesh. Our spirits were revived by this small supply, and the Doctor endeavoured to raise them still higher by the prospect of Hepburn's being able to kill a deer next day, as they had seen, and even fired at, several near the house. He endeavoured, too, to rouse us to some attention to the comfort of our apartment, and particularly to roll up, in the day, our blankets which (expressly for the convenience of Adam and Samandrè) we had been in the habit of leaving by the fire where we lay on them. The Doctor having brought his prayer-book and testament, some prayers and psalms, and portions of scripture, appropriate to our situation, were read, and we retired to bed. . . .

[October 30] After our usual supper of singed skin and bone soup, Dr. Richardson acquainted me with the afflicting circumstances attending the death of Mr. Hood and Michel, and detailed the occurrences subsequent to my departure from them, which I shall give from his journal, in his own words;[32] but, I must here be permitted to express the heart-felt sorrow with which I was overwhelmed at the loss of so many companions; especially for that of my friend Mr. Hood, to whose zealous and able co-operation I had been indebted for so much invaluable assistance during the Expedition, whilst the excellent qualities of his heart engaged my warmest regard. His scientific observations, together with his maps and drawings (a small part of which only appear in this work), evince a variety of talent, which, had his life been spared, must have rendered him a distinguished ornament to his profession, and which will cause his death to be felt as a loss to the service.

Dr Richardson tells of the deaths of Hood and Michel

After Captain Franklin had bidden us farewell we remained seated by the fire-side as long as the willows, the men had cut for us before they departed, lasted. We had no *tripe de roche* that day, but drank an infusion of the country tea-plant, which was grateful from its warmth, although it afforded no sustenance. We then retired to bed, where we remained all the next day, as the weather was stormy, and the snow-drift so heavy, as to destroy every prospect of success in our endeavours to light a fire with the green and frozen willows, which were our only fuel. Through the extreme kindness and forthought of a lady, the party, previous to leaving London, had been furnished with a small collection of religious books, of which we still retained two or three of the most portable, and they proved of incalculable benefit to us. We read portions of them to each other as we lay in bed, in addition to the morning and evening service, and found that they inspired us on each perusal with so strong a sense of the omnipresence of a beneficent God, that our situation, even in these wilds, appeared no longer destitute; and we conversed, not only with calmness, but with cheerfulness, detailing with unrestrained confidence the past events of our lives, and dwelling with hope on our future prospects. Had my poor friend been spared to revisit his native land, I should look back to this period with unalloyed delight.

On the morning of the 29th,[33] the weather, although still cold, was clear, and I went out in quest of *tripe de roche*, leaving Hepburn to cut willows for a fire, and Mr. Hood in bed. I had no success, as yesterday's snow drift was so frozen on the surface of the rocks that I could not collect any of the weed; but, on my return to the tent, I found that Michel, the Iroquois, had come with a note from Mr. Franklin, which stated, that this man, and Jean Baptiste Belanger being unable to proceed, were about to return to us, and that a mile beyond our present encampment there was a clump of pine trees, to which he recommended us to remove the tent. Michel informed us that he quitted Mr. Franklin's party yesterday morning, but, that having missed his way, he had passed the night on the snow a mile or two to the northward of us. Belanger, he said, being impatient, had left the fire about two hours earlier, and, as he had not arrived, he supposed he had gone astray. It will be seen in the sequel, that we had more than sufficient reason to doubt the truth of this story.

Michel now produced a hare and a partridge which he had killed in the morning. This unexpected supply of provision was received by us with a deep sense of gratitude to the Almighty for his goodness, and we looked upon Michel as the instrument he had chosen to preserve all our lives. He complained of cold, and Mr. Hood offered to share his buffalo robe with him at night; I gave him one of two shirts which I wore, whilst Hepburn, in the warmth of his heart, exclaimed, 'How I shall love this man if I find that he does not tell lies like the others.' Our meals being finished, we arranged that the greatest part of the things should be carried to the pines the next day; and, after reading the evening service, retired to bed full of hope.

[*October 10*] Early in the morning Hepburn, Michel, and myself, carried the ammunition, and most of the other heavy articles to the pines. Michel was our guide, and it did not occur to us at the time that his conducting us perfectly straight was incompatible with his story of having gone astray on his way to us. He now informed us that he had, on his way to the tent, left on the hill above the pines a gun and forty-eight balls, which Perrault had given to him when with the rest of Mr. Franklin's party, he took leave of him. It will be seen, on a reference to Mr. Franklin's journal, that Perrault carried his gun and ammunition with him when they parted from Michel and Belanger. After we had made a fire, and drank a little of the country tea, Hepburn and I returned to the tent, where we arrived in the evening, much exhausted with our journey. Michel preferred sleeping where he was, and requested us to leave him the hatchet, which we did, after he had promised to come early in the morning to assist us in carrying the tent and bedding. Mr. Hood remained in bed all day. Seeing nothing of Belanger to-day, we gave him up for lost.

On the 11th, after waiting until late in the morning for Michel, who did not come, Hepburn and I loaded ourselves with the bedding, and, accompanied by Mr. Hood, set out for the pines. Mr. Hood was much affected with dimness of sight, giddiness, and other symptoms of extreme debility, which caused us to move very slow, and to make frequent halts. On arriving at the pines, we were much alarmed to find that Michel was absent. We feared that he had lost his way in coming to us in the morning, although it was not easy to conjecture how that could have happened, as our footsteps of yesterday were very distinct. Hepburn went back for the tent, and returned with it after dusk, completely worn out with the fatigue of the day. Michel too arrived at the same time, and relieved our anxiety on his account. He reported that he had been in chase of some deer which passed near his sleeping-place in the morning, and although he did not come up with them, yet that he found a wolf which had been killed by the stroke of a deer's horn, and had brought a part of it. We implicitly believed this story then, but afterwards became convinced from circumstances, the detail of which may be spared, that it must have been a portion of the body of Belanger or Perrault. A question of moment here presents itself; namely, whether he actually murdered these men, or either of them, or whether he found the bodies on the snow. Captain Franklin, who is the best able to judge of this matter, from knowing their situation when he parted from them, suggested the former idea, and that both Belanger and Perrault had been sacrificed. When Perrault turned back, Captain Franklin watched him until he reached a small group of willows, which was immediately adjoining to the fire, and concealed it from view, and at this time the smoke of fresh fuel was distinctly visible. Captain Franklin conjectures, that Michel having already destroyed Belanger, completed his crime by Perrault's death, in order to screen himself from detection. Although this opinion is founded only on circumstances, and is unsupported by direct evidence, it has been judged proper to mention it, especially as the subsequent conduct of the man shewed that he was capable of committing such a deed. The circumstances are very strong. It is not easy to assign any other adequate motive for his concealing from us that Perrault had turned back, and his request overnight that we should leave him the hatchet; and his cumbering himself with it when he went out in the morning, unlike a hunter who makes use only of his knife when he kills a deer, seem to indicate that he took it for the purpose of cutting up something that he knew to be frozen. These opinions, however, are the result of subsequent consideration. We passed this night in the open air.

On the following morning the tent was pitched, and Michel went out early, refused my offer to accompany him, and remained out the whole day. He would not sleep in the tent at night, but chose to lie at the fire-side.

On the 13th there was a heavy gale of wind, and we passed the day by the fire. Next day, about two, P.M., the gale abating, Michel set out as he said to hunt, but returned unexpectedly in a very short time. This conduct surprised us, and his contradictory and evasory answers to our questions excited some suspicions, but they did not turn towards the truth.

October 15th. — In the course of this day Michel expressed much regret that he had stayed behind Mr. Franklin's party, and declared that he would set out for the house at once if he knew the way. We endeavoured to soothe him, and to raise his hopes of the Indians speedily coming to our relief, but without success. He refused to assist us in cutting wood, but about noon, after much solicitation, he set out to hunt. Hepburn gathered a kettle of *tripe de roche*, but froze his fingers. Both Hepburn and I fatigued ourselves much to-day in pursuing a flock of partridges from one part to another of the group of willows, in which the hut was situated, but we were too weak to be able to approach them with sufficient caution. In the evening Michel returned, having met with no success.

Next day he refused either to hunt or cut wood, spoke in a very surly manner, and threatened to leave us. Under these circumstances, Mr. Hood and I deemed it better to promise if he would hunt diligently for four days, that then we would give Hepburn a letter for Mr. Franklin, a compass, inform him what course to pursue, and let them proceed together to the fort. The non-arrival of the Indians to our relief, now led us to fear that some accident had happened to Mr. Franklin, and we placed no confidence in the exertions of the Canadians that accompanied him, but we had the fullest confidence in Hepburn's returning the moment he could obtain assistance.

On the 17th I went to conduct Michel to where Vaillant's blanket was left, and after walking about three miles, pointed out the hills to him at a distance, and returned to the hut, having gathered a bagful of *tripe de roche* on the way. It was easier to gather this weed on a march than at the tent, for the exercise of walking produced a glow of heat, which enabled us to withstand for a time the cold to which we were exposed in scraping the frozen surface of the rocks. On the contrary, when we left the fire, to collect it in the neighbourhood of the hut, we became chilled at once, and were obliged to return very quickly.

Michel proposed to remain out all night, and to hunt next day on his way back. He returned in the afternoon of the 18th, having found the blanket, together with a bag containing two pistols, and some other things which had been left beside it. We had some *tripe de roche* in the evening, but Mr. Hood, from the constant griping it produced, was unable to eat more than one or two spoonfuls. He was now so weak as to be scarcely able to sit up at the fire-side, and complained that the least breeze of wind seemed to blow through his frame. He also suffered much from cold during the night. We lay close to each other, but the heat of the body was no longer sufficient to thaw the frozen rime formed by our breaths on the blankets that covered him.

At this period we avoided as much as possible conversing upon the hopelessness of our situation, and generally endeavoured to lead the conversation towards our future prospects in life. The fact is, that with the decay of our strength, our minds decayed, and we were no longer able to bear the contemplation of the horrors that surrounded us. Each of us, if I may be allowed to judge from my own case, excused himself from so doing by a desire of not shocking the feelings of the others, for we were sensible of one another's weakness of intellect though blind to our own. Yet we were calm and resigned to our fate, not a murmur escaped us, and we were punctual and fervent in our addresses to the Supreme Being.

On the 19th Michel refused to hunt, or even to assist in carrying a log of wood to the fire, which was too heavy for Hepburn's strength and mine. Mr. Hood endeavoured to point out to him the necessity and duty of exertion, and the cruelty of his quitting us without leaving something for our support; but the discourse far from producing any beneficial effect, seemed only to excite his anger, and amongst other expressions, he made use of the following remarkable one: 'It is no use hunting, there are no animals, you had better kill and eat me.' At length, however, he went out, but returned very soon, with a report that he had seen three deer, which he was unable to follow from having wet his foot in a small stream of water thinly covered with ice, and being consequently obliged to come to the fire. The day was rather mild and Hepburn and I gathered a large kettleful of *tripe de roche*; Michel slept in the tent this night.

Sunday, October 20. — In the morning we again urged Michel to go a hunting that he might if possible leave us some provision, to-morrow being the day appointed for his quitting us; but he shewed great unwillingness to go out, and lingered about the fire, under the pretence of cleaning his gun. After we had read the morning service I went about noon to gather some *tripe de roche*, leaving Mr. Hood sitting before the tent at the fire-side, arguing with Michel; Hepburn was employed cutting down a tree at a short distance from the tent, being desirous of accumulating a quantity of fire wood before he left us. A short time after I went out I heard the report of a gun, and about ten minutes afterwards Hepburn called to me in a voice of great alarm, to come directly. When I arrived, I found poor Hood lying lifeless at the fire-side, a ball having apparently entered his forehead. I was at first horror-struck with the idea, that in a fit of despondency he had hurried himself into the presence of his Almighty Judge, by an act of his own hand; but the conduct of Michel soon gave rise to other thoughts, and excited suspicions which were confirmed, when upon examining the body, I discovered that the shot had entered the back part of the head, and passed out at the forehead, and that the muzzle of the gun had been applied so close as to set fire to the night-cap behind. The gun, which was of the longest kind supplied to the Indians, could not have been placed in a position to inflict such a wound, except by a second person. Upon inquiring of Michel how it happened, he replied, that Mr. Hood had sent him into the tent for the short gun, and that during his absence the long gun had gone off, he did not know whether by accident or not. He held the short gun in his hand at the time he was speaking to me. Hepburn afterward informed me that previous to the report of the gun Mr. Hood and Michel were speaking to each other in an elevated angry tone; that Mr. Hood being seated at the fire-side, was hid from him by intervening willows, but that on hearing the report he looked up, and saw Michel rising up from before the tent-door, or just behind where Mr. Hood was seated, and then going into the tent. Thinking that the gun had been discharged for the purpose of cleaning it, he did not go to the fire at first; and when Michel called to him that Mr. Hood was dead, a considerable time had elapsed. Although I dared not openly to evince any suspicion that I thought Michel guilty of the deed, yet he repeatedly protested that he was incapable of committing such an act, kept constantly on his guard, and carefully avoided leaving Hepburn and me together. He was evidently afraid of permitting us to converse in private, and whenever Hepburn spoke, he inquired if he accused him of the murder. It is to be remarked, that he understood English very imperfectly, yet sufficiently to render it unsafe for us to speak on the subject in his presence. We removed the body into a clump of willows behind the tent, and, returning to the fire, read the funeral service in addition to the evening prayers. The loss of a young officer, of such distinguished and varied talents and application, may be felt and duly appreciated by the eminent characters under whose command he had served; but the calmness with which he contemplated the probable termination of a life of uncommon promise; and the patience and fortitude with which he sustained, I may venture to say, unparalleled bodily sufferings, can only be known to the companions of his distresses. Owing to the effect that the *tripe de roche* invariably had, when he ventured to taste it, he undoubtedly suffered more than any of the survivors of the party. *Bickersteth's Scripture Help*[34] was lying open beside the body, as if it had fallen from his hand, and it is probable that he was reading it at the instant of his death. We passed the night in the tent together without rest, every one being on his guard. Next day, having determined on going to the Fort, we began to patch and prepare our clothes for the journey. We singed the hair off a part of the buffalo robe that belonged to Mr. Hood, and boiled and ate it. Michel tried to persuade me to go to the woods on the Copper-Mine River, and hunt for deer instead of going to the Fort. In the afternoon a flock of partridges coming near the tent, he killed several which he shared with us.

Thick snowy weather and a head wind prevented us from starting the following day, but on the morning of the 23d we set out, carrying with us the remainder of the singed robe. Hepburn and Michel had each a gun, and I carried a small pistol, which Hepburn had loaded for me. In the course of the march Michel alarmed us much by his gestures and conduct, was constantly muttering to himself, expressed an unwillingness to go to the Fort, and tried to persuade me to go to the southward to the woods, where he said he could maintain himself all the winter by killing deer. In consequence of this behaviour, and the expression of his countenance, I requested him to leave us and to go to the southward by himself. This proposal increased his ill-nature, he threw out some obscure hints of freeing himself from all restraint on the morrow; and I over-heard him muttering threats against Hepburn, whom he openly accused of having told stories against him. He also, for the first time, assumed such a tone of superiority in addressing me, as evinced that he considered us to be completely in his power, and he gave vent to several expressions of hatred towards the white people, or as he termed us in the idiom of the voyagers, the French, some of whom, he said, had killed and eaten his uncle and two of his relations. In short, taking every circumstance of his conduct into consideration, I came to the conclusion, that he would attempt to destroy us on the first opportunity that offered, and that he had hitherto abstained from doing so from his ignorance of the way to the Fort, but that he would never suffer us to go thither in company with him. In the course of the day he had several times remarked that we were pursuing the same course that Mr. Franklin was doing when he left him, and that by keeping towards the setting sun he could find his way himself. Hepburn and I were not in a condition to resist even an open attack, nor could we by any device escape from him. Our united strength was far inferior to his, and, besides his gun, he was armed with two pistols, an Indian bayonet, and a knife. In the afternoon, coming to a rock on which there was some *tripe de roche*, he halted, and said he would gather it whilst we went on, and that he would soon overtake us. Hepburn and I were now left together for the first time since Mr. Hood's death, and he acquainted me with several material circumstances, which he had observed of Michel's behaviour, and which confirmed me in the opinion that there was no safety for us except in his death, and he offered to be the instrument of it. I determined, however, as I was thoroughly convinced of the necessity of such a dreadful act, to take the whole responsibility upon myself; and immediately upon Michel's coming up, I put an end to his life by shooting him through the head with a pistol. Had my own life alone been threatened, I would not have purchased it by such a measure; but I considered myself as intrusted also with the protection of Hepburn's, a man, who, by his humane attentions and devotedness, had so endeared himself to me, that I felt more anxiety for his safety than for my own. Michel had gathered no *tripe de roche*, and it was evident to us that he had halted for the purpose of putting his gun in order, with the intention of attacking us, perhaps, whilst we were in the act of encamping.

I have dwelt in the preceding part of the narrative upon many circumstances of Michel's conduct, not for the purpose of aggravating his crime, but to put the reader in possession of the reasons that influenced me in depriving a fellow-creature of life. Up to the period of his return to the tent, his conduct had been good and respectful to the officers, and in a conversation between Captain Franklin, Mr. Hood, and myself, at Obstruction Rapid, it had been proposed to give him a reward upon our arrival at a post. His principles, however, unsupported by a belief in the divine truths of Christianity, were unable to withstand the pressure of severe distress. His countrymen, the Iroquois, are generally Christians, but he was totally uninstructed and ignorant of the duties inculcated by Christianity; and from his long residence in the Indian country, seems to have imbibed, or retained, the rules of conduct which the Southern Indians prescribe to themselves. . . .

On the 28th we rose at day-break, but from the want of the small fire, that we usually made in the mornings to warm our fingers, a very long time was spent in making up our bundles. This task fell to Hepburn's share, as I suffered so much from the cold as to be unable to take my hands out of my mittens. We kept a straight course for the Dog-rib Rock, but, owing to the depth of the snow in the valleys we had to cross, did not reach it until late in the afternoon. We would have encamped, but did not like to pass a second night without fire; and though scarcely able to drag our limbs after us, we pushed on to a clump of pines, about a mile to the southward of the rock, and arrived at them in the dusk of the evening. During the last few hundred yards of our march, our track lay over some large stones, amongst which I fell down upwards of twenty times, and became at length so exhausted that I was unable to stand. If Hepburn had not exerted himself far beyond his strength, and speedily made the encampment and kindled a fire, I must have perished on the spot. This night we had plenty of dry wood.

On the 29th we had clear and fine weather. We set out at sunrise, and hurried on in our anxiety to reach the house, but our progress was much impeded by the great depth of the snow in the valleys. Although every spot of ground over which we travelled to-day, had been repeatedly trodden by us, yet we got bewildered in a small lake. We took it for Marten Lake, which was three times its size, and fancied that we saw the rapid and the grounds about the fort, although they were still far distant. Our disappointment when this illusion was dispelled, by our reaching the end of the lake, so operated on our feeble minds as to exhaust our strength, and we decided upon encamping; but upon ascending a small eminence to look for a clump of wood, we caught a glimpse of the Big-Stone, a well known rock upon the summit of a hill opposite to the Fort, and determined upon proceeding. In the evening we saw several large herds of rein-deer, but Hepburn, who used to be considered a good marksman, was now unable to hold the gun straight, and although he got near them all his efforts proved fruitless. In passing through a small clump of pines we saw a flock of partridges, and he succeeded in killing one after firing several shots. We came in sight of the fort at dusk, and it is impossible to describe our sensations, when on attaining the eminence that overlooks it, we beheld the smoke issuing from one of the chimneys. From not having met with any footsteps in the snow, as we drew nigh our once cheerful residence, we had been agitated by many melancholy forebodings. Upon entering the now desolate building, we had the satisfaction of embracing Captain Franklin, but no words can convey an idea of the filth and wretchedness that met our eyes on looking around. Our own misery had stolen upon us by degrees, and we were accustomed to the contemplation of each other's emaciated figures, but the ghastly countenances, dilated eye-balls, and sepulchral voices of Mr. Franklin and those with him were more than we could at first bear.

Franklin's narrative resumes. . . .

November 1. — This day was fine and mild. Hepburn went hunting, but was as usual unsuccessful. As his strength was rapidly declining, we advised him to desist from the pursuit of deer; and only to go out for a short time, and endeavour to kill a few partridges for Peltier and Semandrè. The Doctor obtained a little *tripe de roche*, but Peltier could not eat any of it, and Semandrè only a few spoonfuls, owing to the soreness of their throats. In the afternoon Peltier was so much exhausted, that he sat up with difficulty, and looked piteously; at length he slided from his stool upon his bed, as we supposed to sleep, and in this composed state he remained upwards of two hours, without our apprehending any danger. We were then alarmed by hearing a rattling in his throat, and on the Doctor's examining him, he was found to be speechless. He died in the course of the night. Semandrè sat up the greater part of the day, and even assisted in pounding some bones; but on witnessing the melancholy state of Peltier, he became very low, and began to complain of cold and stiffness of the joints. Being unable to keep up a sufficient fire to warm him, we laid him down and covered him with several blankets. He did not, however, appear to get better and I deeply lament to add he also died before daylight. We removed the bodies of the deceased into the opposite part of the house, but our united strength was inadequate to the task of interring them, or even carrying them down to the river.

It may be worthy of remark that poor Peltier, from the time of Benoit's departure, had fixed on the first of November as the time when he should cease to expect any relief from the Indians, and had repeatedly said that if they did not arrive by that day, he should not survive.

Peltier had endeared himself to each of us by his cheerfulness, his unceasing activity, and affectionate care and attentions, ever since our arrival at this place. He had nursed Adam with the tenderest solicitude the whole time. Poor Samandrè was willing to have taken his share in the labours of the party, had he not been wholly incapacitated by his weakness and low spirits. The severe shock occasioned by the sudden dissolution of our two companions rendered us very melancholy. Adam became low and despondent, a change which we lamented the more, as we had perceived he had been gaining strength and spirits for the two preceding days. I was particularly distressed by the thought that the labour of collecting wood must now devolve upon Dr. Richardson and Hepburn, and that my debility would disable me from affording them any material assistance; indeed both of them most kindly urged me not to make the attempt. They were occupied the whole of the next day in tearing down the logs of which the store-house was built, but the mud plastered between them was so hard frozen that the labour of separation exceeded their strength, and they were completely exhausted by bringing in wood sufficient for less than twelve hours' consumption.

I found it necessary in their absence, to remain constantly near Adam, and to converse with him, in order to prevent his reflecting on our condition, and to keep up his spirits as far as possible. I also lay by his side at night. . . .

The next day [the 6th] was fine, but very cold. The swellings in Adam's limbs having subsided, he was free from pain, and arose this morning in much better spirits, and spoke of cleaning his gun ready for shooting partridges, or any animals that might appear near the house, but his tone entirely changed before the day was half over; he became again dejected, and could scarcely be prevailed upon to eat. The Doctor and Hepburn were almost exhausted. The cutting of one log of wood occupied the latter half an hour; and the other took as much time to drag it into the house, though the distance did not exceed thirty yards. I endeavoured to help the Doctor, but my assistance was very trifling. Yet it was evident that, in a day or two, if their strength should continue to decline at the same rate, I should be the strongest of the party.

I may here remark that owing to our loss of flesh, the hardness of the floor, from which we were only protected by a blanket, produced soreness over the body, and especially those parts on which the weight rested in lying, yet to turn ourselves for relief was a matter of toil and difficulty. However, during this period, and indeed all along after the acute pains of hunger, which lasted but three or four days, had subsided, we generally enjoyed the comfort of a few hours' sleep. The dreams which for the most part, but not always accompanied it, were usually (though not invari- ably,) of a pleasant character, being very often about the enjoyments of feasting. In the day-time we fell into the practice of conversing on common and light subjects, although we sometimes discussed with seriousness and earnestness topics con- nected with religion. We generally avoided speaking directly of our present sufferings, or even of the prospect of relief. I observed, that in proportion as our strength decayed, our minds exhibited symptoms of weakness, evinced by a kind of unreasonable pettishness with each other. Each of us thought the other weaker in intellect than himself, and more in need of advice and assistance. So trifling a circumstance as a change of place, recommended by one as being warmer and more comfortable, and refused by the other from a dread of motion, frequently called forth fretful expressions which were no sooner uttered than atoned for, to be repeated perhaps in the course of a few minutes. The same thing often occurred when we endeavoured to assist each other in carrying wood to the fire; none of us were willing to receive assistance, although the task was disproportioned to our strength. On one of these occasions Hepburn was so convinced of this waywardness that he exclaimed, 'Dear me, if we are spared to return to England, I wonder if we shall recover our understandings.'

November 7.—Adam had passed a restless night, being disquieted by gloomy apprehensions of approaching death, which we tried in vain to dispel. He was so low in the morning as to be scarcely able to speak. I remained in bed by his side to cheer him as much as possible. The Doctor and Hepburn went to cut wood. They had hardly begun their labour, when they were amazed at hearing the report of a musket. They could scarcely believe that there was really any one near, until they heard a shout, and immediately espied three Indians close to the house. Adam and I heard the latter noise, and I was fearful that a part of the house had fallen upon one of my companions, a disaster which had in fact been thought not unlikely. My alarm was only momentary. Dr. Richardson came in to communicate the joyful intelligence that relief had arrived. He and myself immediately addressed thanksgiving to the throne of mercy for this deliverance, but poor Adam was in so low a state that he could scarcely comprehend the information. When the Indians entered, he attempted to rise but sank down again. But for this seasonable interposition of Providence, his existence must have terminated in a few hours, and that of the rest probably in not many days.

The Indians had left Akaitcho's encampment on the 5th November, having been sent by Mr. Back with all possible expedition, after he had arrived at their tents. They brought but a small supply of provision that they might travel quickly. It consisted of dried deer's meat, some fat, and a few tongues. Dr. Richardson, Hepburn, and I, eagerly devoured the food, which they imprudently presented to us, in too great abundance, and in consequence we suffered dreadfully from indigestion, and had no rest the whole night. Adam being unable to feed himself, was more judiciously treated by them, and suffered less; his spirits revived hourly. The circumstance of our eating more food than was proper in our present condition, was another striking proof of the debility of our minds. We were perfectly aware of the danger, and Dr. Richardson repeatedly cautioned us to be moderate; but he was himself unable to practise the caution he so judiciously recommended. . . .

November 8.—The Indians this morning requested us to remove to an encampment on the banks of the river, as they were unwilling to remain in the house in which the bodies of our deceased companions were lying exposed to view. We agreed to remove, but the day proved too stormy, and Dr. Richardson and Hepburn having dragged the bodies to a short distance, and covered them with snow, the objections of the Indians to remain in the house were removed and they began to clear our room of the accumulation of dirt and fragments of pounded bones. The improved state of our apartment and the large and cheerful fires they kept up, produced in us a sensation of comfort to which we had long been strangers. In the evening they brought in a pile of dried wood, which was lying on the river-side, and on which we had often cast a wishful eye, being unable to drag it up the bank. The Indians set about every thing with an activity that amazed us. Indeed, contrasted with our emaciated figures and extreme debility, their frames appeared to us gigantic, and their strength supernatural. These kind creatures next turned their attention to our personal appearance, and prevailed upon us to shave and wash ourselves. The beards of the Doctor and Hepburn had been untouched since they left the seacoast, and were become of a hideous length, and peculiarly offensive to the Indians.[35] The Doctor and I suffered extremely from distention, and therefore ate sparingly. Hepburn was getting better, and Adam recovered his strength with amazing rapidity. . . .

The natives unexpectedly depart in search of assistance

[*November 14*] On the following day the Doctor and Hepburn resumed their former occupation of collecting wood, and I was able to assist a little in bringing it into the house. Adam, whose expectation of the arrival of the Indians had been raised by the fineness of the weather, became, towards night, very desponding, and refused to eat the singed skin. The night was stormy, and there was a heavy fall of snow. The next day he became still more dejected. About eleven Hepburn, who had gone out for wood, came in with the intelligence that a party appeared upon the river. The room was instantly swept, and, in compliance with the prejudices of the Indians, every scrap of skin was carefully removed out of sight; for these simple people imagine, that burning deer-skin renders them unsuccessful in hunting. The party proved to be Crooked-Foot, Thoo-ee-yorre, and the Fop, with the wives of the two latter dragging provisions. They were accompanied by Benoit, one of our own men.

We were rejoiced to learn, by a note from Mr. Back, dated November 11, that he and his companions had so recruited their strength that they were preparing to proceed to Fort Providence. Adam recovered his spirits on the arrival of the Indians, and even walked about the room with an appearance of strength and activity that surprised us all. As it was of consequence to get amongst the rein-deer before our present supply should fail, we made preparations for quitting Fort Enterprise the next day; and, accordingly, at an early hour, on the 16th, having united in thanksgiving and prayer, the whole party left the house after breakfast. Our feelings on quitting the Fort, where we had formerly enjoyed much comfort, if not happiness, and, latterly, experienced a degree of misery scarcely to be paralleled, may be more easily conceived than described. The Indians treated us with the utmost tenderness, gave us their snow-shoes, and walked without themselves, keeping by our sides, that they might lift us when we fell. We descended Winter River, and, about noon, crossed the head of Round-Rock Lake, distant about three miles from the house, where we were obliged to halt, as Dr. Richardson was unable to proceed. The swellings in his limbs rendered him by much the weakest of the party. The Indians prepared our encampment, cooked for us, and fed us as if we had been children; evincing humanity that would have done honour to the most civilized people. The night was mild, and fatigue made us sleep soundly.

From this period to the 26th of November we gradually continued to improve, under the kindness and attention of our Indians. On this day we arrived in safety at the abode of our chief and companion, Akaitcho. We were received by the party assembled in the leader's tent, with looks of compassion and profound silence, which lasted about a quarter of an hour, and by which they meant to express their condolence for our sufferings. The conversation did not begin until we had tasted food. The Chief, Akaitcho, shewed us the most friendly hospitality, and all sorts of personal attention, even to cooking for us with his own hands, an office which he never performs for himself. Annoethai-yazzeh and Humpy, the Chief's two brothers, and several of our hunters, with their families, were encamped here, together with a number of old men and women. In the course of the day we were visited by every person of the band, not merely from curiosity, I conceive, but rather from a desire to evince their tender sympathy in our late distress. . . . .

In the afternoon of the 6th, Belanger, and another Canadian, arrived from Fort Providence, sent by Mr. Weeks, with two trains of dogs, some spirits and tobacco for the Indians, a change of dress for ourselves, and a little tea and sugar. They also brought letters for us from England, and from Mr. Back and Mr. Wentzel. By the former we received the gratifying intelligence of the successful termination of Captain Parry's voyage;[36] and were informed of the promotion of myself and Mr. Back, and of poor Hood, our grief for whose loss was renewed by this intelligence.[37] The gratification which it would otherwise have afforded, was materially damped by our sincere regret that he had not lived to receive this just reward of his merit and services. The letter from Mr. Back stated, that the rival Companies in the fur trade had united; but that, owing to some cause which had not been explained to him, the goods intended as rewards to Akaitcho and his band, which we had demanded in the spring from the North-West Company, were not sent. . . . .[38]

[*December 14*] In the afternoon of the 14th, Akaitcho, with his whole band, came to the Fort. He smoked his customary pipe, and made an address to Mr. Weeks in the hall, previous to his coming into the room in which Dr. Richardson and I were. We discovered at the commencement of his speech to us, that he had been informed that our expected supplies had not come. He spoke of this circumstance as a disappointment, indeed, sufficiently severe to himself, to whom his band looked up for the protection of their interests, but without attaching any blame to us. 'The world goes badly,' he said, 'all are poor, you are poor, the traders appear to be poor, I and my party are poor likewise; and since the goods have not come in, we cannot have them. I do not regret having supplied you with provisions, for a Copper Indian can never permit white men to suffer from want of food on his lands, without flying to their aid. I trust, however, that we shall, as you say, receive what is due next autumn; and at all events', he added, in a tone of good-humour, 'it is the first time that the white people have been indebted to the Copper Indians.' We assured him the supplies should certainly be sent to him by the autumn, if not before. He then cheerfully received the small present we made to himself; and, although we could give a few things only to those who had been most active in our service, the others who, perhaps, thought themselves equally deserving, did not murmur at being left out in the distribution. Akaitcho afterwards expressed a strong desire, that we should represent the character of his nation in a favourable light to our countrymen. 'I know,' he said, 'you write down every occurrence in your books; but probably you have only noticed the bad things we have said and done, and have omitted to mention the good.' In the course of the desultory conversation which ensued, he said, that he had been always told by us, to consider the traders in the same light as ourselves; and that, for his part, he looked upon both as equally respectable.... After this conference, such Indians as were indebted to the Company were paid for the provision they had given us, by deducting a corresponding sum from their debts; in the same way we gave a reward of sixteen skins of beaver to each of the persons who had come to our relief at Fort Enterprise. As the debts of Akaitcho and his hunters had been effaced at the time of his engagement with us, we placed a sum, equal to the amount of provision they had recently supplied, to their credit on the Company's books. These things being, through the moderation of the Indians, adjusted with an unexpected facility, we gave them a keg of mixed liquors, (five parts water,) and distributed among them several fathoms of tobacco, and they retired to their tents to spend the night in merriment....

Franklin leaves Fort Chipewyan for Hudson Bay

We were here furnished with a canoe by Mr. Smith, and a bowman, to act as our guide; and having left Fort Chipewyan on the 5th [of June], we arrived, on the 4th of July, at Norway House. Finding, at this place, that canoes were about to go down to Montreal, I gave all our Canadian voyagers their discharges, and sent them by those vessels, furnishing them with orders on the Agent of the Hudson's Bay Company, for the amount of their wages. We carried Augustus down to York Factory, where we arrived on the 14th of July, and were received with every mark of attention and kindness by Mr. Simpson, the Governor, Mr. McTavish, and, indeed, by all the officers of the United Companies. And thus terminated our long, fatiguing, and disastrous travels in North America, having journeyed by water and by land (including our navigation of the Polar Sea,) five thousand five hundred and fifty miles.

Notes

[1] Sir John Richardson (1787–1865) was only 32 when he travelled with Franklin; he later attained great eminence as a surgeon and scientist. Richardson returned to the Arctic in 1848 with Dr John Rae to search for Franklin when he failed to return from his third expedition (see LETITIA HARGRAVE). He kept a journal of the first expedition, from which Franklin includes a long excerpt (see below); it was edited by C. Stuart Houston in 1984.

[2] Robert Hood (c. 1797–1821), naval officer, explorer, and artist. Hood joined the navy at 12, and had already served in Europe when he was appointed midshipman on the Franklin expedition. In later years John Hepburn (see below, n. 26) maintained that during the expedition Hood and George Back had almost fought a duel over the attractive native woman known as Green-Stockings. Hood painted a memorable watercolour sketch of her, and she bore him a daughter, whom Hepburn appears to have believed was still alive in 1851. Hood does not mention her in his own journal, which was edited by C. Stuart Houston in 1974.

[3] The Hudson's Bay Company was attempting to drive the North West Company out of the Athabasca region, and Franklin's expedition was fraught with tensions resulting from his need

to remain on good terms with both parties. Angus Shaw, John George McTavish (uncle of LETITIA HARGRAVE), and several others had been ambushed by Governor William Williams in June 1819 at the Grand Rapid on the Saskatchewan River (Grand Rapids in present-day Manitoba). They were imprisoned at York Factory on charges of murder, robbery, and burglary; the ghost of Benjamin Frobisher, who died while escaping, turns up in the *Letter Journal* of GEORGE NELSON. The North West Company was to counter with indictments of its own, but by 1821 the two companies were amalgamated; news of the union reached Franklin near the end of his journey (see below).

[4] Richardson's dilemma is that faced by many early ethnographers: the difficulty of analysing an aboriginal 'honour society' from the sole perspective of Christian European culture; as one of the most learned men ever to explore Canada, he is aware of the problem, but cannot escape it.

[5] Alcoholism troubled nineteenth-century English men and women in the same way the drug trade concerns us today; Franklin and his fellow officers were profoundly shocked by the long-term effects of liquor on the Cumberland House Cree.

[6] Akaitcho was chief of a dwindling band of Copper (or Yellowknife) Indians to whom Franklin was deeply indebted for assistance in establishing Fort Enterprise, and for advice before undertaking his northward journey. It was Akaitcho's people who rescued the dying explorers at Fort Enterprise in November; his own later address to the members of the English party is memorable for its philosophic insight and its gentle irony (see below).

[7] William Wilberforce (1759–1833), British parliamentarian, and a leader in the fight to abolish the slave trade in the British Empire.

[8] Rear-Admiral Sir George Back (1796–1878), naval officer, explorer, artist, and poet. Dashing and sophisticated, not to say vain, he was nevertheless intrepid. He was a member of Franklin's second expedition (1824–27), and despite ill-health undertook two later expeditions of his own, and participated in planning the Admiralty's searches for Franklin in 1847–56. His fifteen-stanza poem on the first Franklin expedition is still in manuscript. He produced many important sketches and watercolours of Arctic life and scenery. For his quarrel with Hood over the native woman Green-Stockings see note 2 above. Franklin seems to have handled Back by giving him independent responsibilities whenever possible.

[9] Any expedition on foot was dependent on a constant supply of moccasins, which wore out quickly; the native and Métis women who made them were an essential part of most travelling parties, including Franklin's in its earlier stages.

[10] Up to this point the 'men' — the voyageurs and presumably John Hepburn (see below) — as distinct from the 'officers' routinely carried all the baggage and supplies.

[11] For 'portable soup', see VANCOUVER, note 9.

[12] Joseph Benoit, voyageur, who survived the journey.

[13] Hoeootoerock, known as Junius, Eskimo translator and canoeman; he was separated from the party when they crossed the Coppermine River at Obstruction Rapid (see below), and presumably perished.

[14] Pierre St Germain, Métis interpreter, whose inventiveness finally made it possible for the party to cross the Coppermine River at Obstruction Rapid (see below). He survived the journey.

[15] Jean-Baptiste Adam, interpreter; he was among those rescued at Fort Enterprise.

[16] Joseph Peltier, voyageur; he died 1 November, at Fort Enterprise.

[17] Throughout this part of its journey, Franklin's party is travelling in the area traversed fifty years earlier by SAMUEL HEARNE; Congecathawhachaga is at the north end of Contwoyto Lake.

[18] Mathew Pelonquin, called Crédit, voyageur; he rejoined the party on this occasion, but eventually died on or about 6 October.

[19]Michel Teroahauté, an Iroquois voyageur; for his fate, see the excerpt from Dr Richardson's narrative included by Franklin, below.

[20]Ignace Perrault, voyageur, who perished some time in October; Michel may have used his body for food (see below).

[21]Voyageur; he eventually reached Fort Providence with Back. To be distinguished from Jean-Baptiste Belanger, who died somewhere near Hood and Richardson on 9 October (see below).

[22]Tattannoeuck, known as Augustus, Eskimo guide. He also participated in Franklin's expedition of 1825–7, and in Back's of 1833–5.

[23]Dip: inclination of the magnetic needle towards the horizon; variation: compass variation.

[24]Registe Vaillant, voyageur; he died 6 October.

[25]Obstruction Rapid.

[26]John Hepburn (1794–1864), seaman, first served under Franklin in 1818. After their return from the Arctic in 1822 he remained fast friends with his Captain, and accompanied him when he became Governor of Van Dieman's Land (Tasmania) in 1836. In 1851 he participated in one of the many expeditions sent to search for Franklin, and his shipboard reminiscences provide some background information on the personal relationships of those who travelled with Franklin in 1819–22.

[27]François Samandré, voyageur; he died on 1 November, at Fort Enterprise.

[28]Gabriel Beauparlant, voyageur; he died 17 October.

[29]Jean-Baptiste Belanger, voyageur; to be distinguished from Solomon Belanger (above). Jean-Baptiste later turned back with Michel to stay with Richardson and Hood, and may have been killed and eaten by Michel (see below) on or about 9 October.

[30]Willard Ferdinand Wentzel, North West Company trader at Fort Providence; he had accompanied Franklin's party as far as the Arctic Ocean, but returned when the party began its coastal exploration eastward.

[31]Vincenza or Antonio Fontano (Franklin uses both names), Italian voyageur; a former soldier in De Meuron's regiment, a unit which was originally Swiss, and later British; when it disbanded in 1816 many of its continental soldiers elected to remain in Canada. Franklin had been forced to leave him behind on 7 October.

[32]See below.

[33]Thus the original edition; the correct date is 9 October.

[34]Edward Bickersteth (1786–1850), evangelical Church of England divine; his *A Scripture Help, Designed to Assist in Reading the Bible Profitably* (London, 1816) had gone into five editions by 1819, and remained popular for many years.

[35][Franklin's note] The first alvine discharges [movements] after we received food, were, as Hearne remarks on a similar occasion, attended with excessive pain. Previous to the arrival of the Indians the urinary secretion was extremely abundant, and we were obliged to rise from bed in consequence upwards of ten times in a night. This was an extreme annoyance in our reduced state. It may, perhaps, be attributed to the quantity of the country tea that we drank.

[36]Sir William Edward Parry, R.N. (1790–1855), Arctic explorer. Parry led three expeditions in search of the Northwest Passage (1819, 1821, and 1824); the news Franklin receives is of the first, which ended in 1820.

[37]Franklin was promoted from captain to commander, Hood and Back from midshipman to lieutenant.

[38]Franklin was deeply embarrassed at his inability to reward the natives, who had not only supplied the expedition, but rescued its survivors.

George Nelson   (1786 – 1859)

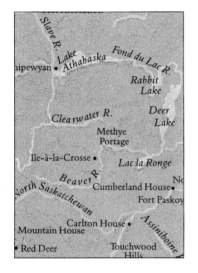

GEORGE NELSON was born in Montreal to an English schoolmaster and his wife who eventually settled in Sorel (William Henry), Quebec. Between 1802 and 1823 he was a clerk with, in succession, the XY Company, the North West Company, and the Hudson's Bay Company. From his earliest years trading in Wisconsin he eagerly observed and recorded native life. Nelson became fluent in Ojibwa, and also learned some Cree; his two wives were both natives. He absorbed as much as he could of native ways, and wrote voluminously about the Cree and Ojibwa with whom he lived and worked. The result has been called 'one of the finest early ethnographic documents of its kind'. Nelson's writings show that he was a literate man with a good education; the books he later came across acquainted him with Enlightenment ideas about the ideal character of humans in their natural state, and he struggled to maintain a balance between these ideas, his knowledge of native religion, and his own Christian faith. The religious practices described here with such extraordinary humour and sympathy were related to his father William in a letter-journal written between March and June 1823 when he was stationed at Lac La Ronge. Made redundant after union, he left the HBC in 1823 and returned to Montreal, where — unsuccessful in business, and often ill — he persevered in recording his experiences in manuscripts which are only now beginning to be published.

Text: *'The Orders of the Dreamed': George Nelson on Cree and Northern Ojibwa Religion and Myth, 1823*, ed. Jennifer S.H. Brown and Robert Brightman. Manitoba Studies in Native History III. Winnipeg: The University of Manitoba Press, 1988.

Dreaming to Conjure[1] and Predict

There are but few individuals (i.e., men) among the Sauteux or Cris or Crees who have not their medicine bags — and [are not] initiated into some ceremoney or other, but it is not *all* of them who can conjur. Among some tribes, most of them can; and among others again, there are but very few. Nor is it every one of them that tells *all truth*, some scarcely nothing but lies, others again not one falsehood, and this depends upon their *Dreamed*, sometimes, but I think may be equally imputed to their own selves, i.e., Presumption, ignorance, folly, or any other of our passions or weaknesses. But to become conjurors, they have rights [rites] and ceremonies to Perform and go through, which, tho' apparently simple and absurd, yet I have no doubt but fully answer their ends. Any Person among them wishing to dive into futurity, must be young and unpolluted, at any age between 18 and 25, tho' as near as I can [tell] born between 17 and 20 years old. They must have had no intercourse with any of the other Sex — they must be chaste and unpolluted. In the spring of the year they chuse a proper place at a sufficient distance from the camp not [to] be discovered nor disturbed. They make themselves a bed of Grass, or hay as we term it, and have besides enough to make them a covering. When all this is done — and they do it entirely alone, they strip stark naked and put all their things a good way off and then return, ly on this bed and then cover themselves with the rest of the Grass. Here they remain and endeavour to *sleep*, which from their nature is no very difficult task. But during whatever time they may remain, they must neither eat or drink. If they want to Dream of the spirits above, their bed must be made at some distance from the Ground — if of Spirits inhabiting our Earth, or those residing in the waters, on the Ground. Here they ly for a longer or shorter time, according to their success, or the orders of the Dreamed. Some remain but 3 or 4 days, some 10, and I have be[en] told one remained 30 days without eating or drinking, such was the delight he received from his Dreams! When I laughed at this, the man was vexed, and the others not a little hurt.

The first thing they do after their return to their friends is to take a good drink of water, smoke the Pipe; and after that eat, but as composedly as if they had but just risen from a hearty meal. Their *Dreamed* sometimes order them to make a Feast; and not uncommonly tell them where to go, where they will find the animal whose flesh is to be served up (i.e., always boiled) &c. They sometimes lie in one Posture, and sometimes in another, i.e. their head to some one of the Cardinal Points. Some have the most pleasant dreams imaginable; others indifferent. When they are to live to a good old age (!!!) they are told — 'You will see many winters! Your head will grow quite white'; or, 'tho' you shall never see your head white, yet you shall live till you are obliged to make use of a stick, and long after' — 'You shall die old, very old, respected and regretted.' If they are to die young . . . 'Thou shalt see the years of a young man'; and so on of the other ages, as well of the manner of life they shall have; and the language is not very dissimilar to that of our version of the Bible. But that stile [style] seems to me to be the language of Nature which *I* always find the more charming the more retired the *speaker* is from the Pompous, bombastic walks of high life, which, tho' they furnish us with more ideas, I do not think adds much to the beauty of the language.

The Spirits, their Shapes, and their Songs

As I have said before, the purpose of these Dreams is to dive into futurity. Every thing in nature appears unto them, but in the Shape of a human-being. They dream they meet a man who asks them (after some preliminary conversation of course), 'Dost thou know me? (who or what I am)?'

'No.'

'Follow me then,' replies this stranger. The indian follows — the other leads him to his abode and again makes the inquiry — the answer is perhaps as before. Then the Stranger assumes his proper form, which is perhaps that of a Tree, a Stone, a fish, &c, &c. and after rechanging several times in this manner, till such times as the 2nd becomes perfectly to know him, then this stranger gives him to smoke, learns him *his* Song, &c, thus addressing him: 'Now don't you remember my Song? . . . Whenever you will wish to call upon me, Sing this Song, and I shall not be far — I will come and do for you what you require.'

They know many of *these* spirits as soon as they see them (in their dreams) by the description the other indians have given to them — some, however, they know from their Nature. When the *Snow* addresses them — he they know, because he is perfectly white. The *Ice* also. The Sun and Moon from their beautifull brilliancy and the elegance of their abode. The Houses of the two last being uncommonly neat and handsome, such as those of the white (i.e., Civilised).

The Supreme Being

The Principal amongst all these [spirits] and every thing in Nature appears at least to some of them, is the Supreme Being, whom they term Wee-suck-a-jaak (the last a's being pronounced as in, all, hawk, &c; the first as ale, bail, &c), i.e. by his Proper name, his common name, Key-shay-mani-to (this is among the Crees Nation) which signifies 'The Greatly charitable Spirit'.[2] He is uncommonly good and kind, addresses them and talk[s] to them as to children whom he most tenderly loves and is extremely anxious for. Thus far every thing is very well, and is perhaps a better *idea* than many of the vulgar christians can give; but on the other hand again their Mythology, or stories relating to him, are many of them absurd and indecent in the highest degree: reducing him to the level of his creatures, and not unfrequently making him their dupe; but become so by such vile, such abominable deception as I doubt to be equalled by the most absurd and romantic of the arabian Tales, for there are many of these Tales the author durst not publish for the abscenity and indecency. There are some obscene passages also in these tales (of the indians) but not more than might be expected from a people yet in a perfect state of nature, as to their mental Powers, to our eternal shame and scandal. This one they love, they love him a great deal, and are by no means afraid of him, because he always addresses them, 'My Little Children, &c' and all the rest of his character is of a piece with this.

Old Nick (Key-jick-oh-kay)[3]

The Next one is Old Nick. Him some term 'Key-jick-oh-kay' (the J being pronounced soft, as Git, or Gil, in french, for I know of no English word where properly speaking the J is of any use and has the sound seemed intended by it) or 'Key-jick-oh-*kaiw*.' I cannot at present give the proper signification of this name, for I am not sufficiently acquainted with the language, but it appears to me as to mean 'he who made the Day or Skies or resides in the Sky.' &c. This one they represent wicked, and terrible, inexorible to the highest degree; always plotting evil, and endeavouring to circumvent the rest of the creation; is always jawing and bawling; but when the other appears he orders him in a peremptory manner, 'hold thy Tongue; Get thee hence, thou deceiver; thou ill-liver.' But these words are uttered on such an authoritative and commanding tone that the Indians themselves are quite astonished, to see so tender and affectionate, even in the choice of his words, assume so suddenly and with so much authority, so much Power over one whose name alone they never utter but with the greatest dread and horor. Their Horor of the Devil is so great, that no one ever utters it but when unavoidable; and if thro' inadvertancy or ignorance one of their children should mention it he is severely reprimanded by all who hear.

Other Beings

There is also the Sea Serpent,[4] a monstrous animal and has much Power; the Mermaid (or Sea Man),[5] the Water Lynx, or rather Tyger[6] — a dreadful character this last, who keeps all the Inhabitants of the deep in the Greatest Subjection — there are however one or two who contend with him; and sometimes he is reduced to the necessity of compounding with them. The Great Turtle,[7] and many others. They have their abodes in the Deep, but perfectly dry and comfortable. Each one of these, and indeed all of them have their stories or Mythology; some I forget intirely, and others remember too incorrectly to mention at present . . . when any one conjures, if he is renouned Medicine Man, they all appear, and Speak to him, mostly in his own language, some few excepted as the Pike (or Jack fish) who speaks french;[8] the Sun and Moon,[9] both speak English; the Bull or Buffaloe[10] is an unknown or at least strange language; but all perfectly intelligible to the Conjuror.

The Sun; Nelson's Dream

I am quite astray — leaving the proper thread of my story to follow one of its branches — I ought to have said that the Sun when he appears to an indian, he is seen in the Heavens, as an Indian (i.e., a Man) '*Walking on the Wind*.' His dress is of a variety of colors and handsome. I had a dream in the month of February, the latter part of which I shall relate to you as it is perfectly descriptive of the manner or form in which the Sun appears. I related it the next day to some of my half-breeds, when one of them replied: 'What a pity! Had you now forborne for a few days mentioning *this*, he would have appeared again to you; and then you would have had a fine opportunity of learning (from the fountain-head, as we may say) how it is the indians come to perform those things the white will never credit': and he continued that it was precisely the form he [the Sun] assumed when he appears to the indians.

In my dream I thought we were travelling a road from which some of our Party had the utmost to dread from the ambush of an indian who could transport himself to what place he pleased. As we were walking I happened to look above and was much struck with the appearance of a man walking in the Heavens. His dress was that of a neat *Southern* [Cree] Indian, composed mostly of red and yellow, but also of a few other colors: The Garters of his leggings were also Neat and handsome and had a tuft of swansdown that had been Powdered with vermillion, attached to the [k]not, on the back part of the leg. To his shoes were attached 2 long Swan quills inclosing the foot thus with a tuft of down at each end and in the middle of both sides, all Powdered with vermillion — with these quills and down, and the down on his Garters buoyed him up in the air. I addressed [him] in broken Cree — he answered in the same broken accent; upon my second address I though[t] he did not understand more of that language than I did myself: The Sauteux seemed to me his proper tongue and I was glad of having an opportunity of speaking that language; so I the third time addressed him in it, asked him from whence he came, whither he was going, &c, &c. He was very hi[gh] insomuch that the others thought it preprosterous in my addressing him — that he could not hear from that distance. Upon this, he came down and talked with us — saying he was an ambassador &c. Such is the habillement, and manner in which the Sun shews himself.

The Thunder also appears to them, in the shape and form of a most beautiful bird (The Pea-Cock).[11]

Roots and Herbs

Roots and herbs also (this ought also to have come in afterwards), i.e., such as are medicinal, appear, and teach their votaries their respective Songs — how they must do, what ceremonies they must perform in taking them out of the Ground, their different application, &c. &c. But these roots, herbs, &c. (medecins), tho' they appear in their Dreams, they do not shew themselves in the Conjuring Hut, box, or frame, that I learn. They are sent, as appears, by Wee-suck-a-jaak, 'to teach indians their use and virtue,' &c, without which 'they would be very ill off, whether to heal or cure themselves, or expell the charms by which other indians may have bewitched them,' &c. And tho' they are acquainted with many of these roots &c, the use and virtue of some of which I can no more doubt than those used by the Faculty[12] in the Civilised world, yet they tell me there are several which they use to different, and some to diametrically opposite purposes.

The Manner of Conjuring

Their manner of conjuring is this — in the first place a number [of] straight poles of 2, or 2¹/₂ ins. diameter and about 8 or 9 feet long are prepared, i.e., cut, branched and Pointed at the lower end — they seldom require so *few* as four, commonly 6 or 8, these are planted in the Ground from 12 to 20 or 24 ins. deep in an hexagon or octagon form, inclosing a space of 3 feet diameter, more or less — these Poles are secured by hoops, 3 or 4 in number, and well tied to each pole, so that none be able to move without the rest. This Hut, square, box, or frame, whatever it may be termed is covered with skins, an oil cloth, or some such sort of thing.[13] The Conjuror is bound hand and foot, not as if he were a man going to *pry* into futurity, but as a Criminal, i.e., a *mere*, pure Devil, and one whom they intend never to loosen, so barricaded and cross-corded is the creature, sometimes all crumpled into a heap. He is tied only with his Cloute on him and thus thurst into the hut, underneath, i.e., by raising the lower covering — his 'she-she-quay'[14] or rather with him. Some of them sing on entering, others make a speech. Here they remain, some several hours, others not 5 minutes, before a fluttering is heard. The rattler is shaked at a merry rate and all of a Sudden, either from the top or below, away flies the cords by which the indian was tied *into the lap of he who tied him.*

The Spirits Enter: Their Names and Natures

It is then that the Devil is at work — Every instant some one or other enters, which is known to those outside by either the fluttering, the rubbing against the Skins of the hut in descending (inside) or the shaking or the rattler, and sometimes all together. When any enter, the hut moves in a most violent manner — I have frequently thought that it would be knocked down, or torn out of the Ground. . . .

Conjuring at Lac La Ronge, June 1823

June 5th. These 3 last days have been busy and turbulent ones for me — it is now considerably past midnight (and of course the 6th of June) but my indians are drinking and as I cannot think of going to bed til they do I shall employ my few remaining *leisure* moments (till next year, please god I live so long) in giving you an account of a conjuring bout I with some difficulty got an indian to make last night (June *4th*). In the evening the hut was prepared at some distance from the houses on account of the Stink as the Spirits cannot, or will not endure any pollution — the hut consisted of 10 Poles about 7 feet out of Ground, well stuck in and somewhat better than 3 feet diameter — the Poles were secured with 2 hoops: they were covered with 2 Parchment skins (of Moose) well bound with many rounds of strong leather line: the *top was covered* with a dressed skin and secured also, to prevent its being carried off (by the wind).

About 10 p.m. (still broad day light with us) we drew up with the conjuror, smoked and chatted some time. After this he took his drum (much resembling a tambourine) and with a stick gently struck it all the time he made a speech: I was almost touching him (all seated) but from the noise of the drum and his low voice, for the man has a dreadful complaint in his lungs, I could only gather, 'take pity upon me; take pity upon me; hear and come; let me not speak in vain, nor become abashed — *show* me charity' &c. &c — it was a moderate and decent prayer. After this *they* (for there were several men) began to sing, using the drum and rattler — they sang among other the moose, horse, Bear, and Dog Songs; about a dozen in number.

When he prepared by taking off his clothes, all to his cloute, and asked who should tie him, I replied that I would, but was afraid of hurting him; another conjuror did beginning with his fingers between the 2 joints nearest the hand as nearly as I can describe it thus giving a double turn to the line between each finger, and the line was new mackerel,[15] small, which I happened to have in my pocket by accident. I drew up to *inspect* and observing the fingers to swell upon his complaining of the tightness I felt a good deal for him. After this his blanket was wrapped around him and tied in such a manner, lengthways, crossways and every way, and a good knot *I* tied at each meeting of the cords; for I assisted in *this*, that I could have laid wager that it was beyond the Power of Spirits themselves, thus tied, to eradicate [extricate] them- selves; and his hands were *under* his hams — as he could no more move than fly, of *himself*, the other conjuror and I put him to the door, but behold! it was with difficulty we could just get his head in, the entry being too narrow by about 10, or 12 ins. screwing and jam[m]ing considered.

'It will do, it will do,' said the conjuror — 'cover me now' — his back was covered with a blanket and we all retreated to our seats, myself about 4 feet distant. The others took the drum and began to sing. I could not help but laughing in myself and pitying the boldness of their vanity, but I had soon occasion to think otherwise and had I not predetermined that reason should conduct me throughout the whole of this, I cannot say how far in the *other* extreme *I* might have gone.

But to return: the conjuror desired the others to sing, they began a short song. I believe it was that of the *Stone*, and the man entered in an instant! I was struck dumb with astonishment; for he appeared to me to *slide* in by something that was neither invisible nor discernible — I heard some thing that for the life of me I cannot account for, and that's all: from the time we covered him (25 past 10 p.m.) to the time we had done hunting for the twine that tied his fingers, not quite 5 minutes elapsed, and not 1 1/2 minutes before his blanket and the cords were thrown out to us! — not one of them, apparently (i.e., one knot) *untied*! My astonishment and apprehensions of his being entirely carried off from us were such, that I was nearly springing up to haul him out, for fear of his being for ever lost. The others continued singing a few other songs and I had the utmost anxiety in hearing [him] repeatedly call out as if in the greatest apprehensions himself, 'enough! enough! Enough of ye I say'; and fre- quently for the space of some minutes repeating the same, and now and frequently for the space of some minutes repeating the same, and now and then calling out, 'do not *Thou* enter.'

The *Stone*[16] was the first one known to us, by his song; for every one almost that entered sang *his* song, to which those (the indians) on the outside would keep chorus.

A vast number entered. I verily beleive upward of an hundred; for upwards of that number of times the frame shook back-and-forwards and very smartly as if to fall; and among the first were some truly terrible characters. I have almost entirely converted myself from these foolish ideas of Ghost and hobgoblins, but I assure you in truth that I more than once felt very uneasy.

The Ice[17] entered — he made a noise extremely resembling that made by a person shivering with cold, loud, and hoarse and *liquid*. The Devil *himself* also entered *a propria persona*, in a very authoritative and commanding manner: I assure you there was no laughing nor giggling outside, all the time he sang and spoke.

The Turtle spoke as an old Jocular man. 'I hate the french; for in their travels when they find me, they kill me and eat me: I shall answer none of their questions,' but this was a joke; for he laughed.

'Speak out, Turtle, speak out, louder, that we hear thee,' said those without.

'I would too,' replied he, 'but my voice is so strong I must contract it thus, otherwise ye could not endure the sound of it. Stop!' continued he, 'I must imitate the drunk,' which he did to the great diversion of us all and concluded with snoring, the natural end of all drunken feasts, and then became quiet, on which another voice (which I also perfectly heard and understood as well [as] the Turtle herself [*sic*]) cried out — 'see! see! if she does not look like a frog stretched out,' and this raised a proper laugh both in and out.

The Dog[18] entered, and spoke perfectly plain and distinct, and with a more elegant and harmoni[o]us voice [than] I ever heard in my life. Bears, of 3 or 4 different sorts,[19] the horse, moose, Skeletons,[20] spirits of departed and *still living friends* entered; but none but the latter and above mentioned were to be understood by any but the conjuror himself.

On the entering of one, 'that is my (*adopted*) Son,' said an Indian seated by me and called out his name to which he readily answered besides questions: this young man and a girl, both living, spoke very plain (you must observe that it is not their bodies, but their Souls or Spirits that enter)—Children almost at the instant of birth, Dwarfs, Giants; but this latter did make a noise indeed.

We all laughted very heartily when the horse entered; for it appears he passed too near the Turtle who called out as the horse was flying about (in the inside) singing and rattling his rattler, 'I wish you would take care of yourself and *not tread on one* River', in allusion to his diminutive size in comparison with that of the horse.

It is somewhat surprising that every one that entered, whether he spoke plain, or was interpreted — their First words were, 'your lands are distressed — keep not on the Gr[an]d River' — sickness, sickness; 'but from amongst *ye here* I shall select only a few aged ones,' said one of the latter, but in a *voice* no one but the conjuror could understand.

As he went out, however, the Conjuror paid him a most bawdy compliment — we all laughed and asked what was the matter. 'Pah! nothing, I am only afraid of him,' said the Conj.

One of them that entered, apparently the Devil himself for he spoke and acted *en veritable maitre*, startled us all a great deal and enquired authoritatively and angrily, 'what want ye of me? — Speak?' Upon several hurried enquiries put to him he said that some things I saw and heard in my house this winter, were by Mr. Frobisher, who expired so dreadfully in 1819[21] — 'he is a Skeleton (Pah-kack); and it is he who built *this* house — he comes to see'!!!

Tho' I did certainly both hear and see, several times this winter, and once in particular, about 2 a.m., yet I do not feel much inclined to add faith to this assertion of Davy's[22] — I must have something more substantial. But I am much inclined to doubt master Davy's assertion and consider this and several others of his sayings at former Periods in the same light as those he delivered at many of [the] Grecian temples;[23] for I have every substantial reason to consider him as the same identical Gentleman: however, a short time hence will decide.

The Turtle said we should have a good deal of rain; but not a *very great deal*, and a very hi[gh] wind, and as soon as the Sun should appear, 'at its setting an indian' (naming him by a very extraordinary and bawdy feature in his person) 'should arrive and bring us meat; *but this you will eat of course, and I shall go without.*' ('Beware of yourselves — Tomorrow night you shall drink and be drunk: drunk and leave the house as soon as you can; *for there are from that wind*' (by which he designated the South) '*who if they drink with ye, ye shall become pitiful,*' alluding to two blackguard half breed brothers, who proud of the bravery of their deceased father are ever and anon insulting and domineering over the other indians: it is worthy of remark that an aged man in the course of this last winter was advertised of the Same, and repeatedly pressed not to drink at the house on their account.)

This is now the 6th (June) the Sun appears, but the wind is very hi[gh]: and we have frequent showers of rain and Snow.

About midnight the Conjuror addressed me and asked if I wished to see any of *them* (the Spirits). I accepted the offer and thrust my head underneath, and being upon my back I looked up and near the top observed a light as of a Star in a Cloudy night about $1^{1}/_{2}$ in. long and 1 broad, tho' dim, yet perfectly distinct. Tho' *they all* appear as lights, some larger and others smaller, this one was denominated the Fisher Star the name by which they designate the Plough. I beleive *we* call it, or Great Bear, from the supposed resemblance it bears to that animal, the fisher.[24]

When I was entering, several of the Indians on the outside called out to the Spirits, 'Gently! gently! It is our Chief who wishes to see ye: do him no evil' &c. I had my apprehensions.

A little after one p.m. [a.m.] one of my men looked in, with several indians, and saw several small lights about as large as the Thumb nail. A few minutes before 2 p.m. [a.m.] being day light, they gave another shaking to the frame and made their exit.

The above is an account of only a small part, for I am too much pressed for time — I cannot therefore enter into particular, nor a larger detail; nor give you my opinion further than a few words. I am fully convinced, as much so as that I am in existance, that Spirits of some kind did really and virtually enter, some truly terrific, but others again quite of a different character. I cannot enter into a detail by comparisons from ancient and more modern history, but I found the consonance, analogy, resemblance, affinity, or whatever if may be termed so great, so conspicuous that I verily believe I shall never forget the impressions of that evening; but above all things that sticks most forcibly in my mind is the unbounded Gratitude we owe, and ought to shew, every instant of our existance to that almighty Power that deigned to scarifice his only Son for us for our Salvation! Oh my God! let me never forget this! and teach me to thank thee not only with my life but with every action of my life! .... &c, &c.

Here I must close and in a few minutes Seal up this for your perusal, sincerely wishing I may find an opportunity, safe, of conveying it to you. How earnestly I wish Rob[er]t had been present and understand the language — this would convi[n]ce the most skeptic.

To Mr. Wm. Nelson, Wm. Henry[25]

G. Nelson

Note: Read these Pages among yourselves, and lend them not out of the house——

Notes

[1] The word 'conjure' as a description of native religious practice was used by most of the fur traders, but natives today quite rightly object to it.

[2] Kišemanitōw: the superior being of subarctic Algonquian cosmology, benevolently inclined towards humans and usually identified as the ultimate creator of the world and of living beings.

[3] Old Nick: English slang for the Devil. By *Kee-jick-oh-kay* (Cree *Kišikohkēw*; Ojibwa *Kišikokkē*) Nelson means the primary evil deity Macimanitōw (Cree), a being conceptually opposed to and subordinate in power to both Kišemanitōw and the trickster Wisahkecahk.

[4] Sea Serpent: (Cree *misikinīpik*; Ojibwa *miššikinēpik*); possesses associations comparable to those of the Great Lynxes (see below), and figures prominently in Algonquian ritual and mythology; like the Great Lynxes, associated with subterranean or underwater spaces usually considered inimical to human beings, and is eternally at war with the Thunder beings of the upper air.

[5] Related to the underwater spirits of Cree, Montagnais, and Ojibwa religion. As underwater creatures they are dangerous and to be feared; they have both male and female forms, and may wield a sexual influence over humans.

[6] Water Lynx, or Tiger: (Cree Misipisiw; Ojibwa Miššipišī): described by an eighteenth century source as 'the god of waters or the master of spirits of lakes, possessing the form of a sea tiger with fins'. A class of malignant aquatic feline beings, as well as the name of their ruler; they control river and lake environments, especially dangerous rapids. The Thunderbirds (see below) are their enemies.

[7] Mee-key-nock (Cree *Miskināhk*, 'turtle'; Ojibwa *Mikkinākk*, 'turtle' or 'snapping turtle'). A spirit being often translated as 'Great Turtle', who functions as messenger or interpreter during the performance of the shaking lodge among most Cree and Ojibwa groups; an amiable and gregarious spirit, as Nelson's account shows.

[8] Another good-humoured spirit who jokes with the audience.

[9] The Sun: One of the major spirits of subarctic Algonquian cosmology, but conceptualized in many different ways (see, for example, HENRY KELSEY). In Nelson's manuscripts he is identified with Euro-Canadian traders; he speaks English, wears English clothing, and can repair

firearms. The Moon: a powerful spirit of the upper air on whom information is sparse. Also identified with the Euro-Canadians by speaking English.

[10](Cree *Mostos*; Ojibwa *Maškotēpišikki*). As observed by Nelson, the Buffalo appears as a stern and formidable alien spirit who resents disparaging remarks from the audience. The fact that it (like some other spirits) communicates in a language intelligible only to the conjuror may reflect its associations with a different environment, the prairie-parklands to the south of Lac La Ronge.

[11]The Thunderbird; their majesty and power was so great the conjurors required them to stay outside the shaking lodge. Could be malignant, but usual benevolent spirits associated with success in war and medicine. They are enemies of the Great Lynxes (see above).

[12]Faculty: doctors educated to practise and teach medicine.

[13]Nelson is describing the making of a 'shaking lodge', a Saulteaux or Cree conjuring hut. The shaking of the hut signified the arrival of the spirit beings.

[14]Ojibwa *šiššīkwē*: 'rattlesnake': probably a metaphor.

[15]Fr. *macle*: line for making net.

[16]The context suggests that this being was recognized as a potential visitor to the shaking lodge; other sources suggest that individual stones might (or might not) turn out to be animate and responsive.

[17]Among the natives at Nelson's post, as among present-day Rock Crees of the Churchill River, the Ice is a malignant being associated with disorder.

[18]Perhaps the Dog's voice reflects its integration into human society.

[19]Among the Algonquians, Bears are the most intelligent, human, and spiritually powerful of terrestrial animals.

[20]Skeletons (Cree *Pakahk*). Nelson gives much detail on ambiguous beings who, though associated with death, sickness, etc. seemed to grant great hunting and curing power to those possessing them as guardian spirits.

[21]Benjamin Frobisher, who died from exposure after escaping from Hudson's Bay Company hands (see FRANKLIN, note 3).

[22]Davy: the Devil.

[23]That is, like the ancient oracles at places like Delphi.

[24]The Fisher Star: the Plough or Great Bear (Ursa Major). Cree *ocīkacahk*, Ojibwa *ocīkanank* or *cīk*.

[25]Sorel, Quebec, then known as William Henry.

Part V: Prelude to Settlement

Frances Simpson   (1812 – 1853)

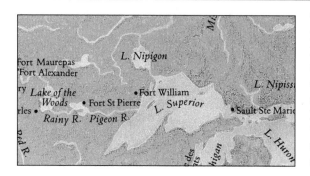

The daughter of a London merchant, FRANCES SIMPSON married her cousin GEORGE SIMPSON, Governor of the Hudson's Bay Company, in 1830. The same spring she travelled with him to Canada, received everywhere with the respect and attention naturally accorded the 'Governor's lady'. The diary of her journey written by this delicately reared eighteen-year-old girl is among the most repressed of exploration documents; unlike the shrewd, inquisitive, and self-mocking LETITIA HARGRAVE, Frances reveals nothing but the most exemplary sentiments as she travels with her fiercely authoritative husband — at what was then top speed — from Lachine to York Fort. Simpson had left a native wife in the west, and there was dismay when he returned with an English bride, but no shadow of this scandal appears in Frances' journal. But even on her ladylike evidence, the trip must have been an exhausting one, as her life with George Simpson in general proved to be; debilitated by frequent pregnancies, she was often an invalid, and died at the age of 41. Her diary of the trip west is an excellent, if somewhat well-bred, account of daily life on an extended canoe journey, and her response to the wilderness bears close comparison with that of Susanna Moodie, her near-contemporary.

Text: 'Journal of a Voyage from Montreal, thro' the Interior of Canada, to York Factory on the Shores of Hudson's Bay' (1830). Winnipeg: Hudson's Bay Company Archives, D6/4. The spelling of the original has been preserved, but some briefer paragraphs have been run together; since entries are day-by-day, ellipses are indicated simply with three dots.

On the 4th of March I arose from my Bed, at 5 AM. (for the first time in my life) with an aching heart, and a mind agitated by the various emotions of Grief, Fear, & Hope. Grief, at parting from my beloved Parents, and a large & united family of Brothers &

Sisters, from whom I had never been separated. Fear, for the changes which might take place among them during my absence, and Hope, which in the midst of my distress, diffused its soothing influence, and acting as a panacea seemed to point to the home of my infancy as the goal at which, at some future period, however distant I should at length arrive. . . .

I can scarcely trust myself, to think of the pang which shot thro' my heart, on taking the last 'Farewell' of my beloved Father, who was equally overcome at the first parting from any of his children. Suffice it to say, that this was to me a moment of bitter sorrow, and one over which in pity to my own feelings I must throw a veil. . . . [en route from New York to Montreal[1]] . . . we were conveyed down the noble river St. Lawrence at the breadth of which I was perfectly amazed, and which added to the views of the Town and the beauty of the surrounding Country would have made a fine subject for an artist.

The first appearance of Montreal from the Water, is striking in the extreme: all the buildings are roofed with tin, which causes it to glitter in the Sun, like a City of Silver. The most conspicuous object is the Roman Catholic Church (the largest place of Public Worship some Cathedrals excepted I have ever seen) situated nearly in the centre of the Town, and which rises with an air of grandeur, to a height which appears almost gigantic. The 'Mountain' (which is one of the chief 'Lions'[2]) is also an attraction on account of the relief its verdure affords the eye. . . . The Country is beautiful, being varigated with Farms, Orchards & Meadows as far as the village in which the house[3] is delightfully situated, having the St. Laurence running in front. It was almost too early in the Season to judge of the productions, and vegetation, but it must be a charming Summer residence.

We remained here 8 days, during which time we were visited by all the principal families, far and near. . . . [the Mountain] is a spot worthy the attention of all Strangers. There are two roads running up each side, till it reaches the summit, from whence the eye is feasted with a magnificent, and extended prospect. The sides exhibit patches of large Timber, clumps of young Trees, Underwood, & ornamental Shrubberies; rich Orchards, & Gardens belonging to several fine houses which overlook the Town, River, & opposite shores.

[Of our voyage to the Interior] I must observe that it was regarded as a wonder, was the constant subject of conversation, and seemed to excite a general interest, being the first ever undertaken by Ladies, and one which has always been considered as fraught with danger. In order to amuse myself, and likewise to refresh my memory on subjects connected with this voyage, at a future period, I determined on keeping a Journal, which I now commence. . . .

May 2nd. Left La Chine at 4 AM in two Canoes manned by 15 hands each, all strong active, fine looking Canadians the passengers consisting of Mr. & Mrs. McTavish,[4] & Maid Servant in the one, & Mr. Simpson Myself & Servant in the other accompanied by Messrs. Keith & Gale who kindly volunteered to favor us with their company for a day or two.

Our Canoe, a most beautiful craft, airy and elegant beyond description, was 35 feet in length, the lading consisting of 2 Water proof Trunks (known by the name of

Cassets) containing our clothes: 1 Basket for holding Cold Meat, Knives & Forks, Towels &c. 1 Egg Basket, a travelling Case (or Canteen) containing 6 Wine Bottles, Cups & Saucers — Tea Pot, Sugar Basin, Spoons, Cruets, Glasses & Tumblers, Fishing Apparatus — Tea, Sugar Salt. &c. &c. — also a bag of Biscuits, a bale of Hams, a Keg of Butter &c. &c.

The provisions for the Crew were Pork & Biscuits: from which circumstance the young recruits are called 'Pork Eaters' to distinguish them from the old Winterers, who feed chiefly on 'Pemican,' a mixture of Buffalo Meat, Tallow, and a due proportion of hairs (but whether the last ingredient is intended to keep the composition together or not, I cannot say) — this is not the most delicate, but it is very substantial food, and more portable than any other, as it is closely packed in a bag made of Buffalo hide. There is also a keg of liquor (called the Dutchman) from which the people are drammed[5] three or four times a day, according to the state of the Weather. In this order we started, the voyageurs singing, and the Canoe almost flying thro' the water — the motion is perfectly easy, & in fine weather it is the most delightful mode of travelling that can be imagined.

At 9 O'clock we put ashore for Breakfast, above the Rapids of St. Ann. The water being too shallow for the Canoes to touch the bank, Mrs. McTavish & myself were carried in the arms, and the Gentlemen on the backs of our sturdy Canadians, which (as may be supposed) caused a hearty laugh both at, and to, such of the company as were novices. Immediately upon landing, the Guide 'Bernard' (an Indian) kindled a fire with his Flint & Steel, and a small piece of Bark & Touchwood, with which the 'Fire Bag' is furnished: two or three men with hatchets, provided wood, — 3 poles tied together were placed over the fire, with a large kettle suspended from them by a chain — the cloth was laid on the grass, & spread with Cold Meat, Fowls, Ham, Eggs, Bread & Butter everyone sat down in the position found most convenient, and each made the most of the time afforded. Mr. Simpson (after looking at his watch) gave the call of 'Take away.' The breakfast party were on their feet in a moment, the things washed, packed, and the Canoe off again, within the 45 Minutes usually allowed for this Meal.

At 11 A.M. we landed at the beautiful Indian village of the 'Lake of Two Mountains,' (where the Company have an Establishment under the charge of Mr. Cameron) from whence, on approaching the shore, we were saluted with a discharge of Artillery, by the Chiefs of the Iroquay, Algonquin, and Nepisang tribes. The Indians decked out in all their finery of Ribbons, Beads, & Silver works, placed themselves in rows, on either side of the path leading to the house, and smiled, and appeared much pleased, when spoken to. The daughter of one of the principal Chiefs (a little Girl about 8 years of age) came forward, and saying a few words in her native language, presented me with a Bouquet of Cherry Blossom very prettily arranged, as a mark of friendly greeting. . . .

3rd. Arose at 2 AM. with aching bones, occasioned by the dampness, and hardness of my couch. The people were roused by Mr. Simpson's well known call of 'Lève Lève Lève,' when they all started up, covered with their Blankets in which they wrap themselves, sleeping all weathers in the open air on the ground. The Canoes were then laden and we embarked at 3 O'clock. Soon after daylight, we came to some heavy Rapids where we were obliged to land, and walk 7 Miles up the banks of the Grenville Canal, till we came to the small village of Grenville, where there is a detachment of Soldiers stationed. The Canoes here joined us, we then travelled till 9 O'Clock, and breakfasted at 'Point Orignal.'

The Sun intensely hot today and the water of the Grand, or Uttowas river as smooth as glass: the Country on either side a thick Forest; the trees near the edge of the Water low, & branching, chiefly Aspen: while those behind were Pine, straight as Arrows, and growing to an enormous height: every thing was calm & quiet, not a sound to be heard excepting the stroke of the paddle, and the clear mellow voice of our principal vocalist Tomma Felix, singing 'La Belle Rosier' and other sweet Voyageurs airs. Dined at 2 O'clock at Pappinoe [Papineau] Island, and travelled till 9 when we encamped at Riviere de Lievres. . . .

5th. The Establishment at which we encamped last night, may be considered the boundary between the Civilized and Savage Worlds, as beyond this point, the country is uninhabited by Whites, except where a Trading Post of the Honourable Hudson's Bay Company occasionally presents itself.

At 3 A.M. the signal for starting was given, & in a few minutes after, the paddle kept time, to the lively song. Our progress however, was soon interrupted by the Portage of the Chats Falls, which we passed before day light, altho' the path which lay across rocks & precipices, was very rugged, and intersected by a small Channel of the River over which I was carried in the arms of one of the men, who waded thro' it, nearly breast-high. At day-break the Sky became cloudy, with the appearance of bad weather, and soon afterwards, rain came on, and continued more or less heavy, until 8 PM. at times in such torrents that we might have fancied we were under a Terrestrial, instead of a Celestial Waterfall: but in defiance of the elements we kept 'en route,' making several Portages in the course of the day, amounting in all, to about 5 miles: thro' Mud & Water, over fallen trees, rocks, up hill & down: — in short such a disagreeable variety in the shape of a walk, I never before experienced.

At Sun set we encamped at the upper end of the Grand Calumet Portage. The Weather cleared up, immense fires were soon blazing cheerfully; a comfortable warm Supper was prepared, and by 10 O'clock there was such a Nasal Serenade set up in the Camp, as to drown the shrill notes of thousands of Bull-frogs, which were luxuriating in a swamp hard by.

6th. We were in the Canoe before 2 this morning, but on pushing off from the Shore, discovered that one of our Crew was missing: a few shots were fired by way of signal, and the people re-landed in order to search for the Deserter, but to no purpose, as he had got clear off into the Woods, where it would be in vain to look for him, so we made a fresh start, his fellow labourers not best pleased at this detention and the additional work imposed upon them.

The morning was cold & disagreeable after the incessant rain of yesterday, but neither that, nor the fatigue of the forced march we were making, served to depress the Spirits of our voyageurs; who paddled, sung, laughed & joked, as if on an excursion of pleasure, until one of them who seemed to feel the force of a joke, which his neighbour indulged in, at his expense, returned it upon him in a still more forcible manner by a blow, which gave rise to a battle in the Canoe. Mr. Simpson was asleep at the time, but the noise awoke him, and put him into nearly as great a passion as the combatants, upon whom, he bestowed a shower of blows with a paddle which lay at hand, and brought about an immediate cessation of hostilities. . . .

[May 7th] . . . another of our crew deserted and while searching for him, his example was followed by a third. These runaways were young Recruits, who were never on the voyage before, and finding the labor greater than they expected, took French leave, which I learn is frequently done by them, but the old experienced voyaguers are all upon honor, & never desert. Precautions were here taken to secure these light-footed gentry, and with the assistance of an old Indian Woman & her children (whom we found on the Portage) got hold of them after a search of 4 or 5 hours. A Court Martial was held upon them, composed of the old voyageurs, the sentence of which, was a dozen lashes with their leather carrying straps; and in spite of their tears, and entreaties would (I believe) have been carried into effect, had not Mrs. McTavish & myself, called to their aid our most persuasive arguments, and obtained their pardon. This incident occasioned the loss of nearly half a day to us. . . .

[May 9th] We left the Grand or Uttowas river at 7 O'clock, and entered a little river falling into it from the South, called the Matowa, on a Portage of which we breakfasted at 8. Made several Portages in the course of the forenoon, in this turbulent little river, and at 2 O'Clock got to one called the 'Talon' Portage, the most wild & romantic place I ever beheld: it reminded me of the description I have read (in some of Sir Walter Scott's beautiful tales) of Scottish Scenery. The approach to this Portage is truly picturesque: the river from being a considerable width, here branches into a variety of Channels, one of which we entered, so narrow as scarcely to leave a passage for the Canoe — on either side are stupendous rocks of the most fantastic forms: some bear the appearance of Gothic Castles, others exhibit rows of the most regular, and beautifully carved Corinthian Pillars: deep Caverns are formed in some, while others present a smooth level surface, crowned with tufts of Pines, and Cedars. From the upper end of the Portage is seen a beautiful Waterfall, which dashes over immense masses of rocks thro' which it had worn itself many a channel foaming & roaring to a considerable distance, the spray glittering in the Sun with all the varied hues of the Rainbow. . . .

[May] 10th. . . . A sharp frost had set in last night, and the morning was exceedingly cold; we got from under our Cloaks in very bad humour, when the Guide roused us for the purpose of making the 'Prairie la Vase' Portage, about a mile & a half in length.

The walking would have been bad in broad daylight, but the darkness of the morning rendered it almost impassable, as it partly lay thro' a Morass knee deep, and blocked up with Wind fallen Timber: we contrived however to wade, and scramble our way to the other end, where a fire was immediately lighted, for the purpose of warming ourselves, & drying our clothes. We then passed thro' a small muddy channel, (in the Canoe) which was terminated by another Portage even worse than the former, (altho' not exceeding ½ a mile in length) as it was not only knee, but waist deep in parts. To cross this, baffled the skill both of Mrs. McTavish & Myself (good walkers as we flattered ourselves to be) and accordingly after mature delibera-tion, it was agreed that each should be carried by a man chosen for the purpose. Tomma Felix took me up in his arms, & Nicholas Monique, an old Indian, volun-teered his services in transporting my companion across the miry portion of road which lay before us. Tomma pushed on, despite of every difficulty making however many stumbles & false steps — but Nicholas' load being rather heavier, he absolutely came to a stand still, in the midst of a bog, and declared he could not take the Lady a step farther in his arms, but if she would get on his back, he thought he might accomplish the journey.

Mr. Simpson who was coming on after us, persuaded Mrs. McTavish (with some difficulty) as a last resource to do as Nicholas recommended, which she at length agreed to, and on the back of Nicholas accordingly mounted: the scene however was so ludicrous, that the by-standers could not resist a laugh, in which Mrs. McTavish joined so heartily, that poor Nicholas was thrown off his equilibrium, stumbled forwards, fell on his face, and gave his unfortunate rider a summerset over his head, into the mud: throwing her into a situation the most awkward, and ridiculous that ever poor Lady was placed in.

After extricating her with much difficulty, she was at length dragged to the end of the Portage, where we all washed & dried ourselves, and had Breakfast, after which we descended a small river, passed thro' Lake Nipisang, about 40 miles in length, then made a Portage, into the French River. . . .

14th The fog did not clear away until nearly 6 AM. when we embarked. The weather became boisterous again, with hail storms, & exceedingly cold; but by great exertion we reached the Sault St. Mary's at 5 PM. where the Company have a small neat Establishment under the charge of Chief Factor Bethune,[6] whose utmost politeness was called forth in his reception of us.

The Sault St. Mary's is a narrow Channel, through which, the waters of the great Lake Superior fall into Lake Huron, forming a line of demarkation between the British & United States Territory here. The Company's Establishment is of course on the British side. On the American side there is a small Garrison, and lower down a village. The appearance of a civilized habitation rising in the midst of a boundless Wilderness, served in a great measure to dissipate a certain feeling of melancholy, which I felt gradually stealing over me at the sight of Nature in her grand, but Savage and uncultivated state of Rock, Flood, & Mountain; without the sign of a living creature to admire the beauties presenting themselves on every side, or to wonder at, and praise the Mighty Power of Him, who had formed those vast, and desolate Forests unknown to Man, and adorned them with many a flower which 'Wastes its sweetness on the desert air.'

It likewise reminded me of the enterprise of Europeans, whom no difficulty could dismay, and who have at last established so extensive, and lucrative a commerce between the Old & New Worlds; providing employment for thousands, taming the ferocious lives of the Indians, and gradually introducing the peaceful occupation of husbandry; the first step towards civilization, before which, the wild & savage habits of the Aborigines must give way. . . .

22nd. Embarked at 1/2 past 1 AM. the weather still boisterous, and very cold. Travelled till 2 PM. when we came to an Establishment called the Pic, on the banks of a large river of the same name. Here I was highly entertained by a visit from a band of Indians who had been waiting our arrival several days.

We were seated at the end of the room, in order to receive the party, who came in without the least ceremony. Some placed themselves on the floor in their usual position of resting on their heels: others leaned against the wall, and such as could not gain admittance crowded into a small passage at the entrance of the house. The Chief (who took possession of a Chair the moment he entered) was dressed in a short Coat of blue cloth, and scarlet cloth Stockings worked with different colored Beads — very large rings in his ears, a silver ornament suspended from his nose, and an immense crooked Knife stuck in a leathern girdle round his waist. His feet were bare. Those of inferior rank were chiefly attired in Blankets; and all had their eyes painted with red ochre.

The Chief, after making a speech, presented some furs, for which he received a large keg of liquor, some Tobacco, red & blue cloth, Beads, a Blanket for his Wife, and a coat for his child, a little creature about 5 years old, who was present, and who expressed his joy in the most lively manner: stripped himself, put on his new dress, laughed, clapped his hands, & danced with real delight. They were then regaled with a glass of wine all round, and took their departure apparently very well satisfied. . . .

May 24th. On awakening this morning, I was surprised to see so thick a coat of Ice on the Lake, that the men were obliged to break it with poles, for the Canoe to pass. . . . Travelled till about 1/2 past 6 PM. when we put ashore for the purpose of dressing previous to landing, at Fort William, where we intended to remain that night & the following day. . . .

May 25th. This Establishment is of considerable extent, and some years ago, was the principal Depot of the North-West Company: but the buildings are going fast to decay, and it is now of very little importance in comparison to what it then was. . . . In the course of the morning we were visited by an old Indian Chief called the Spaniard, who came to presesnt his Furs. He was the most lively, good-tempered looking Indian, I had met with; appeared both surprised & pleased at seeing me, and shook me very cordially by the hand several times. He was very gaily dressed in a Scarlet Coat, with black velvet Cuffs & Collar, edged with gold lace — a White Calico Shirt ornamented with a frill about 1/2 a yard in depth — cloth Stockings worked with beads, an immense Sword dangling by his side, and an enormous Cocked hat, surmounted by a profusion of different colored feathers. He was accompanied by his Son-in-law, who was dressed in a similar style, tho' his clothes were of plainer colors — he was a young Man, and paid great deference to his Father. After making a long speech, and receiving a present of Liquor, Tobacco, Beads & Cloth, they took their departure, apparently very well satisfied.

The large Canoes, in which we left Montreal, were here exchanged for smaller, (or North Canoes) in which we were to embark the following morning. . . .

27th. . . . encamped at 8 O'clock, on the best spot we could find, after much examination: but bad enough, as it was covered with burnt wood, & fallen timber, and accessible only, by clambering over the men's shoulders, which formed a bridge across the deep, slimy mire, of which the bank is formed.

This abominable spot was surrounded by stagnant pools, from which our ears were assailed by the croaking & whistling of thousands of Bull-frogs: and here the Musquito first introduced himself to our notice, exerting his sting vigourously, and giving full employment to our fingers in allaying the irritation occasioned thereby.

28th. Off at 2 AM. This I may say was the most fatiguing day I ever experienced having walked between Breakfast & Dinner (under a scorching Sun) upwards of 7 miles, over the 'Prairie,' 'Middle' & 'Savanne' Portages, the last of which, deriving its name from its character, is formed of a bridge of Logs in a very crazy, & decayed state: so slippery, unsteady & uneven, as to occasion the greatest difficulty in crossing it. This walk (if so it may be called, as it was an operation of 6 hours, of hopping, slipping & climbing) completely overpowered me with fatigue, and on arriving at the end I threw myself upon the grass, unable to move for some time.

The Afternoon exceedingly wet, and uncomfortable, but it was cheering to know that we were now within the Territory of 'Ruperts Land,' as the Middle Portage is the height of land, separating the Waters which run into Hudson's Bay, from those which fall into the Gulf of St. Lawrence. Descended the river Embarras about 2 miles, which takes its name from the frequent obstructions of wind fallen timber, which is carried down by the Spring floods; requiring the constant use of the axe, to cut a passage through it. Encamped on the edge of a filthy Swamp at 1/2 past 7.

29th. Torrents of rain during last night, and a snow storm this morning, which prevented our starting till after breakfast, rather an unfashionable hour 5 AM. Off at 6, and occupied until 11, cutting our way thro' this tiresome little river, which was completely chocked up with Drift-wood: when as ill-fate would have it, our Consort Canoe in following us round one of the points, formed by the winding course of the Stream, ran against a stump, which did not show itself above Water, tore up about 9 feet of its bark, and in a few minutes (altho' all the people were occupied in baling with every vessel they could get hold of from Hats downwards) was up to the Gunwales in water: but Providentially, the river was so shoal where she sunk, that no lives were lost, and we got to her assistance in sufficient time to save what was not perishable of the baggage: so that no evil was sustained by the accident, except the loss of half this day, (occupied in repairing the Canoe) and of a great portion of our Tea, Sugar, & Biscuit.

Employed from 11 till 3 O'clock putting our wreck in a 'Sea worthy state,' which was a very simple process; by introducing a piece of new bark, inside the damaged part, sewing it with the thin fibre of the root of a tree,[7] and covering the Seam with melted Pine Pitch, or 'Gum' which rendered it perfectly water-tight. . . .

[June] 5th. At the last Portage in this river (Winnipeg) the crews of both Canoes shaved, and dressed in their gayest attire, previous to landing at Fort Alexander,[8] where we arrived at 1 AM. [PM.?] and were welcomed with no ordinary degree of kindness by Chief Factor John Stuart,[9] the Gentleman in charge of the

Establishment. Dined here, and took our departure at Sun Set, encamping about a mile below the Establishment.

6th. Mr. Simpson being anxious to get to Fort Garry (about 100 miles distant) today, gave his usual 'Leve Leve Leve' at 12 PM. [AM. ?] and although it blew very hard, occasioning a heavy swell on Lake Winnipeg when we embarked, we got to the mouth of Red River at 11 AM. The beauty of this Stream surpasses that of every other I have yet seen in the Interior. The banks are richly clothed with Timber of larger size, and greater variety than is generally met with, and the soil when properly cultivated as fertile as that of a manured garden. This rich Country forms an immense sea of level plains, which extends upwards of 500 miles back, on the West side to the foot of the Rocky Mountains, on the South to the Missourie, and on the North to the Saskatchawin.

On advancing in the Settlement, signs of civilization began to appear in the form of houses built of Logs, and surrounded by patches of ground which bore the marks of the Plough & the Spade: from this point, cultivation is continued along the banks with very little intermission, as far as nine miles beyond the Fort, which is situated 50 miles from the mouth of the River. As the houses and farms increased in magnitude, & improved in quality, the pleasing & domestic sight of Cattle appeared, which added much to the beauty and interest of the Scene.

About 2 O'clock we came to an Indian Camp, the Chief of which was recognized as 'Peguish' or the 'Cut nosed Chief,'[10] who embarked in his Canoe, attended by six or seven of his followers, to congratulate Mr. Simpson on his return, he being very popular among the Indians, on account of treating them with uniform kindness: which in my humble opinion (except perhaps in extreme cases) is the surest way towards attaining the desired end of improving their condition; as it is far more likely to succeed in weaning them from their Savage life & roving habits, than authority harshly exercised could be — and they are thus frequently induced to give up the fatigue & uncertainty of the Chase, for the more peaceable and certain occupation of husbandry. The Chief welcomed me very cordially in his Native Tongue, to his 'Native Land' — shook me by the hand several times, and promised to come to the Fort next day to pay me a visit.

On stopping to prepare for Dinner, Mr. Simpson gave all the Wine & Liquor that remained to the Men, who made it into Punch in their large cooking Kettle, and regaled thereon, till some of them were 'powerfully refreshed.' This debauch (the first I had seen on the voyage) infused into our Crew a degree of artificial strength & spirits, otherwise we should not have reached the Fort, as they were quite overpowered with sleep and fatigue; but after it began to operate, they paddled and sung, with much gaiety, bringing us to the Establishment at 12 PM. after a hard day's work of 24 hours.

The first respectable looking house to be seen, belongs to Mr. Cocrane,[11] one of the Clergymen of the Settlement, and is situated about 16 miles from the Fort: near it, is his Church,[12] the sight of which, had the most cheering effect, after passing so many Wilds without the smallest trace of a Sacred Edifice, or even of a Civilized habitation, and seemed to raise the Soul to its Creator, who is to be found in the remotest corner of the Globe, and whose Fatherly care, and protection are equally divided, between the poor untutored Savage, and the Monarch who reigns over an enlightened people. This was the first place of Worship I had seen, since leaving Montreal, and I hailed it as a favorable sign of the moral state of the Colony.

Mr. Cocran was from home, but his Wife on seeing us approach, came from the house, and pressed us very kindly to land, which invitation we were obliged to decline, as it was then late in the Evening. A Courier was sent on horseback from the foot of the Rapids, to make known our arrival, and at midnight we landed at 'Fort Garry.' The reception I here met with, convinced me that if the Inhabitants of this remote Region were plain & homely in their manners, they did not want to kindness of heart, and the desire of making every thing appear favorable, and pleasing, to the eye & mind of a Stranger.

7th. The day after arrival was fully occupied in introductions to the different Settlers who came to pay their respects, and offer their congratulations to Mr. Simpson. Among the first was the Revd. Mr. Cocrane, one of the Mission for propagating Christian Knowledge. He is a very respectable good Man, plain, & frank in his manners, and apparently very anxious to succeed in the task he has undertaken: he keeps a School for the instruction of the Indian and Half-breed boys of the surrounding Country, and Mrs. Cocrane in like manner gives instruction to the Girls of the Settlement.

The Revd. Mr. Jones[13] (the Company's principal Chaplain) is a very genteel, highly educated man, pleasing in his manners, and an admirable preacher. He appears to enter very zealously into the humane and laudable objects of reforming the loose & savage lives of the Indians, and of training their Offspring in the paths of Virtue, by instilling into their minds at an early age, the doctrines and precepts of the Christian Religion. Indeed, the whole Colony appears in a flourishing condition in every point of view, and will I have no doubt in the course of time, (when the civilized part of the population shall have increased) form a Settlement which will not only shed lustre on the memory of its Founder,[14] and hand down his name to posterity; but will influence others to follow so bright an example, and settle different portions of this vast Continent, the Interior of which, presents so fair a field to work upon.

There are two Protestant Churches, the lower one (situated near the house of Mr. Cocrane) being the larger on account of the great number of Settlers residing in that quarter: the upper one[15] next the Parsonage House is small, and attended by the Inhabitants of the Fort, who regularly observe the Sabbath with due & respectful deference. Opposite to Fort Garry, across the river, are the Church and House of the Catholic Bishop[16] who is held in high veneration by the Canadian party here resident — he is a clever, sensible man, of majestic stature, fine open countenance, and an easy & pleasing address.

During our short stay here, I experienced the greatest kindness from the Inhabitants of Fort Garry, among whom were Messrs. Finlayson, McKenzie, Todd, & Rae.[17] Mr. McKenzie the Companys principal representative here, has been for many years stationed in the Interior of this vast Country, and is a very clever man, possessing a fund of amusing anecdotes and adventures, with which he entertained me not a little. According to custom, Mr. Simpson gave a dinner before leaving the Colony, to all the respectable Settlers. The Bishop with his retinue of Priests was present, also Mr. Jones (the head of our Church) and his Wife, and Mr. Cocrane (his better half being unable to attend, owing to the illness of one of her Children). The whole party appeared very happy, and enjoyed the good cheer exceedingly. . . .

11th. Left Fort Garry at ¹/₂ past 6 A.M. accompanied by another Canoe, in which were Messrs. McKenzie & Finlayson and arrived at 9 O'clock at Mr. Cocrane's, where we were met by Dr. Todd, & Mr. Rea [Rae] who had travelled across the Plains on horseback. After breakfasting with Mrs. Cocrane, we proceeded to examine the ground for the site of a New Establishment,[18] about to be built at this end of the Settlement, and Mr. Simpson having selected a beautiful spot on a gentle elevation, surrounded by Wood, and commanding a fine view of the River, we took leave of Messrs. McKenzie & Cocrane, and continued our march. . . .

26th. Started at ¹/₂ past 1 AM. descended the Hill River, deriving its name from a Hill about 600 feet in height, which may be seen in clear weather, from the upper end of the river, but is afterward lost, owing to the rapid descent of Country. From this hill, 35 Lakes are visible, intersecting the surrounding Country. . . . Travelled today with great rapidity; the people being told they must reach York Factory before they slept. They accordingly lost no time, and by applying frequently to the Liquor Keg, contrived to keep up both their strength & spirits. We arrived at the Factory at Midnight, and retired immediately to rest, Mr. Simpson having ordered that none of the Gentlemen should be disturbed.

Fond as I am of travelling, I own, I felt pleased at the idea of remaining quiet for two months: having traversed in various ways (since the 8th of March) a distance of 8,000 Miles, which for a Novice, is no small undertaking. I must here observe, that a Canoe voyage is not one which an English Lady would take for pleasure; and though I have gone through it very well, there are many little inconveniences to be met with, not altogether pleasing or congenial to the taste of a Stranger: viz. rising between 1 & 2 AM. sleeping sometimes on swampy ground, sometimes on hard rocks, and at others on Sand, (the worst of all materials for a couch) with no other bedding than a couple of Blankets & Cloaks: — living the greater part of the time on salted provisions without vegetables: — exposed to a Scorching Sun, cold winds, and heavy rain — putting up late some evenings drenched to the skin, and finding the Encampment so wet, as to render it impossible to dry any of our wet clothes, when it became necessary to wear them the following day in the same state. . . .

This Establishment [York Factory] far exceeds every other in the Country both as regards magnitude and appearance. The houses and Stores, are roofed with Tin, and neatly painted, some white, others yellow. The front of the Factory presents 3 sides of a square, comprehending two large buildings, which are the public Mess Room, and the apartments of Chief Factors and Chief Traders, divided by the Old Factory, a low Octagon building over the gateway of which, the Company's arms are displayed. These face the river. The sides are formed by the Stores & Shops. Behind are the houses & workshops of the tradesmen, and Servants of the Establishment.

The Sale shops are provided with goods of almost every description, viz [that is]

Grocery, Haberdashery, Ironmongery, Cutlery, Perfumery, Medicines, etc. supplied by the Annual Ships from England: and the prices I am told, are lower than the same articles could be had at, in any retail shop in London. The whole Establishment is in fine order, and the greatest regularity is observed in every department of the business.

Since my arrival here, I have experienced the greatest kindness from all the Gentlemen: who (tho' perhaps not exactly calculated to shine in polished Society,) are warm-hearted, kindly dispositioned people; who offer to a Stranger, the most cordial, and unaffected welcome, and endeavour to make every thing pleasing & agreeable. . . .

[May 25th] We shall now voyage by Boat,[19] instead of Canoe, being the more commodious, and comfortable mode of travelling for this season; and having nothing further worthy of remark to introduce here, I shall lay aside my pen: trusting, that such of my friends as may take the trouble of perusing the foregoing unconnected Memoranda, will examine them with an indulgent eye; and as they must know that this is my first essay at committing my ideas, or the result of my observations to paper, except in the form of a familiar note, or letter, I feel asssured they will excuse the style, and small degree of merit they possess — it is my intention, however, to continue this narrative (if it deserves that name) during my residence in the Arctic Regions, and hope as it progresses, that it will acquire a greater degree of interest.[20]

Frs. R. Simpson

York Factory — August 25th 1830.

Notes

[1] Frances records that on the Atlantic voyage she endured three weeks of sea-sickness so acute that Simpson proposed to pay the Captain $5000 to put her ashore in Ireland until her father or brother should arrive; in the meanwhile he would go on ahead. Foiled by bad weather, however, they sailed on, landing at New York and proceeding on to Montreal by a water route through northern New York state.

[2] Sights of the city.

[3] Simpson's residence at Lachine.

[4] John George McTavish (c. 1778–1847) is mentioned in several of these excerpts; he was LETITIA HARGRAVE's uncle. His newly married wife was Catherine Turner, and the McTavishes travelled with the Simpsons as far as Michipicoten. For the consternation created by the arrival of McTavish and Simpson with English wives, see John Stuart, below.

[5] Given a 'dram', a portion of liquor.

[6] Angus Bethune (1783–1858) is portrayed in very uncomplimentary terms in GEORGE SIMPSON's *Character Book*.

[7] With spruce roots.

[8] Established in 1793 where the Winnipeg River enters Lake Winnipeg.

[9] John Stuart appears in a number of exploration and fur trade narratives; see among others DANIEL HARMON, SIMON FRASER, LETITIA HARGRAVE. Frances stresses the warmth of the welcome she received, but in fact Stuart and others were shocked and angry that McTavish and Simpson should have married English wives without making any provision for the 'country'

wives they had left behind in the care of Stuart and Daniel McKenzie. Simpson's wife Margaret Taylor had borne him two sons; for her story as rediscovered by her descendant, film-maker Christine Welsh, see 'Voices of the Grandmothers: Reclaiming a Métis Heritage', *Canadian Literature* 131 (Winter, 1991), 15–24.

[10]Peguis (*c.* 1774–1864), noted Saulteaux (Ojibwa) chief. His people are still settled at Netley Creek, south of Lake Winnipeg. Part of his nose had been bitten off in a quarrel about 1802.

[11]William Cockran (1796/7–1865), Anglican missionary and agricultural educator. See also LETITIA HARGRAVE.

[12]St Andrew's on the Red, which Cockran founded in 1829; it still stands north of Winnipeg, near Lower Fort Garry.

[13]David Jones (1796–1844), Anglican missionary at Upper Fort Garry and founder of the Red River Academy. He and the Rev. Mr Cockran did not in fact get on very well.

[14]Thomas Douglas, 5th Earl of Selkirk (1771–1820).

[15]St John's Church at Kildonan, in the north end of present-day Winnipeg.

[16]Joseph-Norbert Provencher (1787–1853), for more than thirty years missionary bishop to the Catholics of the north west; his seat was at St Boniface across the Red River from Fort Garry.

[17]Duncan Finlayson married Frances Simpson's sister, Isobel, in 1838; for her trip to York Fort see LETITIA HARGRAVE. Finlayson, McKenzie, and Todd all appear in the *Character Book* of GEORGE SIMPSON; it was Todd, the most noted doctor in the west in his day, who saw Frances through her first, difficult, pregnancy in 1831. W.G. Rae was a son-in-law of the formidable John McLoughlin; both are in the *Character Book*.

[18]Lower Fort Garry, which stands today, fully restored, near St Andrew's-on-the-Red, north of Winnipeg.

[19]Probably by York boat. First built in 1749 at York Factory, by the late eighteenth century York boats were very important to the Hudson's Bay Company's inland trade routes; they were still in use in the early twentieth century.

[20]If Mrs Simpson in fact wrote another journal, it does not seem to have survived.

George Simpson   (1786/7 – 1860)

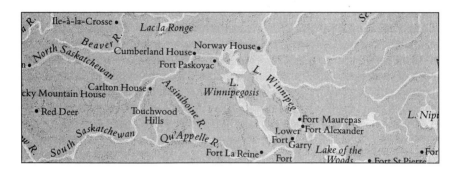

GEORGE SIMPSON was an illegitimate child, but connected with solid merchant families who could give him advancement. The sister of a business partner of his uncle had married the Earl of Selkirk, and as a result of this connection Simpson was put in charge of North American operations for the Hudson's Bay Company in 1820. The HBC had been locked in conflict with the North West Company for a decade, and a cool business head was needed to handle the merger negotiations which appeared imminent. Simpson knew nothing of the fur trade, but he took up his appointment with the fierce energy that characterized everything he did. From 1820 to his death he dominated the life of the Company, making lengthy journeys through its territory (always at breakneck speed), getting to know every personality in it, and superintending its transformation into a modern business enterprise. In 1830 he surprised fur trading society (including his 'country wife' Margaret Taylor) by returning from England with an eighteen-year-old bride, his cousin FRANCES SIMPSON. Her journal of their trip west appears in the anthology. She proved somewhat frail for the frenetic life led by her husband, whether in the west or at his residence at Lachine, where he played a leading role in Montreal business and society. 'The Emperor of the Plains' was knighted in 1841. Sir George travelled extensively, and like most HBC men kept journals, but the most fascinating of his writings (and one of the liveliest in fur trade and exploration literature) is the *Character Book* which he made for his own private use. In it more than 150 of the Company's personalities are gleefully sketched, sometimes in vitriol, sometimes with evident partisanship. However unjust its comments, the *Character Book* provides a brilliant and often scandalously funny panorama of fur trade and exploration culture just before the historic changes which led to the transfer of Rupert's Land to the emerging nation of Canada. The selections here have been chosen for their stylistic verve, or to show the extraordinary range of personalities active in fur trade culture, or because their subjects appear in other excerpts in the anthology.

Text: 'The "Character Book" of George Simpson' (1832), in *Hudson's Bay Miscellany 1670–1870*, ed. Glyndwr Williams. Winnipeg: Hudson's Bay Record Society, 1975. Williams' annotations (greatly condensed here) are rich in detail. In Simpson's original manuscript many names are coded, thus the square brackets used in this selection from among the 157 entries.

Twelve of the Chief Factors, the 'First Class'

No. 1 [COLIN ROBERTSON[1]] A frothy trifling conceited man, who would starve in any other Country and is perfectly useless here: fancies, or rather attempts to pass himself off as a clever fellow, a man of taste, of talents and of refinement; to none of which I need scarcely say he has the smallest pretension. He was bred to his Fathers Trade an operative Weaver in the Town of Perth, but was too lazy to live by his Loom, read Novels, became Sentimental and fancied himself the hero of every tale of Romance that passed through his hands. Ran away from his master, found employment for a few months as a Grocers Shopman at New York, but had not sufficient steadiness to retain his Situation. pushed his way into Canada and was at the Age of 25 engaged as *Apprentice* Clerk by the N W Co for whom he came to the interior, but found so useless that he was dismissed the Service. His age about 55 and his person of which he is exceedingly vain, large, soft, loosely thrown together inactive and helpless to infirmity. He is full of silly boasting & Egotism, rarely deals in plain matter of fact and his integrity is very questionable. To the Fur Trade he is quite a Burden, and a heavy burden too, being a compound of folly and extravagance, and disarranging and throwing into confusion whatsoever he puts his hand to in the shape of business. The concern would gain materially by allowing him to enjoy his situation a thousand Miles distant from the scene of operations instead of being taxed with his nominal Services in the Country.

No. 2 [ALEXANDER STEWART[2]] An easy, mild tempered, well disposed little man about 52 Years of Age; speaks Cree well, and acquires influence over Indians by his kind treatment and patient attention to them; but his diminutive size and retiring diffident manner, unfit him very much for the 'rough & tumble' of the business. He is a man of strict integrity & veracity but 'tis strongly suspected is given to tippling in private.

No. 3 [JOHN GEORGE MCTAVISH[3]] Was the most finished man of business we had in the Country, well Educated, respectably connected and more of the Man of the World in his conversation and address than any of his colleagues. A good hearted Man and generous to extravagance, but unnecessarily dignified and high minded which leads to frequent difficulties with his associates by whom he is considered a 'Shylock' and upon many of whom he looks down; rather strong in his prejudices against, and partialities for individuals, which frequently influences his judgement, so that his opinions on men and things must be listened to with caution: is about 54 Years of Age, has of late Years become very heavy unwieldy and inactive; over fond of good living and I must fear is getting into habits of conviviality and intemperance.

No. 4 [JOHN CLARKE[4]] A boasting, ignorant low fellow who rarely speaks the truth and is strongly suspected of dishonesty; his commanding appearance & pompous manner, however, give him a good deal of influence over Indians and Servants; and his total want of every principle or feeling, allied to fair dealing, honour & integrity, together with is cruel & Tyrannical disposition render him eminently qualified for playing the lawless, cold blooded Bravo in opposition. He is in short a disgrace to the 'Fur Trade'; about 52 Years of Age.

No. 8 [JOHN STUART[5]] About 57 Years of Age, calls himself 47 — 70 winters at least, however, are marked on his countenance, but still very tough & hardy; has undergone a good deal of privation and from his persevering character was at one time the fittest man in the country for exploring Service and severe duty. Had not the advantage of a good Education but being studious improved himself very much and having a very retentive memory is superficially conversant with many subjects. Is exceedingly vain, a great Egotist, Swallows the grossest flattery, is easily cajoled, rarely speaks the truth, indeed I would not believe him upon Oath; lavish of his own means, extravagant and irregular in business and his honesty is very questionable: a good hearted man where he takes a liking but on the contrary [i.e., where he does not] Malicious & Vindictive: fancies himself one of the leading & most valuable men in the Country, but his Day is gone by, and he is now worse than useless being a cloy upon the concern: has many eccentricities, & peculiarities, yet few of them do credit either to the head or heart although they afford him a priviledge of speech and of action which no other man in the Country possesses; in short he is a contemptable body altogether. (May be considered in his dotage and has of late become disgustingly indecent in regard to women.)

No. 10 [JOHN MCLOUGHLIN[6]] About 48 Years of Age. A very bustling active man who can go through a great deal of business but is wanting in system and regularity, and has not the talent of managing the few associates & clerks under his authority: has a good deal of influence with Indians and speaks Siaulteaux tolerably well. Very Zealous in the discharge of his public duties and a man of strict honour and integrity but a great stickler for rights and priviledges and sets himself up for a righter of Wrongs. Very anxious to obtain a lead among his colleagues with whom he has not much influence owing to his ungovernable Violent temper and turbulent disposition, and would be a troublesome man to the Compy if he had sufficient influence to form and tact to manage a party, in short, would be a Radical in any Country — under any Government and under any circumstances; and if he had not pacific people to deal with, would be eternally embroiled in 'affairs of honor' on the merest trifles arising I conceive from the irritability of his temper more than a quarrelsome disposition. Altogether a disagreeable man to do business with as it is impossible to go with him in all things and a difference of opinion almost amounts to a declaration of hostilities, yet a good hearted man and a pleasant companion.

No. 11 [JAMES KEITH[7]] About 47 Years of Age. A scrupulously correct honourable man of a serious turn of mind, who would not to save life or fortune, do what he considered an improper thing. Well Educated, very attentive to business in which he is regular & systematic, indeed both in business and private Life formal to a fault, his whole words and actions being governed by what he considers the strictest rules of propriety but with all I consider him the most faultless member of the Fur Trade.

No. 13 [ANGUS BETHUNE[8]] A very poor creature, vain, self sufficient and trifling, who makes his own comfort his principal study; possessing little Nerve and no decision in anything: of a snarling vindictive disposition, and neither liked nor respected by his associates, Servants or Indians. His Services would be overpaid by the victuals himself & Family consume. About 48 Years of Age.

No. 14 [DONALD MCKENZIE[9]] About 52 Years of Age. A large, heavy, inactive indolent Man, who makes a very bad use of the Talents he possesses, which in some respects are above mediocrity. In business he is perfectly useless and never gives it the smallest attention. His style of writing is Flowery and not inelegant, and in conversation he is smooth & plausable to such a degree that a Stranger or one unacquainted with his artifices is likely to be deceived in him: indeed his whole Life is one uniform system of art, deceit, falsehood, intrigue, suspicion, selfishness and revenge. When I brought him to this place [Red River] it was in the most dismal state of dissension that can be conceived owing to the misconduct of Mr Bulger & Mr Clarke and to the wretched condition of the people; a good deal of address was therefore necessary to prevent them from cutting each others throats, so that his insinuating manner, together with his disingenuous subtlety and talent in lying, rendered him eminently qualified for smoothing them over, and doing such dirty work as a Straight forward honourable conscientious man would not descend to; he was therefore a convenient instrument in the hands of an other, but when left to himself, he had full scope of which he availed himself, for the indulgence of the bad qualities already enumerated to which may be added a degree of vanity, jealousy and malice which it is scarcely possible to conceive. For a length of time I was myself egregiously deceived by his specious reasoning, and he contrived to mystify and pervert facts and to shield himself by his hints, insinuations and falsehoods so effectively that when I came to examine into some of the charges brought against him I thought him more Sinned against than Sinning; but I now know him thoroughly, and have no hesitation in saying, that he is one of the worst and most dangerous men I ever was acquainted with. My presence alone keeps him Sober, but when left to himself he will assuredly become a confirmed Drunkard.

No. 15 [ALEXANDER CHRISTIE[10]] Never were two characters so different from each other as that of the Gentleman I am now describing and of the person I have just noticed. This is one of our best characters, an honourable, correct, upright good hearted man as can be found in any Country; beloved & respected by all who know him, attentive to business qualified to be useful in any branch thereof and a valuable member of the concern. About 49 Years of Age.

No. 19 [JOHN ROWAND[11]] About 46 Years of Age. One of the most pushing bustling Men in the Service whose zeal and ambition in the discharge of his duty is unequalled, rendering him totally regardless of every personal Comfort and indulgence. Warm hearted and Friendly in an extraordinary degree where he takes a liking, but on the contrary his prejudices exceedingly strong. Of a fiery disposition and as bold as a Lion. An excellent Trader who has the peculiar talent of attracting the fiercest Indians to him while he rules them with a Rod of Iron and so daring that he beards their Chiefs in the open camp while surrounded by their Warriors: has likewise a Wonderful influence over his people. Has by his superior management realized more money for the concern than any three of his Colleagues since the Coalition; and altho' his Education has been defective is a very clear headed clever fellow. Will not tell a lie (which is very uncommon in this Country) but has sufficient address to evade the truth when it suits his purpose: full of drollery and humour and generally liked and respected by Indians Servants and his own equals.

No. 25 [DUNCAN FINLAYSON[12]] About 38 Years of Age. A highly upright honourable correct man of good Education and superior abilities to most of his colleagues. Has great influence with and is much liked by his Equals, inferiors and the natives: Speaks Cree, understands accounts, is a good correspondent and is well qualified for the management either of a Depot or Trading Establishment. Firm Cool and decisive, one of our best Legislators and most effective practical Men, and his private conduct & character are models worthy of imitation; in short, he may be ranked high among the most respectable and efficient men of his class.

Nine of the Chief Traders, the 'Second Class'

No. 3 [DONALD MCINTOSH[13]] About 64 Years of Age. A very poor creature in every sense of the Word, illiterate, weak-minded and laughed at by his Colleagues. Very much offended, that he has not been promoted and complains loudly of the neglect he has experienced in that respect altho' his only claim to advancement is his antiquity. Speaks Saulteaux, is qualified to cheat an Indian, and can make & set a Net which are his principal qualifications; indeed he would have made a better Canoe Man or Fisherman than a 'Partner'. 'Tis high time he should make room for a better Man. He is perfectly Sober and honest.

No. 6 [ANGUS CAMERON[14]] About 48 Years of Age. A very active useful Man and steady, regular and œconomical in business. Possesses a description of firmness allied to obstinacy but sound of judgement in most things and on the whole, shrewd sensible correct man who will not do an improper thing nor descend to an untruth: displays excellent management in any business entrusted to his charge, speaks

Algonquin, has much influence with Indians and is generally respected: his prejudices are strong, but he is not blinded by them, and would make a respectable
Member of our board of Direction to a Seat in which he aspires with fine prospects of
success.

No. 7 [SIMON MCGILLIVRAY[15]] About 45 Years of Age. Possesses a good deal of super-
ficial cleverness and is very active but conceited, self sufficient and ridiculously high
minded. Very Tyrannical among his people which he calls 'discipline' and more
feared than respected by Men & Indians who are constantly in terror either from his
Club or his Dirk: Would be a very dignified overbearing man if he was in power; fond
of little *convivial* parties and would soon fall into intemperate habits if he had an
opportunity of indulging in that way. Has a good deal of the Indian in disposition as
well as in blood and appearance, and if promoted would be likely to ride on the top of
his commission and assume more than it is either fit or proper he should have an
opportunity of doing; in short I think he would make a bad use of the influence he
would acquire by promotion, and be a very troublesome man.

No. 9 [ALEXANDER RODERICK MCLEOD[16]] About 50 Years of Age. Has been a stout
strong active Man; a good pedestrian, an excellent shot, a skilful Canoe Man and a
tolerably good Indian Trader, but illiterate self sufficient and arrogant; does not
confine himself to plain matter of fact, annoys every one near him with the details of
his exploits; 'I did this' 'I did that' and 'I did the other thing' continually in his mouth,
but it unfortunately happens that he rarely does any thing well. Even his physical
powers have been greatly over-rated and I have never been able to discover that he
possesses beyond the most ordinary mental abilities: yet his own vanity and the
partiality of Friends have made him an aspirant to a place in the 1st Class to which in
my opinion he has very moderate pretensions as regards merit and if he did succeed
in gaining that stand he would be a most overbearing Tyrannical fellow. is capable of
little man tricks and I suspect is fond of a Glass of Grog in private. Would have made
an excellent *Guide* altho' he adds little respectability to the 'Fur Trade' as a 'Partner'.

No. 11 [SAMUEL BLACK[17]] About 52 Years of Age. The strangest man I ever knew. So
wary & suspicious that it is scarcely possible to get a direct answer from him on any
point, and when he does speak or write on any subject so prolix that it is quite
fatiguing to attempt following him. A perfectly honest man and his generosity might
be considered indicative of a warmth of heart if he was not known to be a cold
blooded fellow who could be guilty of any Cruelty and would be a perfect Tyrant if he
had power. Can never forget what he may consider a slight or insult, and fancies that
every man has a design upon him. Very cool, resolute to desperation, and equal to the
cutting of a throat with perfect deliberation: yet his word when he can be brought to
the point may be depended on. A Don Quixote in appearance Ghastly, raw boned
and lanthorn jawed, yet strong vigorous and active. Has not the talent of conciliating
Indians by whom he is disliked, but who are ever in dread of him, and well they may
be so. as he is ever on his guard against them and so suspicious that offensive and
defensive preparation seem to be the study of his Life having Dirks, Knives and

Loaded Pistols concealed about his Person and in all directions about his Establishment even under his Table cloth at meals and in his Bed. He would be admirably
adapted for the Service of the North West coast where the Natives are so treacherous
were it not that he cannot agree with his colleagues which renders it necessary to
give him a distinct change. I should be sorry to see a man of such character at our
Council board. Tolerably well Educated and most patient and laborious in whatever
he sets about, but so tedious that it is impossible to get through business with him.

No. 12 [PETER SKENE OGDEN[18]] About 45 Years of Age. A keen, sharp off hand fellow of
superior abilities to most of his colleagues, very hardy and active and not sparing of his
personal labour. Has had the benefit of a good plain Education, both writes and speaks
tolerably well, and has the address of a Man who has mixed a good deal in the World.
Has been very Wild & thoughtless and is still fond of coarse practical jokes, but with all
the appearances of thoughtlessness he is a very cool calculating fellow who is capable
of doing any thing to gain his own ends. His ambition knows no bounds and his
conduct and actions are not influenced or governed by any good or honourable
principle. In fact, I consider him one of the most unprincipled Men in the Indian
Country, who would soon get into habits of dissipation if he were not restrained by the
fear of these operating against his interests, and if he does indulge in that way madness
to which he has a predisposition will follow as a matter of course. A man likely to be
exceedingly troublesome if advanced to the 1st Class as the Trade is now constituted,
but his Services have been so conspicuous for several years past, that I think he has
strong claims to advancement.

No. 16 [ROBERT MILES[19]] About 40 Years of Age. The best Clerk in the Country as
regards Penmanship and Knowledge of Accounts, but his Education does not qualify
him for any thing beyond the Mechanical operations of a Counting House; he has
had little or no experience in any other branches of the business and his judgement is
of no great depth. Very fond of good living and if not kept at his Work would become
indolent and devoted to his pot and his pipe. A man of good conduct generally
speaking who will not tell a deliberate falsehood nor act improperly; but not so close
and confidential as a person in his Situation ought to be, fond of finding fault; full of
childish jealousy and ridiculously stiff and stately behind his Desk as also behind his
pipe, in short, a wiseacre who would in England be a Pot House Politician.

No. 17 [COLIN CAMPBELL[20]] About 45 Years of Age. An Excellent Trader who
speaks Several of the Native Languages well, and has the talent of conciliating the
Friendship of Indians. Mild and unassuming in his manners, commands respect
from his people and is esteemed by his colleagues and superiors; his conduct
highly correct and proper, has had the advantage of a plain Education, writes a
good hand, is a tolerable accountant and generally speaking a useful man who
would make a more respectable figure at the Council Board than many who now
occupy seats there.

No. 25 [WILLIAM TODD[21]] About 48 Years of Age. Considered skilful in his profession
and a tolerable Indian Trader, but not regular in business, nor is he an active bustling

man, and his ignorance of the French and Indian Languages disqualify him for many situations in the Service and of Counting House and Depot business he is quite ignorant. A Man of fair conduct, perfectly honest, and will not tell a direct lie: not much liked by his colleagues who think little of him altho' he has a very good opinion of his own abilities and is really a shrewd Sensible fellow, but wanting in the Manner and address which a man of his Profession might be expected to have. Has a tinge of Radicalism about him, is over fond of a Glass of Grog, and would in the Civilized World be addicted to Pot House conviviality altho' not a Drunkard.

Sixteen of the Clerks (here the names were not coded)

No. 1 Annance F. N.[22] About 40 Years of Age. 13 Years in the Service. A half breed of the Abiniki Tribe near Quebec; well Educated & has been a Schoolmaster. Is firm with Indians, speaks several of their Languages, walks well, is a good Shot and qualified to lead the life of an Indian whose disposition he possesses in a great degree. Is not worthy of belief even upon Oath and altogether a bad character altho' a useful Man. Can have no prospects of advancement. Attached to the Columbia Deptmt.

No. 6 Brisbois Chs.[23] A Canadian about 38 years of age, has been 15 Years in the Service. Is a tolerable Trader but not active; deficient in Education and does not speak English: his private character good, but neither his acquirements nor the importance of his services are such as to afford him the least prospect of advancement. Stationed in McKenzies River.

No. 7 Bell John.[24] A Scotchman, about 35 Years of Age, has been 13 Years in the Service. Writes a good hand, but his Education has been very limited. A quiet, steady well behaved Man, but wanting in the Manner address necessary to acquire influence over Indians or Servants, and does not possess any qualification likely to bring him into particular notice: equal however to the management of a smaller Trading Post. Not likely to come rapidly forward to an interest in the business. Stationed at McKenzies River.

No. 11 Bryson L. M.[25] An Irishman. About 42 years of age 13 Years in the Service. Steady and tolerably well conducted, but not a good Clerk or Trader; does not speak Indian and is not particularly active. Was attached to the Commissariat in the Peninsular War, but I should think in one of the lowest capacities. says he has been a 'Mercht' but was unfortunate: is evidently a fellow who has been accustomed to live from hand to mouth by his Wits. deals in the Marvellous but his fiction is harmless: has no hopes of advancement. Attached to the Temiscamingue Deptmt.

No. 12 Brown Nichs.[26] An Irishman, about 35 years of age, has been 4 Years in the Service: a very sharp active little fellow who conducts himself tolerably well, speaks Algonquin and is useful in Opposition. Deficient in Education, not steady, has changed his Masters very frequently and is considered by us merely a temporary Servant. Was picked up accidentally in Canada and does not look forward to promotion. Stationed at the Grand River.

No. 16 Deschambeault George.[27] A Canadian about 27 Years of Age. has been 13 Years in the Service. A well meaning, well disposed, heavy dull slovenly man, who is deficient in Education and can never be particularly useful. Understands a few Words of Cree, has charge of a small Post and does his best to manage it well, which does not require much talent otherwise it would not have been placed in his hands. Can have no pretensions to look forward to advancement. Stationed in English River Deptmt.

No. 17 Douglas James.[28] A Scotch West Indian: About 33 Years of Age, has been 13 Years in the Service. A stout powerful active Man of good conduct and respectable abilities: tolerably well Educated, expresses himself clearly on paper, understands our Counting House business and is an excellent Trader. Well qualified for any Service requiring bodily exertion, firmness of mind and the exercise of Sound judgement, but furiously violent when roused. Has every reason to look forward to early promotion and is a likely man to fill a place at our Council board in course of time. Stationed at the Columbia Deptmt.

No. 21 Erlandson Erland.[29] A Dane. About 42 Years of Age, has been 17 years in the service. Was bred a ship Carpenter in the Dock Yard of Copenhagen and entered the Service as a labourer from one of the Prison Ships at Chatham where he was a Prisoner of War. A steady painstaking well behaved man who has improved himself very much since he came to this country, writes a good hand, expresses himself well in English either Verbally or by Letter for a Foreigner and is a shrewd Sensible Man. Strong, active & useful, liked by his Superiors, esteemed by his Colleagues and respected by Servants and Indians; indeed a superior man in many respects to some of our Councillers, and whom I should like to see promoted in due time as a reward for his meritorious conduct and in order to shew that it is to Character & conduct we principally look in our Elections: but being a Foreigner and raised from the ranks I suspect it will be a difficult matter to get him the number of Votes necessary to put him in Nomination. Stationed at Ungava.

No. 27 Gladman George.[30] A half-breed. About 36 Years of Age, has been 17 years in the Service. Is the principal accountant at Moose Factory, writes a good hand and understands our accounts. Has had no experience as a Trader and knows little about the general business of the Depot. Entertains a very high opinion of himself and would be presuming & forward if permitted. Exceedingly jealous of any little attentions shown his colleagues and disposed to assume authority over juniors: fancies that his time is thrown away in this country, and that he could do much better elsewhere — but I think he has brought his Services to an excellent Market and that he is fully paid for them.

No. 29 Good, Richd.[31] An Englishman about 55 Years of Age, has been 37 Years in the Country. A poor Drunken useless creature, in whom, no trust or confidence can be placed. Quite a Sot from whom it is impossible to keep Liquor as if he cannot purchase or pilfer it from the Stores, he will obtain it clandestinely through the Servants or Indians. Retained in the Service from a feeling of charity alone, as were he discharged he would either Starve or become a Pauper. Stationed at Moose.

No. 31 Grant Cuthbert.[32] A half breed whose Name must long recall to mind some horrible scenes which in former Days took place at Red River Settlement in which he was the principal actor. About 38 Years of Age, during 20 of which he has been more or less connected with the Service. A generous Warm hearted Man who would not have been guilty of the Crimes laid to his charge had he not been drawn into them by designing Men. A very stout powerful fellow of great nerve & resolution but now getting unwieldy and inactive. Drinks ardent spirits in large quantities, thinks nothing of a Bottle of Rum at a Sitting but is so well Seasoned that he is seldom intoxicated altho it undermines his constitution rapidly. A sensible clear headed man of good conduct except in reference to the unfortunate habits of intemperance he has fallen into. Entirely under the influence of the Catholic Mission and quite a Bigot. The American Traders have made several liberal offers to him, but he has rejected them all being now a staunch Hudsons Bay man and we allow him a saly of £200 p Annum as 'Warden of the Plains' which is a Sinecure offered him intirely from political motives and not from any feeling of liberality or partiality. This appointment prevents him from interfering with the Trade on his own account which he would otherwise do in all probability; it moreover affords us the benefit of his great influence over the half breeds and Indians of the neighbourhood which is convenient inasmuch as it exempts us from many difficulties with them. He resides at the White Horse Plain about 16 miles up the Assiniboine River where he has a Farm and only visits the Establishment on business or by Invitation; but is always ready to obey our commands and is very effective when employed as a constable among the half breeds or Indians. Is perfectly satisfied with what has been done for him which is quite sufficient and has no prospect of advancement.

No. 40 Hargrave James.[33] A Scotchman about 32 Years of Age, has been 12 years in the Service. A man of good Education and of highly correct conduct and character and very useful. Expresses himself well either Verbally or on paper, is clear headed and possesses a better Knowledge of general business than might be expected from the advantages he has had. Equal to the management of York Depôt and is better qualified for a Seat in Council than 9 out of 10 of our present Chief Factors. Has every reason to calculate on early promotion and may in due time reach the board of Green Cloth if he goes on as he promises: he has not however had any experience in the Indian Trade, can speak none of the Native Languages, his Health is not very good and his temper is rather Sour. Stationed at York Factory.

No. 53 McKenzie Charles.[34] A Scotchman about 56 Years of Age. 29 Years in the Service. A queer prosing long Winded little highland body, who traces his lineage back to Ossian and claims the Laureatship of Albany District now that Chief Factor Kennedy is gone. Never was a bright active or useful man even when there was a greater Dearth of talent in the country than now, but fancies himself neglected in being still left on the list of Clerks notwithstanding a Servitude of nearly 30 years: his Day is gone by, and I think it would be highly inexpedient to promote such men who have no other claim to advancement than their antiquity. Stationed at Albany District.

No. 62 McKay Thomas.[35] A half breed of the Saulteaux Tribe, about 40 Years of Age has been 20 years in the Service. Lame in consequence of a Deslocation of the Knee notwithstanding which he is very active, one of the best Shots in the Country and very cool and resolute among Indians. has always been employed on the most desperate service in the Columbia and the more desperate it is the better he likes it. He is know to every Indian in that Department and his name alone is a host of Strength carrying terror with it as he has sent many of them to their 'long home'; quite a 'blood hound' who must be kept under restraint. possesses little judgement and a confirmed Liar, but a necessary evil at such a place as Vancouver; has not a particle of feeling or humanity in his composition. Is at the height of his ambition.

No. 80 Simpson Thomas.[36] A Scotchman 3 years in the Service 24 Years of Age; Was considered one of the most finished Scholars in Aberdeen College: is hardy & active and will in due time if he goes on as he promises be one of the most complete men of business in the country; acts as my Secty and Confidential Clerk during the busy Season and in the capacities of Shopman, Accountant & Trader at Red River Settlement during the Winter. Perfectly correct in regard to personal conduct & character.

No. 88 Barnston George.[37] A Scotchman, 12 Years in the Service, about 32 Years of Age. A well Educated man, very active, & high Spirited to a romantic degree, who will on no account do what *he* considers an improper thing, but so touchy & sensitive that it is difficult to keep on good terms or to do business with him, which frequently leads to difficulties: Seems to consider it necessary to make an 'affair of honour' of every trifling misunderstanding; has been a principal in one and Second in another bloodless Duel and would fight anything or any body either with or without a cause. Has a high opinion of his own abilities which are above par, but over rates them. Is sometimes of a gloomy desponding turn of mind and we have frequently been apprehensive that he would commit suicide in one of those fits. It is evident that he is of unsound mind at times; but with all his failings & peculiarities we feel an interest in him. Retired from the Service last year fancying himself neglected or ill used but without any good grounds for so thinking, and re-admitted this Season lest he might connect himself with the Americans and give us trouble or do worse in a fit of desperation (if reduced to distress) out of which a story might be made by designing people to the great annoyance of the Company.

Notes

[1] Colin Robertson (1783–1842). Glyndwr Williams calls this 'the most cruelly unfair of any entry'; Simpson ignores Robertson's energetic contribution to the Hudson's Bay Company during its years of conflict with the NWC to mock the 'rather pathetic figure of the 1830s'.

[2] 'Sandy' Stewart served the NWC from 1796 to union in 1821, and then became an HBC Chief Factor. He retired in 1833 and died in 1840.

[3] John George McTavish (c. 1778–1847) was LETITIA HARGRAVE's uncle. It is not easy to tell from this

entry that McTavish was Simpson's closest friend in the fur-trade country, and the recipient of a remarkably frank private correspondence from Simpson over a long period of time.

[4] John Clarke (1781–1858), a restless man who had moved from company to company and had a reputation for violent and imprudent behaviour.

[5] For John Stuart (1779–1847) see of course SIMON FRASER, whom he accompanied on his journey of 1808 down the Fraser River; also LETITIA HARGRAVE, DANIEL HARMON.

[6] John McLoughlin (1784–1857), along with John Rowand and James Douglas, was among the most formidable men sketched by Simpson. In one of his typical paradoxes, in the same year Simpson praised him unreservedly to the London Committee.

[7] James Keith (1782–1851), a NWC trader who joined the HBC at union; he managed their affairs at Lachine, near Montreal.

[8] Angus Bethune (1783–1858), another NWC trader who had joined the HBC at union. He was in charge Sault Ste Marie when FRANCES SIMPSON passed through in 1830.

[9] Donald McKenzie (1783–1851) was a cousin of Alexander Mackenzie, and an eminent member of the NWC. He joined the HBC at union. He was in charge of Red River 1823–33, and Governor of Assiniboia 1825–33. He retired in 1835.

[10] Alexander Christie (1792–1872) joined the Hudson's Bay Company in 1809. His ability was highly respected; he was Governor of Assiniboia in 1833–9 and 1844–8. He retired in 1853.

[11] John Rowand (1787–1854), a NWC partner who joined the HBC at union. From 1823 to 1854 he was at Edmonton House as head of the Saskatchewan District. He died at Fort Pitt, still in the Company's service, the last to survive of the officers who had been appointed in 1821. Rowand's wife Lisette was a mixed-blood daughter of EDWARD UMFREVILLE.

[12] Duncan Finlayson (c. 1796–1862) married Frances Simpson's sister Isobel. He joined the company as a clerk in 1815 and eventually rose to Chief Factor. He became Governor of Assibiboia and later (a rare honour for an old servant of the Company) a member of the London Committee. See LETITIA HARGRAVE.

[13] McIntosh was with the NWC by 1806 and joined the HBC at union. His career was unremarkable, and he died in 1845.

[14] Angus Cameron (c. 1782–1876), the longest-lived of the old NWC partners. He had joined the NWC in 1801, and was a formidable opponent of the HBC, but became a Chief Trader at union.

[15] Often called 'Junior' to distinguish him from his uncle, the great Simon McGillivray of the NWC. Born in 1790 and entered the NWC in 1813; he joined the HBC at union, and died in 1840.

[16] McLeod (c. 1782–1840) was with the NWC from 1801, but joined the HBC at union. He had a colourful and controversial career, including service on George Back's Arctic Land Expedition of 1833–5.

[17] Black (1780–1841) served both the XY and North West Companies; he was a fierce and intimidating opponent of the Hudson's Bay Company and was one of the few North Westers rejected at union. He later joined the HBC as a clerk, and in 1824 made a notable exploration of the Finlay River. He died at the hands of a native at Kamloops, where he was Chief Trader.

[18] Ogden (1790–1854), like his friend Samuel Black, was originally a NWC man with a reputation for violence; chiefly in its own defence, the HBC allowed him to join the Company two years after union. Between 1824 and 1830 he traded furs in the rich Snake Country south of the Columbia River, under instructions from Simpson to 'ruin' the country for American traders. At the same time he recorded important geographical discoveries in the American north west.

[19] Miles was born in England in 1795 and spent his whole career with the HBC; he died in 1870.

[20] Born in Canada about 1787, Campbell served the NWC and the HBC, rising no higher than Chief Trader; he died in 1853.

[21] Born in Ireland in 1784, Todd joined the HBC as a surgeon, though he was also a trader.

Simpson had reason to be grateful to him, since he had seen Frances Simpson through her first, very difficult, pregnancy in 1831. He earned a distinguished medical reputation in the west, and died in the Company's service in 1851.

[22]François Noel Annance joined the NWC in 1820, and moved to the HBC at union as interpreter and clerk. He retired from the service after a dispute with John Stuart in 1834.

[23]Charles Brisbois joined the NWC in 1816, and transferred to the HBC at union. His post journals and letters are in French. His abilities must have been few, as the Company nearly retired him twice. He died in 1847.

[24]Born about 1799, Bell moved from the NWC to the HBC at union, and spent most of his subsequent career in the Mackenzie River district. In 1839–45 he explored the Peel River and the country to the west. He died in 1868.

[25]Leslie Bryson served the NWC and then the HBC; Company documents support Simpson's estimate of his abilities. He retired in 1834.

[26]Nicholas Brown joined the HBC in 1828, and despite Simpson's low opinion of his abilities acquitted himself well; he stayed with the Company until 1847.

[27]Born in Quebec about 1801, George Deschambeault joined the HBC in 1819. Company records of his abilities vary, and despite Simpson's verdict, he rose to Chief Trader; he died at St Boniface in 1870, still in the Company's service.

[28]Douglas would become one of the most distinguished of the clerks Simpson portrayed. Born in 1803, he joined the NWC in 1819 and the HBC in 1821, rising rapidly to Chief Factor in 1839. He was appointed Governor of Vancouver Island in 1851, of British Columbia in 1858, and was knighted in 1863. He died in 1877.

[29]Born in Copenhagen about 1790, Erlandson joined the HBC in 1814, serving at Moose and on the Eastmain. He played a prominent role in opening up Ungava, but retired in 1848, disappointed at his lack of advancement.

[30]George Gladman Jr (*c.* 1799-*c.* 1863). See LETITIA HARGRAVE.

[31]Richard Good joined the HBC in 1796 but never rose higher than clerk. He died in 1850.

[32]Among the most famous figures of the early west, Grant was born in 1793 and joined the NWC in 1812. Appointed 'Captain General of all the half-breeds in the country', he led a party of Métis in the massacre at Seven Oaks in 1816. Simpson's personal intervention gained him admission to the HBC in 1823, but he retired in 1824, and in 1828 was made 'Warden of the Plains' at Red River, a post he held until 1849. He died in 1854.

[33]For James Hargrave, see LETITIA HARGRAVE.

[34]Born in Scotland in 1774, McKenzie served both the NWC and the HBC, retiring, still a clerk, in 1854. He died in 1855.

[35]A step-son of John McLoughlin, McKay was born in the Indian country around 1796. Before his death in 1849/50 he had served several trading companies, and led an adventurous life (including participation in the California gold rush) on the west coast.

[36]A cousin of GEORGE SIMPSON, born in Scotland in 1808, Thomas Simpson at first refused the Governor's offer to become his secretary, but eventually joined the Company. He served as his cousin's confidential clerk, and then between 1836 and 1840 shared leadership of the Company's Northern Discovery Expedition with Peter Warren Dease. His mysterious death shortly after his return in 1840 caused much gossip among traders and settlers.

[37]Born in Scotland about 1899, Barnston joined the NWC in 1820 and the HBC at union. He complained constantly about his dissatisfaction, but was eventually promoted, and died, a retired Chief Factor, in 1882.

Letitia Hargrave   (1813 – 1854)

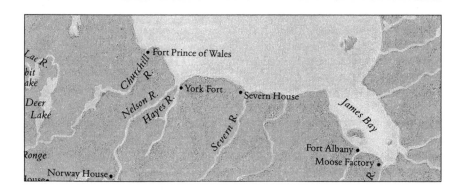

LETITIA HARGRAVE was born into a Scottish family with extensive fur trade connections, including both Simon McTavish (or Mactavish) of the North West Company and her uncle J.G. McTavish, mentioned in a number of these excerpts. In 1840 she married James Hargrave, Chief Trader at York Factory where her brother William was posted. With FRANCES SIMPSON and Isobel Finlayson, Letitia was among the first English women to come to western Canada, but their personalities could not have been more different. Letitia's early letters, written to her mother from London, show her lively and impetuous temperament and her ability to adapt rapidly to new scenes; she was quick to judge and just as quick to withdraw her judgement, sharp of tongue yet as ready to laugh at herself as at others. In her letters home, written over more than a decade, she matures from a gawking, seasick provincial into a shrewd and experienced reporter on the fur trade and all that went on amidst the lively scene of York Fort. She and Hargrave took home leave in 1846, and in 1850 were posted from York Fort to Sault Ste Marie where Letitia died suddenly of cholera in 1854.

Text: Margaret Arnett McLeod, ed., *The Letters of Letitia Hargrave*. Toronto: The Champlain Society, 1947, compared with originals and copies in the National Archives of Canada. Contractions have been expanded. The letter of 1 Sept. 1849 to Dugald Mactavish (not in McLeod) is NAC MG19 A21, Series 1, Vol. 27, No. 42.

(4) To Mary Mactavish
London, Saturday
2 May 1840

My dear Polly:

We arrived here, *viz* [that is to say, at the] George and Vulture[1] at seven o'clock last evening after an agreeable drive through the streets in a coach — London is not so ugly as I expected. . . . Tell Mama I have picked off all my haps [cloaks], it is so fearfully hot, but I must try and describe the George and Vulture. We drove for three miles from the station, passed St Paul's, Newgate and the Mansion House and shortly after the coach entered a sort of long narrow Court down from Lombard Street and there was the George at the bottom of it, a large black house — Hargrave *would* have his dinner though it was eight before we were ready.[2]

While he was working with the luggage the landlady sailed into my room, but as I thought she looked very patronizing and being wearied and rather cross I was stately too and *malgré* all my own exertions I could not help being repulsive and disagreeable so after a polite speech she retired. When Hargrave came up he mentioned that she had asked if I had ever been in town before and on hearing not, she said it might please me to see a little society and she and her sons would feel honored if I would *look* in on them for half an hour. I would not, as I could not be bothered dressing for such a purpose when I was just at the [point of] fainting and I said I must run to my bed. Think of my rage and grief when a very nice looking woman who is upper servant told me her mistress had sent her to enquire if I would like to see the table. On my going with her she took me first into a large room arranged for dancing and then showed me another with a most magnificent supper laid out for upwards of 100!!! I never saw anything like it and fear I never will again. I eat [ate] my dinner with a heavy heart and Hargrave sent me off to my bed, where I was scarcely deposited till the carriages arrived and I cannot tell you the number of times I was out and in. Only one could enter at a time and such a host as there were. I would not have been two minutes in my bed till midnight had I not been disgusted by several gentlemen arriving by themselves in a cab and as I could not distinguish between that conveyance and a coach I was exasperated at their imposing upon me as there was of course nothing remarkable about them save the extreme whiteness of their gloves. The Ladies were well worth the risk of catching a little cold. The flower wreaths in their hair and the grandeur of their gowns were displayed by the bright light of the lamps over the door and as each waited coolly in the court, bare neck, arms and all till she arranged herself, I had lots of time to admire. . . . I have not recovered my sorrow at not knowing that it was not a private tea party. The fete was in honor of the marriage of her son and I much fear Boz[3] would be there. . . .

Old Mr. Stuart[4] is here blackguarding the Queen for dismissing the beautiful Lady Fanny Cooper because Prince Albert spoke to her on approaching the Altar at his marriage. She was disbanded[5] next day.

Make Locky[6] write if you can't. Hargrave joins me in love to you all. I am going out to see the world in a bus as I am very feckless [weak] on my feet and wearied myself out in two hours at Liverpool which is as moully[7] a looking place as I would wish to see. I will write Flora[8] now and Papa and Mama next time as I hope to have seen some thing or other.

(22) To Mrs. Dugald Mactavish   York Factory, September 1840

My dear Mama:

We arrived here on Monday the 10th of August after an unusually short passage. We got on shore, meaning stuck on the bar, on Sunday evening 15 miles from York. Fortunately the bottom was soft mud and except that there was much confusion and the men took the opportunity to get tipsy, the weather being calm we lay quietly although a good deal on one side, and no harm was done. In consequence of our guns, Mr. Finlayson and Willie came off in a small boat about nine at night.[9] They remained all night but William returned at daylight with the despatches. We waited for the afternoon tide and left the ship at four o'clock sticking fast. She got off next morning and reached York in three hours and I can give you very little idea of my feelings as for some days or weeks I had been so wretched that Hargrave thought if I went on shore at all it would have been rolled and carried in a blanket. I could neither eat sleep nor speak and my pulse was often 120. I could not take medicine as I told you we had the cuddy[10] for our cabin and the mess was there and the Captain always in it. My first exploit on being lowered into the yawl, was to turn my back to the company and cry myself sick. After which I began to look about me and feel less disconsolate. I had no sooner got out of the yawl than I felt better and have ever since got stronger, and as for fatness I am getting on well and my neck is as well covered as when I left Stromness.

On reaching the Quay here we found Mr. Gladman[11] and a Mr. Manson Chief trader from Fort Vancouver who goes home by the ship this season. Hargrave introduced them both and then took Miss Ross and me away up. On looking round we found Mr. and Mrs. Finlayson behind together, Mr. Gladman and Miss Allan, and Mrs. Potter and Mr. Manson likewise arm in arm. . . .

. . . I hope that wherever it may be my lot to go I shall never be shut up in a cabin with 3 ladies and servants. The constant clack clack and the impossibility of being one moment alone had worn me out completely. Had I had the power to get a little time to myself I would not have been so miserable, but if I were half dead and lay down on my berth, one or other of them was sure to squat on the ledge of my bed and all out of kindness.

. . . Margaret[12] is very satisfactory and quiet, works very neatly and is a great hand at making drawers, flannels etc. and sorting Mr. H.'s clothes having learned from her father. She will have a very easy time of it as she has nothing to do, but our bedroom and the stove is lighted at 5.A.M. by the butler, an elderly conceited Canadian called *Gibout* an old servant of Uncle's.[13] . . . I like old Gibout best, he is very respectable and the delight he takes in toiling for me is refreshing. . . . The usual dinner for our mess meaning the three ladies and me was: a roast of venison at the top, three geese at the foot, four ducks on one side, six plovers on the other, a large Red River ham (whole leg) and potatoes and mashed turnips or boiled lettuce. For something green when they have broth they put lettuce and the bitterness is surprizing. They have radish and lettuce after dinner. . . .

I only observed one or two half-breeds; one was a woman, the only female except ourselves and Mrs. Potter and Margaret. She had a baby with her and its unhappy legs [were] wrapt up in a moss bag. It looked like a mummy. I have not been near enough to inspect closely but I shall make Margaret fetch a child over without the mother that I may examine it. The moment it is born they get the bag stuffed with soft moss which has been in readiness and stuff the wretch into it up to the neck, bind it tightly round like a mummy, so as to make it as firm and flat as a deal board, then fasten it around their own back and work away about what they have to do. They don't mind the moss being wet and dirty but consider it a great convenience that they have no trouble shifting [it] at least for a long time. The Indians all walk with their feet turned in from this discipline and their arms are as stiff as if there was not a joint in them. While the whites gentle and simple[14] are running about perspiring with haste the Indians stalk along the platforms with their backs bent as if it were entirely for pleasure that they were wheeling barrows. They march so slowly and look so stately that they remind me of people on the stage. The women always come to the Fort in pairs, the older first, the younger behind her, and they also look very dignified and demure. The men wear long blue capots like children's surtouts (very long) and hoods either hanging down or on their head, scarlet leggings not trowsers, and gay scarlet military sashes round their waist.[15] Squaws never move without their blanket, common coarse often dirty affairs. They fold them like a scarf, not a shawl. The wee'est girls have them. One of the pigs comes to my window with red currants in the corner of hers which is black with dirt. Hargrave bought two pounds of peppermint drops at Stromness and they laugh aloud when I give them some. They don't know a word of English or French. When I want flowers or berries I show them a specimen and give them a shove and off they go. It never happens that they fail.

I was much surprised at the 'great swell'[16] the Factory is. It looks beautiful. The houses are painted pale yellow. The windows and some particular parts white. Some have green gauze mosquito curtains outside and altogether the effect is very good. Our house is a good size, one bedroom off each sitting room and men servants' rooms off the kitchen, a very large closet off the dining room. I had nearly forgot my piano.[17] It is a very fine one and the handsomest I ever saw. The wood is beautiful and Mr. Finlayson is croaking for one the same. Mrs. F. does not play except to accompany herself. I was astonished at its appearance as I did not expect the case to be any great thing. The hinge of the lid, and the lock have created a sensation among the geniuses here from the uncommon elegance of their contrivance and mechanism. There was not a scratch upon it nor a note out of tune. The form of the pedal is magnificent and the wood beautifully marked. Mr. Gladman has a barrel organ in which are a drum and some other instruments. It is never silent, the family imagine themselves so fond of music. Willie maintains that it was nothing but weakness and want of sense that made Gladman cause the disturbance between Uncle and Dugald.[18] The whole family make it their duty to gather gossip and to detail it to all and sundry. . . .

(23) To Florence Mactavish

York Factory, 1st [to 5th] September 1840

My dear Flora:

I began and continued a sort of diary but in the hubbub of leaving the ship and my being so unwell that I could do nothing Mr. Hargrave and Margaret lost the sheet containing our adventures in Hudson Straits so that I must remember what I can. On first entering we were becalmed among the ice and lay two days off Savage islands.[19] For 24 hours night and day we were beset with huskies. They were heard shouting for at least two hours and a half before they reached us which they did in light canoes with a hole in the middle. Each holds one man and a few tusks of ivory (walrus teeth) which they brought to traffic. There were 34 canoes. We moved so slowly that they kept up with us all the time. Three hours after their arrival the luggage boats came up manned by women and laden with children, husky dogs, [and] images or dolls in imitation of themselves. There were several large boats holding the various families of the gents in the light ones. Almost every woman had a huge fat child in her hood[20] and when they saw anything in the sailors' hands that they wanted they seized the babies, pulled off their one article of dress, shriek-ing *pilly tay* (give me) threw the weans who squalled like any white back into the hood. If they did not get quiet they put their breasts some how over their shoul-ders and contined their *pilly tay*. When a saw was shown them the whole fleet got into commotion and screamed *cutty swaback*. A gimblet was *billy linga*. They would give any thing for them, but poor wretches except a few seal skins and the walrus teeth they had nothing worth trading. When they get any thing—a broken pair of rusty scissors or horrid old iron off a barrel (the hoop)—they rubbed their tongue over it. They use their boots as you used to do your wide sleeves, that is put every thing into them, pot lids and darning needles. I gave one some needles; he tried to stick them into his trowsers but always pricked his fingers, so after licking both finger and needles, he said *coonah* looking very knowing, and handed them over the ship's side to his coonah (wife). They were evidently quite ignorant of the use of water and nothing more horrible than the old black dirt of the ladies can be imagined. They rub themselves all over with grease and from the hood being always dragged down by the child's weight their necks and shoulders are blackened by wind and weather. I got a doll and will see if it can get a place among the tongues.[21] The hood is on the head and the tail behind is too short, but the car-riage and shoulders are the very thing, and the shape of the face. They keep bawl-ing *Chimoo Chimoo*, signifying good and *aha* when pleased which indeed they always seemed. The men looked well, each in his beautiful canoe, but the women gathered together in the luggage canoes were hideous, the children like Johnnie McBride in feature and color.

While the canoes were round us a shouting and yelling arose and off they all paddled towards a berg, where on looking through a glass an unfortunate seal was discovered. Their clamor stupefied the animal and he stood quietly till they harpooned him on which he fell head over feet off the ice into the water. Any thing like the rapidity of their progress I never saw. All the men's canoes were there. They cut the seal up, eat what they wanted (they don't cook) and then divided the remains faithfully among them. When they returned to the ship each man had a lump of red seal behind him. Every moment they would put a hand back rub it over the store and lick the fat and blood off the paw with great satisfaction. We had great difficulty in getting rid of them, they followed and made such a noise and the smell they left was insufferable all about for days. Although only one man had been allowed to come on board yet he managed to drag his wife up by a leg and arm. Hargrave and I were standing on a pigs' house when she came up and before I could escape she had her arms about my waist dancing and singing till I thought we should have either got over board or down among the pigs. They plait their hair in tails both before and behind and are certainly well sized and not the wretched looking objects they are often represented. They are a little fat I confess, but had they been clean they would many of them have looked well particularly the men who seem very strong. They wear often a queer sort of spectacle to save their eyes, which are probably affected before they put them on by the snow both on land and water. It is a piece of wood this shape [diagram] these narrow slits to see through. Indeed I have given you the idea that the slits are wider than they really are as you would wonder how they could see at all. They all appeared very happy and good natured to each other. . . .

I forgot to say that on Friday we got into some very thick ice and feared that we might have been kept. The bells were kept ringing for a while by the thumps but by dint of management we escaped. A large white bear came out on the ice. We had seen one in the straits and by my running on deck I got a few days threatening of an attack of earache but it was very slight. Mrs. Finlayson's hands and my feet suffered dreadfully from chilblains. They broke and swelled so that I had to wear mocassins and she could not put on her gloves. . . .

. . . Give my love to Hector and Alexander.[22] I often wish very sorely that I could see Alexander and many a good volley Willie gives me for saying it. I know I will like York as well as any other place if I ever get over the constant wish to hear from you. Hargrave I think will go back to Scotland at least if we live but at the very soonest that will not be for ten years. Of course I mean to remain. . . .

Mr. Cochran,[23] chaplain at Red River has written a long letter to Hargrave on the subject of how I should be treated. What ever wrong I may [do] he is to be sure it is half his fault so that I am to [be] in peace and H. is to have all the remorse. When the Governor and Mrs. Simpson were there he had promised [to] dine but as the day was fearful with wind and snow and he had many miles to travel they did not wait so at eight o'clock he made his appearance in their room and they made no attempt to conceal their amazement. So he told them that as his horse could not travel he had come on his cow, having promised that he would do so. So he demanded a cup of tea and said that having seen them he would return immediately. They pressed him to stay all night but he said he had promised his wife that he would go home, so off he set on his devoted cow's back.

(24) To Mary Mactavish

York Factory, 1st September 1840

My dear Polly:

. . . I went into the kitchen today and found Betsy the washing woman busy over a tub with a Stuart tartan gown and her hair dressed for the occasion. She has charge of a family whose mother died in Spring and right in the middle of the floor stood the baby in its moss bag and cradle quite erect. Betsy lived as squaw with a Mr. Randall who went home in the Autumn and whom the people in London have put into the house there.[24] She waited on Miss Ross and told her what she thought of Mr. Randall having gone. She says she has had four or else five husbands, but she will never take another as it will only be for her money that they will ask her. Hargrave looked over her accounts and found she really has gathered £88, which is in the Company's hands. She makes it by washing and never spends a penny of the interest as she has her living from the kitchen and is well behaved. Her kindness to the poor baby is extraordinary. Miss Ross used to hear it squalling all night as it is teething and she soothed and sung to it as if she had been its mother. All this because when its own mother was dying she asked her to take it home and nurse it out of a sucking pipe and be good to it. . . .

Before Mrs. Finlayson went she thought it would be right to call for Mrs. Gladman[25] partly for civility and partly because she wished that Mrs. G. and I should be on civil terms being the only women, and she would not advise me to go to her first lest as they have a way of doing she might sneer and say I was glad to get her company. So over Mr. F and she went, and she very coolly informed her that we were sorry at not seeing her, but it was not customary in England for the lady newly arrived to call for the old settler. So the very day after she left us I perceived Mr. and Mrs. Gladman coming along the platform, the lady as large as a lady can be and dressed to death in a Waterloo blue Merino, moccasins, a straw bonnet lined with lilac satin with a profusion of lilac blue and white ribbon and a cap border of very broad blonde, the same depth all round, no gloves and a silk shawl, the old fashion white around and green pattern. Mr. Gladman said she would have come sooner if she had wished to please him, but she was bashful and did not like to intrude. She is very decent looking and Mrs. Finlayson says her daughters are quite modest-like girls. I shall return the visit tomorrow and see them. Her first husband the Misses Stewart's father is still alive, but she is now fairly married. The two Miss Stewarts live with them and are both past 20 and they have a very large family of Gladmans. All the half castes speak very low and I have always remarked that their voices were pleasant. Mrs. Gladman is fully as vulgar looking as Mrs. Loynachan but speaks well and that is a great help. I rather think she is kindly disposed and looks at any rate good natured. The poor woman must be uncomfortably situated with such a family and no servant, obliged to take what is sent her from the mess kitchen. Willie says they like nothing but animal food so that they will be pleased. As for me I am tired already and have taken to milk porridge for a change and find it very good for me as my bowels don't plague me now at all.

(26) To Mrs. Dugald Mactavish

York Factory, 1st December, 1840

My dear Mamma

Mrs. Gladman and I are getting very gracious. She favored me with her history and that of her mother before her. Her father was partner in the other Company.[26] Her mother, his wife as she considered herself, got a girl in to help her work who prevailed on her father to take her too, so the first got indignant and left him, with Mrs. Gladman's mother, widow of one in the same Company. The father went to England and died, the second squaw having died before him. I wish I could tell it as Mrs. Gladman did. Her mother suffered so much that she had to be bled on the occasion. Her own story was as disastrous. Mr. Stuart, a man who had established steam mills for sawing timber at Moose and who was employed by the Company asked her father for her when she was 12 years old. She was dragged out of her Mother's room and sent away with him. She declares that she never hated man as she did him, and he beat her and maltreated her till her life was a burden. When she had been married six years she had a daughter and then two other children. After living with him nine years he left her and the children and went to Canada where he has been ever since. She waited four years and then 'I went with Mr. Gladman.' She always says 'When I *was sent* with Mr. Stuart' and 'When I *went* with Mr. Gladman.' She was fairly married three years ago and sports a wedding ring. Her two daughters live with them but she sent the boy to his father. There are six little Gladmans. Hargrave's represent-atives at Oxford and Churchill both wish Miss Stuart to marry them, but her Mother declares she will take neither. They are both partners and are coming here at Xmas. They are very wearyful misses and look like death. . . .

. . . The state of society seems shocking. Some people educate and make gentle-men of part of their family and leave the others savages. I had heard of Mr. Bird at Red River and his dandified sons. One day while the boats were here a common half breed came in to get orders for provisions for his boatmen. Mr. H. called him Mr. Bird to my amazement.[27] This was one who had not been educated and while his father and brothers are nobility at the Colony, he is a voyageur and sat at table with the house servants here. Dr. MacLoughlen, one of our grandees, at a great expense gave two of his sons a regular education in England and keeps the third a common Indian. One of them had been for years at the Military College in London but they have both entered the Company's service. I daresay the heathen is the happiest of them as the father is constantly upbraiding the others with the ransom they have cost him. . . .

(33) To Mrs. Dugald Mactavish

York Factory, 14th May, 1842

My dear Mama:

. . . The holidays were what is considered very gay this winter. The gentlemen had two balls in their house and Mr. H. likewise gave two. As there was no fiddler, they took the liberty of unpacking Mr. Gladman's beloved organ, and Willie and the Doctor performed by turns. They kept it in their house and night and day the unfortunate instrument was grinding and all feet dancing. Hargrave gave another ball while Messrs. Clouston and MacKay[28] were here, when it was again in requisition. I did not see any of the exhibitions. The ladies all behaved very well, only my friend Betsy 'got dronk' as she told me and was carried home. Madame Poukie John also forgot herself and stole as much of the supper as she could, till Gibeault spied her. The old lady has been turned out of the Fort for her ultra views of religion. Having turned saint she persuaded her son, our hunter, to become a preacher, so he gave the Indians a deer he had killed [and] got into notoriety among them. The mother pitched a tent for a church. All the Indians here with three or four exceptions went. Mr. Poukie John appeared in full canonicals, being two blankets sewed together with deer sinew and created a sensation. The women took fits, etc., and Madam was turned off with her son next day. It was her daughter who was married last winter and sent a message to her mother to send her some tea and oatmeal as she was sick of fish and potatoes at Oxford. They can't speak any English.

I hope that in seven weeks at the very most I shall hear that you are all well. Somehow I feel as if I did not care what the rest of the world did, but I trust that nothing has gone far wrong among any of my friends. . . .

(35) To Dugald Mactavish, Sr.

York Factory, 8th September, 1842

. . . I suspect there is something not very likely to be agreeable to the people in this country in the Wesleyan reports[29] this year, as Mr. Evans[30] has not given us one though Hargrave asked it, and last season they were poked at us by the quarter of a hundred. It is not Mr. Evans, I am sure, as it is his policy when he can't say what is favorable to hold his tongue, but some of his young preachers I daresay have been inveighing or complaining, and very ill [on] their part it is. There must be some reason, as Evans admits that he has the reports and he presented us with a pamphlet written by Dr. Alder on the rise and fall of Wesleyan Missions,[31] I mean rise and progress. They have got a college of Jesuits among the Blackfeet, and the Company have given Mr. Blanchette[32] the head, £100 a year, whether as a retaining fee, that he may keep the Indians as *we* wish them, or because they wish well to him and his labors, I can't say but I think the former. M. Blanchette is an excellent old man who appears to mind his own affairs, while the Episcopal missionaries here attend only to other peoples. Mr. Smithurst[33] [of] Red River goes about rechristening Indians and children who had been baptized by Mr. Evans, while the Wesleyans revile the Roman Catholic clergy of the Settlement, and there was no minister left in it but old Mr. Cochran, all the others having retired to combat each other amongst the Indians, four Catholics to I don't know how many Episcopals. Mr. Evans says his instructions are to go only where there is no minister of another sect,[34] but the others hate him with all their heart. He has been busy making a tin canoe all the time he has been here. It looks very stylish but I don't know how it will paddle. Last year he was occupied in making an American despatch [box] which he says is a perfect utensil, and when he returns to Norway House he is to begin a printing press, which he seems to have no doubts about being able to construct, and then he is to publish at a great rate.[35]

(39) To Mrs. Dugald Mactavish

York Factory, 10th April 1843.

. . . Hargrave has promised that he will not send him[36] to a boarding school; let the expense be what it may, he will try and get a clergyman of character to train him, if he is spared to go home. The children brought up here are so simple and ignorant that they are apt to get into ways that those at home escape, and require constant watching. . . . Hargrave told me too that he would let me go home with him although it is not likely that he will yet himself. Many things may happen to make my going inconvenient. But it is a comfort to think that I shall not have to let the little creatutre go alone in the meantime. Besides the pleasure of getting back to you again, I have a feeling that I would not like to see anyone but yourselves and poor Mary Hamilton. I am so changed within that I daresay I am much so externally and I would shrink from exposing myself to the cool criticism of Mrs. Worsley who delights in telling me how old people are looking, saying nothing of herself, however. There has been nothing further of John MacLoughlin's murder except that master and men were all drunk, firing at each other till John who was in the condition of a maniac fell dead.[37] It is a fearful thing. The men will be acquitted, as it will be justifiable homicide, but how are ignorant men to be taught the distinction between that and murder, and it is feared that on every petty quarrel the servant will think himself justified in killing his master. The gentlemen here are too apt to thrash and indeed point their guns at their men and Mr. Anderson who came across from Vancouver last year was so detested that they confessed that if he had fallen into the River not one would have held out a stick to him. One gentleman actually was drowned, when he might easily have been saved without a man wetting his foot. The truth of the matter is that it is a hideous country for man to live in and that it is yearly getting worse. Individually I have no fault to find with it, but I pity every gentlemen in it. Hargrave likes this place and is perfectly contented. I am sure there is not a man in it who would not rejoice to leave it if he could. I am as well pleased with York as at first, I only am so from never thinking. You may believe that the eternal barreness of white water and black pines are not very enlivening to the spirits. The sky is always beautiful night or day, the Aurora being magnificent and the stars very bright. I sew from morning till night except standing on the platforms[38] while Beppo is playing about with a host of husky dogs or digging up the snow and going [I go] out every morning with him in the carriole. I do nothing else. There is no house keeping here nor any thing to look after, Gibeault being mistress both of kitchen and cellar. And a very good one he is at least so Beppo and I think.

(42) To Dugald Mactavish

York Factory, 1st September, 1849

. . . The Prince Rupert brought out so little cargo, scarcely anything but the gunpowder and the clergy and their luggage that she is now almost ready to sail again and will doubtless be home sooner than usual. . . . Old Mr. Christy[39] is here on his way to Scotland having retired at last. He says the pensioners at Red River are useless and a much worse body of men and women than the regular soldiers were. The people don't mind them in the least, and the half breeds openly declare that they will not rest until they kill the recorder Mr. Thom.[40] Sir John Richardson[41] passed Norway House about three weeks ago, on his way to Canada and England. No one now expect that poor Franklin or his party are alive but Dr. Rae[42] is to go again to the shores of the Arctic Sea this Summer with one boat and six men. . . . We have now made up our minds to remain at York, during the time it may be necessary for Hargrave to remain in the service.

(63) To Mrs. Dugald Mactavish

York Factory, 29th March 1849

. . . Dr Rae and Sir John Richardson have come from the 'Sea' and did not see nor hear any thing of Captain Franklin. The Gentlemen in the Country all looked very polite and as if Sir John's expedition was a very feasible exploit, but among themselves they either laughed at the whole turn out or seemed astonished that rational beings should undertake such a useless search. It seems they were right and I don't think they will be accused of not doing every thing in their power to aid it. Sir John will return by Canada. Dr Rae is to remain and take charge of MacKenzie's River as Mr. McPherson goes home. The people about the Rocky Mountains write us that gold is got in great abundance and with wonderful ease, inasmuch as a little boy dug a thousand pounds worth with his spoon. The Yankees in the Columbia rushed off whenever they heard of it and left their beautiful wheat fields, some ripe and some cut down, on the ground to rot. I dont know how the speculation will end but it is likely they will have reason to wish they had secured their crop. I expect to hear that Dugald is in the midst of them. He had a notion for California when he only admired its hides and tallow. When diamonds and gold are its staple his partiality will be increased. No disaster has happened in the Northern Department this season. There is however an extraordinary scarcity of animals, fish, flesh and furs. The Indians are starving in every direction and of course the dividends will be small. Even the buffaloes have left the Saskatchewan and there will be no dried meat nor pemmican for next year. Mr. Rowand[43] had been living on hung fish, in the last stage of decomposition for a month. He had heard of buffaloes 100 miles off and sent men and horses out to bring home what they could get, but the Indians attacked the men with arrows and robbed them of their horses and they returned to Edmonton in a miserable plight.

I need not say how we are wearying for the packet to hear how you all are. . . .

I have not written to Doi44, indeed I shrink from attempting it, it is so long now since we heard from him, ten months since the date of his and Mr. Young's letters. He will be able to read my letters himself soon and then we will not let a packet go without availing ourselves.

Notes

[1] A twelfth century inn in George Yard, Lombard Street, much frequented by literary men. At this time the landlady (see below) was a Mrs Warriner.

[2] For a portrait of James Hargrave in 1832, see GEORGE SIMPSON.

[3] Charles Dickens, author of *Sketches by Boz* (1836); his characters in the recently serialized *Pickwick Papers* (1836–7) made the George and Vulture their 'favourite city headquarters'.

[4] John Stuart, who is seen from various points of view in several excerpts in our anthology; see DANIEL HARMON, SIMON FRASER, GEORGE SIMPSON. He had retired in 1839 after 40 years in the fur trade.

[5] Dismissed from her service.

[6] Letitia's brother Lockhart, who was to settle in Australia.

[7] Moully: (Scots) wet or decayed.

[8] Her sister Florence (Flora); she never married, and cared for the Hargraves' daughters between Letitia's death in 1854 and James' remarriage in 1859.

[9] The *Prince Rupert*'s guns announced her arrival in York Road, and a launch put out from shore bearing Duncan Finlayson, husband of Isobel Finlayson who was also travelling outward, and Letitia's brother William McTavish, who would eventually become a governor of Rupert's Land. Isobel Finlayson was the sister of FRANCES SIMPSON, and she also wrote a journal; see 'York Boat Journal', *The Beaver* (September and December, 1951).

[10] A large room aft where the officers and passengers dined.

[11] George Gladman (1800–1863); son of a Company trader and a native woman. At this time he was Chief Trader at Oxford House. In 1857 he led the first Canadian exploring expedition to Red River, accompanied by H.Y. HIND.

[12] Margaret Dunnet, the maidservant who came with Letitia from England.

[13] Edouard Guilbault, a Canadian, had served under Letitia's uncle John George McTavish for both trading companies, and was butler at York until 1845; he had a serious drinking problem, as other correspondence of the period shows.

[14] Both gentry and ordinary folk.

[15] This is the traditional garb that gave rise to the famous 'Red River coat' which was commercially marketed for Canadian children in later years.

[16] Current slang: stylish and up-to-date.

[17] One of the Hargraves' tasks before they left London had been to purchase this piano, which James Hargrave described in a letter as 'a square mahogany piano of $6^{1}/_{2}$ Octaves, made in Vienna'.

[18] Another of Letitia's brothers in the service of the Company, chiefly stationed at Fort Vancouver.

[19] Probably the Lower Savage Islands at the entrance to Hudson Strait.

[20] Vilhjalmur Stefansson confirmed to Margaret Arnett McLeod that Letitia reported the Inuit words with considerable accuracy but that she was mistaken in saying that the naked baby was in the mother's hood; it is actually carried against the mother's naked back.

[21]Smoked buffalo tongues were a Rupert's Land delicacy much prized in Great Britain.

[22]Two more of Letitia's six brothers; Hector entered the service of the Company but drowned shortly after arriving in Canada; Alexander, like Lockhart, settled in Australia.

[23]Reverend William Cockran (1798–1865), Anglican clergyman. He came to Red River in 1825, where he founded historic St Andrew's church in 1831; he remained in Canada for the rest of his life. See also FRANCES SIMPSON.

[24]The house: Hudson's Bay House.

[25]Harriet Gladman, daughter of Thomas Vincent of the Hudson's Bay Company and the native-born Jane Renton. Letitia became very attached to Mrs Gladman, who was godmother to her son Joseph James.

[26]The Hudson's Bay Company before the union of 1821.

[27]Hargrave would not ordinarily address 'a common half-breed' as 'Mister'.

[28]Robert Clouston was in charge at Oxford House in 1841–2; William McKay was post master at Island Lake.

[29]That is, in the *Seventeenth Annual Report of the Missionary Society of the Wesleyan-Methodist Church in Canada, from June, 1841, to June, 1842 (Toronto: for the Society, 1842).*

[30]Rev. James Evans (1801–1846), first superintendent of Wesleyan missions in Rupert's Land (1840–6); his headquarters were at Norway House. For Evans' invention of Cree syllabics, see below.

[31]Robert Alder, *Wesleyan Missions: Their Progress Stated and Their Claims Enforced* (London, 1842).

[32]François-Norbert Blanchet (1795–1883), missionary to the Oregon region and first archbishop of the see of Oregon City (1846).

[33]John Smithurst (1807–1867), from 1840–51 Anglican missionary at Netley, north of St Andrews, on the Red River; he later settled in Elora, Ontario. He never married, and romantic legend connects him with his cousin, Florence Nightingale.

[34]This was standard Hudson's Bay Company policy.

[35]Evans had already prepared a syllabary for Ojibwa, and at Norway House he rapidly learned Cree, prepared a syllabic alphabet, and began translating and printing. He had to cast his own type, for which he apparently used the lead linings of the chests in which tea was shipped.

[36]The Hargraves' son Joseph James (1841–1894), variously called 'Beppo' and 'Doi' in Letitia's letters; he served the company in his turn, rising to become a Chief Trader, and published *Red River* (Montreal, 1871).

[37]John McLoughlin, Jr (1812–1842), surgeon, the native-born son of John McLoughlin (Chief Factor in the Columbia District) was slain at his post, Fort Stikine, by his own men. The case long caused controversy in the Company; Letitia's account tells only one side of the story, for his father succeeded in exposing the crime as a put-up job. However, it took place on Russian territory, which Recorder Thom (see below) ruled was outside Canadian jurisdiction, and McLoughlin could not afford to seek remedy in a British court.

[38]The wooden sidewalks over the mud at York Factory.

[39]Alexander Christie (1792–1872), in the Company's service throughout his life, at York Factory and other posts; governor of Assiniboia 1833–9.

[40]Adam Thom (1802–1890). Born in Scotland, Thom was appointed Recorder at Red River in 1839 to rationalize the informal legal system, but his francophobia and advocacy of repressive measures alienated the colonists. Letitia is referring to the trial of Pierre Sayer in 1849; the issue was the right to trade freely in furs, and the Métis opposition, led by Louis Riel, helped lay the groundwork for the first Riel Rebellion (1869–70).

[41]See JOHN FRANKLIN; Richardson and Rae were in search of Franklin after he failed to return from his third voyage.

[42]John Rae (1813–1893), surgeon, Hudson's Bay Company chief trader, and explorer. Famous for his ability to travel and live like a native, he undertook four Arctic expeditions between 1846–54, and eventually claimed the reward offered by the British government to the explorer who ascertained the fate of Franklin and his men.

[43]For a sketch of the remarkable John Rowand, see GEORGE SIMPSON.

[44]Her son Joseph James (see above).

Henry Youle Hind   (1823 – 1908)

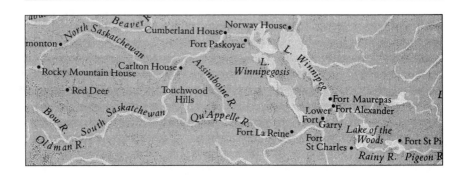

H.Y. HIND was Professor of Chemistry at Trinity College, Toronto, when he was asked to participate in the Canadian government's Red River exploring expedition of 1857, led by George Gladman.[1] Hind was the group's geologist on this expedition, and served as director of the 'topographical and geological' section of the 1858 expedition. From 1852–7 he had been editor of the *Canadian Journal*, a scientific periodical which reflected the growing nationalism of the time, and the serene comprehensiveness of his account of the prairies is part of this sense of growing Canadian identity. Hind's descriptions mingle the close and detailed observations of the geologist-surveyor with the nostalgia of one who is aware the society he is observing has become a mere remnant of its heroic past. His repugnance at the carnage of the buffalo hunt contrasts strongly with the romantic descriptions of earlier travellers.

Text: Henry Youle Hind, *Narrative of the Canadian Red River Exploring Expedition of 1857 and of the Assinniboine and Saskatchewan Exploring Expedition of 1858* (2 vols) London: Longman, Green, Longman and Roberts, 1860.

from Chapter XV, The Qu'Appelle Valley

Three quarters of a mile from the mouth of the little stream joining the second and third Fishing Lakes, the lead showed 44 feet of water. This great depth surprised us, as we had been paddling, since leaving the Mission, in shallows not exceeding four and five feet in depth. Cross sections subsequently made, showed that the lakes were generally deep on the north and shallow on the south side. An abundant growth of green confervæ covered the surface, which, in its aggregations and general distribution, reminded me of a similar profusion on the Lake of Woods during August, in 1857. The hill sides of the valley are deeply ravined and wooded, but the hills they separate are bare; we soon noticed too that the north side began to show far less timber than the south, and of more stunted growth. The snowberry was seen in every hollow. Ash-leaved maple and elm were numerous on the south side of the lake, together with the mesaskatomina.

Two excellent photographs, taken near the Mission, of the lakes and hills, display the chief characteristic of the valley with the fidelity which can only be attained by that wonderful art. . . .[2]

Geese appeared in large numbers in the Fourth Lake, and at its western end we saw a splendid flock of pelicans containing thirty-five individuals; as we approached they sailed majestically round and round, but took flight before we arrived within gunshot. Magpies are very numerous in the thin woods fringing the lakes; so also are grackles, the cat bird, and many smaller birds. The Fourth Lake is very shallow at its western extremity, six feet being the greatest depth recorded. The hills on the north side are quite bare, and trees on the south side are found only in the ravines. The lake is full of weeds and its water emits a very disagreeable odour, but the watermarks show, that during spring freshets, its level is eight feet higher than in the summer season. This is an important fact when taken in connection with the alleged appearance of the whole valley during wet springs; it is then said to resemble a broad river from a few miles east of the Saskatchewan to the Assinniboine. In 1852, a year memorable in Rupert's Land for the great floods which covered an immense tract of country, the Indians represent the Qu'appelle Valley as filled with a mighty river throughout its entire length, flowing with a swift current from the lakelets at the Height of Land, soon to be described, to the Assinniboine, and as a mountain torrent through the short distance of twelve miles, which separates them from the South Branch of the Saskatchewan.

After leaving the Fourth Lake and the marshes at its west extremity, we paddled, sailed, or tracked up a narrow swift stream, four or five feet deep, seventy feet broad, and winding through an alluvial flat in a valley of undiminished breadth and depth. The hill sides were now absolutely bare, not a tree or shrub was to be seen. We had reached the point where timber ceases to grow in the valleys of the rivers except in peculiar situations; the altitude of the banks could not be less than 280 or 300 feet. The prairie on either side is also treeless and arid. On the 21st, after spending a restless night owing to the attacks of multitudes of mosquitoes, we left the canoe in the hands of our half-breeds to track up the stream, and, ascending to the prairie, walked for some miles on the brink of this great excavation. We waited five hours for the canoe to reach us, the windings of the stream involving a course three times as long as a straight line up the valley. The hill sides here began to acquire a more imposing altitude, and probably exceeded 300 feet. White cranes appeared in flocks of four and seven together, but they were so wary that it was impossible to approach them. . . .

. . . On the fourth day after our departure from the lakes we sighted the Grand Forks;[3] leaving the canoe, I hastened on to a point where the men with the carts and horses were to await our arrival, and found them safely encamped on a beautiful meadow, anxiously looking for us. An empty cart and a couple of horses were despatched for the canoe, still some miles below us, and in the evening we were joined by Mr Flemin[4] and the two voyageurs. . . .

. . . Numerous buffalo tracks began to appear before we reached the Forks, and where these animals had crossed the river, they had cut deep roads to the water's edge, and lanes through the willow bushes. The bones of many a young bull and cow were seen sticking out of the banks where they had been mired. . . .

No rock exposure was anywhere to be seen; drift appears to cover the country to a great depth. Where land slips have occurred and exposed an almost perpendicular section, yellow gravelly clay alone is visible. Some of the limestone erratics strewed over the sides of the ravines resemble those frequently seen on the south-east side of Lake Winnipeg.

Near our camp, on the 23rd, were six or seven loghouses, occasionally inhabited during the winter months by *freemen*, that is, men no longer in the service of the Company. The prairie above the freemen's houses slopes gently to the edge of the valley from the distant horizon on both sides. Clumps of aspen vary its monotonous aspect, and though clothed with green herbage, due to the late abundant rains, the soil is light and poor. Some distance back from the valley it is of better quality, the finer particles not having been washed out of it; the grass there is longer and more abundant, but the greatest drawback is the want of timber. . . .

Soon after sunset our camp received an unexpected addition of six 'Bungays',[5] who were on their way to Fort Ellice with dried buffalo meat and pemmican.

They had been hunting between the two branches of the Saskatchewan, and represented the season as very dry and the buffalo scarce. We passed a quiet and friendly night with them, and on the following morning made them a small present and pursued our way to the Grand Forks.

I happened to be about 100 yards in advance of the carts, after we had traveled for about a quarter of an hour, when hearing a loud clatter of horses' feet behind me, I looked round and saw the six Indians approaching at a gallop. One of them, who had represented himself as a chief, seized my bridle, drew the horse's head round, and motioned me to dismount. I replied by jerking my bridle out of the Indian's hand. My people came up at this moment and asked in Cree what this interference meant. 'We wanted to have a little more talk,' said the chief; 'we are anxious to know the reason why you are traveling through our country.' It turned out after a little more 'talk' that they wished to establish a sort of toll of tobacco and tea for permission to pass through their country, threatening that if it were not given they would gather their friends in advance of us, and stop us by force. We knew that we should have to pass through about 100 tents, so there was some little meaning in the threat. The old hunter, however, knowing Indian habits and diplomacy well, at once remarked that we were taking a large present to the chief of the Sandy Hills, and we did not intend to distribute any tobacco or tea until we had seen him, according to Indian custom.

They tried a few more threats, but I closed the parley by unslinging a double-barrelled gun from the cart, and instructing the men to show quietly that they had theirs in readiness. Wishing the rascals good day, we rode on; they sat on the ground, silently watching us, but made no sign. In the evening one of them passed near us at full gallop, towards some tents which we saw in the distance as we ascended the hill at the Grand Forks.

One rather significant statement they made proved to be correct, namely, that the Plain Crees, in council assembled, had last year 'determined that in consequence of promises often made and broken by the white men and half-breeds, and the rapid destruction by them of the buffalo they fed on, they would not permit either white men or half-breeds to hunt in their country or travel through it, except for the purpose of trading for their dried meat, pemmican, skins, and robes.'...

... This afternoon we saw three fires spring up between us and the Grand Coteau.[6] They were Indian signs, but whether they referred to the presence of buffalo, or whether they were designed to intimate to distant bands the arrival of suspicious strangers, we could not then tell, and not knowing whether they originated from Crees, Assinniboines, or Blackfeet, we became cautious. In a few days we ascertained that the fire had been put out[7] by Crees, to inform their friends that they had found buffalo.

The grandeur of the prairie on fire belongs to itself. It is like a volcano in full activity, you cannot imitate it, because it is impossible to obtain those gigantic elements from which it derives its awful splendour. Fortunately, in the present instance the wind was from the west, and drove the fires in the opposite direction, and being south of us we could contemplate the magnificent spectacle without anxiety. One object in burning the prairie at this time, was to turn the buffalo; they had crossed the Saskatchewan in great numbers near the Elbow, and were advancing towards us, and crossing the Qu'appelle not far from the Height of Land; by burning the prairie east of their course, they would be diverted to the south, and feed for a time on the Grand Coteau before they pursued their way to the Little Souris, in the country of the Sioux, south of the 49th parallel.

Putting out fire in the prairies is a telegraphic mode of communication frequently resorted to by Indians. Its consequences are seen in the destruction of the forests which once covered an immense area south of the Qu'appelle and Assinniboine. The aridity of those vast prairies is partly due to this cause. The soil, though light, derives much of its apparent sterility from the annual fires. In low places and in shallow depressions where marshes are formed in spring, the soil is rich, much mixed with vegetable matter, and supports a very luxuriant growth of grass. If willows and aspens were permitted to grow over the prairies, they would soon be converted into humid tracts in which vegetable matter would accumulate and a soil adapted to forest trees be formed.[8]...

Immediately on the banks of the Qu'appelle Valley near the 'Round Hill' opposite Moose Jaws Forks, are the remains of ancient encampments, where the Plain Crees, in the day of their power and pride, had erected large skin tents, and strengthened them with rings of stones placed round the base. These circular remains were twenty-five feet in diameter, the stones or boulders being about one foot in circumference. They wore the aspect of great antiquity, being partially covered with soil and grass. When this camp ground was occupied by the Crees, timber no doubt grew in the valley below, or on the prairie and ravines in detached groves, for their permanent camping grounds are always placed near a supply of fuel.

Making an early start in search of wood, we came suddenly upon four Cree tents, whose inmates were still fast asleep; about three hundred yards west of them we found ten more tents, with over fifty or sixty Indians in all. They were preparing to cross the valley in the direction of the Grand Coteau, following the buffalo. Their provisions for trade, such as dried meat and pemmican, were drawn by dogs, each bag of pemmican being supported upon two long poles, which are shaft, body and wheels in one. Buffalo Pound Hill Lake, sixteen miles long, begins near the Moose Jaws Forks, and on the opposite or south side of this long sheet of water, we saw eighteen tents and a large number of horses. . . . [The natives] announced the cheering intelligence that the Chief Mis-tick-oos, with some thirty tents, was at the Sandy Hills impounding buffalo.[9] Leaving the hospitable Crees after an excellent breakfast on pounded meat and marrow fat, we arrived at Buffalo Pound Hill at noon. The whole country here assumed a different appearance; it now bore resemblance to a stormy sea suddenly become rigid; the hills were of gravel and very abrupt, but none exceeded 100 feet in height. The Coteau de Missouri, particularly the 'Dancing Point', is clearly seen from Buffalo Pound Hill towards the south, while northeasterly the last mountain of the Touchwood Hill Range looms grey or blue in the distance. Between these distant ranges a treeless plain intervenes.

Ponds and lakes are numerous on the Grand Coteau side, and it is probably on this account that the buffalo cross the Qu'appelle valley near the Moose Jaws Fork and west of Buffalo Pound Hill Lake; in the winter they keep towards the Touchwood Hills for the sake of shelter, and the excellent herbage which grows in the beautiful meadows between the aspen clumps. The prairies there too are not so often burned as south of the Qu'appelle, the valley of that river serving as a great barrier to prevent the onward progress of the devastating fires.

We now began to find the fresh bones of buffalo very numerous on the ground, and here and there startled a pack of wolves feeding on a carcass which had been deprived of its tongue and hump only by the careless, thriftless Crees. On the high banks of the valley the remains of ancient encampments in the form of rings of stones to hold down the skin tents are everywhere visible, and testify to the former numbers of the Plain Crees, affording a sad evidence of the ancient power of the people who once held undisputed sway from the Missouri to the Saskatchewan. The remains of a race fast passing away give more than a transient interest to Buffalo Pound Hill Lake. The largest ancient encampment we saw lies near a shallow lake in the prairie about a mile from the Qu'appelle valley. It is surrounded by a few low sandy and gravelly hills, and is quite screened from observation. It may have been a camping ground for centuries, as some circles of stones are partially covered with grass and embedded in the soil. . . .

from Chapter XVI: the Buffalo Hunt of the Plains Cree, 1858

We made ourselves acceptable to the Indians by offering them a present of powder, shot, tea, and tobacco, and in return they invited us to partake of pounded meat, marrowfat and berries. The chief of the band assured us that his young men were honest and trustworthy; and in compliance with his instructions, property would be perfectly safe. . . .

. . . From time to time, scouts would come in and go out towards the Grand Coteau, on the look out for Blackfeet, and as nightfall approached, the wandering horses were gathered closer to the camp. The dogs, however, are their great protection; it is almost impossible for any stranger to approach a camp without arousing the whole canine population; and the passage of bands of buffalo during the night-time is signalised by a prolonged baying, which, however suggestive of sport and good cheer, is most wearisome to those who are anxious to rest. During the night a heavy rain filled the hollows with water, and gave us promise of an abundant supply until we arrived at the Sandy Hills, where the main body of Plain Crees were encamped. On the following day, the 28th, I rode to the Eye-brow Hill range, a prolongation of the Grand Coteau, and distant from the Qu'appelle Valley about four miles. It was there that the Indians told me I should find one of the sources of the Qu'appelle river. After an hour's ride I reached the hills, and quickly came upon a deep ravine at the bottom of which bubbled a little stream about three feet broad. I subsequently followed its course until it entered the prairie leading to the great valley, and traced it to its junction with the main excavation, through a deep narrow gully.

The Eye-brow Hill range is about 150 feet above the prairie, and forms the flank of a tableland stretching to the Grand Coteau, of which it is the northern extension. The recent tracks of buffalo were countless on the hill sides, and in the distance several herds could be seen feeding on the treeless plateau to the south. On the flanks of the Grand Coteau the true prairies may be said to terminate, and the plains to commence. It is doubtful whether the term 'Plain' is not now applicable to a large portion of the country west and south of the Qu'appelle Mission. The destruction of 'woods' by fires has converted into sterile areas an immense tract of country which does not appear necessarily sterile from aridity, or poverty of soil.

The Plains and Prairies of America occupy regions differing widely from one another in physical characteristics. The phraseology of the half-breeds tends to mislead a traveler not familiar with the precise application of the words they use. Such terms as 'woods', 'prairies', and 'plains' are illustrations of this apparent want of precision, which if employed without explanation in a written narrative, would very probably cause considerable misapprehension, and lead to deductions wholly at variance with fact. A tract of country may be described as a 'wooded country', conveying the idea that timber covers the surface and is capable of affording a supply of that indispensable material for building purposes and fuel; but in Rupert's Land, west of the Low Lake Region, and south of the 53rd parallel, the 'woods' consist generally of small aspens very rarely exceeding six inches in diameter or twenty-five in altitude, and most frequently distributed in detached groves, 'bluffs', or belts. The same remark applies to the use of the word 'prairie', and to prairie country; prairies may be level, rich and dry, sustaining luxuriant grasses and affording splendid pasturage; they may be marshy and wet, or undulating — 'stony', 'sandy', or 'salt'. Such indefinite terms as 'open prairie', 'rolling prairie', 'alluvial prairie', not unfrequently employed in describing without limit as to space, the vast unpeopled wastes, — often beautiful and rich, often desolate and barren, — of the Prairies and *Plains* of America, are sometimes both physically and geologically wrong, and serve to convey the impression that the large areas to which they are applied possess, if not a fertile, at least not an unkindly soil, or an arid climate, rendering husbandry hopeless. . . .

In the afternoon I bade farewell to our Cree friends, and riding west joined the carts on the south side of Sand Hill Lake, on the brink of which we travelled until we arrived at the gully through which the stream from the Eye-brow Hill range enters the Qu'appelle valley. It was here nine feet broad, and three deep, having received accessions in a short course through the prairie from the hills where I had observed it scarcely three feet broad. We camped in the valley, and employed the evening in taking levels.[10]

About four miles west of us we saw the Sandy Hills, and could discern the great valley passing through them, and containing, as the Indians had alleged, ponds which sent water both to the South Branch and the Assinniboine; an important physical fact which we afterwards verified instrumentally and by optical proof. . . .

On the morning of the 29th, we prepared to visit the main body of the Crees at the Sandy Hills, and with a view to secure a favourable reception sent a messenger to announce our arrival, and to express a wish to see Mis-tick-oos, their chief. Soon after breakfast we crossed the valley and threaded our way between sand dunes; one dune was found to be seventy feet high, quite steep on one side, beautifully ripple-marked by the wind, and crescent-shaped; from its summit we saw the woods and hills beyond the South Branch of the Saskatchewan, and what was more delightful to us, traced with the eye the Qu'appelle valley apparently with undiminished depth and breadth through the Sandy Hills, until it was lost as it dipped towards the South Branch.

At eight o'clock A.M. we came in sight of the Cree camp, and soon afterwards messengers arrived from Mis-tick-oos, in reply to the announcement we had transmitted to him of our approach, expressing a hope that we would delay our visit until they had moved their camp half-a-mile further west, where the odour of the putrid buffalo would be less annoying. We employed the time in ascertaining the exact position of the height of land, and soon found a pond from which we observed water flowing to the Saskatchewan and the Assinniboine. . . .

. . . [We found it necessary to stop taking levels for] the present, in consequence of the arrival of about sixty Cree horsemen, many of them naked with exception of the breech cloth, and belt. They were accompanied by the chief's son, who informed us that in an hour's time they would escort us to the camp.

They were about constructing a new pound, having literally filled the present one with buffalo, and being compelled to abandon it on account of the stench which arose from the putrifying bodies. We sat on the ground and smoked, until they thought it time for us to accompany them to their encampment. Mis-tick-oos had hurried away to make preparations for 'bringing in the buffalo', the new pound being nearly ready. He expressed, through his son, a wish that we should see them entrap the buffalo in this pound, a rare opportunity few would be willing to lose.

We passed through the camp to a place which the chief's son pointed out, and there erected our tents. The women were still employed in moving the camp, being assisted in the operation by large numbers of dogs, each dog having two poles harnessed to him, on which his little load of meat, pemmican, or camp furniture was laid. After another smoke, the chief's son asked me, through the interpreter, if I would like to see the old buffalo pound, in which they had been entrapping buffalo during the past week. With a ready compliance I accompanied the guide to a little valley between sand hills, through a lane of branches of trees, which are called 'dead men' to the gate or trap of the pound. A sight most horrible and disgusting broke upon us as we ascended a sand dune overhanging the little dell in which the pound was built. Within a circular fence 120 feet broad, constructed of the trunks of trees, laced with withes[11] together, and braced by outside supports, lay tossed in every conceivable position over two hundred dead buffalo. From old bulls to calves of three months old, animals of every age were huddled together in all the forced attitudes of violent death. Some lay on their backs, with eyes starting from their heads, and tongue thrust out through clotted gore. Others were impaled on the horns of the old and strong bulls. Others again, which had been tossed, were lying with broken backs two and three deep. One little calf hung suspended on the horns of a bull which had impaled it in the wild race round and round the pound.

The Indians looked upon the dreadful and sickening scene with evident delight, and told how such and such a bull or cow had exhibited feats of wonderful strength in the death-struggle. The flesh of many of the cows had been taken from them, and was drying in the sun on stages near the tents. It is needless to say that the odour was overpowering, and millions of large blue flesh flies, humming and buzzing over the putrefying bodies was not the least disgusting part of the spectacle. At my request the chief's son jumped into the pound, and with a small axe knocked off half a dozen pair of horns, which I wished to preserve in memory of this terrible slaughter. 'To-morrow,' said my companion, 'you shall see us bring in the buffalo to the new pound.'

After the first 'run', ten days before our arrival, the Indians had driven about 200 buffalo into the enclosure, and were still urging on the remainder of the herd, when one wary old bull, espying a narrow crevice which had not been closed by the robes of those on the outside, whose duty it was to conceal every orifice, made a dash and broke the fence, the whole body then ran helter skelter through the gap, and dispersing among the sand dunes escaped, with the exception of eight who were speared or shot with arrows as they passed in their mad career. In all, 240 animals had been killed in the pound, and it was its offensive condition which led the reckless and wasteful savages to construct a new one. This was formed in a pretty dell between sand hills, about half a mile from the first, and leading from it in two diverging rows, the bushes they designate 'dead men', and which serve to guide the buffalo when at full speed, were arranged. The 'dead men' extended a distance of four miles into the prairie, west of and beyond the Sand Hills. They were placed about 50 feet apart, and between the extremity of the rows might be a distance of from one and a half to two miles.

When the skilled hunters are about to bring in a herd of buffalo from the prairie, they direct the course of the gallop of the alarmed animals by confederates stationed in hollows or small depressions, who, when the buffalo appear inclined to take a direction leading from the space marked out by the 'dead men', show themselves for a moment and wave their robes, immediately hiding again. This serves to turn the buffalo slightly in another direction, and when the animals, having arrived between the rows of 'dead men', endeavour to pass through them, Indians here and there stationed behind a 'dead man', go through the same operation, and thus keep the animals within the narrowing limits of the converging lines. At the entrance to the pound there is a strong trunk of a tree placed about one foot from the ground, and on the inner side an excavation is made sufficiently deep to prevent the buffalo from leaping back when once in the pound. As soon as the animals have taken the fatal spring they begin to gallop round and round the ring fence looking for a chance of escape, but with the utmost silence women and children on the outside hold their robes before every orifice until the whole herd is brought in; they then climb to the top of the fence, and, with the hunters who have followed closely in the rear of the buffalo, spear or shoot with bows and arrows or fire-arms at the bewildered animals, rapidly becoming frantic with rage and terror, within the narrow limits of the pound. A dreadful scene of confusion and slaughter then begins, the oldest and strongest animals crush and toss the weaker; the shouts and screams of the excited Indians rise above the roaring of the bulls, the bellowing of the cows, and the piteous moaning of the calves. The dying struggles of so many huge and powerful animals crowded together, create a revolting and terrible scene, dreadful from the excess of its cruelty and waste of life, but with occasional displays of wonderful brute strength and rage; while man in his savage, untutored, and heathen state shows both in deed and expression how little he is superior to the noble beasts he so wantonly and cruelly destroys.

Mis-tick-oos, or 'Shortstick', is about fifty years old, of low stature, but very power-fully built. His arms and breast were deeply marked with scars and gashes, records of grief and mourning for departed friends. His son's body was painted with blue bars across the chest and arms. The only clothing they wore consisted of a robe of dressed elk or buffalo hide, and the breech cloth; the robe was often cast off the shoulders and drawn over the knees when in a sitting posture; they wore no covering on the head, their long hair was plaited or tied in knots, or hung loose over their shoulders and back. The forms of some of the young men were faultless, of the middle-aged men bony and wiry, and of the aged men, in one instance at least, a living skeleton. I inquired the age of an extremely old fellow who asked me for medicine to cure a pain in his chest; he replied he was a strong man when the two Companies (the Hudson's Bay and the North West) were trading with his tribe very many summers ago. He remembers the time 'when his people were as numerous as the buffalo are now, and the buffalo thick as trees in the forest'. The half-breeds thought he was more than 100 years old.

When Mis-tick-oos was ready to receive me, I proceeded to the spot where he was sitting surrounded by the elders of his tribe, and as a preliminary, rarely known to fail in its good effect upon Indians, I instructed one of my men to hand him a basin of tea and a dish of preserved vegetables, biscuit, and fresh buffalo steaks. He had not eaten since an early hour in the morning, and evidently enjoyed his dinner. Hunger, that great enemy to charity and comfort, being appeased, I presented him with a pipe and a canister of tobacco, begging him to help himself and hand the remainder to the Indians around us. The presents were then brought and laid at his feet. They consisted of tea, tobacco, bullets, powder, and blankets, all which he examined and accepted with marked satisfaction. After a while he expressed a wish to know the object of our visit; and having at my request adjourned the meeting to my tent in order to avoid sitting in the hot sun, we held a 'talk', during which Mis-tick-oos expressed himself freely on various subjects, and listened with the utmost attention and apparent respect to the speeches of the Indians he had summoned to attend the 'Council'.

All speakers objected strongly to the half-breeds' hunting buffalo during the winter in the Plain Cree country. They had no objection to trade with them or with white people, but they insisted that all strangers should purchase dried meat or pemmican, and not hunt for themselves.

They urged strong objections against the Hudson's Bay Company encroaching upon the prairies and driving away the buffalo. They would be glad to see them establish as many posts as they chose on the edge of the prairie country, but they did not like to see the prairies and plains invaded. During the existence of the two companies, all went well with the Indians, they obtained excellent pay, and could always sell their meat, skins, robes, and pemmican. Since the union of the companies they had not fared half so well, had received bad pay for their provisions, and were growing poorer, weaker, and more miserable year by year. The buffalo were fast disappearing before the encroachments of white men, and although they acknowledged the value of fire-arms, they thought they were better off in olden times, when they had only bows and spears, and wild animals were numerous. They generally commenced with the creation, giving a short history of that event in most general terms, and after a few flourishes about equality of origin, descended suddenly to buffalo, half-breeds, the Hudson's Bay company, tobacco, and rum. I asked Mis-tick-oos to name the articles he would wish me to bring if I came into his country again. He asked for tea, a horse of English breed, a cart, a gun, a supply of powder and ball, knives, tobacco, a medal with a chain, a flag, a suit of fine clothes, and rum. The 'talk' lasted between six and seven hours, the greater portion of the time being taken up in interpreting sentence by sentence, the speeches of each man in turn.

During the whole time we were engaged in 'Council' the pipe was passed from mouth to mouth, each man taking a few whiffs and then handing it to his neighbour. It was a black stone pipe, which Mis-tick-oos had received as a present from a chief of the Blackfeet at the Eagle Hills a few weeks before.[12] When the pipe came round to me I usually replenished it, and taking a box of 'vespers'[13] from my pocket, lit it with a match. This operation was observed with a subdued curiosity, each Indian watching me without moving his head, turning his eyes in the direction of the pipe. No outward sign of wonder or curiosity escaped them during the 'talk'. On one occasion the pipe was out when passed to the Indian sitting next to me; without turning his head he gently touched my arm, imitated the action of lighting the match by friction against the bottom of the box, and pointed with one finger to the pipe. They generally sat with their eyes fixed on the ground when one of them was speaking, giving every outward sign of respectful attention, and occasionally expressing their approval by a low gurgling sound. When the talk was over, I went with Mis-tick-oos to his tent; he then asked me to reproduce the match-box, and show its wonders to his four wives. One of them was evidently sceptical, and did not think it was 'real fire' until she had ignited some chips of wood from the lighted match I presented to her. I gave a bundle to Mis-tick-oos, who wrapped them carefully in a piece of deerskin, and said he should keep them safely, — they were 'good medicine'. . . .

At noon I bade farewell to Mis-tick-oos, and joining the carts we wended our way by the side of 'the River that Turns', occupying the continuation of the Qu'appelle valley, to the South Branch of the Saskatchewan. The carts were accompanied by several Indians, who watched with much curiosity the progress of taking the levels, and were very anxious to know what 'medicine' I was searching for when sketching the position of the erratics in the valley.

Now and then a fine buffalo bull would appear at the brow of the hill forming the boundary of the prairie, gaze at us for a few minutes and gallop off. The buffalo were crossing the South Branch a few miles below us in great numbers, and at night, by putting the ear to the ground, we could hear them bellowing. Towards evening we all arrived at the South Branch, built a fire, gummed the canoe, which had been sadly damaged by a journey of 700 miles across the prairies, and hastened to make a distribution of the supplies for a canoe voyage down that splendid river. We were not anxious to camp at the mouth of 'the River that Turns', in consequence of a war party of Blackfeet who were said to be in the neighbourhood of the Cree camp, watching for an opportunity to steal horses, and if possible to 'lift a scalp'.

The Indians who had accompanied us hastened to join their friends as soon as they saw we were ready to embark, and just as the sun set, the canoe containing Mr. Fleming and myself, with two half-breeds, pushed off from the shore; the remainder of the party in charge of the old hunter, retired from the river with the carts and horses to camp in the open prairie, where they would be able to guard against a surprise by the Blackfeet, or the thieving propensities of treacherous Crees. Great precautions were undoubtedly necessary, as sure signs had been observed within three miles of the Sandy Hills, proving that a war party of Blackfeet were skulking about. The Crees, always accustomed when on the South Branch to their attacks, merely adopted the precaution of posting watchers on the highest dunes, about a mile from their camp, but in accordance with the friendly advice of Mis-tick-oos, we embarked at this late hour in the evening with a view to avoid surprise and mislead any watchful eyes that might have taken note of our movements. We drifted a mile or two down the river until we came to a precipitous cliff showing a fine exposure of rock, which proved a temptation too great to be resisted, so we drew the canoe on the bank and camped for the night on the east side of the river, making arrangements to watch in turns.

The first view of the South Branch of the Saskatchewan, fully 600 miles from the point where the main river disembogues into Lake Winnipeg, filled me with astonishment and admiration. We stood on the banks of a river of the first class, nearly half a mile broad, and flowing with a swift current, not more than 350 miles from the Rocky Mountains, where it takes its rise. We had reached this river by tracing for a distance of 270 miles, a narrow deep excavation continuous from the valley of one great river to that of another, and exhibiting in many features evidences of an excavating force far greater than the little Qu'appelle which meanders through it, was at the first blush, thought capable of creating. How were the deep lakes hollowed out? lakes filling the breadth of the valley, but during the lapse of ages not having increased its breadth, preserving too, for many miles, such remarkable depths, and although in some instances far removed from one another, yet maintaining those depths with striking uniformity. What could be the nature of the eroding force which dug out narrow basins 54 to 66 feet deep at the bottom of a valley already 300 feet below the slightly undulating prairies, and rarely exceeding one mile in breadth? It was easy to understand how a small river like the Qu'appelle could gradually excavate a valley a mile broad and 300 feet deep. The vast prairies of the north-west offer many such instances; the Little Souris River, for example, in passing through the Blue Hills; the Assinniboine, for a 150 miles, flows through a broad deep valley, evidently excavated by its waters; the rivers in western Canada often flow in deep eroded valleys; but in no instance to my knowledge are deep and long lakes known to occupy a river valley, where nearly horizontal and very soft rocks preclude the assumption that they may have been occasioned by falls, without bearing some traces of the force which excavated their basins. They seem to point to the former existence of a much deeper valley now broken into detached lakes by the partial filling up of intervening distances. It was certainly with mingled feelings of anxiety and pleasurable anticipation that we embarked on the broad Saskatchewan, hoping during our long journey down its swift stream to find some clue to the origin of the curious inosculating[14] valley of the Qu'appelle we had traced from one water-shed to another.

Notes

[1] For more on George Gladman, see LETITIA HARGRAVE.

[2] The photographer to the expedition was Humphrey Lloyd Hime; his pictures were used as the basis for the 'chromoxylographs' or coloured wood-engravings included in Hind's text. The photographs were sold separately from the volumes of the report, and have since been republished; see Richard J. Huyda, *Camera in the Interior: 1858; H.L. Hime, Photographer*, (Toronto: Coach House Press, 1975). One is reproduced on the cover of our text.

[3] Here, the intersection of the Qu'appelle River and the South Branch of the Saskatchewan.

[4] John Arnot Fleming (1835–1876), surveyor and artist. He had been Hind's assistant when Hind was second in command to George Gladman on the 1857 expedition, and was assistant surveyor and draughtsman on the 1858 expedition.

[5] Hind's note defines 'Bungays' as 'Crees and Ojibways of mixed origin'. The 'six Indians' (see below) were probably speakers of 'Bungee,' the speech used by the descendants of English, Scottish and Orkney fur traders and their Cree or Saulteaux wives.

[6] The Missouri Coteau, the gentle escarpment running from south-east to north-west, from the Mandans in the south towards the North Saskatchewan River; it marks the rise from the second to the third prairie level.

[7] That is, 'set out' or lit.

[8] This issue is still debated today.

[9] Driving buffalo into a circular enclosure; see KELSEY.

[10] Measuring the elevation of the land with surveying instruments.

[11] Thin willow branches.

[12] In Chapter XXIX Hind relates that the Blackfoot chief had given Mis-tick-oos the pipe at a peaceful meeting of Blackfoot and Cree the previous year which had tragically ended in the slaughter of youthful Cree horse-stealers. 'Mis-tick-oos, when relating these adventures, raised the pipe he held in his hand and exclaimed, "This is what my Blackfoot friend gave me one day, the next he killed my young men; he is now my enemy again." I expressed a wish to buy the pipe; the chief's reply was "Take it," handing it to me with a gloomy frown, and silently extending his hand for the Wapekancuspwägän, or clay pipe, which I was smoking at the time.'

[13] Probably a slang variant of 'vestas' or wax matches.

[14] Having a mouth or outlet.

John Palliser   (1817 – 1887)

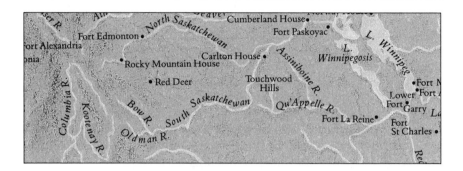

JOHN PALLISER was a member of the Anglo-Irish gentry, cultivated, widely travelled, and with a tradition of public service. He was also an enthusiastic big game
hunter, and in 1847 journeyed to America to hunt buffalo, the result of which was an
often-reprinted book about his adventures. The prairies, however, were ripe for
settlement, and American interests were already exploring railway routes through
the west. In 1856 Palliser submitted plans to the Royal Geographical Society for a
similar exploration of the little-known plains of British North America, to the south
of the area which historically had been the preserve of the fur trade. The wide-
ranging and scientifically significant expedition took place, with the financial support of the British government, between 1857 and 1859, the same years in which H.Y.
HIND was crossing the prairies on behalf of the Canadian government.

Palliser's 'General Report', which introduced the published journals, gives us a
magisterial view of the area between the Laurentian Shield and the Rockies just as
the west of fur-trade culture and early exploration was transforming itself into the
settled land of today. It may seem a dry and detailed survey of the plains, region by
region, but read in the setting provided by KELSEY, LA VÉRENDRYE, THOMPSON, by
HENDAY, COCKING and HENRY, it becomes a magnificently ironic elegy for a world
which was about to die. This is the last thing Palliser intended, of course; as his report
shows, he was full of optimism for the settlements and farms he was sure would rise
in the 'fertile belt'. But within a decade of its publication, Rupert's Land was no
more, and in the year before Palliser's death, the railway crossed the prairies at last.

Text: Irene M. Spry, ed., *The Papers of the Palliser Expedition*. Toronto: Champlain Society, 1968.

From 'The General Report'

I propose in the following remarks, which are introductory to the journals and other detailed papers relative to the Expedition recently under my command, to give a short sketch of the physical features of the country explored, with especial reference to its economic value. These remarks will be principally based upon the facts and observations to be found in detail in the body of the Report.

The portion of British North America examined by the Expedition is contained between the western shore of Lake Superior, in longitude 89°W., and the Okanagan Lakes, in longitude 119°W., and extends from the frontier of the United States, in latitude 49°N., northwards to the sources of the chief rivers that flow to the Arctic Ocean. In other words, it embraces 30° of longitude, and in some place 6° latitude. Some portions of this large extent of British territory were well described previously to the organising of this Expedition, especially the neighbourhood of Red River, where the Selkirk Settlement is situated.

The district stretching from thence to the north-west along the valley of the Assineboine and the North Saskatchewan was also well known, from the Hudson Bay Company having for many years had a chain of trading posts or forts on that river at intervals of about 200 miles, established partly for the trading of furs, but mainly for the purpose of procuring provisions from the vast herds of buffalo, on which their more valuable trading posts in the northern districts depend for subsistence.

It is by the trail passing from fort to fort on this route along the North Saskatchewan river that the few emigrants have travelled, who, besides travellers connected with the fur company, have passed through the country on their way to cross the Rocky Mountains. The southern portion of the country along the South Saskatchewan remained, however, comparatively unknown.

Many years ago, indeed, the Hudson Bay Company had sent an expedition of a hundred men up that river and endeavoured to establish two trading posts;[1] but after a very short trial the attempt was abandoned as too expensive and dangerous, owing to the menacing and often hostile tendencies of the Indian tribes who inhabit that district.

The information we possessed concerning the Rocky Mountains, and the extent to which they truly formed a barrier to the formation of a road across the continent in the most southern latitudes within the British territory, was extremely vague and unsatisfactory. The late Sir George Simpson had, indeed, described the crossing from the Saskatchewan to the source of the Columbia[2] and several parties of emigrants from the Red River Settlement to Oregon, on the Pacific coast, were known to have crossed the Rocky Mountains, under the guidance of the late James Sinclair, by nearly the same route, taking with them not only horses, but also cattle.[3] Nothing was, however, published as to the exact nature of the difficulties encountered by any of these parties, or whether or not these could be easily evaded or removed.

The United States' Government, since 1853, have sent a succession of exploring parties into different parts of the mountain country within their territory, with the immediate object of selecting the best route by which to carry a line of railway to connect the States on the Atlantic with those on the Pacific coast.

The reports and surveys of these expeditions already published fill twelve large quarto volumes, abounding with valuable information of every kind respecting the country, and embellished with views of the scenery.[4]

No one of these surveys, however, offers a favourable prospect for the ultimate construction of a line of railway connecting the Atlantic with the Pacific, principally from the fact that in the central part of the continent there is a region, desert, or semi-desert in character, which can never be expected to become occupied by settlers.

It was, therefore, with considerable interest and anxiety that public attention was turned to our own territories, and the wish to have more exact information concerning their nature and resources induced Her Majesty's Government in 1857 to despatch the Expedition which I had the honour to command. . . .

The general aspect of the northern shore of Lake Superior is precipitous and rugged. Around Thunder Bay, however, and extending for some distance up the valley of the Kaministaquoia there is a considerable extent of rich alluvial land, heavily timbered. The rise to the crest of the rocky district that forms the height of land is almost abrupt, to an altitude of 800 feet above Lake Superior, or 1,400 feet above the sea level.[5]

The country which succeeds to the west and north is wild and rocky, but with no hill more than 300 feet above the general level, so that it cannot be called a mountainous region. It is intersected by long narrow lakes and innumerable watercourses, broken by ridges of rock, across which the traveller has to make tedious portages. The extent of the continuous water communication improves considerably as we descend to the west, and there are some large lakes which would be available for steam navigation in the event of the country ever becoming settled.

As a line of communication with the Red River and the Saskatchewan prairies, the canoe route from Lake Superior to Lake Winnipeg, even if modified and greatly improved by a large outlay of capital, would, I consider, be always too arduous and expensive a route of transport for emigrants, and never could be used for the introduction of stock, both from the broken nature of the country passed through, and also from the very small extent of available pasture. I therefore cannot recommend the Imperial Government to countenance or lend support to any scheme for constructing or, it may be said, forcing a thoroughfare by this line of route either by land or water, as there would be no immediate advantage commensurate with the required sacrifice of capital; nor can I advise such heavy expenditure as would necessarily attend the construction of any exclusively British line of road between Canada and Red River Settlement.

As regards the fitness for settlement of the district traversed by the canoe route, I beg to state that there are only very few and isolated spots where agriculture could be carried on, and that only by the discovery of mineral wealth would this region be likely to attract settlers. At present the considerable number of Indians living in it subsist by hunting, fishing, trapping, and trading furs to the Hudson Bay Company; but the fitness of the country for these pursuits is by no means a proof of its being so for those of civilized man. . . .

The whole territory explored may be naturally divided into three districts, marked by different physical features. Concerning the first of them, the canoe route, it is not necessary for me to enter into further particulars, as it has been made the subject of a minute and able report (already laid before Parliament) by a Canadian Expedition, which had much greater facilities for making an examination of this region than my Expedition possessed. I shall, therefore, pass to the consideration of the central prairie region, and as this is for the purpose of agricultural settlement by far the most valuable portion of the territory traversed by the Expedition, and is also somewhat diversified in its character, I shall be warranted in entering more into detail upon this portion of my subject.

Immediately to the west of the rocky district already referred to succeeds a chain of lakes, the principal of which is Lake Winnipeg, which has the same altitude above the sea level as Lake Superior, viz., 600 feet. From these lakes to the Rocky Mountains the central region may be considered as a plain gradually rising until it gains an altitude of 3,000 feet at the base of the mountain chain. The surface of this slope is marked by steppes, by which successive and decided increases of elevation are effected, accompanied by important changes in the composition of the soil, and consequently in the character of the vegetation.

These steppes are three in number. The first may be said to spring from the southern shore of the lake of the woods, and, trending to the S.W., crosses Red River consequently south of the boundary line; thence it runs irregularly in a north-westerly direction towards Swan River to meet the North Saskatchewan below Fort à la Corne. The general altitude of this first or most easterly prairie steppe may be estimated at 800 to 900 feet above the sea level.[6]

The second or middle steppe, conterminous with the limit of the first just de-scribed, extends westward to the base of the third steppe, which may be defined by a line crossing the United States frontier not far from the 'Roche Percée,' in longitude 104° W.; thence passing in a north-westerly direction to near the elbow of the South Saskatchewan, and northwards to the Eagle Hills, west of Fort Carlton. The mean altitude of this second steppe is about 1,600 feet above the sea level.[7]

The third and highest steppe extends to the base of the Rocky Mountains, and has a mean altitude of 2,700 feet.[8]

The composition of the plains being, to a great depth, of soft materials, these steppes do not influence the river channels, so that the rivers rising in the Rocky Mountains traverse the plains with an uniform current, uncontrolled by the super-ficial features of the country. These rivers have, generally speaking, formed deep rather than wide valleys, their lateral extent being rarely proportionate to their steep and lofty banks; consequently, these valleys do not afford a great extent of alluvial land, or land of first quality, for agricultural purposes; and this is more particularly true of the western plain country, where the rivers traverse the higher plateaus.

The existence of a general law regulating the distribution of the woods in this portion of the continent suggested itself to us during our first summer's explorations, and subsequent experience during the seasons of 1858–9 fully confirmed it.

The fertile savannahs and valuable woodlands of the Atlantic United States are succeeded, as has been previously alluded to, on the west by a more or less arid desert, occupying a region on both sides of the Rocky Mountains, which presents a barrier to the continuous growth of settlement between the Mississippi Valley and the States on the Pacific coast. This central desert extends, however, but a short way into the British territory, forming a triangle, having for its base the 49th parallel from longitude 100° to 114° W., with its apex reaching to the 52nd parallel of latitude.

The northern forests, which in former times descended more nearly to the frontier of this central desert, have been greatly encroached upon and, as it were, pushed backwards to the north through the effect of frequent fires.

Thus a large portion of fertile country, denuded of timber, separates the arid region from the forest lands to the north, and the habit which the Indian tribes have of burning the vegetation has, in fact, gradually improved the country for the purpose of settlement by clearing off the heavy timber, to remove which is generally the first and most arduous labour of the colonist.

All the rivers which intersect the plains traversed by the Expedition east of the Rocky Mountains, with the exception of the Athabasca, flow into Lake Winnipeg and thence into Hudson Bay. The Athabasca, on the other hand, joins the McKenzie, which flows to the Arctic Ocean. . . .

Next in order comes the Red River of the North, so called to distinguish it from a river of the same name in the state of Arkansas.

Although this is not the largest, it is by far the most important river in this portion of the British territories, on account of the great extent of arable land which the lower portion of its valley affords for agricultural development, and much of which is already under cultivation by the inhabitants of the Selkirk Settlement.

Red River has its source in the same direction of marshes and lakes, from which flows also the Mississippi. This district is situated in about lat. $46^1/_2°$, long. 95° W., and is elevated 860 feet above the sea level. The course of Red River is slightly west of north to where it falls into Lake Winnipeg, in lat. $50^1/_2°$ N. and long. 97° W. After crossing the frontier at Pembina, in lat. 49°, it flows with a very serpentine course for about 140 miles through British territory. At 8 or 10 miles from the lake the land on the banks of the river becomes sufficiently elevated to be available for agriculture; it stretches back for many miles on either hand in fine rich savannahs or lightly timbered country. Indeed, the valley of Red River being rarely confined by lofty banks in any portion of its course, is valuable for settlement the whole way up stream and for a considerable distance south of the international line.

Of the prairies along Red River only narrow strips on the top of the banks have been yet brought under cultivation by the colonist, as there the land is naturally rather higher and better drained than that lying further in the rear, both from its proximity to the river and also from the frequent gullies cut in the soft clay soil by the numerous small creeks that carry off the surface water. These gulleys at present reach but a very short distance back from the river, but were they artificially extended so as to serve as main drains, much land at present covered by swamps and marsh would be reclaimed. As it is, however, these marshes are of considerable value to the colonist from the abundant supply of natural hay which they yield. The channel of Red River is from 50 to 60 feet in depth, but occasionally the floods in spring are so high as to raise the river above that level, and to inundate the prairies to a great distance on either hand, devastating the property of the settlers. These floods seem to occur at intervals of 8 or 10 years, the last having occurred in 1852, previous to one which has again damaged the settlement this summer (1861).

It is not improbable that these floods could to a great extent be prevented by attention to the state of the river channel, especially towards its mouth. Both Red River and its large tributary the Assineboine, bring down an excessive quantity of fine sediment that gradually fills up the channels wherever the force of the current is checked.[9]

From this cause these rivers apparently increase in size for a course of years, till at last a flood in the upper country towards their sources happens at the same time that Lake Winnipeg is at a high level, or that its south end is blocked by ice in early spring. The result of this is, that the river, from the sluggishness of its current at its mouth, overflows the lip-like ridges which bound the channel, and submerges the lower country in their rear on either hand. During the remainder of the season in which the overflow occurs, the great body of water which thus accumulates only slowly escapes to the lake, and by keeping the river in high flood for a much longer term than usual, and until the level of the lake has fallen with the advancing summer, the channel is thus scoured out and a second flood is averted, until the river-bed has again been blocked up by the accumulation of sediment. Were this cleansing of the river channel effected artificially, so that there should be always a sufficient depth to allow the flood water to escape with the requisite velocity under all circumstances, the great calamity of periodic floods might be averted from this settlement, especially if these labours were combined with works for raising the banks of the river in a few places where they are below the general level.

Full details and statistics of the Red River Settlement have been recently published,[10] and from the study of these, as well as from my own more limited opportunities for examination, I can entirely coincide in the hopeful views which have been expressed regarding the future development of this settlement as a British Colony.

Its position is, however, too much isolated for it to progress rapidly, unless some arrangement be made to allow of a secure system of traffic through or with the north-western United States, for there can be no question that the natural line of ingress to the country is from the south, by way of St Paul's, Crow Wing, and Pembina. There are two routes from Crow Wing to Pembina, which is a distance of 310 miles; one of which can only be used in winter when the swamps are frozen. The other is some-what longer, but as it passes out into the plains along the border of the Sioux Indians' country, it is sometimes dangerous for travellers unless they form a strong party.

A few years ago these roads were in very bad state, being nothing more than trails, without any attempt at grading or constructing bridges where necessary.

The Hudson Bay Company have however now commenced to bring their goods for the fur trade into the country by this route, and a steamer[11] plies on Red River as high as Grahams Point, which is about 230 miles above Pembina, in connexion with stage waggons that continue the route to St Pauls. The road has doubtless been much improved since I traversed it, and soon no greater difficulty will exist in gaining access to the Red River Settlement than to any of the more western towns of the United States which are not yet reached by railways.

With regard to the climate of the district of Red River and the Assineboine, we are in need of more complete and careful observations than have yet been obtained to justify our speaking with confidence on the subject.

It would appear, however, that the winter is somewhat shorter in this region than in that about Lake Superior. The average time for its commencement is in the beginning of November, and by the middle of the month all the lakes and streams are completely frozen, and the ground covered with snow, which lasts throughout the season.

The winter really lasts till about the second week in April, although during the month of March there are many warm genial days, with hard frosts during the nights; but, in addition to this period of five months, there is a previous frost of two or three weeks, preceding the freezing over of the rivers, and sufficiently severe to stop agricultural operations, so that the winter may generally be estimated at six months' duration. The extreme cold is in the month of February, when the thermometer sometimes falls to about 45° below zero. The winter is the most favourable time for the transport of heavy materials, such as those required for building purposes. Thaws rarely occur before the month of March; but, at this time, the existence of horses and horned cattle becomes precarious, owing to the thaws by day being succeeded by frosts at night, causing a crust on the snow, in many cases, too hard for the animals to remove in order to feed. The inhabitants, however, by the exercise of a little forethought during the previous autumn, might, without any difficulty, provide abundance of the finest natural hay from the adjacent swamps. Horses and cattle, if provided with a sufficiency of hay for only six or seven weeks, will not only survive, but continue useful and serviceable during the whole of the winter and spring. Spring progresses with great rapidity; in a few days snow disappears, and the new grass has already commenced to grow up by the beginning of May. At the end of that month agricultural operations may be commenced. During the month of June, however, severe night frosts frequently occur, rendering the wheat crops very precarious; but the climate is well suited to the growth of barley, oats, potatoes, and garden vegetables. . . .

The chief wealth of the agriculturist would be derived from the rearing of cattle, large quantities of very nutritious grasses abounding everywhere, together with hemp, flax, and hops, which grow admirably. Between the Red River and the Saskatchewan, no river of any great size enters on the west side of Lake Winnipeg. There are indeed several streams which are navigable for boats, but these are merely channels of communication between various lakes. . . .

From the Rocky Mountain House to Fort [à] la Corne, the North Saskatchewan traverses the plains in a valley that varies in depth from 100 to 300 feet, and never exceeds two miles in width. The greater part of this width is occupied by alluvial flats, the river itself rarely exceeding 400 yards in width. The alluvial flats, which form the finest quality of land in this part of the country, are often well timbered, but from the manner in which the river winds from side to side of the valley, the 'points,' as they are termed, are seldom more than two or three miles in extent.

Wherever the banks of the valley slope gently back to the higher prairie level, as at Fort Carlton, there are to be found the most desirable spots for settlement. By inspecting the map it will be observed that the general course of the river is bounded by hills which sometimes recede to a considerable distance. These hills rise two to four hundred feet above the general level, and skirting along their base there is often to be found areas of land of fine quality, while the whole distance, sometimes equal to 30 miles between the hills and the river, is fine grazing land, and as it all lies within the limit of the partially wooded belt of country, there are 'bluffs' that will afford shelter to stock.

The richness of the natural pasture in many places on the prairies of the second level along the North Saskatchewan and its tributary, Battle River, can hardly be exaggerated. Its value does not consist in its being rank or in great quantity, but from its fine quality, comprising nutritious species of grasses and carices, along with natural vetches in great variety, which remain throughout the winter sound, juicy, and fit for the nourishment of stock.

Almost everywhere along the course of the North Saskatchewan are to be found eligible situations for agricultural settlement, a sufficency of good soil is everywhere to be found, nor are these advantages merely confined to the neighbourhood of the river; in several districts, such as N.W. of Carlton, we traversed fine land fit for all purposes, both of pasture and tillage, extending towards the Thickwood hills, and also to be found in the region of the lakes between Forts Pitt and Edmonton.

In almost every direction round Edmonton the land is fine, excepting only the hilly country at the higher level, such as the Beaver Hills. Even there, however, there is nothing like sterility, only the surface is too much broken to be occupied while more level country can be obtained. The places which have been chosen for mission stations are all at a distance from the river, a preference having naturally been given to the borders of the large lakes which lie along the base of the hilly country for the sake of the fine fish which these yield in abundance. The quantity of fish of very fine quality obtained from some of these lakes is enormous. The best fishing season is just as the winter commences, and in the course of a few weeks, some years ago, there were taken in Lake St Ann's alone 40,000 of these 'white fish' (*coregonus albus*), having an average weight of 3 to 4 lbs. each. The fish are preserved during the winter simply by being frozen, and afford a cheap and nutritious article of food.

In the upper part of the Saskatchewan country coal of fair quality occurs abundantly, and may hereafter be found very useful; it is quite fit to be employed in the smelting of iron from the ores of that metal, which also occurs in large quantities in the same strata.[12] Building stone is wholly absent until quite close to the Rocky Mountains, but brick earth and potter's clay may be obtained in many parts of the country. The climate is more irregular than that of Red River, and partial thaws often occur long before the actual coming of spring and do great harm to the vegetation. The winter is much the same in its duration, but the amount of snow that falls decreases rapidly as we approach the mountains.

The North Saskatchewan freezes generally about the 12th November, and breaks up from the 17th to the 20th of April. During the winter season of five months the means of travelling and transport are greatly facilitated by the snow, the ordinary depth of which is sufficient for the use of sleighs, without at the same time being too great to impede horses. If proper roads were formed this facility would be greatly increased, and as a result there would be no season during which the country could be said to be closed for traffic.

Between Carlton and Edmonton there is no valuable timber to be found south of the river, the only trees growing there being small aspen poplars. To the north, however, and along the river above and below these points, the spruce, fir, pine, and birch occur abundantly. There is neither oak, ash, elm, maple, or any of the hardwood trees that are found at Red River in any part of the Saskatchewan. Only a few trees of the false sugar maple, from which the Indians make a coarse kind of sugar, being found in certain places.

The South Saskatchewan, which in its upper part is called Bow River, resembles the North Saskatchewan in size, volume of water, and its general direction, but it passes through a very different description of country.

After leaving the eastern limit of the country that is within the influence of the mountains (which may be considered to commence about 20 miles below where it receives Ispasquehow River),[13] the South Saskatchewan flows in a deep and narrow valley, through a region of arid plains, devoid of timber or pasture of good quality. Even on the alluvial points in the bottom of the valley trees and shrubs only occur in a few isolated patches. The steep and lofty sides of the valley are composed of calcareous marls and clays that are baked into a compact mass under the heat of the parching sun. The sage and the cactus abound, and the whole of the scanty vegetation bespeaks of arid climate. The course of its large tributaries, Red Deer River and Belly River, are through the same kind of country, except in the upper part of the former stream, where it flows through rich partially wooded country similar to that on the North Saskatchewan.

Towards the confluence of Red Deer River and the South Saskatchewan, there are extensive sandy wastes.[14] For 60 miles to the east of this point the country was not examined by the Expedition,[15] but at the elbow the same arid description of country was met with, and it seems certain that this prevails throughout the entire distance. Below the elbow the banks of the river and also the adjacent plains begin to improve rapidly as the river follows a north-east course and enters the fertile belt.[16] From the Moose Woods[17] to its confluence with the North Saskatchewan it in no way differs from that river, which indeed is nearly flowing parallel with it, only 30 or 40 miles distant.

In the midst of the arid plains traversed by the South Saskatchewan, there are isolated patches of table land, upon the surface of which the vegetation becomes luxuriant, and pasture of fair quality may be found. The Expedition spent two weeks at the Hand Hills[18] which form one of these patches, for the purpose of recruiting the horses.

To the south of the river also, in lat. 49° 40' N., at the Cyprées Hills,[19] there is abundance of water and pasture, and also a heavily timbered slope facing the north, where spruce firs, pines, maple, and many kinds of shrubs flourish in abundance, while for hundreds of miles around in every direction there is no appearance of the plains having ever supported a forest growth. . . .

All along the northern districts of the country above described occur very numerous lakes, supplying immense quantities of nutritious fish, among which are pike, sturgeon, cat-fish, gold-eyed carp,[20] and white fish in greatest abundance. I have seen these obtained with the greatest of ease even in winter where holes had to be chopped through the ice in order to catch them. None can so readily appreciate the advantage that a farmer would derive from a certainty of obtaining plenty of fish in the neighbourhood of his farm as those who know the difficulties attending the hunting of animal food, where the settler would have to compete for a bare existence against the Indian trained almost from birth to the tracking and killing of thickwood animals, such as deer, elk, and moose.

Granting even that the colonist is a skilled hunter and able to compete with the man born in the forest, the greater portion of his time would be absorbed in the same pursuit as the Indian, and little time or energy would remain for agriculture.

Add to this the fact that the smoke and the noise attending the home of the white man frightens the game far and near, and so increases the labour necessary to obtain it.

The second advantage found by the settler is the abundance of good food for cattle growing throughout the region, such as goose-grass, pease-grass, vetches, astragalous[21] and other plants, which preserve their nutritious quality through the winter season. Horses and horned cattle would resist the rigour of winter well and continue in good condition, if not poor when turned out at its commencement, and if provided with artificial food in the very early spring when the partial thaws during the day cause a coating of ice over the herbage, which the animals find very difficult to remove in order to feed. I have killed many fat buffaloes in the months of January and February; after which I have invariably found them lean, and sometimes seen the ground sprinkled with blood from the hardness of the surface, which the animal tries to shovel aside with its nose.

If even the buffalo, whose nose is formed by nature for this purpose, finds a difficulty in obtaining his food, how much more difficult must be the task of self-support to the domestic animals. . . .

A third inducement to settlement in the valley of the Saskatchewan is the fact that the settler has not to encounter the formidable labour of clearing the land from timber. The frequent fires which continually traverse the prairie have denuded the territory of large forest trees, indeed so much so as in some places to render their absence deplorable, and the result of these fires is that the agriculturist may at once commence with his plough without any more preliminary labour.

Although throughout the whole of the fertile region, as well as in the subarctic forests of the north and west, there is no timber fit for export, such as the white pine or the gross larch, so highly prized by the lumberer. Yet there is abundance which would serve the purpose of the settler, and suffice to construct houses and furnish him with fuel. Coal, available for smelting purposes, exists abundantly, and iron in very large quantities.

The capabilities of this country and its climate, for the success of the cereals, have hardly been sufficiently tested. But I have seen first-rate specimens of barley and oats grown at many of the forts. Wheat has not been so successful, but I am hardly prepared to say that this was because of the unfitness of the climate to produce it. I have much reason to believe that the seed has been bad, and the cultivation neglected, and the spots chosen not of a suitable aspect. I have not only seen excellent wheat, but also Indian corn (which will not succeed in England or Ireland) ripening on Mr. Pratt's farm, at the Qu'appelle Lakes, in 1857.

Harvest would commence early in September, and its operation would not be seriously interrupted by three or four wet days in that month, taking that as a fair average of the rain that falls at that period; more rain falls in the spring than in the autumn, but even then it is inconsiderable.

The only principal disadvantage accruing from the greater altitude of the region approaching the Rocky Mountains, is the almost continual night frosts[22] during the summer, not severe during that season, but so frequent as to be almost of nightly occurrence; these would probably prove prejudicial to wheat; barley and oats, however, would do well.

The only objection to raising sheep and pigs would arise from the number of their natural enemies, the wolves,[23] which roam everywhere through wood and plain, and this is probably the cause why the sheep of the country are prompted by their natural instinct to shelter in the inaccessible cliffs of the Rocky Mountains. The ewes and lambs are frequently seen feeding at a low altitude, and evince a preference for the grass below, which naturally grows in greater quantities. . . .

I undertook the exploration of the Kananaskis pass myself, accompanied by my secretary, Mr. Sullivan, and after traversing the mountains we returned to the eastern plains again by the British Kootanie pass. . . .

The timber on the western slope of the mountains was somewhat finer than that which we found on the eastern side, and we saw several new pines, together with oak, ash, birch, and larch, but the lands in the valley of the Columbia and Kootanie rivers, as far as I could judge, were neither valuable for their extent nor for their quality.

A ride from the Columbia Lakes to the boundary line sufficed to show me that the difficulties to be overcome in crossing the continent to the westward, without passing to the southward of that line, were far from being overcome. A formidable tract of country still remained to be traversed before a connexion with British Columbia could be effected. . . .

The Kootanie River, which, with its branches, derives its source north of the international line, descends over 40 miles into the American territory, and thence returns to the north to flow into Flat Bow Lake,[24] and finally terminates into the

Columbia. The irregular quadrilateral piece of country thus formed by these two rivers represents a most formidable tract where even the banks of the rivers are cloud-capped mountains. I determined, however, to penetrate it in order to endeavour to discover if the passage of the continent north of the boundary line could be effected . . . .

During my branch exploration by the westward, I was accompanied by an Indian and a half breed,[25] and in addition to the fallen timber I encountered almost insuperable difficulties in the mountainous nature of the country westward of the Columbia River, and although I succeeded in forcing my way and taking the horses across from Fort Shepherd to the place where I met the American Commission upon the boundary line in long. 119°,[26] yet I could not recommend that line of country as one through which it would be advisable to carry a road. Besides, the lateness of the season did not admit of my crossing the Cascade Range, otherwise I should myself have crossed the continent altogether in an unbroken line from Canada to the shores of the Pacific.

Here I met the gentlemen employed under the American Commissioners for laying down the boundary line from the Gulf of Georgia, near the Little Okanagan Lakes,[27] from which point the Hudson Bay Company's trail passes north of the boundary line, altogether crossing the Cascade Range at Mansen's Mountain.[28]

This Hudson Bay trail, which is used for bringing in supplies to Colville from Fort Langley (on the west coast) crosses the boundary line for the first time on the lesser Okanagan Lakes in long. 119° 10′ W. Being already aware of this fact, and being subsequently confirmed in this opinion by Lieut. Palmer, R.E., who made a reconnaissance of the Hudson Bay Company's trail all the way from Fraser River to Fort Colville, I did not think it necessary or justifiable to cross the Cascade Range so late in the season, and to run the risk of losing the horses without obtaining any further knowledge with regard to this old established trail beyond that already known to the Hudson Bay Company, and already supplied to Her Majesty's Government by Lieut. Palmer, R.E.

The connexion therefore of the Saskatchewan plains, east of the Rocky Mountains, with a known route through British Columbia, has been effected by the Expedition under my command, without our having been under the necessity of passing through any portion of United States Territory. Still the knowledge of the country on the whole would never lead me to advocate a line of communication from Canada across the continent to the Pacific, exclusively through British territory. The time has now for ever gone by for effecting such an object, and the unfortunate choice of an astronomical boundary line has completely isolated the Central American possessions of Great Britain from Canada in the east, and also almost debarred them from any eligible access from the Pacific coast on the west.

The settler, who will always adopt the shortest and least expensive route, will undoubtedly follow the line of traverse indicated by the formation of the country.

He will travel by steamer along the Canadian Lakes through Sault Ste Marie to Superior City, situated at the extremity of the 'Fond du Lac' or most western extremity of Lake Superior; and he will then be only 70 or 80 miles distant from Crow Wing, on the high road between Saint Pauls and the Red River Settlement.

American squatters and lumberers are rapidly settling up Red River, and the railway communication (now nearly complete to Saint Pauls), will soon be completed to Pembina, in which case the establishment of a branch line to Superior 'Fond du Lac' would be a positive certainty, thus easy and rapid communication would be established between Lake Superior and the frontier of Red River Settlement.

In the event of railway communication being extended as far as Pembina, it would not be unreasonable then to entertain the prospect that the Imperial Government might feel justified in encouraging the extension of such railway on the British side of the line to the northward and westward, through the southern portion of 'the fertile belt' to the Rocky Mountains; at all events as soon as the country showed symptoms of becoming sufficiently populated to warrant such an effort.

As the case at present stands all communication with the Colony at Red River is through the States.[29] Soon after the publication of my despatch, declaring the navigability of the Red River for steamers, American enterprise established one there;[30] this, as I now understand, plies the whole way from Lake Winnipeg to Graham's Point, above the forks of the Shienne,[31] and, now that the results of the Expedition lately under my command are known, even the Hudson Bay Company have adopted the route *via* St Pauls and Pembina, for bringing their merchandise into this country. As for the importation of horses, cows, and any other species of live stock, all such traffic would be impossible either *via* Hudson Bay or by the canoe route. To the westward of the Rocky Mountains the communication is very arduous; no road fit for carts exists north of the boundary line, nor indeed is there a single portion of the territory that could be traversed by the roughest or strongest cart, from the plains at the entrance of the several Rocky Mountain passes in the east until you come to the western slope of the Cascade range. . . .

We do not apprehend that the Indians along the North Saskatchewan are likely to cause any serious difficulties to the settlement of the 'fertile belt'. The Salteaus, Crees, and Thickwood Assineboines have been for many years on the best of terms not only with the members and servants of the Hudson Bay Company, but with all the free traders, missionaries, visitors, &c., that have visited their country; this may be in some measure accounted for by the justice and good faith which characterize all the dealings of the Hudson Bay Company with them, and also by the number of the company's servants who have adopted their women, and have established with them relationships of which they feel proud.

If white men, or indeed if half-breeds were to settle as agriculturists in the country, I do not say that they would never have serious cause of complaint with the Indians of the North Saskatchewan; quarrels doubtless would arise sometimes out of horse stealing, at other times out of their harmless mischief; but I do not think that any organized system of aggression would be attempted against the settlers, and I even think that many Indians, provided they could obtain farming implements, would follow the examples they saw before them and begin to till the soil themselves.

No doubt it would often happen that the Indians might carry off horses or oxen, and that the white man in pursuit of them would come into deadly collision with them, the result of which would be a regular system of reprisals. But if examples of practical agriculture, and facilities for obtaining agricultural implements were offered to the Thickwood Crees and Mountain Stoneys, I am certain that they would very rapidly commence planting potatoes, and so save themselves from much of the labour and hunger which they have to endure throughout the winter in providing the flesh of the elk, moose, and deer, as food for their large families. First-rate hunters have frequently told me that such hard and constant labour in pursuing thickwood animals for the support of themselves and their families left them neither courage nor time to devote to their traps, and that consequently they could not get furs wherewith to purchase blankets and other comforts for themselves from the company, adding that if they could be sure of a meal of potatoes sometimes they could follow the traps.

The settlers, however, would not find all the Indians with whom they came in contact so friendly as the generality of those that occupy the fertile belt. The country to the southward on both sides of the international line is that of the Blackfeet, Piegans, and Blood Indians, and I should apprehend that these Indians would form large war parties (against the Crees ostensibly), and these war parties, although first organized without any hostile intention against their agricultural neighbours, yet infallibly would end in attacks on the property of the settler and in loss of life to both Indians and settlers. When once the party goes forth to war, its individual members are not very nice in their distinctions who may be the owners of the horses they steal. Add to this the fact of the settler being a friend of their enemies, the Crees, will be accused of having furnished them with ammunition, which will render him liable to be ill-treated when he is in the power of these wilder and more uncertain tribes. In the exploring season of 1859 our Expedition traversed the whole of the British portion of the territory of the Blackfoot, Piegan, and Blood Indians, but such was the general terror of the half-breeds whom I had engaged, that it was with the utmost difficulty I could lead them on, and, indeed if it had not been for the gentlemen and the Americans who had taken service under me, I do not think I could have gone forward at all.

The Hudson Bay Company have long given up the posts[32] they once held in that country as too dangerous to maintain, and since my departure from the country even the Rocky Mountain House, the last of the Blackfoot posts, has been abandoned. . . .[33]

Beyond the immediate neighbourhood of Red River Settlement no money of any coinage whatsoever is in use, and all payments are made in kind; the men, therefore, had to be paid in such articles as coats, trousers, blankets, guns, ammunition, tea, tobacco, axes, knives, &c. and as the Hudson Bay Company's stores never contained a sufficiency of such goods for the purposes of their own trade, I organized a further supply (in anticipation of the payments at the end of each season to men employed by the Expedition). These supplies were forwarded to me from Norway House up the Saskatchewan to Carlton in 1857 and to Edmonton in 1858, along with supplies of tea, sugar, and flour, for the use of the Expedition.

During our canoe route in the commencement of the summer of 1857, we were provided by Iroquois half-breeds, engaged for us by Sir G. Simpson, from La Chine in Canada. These men were only engaged up to the period of our arrival at Red River Settlement. Those engaged for our first season's journeys in the plains were English and French Red River half-breeds, about 12 in all,[34] and their services terminated at our arrival at Carlton, whence they started again on foot to return to Red River, a journey of 600 miles. I paid them for the time consumed on the journey, and allowed them two carts and horses to carry their bedding and provisions.

During the second season's explorations, when we contemplated passing through a portion of the Blackfoot country, previous to crossing the mountains, I deemed it necessary to employ a greater number of men, and therefore engaged 12 from Red River, and directed Dr Hector to procure the services of 12 others from the settlement of Lake St Ann, about 40 miles west of Fort Edmonton. These men were directed to go down from Lake St Ann to Carlton, where they met the men engaged by me, who also started for the same place in March 1858, from Red River Settlement.

During the third season's explorations, I had not only English and French half-breeds in the service of the Expedition, but also employed several Americans who had failed in crossing the mountains in search of the gold already reported to be abundant on Fraser River. Although the men were not experienced in the usages of prairie life, yet I found their assistance most valuable, as I could always rely on their siding with the gentlemen in supporting me, when I insisted on traversing the Blackfoot country, at the time when only one or two of my half-breeds were to be depended on, and had it not been for them, I should have found it impossible to coerce the rest. In alluding to this subject, however, I cannot omit to mention that the gentlemen of the Expedition (Dr Hector and Mr. Sullivan) were ably seconded by my friends, the late Capt. Brisco and Mr. Mitchell, in staunch adhesion to my proposed plan of operations. . . .

From 'Journal No. 2' (14 July–8 October 1857): life on the trail; buffalo hunting in the 1850s.

September 19th, Saturday. The whole of this forenoon was occupied in crossing over a succession of ridges or prairie rolls, among which are a number of lakes. These ridges are composed of light yellowish sand of very fine grain, the sides of many of which supported berry-bearing bushes and a few poplars. We passed a second creek,[35] which, like the one we encamped at last night, takes it rise in a small lake to the south, and is tributary to the Thunder Mountain Creek. At noon an observation for latitude was 50° 27′ 39″ N.[36] During the afternoon we were met by a few Indians, some of whom produced certificates, which they had received from the various trading posts of the Hudson Bay Company, and which were folded and tied carefully in a piece of bark. One of these certificates ran as follows: 'This is to certify that Awaskasoo (the Red Deer) is a good Indian, and a man of some influence in his tribe, and that he has brought many furs to the Company's establishments; he has once traded with the opposition traders, but promises never to do so again.' . . .

September 20th, Sunday — Started early, and not long afterwards came in sight of one or two old buffalo bulls, evidently stragglers; we at once concluded that buffaloes were not far off; we continued our course, and saw bands of bulls, at first small, but increasing in number as we proceeded westwards. Seeing that as yet there was no danger of disturbing any cows in that neighbourhood, I encouraged Mr. Sullivan to mount one of our best horses, and run a band of bulls, in company with Morin, and he acquitted himself very well, rushed in boldly, and bowled over his bull at the first shot. Morin afterwards killed a young bull, of which we were able to eat a little. We were now in hourly expectation of coming upon bands of cows, when we should enjoy fresh meat once more. We were now verging on the neutral ground of the Blackfeet and Crees, and Nichiwa smartened himself up considerably, having obtained from me an old shooting jacket, from the Doctor a pair of corduroys, and from Mr. Sullivan a waistcoat and neckhandkerchief. He never was an imposing or a fine-looking Indian, but now he looked more like a monkey than ever. The country was much the same as we have travelled over since we left the line of woods in the east. We continued to fall in with several bands of bulls, but did not molest them. Rain threatened; camped early; our latitude was 50° 28′, long. 106° 50′. We camped on Thunder Mountain Creek,[37] which rises in two streams from the so named portion of the Coteau; it flows to the east to join Moose Jaw Creek, which runs into the Qu'appelle River.

September 21st — Started early; sent men on in advance to report on the buffalo; passed some bands of bulls. At half-past seven one of the scouts returned to the carts and reported a band of cows not three miles distant. Halted to breakfast at a small swamp, where we took a hurried meal, cooked with some of the fuel still remaining to us out of that which we had taken from Moose Jaw Creek, which wood we used very sparingly, and kept the remainder for the plentiful meal on which we were speculating for the evening. After breakfast McKay and I started to run buffalo, accompanied by Hallet and Morin (two of the best buffalo hunters in Red River Settlement). We found the ground very bad, and full of badger holes, rendering the running of the horses very dangerous, and somewhat similar to riding a steeple chase over a rabbit warren.[38] Our horses were not in very good order, but, of course, I was mounted on the best, my own horse Pharaoh; the next best was given to James McKay; Hallet and Morin completed the hunters. We approached rather close, favoured by some sand hills, and got very near our game. When the race began, the pace was tremendous, because early in the day the cows are far swifter; in less than five minutes we left the bulls floundering in the rear, and were a-head among the cows, Hallet and I riding neck and neck. Seeing a fat one, I ran in, fired, and missed; I slackened, and riding knee to knee with Hallet, asked him for his loaded gun, saying 'You cannot come up.' He, a little piqued, swerved from me. McKay, who was in the rear, came up and said, 'Captain, my horse cannot do it, I shall injure the horse, and do no good; take my loaded gun, give me your empty one.' I, who had been reining in, took McKay's gun, and, just as I was again passing Hallet, his horse put his foot into a hole, and horse and rider got a fearful fall. I passed on, got a second shot, and killed a fine cow; slackening again, McKay came up to me a second time, and handed me a loaded gun. I rushed again into the band and got a third short, but my gun missed fire. My horse was wonderfully fresh, and I was debating on another race, when Beauchamp, a very good hunter, came riding up. He was a light weight, so I called him, and leaped off my horse; he jumped on, and very soon picked out and brought down another fat cow. Morin also killed a good cow. Our race was westwards, and at its termination we found ourselves in view of the bluffs of the South Saskatchewan.[39] By the time we had cut up our meat the carts had arrived, and we camped on a small stream tributary to the South Saskatchewan, where we found wood, water, and grass. This creek is winding, and depressed considerably below the prairie level, and its sides are strewn with boulders.[40] The plants do not materially differ from those at Moose Jaw Creek. Here we, for the first time, met with the sage (*artemesia tridentifolia*) which is a low shrub, characteristic of the great American deserts. We gave this little tributary of the South Saskatchewan the name of Sage Creek. Although the country throughout was arid and sterile, still muddy swamps very frequently occur, in which are to be found wild fowl in great abundance; out of one of these (a very small swamp) we were surprised at starting a flock of geese, in numbers quite disproportioned to its area. Buffalo were also here in great numbers, as well as their constant attendants the wolves, ever ready to attack a worn-out or wounded straggler, or some stray calf. The abundance of game here is accounted for by its being the neutral ground of the Crees, Assineboines, and Blackfeet; none of these tribes are in the habit of resorting to its neighbourhood except in war parties. The grass in this arid soil, always so scanty, was now actually swept away by the buffalo, who, assisted by the locusts, had left the country as bare as if it had been overrun by fire; even at the edge of Sage Creek we could obtain but very little grass for our horses.

We guarded the horses carefully each night, especially near daylight, the favourite moment for an attempt to steal them. Buffalo sometimes fed close to our horses at night, and bands of wolves howled piteously along the plains above. We could plainly distinguish them passing backwards and forwards by the light of the moon which shone on the bluffs above us.

Notes

1. Chesterfield House, 5 miles below the forks of the South Saskatchewan and Red Deer; and Bow Fort, alias Peigan Post, at the Bow River and Old Fort Creek.
2. Sir GEORGE SIMPSON, *Narrative of a Journey Round the World* (1847), 106–30.
3. James Sinclair (1811–1856), a private trader at Red River descended from an HBC family. When the Company began to feel population pressure in the Red River Colony he led a party of emigrant families from the settlement to the Columbia. An energetic merchant, he also functioned virtually as a secret agent of the Company; he was eventually killed in a native attack in Oregon.
4. Palliser has in mind the United States Pacific Railroad Surveys.
5. Lake Superior is 602.23 feet above sea level; Dog Lake (from which the Kaministikwia River flows) is 1,380 feet. The height of land rises to over 1,500 feet.
6. This first prairie level is the Manitoba Lowland or Red River Plain, bounded on the west by

Pembina Mountain, Riding Mountain, Duck Mountain, Porcupine Mountain, and the Pasquia Hills.

[7]The Saskatchewan Plain, stretching southwestward to the foot of the Coteau, also known as the Coteau des Prairies or Missouri Coteau.

[8]Now known as the Alberta Plateau.

[9]In actuality the major cause of flooding is not silt, but heavy precipitation in the autumn, saturating the ground before freeze-up, or in the winter, especially just before break-up; a cold winter with no thaws; a late spring with high temperatures during break-up so that run-off is fast; and heavy rainfall during break-up.

[10]By H.Y. HIND, 6 February 1858, in *Canadian Report*, pp. 301–424.

[11]The *Anson Northup*, launched 19 May 1859.

[12]So far no iron ore has been mined in this area.

[13]Highwood River, the Stoneys' 'river-where-the-wood-grows-high'.

[14]The Middle Sand Hills.

[15]Palliser's editor, Irene Spry, observes 'more likely 100 miles or more.'

[16]The great arc of fertile land (also called the 'park belt') stretching north and west from Red River to Saskatoon and Edmonton. It was into this country that HENRY KELSEY had travelled nearly two centuries earlier.

[17]South of modern Saskatoon in the area which is now the Dundurn Forest Reserve.

[18]East of Drumheller, Alberta.

[19]Now Cypress Hills, named for their forests of lodgepole pine which, along with other conifers, the voyageurs called *cyprès*.

[20]The gold-eye (*Amphiodon alosoides*), which is not a carp.

[21]*Astragalus*, the large family of milk vetches.

[22]Dr. Hector, in his copy of the *Report*, corrected this to 'are the occasional night frosts'.

[23]The timber wolf and the coyote.

[24]Kootenay Lake.

[25]This was Pichena, 'an old Blackfoot half-breed hunter'.

[26]At Midway, British Columbia, in 118° 45′ W. This was one of the two American astronomical parties of the North West Boundary Survey, led by Joseph S. Harris.

[27]Lake Osoyoos. The meeting was about 30 miles east of the lake.

[28]Manson Ridge, east-southeast of Fort Hope and west-southwest of Princeton.

[29]In fact, the route from Britain through Hudson Bay was still in use. Even from Canada there was some communication by the old canoe route, such as SIMPSON's journeys and the efforts made by the North West Trading and Colonisation Company to establish a mail service. Troops were sent to Red River Settlement in 1857 from Canada via Hudson Bay.

[30]Palliser's editor, Irene Spry, calls this suggestion of a causal relationship questionable.

[31]The Sheyenne joins Red River at modern Fargo. The *Anson Northup* plied as far upstream as Fort Abercrombie (some miles north of Breckenridge) before Georgetown was established as the Hudson's Bay Company post at the head of navigation in Red River.

[32]Chesterfield House and Peigan Post (Bow Fort).

[33]When Palliser wrote this, Rocky Mountain House was temporarily closed.

[34]Six of the twelve are mentioned by name in the published documents: John Ferguson, the head guide; 'Old Henry' Hallet, second guide; Pierre Beauchamp; [Antoine] Morin; John Foulds (or Fowlds); and Joseph Boucher or Bouchi [known as Musqua]. Others are named in the Expedition's and Company documents: Samuel Ballenden (or Ballendine); George Daniel; Baptiste Degrace; Pierre Falcon; Amable Hogue; Donald Matheson; George Morrison; Charles Racette; John Ross; John Simpson; Thomas Sinclair; Robert Sutherland; George

Taylor; Joseph Vermette, and Pascal. In fact Palliser, in a letter of September 13, 1857, says that when he reached the Qu'Appelle Lakes Post he had fourteen men, besides Nichiwa and McKay.

[35]Probably Sandy Creek.

[36]This was very near Mortlach.

[37]This would be south of Darmody. Thunder Creek rises near a part of the Coteau now know as Vermilion Hills.

[38]Hector's diary notes that McKay 'plagued' a herd of buffalo till he made them charge right for the carts.

[39]'Bluffs' in the west means clumps of wood, but Hector's sketches show none here; undoubtedly Palliser is using it in the common English sense of cliffs.

[40]Probably Sage Creek, about halfway between Riverhurst and the Elbow.

Suggestions for Further Reading

For standard or current editions of specific writers, see the 'Textual Note' to each selection.

Two fundamental sources are *The Dictionary of Canadian Biography* (Toronto: University of Toronto Press, 1966—) and Vol. I of the *Historical Atlas of Canada: From the Beginning to 1800*, ed. R. Cole Harris and Geoffrey J. Matthews (Toronto: University of Toronto Press, 1987); Vol. II, covering the nineteenth century, is forthcoming.

There is an extensive and easily accessible historical and biographical literature on the explorers of early Canada. This brief and very selective list focuses chiefly on literary and cultural studies of writers in English.

Adams, Percy G., *Travel Literature and the Evolution of the Novel*. Lexington: University Press of Kentucky, 1983.

Belyea, Barbara, 'Captain Franklin in Search of the Picturesque', *Essays on Canadian Writing* 40 (Spring, 1990), 1–24.

———, 'Mackenzie Meets Moodie at the Great Divide', *Journal of Canadian Studies* 23 (1988), 118–29.

Bentley, D.M.R., '"Set Forth as Plainly May Appear": the Verse Journal of Henry Kelsey', *Ariel: a Review of International English Literature* 21 (1990), 9–30.

Bibeau, Donald F., 'Fur Trade Literature from a Tribal Point of View: a Critique' in *Rendezvous: Selected Papers of the Fourth North American Fur Trade Conference, 1981*, ed. Thomas C. Buckley (St Paul, Minn.: North American Fur Trade Conference, 1984), 83–91.

Brown, Jennifer S.H., *Strangers in Blood: Fur Trade Company Families in Indian Country*. Vancouver: University of British Columbia Press, 1980.

Cole, Douglas and Maria Tippett, '"Pleasing Diversity and Sublime Desolation": the Eighteenth Century British Perception of the Northwest Coast', *Pacific Northwest Quarterly* 65 (1974), 1–7.

Daniells, Roy D., 'The Literary Relevance of Alexander Mackenzie', *Canadian Literature* 38 (1968), 19–28.

Davey, Frank, 'The Explorer in Western Canadian Literature', *Studies in Canadian Literature* 4 (1979), 91–100.

Davis, Richard C., ed., *Rupert's Land: a Cultural Tapestry*. Waterloo: Wilfred Laurier University Press for the Calgary Institute for the Humanities, 1988.

————, 'Exploration and Travel Literature in English', *The Canadian Encyclopedia*, 3 vols. Edmonton: Hurtig, 1985 (I, 605); second ed., 4 vols. Edmonton: Hurtig, 1988 (II, 735–6).

Dickason, Olive, *Canada's First Nations: A History of Founding Peoples from Earliest Times.* Toronto: McClelland & Stewart, 1992.

Duchemin, Parker, '"A Parcel of Whelps": Alexander Mackenzie Among the Indians', *Canadian Literature* 124–125 (Spring–Summer, 1990), 49–74.

Francis, R. Douglas, *Images of the West: Changing Perceptions of the Prairies, 1690–1960.* Saskatoon: Western Producer Prairie Books, 1989.

Franklin, Wayne, *Discoverers, Explorers, Settlers: The Diligent Writers of Early America.* Chicago: University of Chicago Press, 1979.

Galinsky, Hans, 'Exploring the "Exploration Report" and its Image of the Overseas World: Spanish, French and English Variants of a Common Form Type in Early American Literature', *Early American Literature* 12 (1977), 5–24.

Galloway, David, 'The Voyagers' in *The Literary History of Canada*, 2nd ed., vol. I, ed. Carl Klinck *et al.* Toronto: University of Toronto Press, 1976.

Giltrow, Janet L., 'Westering Narratives of Jonathan Carver, Alexander Henry and Daniel Harmon', *Essays on Canadian Writing* 22 (Summer, 1981), 27–41.

Glover, Richard, 'The Witness of David Thompson', *Canadian Historical Review* 31 (1950), 25–38.

Green, L.C. and Olive P. Dickason, *The Law of Nations and the New World.* Edmonton: University of Alberta Press, 1989.

Greenblatt, Stephen, *Marvellous Possessions: The Wonder of the New World.* Chicago: University of Chicago Press, 1991.

Greenfield, Bruce R., 'The Idea of Discovery as a Source of Narrative in Samuel Hearne's *Journey to the Northern Ocean*', *Early American Literature* 21 (1986–7, 189–209.

————, *Narrating Discovery: The Romantic Explorer in American Literature.* New York, Columbia University Press, 1992.

Gross, Konrad, 'Coureurs-de-bois, Voyageurs & Trappers: The Fur Trade and the Emergence of an Ignored Canadian Literary Tradition', *Canadian Literature* 127 (Winter, 1990).

Hamilton, Mary E., 'Samuel Hearne,' in *Profiles in Canadian Literature* 3, ed. Jeffrey M. Heath. Toronto: Dundurn Press, 1982, 9–16.

Hodgson, Maurice, 'The Exploration Journal as Literature', *The Beaver* 298 (Winter, 1967), 4–12.

————, 'Initiation and Quest', *Canadian Literature* 38 (Autumn, 1968), 29–40.

Hopwood, Victor, 'Centenary of an Explorer—David Thompson's *Narrative* Reconsidered', *Queen's Quarterly* 64 (1957), 41–9.

————, 'Explorers by Land (to 1867)', and 'Explorers by Sea: The West Coast' in *The Literary History of Canada*, 2nd ed., vol. I, ed. Carl F. Klinck *et al.* Toronto: University of Toronto Press, 1976.

Lang, George, 'Voyageur Discourse and the Absence of Fur Trade Pidgin', *Canadian Literature* 131 (Winter, 1991), 51–63.

Lewis, G. Malcolm, 'La grande rivière et fleuve de l'ouest / The realities and reasons behind a major mistake in the 18th-century geography of North America', *Cartographica* 28 (1991), 54–87.

Long, John S., 'Narratives of Early Encounters Between Europeans and the Cree of Western James Bay', *Ontario History* 80 (1988), 227–45.

MacLaren, Ian S., 'Alexander Mackenzie and the Landscapes of Commerce', *Studies in Canadian Literature* 7 (1982), 141–50.

———, 'David Thompson's Imaginative Mapping of the Canadian Northwest, 1784–1812', *Ariel: A Review of International English Literature* 15 (1984), 89–106.

———, 'Retaining Captaincy of the Soul: Response to Nature in the First Franklin Expedition', *Essays on Canadian Writing* 28 (Spring, 1984), 57–92.

———, 'Samuel Hearne and the Landscapes of Discovery', *Canadian Literature* 103 (1984), 27–40.

———, 'The Aesthetic Map of the North, 1845–1859', *Arctic* 38 (1985), 89–103.

———, 'Aesthetic Mappings of the West by the Palliser and Hind Survey Expeditions', *Studies in Canadian Literature* 10 (1985), 24–52; 11 (1986), ii-iv.

———, 'John Franklin', in *Profiles in Canadian Literature* 5, ed. Jeffrey M. Heath. Toronto: Dundurn Press, 1986, 25–32.

———, 'Touring at High Speed: Fur Trade Landscapes in the Writings of Frances and George Simpson', *Musk-Ox* 34 (1986), 78–87.

———, 'Literary Landscapes in the Writings of Fur Traders', in *Le Castor Fait Tout: Selected Papers of the Fifth North American Fur Trade Conference, 1985*, ed. Bruce G. Trigger *et al.* Montreal: Lake St Louis Historical Society, 1987, 566–86.

———, 'Creating Travel Literature: the Case of Paul Kane', *Papers of the Bibliographical Society of Canada* 27 (1988), 80–95.

———, ' "I came to rite thare portraits": Paul Kane's Journal of his Western Travels, 1846–1848' (with an edition of the journal), *The American Art Journal* 21, 2 (1989).

———, 'George Back', in *Profiles in Canadian Literature* 7, ed. Jeffrey M. Heath. Toronto: Dundurn Press, 1991, 9–17.

———, 'Samuel Hearne's Accounts of the Massacre at Bloody Fall, 17 July, 1771', *Ariel: A Review of International English Literature* 22 (1991), 25–51.

———, 'Exploration/Travel Literature and the Evolution of the Author', *International Journal of Canadian Studies/Revue internationale d'études canadiennes* 5 (Spring/printemps, 1992), 39–68.

MacLulich, T.D., 'The Explorer as Sage: David Thompson's *Narrative*', *Journal of Canadian Fiction* 4, 4 (1976), 97–107.

———, 'The Explorer as Hero: Mackenzie and Fraser', *Canadian Literature* 75 (Winter, 1977), 61–73.

———, 'Hearne, Cook and the Exploration Narrative', *English Studies in Canada* 5 (1979), 187–201.

————, 'Reading the Land: the Wilderness Tradition in Canadian Letters', *Journal of Canadian Studies* 20 (1985), 29–44.

————, 'Canadian Exploration as Literature', *Canadian Literature* 81 (Summer, 1979), 72–85.

————, 'Alexander Mackenzie' in *Profiles in Canadian Literature 5*, ed. Jeffrey M. Heath. Toronto: Dundurn Press, 1986, 17–24.

Marshall, P.J. and Glyndwr Williams, *The Great Map of Mankind: Perceptions of New Worlds in the Age of Enlightenment*. Cambridge, Mass.: Harvard University Press, 1982.

Pratt, Mary Louise, *Imperial Eyes: Travel Writing and Transculturation*. London and New York: Routledge, 1992.

Ruggles, Richard I., *A Country So Interesting: The Hudson's Bay Company and Two Centuries of Mapping, 1670–1870*. Montreal: McGill-Queen's University Press, 1991.

Trigger, Bruce, *Natives and Newcomers: Canada's Heroic Age Reconsidered*. Kingston: McGill-Queen's University Press, 1985.

Van Kirk, Sylvia, *Many Tender Ties: Women in Fur Trade Society in Western Canada, 1670–1870*. Winnipeg: Watson and Dwyer, 1980.

Warkentin, Germaine, 'David Thompson' in *Profiles in Canadian Literature 1*, ed. Jeffrey M. Heath. Toronto: Dundurn Press, 1980, 1–8.

————, 'Exploration Literature in English', in *Oxford Companion to Canadian Literature*, ed. William Toye. Toronto: Oxford University Press, 1983, 242–9.

————, '"The Boy Henry Kelsey": Generic Disjunction in Henry Kelsey's Verse Journal' in *Literary Genres/Genres littéraires*, ed. I.S. MacLaren and C. Potvin. Edmonton: Research Institute for Comparative Literature, 1991, 99–114.

Warkentin, John, *The Western Interior of Canada: A Record of Geographical Discovery*. The Carleton Library, no. 15. Toronto: McClelland and Stewart, 1964.

Warwick, Jack, 'Writing in New France, Part I: Exploration' in *Oxford Companion to Canadian Literature*, ed. William Toye. Toronto: Oxford University Press, 1983, 552–6.

Waterston, Elizabeth *et al.*, *The Travellers — Canada to 1900: An annotated bibliography of works published in English from 1577*. Guelph: University of Guelph, 1989.

Wiebe, Rudy, *Playing Dead: A Contemplation Concerning the Arctic*. Edmonton: NeWest, 1989.

Welsh, Christine, 'Voices of the Grandmothers: Reclaiming a Métis Heritage', *Canadian Literature* 131 (Winter, 1991), 15–24.

Williams, Glyndwr, 'Andrew Graham and Thomas Hutchins: Collaboration and Plagiarism in Eighteenth-Century Natural History', *The Beaver* (Spring, 1978), 5–14.

————, 'The Puzzle of Anthony Henday's Journal, 1754–55', *The Beaver* (Winter, 1978), 40–56.

Wright, Ronald, *Stolen Continents: the Americas Through Indian Eyes Since 1492*. Boston: Houghton Mifflin, 1992.

Index of Proper Names